D1436259

PRINTED IN GREAT BRITAIN
AT THE UNIVERSITY PRESS OXFORD
BY VIVIAN RIDLER
PRINTER TO THE UNIVERSITY

HIS MAJESTY'S
OPPOSITION
1714–1830

Oxford University Press, Amen House, London E.C.4

GLASGOW NEW YORK TORONTO MELBOURNE WELLINGTON
BOMBAY CALCUTTA MADRAS KARACHI LAHORE DACCA
CAPE TOWN SALISBURY NAIROBI IBADAN ACCRA
KUALA LUMPUR HONG KONG

HIS MAJESTY'S OPPOSITION

1714–1830

BY

ARCHIBALD S. FOORD

Master of Calhoun College, Yale University
Associate Professor of History

OXFORD
AT THE CLARENDON PRESS
1964

PRINTED IN GREAT BRITAIN

To my mother

MADELEINE B. FOORD

*whose selfless devotion has
comforted and strengthened her sons
and enriched their lives
beyond all measure*

ACKNOWLEDGEMENTS

I TAKE pleasure in expressing my gratitude to the many kind and generous people who have given me assistance in the preparation of this volume. Its flaws must be attributed not to them but to the author.

My greatest debt is to Lewis P. Curtis of Yale University. His eloquent and learned lectures first aroused my interest in eighteenth-century Britain, and he has been a guide and an inspiration for more than twenty years. Out of his keen perception, broad knowledge, and mastery of English prose he has contributed more to this work than I can well estimate. Like the numerous others who have been so fortunate as to have Professor Curtis as their preceptor, I acknowledge my obligation to him with warm affection and deep respect.

Among my other colleagues in the field of history I owe particular thanks to Wallace Notestein and William H. Dunham, Jr. for their encouragement and wise advice, and to Basil D. Henning, Thomas C. Mendenhall, Robert Walcott, Jr., and David Elliot for their criticism and helpful suggestions.

For assistance in compiling statistics and checking references I thank my bursary aides Robert A. Divine, Edward A. Stoll, Richard H. Hiers, Ulf P. Sudeck, and Jonathan Russin. The typescript was prepared by Mrs. Winifred A. Murck, Mrs. Lydia Romanik, and Mrs. Carol B. Pearson, whose labour and skill are much appreciated.

The staffs of the Yale University Library, the Huntington Library, the British Museum, the Public Record Office, and the Bodleian Library have been unfailingly courteous and obliging. I remember with gratitude the particular kindness of the late R. L. Atkinson, Secretary of the Historical Manuscripts Commission; the late Col. G. E. G. Malet and Miss W. D. Coates of the National Register of Archives; and A. J. Collins, formerly Keeper of Manuscripts in the British Museum.

I acknowledge with thanks my debt to His Grace the Duke of Portland and the University of Nottingham for permission to use the Portland Papers, to His Grace the Duke of Marlborough for permission to use the archives at Blenheim Palace, to Earl Fitzwilliam and Earl Fitzwilliam's Wentworth Estates Company for permission to quote from the Rockingham and Fitzwilliam Papers in the Sheffield City Library, to Lieut. Col. John H. Busby for permission to use the diary of Mrs. Charles Caesar, and to Wilmarth S. Lewis for allowing me to use his valuable collection of eighteenth-century material.

The research for this volume was made possible by a grant from the John Simon Guggenheim Memorial Foundation. A Senior Faculty Fellowship awarded by the President and Fellows of Yale University enabled me to complete the writing. My warm appreciation is due them for these indispensable benefactions.

My wife has loyally sustained me with sympathy and encouragement during the years this book has been in preparation. My daughter Bonnie and my son William have given me assistance in many ways. I thank them with love and devotion.

ARCHIBALD S. FOORD

Calhoun College
Yale University
1 November 1962

CONTENTS

I

INTRODUCTION

THE expression 'His Majesty's Opposition' was originally
a bit of parliamentary persiflage. Its author was a radical
statesman of moderate distinction, Sir John Cam Hobhouse,
whose political career opened with a dozen years of opposition
to the Governments of Liverpool and Wellington. During a
debate on the Civil List Act in 1826, Hobhouse declared himself obliged to oppose the report of the Bill in order to maintain
the principle that the number of government officers sitting in
the House of Commons should not be increased. 'It was said to
be very hard on His Majesty's ministers to raise objections to
this proposition', said Hobhouse. 'For my own part, I think it is
much more hard on His Majesty's Opposition to compel them
to take this course.'[1]

Laughter followed this sally, and in his retort Canning drew
another laugh by repeating the phrase. It was picked up
shortly afterward by a leading Whig, George Tierney, who
thought Hobhouse had said 'the King's Opposition':

My honourable friend [said Tierney] could not have invented a
better phrase to designate us than that which he has adopted, for we
are certainly to all intents and purposes a branch of His Majesty's
Government. Its proceedings for some time past have proved that,
although the gentlemen opposite are in office, we are in power. The
measures are ours, but all the emoluments are theirs. [Cheers and
laughter.][2]

Tierney's interpretation of the phrase was apt enough to gain
him repute in some quarters as its author. A year later Hobhouse noted, 'The Times of today gives to Tierney my joke of His
Majesty's Opposition.'[3] Within a short space of time, indeed
within the lifetime of those who first heard it, the humorous
origin of the phrase was forgotten, and 'His Majesty's Opposition' was applied to an important constitutional concept.

[1] Lord Broughton, *Recollections of a Long Life* (London, 1909–11), iii. 129–30;
Hansard, 2 s., xv. 135–50. For the use of 'Opposition' see Chapter IV below.
[2] *Hansard*, 2 s., xv. 150. [3] Broughton, *Recollections of a Long Life*, iii. 191.

B

This concept has often been stated and defined. No work on British Government can ignore it. Since the middle of the nineteenth century the definitions have possessed a general uniformity.[1] 'His Majesty's Opposition' is a political party or group of parties out of office, whose primary function is to criticize and attack the party or parties in power. The composition and organization of parties may vary greatly, from the Whigs of Russell to the Labourites of Attlee, but a group of politicians with some seats in Parliament and a following in the country, possessed of some form of cohesion for common political action, is generally deemed to be a party. Ideally, in the minds of most, there should be two overwhelmingly dominant parties, one in office and one constituting 'His Majesty's Opposition', but even within the last century the facts have not always corresponded to the ideal. The immediate purpose of Opposition criticism is to check, prevent, and rectify any abuses of which government may be guilty. The ultimate purpose is to replace the party or parties in power by the Opposition, either as the result of a shift in parliamentary opinion or as the result of a general election which gives the Opposition a majority. To impel and to justify such a turnover of power, the Opposition normally advocates a programme of action which differs, though not necessarily in every detail, from that of the Government, and which the Opposition pledges to effectuate when able to do so. The Opposition employs none but such peaceful means to achieve power. It operates wholly within the laws and conventions of the state, to which it is completely loyal. The Opposition is a responsible body, obliged not to take any action calculated to drive the country into chaos, and equally obliged to take office should its activities make government by those in power unfeasible or impossible. The assumption of loyalty and responsibility by the Opposition convert it from mere political faction into 'His Majesty's Opposition'.

---

[1] The best mid-nineteenth-century study is 'Parliamentary Opposition' in the *Edinburgh Review*, ci (1855), 1–22. For a classic treatment of the subject half a century later, see A. L. Lowell, *The Government of England* (New York, 1908), i. 435–47. Excellent recent analyses of opposition are to be found in two volumes by Ivor Jennings, *Cabinet Government* (Cambridge, England, 1936), pp. 384–8; and *Parliament* (Cambridge, 1940), pp. 152–70.

He who conceives of the institution in these terms belongs to that school of Western thought generically classified as liberal: a school which counts among its adherents the great majority of the English-speaking world. The concept itself rests upon the idea, common to all types of Western liberalism, that men possess certain basic human rights, among which freedom of speech furnishes the citizen with liberty to criticize his rulers. For the effective guarantee of his rights, the liberal holds representation, though not necessarily universal suffrage, to be indispensably necessary and party to be a useful means of bringing public opinion to bear upon the conduct of government. Within the framework of the state, a loyal and responsible Opposition performs in the main two beneficial functions. First, as representative of the minority, it strives to protect minority rights, to reduce administrative injustice and inefficiency by ruthless criticism, and to modify Government policy, both legislative and executive, in line with its own programme. In this sense the Opposition sustains the work of an *advocatus diaboli*, vigilant, earnest, and pitiless. Second, as an alternative Government, the Opposition provides a means for peaceful change of administration, the overthrow of those in power without resort to violence or revolution. In this sense, the institution affords a practical solution to the age-old problem of political stability. Liberal theory does not insist that the institution is without fault. Indeed, it is readily admitted that opposition may act viciously and obstructively, submitting the administration to unmerited obloquy and crippling the machinery of state. Upon occasion opposition may prove unable to form a stable alternative Government, and a period of confusion may ensue. But institutions can be no better than the men who embody them, and upon the whole during the last century 'His Majesty's Opposition' has in practice performed its theoretical functions with remarkable success.

At times when circumstances do not submit society to unusual stress and strain, Britain takes the successful operation of the institution for granted. Men do not dwell upon the happy fact that British politicians out of office are fair, loyal, and responsible: they assume, as did Redlich in the complacent Edwardian era, that British history has been and will continue to be 'a history of parliamentary opposition, finally victorious, but always moderate in the hour of victory and always legal in its action'.[1] But when Britain finds herself in conflict with the forces of tyranny, 'His Majesty's Opposition' stands out as the very symbol of ordered freedom. So it was in 1855, while British forces in uneasy alliance with Bonapartist troops lay before Sebastopol, that the *Edinburgh Review* observed:

The main characteristic of European despotisms at present is that they suppress all manifestation of opinion adverse to their acts and policy—that they permit no unfavourable criticism of their proceedings, either by speech or by writing, either in parliamentary bodies, in public meetings, or through the press. . . . On the other hand, the distinctive mark of a free Government is, not so much the mildness, moderation, and equity of its administration (although it in general avoids the measures of harshness and cruelty which occur from time to time in despotic states), as its permission of a free discussion of its measures—of its toleration of adverse criticism in Parliament, at public meetings, in newspapers, pamphlets, and books. It is the legal and acknowledged existence of an organized opposition to the Government which is, in these times, the most salient characteristic of a free country and its principal distinction from despotisms. . . .

It is natural that the Emperor Nicholas should consider all constitutional restraints upon the will of the hereditary chief of a state as pernicious, and that he should proscribe them by his imperial anathema. Experience has, however, proved that a constitutional monarchy is a far more solid, durable, and substantial form of government than an absolute monarchy; and that a political opposition, though it may be an institution highly distasteful to a reigning despot, is a necessary condition for freedom and political progress.[2]

And so it was nearly a century later, while England was involved in a cold war with the Tsars' successors in the Kremlin, that Prime Minister Attlee catechized a meeting of Yorkshire miners, 'wherever you find the right of opposition denied, wherever you find such devices as the single list of candidates, wherever you find a Government that cannot be removed by the method of the ballot box, there is no true democracy, there is no true freedom'.[3]

Upon occasion the despot has envied the results of free

[1] Redlich, *Procedure of the House of Commons*, i. 58.
[2] *Edinburgh Review*, ci. 1, 2, 22.
[3] *New York Times*, 22 June 1947. Cf. the exchange of articles on this point between Herbert Morrison and *Pravda* as reported in ibid. 1 Aug. 1951.

discussion in liberal lands. Alexander I was sufficiently impressed during a visit to England in 1814 to declare that when he returned to Russia he 'would have an opposition'.[1] But such institutions are not created by fiat. The despot faces opponents of another sort: those who ironically styled themselves 'His Majesty's most loyal Opposition' in Nazi Germany were the conspirators who endeavoured to assassinate Hitler in 1944.[2] The way of despotism to political stability is inevitably the path of repression, from which there can be no deviation but by violence and revolution. Perhaps the oddest paradox of the twentieth century lies in the fact that Communist Russia, whose doctrine rests on a dialectic that finds progress only in a conflict of opposites, savagely stifles all opposition; while in Western lands, where faith in human reason leads men indefatigably to seek grounds for the reconciliation of opposing interests, the structure of politics requires a permanent organized Opposition. The contrast is most vividly depicted by an American cartoon in which a European peasant, glumly observing the erection of a gallows, remarks to his companion, 'Must be election time. Ze Government is building ze Opposition party's platform.'[3]

As 'His Majesty's Opposition' is anathema in the monolithic state, so has it long been a matter for admiration and emulation in liberal lands. A century ago, Ralph Waldo Emerson, whose British journeys taught him that 'Congress is not wiser or better than Parliament', lauded Britain for having 'hit on that capital invention of freedom, a constitutional Opposition.'[4] We may no longer share Emerson's belief that all the world 'is aiming to be English', but his attitude toward English government persists in America. After the presidential election of 1940 the defeated candidate, Wendell Willkie, exhorted the Republicans to follow the British example by constituting themselves 'a vigorous, loyal, and public-spirited Opposition party.'[5] Moreover, where free government has proved weak or a failure, political scientists often detect as a major cause the absence of an Opposition similar to that in Britain. Such was the common criticism of the

[1] Strachey and Fulford, eds., *The Greville Memoirs*, i. 241; cf. Hardcastle, *Life of John Lord Campbell*, i. 304–5.
[2] *The von Hassell Diaries*, 1938–44 (London, 1948), pp. 181–2.
[3] Bill Mauldin, *Back Home* (New York, 1947), p. 233.
[4] *English Tracts* (1856), chs. v, xviii.   [5] *New York Times*, 12 Nov. 1940.

Third French Republic.[1] Friedrich Sieburg saw the Weimar
Republic succumb to Hitler because 'German democracy
neither displayed toleration within its own ranks nor had the
courage to assign to the Opposition its proper role'.[2] The
existence of a loyal Opposition is generally considered to be
indispensable to the proper working of modern democracy.

None but the most naïve, however, believe that man can
successfully transplant political institutions in their entirety.
Constitutions do not function like machines which may operate
in precisely the same fashion wherever located. A weak, corrupt,
or tyrannical state cannot be transformed into a free and beneficent one merely by decreeing that a loyal Opposition shall
exist—not, that is, unless the decree be the will of the political
community. For a loyal Opposition, like similar institutions,
is not 'created' in the formal sense. It is a product of growth
and political education. 'His Majesty's Opposition', the great
prototype, did not suddenly spring into existence at any date in
history. Britain did not, in a flash of inspiration, 'hit on' the
concept, as Emerson suggested. The institution evolved only
after a long period of development. Indeed, it grew out of an
atmosphere in which any form of organized opposition stood
condemned as faction and disloyalty. Perhaps the Tories merely
indulged in self-pity when they lamented that, under the
Whig Junto in Anne's reign,

if a gentleman stands up to complain of grievances, although this
House meets in order to redress them, he is represented as a person
that obstructs Her Majesty's business; if he finds fault with the
Ministry, he is said to reflect upon the queen; if he speaks against
the continuance of the war, to prevent the beggary of the nation . . .,
then he is to be no object of Her Majesty's favour and encouragement.[3]

But in the eighteenth century such was still the position of the
Crown that the sovereign did not conceal aversion to critics of
the Ministry and its measures. George II habitually referred
to Walpole's opponents as rascals and knaves, puppies and

[1] For example, see F. J. C. Hearnshaw, *Democracy at the Crossways* (London, 1918),
pp. 409–10.
[2] *Germany: My Country* (London, 1933), p. 122. Cf. Ramsay Muir, *Future for
Democracy* (London, 1939), p. 123.
[3] Townsend, *Memoirs of the House of Commons*, i. 309.

scoundrels.[1] After eighteen years on the throne, George III recorded 'an opinion I have long had that men who have been active in opposition rarely make useful servants to the Crown',[2] and he consistently maintained the unconstitutionality of any 'attempt to wrest the executive government into the hands of the House of Commons by opposition'.[3] In 1762 Lord Hardwicke warned the Duke of Newcastle against taking action which would 'give a handle to suspicions, insinuations, and malicious reports of caballing and concert in order to opposition, and what will be traduced with the name of faction, however unjustly';[4] and the politicians of that period generally professed to regard an Opposition designed to overthrow the Ministry with loathing and horror.[5] As late as 1830, Bagehot observed, something of this attitude still persisted. About this time a gentleman, contemplating the idea that the Crown should invite a successful Opposition to take office, remarked, 'Sir, I would as soon choose for a new coachman the man who shied stones best at my old one.'[6] Yet while politicians abhorred opposition in theory, they gradually developed the institution in practice. The concept of 'His Majesty's Opposition', as is so often true in political theory, was the rationalization of an existing fact.

It is probably impossible to determine the historical moment when organized opposition first appeared in Parliament. A noted medievalist refers to Simon de Montfort as 'a prominent member of the Parliamentary Opposition',[7] and perhaps careful construction could make a case for the Provisions of Oxford, and even Magna Carta, as successful opposition programmes, complete with new measures and new men. But it should be superfluous to point out that the battle-axe, not the ballot, was the instrument of the medieval barons, and that the modern concept of opposition depends upon the existence of an elected assembly which possesses freedom of debate. Even after the establishment

---

[1] Sedgwick, ed., *Memoirs of Lord Hervey*, pp. 160, 170, 755 and *passim*.
[2] Add. MSS. 37,833, f. 216: George III to Robinson, 7 Feb. 1778.
[3] P.R.O. Chatham MSS., 104: George III to Pitt, 11 Apr. 1797.
[4] Add. MSS. 32,939, f. 54.
[5] Cf. Namier, *England in the Age of the American Revolution* (London, 1930), pp. 55–59.
[6] Walter Bagehot, *The English Constitution and Other Political Essays* (New York, 1911), p. 396.
[7] Carl Stephenson, *Mediaeval History* (New York, 1935), p. 559.

of the House of Commons there ensued a prolonged struggle between Crown and Parliament over the issue of free speech, which was not finally resolved until 1660. The records make clear that from the fourteenth century onward Members of Parliament criticized the executive and its policies—in this sense opposition is of medieval origin—and during the seventeenth century Eliot, Wentworth, and Pym occasionally acted very much like the leaders of a modern Opposition. But as long as the sovereign exercised the right to punish critics in Parliament, and ultimately to call out an army against them, a constitutional Opposition in the modern sense could not develop. Another block to its development, which still existed after 1660, was the practice of pursuing fallen ministers to the dungeon or into exile. Peaceful changes of government could not take place if vengeance followed dismissal, even though the avenger was Parliament rather than the Crown. Nor could peaceful change become the norm before agreement on fundamentals made resort to revolution unnecessary. Not until after 1688, therefore, did the basic conditions obtain for the natural development of 'His Majesty's Opposition', and not until 1714 were there established certain ancillary conditions which made possible its development upon a stable political foundation.

In 1714 Britain finally settled her dynastic problem. Some time was required, of course, to make the settlement secure, for two Jacobite invasions and one Jacobite plot followed within eight years of the Hanoverian accession. During that period, and for a generation afterward, the Court party made political capital out of identifying opposition with Jacobitism, but in actual fact, as the Ministry well knew, very few members of either House of Parliament were involved in treasonable activity. The proscription of Tory leaders and the rebellion of 1715 were the last manifestations of the forms of violence that characterized restoration politics.[1] The Whigs had apparently

---

[1] In his essay on Mackintosh, Macaulay pointed out that important conditions for the development of opposition were secured by the provisions in the revolution settlement guaranteeing the tenure of judges and regulating treason trials. Previously the Crown could eliminate opponents 'by means of perjured witnesses, packed juries, and corrupt, hard-hearted, brow-beating judges', making it 'as safe to be a highwayman as to be a distinguished leader of opposition'. Since the enactment of these provisions, Macaulay contended with but slight exaggeration, 'no statesman, while engaged in constitutional opposition to a Government, has had

considered the assassination of their opponents in 1714, but upon Anne's sudden death, they chose instead to move by more cautious methods.[1] When Oxford, Bolingbroke, and Strafford were impeached, politicians were not surprised but calmly compared their fate to that of Clarendon and Danby.[2] Yet the phenomenon was never to recur. Walpole faced the threat of impeachment in 1742, Newcastle was worried in 1762, but England had abandoned political proscription after 1715. Thereafter, also, rebellion soon became a forlorn hope, rather than an ever-present menace. When Prince Charles came over the water in 1745, a few members acted rather equivocally in Parliament, but no prominent statesman, soldier, or divine rallied to his standard. Moreover, the advent of the Hanoverians coincided closely with the conclusion of that long series of desperate wars with France which had intimately affected British political life since the reign of Charles II. No major conflict intervened again for a generation. The date 1714, therefore, marks the commencement of a period of relative peace, both internal and external, which enabled British statesmen to dispense finally with political procedures that prevented the growth of a constitutional Opposition.

At roughly the same time several subsidiary factors were introduced which influenced political life for years to come. In 1707 the Act of Union placed forty-five Scots in the House of Commons and sixteen Scottish peers in the House of Lords. The electioneering activity of the Court after 1714 was often to turn them into important blocs of support for the Ministry. Its measure of control over Scottish members was a vital index to the strength of a Government until the Reform Act. The Septennial Act of 1716 stabilized the life-cycle of Parliaments for two centuries. In general, only the demise of the Crown or an abnormal crisis interrupted the specified seven-year span, a significant factor in the growth of party and electioneering methods. In 1717 the prorogation of Convocation, not to meet again with one brief exception until the middle of the nineteenth

the axe before his eyes. The smallest minorities, struggling against the most powerful majorities, in the most agitated times, have felt themselves perfectly secure': Trevelyan, ed., *The Works of Lord Macaulay* (London, 1871), vi. 127–30.

[1] *H.M.C., Egmont Diary*, ii. 509.

[2] Egmont MSS. 234: Diary, 30 Mar. 1715 and ff. For an explanation of references to the Egmont MSS. see Bibliographical Note.

century, signalized the disappearance of fierce theological controversy from political life. Sporadically thereafter religion became a major issue—the Jew Bill of 1753, the Gordon Riots of 1780, Catholic Emancipation after 1800—but the clerical disputes which had produced revolutionary cleavages in British society were silenced. Henceforward political parties were not to be based upon religious differences.

The advent of the Georges also produced two changes peculiar to themselves. Their possession of the Electorate of Hanover made it a major factor in domestic politics and foreign policy for two reigns and a minor factor until 1837. More important, the Hanoverian accession ushered in a line of kings who in all their acts were completely loyal to the Constitution, a prerequisite for a similar loyalty on the part of all the statesmen who served them. Even William III and Anne had been deeply suspected of a desire to overturn certain aspects of the Revolution settlement, and Anne's equivocal attitude had apparently done much to encourage Jacobitism. But such occasional bitter accusations, as that George II and Cumberland intended to erect a military Government in England, and that George III sought to revive absolute monarchy, were merely the biased taunts of party strife and known to be so by the men who made them. The accusers, indeed, frequently lamented their inability to convince others. Hanoverian rule rightly engendered not suspicion but trust, an element indispensable to peaceful constitutional development.

The existence of the conditions necessary for the growth of 'His Majesty's Opposition' did not mean, of course, that the institution quickly sprang into existence. Old political attitudes die hard, and the pressure of events often diverts institutional development from what later may seem to have been the logical course. The growth of constitutional Opposition after 1714 was slow and uneven, until the concept was formalized in the middle of the nineteenth century. By 1830, however, the institution had reached maturity. Then for the first time occurred the procedure for a change of ministry which, with variations, has since obtained. Wellington's Government lost a general election, and after testing opinion in Parliament, the Prime Minister resigned for all his colleagues, recommending the chief Opposition leader as his successor. William IV authorized Grey to form a new ministry with '*carte blanche* as to all offices both in Government and the Household but Brougham'.[1] Grey, having overcome the difficulty with Brougham by making him Lord Chancellor, assembled a Cabinet from among the Opposition parties and embarked upon his programme of parliamentary reform. After some hesitation Wellington and Peel formed an Opposition which later fought its way back into office. Before 1830 no change of ministry had conformed in essentials to modern procedure, a fact which renders that date of considerable significance in constitutional history.

The years 1714 and 1830, therefore, make natural terminal dates for a study of 'His Majesty's Opposition'. The 115 years that lay between constitute the germinating period of the modern institution. A study of its germination must necessarily concentrate upon the House of Commons. Not that the Lords were a negligible element in the Constitution. George III used the defeat of Fox's India Bill in the House of Lords as his reason for dismissing the coalition in 1783, and in 1788 Pitt threatened to resign if Dolben's Slave Trade Bill did not pass the Upper House. Even in 1809 Wellington exaggerated when he exclaimed, 'Nobody cares a damn about the House of Lords; the House of Commons is everything in England and the House of Lords is nothing.'[2] But it being an essential corollary of the modern concept of Opposition that it operates in an elected assembly, through which government is responsible to the people, the peers inevitably play a secondary role. It is, then, mainly at St. Stephen's that we shall trace the irregular and often illogical development of the institution.

At the outset, a detailed analysis of George I's first few months on the throne, set against the background of generally received views on the political structure of eighteenth-century Britain, is necessary to explain the situation out of which 'His Majesty's Opposition' grew. The treatment of the subject is then proportioned in large measure to the degree of illumination shed upon it by previous scholarship. For the first forty years of the Hanoverian era there is much to be learned from manuscripts, printed documents, pamphlets, and parliamentary records. The Jacobite parliamentary party from 1716 to 1722, significant as

---

[1] Trevelyan, *Lord Grey*, p. 241.   [2] Green, *The Hanoverians*, p. 50.

the last disloyal Opposition, has hitherto been neglected, and the Leicester House Opposition from 1717 to 1720 needs to be placed in proper perspective. Although a great deal has been written about the patriots who defeated Walpole, their striking achievements in theory and practice require full exposition and considerable reinterpretation. The age of 'broad bottom' from 1742 to 1760 was not quite as sterile as it has seemed. A study of the interplay of faction reveals much of intrinsic interest about the period, both as the aftermath of Walpole's fall and as the prelude to the reign of George III. Thereafter the enormous volume of data and the mass of scholarship leave no doubt about the central facts of political history, and it is unnecessary to re-examine them in detail. For the reigns of the last two Georges the historian's task is to concentrate upon the crucial episodes and important ideas that produced the party system as it existed in 1830.

II

THE OPPOSITION AT THE HANOVERIAN ACCESSION

I AUGUST 1714–15 JANUARY 1715

II

THE OPPOSITION AT THE
HANOVERIAN ACCESSION

I AUGUST 1714–15 JANUARY 1715

I. THE CROWN AND ITS MINISTERS

UPON the accession of George I there ensued a marked overturn in British politics. Events moved at an uneven pace, but the change was thorough and the result decisive. Anne's last Parliament met the day she died, 1 August 1714, and her last Ministry carried through in the following three weeks the measures necessary for the establishment of the new reign. Parliament was then prorogued, and a week thereafter began the replacement of all the principal officers of state with their political opponents. By the time of the coronation on 20 October the process was practically finished, to be followed by similar shifts in the royal household, army, navy, law, and local government over the next three months. Then on 15 January 1715 George I called a general election by a proclamation in which the leaders and the majority in the old Parliament were clearly, if obliquely, stigmatized as traitors. Thus, without a defeat in Parliament or the country, without any major crisis in national affairs or breakdown in the management of the state, a ministry and its followers who had loyally served the reigning monarch were cast into opposition.

The manner in which the overturn took place may be explained to some extent by the circumstances attending the succession. Anne had died after a brief mortal illness. George was at Hanover, a minimum of six days' journey from England. A Stuart Pretender residing in Lorraine threatened the Protestant succession. An Act of 1708,[1] whose authors foresaw such a situation, laid down the procedure for the transition from one reign to the next. By its provisions, the governance of the realm

---

[1] 6 Anne c. 7.

was entrusted to a group of Lords Justices, seven designated by office, others to be named by the heir. Under their direction, Privy Council and Parliament were to meet immediately and to carry on their functions for six months, unless the new monarch altered these arrangements after his accession. George I did not alter them. As required by law, he had appointed the additional Lords Justices before Anne's death, and for seven weeks after his accession, until his arrival in England on 18 September, he allowed his regents to govern the kingdom with only occasional directions from Hanover. The Act of 1708 determined, therefore, that the first Acts of George's reign should be carried out in Anne's Parliament by Anne's ministers. It seems logical enough that ministerial changes should await the sovereign's advent into his new realm, and, parliamentary business having been accomplished, that the dissolution should take place near the legal limit.

But neither the dynastic situation nor the technicalities of the succession explain how such a political *bouleversement* could occur or why in fact it did. In the absence of the critical factors that customarily make possible a change of government in a parliamentary state, what enabled the Opposition to displace the Ministry? Given the possibility of a political overturn, what brought about the 'change of hands' in 1714? The answer to these questions, fundamental to an understanding of the development of 'His Majesty's Opposition', must be sought within the framework of certain well-established facts and current hypotheses concerning the power of the Crown and the nature of politics in eighteenth-century Britain.[1]

Despite the numerous limitations placed upon the royal power since 1660, the king remained the dominant figure in political life. The Constitution endowed the monarch, as chief executive, with control of Government patronage and national policy, a share in one or both of which is ever the goal of the aspiring politician. He who would secure place, honour, pension, or other favour must go to Court. He who would influence the great decisions of state must first convince His Majesty. It should

---

[1] Scholars still disagree to some extent over the precise emphasis to be placed upon certain factors in the current hypotheses: see W. R. Fryer, 'The Study of British Politics between the Revolution and the Reform Act' in *Renaissance and Modern Studies*, i (1957), 91–114.

be said, however, that in neither of these areas was royal power absolute. Though the king theoretically appointed every official in army, navy, church, and state, in actual practice his free choice was frequently hampered by numerous factors: life-grants and reversions issued in earlier reigns, freehold rights asserted by the incumbents of certain positions, claims of higher officials to elect their own subordinates, the traditional exercise of powers of appointment by the chief officers of the Crown. Though the Constitution made no distinction between royal policy and national policy, the king could not carry out decisions strenuously disapproved by a parliamentary majority and devoid of the necessary financial support. On the other hand, to obtain a favour or to implement a design opposed by the monarch was extremely difficult. Nothing but heavy pressure from external circumstances could ordinarily force the king to act against his will. If not absolute, therefore, royal control of policy and patronage was at once so extensive in its scope, so pervasive in its influence, and so concentrated in the king's person that politics inevitably revolved about the throne.

Of the powers which thus remained vested in the Crown, the most vital was the monarch's constitutional right to choose his own ministers. The choice of the Ministry was, in effect, the key to the exercise of all the other prerogatives. Through his ministers the king distributed patronage and executed policy. They were his servants in the management of the state, placed in office to give advice but to do his bidding. Were he to lose control of them, he would inevitably lose also the powers which they exercised in his name. Realizing its importance, the kings of England had fought off every attack on this prerogative from the days of Simon de Montfort through those of John Pym. In one particular only had the royal power of appointment suffered modification. The Act of Settlement of 1701 had incapacitated the alien-born, except a child of English parents abroad, for membership in Parliament, the Privy Council, and 'any office or place of trust, either civil or military'.[1] With this exception,

---

[1] 12 and 13 William III c. 2. This Act also barred all placemen from the House of Commons after Anne's reign, but 'West's expedient', incorporated in 4 Anne c. 8 and confirmed by 6 Anne c. 7, permitted them to sit if elected or re-elected after their appointment. In a sense this provision placed an additional check on the prerogative, as general practice required that all important ministers be members of one of the Houses of Parliament. Lord Perceval, indeed, once expressed the

the prergoative of free ministerial choice was denied by no one
in 1714. When George I carried out his wholesale changes
upon his first arrival in England, even those who most disapproved did not deny his right to do so.

Parliament, it is true, possessed constitutional weapons with
which to assault unpopular ministers. Either House might
petition the king to remove a man from his councils. Impeachment or attainder drove a minister from office. In fine, the
legislature, while it could not dictate appointments, had means
to undo them. But Parliament's weapons were largely ineffective. Nothing obliged the Crown to grant a petition against a
minister; indeed, Charles II had ignored such moves with
impunity. A Bill of Attainder could not pass without the royal
assent, nor could a Bill of Pains and Penalties. Impeachment
was a clumsy process which required legal evidence as well as
political animosity to be successful.[1] Both attainder and
impeachment worked better as measures of vengeance against
fallen ministers, or those with whom the king was willing to
part, than as methods of removing those in favour. Hence, in
1714 a minister who enjoyed the king's confidence had little to
fear from attacks of this nature in Parliament.

The Crown's control of patronage, moreover, gave the king
and his chosen ministers an influence over Parliament which
normally prevented that body from acting contrary to their
wishes. Beginning in the reign of Charles II, the Court had
gradually developed a system of distributing its favours so as to
produce a majority for ministerial measures in both Houses.[2]
The system never reached perfection; at no time was Parliament

opinion that 'West's expedient' constituted a positive admission that the electorate
should have a voice in the selection of royal advisers ('Danger of a New Opposition
after this Change' (1742), P.R.O., Egmont MSS. 212, f. 15ᵛ). Legally, of course,
the king could circumvent this difficulty by his prerogative of creating peers.

[1] The ineffectiveness of impeachment seems to have been broadly recognized,
especially after the failure of the prosecutions of 1715. In a pamphlet published in
1719 Lord Peterborough declared that ministers 'have nothing to fear but an
impeachment from the House of Commons, which I compare to a great wind
whistling amongst trees, making a noise amongst them but blowing none of them
down' (*Remarks on a Pamphlet entituled 'The Thoughts of a Member of the Lower House'*,
p. 7). In 1721 the Master of the Rolls stated that impeachment had become 'ineffectual' as a means of punishing corrupt ministers (Coxe, *Walpole*, ii. 212).

[2] On the early development of the 'Court party', see Andrew Browning,
'Parties and Party Organization in the Reign of Charles II', in *Trans. R. Hist. Soc.*
4th ser. xxx. 21–36.

corrupted into abject compliance with every design of the executive. But, except in unusual circumstances, so great was the 'influence of the Crown' that when allied with the 'interest' of those in office and wisely managed, it assured any ministry of the parliamentary strength necessary to get 'the king's business' done. In 'An Impartial History of Parties' addressed to George I upon his accession, Lord Cowper accurately advised the king of his power to guarantee 'a clear majority in all succeeding Parliaments' to the ministry of his choice 'by showing your favour in due time (before the elections)'.[1] No Opposition, as Swift reminded that of 1712, could reasonably hope to destroy a Government supported by the monarch.[2]

The 'influence of the Crown' thus gave the king wide discretion in the practical exercise of his theoretical right to choose his ministry. The political overturn of 1714 took place because George I wished it. There was no need of any crisis to force 'a change of hands'. Parliamentary elections followed, rather than preceded, ministerial alterations, and a Government possessed of the king's confidence could normally withstand defeats in Parliament and national disasters. When George ascended the throne, his choice of ministers was limited, in effect, only by the availability of talent. He had to choose from among the politicians in the two Houses of Parliament,[3] and he had to choose those who would serve together. Men frequently refused office, or agreed to accept only on difficult conditions, or aspired to a post other than the one offered. The king could not coerce one whom the promise of power and emolument did not lure. Within these restrictions, his choice was free.

2. POLITICAL PARTIES

The politicians available for office in 1714 were generally classified as Whigs and Tories. In a vague way contemporaries

[1] John Lord Campbell, *Lives of the Lord Chancellors*, 2nd ser. iv. 429. Cf. Paul Rapin-Thoyras, *Dissertation sur les Whigs et les Torys* (The Hague, 1717), pp. 156–8; [Richard Harley], *Faults on Both Sides* (London, 1710), pp. 10, 20.

[2] [Jonathan Swift], *Some Reasons to Prove that no Person is Obliged by his Principles as a Whig to Oppose Her Majesty or her Present Ministry* (London, 1712), p. 18. Cf. *H.M.C., Bath MSS.* i. 74–75.

[3] This restraint was imposed by practice and utility rather than by law. Bute was the only significant exception to the rule in the eighteenth century; cf. Richard Pares, *King George III and the Politicians* (Oxford, 1953), p. 100.

assigned to these terms a distinction of political principle. The Tory was said to support the prerogatives of the Crown, the Church of England, and the landed interest, against the Whig's predilection for the liberties of the subject, toleration of dissent, and the commercial interest.[1] During Anne's reign the contrast between the two labels had some meaning as reflected in what were called 'Whig points' and 'Tory points' of policy. Whig and Tory had differed as to the constitutionality of Anne's use of the prerogative in creating twelve peers to secure the passage of the treaty of Utrecht. Some Tories had favoured the Schism and Occasional Conformity Acts as a means of protecting the Church, and some Whigs had opposed them as intolerant. Some Tories had projected a commercial treaty with France, and most Whigs had attacked it as harmful to English trade. But such 'points' were not altogether reliable indications of principle. In each case there were to be found Tories who sided with Whigs, and Whigs voting with Tories. As Lord Molesworth observed at this time, 'there has been such chopping and changing both of names and principles that we scarce know who is who'.[2] The principles supposedly dividing Whig and Tory were, in reality, little more than general tendencies or traditional prejudices. Where a politician took his stand upon an issue depended much more upon whether he was in or out of office than upon what label was attached to him.

For Whigs and Tories did not constitute political parties as they came to be in the late nineteenth and twentieth centuries. Those labels were often adopted by, or foisted upon, men who had little in common and few or no real ties. In 1714 and for many years thereafter, the basic political unit was the group or connexion, often called a party, formed under the leadership of a successful politician.

Whoever in the eighteenth century had the 'attractive power' of office received an accession of followers, [writes Sir Lewis Namier]

---

[1] Contemporary views are reflected in Princess Caroline's remarks to Lady Cowper (*Diary of Mary Countess Cowper* (London, 1844), pp. 65, 98) and in tracts such as Rapin-Thoyras, *Dissertation sur les Whigs et les Torys* (The Hague, 1717).

[2] [Robert Viscount Molesworth, trans.], *Franco-Gallia: or, An Account of the Ancient Free State of France . . . by the famous civilian Francis Hotoman* (2nd ed., London, 1738), p. vii. Cf. [John Toland], *The Art of Governing by Partys* (London, 1701), pp. 51–54; *Memoirs of Thomas Earl of Ailesbury, written by himself* (Roxburghe Club, 1890), ii. 651.

and whoever retained it for some time was able to form a party; such parties, barring cases of exceptional mismanagement, would not break up at once on the loss of office: for it was natural for those who had held and lost their places together to remain united, bound as they were by common friendships and hostilities. But while some remained true to their friends from disinterested motives, and others because they believed in collective bargaining and expected to do better by going in and out as a group, there were always some who could not, or would not, wait, and made, therefore, their individual agreements. Thus every single group in opposition was bound to melt, even if opposition as a whole was on the increase: for the basis of the various groups was eminently personal.[1]

Three general categories comprise the personal factors that enabled a politician to acquire the 'attractive power' of office, and hence to form a party. The sovereign's particular favour normally assured high position to a man of general competence. The Duke of Marlborough, for example, had attained a leading role in national affairs through Anne's personal affection for him and his wife, and when the Queen's love died, Marlborough fell from power. There were frequent occasions when circumstances obliged a monarch to part with personal favourites, but if they remained his favourites, even though out of office, they had a good chance of returning. Thus a politician deemed high in royal regard never failed to attract a following.

Possession of a parliamentary 'interest', the power to elect members and control their votes, was also an important asset. Seats commanded by an 'interest' constituted the core of such a party; they were also 'marketable ware', as Henry Pelham once observed, and a Government in search of a stable majority often bought wholesale.[2] The nature of the unreformed Parliament made it possible for wealth and ambition to amass an 'interest' with constant vigilance and attention. The

---

[1] L. B. Namier, *England in the Age of the American Revolution* (London, 1930), pp. 242–3. Cf. the comment of Lord Perceval upon the prospective fate of the Tory groups in August 1714: '. . . they must behave themselves with much dutifulness or else (as they will certainly be a minority in the next Parliament), they will ruin themselves irretrievably, for though they endeavour to keep together, yet people fall every day from them, and if under the present prejudice against them, they should be troublesome and yet a minority, they will be neglected and dwindle to nothing' (Perceval to George Berkeley, 31 Aug. 1714, P.R.O., Egmont MSS. 234).

[2] H. P. Wyndham, ed., *The Diary of the late George Bubb Dodington* (London, 1785), p. 308.

electorate was small and subject to pressure, the tenant by his landlord, the tradesman by his customer. By exerting his influence, the affluent property-holder might turn a narrow constituency into a 'pocket' borough, whose members he nominated. He might exercise great influence in larger 'open' boroughs and counties. In Anne's reign, for example, Lord Wharton was reputed to own five pocket boroughs and to exercise a powerful influence in eight other boroughs and three counties.[1] Though few could rival Wharton, there was among the nobility and gentry of Britain a sizeable number of magnates who inherited or acquired the wealth, primarily in land, to establish parliamentary 'interests' on a lesser scale. The number and strength of 'interests' varied at different times, for they were neither eternal nor absolute. Redistributions of family property consequent upon death and distress tended to break up some interests and create or augment others. The existence in some constituencies of rival 'interests', often quite evenly balanced, provoked continual conflicts, in which evanescent victories went now to one party, now to another, now to a new invading 'interest'. The political advantages conferred by a parliamentary following made the clash of interests, in this sense, the very essence of electoral warfare.

The need of every administration for able speakers to pilot its measures through Parliament meant that a group usually tended to form about the person of the able parliamentarian. He attracted alike the unattached member and the interest seeking a star for its wagon. Most important, like the nuclei of other groups[2]—the royal favourite and the magnate with an interest—he attracted, in the first instance, his personal friends and relations. In the small political world of eighteenth-century England nearly every politician found numerous others bound to him by private associations. 'For a member, like Joseph Ashe in 1710,' writes one historian, 'to have fifty relatives who were

---

[1] Robert Walcott, Jr., 'English Party Politics (1688–1714)' in *Essays in Modern English History in Honor of Wilbur Cortez Abbott* (Cambridge, Mass., 1941), pp. 116–17. Wharton's heir boasted in 1716 that he could return fourteen 'friends' to the House of Commons: *H.M.C., Stuart Papers*, ii. 471.

[2] It should be observed that these categories were not mutually exclusive. The elements of all three might be found in a single party, as in the Walpole–Townshend group in the early days of George I.

M.P.'s was a commonplace.'¹ It was natural that a political leader should draw to his standard those with whom he had personal ties. So vital was this element that contemporaries were wont to designate parties by such terms as 'Newcastle's friends' or 'the Grenville clan'.

From this fact emerges another aspect of the 'eminently personal basis' of party organization. Not only were connexions formed around the person of a politician with the 'attractive power of office', actual or potential, but also they were formed largely by his schoolfellows, neighbours, associates, and relatives by blood or marriage. This is not to say that party rested solely upon a social or family foundation. On the one hand, most connexions included men whose real ties were primarily political. On the other, separate interests and private feuds split friends and families periodically for years and sometimes for generations. One can never assume that all Pouletts, Wentworths, and Pitts belonged to the same group. The instability of human relations, as well as depressions in political fortune, contributed to the mutability and evanescence characteristic of party. But by the same token it was the positive side of each factor, private connexion and political success, that gave to every group its basic, if temporary, cohesion.

The parliamentary parties comprised most of the active politicians, those engaged in the quest for the favours and offices distributed by the Court. They did not include all Members of Parliament. At the end of Anne's reign it is estimated that men unconnected with any group held nearly 200 of the 558 seats in the House of Commons.² These were the independents, squires, and merchants elected each on his own 'interest', little concerned in national politics, irregular in attendance, unambitious for place. The independent was nevertheless a factor in politics. Parliamentary leaders courted his prejudices and sought his vote, especially during struggles over major issues, when the opinion of the unconnected members often decided the fate of a measure.

¹ J. H. Plumb, *England in the Eighteenth Century* (Harmondsworth, Middlesex, 1950), p. 41.
² *Essays in Modern English History in Honor of Wilbur Cortez Abbott*, p. 130. See the incisive comments of Professor Pares on the independents in *King George III and the Politicians*, pp. 10–15.

Among the parties and independents of which Parliament was composed at the time of the Hanoverian accession there existed certain roughly defined political tendencies derived from personal interest and native conviction.[1] The poles of attraction were Ministry and Opposition, or, in contemporary phraseology, 'Court' and 'Country'. Every individual and group, regardless of party label, was drawn with greater or lesser force in one direction or the other. The Court possessed a bloc of steady adherents, lesser officials and 'Government members' elected for constituencies controlled by the Court, who voted for the ministry of the day no matter what its composition. Closely drawn to the Court also were some independents who thought it their duty to support the sovereign's chosen servants unless Government policy violated their deepest convictions. The political groups included several, bearing one or the other party label, whose primary concern was royal favour. Devoid of other guiding principle, 'Court Whig' groups led by Somerset and Newcastle and 'Court Tory' groups led by Lindsey, Radnor, Pembroke, and Derby, all trimmed their sails to ride before the prevailing political breeze. Throughout the ministerial changes of Anne's reign, they clung consistently to office, co-operating with whomever the Queen called into her service. Altogether, the Court could round up the votes of 100 to 125 'Queen's Servants' in the Lower House.

From these elements so closely attached to the Court, there was a general shading-off to parties with various programmes and loyalties. All would be at Court but not under all conditions, and the intensity of their convictions amid changing circumstances determined whether Court or Country attracted them most strongly. Those labelled Tory, arranged in declining order of docility to the Court, were the connexions led by Marlborough, Oxford, Rochester, Nottingham, and the 'October Club' group of Bolingbroke. On the Whig side, in similar order, stood the Walpole–Townshend party and the galaxy of clans guided by the 'Junto Lords' Halifax, Orford, Somers, Wharton, and Sunderland.

---

[1] The following section is based on Walcott's ground-breaking essay in *Essays in Modern English History in Honor of Wilbur Cortez Abbott*, pp. 81–131. A fuller exposition by the same author is to be found in *English Politics in the Early Eighteenth Century* (Cambridge, Mass., 1956).

Finally came the independents drawn inveterately to opposition, the 'Country members'. Possessed, it would seem, of an instinctive hatred of courts and a rooted distrust of Government, they invariably supported attacks upon the Ministry of the day, usually with a silent vote. 'Country Whigs' and 'Country Tories' tended to vote with others of the same designation but always against the Court. Plain 'Country members', who defied any classification, gave their negatives in every division at which they were present to all ministerial measures.

These were the elements, groups and independents with distinct political tendencies, from whom the sovereign must choose his ministry. At the accession of George I the British Parliament, as Professor Walcott writes,

was divided not into two parties, but into four major segments: Country, Whig, Tory, and Court. Each of these segments was composed in turn of groups of stalwarts together with various border-groups. It is possible, in other words, to read the roster of party groups as though we were boxing the compass: Courtiers, Court Tories, Churchill Tories, Harley Tories, Rochester Tories, Nottingham Tories, October Club Tories, Country Tories, Country members, Country Whigs, Junto Whigs, Walpole–Townshend Whigs, Court Whigs, and so back to the Courtiers. The architects of parliamentary majorities worked within this framework, seeking to combine as many allied groups as possible.[1]

The possibilities were numerous, for the distinction of party names did not prevent Whig and Tory groups from serving in the same ministry. Indeed, under William and Anne the Government included connexions of both types more often than not. Hence the fact that Tories were to be found voting with Whigs against other Tories, as well as the reverse. For the political groups, one must reiterate, their position in or out of office meant more than party label.

In these circumstances every Ministry was necessarily a temporary coalition, and every formed Opposition a rival alliance equally transitory in character. A single connexion might dominate either confederacy, but owing to the personal nature of eighteenth-century party, none could be large enough to comprise the whole. As a rule, however, rival coalitions did not go in or out of place *en bloc*. The seams binding group

[1] *Essays in Modern English History*, p. 131.

alliances, fashioned only for immediate political advantage, wore thin and parted easily under the stress of competition for the prizes of office.[1] Each group sought its fortune by making the most of opportunities as they offered. It was not uncommon for one party in the ministerial coalition to jockey an ally out of office and bring in an opposing clan in order to secure a redistribution of places that enhanced its power. In the same way a group frequently deserted its allies in opposition to seize an offer from the Government, just as the individual members of a group in the political wilderness often abandoned their leader for a more successful rival. Though many a politician clung to his loyalties in the face of misfortune, the normal process was for a party to disintegrate and an alliance to dissolve as soon as the advantages for which they had been formed had disappeared. A change of ministry, therefore, generally took place in the form of a 'reconstruction' rather than a wholesale sweep. Courtiers and Court parties made up a more or less permanent core, about which the sovereign assembled varying combinations of other connexions to form a Government. The combinations were altered at the monarch's will as personal relations and political events made a new coalition expedient. Rarely did more than one or two parties enter the Government at one time, and change usually was moderate and continual, rather than violent and abrupt.

For a wholesale sweep, like that which occurred in 1714, there was only one immediate precedent, but it directly set the stage for the action taken by George I. In 1710 Anne had replaced a coalition composed of Churchill Tories, Court groups, Walpole–Townshend Whigs, and Junto Whigs with a combination of Courtiers and Tory connexions led by Oxford, Rochester, and Bolingbroke. This was the most thoroughgoing overturn since the Revolution. The new Ministry, having persecuted the old with charges and imprisonments, carried out the policy its predecessors most detested by making peace with France. The peace found as little favour with the Elector of Hanover. A member of the anti-French alliance, he considered England a deserter from the common cause. He opposed

---

[1] Swift once referred to 'the old maxim which pronounces court friendships to be of no long duration': Walter Scott, ed., *The Works of Jonathan Swift* (Edinburgh, 1814), vi. 20.

negotiations from the outset;[1] and the final treaties did not satisfy Hanoverian pretensions.[2] Subsequent difficulties over paying off the electoral troops subsidized by Britain further chagrined the future George I.[3]

To these grievances was added the growing suspicion that Oxford's Ministry was preparing the ground for a Jacobite restoration. As early as January 1713 the Elector's private secretary, Robethon, had become deeply concerned in measures to secure his master's claim to the throne and to 'unmask' the Queen's servants.[4] By the same time it is clear that Robethon acted in concert with the parliamentary Opposition. He urged 'Lord Halifax and other friends' in January to propose a Bill to exclude the Pretender 'even though he should become a Protestant'.[5] From March until Anne's death in the following year Hanoverian agents in England, under Robethon's direction, kept in constant communication with Halifax, Townshend, Sunderland, Orford, Somers, and other Whig Opposition leaders, who were always denominated 'our friends'.[6] Meanwhile Marlborough, then in exile on the continent, corresponded frequently with George, from whom he received in April 1713 a secret commission 'to act for the service of your Electoral Highness' when the Queen died.[7] And in April 1714 the Tory Opposition leaders, Nottingham, Anglesea, Hanmer, and the Archbishop of York, joined the cabal of Whigs and Hanoverian agents in London.[8]

---

[1] W. S. Churchill, *Marlborough: His Life and Times* (New York, 1933–8), vi. 475–6, 486–8, 544.

[2] Hanover, along with the other princes of the empire, could not be brought to peace terms until seventeen months after Britain had concluded negotiations. The Treaty of Utrecht was signed on 22 Apr. 1713; the Treaty of Baden on 18 Sept. 1714.

[3] Britain did not make provisions for paying the arrears until after George I's accession: *Parliamentary History*, vii. 7–8.

[4] James Macpherson, *Original Papers; Containing the Secret History of Great Britain, from the Restoration to the Accession of the House of Hanover* (London, 1776), ii. 465, 468, 472. Hanoverian suspicions were not without foundation, though politicians of all hues attempted at this time to 'insure' themselves against a Jacobite restoration by giving fair words to the Pretender: see H. N. Fieldhouse, 'Bolingbroke's Share in the Jacobite Intrigues of 1710–14' in *E.H.R.* lii (1937), 443–59.

[5] Macpherson, *Original Papers*, ii. 464.

[6] Ibid. 475 ff.

[7] Ibid. 488. Cf. W. Coxe, *Memoirs of the Duke of Marlborough* (3rd ed., London, 1847–8), iii. 351.

[8] Macpherson, *Original Papers*, ii. 587–9, 592.

This group took every occasion to fortify the Elector's resentment against the British Ministry. Their masterstroke was to persuade Sophia in April 1714 that she should request the Lord Chancellor to issue a writ of summons to the House of Lords for the Electoral Prince, on the grounds that the presence in England of a member of the Electoral family was necessary to secure the Protestant succession. The sensitive Anne, outraged at the proposal as an impeachment of her integrity and sovereignty, sent a bitter remonstrance to Herrenhausen and forbade the Hanoverian Resident to appear at court.[1] The writ was issued, but the Electoral Prince dared not answer it. For Anne's strong measures her ministers suffered the blame. The objection to the residence of Sophia's grandson gave heightened colour to charges that they laboured for a Stuart restoration.

The Ministry endeavoured to efface the impression made by their opponents. Oxford dispatched his brother as special envoy to Hanover. Both he and Strafford wrote professions of undying attachment to the Electoral family.[2] Neither measure appears to have achieved any success, and as the Queen's death approached, the intensification of a long-standing feud between Oxford and Bolingbroke further weakened the Ministry's position. On 27 July 1714 Bolingbroke secured the dismissal of Oxford as Lord High Treasurer. There followed three days of intrigue and indecision as Anne lapsed into her mortal illness. At last on 30 July the Privy Council persuaded the dying Queen to confer the white staff upon the Courtier Shrewsbury. Within less than forty-eight hours she was dead.

George I thus encountered at his accession a ministry in the process of reconstruction. With his partisans among the Lords Justices in full control, the new King halted further change until Parliament had voted supply and was prorogued.[3] Then the rout of the old Court party began with the dismissal of its leading member. In accordance with instructions from Hanover the Regents deprived Bolingbroke of the Secretary's seals on

---

[1] Macpherson, *Original Papers*, ii. 599, 621. Cf. J. M. Kemble, *State Papers and Correspondence* (London, 1857), pp. 519–28.

[2] Macpherson, *Original Papers*, ii. 567–8, 593–4, 600–3.

[3] 'The parliament being dissolved,' wrote a Hanoverian agent to Robethon on 27 Aug., 'the king will not be troubled with it on his arrival, and will have time to take his measures before he calls another' (ibid. 648).

31 August. A later dispatch conferred them upon Townshend, who was sworn to office on 17 September. Upon his arrival the next day the King treated the old ministerialists with studied frigidity and their opponents with marked favour. Dismissals and appointments ensued almost daily, until by mid-October the Court coalition, except for a few individuals in lesser posts, had been thoroughly reconstituted.[1] The roster of groups in office now read Nottingham Tories, Churchill Tories, Courtiers, Walpole–Townshend Whigs, and the Whig clans of the old Junto. The Opposition confederacy, the chief advisers of Hanoverian policy in England before the accession, had become the Ministry of the new monarch.

3. TYPES OF OPPOSITION

The overturn at Court presented the fallen ministers—the Tory connexions led by Oxford, Rochester, and Bolingbroke—with the alternatives of passive acceptance or the traditional activities of opposition. The former spelled political extinction. The latter kept open the possibility of a return to power. There were in general three types of opposition which had brought success in the past. Each had numerous variations, and they were not mutually exclusive. An individual or a party might indulge in more than one variety at the same time. Contemporaries seldom made formal distinctions among them, for under the existing conditions of political warfare, all types seemed logically complementary methods of achieving the Opposition goal—office under the Crown.

The central position of the king in politics made intrigue at Court, the oldest of all devices, the primary resort of all ambitious men. Those in opposition did not cease to seek royal favour merely because they were temporarily out of place. They continued to explore every channel open to them and to try any means to discredit their rivals or promote their own advantage. For such activity direct contact with the king in person was eminently desirable though difficult to establish. Any peer

---

[1] For a record of these events in the early weeks of the reign, see the journalistic accounts put together by John Oldmixon in his *History of England during the Reigns of King William and Queen Mary, Queen Anne and King George I* (London, 1735), pp. 569–78.

of the realm, provided he was not expressly banned from Court, had the right to demand a royal audience, but, in contemporary idiom, ministers always endeavoured to 'engross the closet'. They looked with a jaundiced eye upon anyone seeking 'the king's ear'. To the best of their ability they obstructed all confidential communication between their master and their rivals and opponents. Furthermore, a minister dismissed from office still bore a few vestigial traces of the 'disgrace' formerly attached to the fallen courtier. He might attend the formal ceremonies to which men of his rank were admitted, but he always risked insult and humiliation by appearing at Court. From the outset George I placed marks of his personal displeasure upon the members of Anne's last Ministry. In his case also the language barrier made communication doubly difficult, for the King, of course, knew no English.

Under such circumstances a party in opposition turned to one of the customary variants: the search for a friend established at Court to lend a helping hand. Possible intermediaries were always numerous in the sovereign's crowded suite. Members of the Government itself might serve the purpose, especially at times when rivalries within the Court coalition subjected it to unusual strains. An active Opposition never ceased to probe for weaknesses in the Ministry, and to negotiate for an ally among the dissentients, for at any breach a friend in the garrison might assist one to a foothold from which to penetrate further as opportunity offered. In the early months of George's reign the bitter political animosities between 'ins' and 'outs', and the general solidarity of the groups in royal favour, made the success of such manœuvres extremely improbable.

But like all his predecessors, the new King surrounded himself with a personal entourage whose interests frequently got entangled in politics. The long train of courtiers and servants that followed George from Herrenhausen included various types, from German nobility to Turkish body servants. Two types were of particular political importance: the Hanoverian ministers and the royal mistresses. The most influential of the former were Bernsdorff, the Hanoverian First Minister of State, Bothmer, the Hanoverian Resident in England, and Robethon, private secretary to the King. Robethon in particular had a good knowledge of English politics. He had served under

William III, and through his correspondence with the Electoral emissaries in England from 1710 to 1714 he had kept abreast of British developments. Bothmer, as chief Hanoverian agent in London immediately before Anne's death, had acquired an extensive acquaintance among the leading British politicians. All three were men of ambition, anxious to profit by the Hanoverian accession. The Act of Settlement excluded them from office, but their private influence with the King made them important intermediaries in Court intrigue.[1]

The royal mistresses, according to general estimate, were distinguished for neither their physical nor their intellectual qualities. But they were indefatigable busybodies at Court. Baroness von der Schulenberg and Baroness Kielmansegge had come to England to improve their fortunes, financially and socially. The only asset of each was her favour with the King, a fact which provoked a natural rivalry between them. Their rivalry in turn made them a prey to contending factions, as indeed contending factions became pawns in their game. The mistresses were willing to espouse the cause of a party with the King in return for suitable rewards.[2] Parties kept a vigilant look-out for opportunities to please one or another of the mistresses. Success at Court was presumed to depend upon rendering the proper service to the lady in highest favour at the moment.

To intrigue at the royal Court there was a generic alternative or perhaps concomitant: intrigue at another court. Such activity constituted a second basic type of opposition. Its methods did not differ in kind from those of the first, but its hopes of fulfilment lay, not in the present reign, but in the future. The other courts to which an Opposition might turn were the retinue of a rival for the Crown and the household of the heir to the throne. Favour in either of these quarters promised success at some indefinite date when the existing régime came to an end through rebellion or the demise of the Crown. Hence, the dimmer a party's chances of achieving its goal at the royal Court, the greater was its activity at one or both of the others.

Support of a rival claimant to the Crown involved *de facto*

---

[1] Wolfgang Michael, *England under George I: The Beginnings of the Hanoverian Dynasty* (trans. L. B. Namier, London, 1936), i. 90–92, 103–6.

[2] Ibid. 81–83.

treason. In the final analysis success depended upon armed force. Historically its nature was essentially feudal. John's barons had turned to Prince Louis, the magnates of Richard II to Henry of Lancaster. Opposing factions had seated and deposed their royal candidates for a generation in the fifteenth century. The most recent examples were the disastrous rebellion of 1685 and the successful Revolution of 1688. At the Hanoverian accession the Jacobite camp in Lorraine afforded a rival court for Opposition intrigue. Statutes made it treason even to correspond with James the 'Old Pretender', but the law was hard to enforce. Jacobite agents kept open the line of communications to Bar-le-Duc, where the 'Chevalier de St. George' held out his hands for aid from every quarter.[1] Any opponent of the Hanoverian Court could be sure of a welcome, perhaps a place or title, and promises of rich rewards upon a Stuart restoration. The hazards were great, but in 1714, at the end of three generations of political turmoil and instability, another 'glorious revolution' did not seem beyond the bounds of possibility.

The lawful heir to the throne offered brighter and less perilous opportunities. Barring revolution or premature death, he must one day succeed. The older the reigning monarch, the sooner would the heir come into his patrimony. He was, as politicians later called him, a 'reversionary resource', and his Court naturally tended to become a veritable cave of Adullam. Historians have attempted in many ways to account for the constantly recurring animosity between the English monarchs and their heirs, and the Hanoverians have undergone especial criticism as shabby fathers and fractious sons. But whatever may have been their innate qualities, the nature of political warfare did much to force divisions between them. 'Future interests' drew opposition groups to the heir's Court, and for them to accentuate every difference was the surest means of guaranteeing that the son on his accession would displace his father's ministers in their favour. This practice, moreover, had solid precedents in the immediate past. The groups clustered about the Princess Anne in William's reign had stirred her to an abiding discontent at the King's treatment, and they had

---

[1] The chief Jacobite agent in England, the Abbé Gaultier, returned to the Continent at the end of August 1714, but correspondence with the Pretender's Court continued: see *The Lockhart Papers* (London, 1817), i. 484.

reaped a bumper crop of rewards when she came to the throne.[1] In similar fashion had the coalition placed in office by George I secured his favour while he was yet only heir presumptive. Not only was this a successful way to power, but it had the additional advantage of being free of any treasonous taint. In an age of disputed successions, nothing gave greater proof of loyalty than an attachment to the rightful heir.

George Augustus, Duke of Cambridge, accompanied his father to England. Seven days after their arrival the son was created Prince of Wales by a patent in which the King declared him 'a prince whose eminent filial piety has always endeared him to us'.[2] No evidence existed to refute the formal statement. But as the natural object of attention from the Opposition, George Augustus had little chance of maintaining his reputation.

The location of powers in the Constitution made favour at Court so vital a factor in political success that, at first blush, it may seem anomalous for there to have been any form of opposition which invited royal displeasure. Yet the third type, opposition in Parliament, clearly ran that risk. The odds lay heavily against the King's patronizing of his own free will those who attacked his ministers and their policies. The sovereign inevitably tolerated the ceaseless intrigue for place that went on about his person, but under the conventions of the Constitution, not to mention human inclinations, he could hardly be expected to open his arms to the avowed enemies of his chosen servants. For the unambitious 'Country member' to exercise his right of free speech by criticizing the Government was natural enough; he had nothing to lose. A group which had cast its lot wholly with a pretender or a disgruntled heir might logically gamble on resistance *à outrance* to the existing régime; in such a case royal enmity could be an advantage. But, in defiance of conventional reason, parties in quest of immediate preferment constantly laid themselves open to proscription at Court by conducting a 'formed general opposition' in both Houses of Parliament.

It was a calculated risk. The first Lord Clarendon expressed it best in his analysis of the Opposition to Charles I in 1641:

---

[1] See *An Account of the Conduct of the Dowager Duchess of Marlborough, from her First Coming to Court to the Year 1710* (London, 1742).

[2] Oldmixon, *History of England*, p. 577.

'they endeavoured', he wrote, 'by doing all the hurt they could to make evident the power they had to do him good.'[1] Parliamentary opposition was, in other words, a form of advertisement, with several contingencies in mind. A king sometimes bought off an able opponent: so Charles I had taken Wentworth into his service. Persistent and resolute opposition had high 'nuisance value'; if the king's affairs in Parliament were sufficiently distressed, he might find it expedient to calm the turmoil by placating its agitators. So in 1640 Charles I had sworn to the Privy Council in a single day seven of the Opposition Lords, all of whom were in 'visible disfavour' at Court, and Pym and Bedford envisaged even greater results from continuing the assault on the Government.[2] Moreover, parliamentary opposition provided the Crown with obvious candidates for office in the event of a change in royal policy. As in Anne's reign, the opponents of a war could be called in to make peace. There was sound method in the seeming madness of abusing the royal policy and its advocates.

Yet, because of the risk involved, parliamentary opposition was not to be entered upon for light and transient causes. A deposed ministry did not automatically engage in sustained assault upon its successors. Other tactics might prove wiser, at least until the king's disposition and the Ministry's plans became evident beyond mistake. Furthermore, to be effective, opposition had to be organized, and in the state of party, organization was a difficult and laborious task. Unlike the Ministry, Opposition had no facilities for co-ordinating its efforts. Government members met at the Cockpit in Whitehall; scribes at the Treasury or the Secretary of State's office provided them with a secretariat; the royal mails carried their communications; Government funds and patronage constituted a 'war chest' for the Court party. An Opposition had to rely upon its own resources: a private house or tavern for meetings; personal secretaries or their own hands for correspondence; their own pockets for funds; and often their own servants for communication because the Post Office opened the mail of Government opponents. In the face of such difficulties it

---

[1] Earl of Clarendon, *The History of the Rebellion and Civil Wars in England* (Oxford, 1888), bk. iv, para. 77.
[2] Ibid., bk. iii, paras. 49–50.

required leadership, tact, and vision to achieve cohesion among several groups which often had little in common save being out of office. Long-range plans were impossible, with the result that party co-operation seldom survived a session, and Opposition had to be new-modelled before the next meeting. At the opening of Parliament the question faced by the Ministry often was not what the Opposition would do, but whether there would be an Opposition.

Nor did there exist any conventions to facilitate the formation and functioning of an organized Opposition. Parliamentary procedure, it is true, was 'a procedure of opposition, designed to protect a minority'.[1] The rules allowed free criticism of the Government and provided ample means for obstruction and debate. Herein consisted the basic condition for the development of parliamentary opposition. But the employment of the opportunities offered under the rules of procedure depended entirely upon the initiative of the opposer, whose activities never received positive encouragement from the Speaker, normally a Government partisan up to this time.[2] Nothing called an Opposition into existence as a matter of form. Neither orders nor usage assigned any responsibilities to those out of office. No 'question hour' provided a regular means of raising embarrassing issues. Neither House accorded the Opposition a place to sit, a condition that hindered co-ordination of effort and gave the Government a considerable advantage over its opponents.

Since the sixteenth century the Ministry had pre-empted the most desirable seats. Hooker's treatise, written about 1586, states, 'Upon the lower row on both sides the Speaker sit such personages as be of the King's Privy Council or of his chief officers, but as for any other, none claimeth nor can claim any

---

[1] Sir William Holdsworth, *A History of English Law* (London, 1903–38), x. 536. Cf. C. Strateman, *The Liverpool Tractate* (New York, 1937), pp. lxi–lxii.

[2] By the reign of James I it had been clearly established that the Speaker should enforce the rules of the House without partiality (Hatsell, *Precedents of Proceedings*, ii. 227, 231). In the overwhelming majority of cases, however, he continued to be a nominee of the Court, often holding concurrently a place of profit under the Crown, and maintaining his control over the proceedings of the House, he co-operated closely with the ministers in putting Government Bills through. Thus, though perforce a jealous guardian of parliamentary rights and privileges, the Speaker could hardly be expected to have any inclination to forward the establishment of a favoured position for Opposition.

place, but sitteth as he cometh.'[1] Some evidence near the end
of Elizabeth's reign suggests that the opponents of Government
had established a 'rebellious corner in the right hand of the
House', that is, on the Speaker's left.[2] No general usage developed, however. In the Long Parliament of Charles I the
root-and-branch men apparently tended to cluster on the
south side of the House, opposite the Treasury Bench, but Pym
and Hampden led the Opposition from cross benches facing the
chair.[3] After the Restoration the debates afford numerous
indications that, on specific occasions, the 'Country party'
occupied seats on the Speaker's left.[4] The poet Marvell in 1667
described 'the Court and Country both set right on opposite
points', like 'the black against the white' on a backgammon
board.[5] An Opposition nevertheless had established no pre-
scriptive right to its future location, as by courtesy the House
allotted the Treasury Bench to the Ministry. The benches next
to the table on the Speaker's left, prized because of the advantages they gave in debate, went to those who claimed them first.

The absence of procedural conventions underlines the fact
that in 1714 parliamentary opposition had no recognized institutional existence. For generations men in Parliament had attacked royal policy, not merely from prejudice or conviction,
but with a view to attaining office; yet so irregular had been
their activities, so fragmentary and evanescent the nature of
party, that no permanent impression had been made upon the
British Constitution. Nothing in parliamentary practice assumed
or required the presence of an Opposition, nor had it even
acquired its name. Contemporary idiom spoke of 'opposition'
to a Bill, a policy, a ministry, the Court; a candidate encountered 'opposition' in an election.[6] The parties intent upon

---

[1] *Holinshed's Chronicles of England, Scotland, and Ireland* (London, 1807–8), vi. 352.
[2] A. F. Pollard and M. Blatcher, 'Hayward Townshend's Journals', *Bull. Inst.
Hist. Res.* xii. 20.
[3] G. M. Trevelyan, *England under the Stuarts* (London, 1930), pp. 212–13.
[4] B. D. Henning, ed., *The Parliamentary Diary of Sir Edward Dering* (New Haven,
1940), pp. 128–9; Anchitel Grey, *Debates of the House of Commons from the Year 1667
to the Year 1694* (London, 1769), ii. 52; iii. 342; v. 314–15; W. D. Christie, ed.,
Letters Addressed from London to Sir James Williamson (Camden Soc., 1874), ii. 156.
[5] H. M. Margoliouth, ed., *The Poems and Letters of Andrew Marvell* (Oxford, 1927),
i. 143.
[6] For some examples, see *Harleian Miscellany*, vi. 304; viii. 186; *H.M.C., Portland
MSS.* v. 311, 351–3, 384.

wresting power from the Ministry were never designated 'the Opposition'.[1] Various other terms described them: 'the Country party' or the 'discontented party', 'patriots', 'malcontents', or 'grumbletonians' were the appellations in commonest use. To 'Country party' was attached a certain dignity. It was the term 'Opposition' applied to itself, as establishing a claim to represent the interests of the Country against those of the Court. Ministerialists regarded the distinction as invidious and the dignity as false. The other appellations were deliberately opprobrious, the inventions of the Court party. None implied that opposition was a permanent institution of government.

4. POLITICAL THEORY

Such an implication must, in any case, be somewhat illogical in the light of reigning political theory. All men agreed in the abstract that party was no more than faction, an evil to be surmounted and eventually destroyed. The prevalent ideal called for national unanimity beneath the sovereign, not party rivalry among his subjects. Furthermore, if the King rightfully made national policy and chose the ministers to be its executors, the Constitution had no place for an element designed to force his hand. Oppositions had struggled for years with this difficulty, how to square practice with theory. Clearly they could not admit that their actions were unconstitutional. They had to find a plausible way to circumvent the indefeasible royal prerogative. Under the Stuarts they slowly evolved a doctrine of justification out of legal axioms, political theory, and 'enlightened reasoning'. The doctrine remained imperfect and full of contradictions in 1714, and it had by no means gained general

---

[1] The *Oxford English Dictionary* finds the first modern usage of the term in a letter by Charles Davenant in 1704: 'They who shall form oppositions hereafter will be thought to be bribed by France' (Sir H. Ellis, *Original Letters Illustrative of English History* (London, 1825–46), 2nd ser. iv. 244). But the sentence refers to the Scottish Parliament, and from the context it appears that Davenant conceived of 'oppositions' as 'formed' against measures or policies rather than against the Government with a view to its dissolution. At this time 'opposition' still bore a rather sinister connotation; somewhat akin to 'resistance', in the manner used by Locke: 'That force is to be opposed to nothing but unjust and unlawful force. Whoever makes any opposition in any other case draws on himself a just condemnation, both from God and man': *Of Civil Government* (Everyman ed., p. 220). Cf. Wake MSS. xv, cited in Basil Williams, *Stanhope* (Oxford, 1932), pp. 399–400.

acceptance. Rather, it served as a working hypothesis for parliamentary opposition.

At the core of the doctrine lay the medieval maxim, 'the king can do no wrong'. Originally the embodiment of the principle that the sovereign cannot take illegal action against his subjects, the aphorism had undergone a reversal of meaning by the seventeenth century. Its revised construction possessed a two-fold significance: no wrongful act or intent can be attributed to the king, and if evil be designed or done in his name, the blame rests upon his agents, who are responsible for their actions and liable to punishment at law. Accurate interpretation of this principle applied it to strictly legal matters, but Oppositions transferred its application to politics. They thereby established the important fiction that any royal policy which they opposed as evil was an emanation, not of the king, but of his servants; and an attack upon the Ministry and its measures became compatible with unswerving loyalty to the Crown.[1] The deist Toland summarized the concept in these words: 'none are truer friends to His Majesty than such as most vigourously oppose the men who thus plainly abuse him. They are heartily for the present Government, though not always for the present way of governing.'[2] Construed in this fashion, the ancient legal maxim opened the way for an assault on 'evil advisers', whom Parliament should in duty pull down and submit to condign chastisement.

Thus far the argument met with little resistance, nor did it trench directly upon the royal prerogative. The Duchess of Marlborough stated it clearly in 1718 when she wrote 'that Parliaments should punish ill ministers, and by that means oblige weak or bad princes to keep their coronation oaths, and for their rewards I think they should bestow them as they please without being imposed upon by the tenders of either party.'[3] In this form the doctrine did no more than to justify the already legal but ineffective machinery for impeachment, attainder, and addresses for the removal of a minister. Yet within it lay one glaring contradiction. If one cannot impute

---

[1] See B. Behrens, 'The Whig Theory of the Constitution in the Reign of Charles II' in *Cambridge Historical Journal*, vii (1941), 56–57.

[2] *The Art of Governing by Partys*, p. 103.

[3] *H.M.C., Morrison MSS.* (Rep. 9, App. ii), p. 474.

wrongdoing or evil intent to the king, how can one assume that he may be 'weak or bad'? Is the king, to whose care the welfare of the realm is entrusted, incapable of recognizing evil advice?

They are greatly mistaken, [wrote Toland in William's reign], who think the actions of any prince will be excused by laying the blame on his ministers: 'tis a common manner of speaking indeed, but at bottom a modest way of censuring the prince himself, who, if he did not approve their conduct, might easily make a better choice. We find all things laid to the charge of evil counsellors in His Majesty's [William III's] own declaration; yet King James was justly deposed, and his counsellors ought as justly to have been hanged at that time, instead of being at any time since or now preferred.[1]

Oppositions found two ways to resolve the incongruity. One was to ignore it. 'Evil counsellors' was so ancient and honoured a battlecry that it required no justification. The second was to construct another fiction: weak or bad kings have lived in the past and may appear in the future, but the reigning sovereign is so pure and innocent that bad men can impose upon him. The best of kings might have the worst of counsellors. This brittle proposition afforded a reasonably tenable position in parliamentary debate,[2] but the incongruity continued to plague Oppositions for years to come. The Hanoverians found it hard to accept a theory that made them witless dupes and their policies the work of vicious rogues.

Yet freedom to attack the Government, and no more, gave Opposition only a passively critical role, with the constitutional right to participate in the chastisement of the guilty. At this point the 'Country member' was willing to stop. For the office-seeker the battle had just begun. He had necessarily to push Opposition doctrine one step further. Since the king still possessed in practice the power to retain 'evil advisers' and in theory the right to replace any duly convicted, nothing guaranteed that the supposed maladministration should not continue. In other words, even if Parliament pulled down a courtier and his associates, an Opposition had no assurance that it would succeed them in office. In an effort to get over this difficulty, politicians had resort to a simple line of reasoning. 'The great

---

[1] *The Art of Governing by Partys*, pp. 110–11.
[2] For example, see *Parliamentary History*, vii. 53, 565–6.

patriots', wrote Clarendon of Pym's party in 1641, 'thought
that they might be able to do their country better service if they
got the places and preferments in the Court, and so prevented
the evil counsels which had used to spring from thence.'[1] What
more natural than that those who had detected and perhaps
rooted out an evil to which the king had been blind should take
a place in the management of national affairs? Must not the
opposers of wrong themselves be right? Did not His Majesty lie
under moral obligation to employ those who sought to rescue
him from evil that they might do good? When so framed, the
questions answered themselves.

Oppositions had employed this line of reasoning indirectly
in specific cases. When excoriating pernicious counsels, pamphleteers referred to the excellence and public spirit of the
ministerial talent neglected by the Crown.[2] In partisan debate,
ex-ministers compared the laudable policies they had pursued
in office with the disastrous measures now in train, to establish
by implication a virtuous claim to employment.[3] But, within
the limits of accepted constitutional doctrine, it was impossible
to insist as a general principle that any putative moral obligation bound the sovereign in his use of the prerogative. The
imposition of restrictions smacked of republicanism, as in the
argument developed by John Toland out of pseudo-history and
Algernon Sidney's *Discourses*:

> Machiavel says very truly [Toland wrote in 1701] that the wisdom
> of a prince never takes beginning from the wisdom of his council,
> but the wisdom of the council always from the wisdom of the prince.
> If, therefore, our future kings either want the mind or the ability to
> choose the fittest persons into their ministry to serve the nation, the
> Parliament will be obliged to recommend such as shall be answerable
> to the public for their actions: and yet do nothing herein but what
> (as has been often proved) their ancestors have commonly practised:
> for the Lord Chancellor of England, the Lord High Admiral of
> England, the Lord Treasurer of England, the Lord Chief Justice of
> England, and all the officers that have the name of England added

---

[1] Clarendon, *History of the Rebellion*, bk. iii, paras. 83–84.

[2] For examples, see *Somers Tracts* (2nd ed., London, 1815), xiii. 75–85, 120–40,
245–87. As an interesting variant, see *Some Reasons for a Change in the Ministry*
(London, 1717).

[3] Such was the general line of the Whig 'outs' from 1710 to 1714; in particular,
see the utterances of Marlborough, Godolphin, and Argyll in *P.H.* vi. 1146–7, 1336.

to them, were formerly nominated (as a late author tells us) by the representatives of the people of England assembled in Parliament. Nor would it be any wonder should they resume this power, if ever the worst ministers of the late reigns, the declared enemies of the present Government, or any of those evil counsellors so dreadfully described in His Majesty's declaration, should be thought the only men fit to serve him: while those are neglected or mistrusted who invited him hither, placed the crown on his head, and faithfully served him against all his enemies at home and abroad.[1]

The doctrine of popular election clearly implicit in Toland's words was too radical for general acceptance in 1714, for so indefeasible was the king's right to chose his own ministers that no office-seeker could openly avow an argument which subjected it to non-legal restraint. The 'Country party' had perforce to assume the formal pose of unambitious and selfless devotion to the commonweal, declaring perhaps a loyal willingness to accept a summons to service, but denying emphatically every intention of forcing the king's hand.

Organized parliamentary opposition, designed to make its way into office, was thus driven into an extra-constitutional position. The pleas made in its justification could not stand up against the prevailing interpretation of the Constitution, for parliamentary freedom to criticize government, the hard-won privilege of the individual conscience, did not extend to premeditated obstruction or aggressive opposition. The world of politics recognized the actual existence of political discord but with lamentation and regret. In the first days after George I's accession Sir John Perceval expressed a trite sentiment with a Whiggish tinge when he wrote to a Tory correspondent

there can justly be no reason to keep up our divisions when the King is once happily seated on the throne, but . . . parties are exceeding high, and the disdain to see the opposite side enjoy most favour, together with the practices of some leading Tories who have no preferment and now despair of any or think to lose those [*sic*] they have, will certainly occasion the continuance of our parties for some time.[2]

There never seemed to be any immediate way to prevent the

---

[1] *The Art of Governing by Partys*, pp. 111–12; cf. Algernon Sidney, *Discourses Concerning Government* (London, 1698), ch. ii, sect. xx.

[2] P.R.O., Egmont MSS. 234: Perceval to George Berkeley, 31 Aug. 1714; cf. *H.M.C., Marchmont MSS.*, p. 162.

continuance of organized opposition, since, in the philosophic view, it too often arose from the envy, malice, and greed of man. However much one might applaud parliamentary resistance to tyranny in general, or the attack upon some policy or ministry in particular, one could not sanction a permanent separation of the political nation into warring camps. In 1714 the common attitude of preceding generations still obtained: Britain did not feel the development of parliamentary opposition would be a beneficent institution, but looked forward rather to the coming of a king whose virtue and wisdom would 'heal our unhappy divisions'.

5. THE TORIES' DESCENT INTO OPPOSITION

The Tory groups composing Anne's last Ministry had when in office taken the customary strong stand against opposition. The most systematic exposition of their defence is contained in a pamphlet of 1712 attributed to Jonathan Swift and entitled *Some Reasons to Prove that No Person is Obliged by his Principles as a Whig to Oppose Her Majesty or Her Present Ministry, in a Letter Addressed to a Whig Lord.* No basic principle split the contending parties, Swift argued, for 'the dispute at present lies altogether between those who would support and those who would violate the royal prerogative'.[1] Upon this point there could be no honest debate:

The two chief, or indeed the only, topics of quarrel are whether the Q[ueen] shall choose her own servants? and whether she shall keep her prerogative of making peace? And I believe there is no Whig in England that will openly deny her power in either. But I suppose, my Lord, you will not make a difficulty of confessing the true genuine cause of animosity to be that those who are out of place would fain be in; and that the bulk of your party are the dupes of half a dozen who are impatient at their loss of power.[2]

If you fail to support these selfish leaders, Swift continued, you fear the charge of 'forsaking your friends', but that is 'a new party-figure of speech which I cannot comprehend'. It can have no legitimate meaning, for 'will you declare you cannot serve your Q—— unless you choose her m——ry?'[3]

---

[1] *Some Reasons to Prove*, p. 4.   [2] Ibid., pp. 9–10.
[3] Ibid., p. 12.

Having demolished any justification for the Opposition, Swift went on to condemn its methods by comparison with those previously employed by his own party:

If your Lordship will please to consider the behaviour of the Tories during the long period of this reign while their adversaries were in power, you will find it very different from that of your party at present . . . you cannot give a single instance where the least violation hath been offered to Her Majesty's undoubted prerogative in either House by the Lords or Commons of our side. We should have been glad indeed to have seen affairs in other management; yet we never attempted to bring it about by stirring up the city, or inviting foreign ministers to direct the Q—— in the choice of her servants, much less by infusing jealousies into the next heir. Endeavours were not publicly used to blast the credit of the nation and discourage foreigners from trusting their money in our funds. Nor were writers suffered openly and in weekly papers to revile persons in the highest employments. In short, if you can prove where the course of affairs under the late Ministry was any way clogged by the Church party, I will freely own the latter to have so far acted against reason and duty.[1]

Such disloyal activity, the argument proceeded, is made worse by the pettiness of its character and the meanness of its motive:

Why all this industry to ply you with letters, messages, and visits for carrying some peevish vote, which only serves to display inveterate pride, ill nature, and disobedience without effect? Though you are flattered it must possibly make the Crown and Ministry so uneasy as to bring on the necessity of a change: which, however, is at best a design but ill becoming a good subject or a man of honour.[2]

Finally, concluded Swift, Opposition cannot hope for success because the Queen has resolutely determined to support her servants with all her royal influence.[3]

Now upon Anne's demise the ministerial coalition, whom Swift had exalted above the base arts of opposition, faced a calamitous situation. The feud between Bolingbroke and Oxford had divided their ranks and deprived them of authoritative leadership. Serious differences of opinion hampered any effort to renew close co-operation, for the component parties included convinced Jacobites, equally determined advocates of the Protestant succession, and others racked by indecision at the

[1] Ibid., pp. 14–15.   [2] Ibid., p. 16.   [3] Ibid., p. 18.

demoralizing suddenness of the Queen's death. Of one thing only were all equally certain: the inveterate hostility of the new King. George had made no secret of his dislike for their measures, and they could anticipate little favour upon his accession. The King's nomination of Lords Justices, known early in the morning of 1 August, confirmed their fears. Though five members of the Ministry sat on the Regency by virtue of their offices, the King's list of nineteen included but two members of the Court coalition: the Courtier Shrewsbury and Anglesey, who was a member of the Hanoverian cabal. Since hasty overtures made separately by Oxford and Bolingbroke to the expectantly triumphant Whig groups during Anne's dying days had met with a cold response, no quarter could be expected at their hands. The sovereign's absence deepened the dilemma and prolonged the suspense. Had George I, whether in England or Hanover, taken immediate steps to dismiss the Queen's servants, he might have driven them into some united course of action. The delay left them uncertain in the face of a paradoxical conjuncture where the 'Country party' was out of place but the 'Court party' was out of power.

Less than two hours after the Queen's death, six of the leading Tory Courtiers met to consider what lay before them. Bolingbroke, Harcourt, Ormonde, Bathurst, and Wyndham seem to have been hesitant and uncertain. Only Francis Atterbury, Bishop of Rochester, had a positive plan: to proclaim the Pretender, marshal a military force under the Captain-General Ormonde, and seek aid from France to secure a Stuart restoration. It was a natural opposition platform, 'opposing a Tory king to a Whig king', as Bolingbroke later called it.[1] Furthermore, although none of them seems to have committed himself to any explicit plot upon the Queen's death, these Tory leaders had dallied for years with the Jacobites and their agents. But Bolingbroke himself demurred—'all our throats would be cut'— and filibustered till Atterbury quit the meeting in dudgeon and despair.[2] The remainder apparently took no resolution. If they

---

[1] 'A Letter to Sir William Wyndham' in *The Works of Lord Bolingbroke* (Philadelphia, 1841), i. 166; G. H. Rose, ed., *A Selection from the Papers of the Earls of Marchmont* (London, 1831), i. 185–7.

[2] This account of the Tory meeting was given by the Jacobite admiral George Camocke to William Stanhope, British Ambassador to Spain, at Madrid, in August 1722 (Add. MSS. 35837, ff. 509). Thomas Carte recorded in 1725–6

did, their subsequent actions indicate that it must have been to talk and act loyally, await events, and salvage what they could from the wreckage.[1]

All the Tory ministers took their new oaths of office, and at one time or another in the ensuing weeks every one of them, in writing or in speech, declared his submission and devotion to the Hanoverian King. But, like feudal barons making their homage, each one spoke for himself alone. Atterbury urged Harcourt 'to write, not merely as a single person, but in some measure as the head of an interest; this I could wish your lordship would do; and would take steps proper to enable you to do it, but I do not find your lordship so disposed'.[2] Nor was any besides Harcourt willing to assume the lead. Each seems to have thought his best interests lay in acting an individual part, and at one juncture the Earl of Mar stated his hopes and plans quite frankly. When informed that his friends in Scotland were going to desert him, Mar wrote to his brother on 7 August:

> Though I say it who should not, I can make as good terms for [*sic*] the other side for myself as any of them, and I will not be made the fool of the play; though they shall not have me to complain of first. That of Jacobitism, which they used to brand the Tories with, is now I presume out of doors, and the King has better understanding than to make himself but king of one party, and though the Whigs may get the better with him at first, other folks will be in safety, and may have their turn with him too. I know very well people have been at pains to represent me very unfavourably to the King for some years past, but as that was all calumny and out of party design, he will find in time that there was nothing in it; and one prince seldom likes a man the worse for serving his predecessor faithfully and with zeal. For several reasons I do not expect to continue in the post I now hold [Secretary of State for Scotland], but if I be paid my arrears, which I have reason to hope I will, I shall not much regret that loss. And then I must do the best I can for myself.[3]

---

that some of the Jacobites thought Bolingbroke so lukewarm for the cause in 1714 because he had on foot a scheme to secure the favour of the House of Hanover (Macpherson, *Original Papers*, ii. 529–34).

[1] Later that day all but Atterbury signed the document proclaiming the new King and took part in the procession behind the heralds who read the proclamation at four places in London and Westminster (Oldmixon, *History of England*, p. 564).

[2] J. Nichols, ed., *The Miscellaneous Works of Bishop Atterbury* (London, 1789), ii. 13.

[3] *H.M.C.*, *Mar and Kellie MSS.*, p. 505.

Events were to reveal a tenuous solidarity within some groups of the coalition, but the words and deeds of the chiefs suggest that, *mutatis mutandis*, their designs did not differ from that of Mar. Their declarations to the King, in keeping with their intentions, breathed the common sentiments of the faithful but unselfish courtier: an eagerness to serve the new King, as they had the late Queen, 'with constancy and fidelity . . . whether at Court, in Parliament, or in my Country'.[1]

The ministerial Tories lived up to their professions in the brief session of the old Parliament. They moved to add £300,000 to the Civil List, but gave it up as overzealous. They supported a motion to pay the arrears due the Hanoverian troops, with elaborate apologies for having previously voted against it. They tactfully submitted to a proposal to offer a £100,000 reward for apprehending the Pretender. Although there was a mild dispute over the chairmanship of the Committee of Supply, not a single division marred the proceedings.[2] Toward the end of the session, Lord Strafford's brother observed:

At present the strife is who shall show themselves the most zealous for the present King George, which is some disappointment to the leading Whigs, for they did expect some opposition in the manner of granting the Civil List, which the less experienced Tories were ready to give, but they were better advised by the wiser, who are for proposing everything that's for the honour and dignity of the Crown, so much that some people out of doors of both parties begin to fear that we shall have the rights and liberties of Englishmen complimented away.[3]

This superficial unanimity clearly portended that, until the King further showed his hand, there would be no opposition. Throughout August the Tories kept their hopes up,[4] and some at least among their opponents thought the King would not turn out the entire Ministry. On the day of Bolingbroke's dismissal, Sir John Perceval prophesied that all the Secretary's friends must go, but 'so many Tories have withdrawn

---

[1] Gilbert Parke, *Letters and Correspondence, Public and Private, of the Right Honourable Henry St. John, Lord Viscount Bolingbroke* (London, 1798), iv. 646; *H.M.C., Dartmouth MSS.*, p. 320; [Thomas Stackhouse], *Memoirs of the Life and Conduct of Dr. Francis Atterbury* (London, 1723), p. 73.

[2] *Parliamentary History*, vii. 3–11. Cf. Add. MSS. 22221, f. 127.

[3] J. J. Cartwright, ed., *The Wentworth Papers, 1705-39* (London, 1883), p. 415.

[4] F. E. Ball, ed., *The Correspondence of Jonathan Swift* (London, 1911), ii. 220–37.

themselves [i.e. their support] from the late Ministry that His Majesty must needs be convinced there are those of that name who will deserve his favour, and such I believe will meet with it'.¹ Bolingbroke himself despaired and looked about for the materials to form an Opposition. 'I see plainly that the Tory party is gone,' he wrote, 'numbers are still left, and those numbers will be increased by such as have not their expectations answered. But where are the men of business that will live and draw together?'² His question went unanswered, as his former colleagues clung to their offices and upon the King's arrival 'pressed with equal zeal to demonstrate their affections to His Majesty's person as could the other party'.³

George I's cold reception of their advances and his prompt dismissal of the other leading ministers dampened their hopes. Many of their old supporters, sensing the trend, fell away from them. 'The Queen's poor servants,' wrote Arbuthnot on 19 October, 'are, like so many poor orphans, exposed in the very streets, and those, whose past obligations of gratitude and honour ought to have engaged them to have represented their case, pass by them like so many abandoned creatures'.⁴ Still no one resigned, for it might 'be thought to slight the service'.⁵ While they took some comfort from reported quarrels among the Whigs over the division of the spoils, each awaited with feigned composure the notice that the King had no further use for his services. As late as November Bathurst still hoped to turn the tide if only they could get someone next to the King 'who might show him the true interest of the nation'. He wrote to Strafford, then still acting as plenipotentiary to the States General at The Hague,

I own I heartily wish that your lordship were in England. You cannot easily imagine of what consequence it might be, but when you consider that there has not yet been above one person of consideration who has had any opportunity of laying the true status of matters before him, you will be more inclined to believe what I say. The Duke of Sh[rewsbury] is the only man that I know that has had

¹ Perceval to George Berkeley, 31 Aug. 1714: P.R.O., Egmont MSS. 234.
² F. Williams, ed., *Memoirs and Correspondence of Francis Atterbury* (London, 1869), i. 279–80.
³ Perceval's Diary, October 1714: P.R.O., Egmont MSS. 234.
⁴ Ball, ed., *Correspondence of Swift*, ii. 245–6.
⁵ *Wentworth Papers*, pp. 426–8.

it in his power to talk with him of our side, and whether he has had any great opportunity, or made all the use of it that he might have done, is what I can't determine. The advantage your lordship had of an easy conversation with him abroad and of being master of the languages he speaks (which by the by has been a sad defect in some of our friends) might have had considerable effects.[1]

Only with the greatest reluctance could an Opposition surrender the hope of achieving results by improved relations at Court.

Shortly before the Coronation, however, a minor transaction had revealed a stiffening of the Tory attitude in at least one quarter. Apparently under the influence of Bothmer's moderating councils, the King offered lucrative posts in the Exchequer not only to Sir Thomas Hanmer, a Tory member of the Hanoverian cabal, but also to William Bromley, who had been Bolingbroke's colleague as Secretary of State. Both 'wavered extremely at the beginning', Perceval was informed,

figuring undoubtedly to themselves that we now are under a reign that would govern with steady hands, and not be turned and disconcerted by the opposition which a party should make to his [*sic*] Ministry, and consequently that if they should now refuse the favour of the Crown, they could not justly or reasonably expect ever for the future to be taken into play. . . .

However, these two gentlemen were prevailed on by the tempting ambition of appearing generals of a party, and the hopes after distressing the Government to have their choice of the best offices; their party having assured them that they would stand fast to them, and laying before them the justice due to themselves, and the interest that would accrue by making their bottom broader when in place by the support of all their friends coming into employment with them. These and such like arguments were successfully urged to them,

and so Hanmer and Bromley declined the offers with elaborate excuses.[2]

In view of the advantages to be gained by having a foothold at Court it may seem surprising both that their friends took such a stand and that they themselves succumbed to such pressure. But the posts offered did not give their holders direct

---

[1] Add. MSS. 22221, ff. 129–30.
[2] Perceval's Diary, October 1714: P.R.O., Egmont MSS. 234.

access to the King, and all evidently dreaded the break-up of their connexion more than they prized the limited benefits of minor offices. The party feared that the comforts of profitable but uninfluential places would seduce the leaders from their political allegiance, depriving the followers of all chance for preferment. Hanmer and Bromley regarded isolation in office with alarm. The former told 'his intimate friends', according to Perceval, who was one of them, that 'he could not in prudence accept places which did not admit him into His Majesty's schemes of government, but when conferred on him, would lose him the dependence of his friends and then leave him at the mercy of his enemies'.[1]

The event clearly suggests that by early October some among the Tory groups had resolved upon the eventual necessity of parliamentary opposition. Their electoral activity confirms the impression. Whether in or out of office, the members of all parties, knowing that a dissolution must come within the first six months of the reign, naturally 'made interest' promptly in their constituencies. Electioneering had begun immediately following the prorogation in August.[2] After the ministerial changes executed upon the King's arrival in mid-September, activity was intensified. The Whigs and their allies accompanied savage charges of treason and sedition against 'the late Queen's servants' with the wholesale removal of opponents from numerous minor offices which commanded considerable influence in elections.[3] The new Government obviously intended to exert the full force of the 'influence of the Crown' against the old Court party. In the face of such an attack, the ousted Tories found it impossible to maintain the pose of courtly resignation which they had adopted both in Parliament and in their declarations to the new monarch. The ministerial campaign constituted a threat not only to their political careers but also to their electoral 'interests', their property, their 'estates'

---

[1] Idem. The only prominent holdovers from Anne's last ministry were Sir Edward Northey, the Attorney-General, and Shrewsbury, who remained Lord Chamberlain though he resigned as Lord Treasurer and Lord Lieutenant of Ireland. Neither of them lasted long. Shrewsbury quit in 1715, and Northey was ousted in 1718.

[2] Perceval to George Berkeley, 31 Aug. 1714: P.R.O., Egmont MSS. 234.

[3] On 9 Oct. the remodelling of local government began with changes in the lord lieutenancies of the counties. Other alterations followed rapidly.

in the Lockean sense, which they must defend against ruthless encroachment.[1] Like other Oppositions before and after them, the Tories tended to overlook the fact that many of their 'interests' had been built up with the aid of the 'influence of the Crown' when they were in office.

In the constituencies and the public press they anticipated the Government assault and met it with vigorous counter-attack. A communication to *Dawks' News Letter*, dated early in October, reported that in Windsor 'both sides are eating and drinking for the Parliament', and similar activity was taking place throughout Great Britain.[2] Those opposed by ministerial candidates had to drop the mask of cheerful compliance with the wishes of the Court. Some went so far as to invite the imputation of Jacobitism. When Whig candidates employed the Coronation day for loyal political gatherings, Opposition mobs stormed their premises shouting Tory slogans and the names of Tory candidates. At Reading the cry was 'No Hanover, no Cadogan, but Calvert and Clarges'. At Birmingham it was 'Sacheverell for ever, and down with the Whigs'.[3] There can be no doubt that the Opposition exploited High Church prejudice and Jacobite sentiment against Government partisans. Their pamphlets took the same line. So many 'scurrilous libels' had been circulated by 8 November that the magistrates of London issued orders to apprehend the hawkers and peddlers who cried them, a measure publicly approved by Townshend, the Secretary of State.[4] New brochures nevertheless continued to appear at frequent intervals.

The most notorious, which summed up the Tory position, was Atterbury's *English Advice to the Freeholders of England*.[5] He poured scorn upon 'the coward's maxim, that a man should suffer his enemies to destroy him for certain and without opposition, because there is a chance that if he should oppose them, he might possibly come to the worst'.[6] The Tories can no

---

[1] *English Advice to the Freeholders of England* (London, 1714), pp. 2–3.

[2] W. T. Morgan, 'Some Sidelights on the General Election of 1715' in *Essays in Modern English History in Honor of Wilbur Cortez Abbott*, pp. 148 ff.

[3] *Annals of King George* (London, 1716), i. 261.

[4] Boyer, *Political State*, viii. 446–8.

[5] This pamphlet, which appeared late in 1714, was said to have been written in co-operation with Bolingbroke and his clique (Williams, *Memoirs of Atterbury*, i. 289). Since Swift had been in Ireland since early September, the allegation that he shared in the composition seems unfounded.   [6] *English Advice*, p. 5.

longer hope that compliance and passivity will gain them 'the benefit of an indulgence' from the powers at Court, 'for Whiggish moderation, like death, sooner or later strikes all that come in its way'.[1] Atterbury then trumpeted the ancient opposition war-cry that the King must be rescued from evil advisers. He pointed out that in 1710 the Tories had delivered Anne out of the hands of the Whigs who 'neither allowed her the liberty to speak her grievances nor choose her servants'.[2] Hanmer and Bromley provided an inspiration for all, he continued, by 'that unshaken firmness and integrity' with which they had refused to be numbered among the hateful counsellors who imprisoned the monarch.[3] There followed a lengthy justification of all the policies carried out by 'the late Ministry', whose shining virtues illuminated the baseness of their adversaries. Had Atterbury stopped there, he would have done no more than adapt the stock arguments of opposition to the situation in 1714. But the old Jacobite could not refrain from implying, in direct contradiction of his other statements, that the King was secretly in league with the Whigs to overturn the Constitution, and he audaciously referred to the fate of Count Koenigsmarck, reputedly executed by George for alleged fornication with his wife.[4] This sort of language lent colour to the Whigs' charges of sedition, and laid the Tories open to the customary taunt that the traditional righteous pose of Opposition was no more than a hollow pretence of unprincipled scoundrels.[5]

As the old ministerial coalition fell from power, therefore, it became the victim of circumstances that militated against the formation of a loyal Opposition. The King was an obvious partisan. The Whig groups from the very outset spared no effort to identify Toryism with Jacobitism. When the new Government began to employ the 'influence of the Crown' in the usual fashion to win the coming election, the Tories' natural

---

[1] Idem.   [2] Ibid., p. 6.   [3] Ibid., p. 14.

[4] Ibid., p. 10. Perceval thought that Atterbury's 'sedition, personal reflections on the royal family, and notorious untruths' were the factor that finally convinced George I that he must have no dealings with the Opposition Tories (Perceval's Diary, 26 Jan. 1715: P.R.O., Egmont MSS. 234).

[5] For example, see *Remarks on a Libel Privately Dispersed by the Tories, Entitled 'English Advice', etc., Showing the Traiterous Designs of the Faction in Putting out that Villainous Pamphlet, on Occasion of the Ensuing Elections* (London, 1715).

defence of their 'interests' was compromised by the extremists
of their own side. The Pretender cast further suspicion upon
them by circulating a manifesto early in November in which he
referred to 'the Princess our sister, of whose good intentions
towards us we could not for some time past well doubt'.[1] So
damning was this imputation that the Tories at first thought
the manifesto 'a contrivance of the Whigs to asperse the late
Ministry and influence future elections for Parliament men'.[2]

None of the existing evidence proves that Opposition had contemplated a Stuart restoration after the rejection of Atterbury's
wild scheme on the 1st of August. Indeed, their recorded
actions until at least the end of the year indicate that their
leaders intended to operate within the traditional limits of loyal
Opposition. They did their best to curry favour at Court, though
without success. As these efforts gave less and less promise of
reward, some made tentative moves toward the Prince of
Wales.[3] Concurrently they 'made interest' for elections, with a
view to putting up a good show of strength in the next Parliament, and, despite their feuds, there are some indications of
endeavours to re-establish co-operation for a parliamentary
campaign among the chief Tories.[4] But the activities of resolute
enemies, imprudent friends, and a tactless Pretender hindered
their progress at every step and increased the ever-present
temptation to cast their lot with the rival claimant to the throne.

Their true position at Court, furthermore, became apparent
beyond a doubt with the issue of the proclamation summoning a
new Parliament on 15 January 1715. In this document the new
sovereign declared it a miracle that he had come 'safe to the
Crown of this kingdom, notwithstanding the designs of evil men'.
Owing to the 'miscarriages of others', it went on, he had succeeded to a realm which lay 'under the greatest difficulties as
well in respect of our trade and interruption of navigation, as
of the great debts of our nation, which we were surprised to
observe have been very much increased since the conclusion of

---

[1] [H. R. Duff, ed.] *Culloden Papers* (London, 1815), pp. 30–32.

[2] Oldmixon, *History of England*, p. 581. Cf. *Diary of Mary Countess Cowper*, p. 20.

[3] From Lady Cowper's account of intrigue at the Prince's Court, it appears that
several of the Opposition Tories endeavoured to insinuate themselves into favour
there (ibid., pp. 16–41).

[4] *H.M.C.*, *Dartmouth MSS.*, pp. 320–2; *E.H.R.* lii. 673–5; Ball, *Correspondence of
Swift*, ii. 214–40; Boyer, *Political State*, ix. 15, 80.

the last war'. To remedy the ills of political disaffection and economic dislocation, thus unmistakably attributed to the old Tory coalition, the King urged his people to 'have a particular regard to such as showed a firmness to the Protestant succession when it was in danger.[1] The Tories might well believe that their worst fear—that George would become 'king of one party'—had been realized.

Thus it was that the Court party which had faithfully served the King at his accession moved out of power and into opposition. Everything occurred in strictly orthodox fashion. The King allowed a disintegrating coalition to conduct the business of one brief session under the control of his Regency. He then proceeded to replace the old counsellors one by one, and having put the 'influence of the Crown' at the disposal of his new Ministry, he called a general election which was to assure them of a parliamentary majority. The late courtiers slipped into opposition hesitantly and with reluctance. They used every channel of intrigue open to them, and not until fully convinced of the King's hostility did they accept as inevitable the necessity of bold resistance to the Court. Their attitudes and their methods conformed closely to those of preceding generations. There is nothing to support the theory, stated in its most extreme form by Wolfgang Michael, that Opposition underwent an abrupt change at the Hanoverian accession, converted by a sharp decline in royal power from antagonism against the King to fierce but fraternal rivalry with his ministers.[2] George I's view of his functions unquestionably differed from his predecessors', and he soon displayed somewhat different methods of dealing with parliamentary politicians. But the location of powers in the Constitution suffered no alteration upon Anne's death. The structure of party and the character of politics

---

[1] *Commons Journals*, xviii. 14. 'The Tories, I say, find fault with the wording of the proclamation as influencing of elections', wrote Perceval, 'but they don't remember the late queen was wont in her proclamations to express herself much more freely of one part of her people, calling them a faction and recommending to the electors to choose the same set of men who had done the dirty work of her Ministry' (Perceval's Diary, 26 Jan. 1715: P.R.O., Egmont MSS. 234). The election proclamations printed in the *Commons Journals* do not support this charge against Anne, but some of her speeches from the throne reflected sharply upon the Opposition: *P.H.* vi. 1173, 1235–6, 1256–8. Cf. *Somers Tracts* (2nd ed.), xiii. 560.

[2] Wolfgang Michael, *Englische Geschichte im Achtzehnten Jahrhundert* (Leipzig, 1896–1945), iv. 47–48.

remained the same. The Opposition continued to direct its time-honoured activities in the age-old fashion.

In the chronicles of opposition the significance of the Hanoverian accession is that it soon resulted in a period of stability and an atmosphere of fundamental agreement which permitted the tranquil growth of political institutions. The history of Opposition from this point forward is in essence the record of how loyal parliamentary Opposition, able to flourish amid peaceful domestic conditions, came gradually to supersede and supplant the other types. For such a development, multifarious changes had to occur in many aspects of British politics: a decrease in the 'influence of the Crown', the evolution of a satisfactory and consistent doctrine of loyal Opposition, revisions in parliamentary practice and procedure, broader organization of political parties, the spread of a more enlightened political consciousness to the lower classes through education and the press. The changes in all of these areas did not proceed at the same pace, and the interaction among them was complex. At times it seems as if retrogression rather than growth took place. There are no imposing landmarks to delimit 'stages of progress'. In subtle and infinitesimal ways the factors that put a premium upon intrigue at one or another of the courts gradually disappeared, while those that encouraged guerrilla warfare in Parliament grew in importance to produce the institution of 'His Majesty's Opposition'.

III

TORIES, GRUMBLETONIANS, AND MALCONTENTS

1715–1725

III

TORIES, GRUMBLETONIANS,
AND MALCONTENTS

1715–1725

I. THE STORMY DECADE

Significant Developments

THE first ten years of George I's reign were those in which
Britain slowly settled down to peaceful constitutional
development. Thus long did it require to play out the
heritage of Stuart times: to break down the old political pattern,
discard some elements, and redistribute others for the construction of new designs. It was a stormy decade. Jacobitism
fostered a rebellion, an invasion, and two projected invasions
which were dissipated by the Government's vigilance. The
bursting of the South Sea Bubble set the nation in an uproar
that did not subside for more than a year. The furor over the
Bangorian controversy at length forced the Government to
close down Convocation. Trials for treason and sedition, libel
and peculation were commonplace occurrences. Contemporary
tracts of all political hues poured forth continual lamentations
upon 'our heats and animosities' and 'the present discontents'.

Perhaps it was by their very intensity that the old fires con-
sumed themselves. Certainly by midsummer 1725 many of the
passions which had stirred Britain to strife lay in ashes, and the
political alignments of that year bore witness to the disruption
of the pattern existing at the accession. The natural operation
of politics over a decade produced the usual results. Death,
proscription, and retirement removed politicians at every level;
minor figures rose to prominence; alterations in the Ministry
jumbled men and parties, old and new. Different combinations
put a different face on things. But from out the normal process
of change emerge two points of importance for the history of the
Opposition.

The more significant was the decay of Jacobitism as a force in practical politics. The period witnessed a mortifying continuance of frenetic and futile Jacobite activity, the sole uncompromising line of opposition, followed by a cataclasm of personnel and an erosion of hope. After 1725 no politician or party of any consequence placed any reliance on a Stuart restoration. The 'King across the water' (and now across the Alps) no longer provided a rival court to which the 'outs' might turn. Thereby disappeared one of the alternative forms of opposition, and with its disappearance came into existence a basic condition for the development of a 'loyal' Opposition. Henceforward the aspiring politician bent his hopes upon success at home without resort to revolution.

Of less permanent importance, but momentous as an augury for the immediate future, was the situation of the Government in 1725. There existed a stable ministry under the management of one man, possessed of the confidence of the monarch and capable of carrying necessary measures in Parliament. With the usual minor reconstructions, the Ministry was to stand, its essential characteristics intact, for a long term of years. This type of government dominated the scene under the four Georges. In contrast to the relatively short-lived terms prevalent in the late Stuart and the Victorian eras, five ministries of ten or more years' duration occupied approximately 65 per cent. of the time between 1714 and 1830. Three of the five ended, not in political defeat, but in the death or resignation of the leading minister with his power unimpaired.[1] In each instance the monarch viewed the loss of his chief manager with regret. Thus by 1725 the first Hanoverian had established a tendency that was to prove characteristic of all the others: to accept a general superintendent or steward, to support him with personal influence and the 'influence of the Crown', and to retain him in office as long as possible. The majority of the briefer ministries which obtained during the remaining 35 per cent. of the period

---

[1] The ministries of Walpole, Pelham, North, Liverpool, and the first Ministry of the younger Pitt lasted for a total of roughly seventy-five years. The three not ended by defeat in Parliament were those of Pelham, the younger Pitt, and Liverpool. There were times, of course, when some of these ministers cannot be said to have possessed the confidence of the monarch: notably Pelham from the fall of Carteret in 1744 through the 'forty-eight-hour ministry' of 1746. But such instances were the exception rather than the rule.

would have endured had the King's wishes prevailed. Demise or demission destroyed many. Internal weakness broke up a few, despite all the King could do to save some of them. Only occasionally did the Hanoverians deliberately set out to subvert their ministers, either for personal reasons or for reasons of policy.[1] At the end of this first decade, therefore, Opposition had already encountered the indisposition of the Court to 'a change of hands', a factor that would affect the thought and action of ministerial opponents for over a century.

Political Shifts

The general tendency to stability had developed despite the occurrence of frequent change from 1715 to 1725. No two years passed without some noteworthy shift in political alignments. There were, however, no wholesale overturns like those of 1710 and 1714. All were minor reconstructions which gradually produced a strong and competent government under Sir Robert Walpole. The reverse of the coin was an Opposition varying in composition, fluctuating in strength, and divergent in purpose.

The Tory groups cast into opposition by George I underwent severe deprivations in 1715. The general election reduced their voting strength in the House of Commons to about 160. The vengeance of the new ministers weakened Tory leadership. In fear of imminent impeachment Bolingbroke and Ormonde fled to the Pretender and were attainted in the sequel. Strafford and Oxford were impeached, and Oxford went to the Tower for two years. The shadow of disaffection fell on all of the Opposition who had supported Anne's last Ministry. Six of their leaders in the Commons and two peers were ordered arrested for complicity in the Jacobite insurrection. One, Thomas Forster, eluded detection only to surrender as commander of the rebel forces at Preston and thereafter to confirm the suspicions of

---

[1] Each new king had a natural inclination to rid himself of his predecessor's managers, and politicians always expected a 'change of hands' at the opening of a reign. George I and George III lived up to expectations, but George II and George IV retained their fathers' ministers. William IV kept Wellington until forced to part with him. After the establishment of George I's first Ministry, therefore, George III's 'massacre of the Pelhamite innocents' is the only departure from a general tendency to stability so strong that it overrode the personal prejudices of an incoming sovereign. And even George III did not intend to swim against the current; he only wished to set up a stable ministry of his own choosing: see below, Chapter VII.

Government. 'He does not own any concert with other people', ran a report to the Secretary of State in November, 'but says in general he looked on the whole body of the Tories to be in it'.[1]

The upshot of Government persecution and the '15 was the disruption of the ministerial coalition of Whig and Tory elements. In June 1715 Shrewsbury gave up the Chamberlain's staff in protest against the impeachment proceedings. Somerset quit as Master of the Horse in September when his son-in-law, Sir William Wyndham, was arrested. Early in 1716 the Nottingham connexion was ousted from the Ministry in a dispute over the treatment of the rebel lords. Except for the Churchill interest, closely allied with the Whig Sunderland, all groups denominated Tory were now in opposition. The session of 1716 witnessed one of those hitherto rare junctures when the line between Government and Opposition corresponded closely with the division of party names. But it was not to last long.

Rivalries within the Ministry, which had resulted in the Tory dismissals, went on to produce the ouster of several Whig connexions. From 1716 to 1720 the Ministry gradually weakened itself by driving allies out of office without procuring comparable accessions of strength. The same period marks the emergence of the Prince of Wales as leader of the Opposition. In succession to the shattered and demoralized Tory clans there arose in consequence a formidable, if jarring and unreliable, body of Tories, grumbletonians, and malcontents antagonistic to the Ministry. It was to become the first successful Opposition of the Hanoverian era.

In June 1716 the Duke of Argyll and his adherents fell from power. They immediately attached themselves openly to the Prince of Wales, in whose court the Nottingham and other Tory interests were already at work.[2] Six months later the machinations of Sunderland brought about the transfer of Townshend from Secretary of State to Lord Lieutenant of Ireland, and in April 1717 Townshend was dismissed. His own connexion and his closest allies thereupon resigned. The Walpoles, Cavendishes, Russells, Manners, and Pulteneys, along with Paul Methuen, the Duke of Grafton, and other

[1] *H.M.C., Townshend MSS.*, p. 171.
[2] *Diary of Mary Countess Cowper*, p. 69; Coxe, *Walpole*, ii. 61, 66–67.

individuals, all threw up their offices and repaired to the heir apparent. The Prince's relations with his father had been deteriorating since the middle of 1716, when the King had become displeased with his son's conduct as guardian of the realm during the royal *Hannoverreise*. A dispute about a god-father for a newborn son of the Prince in November 1717 provoked an open breach. The King forbade anyone who attended the heir's Court to appear at his own, and those who held offices in both Courts were ordered to make a choice be-tween them. The royal edict also denied the Prince a residence in town. In January 1718, therefore, he purchased a house in Leicester Square to serve as a centre for his social and political activities. As 'the pouting place of princes', it was to be the home of 'Leicester House Oppositions' through four genera-tions.[1]

During this open schism in the royal family there occurred only two notable shifts in the established political alignments. Lord Cowper, long a confidant of the Prince, gave up the Chancellor's seals in March 1718. He possessed no political following, but his parliamentary abilities made him an im-portant addition to what was now generally termed 'the dis-contented party'. In February 1719 the Duke of Argyll broke with the Prince and returned to Court. The struggle for favour and influence at Leicester House was as intense as at St. James's. Argyll lost to Robert Walpole in a contest for the chief place in the counsels of His Royal Highness and found the right channels to make his way back into the King's good graces.[2] But his defection did not seriously weaken the Prince's party. The period of the royal schism, therefore, was one in which a motley group of malcontents, excluded from the monarch's favour, presented an erratic but powerful Opposition to the 'Narrow-bottom Ministry' of Stanhope and Sunderland. Under Walpole's leadership the discontented party won several minor skirmishes and a major triumph in the defeat of the Peerage Bill of 1719. They kept Government in a state of continual worry about its parliamentary strength, and their intrigues produced

[1] G. H. Cunningham, *London* (London 1927), pp. 404–5.

[2] *Cathcart Journal*, 1–13 Feb. 1719: P.R.O., Cathcart MSS. 5/48. At about the same time the Government apparently brought Somerset and Buckingham into the fold. They were the chief promoters in Parliament of the two Peerage Bills of 1719. See *P.H.* vii. 589, 606–9.

a tense atmosphere of uneasiness and suspicion among the courtiers.

This combination of activities brought success to Opposition in the spring of 1720. The nature of the transaction is particularly significant in the history of eighteenth-century politics, for it established a precedent long remembered, and the pattern of change was to recur again and again under the Georges. In the midst of its considerable difficulties the Ministry faced the necessity of buying off some of the malcontents. The furious intrigue at Court provided numerous possibilities. Lady Cowper, a lady-in-waiting to the Princess of Wales, recorded four 'schemes' for ministerial reconstruction and concluded bitterly that 'there was not a rogue in town that was not engaged in some scheme or project to undo his country'.[1] The different groups at Court sought to secure and improve their positions by caballing to bring in allies from the outside, and the Opposition groups, eager to find the right road back to favour, entered into the plans projected by royal mistresses, German favourites, and English ministers.

The Walpole–Townshend connexion eventually carried the day. Their success well illustrates a contemporary dictum of Lord Ilay: 'Politics is a continual petty war and game, and as at all other games, we will sometimes win and sometimes lose, and he that plays best and has the best stock has the best chance.'[2] Robert Walpole, who seems clearly to have led the negotiations,[3] played a very skilful game with Stanhope and Sunderland, carefully concealing his manœuvres from all rivals on both sides except the most influential of the royal mistresses. He possessed the best stock: not only did his group offer valuable ability and strength in Parliament, but being in the ascendant at Leicester House, he could bring in to the 'treaty' the most powerful figure in Opposition, the Prince of Wales.

On 23 April 1720, therefore, Walpole brought about a

---

[1] *Diary of Mary Countess Cowper*, pp. 141–5. Cf. *H.M.C., Portland MSS.* v. 594–6; *H.M.C., Townshend MSS.*, pp. 104–6.

[2] *H.M.C., Bute MSS.*, p. 618.

[3] Tindal lists Devonshire and Walpole as the two chief negotiators (*History of England*, vii. 244). Devonshire was unquestionably one of the inner circle, but he apparently was out of town during the final stages of the intrigue (*Diary of Mary Countess Cowper*, pp. 133, 135). Tindal's estimate of his importance may stem from the fact that Devonshire House served as headquarters for the Opposition clique throughout the negotiations.

reconciliation between the King and his son. Ministers were jubilant. Stanhope, meeting Bothmer and Bernsdorff in an antechamber outside the room in which the Prince was making his submission, screamed shrilly, 'Ah there, sirs, the peace is made, the peace is made!' 'Have the dispatches arrived [from Spain]?' asked Bothmer. 'No, no, it is peace here,' shouted Stanhope; 'we are going to see our prince again.' Taken aback, Bothmer exclaimed, 'Our prince?' 'Yes, yes, our prince, our prince; we are waiting for him to be reconciled with the King.' 'Sir,' answered Bothmer, 'you have been very secret in your affairs.' 'Yes, yes, we have been, . . . secrecy is always necessary to do good things.' And Bothmer is said to have wept at his rivals' success.[1]

But George I, who was most reluctant to readmit his son to favour, appears not to have understood the importance of 'taking off' the Prince of Wales. Lady Cowper reports that the King demanded, 'Can't the Whigs come back without him?' He was told 'that the Whigs don't desire any places, only to be friends again'. The King's perplexity did not diminish. 'What did they go away for?' he said. 'It was their own faults.'[2] This account probably explains in part the amount of time required to complete the transaction.[3] The Walpole–Townshend group abruptly ceased opposition in Parliament, but they did not receive their rewards until seven weeks later. Then Townshend, Grafton, and Walpole returned to posts in the Ministry, and most of their followers were satisfied with favours, jobs, and promises. History does not record the King's reaction to the appointment of these men who desired nothing but friendship.

The 'treaty' of 1720 made it clear that the Prince of Wales was more than a 'reversionary resource'. The device of effecting a reconciliation after strenuous opposition, apparently first conceived by Walpole, made the heir a useful tool even in his father's lifetime. The lesson was not lost upon the politicians of the future. But the 'treaty' brought success to only a fragment of the Opposition, since Walpole had contracted for none but his

---

[1] *Diary of Mary Countess Cowper*, p. 145.

[2] Ibid., pp. 145–6. Cf. the King's letter to his daughter, 6 July 1720, printed in *E.H.R.* lii (1937), 497.

[3] On 6 May Bernsdorff told Lady Cowper that 'they dare not tell the King what they have promised'. The German minister seems to have thought it possible to defeat the 'treaty' until the appointments were finally made (ibid., pp. 162, 172–4).

own connexion and their closest allies. He had been willing to use malcontents of every other hue to muster strength in Parliament, but he assumed no obligation to bring them into office. The result was a commonplace reconstruction of the Ministry by the admission of a segment of the grumbletonians, while the rest of the Opposition lingered in the wilderness. As long as Opposition was composed of discordant elements, bound to each other by no firm commitments, this would remain the customary pattern of change.

The Walpole–Townshend group went on to make the most of the foothold they had gained at Court. Despite the difficulties of managing Parliament through the South Sea crisis and of overcoming the intrigues of rival ministers, Sir Robert gradually established his ascendancy during the next five years. The election of 1722 returned a comfortable majority for the Court coalition. Death carried off Stanhope, Sunderland, and the two Craggs, and Walpole himself subdued or ousted his other most troublesome competitors. With the death of Carleton and the dismissal of Cadogan, Roxburghe, and the Pulteneys in 1725, Walpole clearly emerged as the first of the great chief ministers of the Hanoverian dynasty.

The Opposition he had abandoned fell back into a condition similar to that existing before the breach in the royal family. Lord Cowper, it is true, had declined to profit by the treaty of 1720, and until his death three years later he provided vigorous Opposition leadership in the House of Lords. But the troops he had to lead were the demoralized Tory connexions, still further broken up by the destruction of the Atterbury plot in 1722, and the occasional outcasts from the Court party, none of whom brought any significant addition of strength. Over the first ten years of George I's reign, therefore, there had been no permanent achievement toward the development of a loyal Opposition party. Rather, a splintering of the existing groups had taken place, whereby opposition in 1725 became less well organized than it had been in the days of Anne.

Government and Opposition

The Government was in large part responsible for producing this situation. The policy of the Court party normally determined the activities of the Opposition throughout the eighteenth century, and the years 1715–25 provide good illustrations of the importance of this factor in parliamentary politics. The first Ministry of the reign set out to annihilate its enemies. The personal coldness of the King to Anne's ministers and the impeachment proceedings in Parliament were designed to wreck the Tory coalition. Bolingbroke and his cohorts always insisted that 'Whig vindictiveness' goaded them into Jacobitism.[1] Given the prevailing climate of politics, they spoke the truth. Despite their equivocal conduct in office, there is no reason to believe that most of them would not gladly have accepted office under the new King. The Court policy convinced them that the only road back to power lay in the hazardous journey, in body or in spirit, to Bar-le-Duc. The Government resolved to damn them as Jacobites, and Jacobites most of them became. As always, the generalization applies primarily to the most ambitious. The 'whimsicals' did not succumb to the temptation. But Bolingbroke, Ormonde, Mar, and Forster would not have fought for the Pretender had they not found St. James's locked against them.

The ministerial policy of condemning all opposition as Jacobitical continued even after the defection of Townshend and Walpole. In October 1719 Newcastle wrote to Stanhope,

> The great point I think we ought to aim at is, that there should be but two parties, that for and that against the Government, and I cannot but think that by a new election, Mr. Walpole and the few friends his party will be able to bring in will be so incorporated with the Jacobites that we shall have but little difficulty in dealing with them.[2]

The Court party's ideal was to have all malcontents excluded under a cloud of treason. Perhaps it is another measure of Walpole's greatness that in opposition he never wavered in his support of the Protestant succession, despite the taunts of the Government and the blandishments of the Jacobites.[3] During

---

[1] Bolingbroke, *Works*, i. 128–34; cf. *P.H.* vii, 58, 445–6; *Correspondence of Jonathan Swift*, ii. 341–2.

[2] Williams, *Stanhope*, p. 460.

[3] In *H.M.C.*, *Stuart Papers*, iv–vii (esp. iv. 331–2, 396; v. 158–9, 240), there are numerous references to Jacobite offers to Walpole but no indications that he ever considered them. I can find no evidence to suggest that he even momentarily flirted with the Pretender. Pulteney and Byng seem to have been equally adamant (ibid. iv. 401; v. 458); but Orford may have dallied briefly with Jacobitism (ibid. v. 556).

those critical years he may well have done the dynasty as great a service out of office as in. Some of the Tories nevertheless persisted in their support of James. The Gyllenborg plot of 1717 and the Atterbury plot of 1722, which involved only a few of the more desperate among them, gave the Government continuing opportunities to tar all with the same brush, and upon his return to office Walpole resumed the standard tactic. In the words of Speaker Onslow, the Chief Minister

always aimed at the uniting of the Whigs against the Tories as Jacobites, which all of them gave too much handle for on this [1722] and many other occasions, and making therefore combinations between them and any body of Whigs to be impracticable; and it had that effect for some time.[1]

After the original persecution, however, the Government no longer took vengeance upon those against whom there lay no legal evidence. The release of Oxford and the Act of Grace in 1717 mark the end of that phase.[2] Thereafter the charge of disaffection degenerated into a general smear which did not profoundly affect the conduct of the Opposition, and a new factor appeared to alter the prevailing attitude of both sides. The weakening of the Court party as a result of the dismissals of 1716–17 obliged ministers to cast about for new strength. Shortly after Argyll's fall rumours began that Marlborough and Sunderland were plotting to bring in a group of Tories led by Lord Carnarvon.[3] Such reports continued as the Townshend–Sunderland feud rose to a climax,[4] and the ousting of Townshend and his following set the Court upon an earnest search for replacements. Secretary Craggs wrote to Stair in September 1717,

I agree with you entirely that we stand on a narrow bottom, that it would be right to enlarge it, that violent measures are at all times bad, that moderate knowing men should be courted, and that we may have people among us who are for driving too fast. . . . I would have His Majesty receive not only every honest well-meaning man, but every Jacobite that comes over to his interest. . . . As to moderate

---

[1] *H.M.C., Onslow MSS.*, p. 462.

[2] The Government's lenient treatment of its opponents was remarked by Dubois on his diplomatic mission to England in the autumn of 1717: Williams, *Stanhope*, p. 284.

[3] *Diary of Mary Countess Cowper*, pp. 118–22; *H.M.C., Stuart Papers*, iii, 44–45.

[4] Ibid. 428.

knowing men, I wish to God He would send us a crop of them, for I can swear by Him I don't know them. I don't see a man but is engaged in some cabal or other. I don't see a man that inquires after the public but as he thinks it a popular handle to support his own or distress his enemy's designs.[1]

In the quest for support the King played his part as well. At the Newmarket races in October he was 'particularly civil' to Devonshire, Rutland, Grafton, Orford, and Methuen, all of whom had resigned in April, 'but turned his back to Mr. Walpole and ordered the Lord of the Bedchamber to invite everybody to dine but him and his brother Townshend'.[2] Craggs was still writing to Stair in September 1718,

I think it the rightest measure on earth to hold out one's hands to all people, but in short they must come in to the King's measures, while they are right ones for the public; and upon my word he told me himself but two days ago, in these words, 'Je veux toujours récompenser ceux qui feront bien, mais ceux qui voudront braver se trouveront éloignés de compte avec moi. Qu'est que c'est et de quoi plaint-on?'[3]

The Sunderland–Stanhope Ministry manœuvred continuously throughout its brief tenure 'to enlarge the bottom'. Sunderland appears to have carried on an endless intrigue with various Tory groups, and rumour-mongers constantly expected the Government to take in some of the Opposition until it finally happened in 1720.[4]

The return of the Walpole–Townshend connexion did not stop the rumours, but it brought a noteworthy change in the Government's attitude to the Opposition. Sir Robert's policy, evident from the outset and consistently pursued, was best expressed in this bit of advice he gave to Henry Pelham years later:

Whig it with all opponents that will parly; but 'ware Tory! I never mean to a person or so; but what they can bring with them will prove a broken reed.[5]

The ministers were pleased to call the treaty of 1720 a 'Whig

[1] *Annals of Stair*, ii. 37–39.   [2] Ibid. 41.   [3] Ibid. 374.
[4] MS. Journal of Mrs. Charles Caesar, ii (in the possession of Lieut.-Col. John H. Busby of Harpenden, Herts.); Paul Baratier, *Lettres inédites de Bolingbroke à Lord Stair, 1716-1720* (Paris, 1939), pp. 65–66; *H.M.C., Stuart Papers*, iii. 447–8; vi, 448 ff.
[5] Coxe, *Pelham*, i. 93.

reunion', and Walpole and Townshend were wont to remind each other that it was 'absolutely necessary for us to rest on the Whig bottom'.[1] They displayed a willingness to treat with Whig connexions that would 'parly'; and also a ruthless determination to exclude those which would not acknowledge their leadership. At the same time they occasionally plucked a submissive Tory out of opposition but refused to admit any Tory group. Thus in 1720 Sir Robert Raymond, Solicitor-General in Oxford's Ministry, was made Attorney-General. Walpole bought Harcourt in 1721 with an increased pension and a step in the peerage. Lord Finch of the Nottingham clan, destined to become the 'Whig' Lord Winchilsea, joined the Court party as Comptroller of the Household in 1725.[2] But when a cabal of Tory peers offered their support in return for suitable rewards in 1723, Walpole 'cut short all treaties of that kind at once'.[3]

These shifts in ministerial policy produced corresponding changes in the activities of opposition. The State's vigilance made a dismal failure of Jacobitism, and as it became clear that the King and his managers would smile upon the return of lost sheep, provided their tails were dragging appropriately, most of the malcontents turned their faces again toward the royal Court. With groups and individuals in quest of accommodations for themselves regardless of others, there was little possibility of building a strong Opposition coalition. Government tended to pick off the ablest leaders, thereby casting their followers adrift, and opposition alliances were not proof against the disintegrating effect of the Court manoeuvres.

In this manner Government was partly responsible for the disorganization of its opponents. For the rest, the very nature of the malcontent groups made cohesion difficult. The old Tory feuds of Anne's time prolonged themselves into the next generation. The Oxford and Bolingbroke connexions never forgave

---

[1] Stowe MSS., ff. 6, 21; Add. MSS. 32686, f. 269.

[2] Efforts to 'bring off' individual Tories met with two noteworthy and interesting failures in this period. In 1720 the Government offered the notorious Jacobite William Shippen a deal whereby he could make a £10,000 profit on an investment of £4,000 in South Sea stock, but Shippen refused to bite (Egerton MSS. 2618, ff. 221–6; *H.M.C., Leyborne-Popham MSS.*, p. 253). Two years later Atterbury declined Walpole's offer of the bishopric of Winchester, a £5,000 pension until the see fell vacant, and a tellership of the Exchequer for one of his relatives (Williams, *Atterbury*, i. 377).

[3] Stowe MSS., f. 23.

each other, and the Finches distrusted them both. To personal differences were added differences of principle. Staunch Hanoverians like Anglesey or Hanmer viewed with suspicion such lifelong Jacobites as Shippen and Caesar, and the Opposition Whig groups once voted to send Shippen to the Tower.[1] Disputes over electoral interests divided them also. For example, a Harley fought a Lewis at New Radnor in 1715, and there was a three-cornered battle seven years later in Hertfordshire when a Freeman, a Sebright, and a Caesar went to the poll. Even at Oxford University, the holy of Tory holies, William King stood against George Clarke and William Bromley in 1722. In short, to a remarkable degree history bore out Bolingbroke's plaintive prophecy of 1714:

I see plainly that the Tory party is gone [he wrote to Atterbury in September]. Those who broke from us formerly continue still to act and speak on the same principles and with the same passions. Numbers are still left, and those numbers will be increased by such as have not their expectations answered. But where are the men of business that will live and draw together?[2]

Yet the annals of parliamentary opposition during this stormy decade are something more than an account of divided counsels and divergent aims. Despite all their differences, the 'outs' exhibited certain clearly discernible patterns of behaviour, which reveal a tendency to greater coherence in action than in purpose. A nettled Government leader complained in 1718 that 'such is the nature of Opposition, they can all unite to do mischief although they could not agree a week to do good'.[3] By and large, Opposition activities constitute a continuation of traditional practices and ideas adapted to the immediate circumstances. Along some lines they played an old game out to its ultimate conclusion; along others they worked out a significant legacy for the future. All grumbletonians contributed in some measure to the development of the period, but for a variety of reasons that will become evident, we must accord first consideration to the followers of the Old Chevalier.

[1] *P.H.* vii. 511; *H.M.C., Portland MSS.* v. 544–5. On the divisions among the Tory connexions and between them and Whig dissidents, see *H.M.C., Stuart Papers,* v. 245, 286, 298, 307, 419; *Annals of Stair,* ii. 373, 376; Baratier, *Lettres inédites,* pp. 47–53; Coxe, *Walpole,* ii. 216.

[2] Williams, *Atterbury,* i. 279–80.

[3] *Annals of Stair,* ii. 364.

2. THE CONDUCT OF OPPOSITION

Jacobite Policy

The Jacobites' opening gambit in 1715 was an endeavour to commit all the ousted Tory clans to the Pretender's cause.[1] It failed, partly because some were sincerely attached to the Protestant succession, partly because the rising did not achieve enough success to bring over the waverers. But the Government's policy of excluding and damning them all led Stuart partisans to hope that no other course lay open to them. 'I shall be sorry if the Tory party in England be so divided and disjointed that the King [James III] cannot lay hold on them', wrote Mar in April 1716. 'I see no other they have to lay hold on but the King.'[2] In the aftermath of rebellion, therefore, the Jacobites formulated the programme which they would follow till their movement in England foundered: to use the Opposition as a fifth column in Parliament. At some time in the future Sweden or France or Spain, or all of them, could be persuaded to provide arms and soldiers for another attempt, and in the meantime the role of opposition was to weaken the enemy, to multiply its own forces, and to prepare to open the gates of Britain at the critical moment.

Scarcely had the plan emerged than it met with a series of checks. Jacobite agents reported that Argyll's dismissal in June 1716 had set rumours flying of 'some kind of a coalition in the Ministry which may appease and bring in the Tories and be of bad consequence for us'.[3] None resulted, but the growing change in Government policy and the patent willingness of opposition groups to enter into a treaty set James's adherents to worrying about the reliability of their fifth column. Then in September came the first news of the triple alliance, in which France guaranteed to give no support to the Stuarts and to induce the Pretender to reside beyond the Alps: 'The *coup de grâce* to Jacobites and Tories', wrote a spy from London.[4] And so hopes turned to Sweden. A memoir of September assured the northern Court that the Pretender had 'positive and repeated assurances from the heads of the English Church and the heads of the

---

[1] *H.M.C., Stuart Papers*, i. 404–5, 447, 520.
[2] Ibid. ii. 127; cf. ibid. v. 616.   [3] Ibid. ii. 278–9, 312.
[4] Ibid. iii. 23–25, 28, 46, 107.

Tories, who together form three-quarters of the kingdom, that they will unanimously join him', if he be supported by 6,000 men and arms for 30,000.[1] At about the same time the Swedish ambassador in London, Count Gyllenborg, undertook active measures. He conferred with Jacobite leaders, wrote pamphlets to stir up dissension, and got under way plans for a Swedish force to land on Britain's east coast in March 1717.[2] The role of Opposition was to press in Parliament for a reduction of troops so that the invasion would face the least possible resistance.[3] But Gyllenborg was arrested and his papers seized at the end of January, and the plot died stillborn.

The fall of the Walpole–Townshend group in April gave them renewed hope, and the widening breach in the royal family throughout the year opened the way for a Stuart restoration via an unexpected route. Two extreme views appear in the Jacobite correspondence. One looked to a powerful coalition of Tories and grumbletonian Whigs, all converted to the cause, which would drive the weakened Ministry from office and bring in James III.[4] The other saw the angry royal father badgered by a powerful Opposition led from the Prince's Court to a point at which he would be willing to exclude his son from the throne in favour of the Pretender.[5] Mar thought so well of this idea that he wrote directly to Sunderland in September with the offer of a treaty reminiscent of that made between Stephen and Henry of Anjou: if George I would guarantee the succession to James, the latter would leave England tranquil during George's lifetime.

Opportunities are precious [Mar warned Sunderland], and what is in your power today may not perhaps be in a little time hence. A minister is not always sure of a Parliament if he were of his master, and when that turns against him, it is not in his master's power to save him, however much he may have a mind to it.[6]

[1] Ibid. ii. 427.
[2] See ibid. iii, *passim*; 'Papers Relative to the Intended Invasion from Sweden' printed in *P.H.* vii. 397–421; J. F. Chance, 'The "Swedish Plot" of 1716–17' in *E.H.R.* xviii. 81–106.
[3] *H.M.C., Stuart Papers*, iii. 326.
[4] Ibid. iv. 222.   [5] Ibid. v. 558, 566–7.
[6] Add. MSS. 34518, ff. 117–19. An almost identical letter of the same date was sent to Cadogan: *H.M.C., Stuart Papers*, v. 50–52. The idea of such a treaty seems to have been first suggested by Atterbury, who may have known that James III had made a similar offer to Anne and her ministers in March 1714: Felix Salomon,

Both these happy visions went up in smoke, but hopes for the
success of fifth column tactics increased. The years of the royal
schism proved to be the heyday of Jacobite efforts to serve their
cause 'in a parliamentary way'.

The function of Opposition was 'to make the Government
impracticable to the present ministers but not to go so far as to
force it into stronger hands'.[1] By a curious twist of the normal
procedure, serving a rival king required the Opposition to stay
out of office. 'The Jacobite method', wrote James Murray, 'is to
manage things in both Houses of Parliament so as thoroughly
to divide the Whigs, and to prevent a union betwixt the Tories
and any part of them in order to form a new administration'.[2]
Hence the Jacobites sought to use all elements of opposition,
converting as many as possible, to harass the 'Narrow-bottom
Ministry' and soften Britain for a future blow. In May 1717 Sir
Redmond Everard, Ormonde's agent in England, reported that
the party had concocted measures

in a parliamentary way, which they think will be of immediate
service to the King, and yet will not be refused by the discontented
party of Whigs in the heat they are now in against the Court.

They have already in good measure agreed to address against any
foreign war, which address may, as it is hoped, produce a good effect;
we are also in hopes to bring them into a measure to break the army,
which would be an apparent service; in short, the Tories are resolved
to do everything to increase the discontents of the people at home,
and to satisfy those abroad that they have the King's interest sincerely
at heart and are proof against all temptations to divert them from
it.[3]

Wishful thinking characterized the Jacobite mentality to an
unusual degree. James's agents counted far too much on the
co-operation of Hanoverian Tories and Whig malcontents, but
perhaps it was their blind faith that led them, despite an
occasional complaint of inadequate direction from Rome,[4] to

Geschichte des letzten Ministeriums der Königin Annas von England (Gotha, 1894),
pp. 337–42.

[1] *H.M.C., Stuart Papers*, v. 557; vii. 241.

[2] Idem. Atterbury reported to Mar in December 1717, that he would 'leave
nothing unattempted toward keeping every single Tory, that may have his eye on a
place at Court, from closing with any notion of that kind' (J. H. Glover, *The
Stuart Papers* (London, 1847), p. 13).

[3] *H.M.C., Stuart Papers*, v. 543–4.

[4] Ibid. 617. On the Pretender's leadership, see below, p. 86.

pursue this course with such consistency. They tried to keep Byng's fleet out of the Mediterranean, so that Spain could afford them more aid. To weaken British resistance to the Spanish expedition that invaded Scotland in 1719, they fought to have the army reduced.[1] They wrote pamphlets to gain public support for their measures in Parliament,[2] and they stirred up merchants to protest against the Government's retaliatory prohibition against trade with the conspiring Swedes.[3] It was a hazardous game, and they knew it. Mar predicted as early as 1718 that if the Jacobites did not play a careful 'balancing act' between the ministerial and opposition Whig sections, the policy would fail; 'for', he wrote to one of his spies in England,

should they join entirely with the son's people and push the present managers to extremity, it would not better their own condition; but rather make it worse by occasioning, as it certainly would, a change of ministry into the hands of a stronger party and force the father to make up with the son.[4]

In the end their activities contributed to that eventuality, and the treaty of 1720 forced a revaluation of their tactics. Atterbury wrote to the Pretender on 6 May,

The Tories have now lost their balancing power in the House of Commons, and must either by continuing wholly unactive, sink in their spirit and numbers, or by making attacks, hazard a stricter conjunction between their enemies. On either hand their situation is nice and hazardous; and great prudence as well as resolution is requisite so to conduct them through these difficulties, as neither to forfeit their reputation nor draw upon themselves the united resentment of the new powerful party—who, if ever they agree in good earnest, will be more irresistible than they were before the breach. 'Tis true there is but little time for such experiments before the session will close; and the less there is, in my humble opinion, the better. Ere another is opened, new distastes may arise, and new parties be formed, which may give the Tories matter to work and a foundation to stand upon. The last of these they now evidently want, and for want of it dare hardly, and scarce can prudently, make use of the other.[5]

---

[1] Ibid. iv. 262, 266; *P.H.* vii. 505–22, 534–48.
[2] *H.M.C., Stuart Papers*, vii. 240, 526.
[3] Ibid. vi. 84, 104–7; *P.H.* vii. 548–50. [4] Ibid. 241.
[5] Glover, *Stuart Papers*, pp. 52–53.

For two years the Jacobites tried to erect a new base of operations. The Pretender issued a declaration in the midst of the
South Sea crisis by which he hoped to sow dissension and, by
announcing the pregnancy of his queen, to build new hopes.[1]
But nothing came of it. So well did Walpole provide for his
adherents and protect his rivals that no schism developed in the
Ministry, and the Stuart cause gained only one prominent
adherent. This was Lord Cowper, whom historians have hitherto considered a staunch Hanoverian despite the equivocal
conduct of his declining years.[2] Disgruntled by the reconciliation in 1720, he withdrew his support from both courts and for
a year or so played a lone hand. Then in 1722 Lady Cowper
struck up a friendship with her Jacobite neighbour in Hertfordshire, Mrs. Charles Caesar. Mrs. Caesar introduced Lord
Cowper to Lord Oxford, and, as so often happened in the eighteenth century, a political alliance was built upon a private
attachment. Lord Cowper signalled his conversion to Jacobitism
one day in a casual conversation with Mrs. Caesar; viewing
the Pretender's portrait and some 'restoration hangings' at
Bennington, he turned to her and said, 'They that once thought
they served their country by endeavouring to keep him out
found they had no way to save it but by bringing him home.'[3]

Cowper brought to the cause little but debating power and
a remarkable valetudinarian vigour, however, and in their
search for an effective policy the Jacobites were torn between
two extremes. The one was to abandon all reliance on a weak
Opposition and to gamble altogether on a rising supported from
abroad. The other was to work for the revival of a strong
Opposition and wait upon events. Exponents of the first course
began preparations in mid-1721 for what became known as the
Atterbury plot. Originally designed to break out during the
general election of 1722, it was later postponed till the time

[1] *H.M.C., Var. Coll.* v. 242–3.

[2] Campbell, *Lives of the Lord Chancellors*, iv. 400; Realey, *Early Opposition to Sir
Robert Walpole*, p. 124.

[3] MS. Journal of Mrs. Charles Caesar, i (in the possession of Lieut.-Col. J. H.
Busby of Harpenden, Herts.). This naïve and amusing document gives a valuable
insight into the attitudes and connexions of a Jacobite county family from roughly
1720 to 1740. It makes clear that Cowper intended the Caesars and their friends
to think that he had become a Jacobite, and in conjunction with Oxford, Strafford and others who were in correspondence with the Chevalier, Cowper worked
out the Jacobite 'party line' in Parliament.

when George I had departed for his usual sojourn in Hanover. An insurrection was to seize strategic points in London and arrest the Ministry, while an expedition from Spain, led by Ormonde and joined by the Pretender, would land with a force requisite to take over the country. The more cautious scouted the plan as impractical. One of the plotters later deposed that when he had consulted the timid Orrery about what to do in late summer, 1722, that lord replied that 'he feared nothing could be done but in a parliamentary way', and there was some chance of success because 'Lord Cowper had told him that two hundred Tories and ninety grumbletonian Whigs who are in the House of Commons would try their last efforts'.[1] It was a forlorn hope. Cowper disowned the statement under oath, though he never denied that he planned a strenuous Opposition,[2] but only ignorance or self-deception could put the effective number of malcontents at 290.

In the event the Government thwarted the plot, and the campaign at St. Stephen's came to naught.[3] Therewith died parliamentary Jacobitism as an element in Opposition politics. Atterbury was driven into exile in June 1723. Within a month a group of the Tory leaders who had been deeply involved in the Pretender's schemes since the accession made overtures to the Government. Bathurst, Wyndham, Gower, Kinnoul, and their connexions declared themselves 'ready to enter into any measures' with Walpole and Townshend for they 'were desirous to rid themselves of the disagreeable situation they were in by renouncing Jacobitism'.[4] As we have seen, Walpole refused to take them in *en bloc*, but for a 'scrub pension' he soon bought Kinnoul, who then revealed secrets of Jacobite correspondence;[5]

[1] *A Report from the Committee appointed by order of the House of Commons to examine Christopher Layer and others* (London, 1722–3), Appendix B, pp. 11, 14.

[2] *P.H.* viii. 404–5.

[3] In October 1722 the Pretender issued another declaration, perhaps as a gesture of despair, in which he proposed that 'if King George will quietly deliver to him the possession of his throne, he will in return bestow upon him the title of King in his native dominions and invite all other states to confirm it, with a promise to leave to him his succession to the British dominions secure, whenever in due course his natural right shall take place'. Parliament issued joint resolutions, passed unanimously in both Houses, which condemned the declaration to be burned by the common hangman. There followed a joint address of loyalty to the King, also passed unanimously. See *P.H.* vii. 47–51.

[4] Stowe MSS. 251, f. 14.

[5] *Lockhart Papers*, ii. 132, 134; Glover, *Stuart Papers*, p. 98, app. pp. 48–56.

and though the others received no accommodation from the Government, they never returned to their old allegiance. Then in October came the death of Cowper, whose last letter to his wife contained the cryptic but symbolic message that he had '3,000 dead to dispose of'.[1] The ensuing two sessions of Parliament were among the quietest ever managed by Walpole. A heavy tax imposed on papists and non-jurors in 1723 apparently broke Jacobite finance, and another flood of desertions from the Stuart cause in 1725 left the Pretender with no parliamentary following of any consequence.[2]

Jacobite policy makes the central theme of opposition activity from 1715 to 1725. There was jangling enough among the Pretender's supporters, and certainly they executed their plans in a clumsy and impractical fashion. But till defeats and desertions finally wrecked their hopes, they constituted the only *bloc* in opposition with a consistent programme and a single aim. The other groups and individuals who shuffled in and out of place during this period pursued the traditional guerrilla tactics for their own conflicting and short-term interests. There is no evidence to show that any of them developed a set of political principles accompanied by a scheme for their promotion. All simply sought office on satisfactory terms, and to this end they intrigued at Court, dallied with the Prince of Wales, and combated ministerial measures in Parliament 'to distress the King into a change of hands'. When any of them succeeded, like the Walpole–Townshend connexion in 1720, they quickly

---

[1] Campbell, *Lives of the Lord Chancellors*, iv. 411.

[2] Realey, *Early Opposition to Sir Robert Walpole*, pp. 150–1. The Jacobites were still capable of opposing and thwarting the Government by activity outside of Parliament, as, during the session of 1724–5, they raised such a storm in Scotland over a proposed new tax on Scottish ale that Walpole was obliged to abandon the scheme. It seems clear that by this time, with the dwindling of his adherents at Westminster, the Pretender had come to accept such 'extra-parliamentary opposition' as the only feasible means of keeping the cause alive in Britain. To George Lockhart, who had done much to stir up the ale-tax furor, the Chevalier wrote in March 1725, 'It is but too manifest in this conjuncture nothing but a foreign force can do the work effectually. . . . It is my friends' business to lie quiet, and to preserve themselves in a condition of being useful on a proper occasion, 'tho that ought not to hinder them from using their utmost endeavours to thwart and oppose the measures of the Government in as far as that can be done without exposing themselves to the lash of the law; and indeed so far it is necessary they should exert themselves, since there is no other way left at present to keep up the spirit of the nation and support the credit of the cause, which requires vigour as well as prudence in those concerned in it' (*Lockhart Papers*, ii. 150).

abandoned those with whom they had voted and thereafter displayed no invincible disinclination to support measures of the kind they had previously opposed.[1] Grumbletonians came and went without a trace, but everyone cast into opposition found there the sanguine, eager Jacobites, anxious to fall in with any malcontents, who might 'perhaps be driven', as Atterbury once observed, 'to help forward what they never intended'.[2]

The Country Party Programme

At any given moment, therefore, the Jacobites could be counted on to resist Government proposals, and depending on the nature of the issue, they received a varying amount of support from the other 'outs'. The narrowest area of agreement was that which brought together only the Tory clans of Oxford's Ministry. Hanoverian or Jacobite, they would all on every occasion vote to dispute any reflections on Anne, the Treaty of Utrecht, or the general policies pursued from 1710 to 1714. As questions worthy of a rousing debate, these tended to disappear after the Act of Grace, though as late as March 1718 the House of Lords was the scene of an impassioned argument, concluded by a sizeable division and a protest, because the preamble of a Bill to reconstruct the parish church of St. Giles-in-the-Fields failed to refer to Anne as 'of pious memory'.[3] The old battlecry of 'the Church in danger' still possessed some appeal as well. The Tory members threw all their strength against the repeal of the Schism and Occasional Conformity Acts in 1719, and in this division their numbers were swelled by Whig dissidents willing to embarrass the Government on any issue.[4] But defence of the Church was disappearing as a rallying point. A Tory Blasphemy Bill died a quick death in 1721.[5] The Quaker Affirmation Bill of 1722 went through the Commons without a

---

[1] In 1718 Government leaders taunted Argyll and Walpole with the charge that they 'changed their opinions according as they were in or out of place': *P.H.* vii. 534, 538. It should be added, however, that Walpole displayed some evidence of responsibility in opposition. He supported financial measures which he had framed when in office (ibid. 442–3, 446), and after leading an unsuccessful effort in 1718 to have mutiny and desertion punished by the civil magistrate, he voted for the Mutiny Act on the grounds that 'he had rather those crimes be punished by martial law than not punished at all': ibid. 537–8.

[2] *H.M.C., Stuart Papers*, v. 609.

[3] *P.H.* vii. 551–2.

[4] Ibid. 584–9.

[5] Ibid. 893–5.

recorded division, and Atterbury's attempt to prove 'that the Quakers were no Christians' seems to have stirred little excitement and less support in the Lords.[1] The degree of loyalty evoked by the Tory standards of Anne's reign is a measure of the breakdown of the pre-existing political pattern. For a time the remnants of the Oxford–Bolingbroke coalition found occasional unity in a revival of their former slogans, but changing conditions submerged the old issues, and dying memories make a poor platform for decisive political action.

There were broader issues, also linked to the past though not so closely connected with the history of particular groups, that normally attracted the support of all Anti-courtiers. Reduced to fundamentals, they were two: the security of Britain against foreign and domestic enemies, and the liberty and property of the subject. On any question which could be made to involve either of these points, all malcontents could present a united front. Now, as we generally view the reign of George I, his ministers took very few dangerous or repressive measures, and by the standards of his own time the Government was mild and lenient. All the Jacobite plots produced but a handful of reprisals. There was no conflict between Crown and People to produce general apprehension about the rights and liberties of Englishmen. Probably the most dubious proposals of George I's Ministries, aside from the impeachment proceedings of 1715, were the Septennial Act, the war with Spain, the Peerage Bills, the tax on papists and non-jurors, and two brief suspensions of habeas corpus. All these provided grist for the Opposition mill, and the Government had to face crucial debate on each occasion. But such matters arose irregularly, and they did not constitute a weak or tyrannical policy. As a result, the Opposition generally raised the issues of security and liberty upon the routine proposals of the executive for the armed forces, taxation, and foreign affairs. Here it was possible to evoke the Briton's immemorial dread of standing armies, summary justice, vexatious impositions, costly alliances, and subservience to foreign powers—spectres which all grumbletonians could easily agree to abhor.

In the light of Government policy, it must be seen that these issues were artificial, manufactured as debating points for the

[1] *P.H.* vii. 938–42.

purposes of opposition. Moreover, the alternatives to the administration's measures generally proposed by the Opposition
were unrealistic and unfeasible. Instead of maintaining or
increasing the army, they advocated reliance on the navy and
militia; instead of the intended levies, they recommended
economy by the reduction of pensions and other extravagances;
instead of a foreign policy condemned as ruinous to British
interests, they insisted upon a change or reversal as certain to
enrich and strengthen the realm.[1] The malcontent orators had
probably no intention of putting their proposals into effect if
they attained office. In the event, at least, new ministers
normally continued the measures of their predecessors because
executive policy was usually determined by logical necessity,
but this did not deter the Opposition from maintaining the
same line session after session.

Herein lay an important political factor, of ancient development and long enduring: as a general rule there existed a consistent and undeviating 'Country party' programme advocated
by men without administrative responsibility and not designed
for execution. This programme had nothing to do with the
supposed principles traditionally connected with party names.
It was a product, not of ingrained or abstract principles, but
of Opposition politics regardless of who was in Opposition.
Tories, for example, were presumed to favour the Prerogative,
but out of office this favouritism was scarcely apparent. Sir
Thomas Hanmer, prominent Tory leader in the Commons,
used the following argument against entrusting the Crown
with an army of 16,347 men in 1717:

For the taking this dangerous step, the only justification I hear gentlemen offer for themselves, the shelter they fly to, is the great confidence
which is to be reposed in His Majesty's just and gracious intentions;
of those I will entertain no doubt: I believe His Majesty is too good
to be suspected of any arbitrary designs. But yet there is a general
suspicion, which I will never be ashamed or afraid to own; because
it is a suspicion interwoven in our Constitution; it is a suspicion upon
which our laws, our Parliament, and every part of our Government
is founded; which is, that too much power lodged in the Crown,
abstracting [*sic*] from the person that wears it, will at some time or

[1] For representative examples in this period, see ibid. 57–60, 512–22, 924–6,
935–6, 949.

other be abused in the exercise of it, and can never long consist with
the natural rights and liberties of mankind.[1]

This is the pure milk of the doctrine said to be Whig, but in
truth it was a standard debating point for any grumbletonian.
The conflict between the so-called party principles and the
standpoints of Government and Opposition sometimes bemused
contemporaries as it has bewildered historians. Reporting a
debate in the Lords on the Septennial Bill, a Jacobite agent
observed,

The most remarkable thing was that the Tories talked like old
Whigs and republicans, against monarchy and ministers, etc., and
the Whigs magnified the advantages of unlimited absolute power
and prerogative, vilified the mob, ridiculed the people, and exalted
the Crown.[2]

This was an exaggeration of both arguments, though the debate
does appear to have gone to extremes.[3] The confusion of
theoretical positions in the debates of this period was indubitable,
but the positions taken by Court and Country were standard.

The 'Country party' programme provided a basis of unity
for the disparate malcontent groups upon the occasion of major
divisions in Lords and Commons. The Jacobites were reasonably sure that they could count on support from all the grumbletonians whenever they forced a 'Country' issue, and those
concerned to distress the Ministry with a view to office knew
likewise that all Anti-courtiers would divide with them if they
took the initiative on such questions. Hence the façade of Opposition unity in many of the great parliamentary battles from 1715
to 1725, and hence the Government's complaint that their opponents could all unite to do mischief. But, though sufficient to
bring them together for the purposes of debate, the 'Country
party' programme—negative, impractical, and of doubtful
sincerity—did not suffice to weld them all into an Opposition
coalition, even had they wished it. There is no evidence to
suggest that any effort was made to form all the 'outs' into an

---

[1] *P.H.* vii. 521. The accuracy and correctness of attribution of the speeches in the
P.H. is always open to doubt. In this case Hanmer's speech is printed in quotation
marks, the common practice when a speaker released the text of his address for
publication.

[2] *H.M.C., Stuart Papers,* ii. 122.

[3] *P.H.* vii. 292–308.

alliance prepared to take office, and under the conditions prevailing at the royal Court there was no reason to believe that a confederacy could achieve a *bouleversement* similar to those of 1710 and 1714. Such party organization as existed, therefore, resided in limited associations of individual groups, each of which inevitably tried to mass its strength for its own aims, normally as we know in conflict with those of the other connexions.

The paleontology of these party structures is inexact because there were so few hard parts to fossilize. Our evidence is fragmentary and often unreliable. We can see political organizations at work only in specific, scattered instances, and from them we can do no more than infer what may have been their character and composition. Most party alliances seem still to have been the product of informal private initiative taken shortly before or after the opening of a session. Charles Kinnaird remarked in January 1717, 'that all hands are at work to form new parties against the Parliament meet',[1] a common observation at that juncture in most any year. In 1723 Sir Robert Walpole urged the Crown to summon Parliament for the coming January, rather than to have a short session before Christmas, because 'I always thought the adjournments at Christmas tended more to cabals than all other occasions'.[2] There appears to have existed among some parliamentarians bound by friendship or common experience a distinct predisposition to concert plans year after year. Scattered evidence suggests, for example, that the so-called 'moderate Tories' led by Carnarvon, Anglesey, the Archbishop of York Sir William Dawes, and Sir Thomas Hanmer, who had opposed the commercial clauses in the Treaty of Utrecht and joined the 'Hanoverian cabal' shortly before the accession, met to 'scheme for the winter campaign' from 1716 until at least 1720.[3] By and large, however, such alliances constituted more or less ephemeral 'flying squadrons', the basis of whose formation was likely to dissolve as a result of changes in the political pattern and the loss of members to death or the Court. On the whole it seems clear that only two fixed centres of organized parliamentary opposition were in operation at any time during the period. They were, as might be expected,

[1] *H.M.C., Stuart Papers*, iii. 428.   [2] Coxe, *Walpole*, ii. 293.
[3] Glover, *The Stuart Papers*, p. 33; *Diary of Mary Countess Cowper*, pp. 122, 144–5.

the Pretender's Court from about 1716 to 1723, and the Court of the Prince of Wales from 1717 to 1720. In the years of their effectiveness each regularly formed and executed plans to distress the Government, and from their activities we can glean some knowledge of how cabals of malcontents went about their business.

The Jacobite Party

The Jacobite party in Britain was but one element of an extensive network of conspiracy that spread out over western Europe from the Boyne to the Danube. Resident Jacobite agents were established in most of the great capitals. Couriers posted frequently from one to another, and occasionally special emissaries made their way off the beaten tracks to Sweden and Muscovy. Headquarters for the conspiracy was, of course, the court of the Old Chevalier, which was slow to find a stable location. Expelled from Lorraine early in 1716, James removed to Avignon, only to be driven within a year to papal territory in Italy. He settled temporarily at Urbino, and finally at the end of 1718 he established his retinue in Rome, where the Palazzo Muti became his permanent residence. Despite these peregrinations the Jacobite organization continued to function under the formal direction of James and his chief minister, the Secretary of State. The Earl of Mar, who succeeded Boling-broke in that post in April 1716, retained it until February 1719, when 'bobbing John' resigned abruptly as James was about to join the abortive expedition that collapsed at Glen-shiel.[1] For more than five years thereafter no one held the Seals, but the chief favourite of the moment, the quarrelsome James Murray of Stormont, performed the work of the office for eighteen months, to be followed by John Hay, the titular Earl of Inverness, who was finally invested with the Seals at the close of 1724.[2] The efficiency of the organization, such as it was, however, probably owed less to the management of these Courtiers than to the steady industry of the Pretender's 'Clerk of the Bills' or private secretary, James Edgar. He conducted

[1] A. and H. Tayler, *The Stuart Papers at Windsor* (London, 1939), pp. 45–49, 56–57; H. Tayler, *The Jacobite Court at Rome in 1719* (Edinburgh, 1938), pp. 113, 128, 143–6. Maurice Bruce, 'The Duke of Mar in Exile, 1716–32' in *Trans. R. Hist. Soc.* 4th ser., xx (1937), 61–82.

[2] Tayler, *Jacobite Court at Rome*, pp. 116, 129, 134.

the royal correspondence, as well as a vast correspondence of his own, and with a single exception he kept constantly on cordial terms with all the many figures in the conspiratorial network.[1]

The formal organization of the British branch was simple in structure. After the failure of the '15, the Chevalier appointed two officers, one military and one civil, to carry on his affairs in his kingdoms until the restoration: the Earl of Arran became 'commander-in-chief of all his forces both by sea and land in England and Scotland', and Atterbury was constituted 'his resident in England to and by whom he will from time to time transmit his pleasure, commands, and directions to all his subjects of that kingdom'.[2] Beneath the leaders were two chief agents, Harry Straiton in Edinburgh and John Menzies in London, whose business it was to manage the routine tasks of administration: reporting general intelligence, forwarding correspondence, transmitting funds, and maintaining liaison among the different elements of the party.[3] They employed as many assistants as they needed or could afford, and it was they who really kept the organization functioning.

In the operation of the parliamentary party, the London agent was the key man. Despite his commission from the Pretender, Atterbury did not command the allegiance of all English Jacobites; only his own small following, represented by Arran and the remnants of Ormonde's clique, fully accepted his lead. Sickly and cantankerous, the ageing Bishop worked fitfully, suspected his collaborators, and quarrelled furiously on the slightest provocation. Though Oxford had nominated Atterbury to the Pretender for the post as head of the party,[4] the former Treasurer found it impossible to co-operate cordially

---

[1] Ibid., pp. 40–42; Tayler, *Stuart Papers at Windsor*, pp. 190–2.

[2] *H.M.C., Stuart Papers*, ii. 305, 466–7, 469. There was no official Jacobite resident in Scotland. Until 1720 the non-juring Bishop of Edinburgh acted unofficially in that capacity; thereafter Scottish affairs were managed by a 'Board of Trustees' set up by the King on the suggestion of the Bishop and George Lockhart: *Lockhart Papers*, ii. 25–31.

[3] Though for long infirm, Straiton served as agent throughout this period and died in office in 1725: ibid., pp. 121, 143, 154. Menzies apparently had to flee England late in 1719 or early in 1720. Thereafter his duties were probably divided between James Hamilton and Charles Caesar. Menzies was reported to be 'almost starving' in Paris in 1724: Tayler, *Jacobite Court at Rome in 1719*, p. 130.

[4] *H.M.C., Stuart Papers*, v. 416.

with him, and Bolingbroke's followers, now led by Wyndham, stood at as frigid a distance from 'Old Ruffian' as they did from the detested Oxford. Hence the three main Jacobite elements had but tenuous connexions, and all, including converts like Wharton and Shrewsbury, circumvented Atterbury's authority when they chose, by corresponding directly with the Chevalier. It fell upon John Menzies, therefore, to find means to make them draw together, and in this he was indefatigable. He wrote voluminously, and galloped about in person when necessary, to get agreement among the leaders. He scolded Atterbury about his groundless jealousies, and though Menzies never met Oxford, he persuaded the Earl's bustling mistress, Anne Oglethorpe, to act as go-between with the Bishop.[1] At times he grew discouraged, which led lordly party members to call him 'peevish', but on the whole he was justly characterized as 'very honest, careful, and zealous'.[2]

Liaison between the British party and headquarters at James's Court was sustained but irregular and uneven. Since the law made it high treason to correspond with the Pretender or his agents, nearly all letters went in code. There were different ciphers for different channels of correspondence, and all codes had to be altered now and again when it was believed that the Government had broken them.[3] Despite these precautions, it was always risky to use the regular mail: 'We never write nor receive that way without great doubt and anxiety', Menzies once wrote to Mar, and all the conspirators were well aware that the Post Office opened their letters.[4] To avoid the dangers of discovery the Jacobites endeavoured to operate a postal system of their own. Constant efforts were made to keep a special packet boat running between Britain and the Channel ports, where refugees and sympathetic Catholic clergymen acted as forwarding agents. On the Continent the chief distribution point was the Paris agency of Lieutenant-General

[1] For representative samples of Menzies's activities, see *H.M.C., Stuart Papers*, ii. 343, 419, 459; iii. 169, 196, 219, 234, 236, 249, 285–8, 307, 354, 378, 430, 446, 493, 512; iv. 299, 533.

[2] Ibid. vi. 268.

[3] On the Jacobite codes, see ibid. i. xciv–cii; ii. xxxvii–xlv; iii. xli–xlvii; iv. xxxvii–xli; vi. xxviii–lxxxix.

[4] Ibid. ii. 140, 416, 485; iv. 220, 335; vi. 238, 327. Apparently the Jacobites used the Spanish and French diplomatic pouches upon occasion: ibid. ii. 242, 297; vi. 119–20.

Arthur Dillon, a Jacobite officer in the French service. Menzies and Straiton distributed and dispatched the packets received at London and Edinburgh.

The system never worked smoothly. Faithful captains and crews were hard to find. Indeed, one packet boat was put out of service in 1717 by a mutiny. Funds to support these expensive operations were always short, and an attempt to finance the system by smuggling did not prove successful. There was always the possibility as well that custom house officers would search private packets, which meant that correspondence was jettisoned or captured.[1] Moreover, Atterbury and Oxford, distrustful of each other and ever fearful of betrayal, preferred their own 'puckles' or couriers to Menzies and his messengers. Oxford generally used a captain John Ogilvie, whom James III thought 'quite mad', though sometimes the Earl's beloved Anne Oglethorpe carried his correspondence. Atterbury employed Ormonde's agent, the youthful and captious Sir Redmond Everard, known in cipher as 'the little knight'. Neither Earl nor Bishop would entrust his packets to the courier of the other, and so there were at most times three distinct and mutually antagonistic postal systems.[2] In addition, at various seasons appeared numerous individual emissaries, on special mission or simply self-appointed: the exasperated Menzies was provoked to inform Mar in the spring of 1718,

> The vast multitude of couriers, messengers, plenipotentiaries, etc. of late have confounded everything and ruined all secrecy. Every Irish courier has been an absolute minister, however unfit and poisoned with the prejudices of the little party he likes best, and makes that his chief business. It is not in words or any colours to paint our disorders.[3]

Distance created problems too. After James moved to Italy it was rare for a letter to complete the weary passage between Rome and London in less than six weeks, and recipients do not seem to have been surprised when the time *en route* was twice as

---

[1] On the operations of the Jacobite postal system, see especially ibid. iii, 79, 110–11, 139; iv. 507, 524; v. 143, 211, 296, 390, 422, 430, 441, 522, 569; vi. 331–2, 392–4.

[2] See ibid. v. 291, 555; vi. 111, 125, 209; vii. 517. Oxford's system was more efficient than Atterbury's, so that letters to the Earl from the Chevalier's Court arrived before those to the Bishop, a fact which evidently annoyed the latter intensely: vi. 347.   [3] Ibid. vi. 299.

long. The British party found that 'such a slowness of correspondence . . . is of infinite disadvantage' but were powerless
to rectify it.[1]

Yet, in spite of confusion, interruption, loss, and delay, an
extensive correspondence did go on between the British
Jacobites and the court in exile. To James it was essential that
the party leaders should know and approve his schemes, for not
only did he urgently need their financial contributions, but he
could hardly hope to accomplish his restoration in a manner
which they opposed. Thus he tried to keep them well informed
of all his intricate manœuvres abroad and never ceased to express his desire for their advice and counsel. But James was
careful not to dictate policy to his touchy followers. He suggested, recommended, urged, but did not command, measures
designed to support his current plot, ever recognizing that
conditions in Britain of which he was unaware might make
modifications necessary. The parliamentary leaders deferred to
advices from the Court and seem generally to have pursued
them as far as was possible and practical.[2] There can be little
doubt but that the policies of the Jacobite Opposition were
influenced by the leaders' knowledge of the plans on foot abroad,
though it is equally clear that their actions were naturally
determined by the logic of the situation in which the proponents
of a restoration found themselves. For this there can be no
better proof than the fact that all the different and antagonistic
elements generally voted together in Parliament.

Party discipline, however, was the despair of the Jacobite
managers. The general meeting place in London was the Cocoa
Tree in Pall Mall, as it had been in Anne's time.[3] There seems

---

[1] *H.M.C., Stuart Papers*, v. 323; vi. 166, 207, 510.

[2] For representative examples of exchanges of information and advice between
James and the party, see ibid. iii. 8–14; iv. 177; v. 248, 278–81, 323, 325, 557–60,
564–9, 602–3, 617.

[3] John Timbs, *Club Life of London* (London, 1866), i. 81. Because the Cocoa Tree
was so well known as a Jacobite meeting place, the party constantly feared the
presence of Government spies. Loose talk at the Cocoa Tree led to the flight of
Ogilvie in 1718: *H.M.C., Stuart Papers*, vii. 396, 682. The investigation of the
Atterbury plot in 1722 turned up some evidence to indicate the existence of an
organization of Tory peers and gentlemen under the presidency of Lord Orrery
known as 'Burford's club', but it seems more likely that this was simply a Jacobite
code name for the Tory party in England: *P.H.* viii. 127, 136, 225, 227. Other
code names for the party were 'Mr. Juxon's family' and 'Bernard's family': *H.M.C.,
Stuart Papers*, ii. 62, 447.

clearly to have been something resembling a party 'Whip', for letters went out to prompt a good attendance before each session and sometimes at critical points during a session.[1] But response to the party's call was ragged and uneven. Although the leaders estimated that their numbers were about 160 in the Parliament of 1715–22 and 170 in that elected in 1722,[2] they seldom could muster their full strength. Attendance was relatively good early in the session of 1715, when around 130 regularly showed up for important divisions, but over the hot summer months they dwindled rapidly.[3] So few Tories appeared in January 1716 that it was called a 'Rump Parliament', though the repeal of the Triennial Act in April provoked an attendance close to the maximum.[4] Menzies's letters for the session of 1717–18 are filled with bitterness and disgust. A month after the opening he wrote:

Seventy of the Tories are still absent, hunting the fox and drinking strong beer. Those here are reeling in confusion and factions, the undertakers and leaders changing their maxims every hour of the day, very visionary, very shallow, and very hot, but more Tories are soon expected in town on better advice.[5]

Those present evidently took the duty of attendance very lightly, for during the critical divisions on the army, when the Government won by small majorities, some Tories were in bed, others were drinking in taverns, and still others were carousing with the imprisoned Shippen in the Tower of London.[6] After Christmas, numbers increased somewhat, as Menzies had predicted, but by the third week in February, with a month of the session still to run, they were on their way out of town again, being

---

[1] Ibid. ii. 84; iii. 428; v. 545; vii. 239–40, 261, 424, 551; Coxe, *Walpole*, ii. 162; *H.M.C., Sutherland MSS.*, p. 189. One of the problems involved in the co-ordination of Jacobite activities was to prevent timing the outbreak of a plot or rising with a summons to maximum attendance at Parliament. One of Mar's arguments for postponing the '15 until September was that 'the members of Parliament in the King's [Pretender's] interest, being released from their attendance, shall be at liberty to influence their neighbours in the country and unite their strength by proper measures': *H.M.C., Stuart Papers*, i. 523. The same factor played an important part in planning the abortive *coups* of 1717 and 1722.

[2] Ibid. v. 307; *H.M.C., Sutherland MSS.*, p. 190.

[3] P.R.O. Egmont MSS. 234: Diary, 17 Mar., 23 June, 15 July, 21 Aug. 1715; *H.M.C., Portland MSS.* v. 508; *P.H.* vii. 52.

[4] Ibid. vi. 372–4; *H.M.C., Dropmore MSS.* i. 51.

[5] *H.M.C., Stuart Papers*, v. 298.

[6] Ibid. v. 302, 307.

'assured that nothing is to be attempted this year against the Church'.[1]

What was true of these sessions remained so in those that followed. The bulk of the party arrived late and left early. Upon occasion ministerial trickery may in part have accounted for this: false rumours of further prorogations were circulated in 1718 to discourage prompt arrival,[2] and in 1721 it was charged that the Government deliberately 'spun out' the session 'to that vast length that nothing can keep the country members in town'.[3] But their attendance seems generally to have been lackadaisical except when they were aroused by the emergence of issues which affected their susceptibilities. Then they combined a low boiling-point with a high rate of evaporation.

In the two general elections during this period the Jacobites displayed notable vigour. The exact nature of their electoral organization is indiscernible, but it is clear that the leaders took counsel among themselves and endeavoured to co-ordinate their interests. For the election of 1722 Shippen and Lockhart, with the blessing of the Pretender, made an effort to 'settle an union and correspondence betwixt the Scots and English Tories'. They first met at Newcastle in 1721 to consider proposals of co-operation from Sunderland and Argyll, who were working against Walpole within the Ministry, and there was considerable communication between them thereafter.[4] Each was empowered to speak for an organized group in his own country, but the details of electoral campaigning do not emerge from the records. Although the Jacobites were continually at work to raise funds, their collections seem to have been transmitted abroad or expended on their postal system and publications rather than devoted to the purchase of boroughs or county electors. It is possible that exertions were made to find seats for members of the party cliques, but there is no evidence for it. On the contrary, despite some sanguine expressions of hope for a 'Tory Parliament', the impression is strong that the Tory organization, such as it may have been, existed for defensive purposes, to maintain their existing 'interests' in the traditional fashion, and

[1] *H.M.C., Stuart Papers*, v. 510; vi. 164.
[2] Ibid. vii. 569.
[3] Coxe, *Walpole*, ii. 216. Cf. *H.M.C., Clements MSS.*, pp. 318–19.
[4] *Lockhart Papers*, ii. 63–90.

not to capture a majority by a large-scale invasion of constituencies controlled by Whig clans or the Government.

The elections of 1715 and 1722 were nevertheless hard-fought contests, by one standard of measurement the most spirited of the Georgian era. An eighteenth-century election went through four stages, which constituted a gradual process of elimination. First came the period of 'nominations' and the decision of candidates to stand. Either no one challenged the reigning 'interest', or rival 'interests' agreed to 'divide' the constituency for the peace of the borough or county, or rival candidates issued their requests for favour and support. Then came the campaign, which lasted till the moment of polling. Sometimes new candidates appeared, but more often one or two of the contestants, seeing the trend running strongly for their opponents, 'withdrew their pretensions and declined the poll'. Where no rivals existed, no poll took place. Where competitors were still in the field, the third stage occurred, namely, the poll, a scrutiny if demanded by the defeated candidates and allowed by the returning officer, and the return of the writ to Chancery. There was a final stage if the loser on the poll or his supporters petitioned Parliament against an unjust return, and only with the decisions in the House of Commons on the petitions can a general election be said to have ended.

Now it is impossible to get accurate statistics for the first two stages in all or even a majority of the constituencies. Many of the agreements and decisions were probably never recorded. But for the last two stages there is evidence for very close approximations, and judging both by the number of constituencies that went to the poll and the number of petitions presented to Parliament, the general election of 1722 was the most hotly contested under the four Georges, and 1715 ranks second. The numbers in both cases are not high proportions of the 270 constituencies in England and Wales, but they are higher than for any of the other twenty general elections. In 1715 there were 12 counties and 82 boroughs which went to the poll, and in 1722 the figures are 15 and 88 respectively. In the former year 76 petitions were presented, in the latter 80.[1] Not all these

---

[1] The Jacobites decided to forfeit the elections in Scotland in 1722, 'knowing well that few or none of them would be returned, 'tho elected by ever so great a majority': *Lockhart Papers*, ii. 82. Statistics on election contests are based upon the

contests, of course, were between Jacobites and Government supporters. As noted earlier, rival elements within the party fought each other, and Whig connexions had their conflicts as well. Yet there can be little doubt, as one scrutinizes the names of the contestants, that conflicts of 'interest' frequently coincided with differences of political allegiance.

Perhaps the most perfervid aspect of Jacobite party activity was journalism, despite the severest kind of discouragement. Very shortly after the succession Swift retired to Ireland and Defoe sold his pen to the Ministry. The Government bore down hard on all opposition in the Press:

> By 1718 three satisfactory methods of controlling the Press were in use; offenders were being arrested and imprisoned, papers and manuscripts were being destroyed in printing shops or in coffee houses, and first class writers for the Opposition were getting state pensions.[1]

Still the shops were filled with Jacobite effusions. In the autumn of 1717 Joseph Addison remarked upon 'the unusual spirit got into the enemies of the Government, which discovers itself in the falsehood and virulence of their discourses, newspapers, clandestine prints and letters'.[2] Six years later a Government survey of English printers revealed that in London and Westminster there were 34 'known to be well affected to the King George', whereas there were 3 'non-jurors', 4 'Roman Catholics', and 34 'said to be high flyers'.[3] The compiler of the survey noted that Opposition printing houses 'are daily set up and supported by unknown hands', and he observed that the 'country printers', the twenty-eight presses in corporate provincial towns, 'in general copy from the rankest papers in London; and thus the poison is transmitted from one hand to another through all His Majesty's dominions'.[4]

---

standard compilations of H. S. Smith, *The Parliaments of England* (3 vols., Leeds, 1844–50) and poll figures of W. W. Bean printed in *Notes and Queries*, 8 ser. ii–vi, supplemented and corrected by information gathered from local histories, newspapers, journals, memoirs, letters, &c. The presentation of election petitions and the decisions thereon are recorded in *Commons Journals*.

[1] D. H. Stevens, *Party Politics and English Journalism, 1702–1742* (Chicago, 1916), p. 107.

[2] Graham, *Annals of Stair*, ii. 27.

[3] John Nichols, *Literary Anecdotes of the Eighteenth Century* (London, 1812), i. 288–312.

[4] Ibid., p. 289.

Many of the newspapers of the time were publications of very brief duration. They appeared for a few numbers, often to serve some specific and transitory purpose, and then were abruptly discontinued. One typical life-cycle was that of the *Britons* in 1723–4. The Jacobite Duke of Wharton subsidized the *True Briton* to assault the Ministry, beginning in June 1723. In August the Government brought out the *Briton* to keep up a running counter-attack. After six months of combat the Government decided to put the *True Briton* out of business, which was accomplished by prosecuting Payne, its printer and publisher, for libel against the Administration. The *True Briton* ceased publication on the 17th of February, Payne was found guilty on the 24th, and on the 26th the *Briton* fired a parting shot over its adversary's grave. For a few weeks the Government then ran the *Honest True Briton*, apparently to exorcise the evil spirits raised by Wharton's sheet, and approximately a year after its inception this journalistic episode was over, leaving the field to the more celebrated *Britons* of the future.[1] Not all Opposition papers succumbed in this fashion, however, for after a decade of state persecution, the 'high-flying' journals nearly matched the Government's in number. In 1724 the Tories were reported to control 2 of the 3 London dailies, 4 of the 10 tri-weeklies, and 3 of the 6 weeklies.[2] The Jacobites evidently put great effort into their Press and had great hopes of its influence: 'it was indeed well said of Mr. Locke', John Menzies once remarked, 'give me but the power of the newspapers and the ballads and pamphlets, I will give any man that will the power of the laws'.[3]

Had the Jacobite prints been as influential as they were numerous, this pronouncement might have been put to the test. As it was, 'the power of the laws' proved too strong not only for the Press but for all the forces which the Jacobite Opposition could bring to bear. For this reason it became the last Opposition of its kind rather than a prototype for the future. One can easily imagine the course of events if the Chevalier's followers

---

[1] Add. MSS. 27980, ff. 281, 283, 287–9; Stevens, *Party Politics and English Journalism*, p. 115.

[2] Nichols, *Literary Anecdotes*, i. 312.

[3] *H.M.C., Stuart Papers*, vi. 503. The emphasis placed upon the press by the Jacobite party seems a clear continuation of the policy developed by the Tory clans of Anne's last Ministry, whereby 'Oxford made the journal a fundamental part of his political organization': Stevens, *Party Politics and English Journalism*, p. 80.

had achieved a Stuart restoration at any time during this period: the logical reaction would have been a Hanoverian Opposition of the same character as the Jacobite, and a natural prolongation of the age of political conspiracy. The failure of Jacobitism, however, did not mean the extinction of its attitudes and its methods. They survived to serve the loyal Oppositions of the succeeding era.

The Leicester House Opposition

The organization of the Leicester House Opposition from 1717 to 1720 inevitably differed radically from that of the Pretender's party. Since the Prince of Wales dwelt so conveniently in London, communications were easy. His Court was the natural headquarters of his group, and the town residences of the discontented magnates, Devonshire House in particular, served as secondary centres. These malcontents never had to face a general election and probably never had any plans for doing so. They appear to have been organized only for intrigue and parliamentary activities.

When the Prince first embarked on his opposition, and a variety of connexions gathered about him, he had to cope with much conflicting advice. At first he seems to have relied most heavily upon Argyll, but early in 1718 the Walpole–Townshend group gained a monopoly of the Prince's confidence. By March the Tories who had flocked sporadically to Leicester House ('our occasional conformists', Lord Cathcart called them) gave up their dalliance with the Hanoverian heir, and the disgruntled Argyll, after opening a flirtation with the Jacobites, caught on again at the royal Court.[1] For most of its existence, therefore, the Leicester house Opposition was in the hands of Walpole's Junto.

There appears to have been a directing council which made decisions of policy. At the time of the tense battle over the Army Bill in 1718, Lord Cathcart, an assiduous courtier at Leicester House, recorded in his journal: 'Il y eut cabinet de

---

[1] On the arrival and departure of various groups at the Prince's court, see P.R.O. Cathcart MSS. 5/47, Journal: 27 Dec. 1717, 1 Mar. 1718; Coxe, *Walpole*, ii. 61; Graham, *Annals of Stair*, ii. 87–88; *H.M.C., Stuart Papers*, v. 381, 447. On Argyll's flirtation with Jacobitism, see ibid. v–vii *passim*; *Lockhart Papers*, ii. 11 ff. Negotiations went so far that in 1718 a patent of Jacobite nobility was made out for Ilay, Argyll's brother, and even after he returned to Court, he continued to give Lockhart and others reason to believe that he could still be gained to 'the cause'.

Walpole, Compton, Townshend, et Rutland chez mon maistre.'[1] In the following year, according to Onslow's account, Walpole had to persuade such a gathering to oppose the second Peerage Bill,[2] and as noted earlier, the 'treaty' of 1720 was made by a small cabal of leaders. Like the Jacobites they had a party Whip. Cathcart mentions 'notre opérateur' who circularized the Prince's friends upon his decisions, and Leicester House was able to make very accurate predictions of party strength in the House of Commons.[3] Their own numbers were small—one estimate put their voting strength in the Lower House at 28[4]—but of course they generally manœuvred to enlist the support of the other Anti-courtiers.

The Prince's party seems never to have bought or established a daily or weekly journal. They relied upon pamphlets, issued singly and in profusion, to defend themselves and to assault the Ministry as critical issues arose. When Sunderland's writers attacked the 'resigners' in 1717, the Walpole–Townshend connexion riposted vigorously to every thrust.[5] Their literary campaign against the Peerage Bills provoked one of the bitterest pamphlet wars of the century. Not only did the Opposition issue single pamphlets like Walpole's celebrated *Thoughts of a Member of the Lower House*, but they also promoted the device of a pamphlet series to be carried on till the controversy closed. Steele's *The Plebeian. To be continued Weekly* opened the battle for the Opposition. In reply came Molesworth's *The Patrician. To be continued Weekly*, Addison's *The Old Whig* and *The Moderator. To be continued Occasionally*.[6] Journalism of this sort was best suited to the kind of opposition put up by Leicester House. Walpole and Townshend were not concerned to keep alive a cause, as were the Jacobites, by the issue of regular and familiar sheets. The Whig clans sought rather to force the Ministry to an accommodation by strenuous contention on issues selected to provide the best battleground.[7] Pamphlet and pamphlet series

---

[1] P.R.O. Cathcart MSS. 5/47, Journal: 17 Feb. 1718.

[2] *H.M.C., Onslow MSS.*, p. 459.

[3] P.R.O. Cathcart MSS. 5/47, Journal: 11 Jan., 4 Feb., 17 Feb. 1718.

[4] *H.M.C., Portland MSS.* v. 546.

[5] See the pamphlet bibliography in Williams, *Stanhope*, p. 251, n. 1.

[6] See the bibliography and commentary given by E. R. Turner in 'The Peerage Bill of 1719', *E.H.R.* xxviii (1913), 250–1, notes 56–69.

[7] Cf. Craggs' comments on the Court's reaction to this type of campaign, quoted in *Diary of Mary Countess Cowper*, p. 161.

allowed of complete concentration upon the measures chosen, without any need for consistency. Their loyalty guarded by their attachment to the Prince, this Opposition could speak with greater virulence than any Jacobite dared to use, and the pamphlet was much harder to prosecute than the newspaper.

Now, as we are already aware, no coalition ever took place between the parties of Prince and Pretender. Their organizations, like their aims, remained distinct.[1] But their methods of parliamentary warfare, being largely determined by traditions inherited in common and the immediate circumstances which encompassed them both, bore many close resemblances. As there was a 'Country party' programme, so was there also a set of more or less standard 'Country party' tactics.

Country Party Tactics

From an examination of the debates and divisions of the period, it seems clear that all 'outs' made their main business to oppose, not to propose. To this general practice the exceptions were few. Sometimes an individual, like the economist Archibald Hutcheson, advanced schemes for extinguishing corruption in the army or in elections.[2] The party leaders, however, never introduced measures of constructive legislation. Whenever they took the initiative, it was to open an assault on ministerial policy. In 1715 and 1716 the Tories urged inquiries into the granting of pensions and the keeping of public accounts.[3] In 1717 the Walpole–Townshend group pushed an investigation of peculation in the subsidies to Dutch troops,[4] and the following year the Jacobites organized a merchants' petition against Swedish trade restrictions, upon which they forced two divisions in the House of Commons.[5] But Opposition proposals amounted to little more than these, and after 1718 the records are bare of similar manœuvres of any consequence. The Country party's

[1] The Jacobites earnestly desired to bring the Walpolians into their camp, but though there appears to have been some loose and gingerly co-ordination upon occasion, close co-operation was never achieved: *H.M.C., Stuart Papers*, iv. 262, 266, 331; v. 221, 419; vii. 570; *H.M.C., Carlisle MSS.*, pp. 22–23; *Annals of Stair*, ii. 373.

[2] *P.H.* vii. 534, 948–52; cf. *H.M.C., Stuart Papers*, vii. 314, 526.

[3] *P.H.* vii. 60; *Commons Journals*, xviii. 138–9, 430.

[4] *P.H.* vii. 451, 466–8.

[5] *Commons Journals*, xviii. 729, 756.

only success along these lines was on a point dear to Tory hearts but of scant political importance: by ten votes they carried a motion to have a sermon preached before the House on 29 May 1717 by Andrew Snape, foremost champion of High Church principles against the Bishop of Bangor's innovating doctrines, and though the Ministry thereupon had Snape struck off the list of royal chaplains, the Anti-courtiers secured a resolution of thanks for his address by sixteen votes.[1]

Opposition tactics, therefore, were primarily defensive in character. The country awaited the Court's measures and then selected a line of resistance.[2] The degree and timing of the resistance varied greatly from one session to another—much seems to have depended upon such factors as the size of attendance and the state of public feeling about the outstanding events, foreign and domestic, of the moment—but on the whole we may say that the Opposition tended to take a stand upon occasions which may be placed under three general classifications.

Any ministerial assault upon the persons or interests of the 'discontented party' was almost certain to encounter a strenuous defence, no matter how forlorn the cause. Of this there were four major instances and numerous minor ones during this period. The Tories fought their first general action against the proceedings to prosecute Anne's last Ministry, on which they divided not less than fourteen times in the first session of 1715.[3] The next year they combated the Government's method of

---

[1] Ibid. xviii. 571; *P.H.* vii. 452–3; *H.M.C., Stuart Papers*, iv. 316. The Whig malcontents supported this move, for Snape, a Cambridge man and later Provost of King's, was tutor to the children of Walpole, Townshend, and Devonshire.

[2] An examination of the recorded divisions during this period indicates that the Opposition might choose any stage of a Bill's passage on which to divide. Many critical divisions were taken on the motion to commit and on the third reading. During the debates on the Septennial Act, Shippen is reported to have said after the second reading that 'this Bill . . . hath already got through the most difficult part of its passage' (*P.H.* vii. 313), and the convention that the second reading was the stage for the major battle over the principle of a Bill may already have been established.

[3] *Commons Journals*, xviii. 59, 183, 219, 256, 258, 269, 271; *P.H.* vii. 65–66, 68–73, 128. All divisions in the House are recorded in the *Commons Journals*, but divisions in committee can only be discovered from the incomplete reports in the *P.H.*, news-letters, newspapers, and fragmentary references in private correspondence and diaries. Thus, any statement about the total number of divisions on any issue must be made with the proviso that there may well have been more unnoticed or unrecorded.

trying the rebel lords,[1] and from 1717 to 1720 they divided the House twenty times on the disposition of the forfeited estates.[2] The last big battle came over the crushing of the Atterbury Plot in 1723, when the Opposition forced a dozen divisions.[3] Defensive actions along these lines were rather compromising for a party engaged in treasonable conspiracy, and they never succeeded in blocking the course of ministerial action. But it was always possible that obstreperous resistance might deter the Government from taking more extreme measures,[4] and surely it was better to go down fighting than to lose by default. Perhaps also the Jacobite gentry took some measure of release from frustration by solemnly trooping out to vote that the Bishop of Rochester was not engaged in a popish plot, and that Shippen's calling the King a 'stranger to our language and Constitution' was not an unjust reflection upon the hated Hanoverian.[5]

In the second place, new legislation proposed by the Ministry frequently afforded an opportunity for spirited counter-attack. Measures like the Septennial Act, the repeal of the Schism and Occasional Conformity Acts, and the Peerage Bill raised constitutional, religious, and social issues upon which the Government was particularly vulnerable. Herein lay the best possibilities for striking success. The Opposition could truly pose as the defenders of the established laws of the realm, and ministerial supporters might desert the Court on sensitive points. Despite vigorous opposition, the Government triumphed in the first two instances,[6] but Walpole saw hope for better success when the Peerage Bill was introduced:

He told them [the Leicester House 'Cabinet'] it was the most maintainable point they could make a stand upon in the House of

---

[1] *Commons Journals*, xviii. 367, 377; *P.H.* vii. 291–2.

[2] *Commons Journals*, xviii. 448, 456, 460–1, 470–1, 568, 734, 754–5, 757; xix. 88, 94, 104, 107, 114, 243.

[3] Ibid. xx. 160, 164–5, 184, 186–7; *P.H.* viii. 195–7, 208–9, 213. It should be noted in this connexion that the Jacobites naturally opposed the suspension of habeas corpus both in 1716 and 1722 (ibid. vii, 276; viii. 38–41; *Commons Journals*, xx, 14), and they fought with some success to moderate the Government's vengeance upon papists and non-jurors in 1723 (Add. MSS. 27980, ff. 38–43; *Commons Journals*, xx. 209–10, 214, 217; *P.H.* viii. 51–53, 354–62).

[4] See *H.M.C., Portland MSS.* v. 554; *Annals of Stair*, ii. 27.

[5] Ibid. vii. 511–12; *Commons Journals*, xx. 165.

[6] Ibid. xvii. 429–30, 432; xix. 48–50; *P.H.* vii. 310–67, 584.

Commons against the Ministry [wrote Speaker Onslow]. He was
sure he could put it in such a light as to fire with indignation at it
every independent commoner in England; and that he saw a spirit
rising against it among some of the warmest of the Whigs that were
country gentlemen, and not in other things averse to the Administration. That the first discovery of this to him was from what he overheard one Mr. ——, Member for —— say upon it, a plain country
gentleman of about eight hundred pounds a year, of a rank equal to
that, and with no expectations or views to himself beyond what his
condition at that time gave him. But this person talking with another
Member about this Bill, he said with heat and some oaths (which
was what Mr. Walpole overheard and catched at) —'What, shall I
consent to the shutting the door upon my family ever coming into
the House of Lords!' This, Mr. Walpole told the company, struck
him with [the] conviction that the same sentiment might easily be
made to run through the whole body of country gentlemen, be their
estates then what they would. And so it proved, to a very thorough
defeat of the ministers in this instance.[1]

The Opposition also made use of popular indignation to harry
Walpole himself when he set about resolving the South Sea crisis.
They fought his engraftment scheme at every stage, and altogether there were at least thirty-eight divisions on this issue in
the session of 1720–21.[2] The Government did not carry them all
and sometimes found it wise to give in on minor matters without
a division. On the whole, however, Walpole proved more
fortunate than Sunderland had been, for on this occasion he
achieved the substance of his programme.[3]

Opposition did not restrict its attacks on new proposals to
flamboyant issues alone. They also divided on such minor
questions as a Bill to allow the Crown to issue letters of in-
corporation, a revision of the law on insolvent debtors, a
measure extending the power of the Royal College of Physicians
to examine drugs, and a set of regulations for the leasing of
ecclesiastical estates.[4] On most occasions of this sort there is no

[1] *H.M.C., Onslow MSS.*, p. 459. It seems to have been widely believed that a
good part of Walpole's success was owing to the judicious use of a large sum of
money laid out by the Prince of Wales: *Lockhart Papers*, ii. 58; Coxe, *Walpole*, ii. 172.
[2] *Commons Journals*, xix. 392, 395, 416–17, 422, 454, 462–3, 476, 482, 533, 590,
620–1, 644–5; *P.H.* vii. 685–6, 689–91, 693–5, 709–11, 747, 751–2, 755–6, 759–60,
791–6, 800–2, 827–33, 847–56, 906–11.
[3] Realey, *Early Opposition to Walpole*, pp. 16–30, 69–76.
[4] *Commons Journals*, xix. 356; xx. 157, 316, 327.

record of debate, and consequently we cannot discover the reasons for opposition. It may well have been that the Anti-courtiers endeavoured to capitalize upon aggrieved economic interests, for we have seen in the question of trade with Sweden that they understood the use of this kind of tactic. But the consistency with which the Country party took up a stand leaves the impression also that the Opposition was opposing for the sake of opposition, simply to harass the Ministry, whether or not principle or interest was involved. The impression is deepened by Lord Cowper's frankly stated policy: 'When one could not capture an enemy fort, one had to bombard it at least';[1] and we have the record of one outstanding case in which the Jacobites battled against their own convictions for no other purpose than to cast reflections upon the Court. This took place upon a Government motion to approve Byng's unprovoked assault on the Spanish fleet off Cape Passaro, with a view to preparing the way for a declaration of war. 'The Jacobites universally are as glad in their hearts at this war as the Court is,' wrote Menzies, 'and so for once these two agree.' Yet, in conjunction with the malcontent Whigs, they debated the question until 9 o'clock at night and finally went to a division, having 'struggled as having a mind to be ravished'.[2]

The steadiest opportunities for badgering the Court were the occasions that fall under our third classification, the routine measures necessarily introduced by the Executive, which it could be anticipated would appear regularly every session. The Country party could never foresee with certainty what 'terrible new Bills' the Ministry would bring in, but there must always be a speech from the Throne and an address of thanks, a Mutiny Act, Bills for the land tax, the malt tax and sundry excises, and appropriations for the army, the navy, and the service of the debt.[3] To these propositions the 'Country party programme'

---

[1] Realey, *Early Opposition to Walpole*, p. 83. In 1721–2 Cowper pushed his inveterate opposition to the point of entering protests in the Lords upon every possible occasion. He then had the protests printed and distributed for the purpose of influencing opinion against the Government. Sunderland quickly put a stop to this device by introducing a new standing order requiring that protests be entered and signed before adjournment on the day following that upon which the issue had arisen in the house: ibid., pp. 84–85.

[2] *H.M.C., Stuart Papers*, vii. 570, 574.

[3] The Civil List was voted at the accession for the entire reign and did not again come under consideration except when the necessity arose to supplement it or pay

could be opposed with uniform consistency, and, with some variations depending upon what other opportunities the Ministry offered for *causes célèbres*, the malcontents customarily selected issues from this classification for at least one major struggle every session.

The army made one of the most popular subjects for vigorous opposition. This was probably owing in part to Britain's long-standing prejudice against a standing military force and in part to the Jacobites' desire to keep the country weak in the face of the ever expected invasion by the Chevalier. Strenuous debate normally took place on the Mutiny Act and the Army Appropriation, and the Anti-courtiers forced a trial of strength on the former in three sessions and on the latter in seven.[1] The most important battles over taxation probably occurred in committee, for which our records are so scanty that it is impossible to tell how persistently the Country party divided on Supply. The most that can be said is that our data suggest that divisions in committee may have taken place frequently, and we know that the House divided on financial measures in six sessions.[2] On the address of thanks debate was usual, but divisions were rare. The Commons had apparently come formally to regard the King's speech 'as the composition and advice of his Ministry'—so Shippen stated without contradiction in 1717[3]—and its customary reflections on the Opposition were a challenge to battle. But for two reasons the Country party seldom elected to pick up the gage. On the one hand, parliamentary tacticians saw a division on the address as a trial of strength at the opening of the session, and as we know, the malcontents hardly ever had a muster sufficient to hazard an engagement. On the other, they chose to look upon the address

off its debts (*P.H.* vii. 57–60; viii. 454–5; *Commons Journals*, xx. 484, 493). At rare intervals there were Bills for the reorganization of customs and excise (ibid. xviii. 762; xx. 471), and measures of extraordinary supply (*P.H.* vii. 437–40, 446–7, 846–7; *Commons Journals*, xviii. 530, 537).

[1] Ibid. xviii. 149, 653, 661, 674, 699; xx. 154; *P.H.* vii, 424, 505–23, 536–8, 627, 918; viii. 46, 377–8, 404–10. Opposition questioned the administration of the navy when funds were required to pay off its debt in 1721, but they allowed a motion for £1,000,000 to pass *nem. con.* (*P.H.* vii. 917), and they never sought to reduce the naval Appropriation.

[2] Add. MSS. 27980, ff. 276, 309; *P.H.* vii, 523; *Commons Journals*, xviii. 369, 524, 579–80; xix. 92, 606; xx. 280.

[3] *P.H.* vii. 508.

as a 'matter of compliment' so conventional as not to be worth inviting a severe defeat.[1] In consequence, they divided on this occasion only three times during this period.[2]

As a general rule, however, it cannot be said that the Country party dreaded defeat. They simply disliked to make a poor showing. They rejoiced in their occasional victories, small ones for the most part, but they knew full well that victories, even great ones, would not overturn the Ministry. During the battle over the Peerage Bill, Sunderland called in Lord Midleton and 'used words of the King's being obliged to change hands' if the measure failed, but, recounted that Lord, 'I could not see any such consequence of throwing the Bill out.'[3] Opposition victories helped to unsettle the Ministry—that was their real function—and so did continual Opposition defeats, if the margin were narrow enough. For different reasons, as we know, both Jacobites and Whig malcontents employed parliamentary opposition to debilitate the Ministry, and a resolute and sizable minority, even if a minority always, was calculated to contribute much to this end.

There appears to have been a rough rule-of-thumb by which to measure the effect of Opposition tactics. Lord Sunderland is reported to have said 'that whenever an English minister had but 60 majority in a House of Commons, he was undone'.[4] This may have been merely a comment upon the fact that he was acquitted in the South Sea affair by precisely that figure, but perhaps it represented a dangerous minimum, a point at which the Government felt insecure. Certainly a strikingly large number of critical divisions during the tenure of the 'Narrow-bottom Ministry' were marked by a difference of approximately sixty. As far as can be judged from random remarks about the

[1] *P.H.* vii. 605; *H.M.C., Stuart Papers*, v. 249.

[2] *P.H.* vii. 47–50, 562, 680–4; *Commons Journals*, xviii. 22; xix. 4, 378. Possibly one should include the division on the address after a brief adjournment in April–May 1717 (*P.H.* vii. 451).

[3] Coxe, *Walpole*, ii. 171–2, 180. Coxe reports that Walpole urged his followers to vote for the exoneration of Sunderland in 1721 because 'if they gave their votes against Sunderland, and he was disgracefully removed, their cause would suffer, and the Tories be called into power' (ibid. i. 264). Midleton recognized this threat as an old manœuvre of party leaders to keep their followers in line (ibid. ii. 214).

[4] *H.M.C., Egmont Diary*, ii. 150. Cf. *Marchmont Papers*, ii. 67, where Marchmont, looking back upon Sunderland's administration fifteen years later, observed, 'No administration can be supported by a majority of fifty or sixty'.

size of divisions, the Government seems generally to have been uneasy when their majorities on major issues fell much below 100. Anything over 100 was usually termed a 'great' or 'vast' majority, which constituted a parliamentary triumph.[1]

The significance of numbers, however, lay not so much in their relation to any formulae of abstract political arithmetic, as in what they indicated about the alignment of live political forces. Who voted on either side in a division was no less important than how many. In a House of Commons composed of small, shifting parties and many independents, every division tested allegiances anew and marked trends for or against a change in the existing pattern. The Government was ever fearful of alienating support, not only by the pursuit of unpopular schemes, but also by a display of weakness that might lead uncertain friends to seek sturdier allies. Significant majorities fostered the kind of prestige that helped to keep a ministerial coalition intact.

The role of this factor in parliamentary calculation is nowhere better illustrated than in two analyses of the effects of divisions during the Sunderland administration. The first came in June 1717, when the Walpole–Townshend group, recently withdrawn from the Court coalition, forced a trial of strength by a motion accusing Lord Cadogan of embezzlement in the transportation of Dutch troops to aid in suppressing the '15. Following is an extract from the account of the struggle written by Joseph Addison, then Secretary of State:

Yesterday we look upon to have been the decisive day of this session. Both parties made their utmost efforts and summoned all their friends that could be got together from every quarter of the nation. . . . the whole body of the Tories were there, and not a single man among them voted for us. . . . All the Prince's Court was against us, and 78 Whigs, among whom several in places. But upon the division we were 204 to 194. As this was the utmost effort of all parties united against the present interest, I believe it is not hard to guess which of

[1] For examples of comments, see P.R.O., Egmont MSS. 234, Diary, 23 June 1715; *H.M.C., Portland MSS.* v. 522, 575–6; *H.M.C., Stuart Papers*, ii. 144–5; *Annals of Stair*, ii. 147. In his observations upon the session of 1722, written about forty years later, Speaker Onslow noted that the majority on the suspension of habeas corpus, which was 53, was a precarious one, but that the other majorities on the prosecution of the Atterbury Plot, which ranged from 133 to 189, were 'the greatest disproportions in the numbers upon the divisions in the House of Commons I ever knew there' (*H.M.C., Onslow MSS.*, p. 513).

the sides is likely to grow the strongest [*sic*] for it. Those who lost the
day are amazed at their ill success, and wonder from whence such
a body could be drawn together against 'em, for it was their own
and the common opinion of the town that they would carry it by 50
or 60 voices. But they could not have fallen on any other man
[Cadogan] that could have so well bestirred himself in his defence,
tho' at the same time none appeared in it who, I believe, would not
be ready to promote His Majesty's service with the utmost zeal and
diligence in all other points, as I believe several of those who appeared
against his lordship will do for the future.[1]

Though the majority was slim, the Government had achieved
a noteworthy triumph in the circumstances, and the result for
the immediate future was as Addison had predicted.

Bolingbroke's startled comment on the loss of the Peerage
Bill illuminates the reverse of the coin:

I confess to you, my dear lord [he wrote to Stair], the ill success
of the Peerage Bill astonishes me. To open the session with such an
attempt, and not to have told noses better, is most unaccountable
management. There is no room to expect that the ministers after
this defeat should be able to exert much influence over their party.[2]

Again it was as the writer had foreseen. After this event the
Government carried its measures by thin majorities, and the
resulting instability encouraged the frantic intrigue which
ultimately produced the treaty of 1720.

The parliamentary tactics of the 'Country party' may thus be
compared, as Cowper and others frequently compared them, to
those of a weak besieging force.[3] Since the attackers could not

---

[1] *Annals of Stair*, ii. 20–22.

[2] Baratier, *Lettres inédites*, p. 99. Cf. Coxe, *Walpole*, ii. 173. In point of fact Sunderland's papers (Blenheim MSS. viii (23) and xiii (46)) and Craggs's (Stair MSS.
247, ff. 184–99) indicate that the Government 'told noses' very carefully. The
forecast was pro 211, con 223, doubtful 122; which makes it appear that they
gambled on more support from the last group than they received. Cf. the Stanhope–
Newcastle correspondence on the strategy of introducing the Bill in Add. MSS.
32686, ff. 151–3, 155–6.

[3] It is interesting to observe that throughout the eighteenth century the Opposition customarily employed the military metaphor: the Court was a fortress invested
by the troops of the Country party. Hence the development of the celebrated
phrase, 'storming the closet' (see below, Chapter IV). On the other hand, while
ministers sometimes thought of the Court party as a building or structure (examples in Coxe, *Shrewsbury Correspondence*, p. 552; *Annals of Stair*, ii. 40), they much
more commonly adopted a naval metaphor: their coalition was a 'system' or
'ship' upon which they were 'embarked'. Hence the concept of a 'Narrow-bottom'

hope to take the citadel by storm—nor to hold it against counter-attack if taken—they depended primarily upon steady sapping and mining, intermittent bombardment, and occasional scaling parties. The prevalence of such tactics reflects not only the purposes of Opposition and the actual conditions of political warfare, but also the state of contemporary Opposition, even though all men readily acknowledged the unfortunate fact of its existence. Perhaps the best expression of the orthodox view is contained in the King's Speech which closed the session in June 1720: the Leicester House Opposition having recently succeeded, George I was made to say,

I could wish that all my subjects, convinced by time and experience, would lay aside those partialities and animosities which prevent them from living quietly and enjoying the happiness of a mild legal Government: it is what I choose to recommend at this time, when I am sensible that all opposition to it is become vain and useless and can only end unfortunately for those who shall still persist in struggling against it.[1]

As one can readily observe, the statement bristles with *double entendres* in terms of the contemporary situation; but its general application is quite in keeping with the traditional attitude upon the uselessness as well as sinfulness of endeavours to thwart the policies of His Majesty's chosen servants.

3. CONSTITUTIONAL THEORY

In view of the character of the Anti-courtiers and their aims during this period, it is little wonder that the customary interpretation of Opposition resisted revision. The Prince of Wales frankly acknowledged that the chief goal of his Opposition was to 'bring in my friends with honour',[2] and the Jacobites, though difficult to prosecute under the safeguards of English law, drew but a thin veil over the treasonable nature of their activities.

The contemporary theory of 'balanced government', moreover, tended to block any development of the idea that parliamentary Opposition possessed a legitimate role as defender of

or 'Broad-bottom' Ministry, and Rockingham's celebrated reference to his Ministry of 1765 as a 'frail green vessel' (*H.M.C., Lothian MSS.*, p. 258).

[1] *P.H.* vii. 651.

[2] P.R.O., Cathcart MSS. 5/48: Journal, 4 Aug. 1720; *Diary of Mary Countess Cowper*, pp. 148–9.

the subject's rights and privileges. This was the function of opposition of another sort, that among the three Estates of the Realm. The general acceptance of this concept came out most clearly in the fierce pamphlet warfare over the Peerage Bill, when 'balanced government' made the basis of argument on all sides of the question. A good example may be taken from a brochure attributed to Lord Peterborough:

Without enlarging upon the nature of our Constitution . . . it would suffice to say, it would be better in all respects that it consisted but of one branch or authority than of many; unless the different parts of the Government were calculated to be a proper balance one against the other; if there was not force enough for a regular, sufficient and decent Opposition in the several parts of this compound Government, it would be liable to many objections. Whereas upon this supposition it is allowed to be the best of all, no one part of this Government must be permitted, like Moses' serpent, to be capable of devouring the others. A weak and insignificant contest would be detrimental to action, and no contest would be fatal to liberty.[1]

The deep-rooted nature of this political concept, and the equally well entrenched right of the King to choose his own servants, left the Opposition still ensconced in a defensive posture theoretically as well as tactically. The relationship between the two aspects of the position was direct and functional. Lacking any broad constitutional justification for their activities, malcontents fell back upon the argument that, in resisting the measures proposed by the Ministry, they were seeking prevention or redress of grievances. Any reflection upon the legitimacy of opposition was likely to evoke a response of this sort, and in such responses it would seem that the Country party was coming imperceptibly to lay increasingly greater emphasis upon one strain of a time-honoured theme. All its basic elements are to be found in this argument of Archibald Hutcheson against Septennial Parliaments in 1716:

I believe it will not be denied that it is very possible for a ministry, by pensions and employments to some, and by the expectations raised in others, and by the corruption of electors and returning officers, to obtain a very great majority, entirely and blindly at their

---

[1] *Remarks on a Pamphlet Entituled The Thoughts of a Member of the Lower House* (London, 1719), p. 20.

devotion even at the very first meeting of a Parliament, and that by a committee of elections and other proper helps, their party may daily increase; and that such a parliament may be so far from protecting the liberties of their country, or from being a terror to evil ministers, as to become themselves the tools of oppression in the hand of such a ministry, and by their authority to consecrate the worst of actions and to declare every honest patriot, who has the courage to attempt to stem the tide of wickedness and to stand up for the liberties of his country, to be its greatest enemy; and those who are ready to give it up to be the only true friends of our Constitution.[1]

Such an argument represents a subtle mutation of the ancient cry against bad and corrupt ministers. Hutcheson intended, of course, to describe the actual situation in hypothetical terms, and his angle of emphasis accents a train of reasoning which provides a constitutional function for the Country party: the demand for redress of grievances was a duty once performed by the collective body of the House, but now that the 'influence of the Crown' has made possible the creation of a Court party completely subservient to the executive, the traditional obligation of the whole House has devolved upon that portion of it which remains independent and public spirited, namely those in opposition.

The clearest recognition of the development of this line of thought is the Ministry's effort to combat it. When the Government acquired control of the *London Journal* in 1722, three successive numbers were devoted to direct counter-attack. 'I know it may be said by some', wrote the *Journal's* 'Britannicus', 'that I have carried the matter too far, when I have talked as if the resolutions of any persons were stretched to that degree as to extend to a constant and determined opposition to a ministry, and even to make that the strongest and most infallible note of a true patriot.' 'Yet', he went on, 'this is the current shibboleth of dangerous malcontents who oppose His Majesty's interest.'[2] Government was evidently most concerned to condemn the two points singled out by 'Britannicus': that steady and systematic opposition was a duty and that participation therein was the hallmark of true loyalty. These points

---

[1] *P.H.* vii. 343. The text of this speech appears to have been released by the author, a common practice with Hutcheson. For another example of this type of argument, see ibid. 436–7.

[2] See *London Journal*, nos. 164–6 (15, 22, 29 Sept. 1722).

would become fundamental to an expertly contrived Opposition doctrine in the years just ahead.

Grumbletonians made no progress, however, in establishing a theoretical claim to office by virtue of their opposition. When the Walpole–Townshend connexion pulled out of the Court coalition in 1717, the Ministry immediately charged them with an intention to force a change of hands. '. . . We have an old proverb', ran one Government pamphlet, 'that falling favourites are generally the beginners of a new faction.'¹ 'Quitting of places is no crime', said another, 'but if several cabal to throw up, when the Government has most occasion for their service, in order to force it to comply with their unreasonable demands, this is a very criminal conspiracy.'² To this the resigners replied they had given up their offices as a matter of principle.³ They emphatically disclaimed any thought of imposing themselves on His Majesty, and Walpole is reported to have declared in the House of Commons that 'the tenor of his conduct would show that he never intended to make the King uneasy or to embarrass his affairs'.⁴ Walpole's actions from that moment forward gave the lie to his profession, but in the general state of opinion he evidently could not admit what everyone knew to be his true purpose. During the South Sea crisis, when Parliament raised a hue and cry after Sunderland, an Opposition pamphlet insisted that, with a nation in ferment, a prince would do well 'to give up those that are disgustful to his people'.⁵ But as for

---

¹ *An Answer to the Character and Conduct of R[obert] W[alpole], Esq.* (London, 1717), p. 40.

² *The Defection Considered* (London, 1717), p. 20. This pamphlet, attributed to Matthew Tindal, stressed the theoretical absurdity of recognizing an Opposition's claim to office: 'But let us for once suppose an impossible thing, that they now in administration should be turned out to make room for those who lately threw up; would not the disobliged be at least as great a number as the obliged; and if they, encouraged by this precedent, should take the same methods to be restored, what other effect could it have but putting the Government under a necessity of cashiering both sides, since either one or the other would always be opposing it[?]' (p. 25).

³ See *The Resigners Vindicated*, parts i and ii (London, 1718); *Some Persons Vindicated Against the Author of the Defection* (London, 1718); *The Defection Detected* (London, 1718).   ⁴ *P.H.* vii. 449. Cf. Coxe, *Walpole*, ii. 156, 162–5.

⁵ 'The Sense of the People concerning the present State of Affairs, with Remarks upon some Passages of our own and the Roman History' in *A Collection of Tracts by the late John Trenchard, Esq; and Thomas Gordon, Esq.* (London, 1751), ii. 21. The authors went on to revive the time-honoured argument based on the maxim that the King can do no wrong, which makes the dismissal of erring counsellors mandatory in times of crisis.

the selection of a better ministry, none would openly go further than the proposal of the Jacobite *True Briton* for an addition to the litany which should read, 'Lord . . . deny not sovereign princes that spirit of conduct which is fit for them to govern by, give them understanding enough to counsel themselves well and to choose their councillors as they ought.'[1]

Given the scant development in constitutional theory and the character of the Country party, little change could take place in the nomenclature and conventions of the Opposition. The word 'opposition' was still used only to describe the act of opposing, not the opposers. When in 1718 Craggs wrote, '. . . such is the nature of Opposition, they can all unite to do mischief',[2] he may have meant to apply the term to the opponents themselves, but if so, this is an isolated example. We also have rare instances of 'opposers' and 'the opposite party',[3] and the French ambassador once referred to 'la liste du party opposé à la cour'.[4] For the most part, however, the terms in current usage were those inherited from Stuart times: Country party, the discontented party, the malcontents, and sometimes the grumbletonians or the patriots. They still had not acquired a claim to the benches on the Speaker's left. Allusions to the location of members are too vague and infrequent to give us any information about party alignments.[5] It is possible that some silent progress took place in the conventions of seating, but it is much more likely that, amid the turbulent shifting of connexions and individuals, the Opposition remained as much waifs in the Houses of Parliament as they were in political terminology and constitutional theory.[6]

---

[1] *True Briton*, 30 Aug. 1723. The duty to pull down and punish evil counsellors was never questioned during this period. In fact, the prosecution of Anne's last Ministry by George's first Ministry kept this principle fully alive for future use by the Opposition. For examples of the arguments used, see [Daniel Defoe], *Reasons for Im[peaching] the L[ord] H[igh] T[reasure]r* (London, 1714); [John Toland], *Acts of Parliament no Infallible Security to Bad Peacemakers* (London, 1714); Thomas Burnett, *The Necessity of Impeaching the Late Ministry in a Letter to the Earl of Halifax* (London, 1715); *Burnet [sic] and Bradbury, or the Confederacy of the Press and the Pulpit for the Blood of the Late Ministry* (London, 1715); *Somers Tracts*, xiii. 559–97.

[2] *Annals of Stair*, ii. 364.

[3] Baratier, *Lettres inédites*, p. 95; *H.M.C.*, *Sutherland MSS.*, p. 191.

[4] Realey, *Early Opposition to Walpole*, p. 24.

[5] For example, see *H.M.C.*, *Onslow MSS.*, p. 515; *H.M.C.*, *Portland MSS.* vii. 305.

[6] Despite his anomalous position during this period, the Speaker seems to have taken no hand in encouraging conventions favourable to the Opposition. Like most

On the whole, then, the first decade of the Hanoverian era saw no great and spectacular advances in the ideas and practices of parliamentary opposition. The developments that pointed the way to future progress represent slight modifications or subtle shifts of emphasis within the framework of Stuart traditions, and for the rest the malcontents did little more than keep alive the procedures of the past. Yet this was significant in itself. The extinction of Jacobitism and its policies must be counted a positive gain, but Walpole's relentless destruction of a treasonable conspiracy might have withered or uprooted the forms and usages of parliamentary opposition which the Pretender's party had done so much to maintain. Nevertheless, however much he may have wished it, Walpole could not break the spirit or annihilate the will to power of those whom he excluded from the Court, and in them the traditions survived. During the hapless days at the end of 1723, when the Ministry had disrupted the Jacobite organization and refused an accommodation with a group of its repentant leaders, William Bromley wrote to Lord Oxford,

The time being appointed for the meeting of Parliament . . . , I fear many of both Houses will be very remiss, because they are discouraged, despond, and conclude they can do no service by their attendance. But I have learnt *non est desperandum de republica*, and no one can foresee the opportunities that may offer.[1]

Bromley's tenacity characterized many more than himself.

of his predecessors, Spencer Compton was a Court nominee, and during his second term from 1722 to 1727 he also held the lucrative post of Paymaster of the Forces. At the same time, however, he was the chief personal favourite of the Prince of Wales. He was a member of the Opposition 'Cabinet' at Leicester House from 1717 to 1720, and upon one occasion he spoke in committee against a Money Bill (*P.H.* vii. 439). Although royal father and son remained on cold and distant terms after the treaty of 1720, Compton successfully kept a foot in both camps. As far as I can discover, neither ministers nor their opponents ever complained of his régime in the House. Perhaps his dual role helped him to sustain an attitude of uncompromising neutrality when in the chair.

   [1] *H.M.C., Portland MSS.* v. 637. Bromley's Latin tag was, in variant forms, popular with Opposition writers. Pulteney preferred the imperative *nolite desperare de republica* (*An Humble Address to the Knights, citizens, and Burgesses elected to represent the Commons of Great Britain in the Ensuing Parliament*, London 1734, p. 11). The tag was doubtless inspired by the stirring passage at the close of the twenty-second book of Livy, where he describes how, in the aftermath of Cannae, the Roman citizenry flocked to give thanks to the defeated Varro 'quod de re publica non desperasset' Lord Morton quoted Livy correctly in defence of the Ministry in 1743 (*P.H.* xiii 278). Whitbread misquoted him in defence of Opposition in 1792 (ibid. xxx. 105)

Though shattered and disorganized, the 'outs' continued to present Walpole with a stubborn, if apparently hopeless and ineffective, Opposition throughout the sessions of 1724 and 1725.[1] Bolingbroke had predicted at the beginning of the decade that numbers to oppose would not be wanting, but he looked about in vain for competent leaders. Now numbers still were left, and the traditions of opposition which they had conserved would soon be seized and enlarged upon by a new and vigorous leadership, in which Bolingbroke himself was to play a major part.

[1] See Realey, *Early Opposition to Walpole*, pp. 126–7, 136–7. It should be noted that Realey underplays the vigour of the Opposition in the session of 1724. He notes only one division, but, not including election petitions, at least sixteen are recorded: see Add. MSS. 27980, ff. 260, 289, 295–6; *Commons Journals*, xx. 252, 274, 280, 284–7, 291, 294, 316, 327.

IV

THE SPIRIT OF PATRIOTISM

1725–1742

---

1. *The Formation of the Patriot Coalition*

Bolingbroke and the Political Ecology of 1725–6. The
Elements in Opposition. The Original Camarilla of
1726.

2. *Expansion and its Causes*

The Position and Policy of the Chief Minister. The
Actions of the Royal Family. The Decay of Walpole's
Strength. The Nature of Expansion.

3. *The Principles of the Opposition Blocs*

The Tories. The Pulteney–Carteret Bloc. The New
Doctrine of 'Broad Bottom'. The Progress of
Opposition Theory.

4. *The Institutional Legacy of the Patriots*

IV

THE SPIRIT OF PATRIOTISM

1725-1742

I. THE FORMATION OF THE PATRIOT COALITION

Bolingbroke and the Political Ecology of 1725–6

WHEN in June of 1723 the exiled Atterbury disembarked
at Calais—so runs a persistent legend—he heard that
the pardoned Bolingbroke had just arrived to take
passage for England. A smile lit up the aged Bishop's melancholy features. 'Then I am exchanged!' he exclaimed.[1] The
story may be apocryphal, for *H.M.S. Aldborough* had orders to
land Atterbury at Ostend.[2] But whatever the fact, the alleged
remark expressed an eloquent truth. The Jacobite Opposition
of which the Bishop had been the leader and the symbol was
soon to be exchanged for an Opposition first organized and
greatly inspired by the wayward genius of Bolingbroke.

He had lived abroad under the shadow of his attainder for
eight years, the first few months fruitlessly expended in the
service of the Pretender and all the rest in anxious solicitation
for a remission of his political sins. Delay and discouragement
never quenched his ardent ambition for a return to the political
stage where his early career had signalled a future adorned with
prominence and power. At length his ceaseless intrigue secured
a royal pardon, though not a return of his patrimony or his
title, and he came back to lay a formal claim to the indulgence.

[1] The numerous versions of the legend probably stem for the most part from the
undocumented anecdote in Coxe, *Walpole*, i. 196.

[2] Walter Sichel, *Bolingbroke and His Times* (London, 1902), ii. 192. G. W. Cooke
in his *Memoirs of Lord Bolingbroke* (London, 1835), ii. 59, states that in a letter
found among the Townshend papers Bolingbroke anxiously explained to Townshend that the meeting with Atterbury at Calais was accidental and that he
detested the old Bishop. Cooke apparently takes this to mean that the legend of
Atterbury's exclamation is accurate. From Cooke's description of the letter, however, it appears to be the one printed in Coxe, *Walpole*, ii. 325–7, which has to do,
not with this incident, but with a rumour that Bolingbroke visited Atterbury at
Brussels in the autumn of 1723.

Such, at least, was his ostensible purpose, but scarcely had he landed when his hand was deep in politics. A news-letter of 9 July noted that Lord Bolingbroke had taken lodgings 'near the Cocoa Tree in Pall Mall', the traditional Tory meeting-place.[1] Within two weeks he was acting as emissary to Walpole for his old Tory clique, then in search of a treaty with the Minister.[2] Walpole's flat rebuff, accompanied by a stern admonition to desist from such measures if he wished Parliament to reverse his attainder, sent Bolingbroke once more into cautious seclusion across the Channel.

From watering places, Paris, and country houses abroad he resumed his former tactics to obtain a full rehabilitation. He dabbled in diplomacy, sent repeated applications to his old friend Harcourt and bribes to the Duchess of Kendal. In May of 1725 came his reward. Parliament passed an Act which restored his estates but maintained his incapacity for a seat in the House of Lords and employment under the Crown. He was to have everything but what he wanted most. Back he came again to study the situation and discover what resources he could exploit. A full year passed before his future course of action was set. He would not abandon hope that his old methods might produce results, but under existing circumstances they offered little promise. His interest demanded a vigorous and resolute parliamentary opposition.[3]

The situation which determined Bolingbroke's decision was a

---

[1] Add. MSS. 27980, f. 92.   [2] Coxe, *Walpole,* ii. 264–5.
[3] Bolingbroke frequently expounded the 'principles' upon which he based his conviction that 'steady opposition' was necessary in 1726. One of the best examples is to be found in his reflections on the death of Wyndham in 1740 in Phillimore, *Lyttelton,* i. 153–6. He always decked out these declarations in the language of Opposition oratory, but such verbiage did not disguise his underlying belief that the situation which then existed forced this course of action upon a man of spirit and ambition. That he had not renounced other means, however, is made clear by such incidents as his interview with George I in 1727, secured by the Duchess of Kendal, in which he tried to persuade the King to turn out Walpole (Coxe, *Walpole,* i. 264–5); and his urging Bingley to accept office in 1730 as a method, so his enemies thought, of getting a foothold at Court (MS. Journal of Mrs. Charles Caesar, iv). At one point he insisted that his open opposition actually took its origin from backstairs intrigue: in a letter to Wyndham in 1736 (Coxe, *Walpole,* ii. 340) Bolingbroke asserted that, when he embarked upon opposition, George I 'durst not support me openly against his ministers', but 'he would have plotted with me against them'; and that when George II came to the throne, Bolingbroke continued in opposition primarily out of loyalty to the party which 'I had contributed to form'.

product of Walpole's ascendancy. The triumph of the great Minister had brought about notable modifications in Britain's political ecology. Owing in great part to his favour with the King, Sir Robert had established a large measure of control over the customary channels of intrigue. Since the Treaty of 1720 he had been able to prevent the Hanoverian ministers from undermining his position or thwarting his policies. That they were still a threat is clear from their scheming against the Treaty of Hanover in the spring of 1726, but while Bolingbroke was still making his estimate of the situation, Walpole intercepted diplomatic correspondence and shrewdly counteracted their activities.[1] He could not obliterate the influence of the German mistresses. The Duchess of Kendal in particular could still secure extraordinary boons from His Majesty, and it was probably she who had done most to obtain the indulgences to Bolingbroke. Sir Robert, however, had successfully blocked his total restoration, and it appears that in general he could limit the ladies' meddling to non-essentials.[2] The existence of these influences meant that he did not 'engross the closet', as his enemies often charged, but his credit was clearly great enough to cope both with them and with the rival factions at Court. Having ousted the most recalcitrant and bundled Carteret off to Ireland when he caught him encouraging the Tories to attack the Minister, Walpole had for the moment subordinated the rest. A change of fortune might alter the picture at any time, and an astute Opposition would not ignore that possibility, but in 1726 the chances of toppling Sir Robert by Court intrigue must have seemed remote.

[1] Ibid. ii. 498–512. Onslow noted that German influence kept in office a knot of Sunderland's followers, 'small but of considerable rank' who, during the life of George I, devoted their time to 'waiting and watching for every opportunity to ruin' Walpole: *H.M.C., Onslow MSS.*, p. 465.

[2] In his *Memoirs of Horatio, Lord Walpole* (London, 1820), p. 125, Coxe asserts that he has seen 'some papers' which 'prove that the Minister was threatened with dismission if he did not promote the return of Bolingbroke, and that he compromised the business by consenting to the restitution of his family estate, but prevented his complete restoration'. There can be little doubt that heavy pressure was brought to bear on Walpole in this affair, and no doubt whatsoever that his influence defeated a full rehabilitation of Bolingbroke. But Coxe does not give any clue to the identity of the papers he saw, nor does he say who made the threat of dismissal, and it must be said that for George I to have made it would have been quite inconsistent with all we know of his treatment of his First Minister. That the Duchess's importunities alone could have brought down the Minister defies belief.

As he had crushed Jacobitism, so he had tamed the other rival court. The reconciliation of King and Prince in 1720 had not been altogether cordial, and a foreign observer noted in 1726 that the heir habitually treated Walpole 'very distantly and coldly, to say the least of it, and shows his dislike to him on every possible occasion'.[1] But the Minister prevented any new rupture by vigilant tact and an occasional distribution of favours to the Prince's followers.[2] Bolingbroke put in an appearance at Leicester House immediately upon his second return in 1725,[3] and, whether upon his account or not, shortly thereafter the tension between the two courts mounted again. By spring of 1726, however, the difficulties had been smoothed over and a peaceful *modus vivendi* re-established between the Prince and the Ministry.[4] His Royal Highness's coldness apparently did not portend a revival of his opposition.

At first glance the prospects for a successful coalition of malcontents in Parliament probably seemed no brighter than the possibilities of the other ploys already considered. Early in 1725 Bolingbroke had ruefully acknowledged the truth of Wyndham's estimate of those in opposition as 'people who expect they know not what, who are ready to be angry they know not why, and eager to act, tho' they have neither plan nor concert'.[5] But their last failing was one that Bolingbroke knew he could remedy. He had ever expressed a resilient faith in the powers of leadership. At one time he likened the parties in Parliament to sheep who 'will stand sullen and be run over, till they hear the bell-wether, and then they follow without knowing very well where';[6] and another to hounds who grow 'fond of the man who shows them game and by whose halloo they are used to be encouraged'.[7] With such an attitude he need not despair if he could find colleagues to lead those 'eager to act' in the chambers from which he was barred.

---

[1] Cesar de Saussure, *A Foreign View of England in the Reigns of George I and George II* (London, 1902), p. 175.
[2] Coxe, *Walpole*, ii. 306.
[3] P.R.O., Cathcart MSS. 7/19: Journal, 3 May 1725.
[4] Ibid. 6/37: Journal, 4 Mar. 1726; 6/38, 20 Apr. 1726.
[5] Coxe, *Walpole*, ii. 332.
[6] Baratier, *Lettres inédites*, pp. 47–48.
[7] Bolingbroke, *Works*, i. 117. Cf. Ball, ed., *Letters of Swift*, iv. 136.

The Elements in Opposition

The materials at hand, upon close inspection, were not unpromising. Ten years in the wilderness had not altogether dissolved Bolingbroke's own connexion, which still comprised members of noteworthy parliamentary talent. There were men of the second rank like the ageing but ambitious Bingley and the indolent but able Gower. In the front rank stood Sir William Wyndham and Lord Bathurst, whom a decade of assiduous opposition had made into effective speakers and skilled tacticians. Oxford's group had survived his death, to be carried on by his sons and kinsmen, loyally supported by such old comrades as William Bromley, Strafford, Bruce, and Berkeley of Stratton. The remnants of other Jacobite clans included figures of note as well. Orrery, who had succeeded Atterbury as titular head of the Chevalier's interest, was not a commanding person, though faithful enough in attendance. Scarsdale and Lichfield took a more vigorous lead in the painted chamber, and at St. Stephen's the old warrior Will Shippen, who came to the House drunk or sober to cast invective from behind his muffling glove upon every Hanoverian ministry, received increasing support from younger Jacobites, Sir John Hynde Cotton, Sir Watkin Williams Wynn, and Lord Noel Somerset. The Hanoverian Tories also were still a distinctive group under the leadership of Abingdon, Compton, and the venerable Sir Thomas Hanmer.

To form a confederacy of these elements would have been, in the broadest sense, to reconstruct the ministerial coalition of 1710 to 1714. The desirability of such an achievement was probably as dubious as the possibility. Time had not obliterated their ancient feuds, and the Jacobites in particular detested Bolingbroke, the fallen angel.[1] Furthermore, the public memory of the old Tory coalition was still officially tainted with disaffection, and, though he had granted occasional indulgences to individuals, George I had given no indication of having abandoned his old prejudice against the Ministry which had made the peace of Utrecht and displayed no zeal for the Protestant

---

[1] The Jacobites had taken a prominent part in opposing Bolingbroke's restitution, and in a meeting of party chiefs upon this issue Wharton had insisted that a vote for Bolingbroke was a vote against the Pretender, a point which he thought had profoundly impressed the gathering (Stanhope, *History of England 1713–1783*, 2nd ed. rev., ii, app. xvi). The persistently hostile attitude of the Oxford connexion comes out clearly in the MS. Journal of Mrs. Charles Caesar, i–ii.

succession when it was in danger. British politics, it is true, had witnessed stranger events than an amicable reconciliation between a king and a knot of men whom he had cashiered and condemned. But with the intransigent Walpole so firmly entrenched, the odds against it were long indeed.

The aspiring architect of an Opposition confederacy must needs utilize the talent and the votes of these ostracized, disjointed Tory clans; but to become an effective and respectable force they required both an addition of strength and an infusion of some element of impeccable loyalty to symbolize fidelity to the existing settlement.

Since the heir to the throne, conventional recourse at such a juncture, offered scant hope of assistance, Bolingbroke was naturally drawn to the only other quarter from which such aid could be secured, the motley crowd of dissident Whigs whom Walpole's policies had turned against the Ministry.

Among them were to be found only a small amount of voting strength but a rich supply of debating power and an unquestioned attachment to the Hanoverian dynasty. The two Pulteney cousins stood pre-eminent. William had been an old ally of Walpole, resigning with him in 1717 and returning to office as Cofferer of the Household after the Treaty of 1720. In opposition he had firmly declined all overtures from the Jacobites, and in place he had headed the committee which investigated the plot of 1722 and prosecuted Atterbury. But he and Walpole had gradually grown apart, and after several manifestations of mutual hostility, William had been dismissed in 1725.

It is usually said that he thought his outstanding abilities and notable services insufficiently rewarded and so had broken with the First Minister.[1] For this view the evidence is convincing, but it seems also that his cousin Daniel had much to do with inflaming his resentment and leading him into open opposition.[2] Daniel was warmly attached to the interest of Lord Sunderland, to whom he was brother-in-law and through whose influence he had become a junior Lord of the Admiralty in 1721. After his patron's death he carried on incessant intrigue against Walpole 'in whispers and insinuations and raising private prejudices'

---

[1] See Realey, *Early Opposition to Walpole*, pp. 163–7.
[2] *H.M.C., Onslow MSS.*, p. 466.

until William was cashiered, when Daniel threw up his office and joined his cousin in undisguised assault upon the Ministry.[1] Both were reputed brilliant orators, and political opinion quickly accorded them a leading role in opposition. In September 1725 the Scottish historian Wodrow noted that William 'is reckoned the head of the discontented party in England'.[2]

With Daniel Pulteney were other disgruntled members of Sunderland's old following. Bristol, Coventry, and Lechmere, who hankered after the Woolsack, persistently attacked the Ministry with speeches and protests. The Scottish 'squadrone' headed by Roxburghe, squeezed out of the management of northern politics by Walpole's patronage of Argyll and Islay, made no secret of their vexation. Early in 1726 they were being courted by another connexion of indignant peers, notably Montrose, Tweeddale, Stair, and Marchmont, who had 'joined interests' against the hated Campbells.[3] These veteran political elements found themselves in the same camp with various individuals whose stand seems to have been determined by less obvious motives. Some Whig interests were split. Lord Morpeth and Lord William Paulet, for example, regularly spoke and voted against a ministry which bestowed dignities and favours upon their fathers. There were *soi-disant* country Whigs like Sir Wilfred Lawson, Sir Thomas Pengelly, and Samuel Sandys, who professed a conscientious dislike to Court measures, and Sir Joseph Jekyll, secure in his post as Master of the Rolls, who always spoke his convictions, which were usually anti-ministerial.

The Original Camarilla of 1726

William Pulteney had made strenuous efforts to weld the grumbletonians into a formed Opposition during the session of 1726. To bring into focus all shades of discontent he had developed a vigorous plan of attack upon the policies of the Ministry, for which he directly solicited the support of Tory groups. The result was utter failure.[4] Some time during the

[1] Ibid., pp. 465–7.
[2] Robert Wodrow, *Analecta: or Materials for a History of Remarkable Providences* (Maitland Club, 1842–3), iii. 233. He also reported rumours of meetings at Woodstock Park, headquarters of the Sunderland interest, 'under the notion of huntings'.
[3] Ibid. 290.
[4] Realey, *Early Opposition to Walpole*, pp. 187–92.

summer of 1726, however, Bolingbroke decided to take a hand, and by autumn the foundations had been laid for the alliance that was to harry the Government for seventeen years.

Whether the negotiations began upon Bolingbroke's initiative or upon that of Pulteney the records do not make clear. That Bolingbroke was the chief negotiator is beyond dispute. Parleys took place at Dawley, his country estate, whither came the two Pulteneys and Bathurst in company with such opposition wits as Pope, Arbuthnot, Swift, and Gay.[1] Wyndham never put in an appearance, but Bolingbroke later observed that Sir William, who had declined co-operation with Pulteney in the previous session, 'came into the scheme of coalition as soon as it was proposed to him in 1726'.[2] The symbol of the summer's achievement was the issue on 5 December of the first number of *The Craftsman*, a bi-weekly, single-essay periodical jointly devised by Bolingbroke and William Pulteney, designed to expose 'how craft predominates in all professions' and particularly 'the mystery of statecraft'.[3]

At its inception the coalition seems to have been primarily a union of Bolingbroke's friends with the Pulteneys and their allies among the Sunderland connexion. Perhaps they established a liaison with some of the Jacobites before Parliament was next convened. Bolingbroke remarked long afterward that Shippen 'disliked the coalition from the first',[4] but during the ensuing session he co-operated closely with William Pulteney in the House of Commons. The new alliance, however, did not comprehend all dissident elements, nor did it possess any tightly knit formal organization. Our evidence concerning its formation and early operation suggests that in its original character it was a personal working agreement between the two constituent factions for relentless assault upon Walpole, to which purpose they sought, by direct negotiation and the exploitation of popular issues, to gather support from all other malcontents both within and without the Ministry. No specific contract bound its members, and within its counsels lurked no 'shadow Cabinet'. Its oracles alleged the customary reason for opposition,

---

[1] Realey, *Early Opposition to Walpole*, pp. 193–5.
[2] Phillimore, *Memoirs of Lyttelton*, i. 153–4.
[3] *The Craftsman, by Caleb D'Anvers of Gray's Inn, Esq.* (London, 1731), i. 5–6.
[4] Rose, *Marchmont Papers*, ii. 246–7.

the need to purify a corrupt Government, and everything pointed to a desire for preferment, regardless of others, as the true motivation in the hearts of most. In short, this was a conventional type of cabal, distinguished rather by the brilliance and determination of its leadership than by any novelty of method, plan, or doctrine. From this beginning the Bolingbroke–Pulteney Camarilla broadened into a loose confederation of many factions with many views, its personnel undergoing frequent changes as original members dropped out and new ones adhered, its single bond an inveterate hostility to the great Minister.

2. EXPANSION AND ITS CAUSES

The Position and Policy of the Chief Minister

The expansion of opposition was made possible by the continual modification of the circumstances under which the original coalition had been formed. The impact of a steady succession of events gradually dilated the straitened situation of 1726, giving increasing opportunity to the malcontents and making their activity steadily more effective. By a paradox not uncommon in historical causation, the single factor productive of the greatest change was also the most stabilizing factor, namely the position and policy of Sir Robert Walpole.

Throughout his long tenure of power Sir Robert retained the confidence of the King. He faced his greatest crisis at the accession of George II, when the new monarch's favourite, Spencer Compton, might have succeeded had he been more competent and Walpole less adroit.[1] At times thereafter King and Minister had serious differences and, in the words of Hervey, Walpole was 'often obliged to purchase great points by yielding in little ones'.[2] But despite ever-present rumours of his imminent fall, he appears never to have lost his credit in the royal closet.

[1] The numerous accounts of how Walpole outmanœuvred Compton differ in some details, but the main outlines are the same. For examples, see Coxe, *Walpole*, ii. 519–20, and *H.M.C.*, *Egmont MSS.* ii. 156–7. Horace Walpole, fourth Earl of Orford, has written an interesting marginal note on this affair in his own copy of Philip, second Earl of Harwicke's *Walpoliana* (London, 1781), pp. 6–7. (This volume is in the library of the King's School, Canterbury. I am indebted to Mr. Wilmarth S. Lewis of Farmington, Conn., for the use of his photostatic copy.)

[2] Sedgwick, ed., *Memoirs of Lord Hervey*, pp. 445–6.

One can, nevertheless, make too much of his 'security' at Court. He had to cope not only with strident vilification from the Opposition but also with a continuance of unending intrigue by colleagues who sought to undermine his position. In the early years of George II's reign the major trouble came from Compton, who became Lord Wilmington, Dorset, and Dodington, and later from Newcastle, Pelham, and Hardwicke.[1] Sir Robert was greatly aided by the royal attitude toward administration, the Hanoverian tendency to sustain a stable Government, nowhere more explicit than in a scolding given to Newcastle by the Queen in 1737:

> The business of princes is to make the whole go on, and not to encourage or suffer little, silly, impertinent, personal piques between their servants to hinder the business of government being done; there will always be opposition enough given by the enemies of the King to his measures and his ministers; and you may depend upon it he will never bear it from those who ought to be his friends.[2]

The King himself expressed similar sentiments on other occasions;[3] yet notwithstanding such admonitions, Walpole had to wage a continuous running battle with those who, as he told Dorset, 'betray me whilst you act with me'.[4]

In consequence Sir Robert adhered closely to the policy which had brought him success from 1721 to 1726. By constant vigilance he sought to thwart his enemies within the Ministry, a task facilitated no little by the termination of German influence upon the death of George I.[5] Whenever private caballing took a form which seriously threatened Walpole's leadership, particularly open opposition in Press or Parliament, he generally employed disciplinary measures. These did not

---

[1] For comments on this intra-ministerial intrigue, see Sedgwick, ed., *Memoirs of Lord Hervey*, pp. 701, 830; Graham, ed., *Annals of Stair*, ii. 228; *H.M.C., Egmont MSS.* i. 31–32, 93–94, 279; ii. 178–9, 363, 486; iii. 28, 141; *H.M.C., Stopford-Sackville MSS.* i. 375–80; Coxe, *Walpole*, iii. 201, 506–7, 588–9; Coxe, *Pelham*, i. 22–25. [2] Sedgwick, ed., *Memoirs of Lord Hervey*, p. 718.

[3] Coxe, *Walpole*, iii. 144–5; *H.M.C., Egmont MSS.* iii. 235–6; Sedgwick, ed., *Memoirs of Lord Hervey*, pp. 151–2.

[4] Ibid., pp. 653–4.

[5] The Hanoverian Lady Walmoden became George II's mistress in 1735, and he brought her to England in 1738 after the Queen's death. Madame Walmoden's excursions into Court intrigue did not extend to ministerial politics, however, and the King did not permit her to work behind Walpole's back: e.g. *H.M.C., Egmont Diary*, iii. 259–60.

always go the full length of dismissal. If a dissident had strong influence at Court or a powerful interest in Parliament, the Minister often resorted to milder means. In general he seems to have been averse to drastic action. The picture sometimes given of Walpole as a tyrant bent upon the ruthless extirpation of disagreement in all Government services does not correspond with his actions. His disciplinary measures were calculated to sustain the solidarity and morale of the Court party, not to bolster his dignity or gratify his resentments. In domestic politics as in diplomacy his record indicates that he always preferred peaceful accommodation to heroic defiance. To take a flagrant case, he had put up with William Pulteney's provocations for at least two years before removing him as Cofferer of the Household; Walpole then made several efforts at reconciliation over three years before sacking Pulteney from his Lord Lieutenancy.[1] In another instance, the Duke of Dorset's sole punishment for nearly a decade of underhand plotting with Wilmington was a transfer from the Lord Lieutenancy of Ireland to the Lord Stewardship of the Household.[2] Wilmington, who required careful handling because of his favour with George II, successfully evaded any retribution for his part. Newcastle also retained his place, so Egmont rightly guessed, partly because 'the Duke makes by his influence about fourteen Members of Parliament who are all at the devotion of the Court';[3] his extensive connexions within the Government were an equally strong deterrent to disciplinary action. But Sir Robert was lenient to smaller fry as well. Where threats and family pressure would serve, he did not exact the ultimate penalty for insubordination.[4] Furthermore, some were cashiered at the direct instance of the King or Queen,[5] and in at least one

---

[1] Realey, *Early Opposition to Walpole*, pp. 163–4, 187–8; *H.M.C., Carlisle MSS.*, p. 54; Coxe, *Walpole*, ii. 246. It might be added that Pulteney's name was not stricken from the Privy Council list and the Commissions of the Peace until after his duel with Hervey in 1731.

[2] *H.M.C., Egmont MSS.* i. 193; Graham, ed., *Annals of Stair*, ii. 228; Coxe, *Walpole*, iii. 201; Sedgwick, ed., *Memoirs of Lord Hervey*, pp. 653–4.

[3] *H.M.C., Egmont MSS.* ii. 486.

[4] Ibid. 161 contains Egmont's account of the disciplining of Captain Robert Douglas. In the event, Douglas retained his commission, rose to Lieutenant-Colonel in 1740, later became aide-de-camp to the King, and gave his life at Fontenoy. Sedgwick, ed., *Memoirs of Lord Hervey*, p. 454, records Walpole's reply to Hervey's accusation that he was over-indulgent.

[5] *H.M.C., Egmont MSS.* i. 374.

recorded case the Minister saved a mutineer from the royal wrath.[1]

But it remained true none the less that on critical matters Walpole would not truckle to insurgents, no matter how highly placed. Hence the series of celebrated dismissals that mark the last ten years of his régime. For their desertion of the Government on the Excise Bill of 1733 such prominent figures as Chesterfield, Bolton, Stair, Montrose, Marchmont, and Cobham lost their posts in the Government and the army. Walpole cashiered several, including Sir George Oxenden from the Treasury Board and Lord Westmorland from the Horse Guards, because they voted with the Opposition on the Prince of Wales's allowance in 1737. The fractious Duke of Argyll joined the advocates of a Spanish war in 1739, and after a year of fruitless negotiation he was turned out of all his eight employments. In every instance the provocation was extreme, the action decisive and irrevocable.[2]

Walpole's policy had a twofold significance for the development of the Opposition. On the one hand, his leniency, coupled with the impossibility of eradicating all rivalry within a ministry, meant that there continued to be refractory elements amenable to a deal with the 'outs' or some portion thereof. The time had not yet come when a minister could normally rely upon the loyalty of his colleagues in office. This fact lent encouragement to the malcontents. At the same time it helped to keep them divided, by giving rise to fears that one group might enter upon a treaty to the exclusion of the rest. On the other hand, as is readily discernible, the dismissals contributed to the talent and numbers of Sir Robert's implacable foes.

Their ranks were swelled also by other causes directly

[1] Sedgwick, ed., *Memoirs of Lord Hervey*, p. 743.

[2] The case of William Pitt, cashiered from his Cornetcy of Horse for a parliamentary speech in 1736, may be regarded as an instance of Walpole's lenity rather than his severity. Pitt was a protégé of Cobham, an avowed member of the Opposition clique organized from Stowe, and had acted as teller for the minority before his notorious oration. Walpole left him untouched until Pitt's offensive remarks forced his hand. It may be, as reported, that Sir Robert declared, 'We must muzzle this terrible Cornet of the Horse', but it is hard to believe that so experienced a minister could have seriously expected dismissal to shut Pitt's mouth. An example of this kind was more likely intended *pour encourager les autres*. The furor raised over the affair, kept alive by Lyttelton's verse and Pitt's own histrionics, illustrates the continuing efforts of Walpole's enemies to create an Opposition martyrology.

connected with his position and policy. Colonel James Oglethorpe told Walpole in 1737 'that he was in the case of all ministers who have held the reins for a long time; they [his opponents] were tired of his administration; and the ambitious among them were for coming into place'.[1] Many found their expectations unanswered, in great things or in little, and saw no hope but in his fall. There were outstanding figures like Carteret who, as the Queen reported to Walpole, remarked

that he found you were too well established in my favour for him to hope to supplant you; and upon finding he could not be first, that he had mortified his pride so far as to take the resolution of submitting to be second; but if you would not permit him even to serve under you, who in this House could blame him if he continued to fight against you?[2]

Lesser men like Sandys, Rushout, and Windham turned to opposition upon the disappointment of lesser demands.[3] Some resented the Court's invasion of their electoral interests.[4] Others nursed old grudges for past injuries: 'All Stanhopes and Spencers', wrote Hervey, 'are taught to look on a Walpole as one they are to hate by inheritance.'[5] Various aspects of Government activity alienated still more. Lord Scarborough, an old favourite of the King, quit as Master of the Horse in dudgeon over the dismissals following the Excise Bill.[6] The Duchess of Queensberry was forbidden the Court in 1729 for soliciting subscriptions to Gay's 'Polly', a libel on the Ministry, whereupon her husband resigned as Admiral of Scotland.[7] The revival of the salt tax in 1732 drove Walter Plummer into opposition because it prevented the development of salt works on his estate.[8] The Duke of Rutland fell foul of Walpole in 1735 over the disposal of patronage in the Duchy of Lancaster and threw down his place.[9] Such occurrences were commonplace, and Lord Townshend, who finally fell out with his brother-in-law

---

[1] *H.M.C., Egmont MSS.* ii. 341.

[2] Sedgwick, ed., *Memoirs of Lord Hervey*, p. 702.

[3] *H.M.C., Egmont MSS.* i. 245–6.

[4] Ibid. i. 433, 453, 457, 459, 467; ii. 99, 132; 'An Apology for the Hon. Col. Charles Leslie's quitting the British Service and entering into the Dutch' in P.R.O., Chatham Papers 48.

[5] Coxe, *Walpole*, iii. 312.   [6] *H.M.C., Egmont MSS.* ii. 33–34.

[7] *H.M.C., Downshire MSS.* i, part 2, 909; Sedgwick, ed., *Memoirs of Lord Hervey*, p. 100.

[8] *H.M.C., Egmont MSS.* i. 246.   [9] Ibid. ii. 272.

in 1730, was the rare exception in that he devoted the remainder of his life to agricultural experiment instead of violent recrimination.[1]

The Actions of the Royal Family

The fact that the King and Queen staunchly supported Walpole strengthened his hand but aggravated discontent. Though the blame often redounded to the monarch personally, in an age which habitually regarded high public officials as the chosen instruments of the Crown, the result was usually an addition to the opponents of his Ministry.[2] Lord Burlington, for example, insisted that he had accepted the Captaincy of the band of Gentleman Pensioners upon George II's personal promise that he should have the first vacant ministerial post, and when Lonsdale succeeded to the Privy Seal in 1733, Burlington threw up all his employments 'and listed himself immediately in the Opposition'. His resignation, he declared, 'did not proceed from any dislike to the measures of the administration, or any quarrel with ministers, but that his sole objection was to the King, who had told him a lie and broke his word'.[3]

Both George II and Caroline made occasional endeavours to engage peers in support of Court measures—'closeted, schooled and tampered with' them, in Hervey's phrase[4]—and the King treated opponents with studied discourtesy. Once at

---

[1] It is interesting to note that Townshend's refusal to engage in politics after his retirement was owing to his fear of being driven like Cowper into Jacobitical extremes: Coxe, *Walpole*, i. 338. Horace Walpole gives an interesting account of the quarrel between Townshend and Walpole in a marginal note to his copy of Hardwicke's *Walpoliana*, p. 11. It may well have been, as Plumb avers in *Walpole*, ii. 199, that Townshend placed his vote at the disposal of the Opposition, but I know of no instance in which it was employed. Townshend's signature was not appended to any of the Lords' protests during his retirement.

[2] In this connexion it is interesting to observe the attitude expressed by Egmont when Walpole checked that Lord's efforts to extend his 'interest' in the Government borough of Harwich. Egmont complained of his 'ill usage' to one of Walpole's agents, Augustus Schutz, who 'said he was sure I would not act in the House contrary to the Government for this, for the King would know nothing of it, and my professions and obligations to the King would not suffer it. I replied,' Egmont concludes, 'where I could separate Sir Robert from the King, I should.' *H.M.C., Egmont MSS.* i. 457.

[3] Sedgwick, ed., *Memoirs of Lord Hervey*, pp. 188–9; *H.M.C., Carlisle MSS.*, pp. 114–15.

[4] Sedgwick, ed., *Memoirs of Lord Hervey*, p. 190.

a levee he turned his back upon Lord Falmouth, an act which led in 1734 to the foundation of 'The Liberty or Rumpsteak Club', composed of twenty-seven peers who had been similarly greeted by George's buxom posterior.[1] In the same year the King's refusal to allow Carteret and Sunderland to kiss hands 'highly disgusted several great families', reported the mild and judicious Egmont, who added

It were to be wished the King had more affability, and that the sincerity in showing his resentment where he is displeased with his subject's conduct did not prejudice His Majesty's affairs after this manner. For the nobility of England are proud, and presently take fire at any slight the Crown casts upon them; besides there are conjunctions of time when kings should take some pains to please.[2]

Furthermore, when he chose to be gracious, His Majesty customarily spoke only to titled persons at Court, which aggrieved his loyal commoners. In a long list of complaints about the King's conduct in 1730, a worried Court member named Anthony Duncomb included

the King's not speaking to the country gentry when they come to Court, which tries them and makes them declare they have no business to come here, since they are not regarded, and so they betake themselves to the discontented party.[3]

Personal pique at His Majesty's treatment also gave expanding opposition its greatest asset, the Prince of Wales. He had come to England in 1728, and within a few months there was talk of tension between him and his father.[4] The heir desired a wife and, as always, thought his establishment inadequate. No serious rift developed for some time, but in 1734 rumour had it that the malcontents intended to propose a parliamentary address to the King for an increased allowance of £100,000 for the Prince.[5] The affair came slowly to a head over three years, intensified particularly after Frederick's forlorn marriage in 1735. Some of his friends tried to persuade him not to make the allowance a political issue,[6] and as a crisis approached, the Government made strenuous efforts at conciliation.

---

[1] Rose, ed., *Marchmont Papers*, ii. 19–20; Graham, ed., *Annals of Stair*, ii. 226; *H.M.C., Egmont MSS.* ii. 14. When he heard of this club, the startled and angry King is said to have exclaimed, 'Quoy? est qui se moque de moi?' (ibid. 53).

[2] Ibid. 34.   [3] Ibid. i. 41.

[4] *H.M.C., Carlisle MSS.*, p. 56.

[5] *H.M.C., Egmont MSS.* ii. 7.   [6] Phillimore, *Lyttelton*, i. 77.

Nothing would avail, for Frederick declared the Court had waited too long; he was committed to a parliamentary address which Pulteney and Carteret duly presented in February 1737. The Ministry carried the day, but the Opposition had captured the Prince. Then in the ensuing summer Frederick performed the notorious act of removing his wife while in labour from Hampton Court to St. James's, and his enraged parent pursued the course taken by George I twenty years before: the Prince was banished from the Court and notice given 'that whoever goes to pay their court to their Royal Highnesses the Prince and Princess of Wales will not be admitted to His Majesty's presence'.[1] Thereafter Frederick refused to entertain any overtures till Walpole should be dismissed.[2]

As in 1717 the Prince's descent into uncompromising opposition notably affected the character and alignment of political forces. His Royal Highness's 'interest' now shifted largely to the minority,[3] his Court became a centre of malcontent activity,[4] and his name in their midst authenticated the Anticourtiers' insistent claim to patriotism. Lord Chancellor Hardwicke, who had participated in the abortive negotiations of the Government with the Prince in 1736–7, accurately foresaw the new situation:

Before this the Whigs in opposition wanted a head, because liable to the disagreeable imputation of constantly acting with the Jacobites; and had no prospect of ever coming into any share of power but by

[1] *H.M.C., Egmont MSS.* ii. 432.

[2] Ibid. iii. 238–9; Coxe, *Walpole,* iii. 585–6.

[3] As Frederick moved into opposition, Hervey reported (*Memoirs,* pp. 850–1) that several trimmers among his courtiers—Carnarvon, Baltimore, Herbert, Montagu, and Evelyn—informed him that they would always vote for his personal measures but in other matters would support the Government. The Prince's answer was not known, but from what can be learned of their parliamentary activities, he appears to have allowed them to maintain this equivocal stand. They seem clearly to have been exceptions to the general rule that the Prince's Court voted with the Opposition. See also Hervey's report on Walpole's concern about the loss of the votes of 'the Prince's family': ibid., p. 772. For the strength of Frederick's 'interest', see A. N. Newman, 'The Political Patronage of Frederick, Prince of Wales', *Historical Journal,* i (1958), 68–75.

[4] Upon his expulsion from St. James's, the Prince established his town residence at Norfolk House. He set up his political headquarters, however, at Carlton House, which he had purchased in 1732. After the reconciliation with his father in 1742 he removed both his family and his Court to Leicester House, where he remained until his death. His country residences at Kew and Cliveden often sheltered Opposition gatherings as well.

reuniting with their old friends. They will now find a head in the Prince, and he being the immediate successor in the Protestant line will be an irrefragible answer to the reproach of Jacobitism.[1]

This development consequently weakened the effectiveness of one of Walpole's chief counter-measures against expanding opposition, the traditional accusation of disloyalty.

The Decay of Walpole's Strength

Now few if any knew better than Sir Robert the character and resources of the Jacobites. Not only did he maintain an active espionage system throughout Europe and the British Isles, but he conducted an extraordinary communication with the head of the Pretender's interest in London. This was Colonel William Cecil, who had succeeded Orrery in 1731. According to the Oxford Jacobite William King, Walpole duped Cecil into believing that he might at some propitious moment engineer a Stuart restoration; and Cecil thereupon kept the Minister well informed of the designs of the Chevalier and his followers.[2] It was probably Sir Robert's confidence in the reliability of his intelligence, and the weaknesses which it revealed in the enemies' camp, that led him to treat the 'true blue' Jacobites with such genial forbearance. At various times in the 1730's he granted a personal request to spare an incriminated friend of Shippen, whom he frequently complimented as incorruptible; twitted Barbour about a guilty visit to the Pretender; and joked with Caesar over his implication in the Gyllenborg Plot.[3] In return many of the Jacobites, apparently unaware of Walpole's connexion with Cecil, cherished an unconcealed regard for their inveterate foe.[4]

---

[1] Hardwicke's narrative of the negotiations, from which this quotation is taken, is in Add. MSS. 9198, ff. 1–26 (ff. 32–42 are a fair copy).

[2] William King, *Political and Literary Anecdotes of His Own Time* (Boston, 1819), pp. 37–39. Cf. Hardwicke, *Walpoliana*, p. 7. This little game went so far that in 1739, upon presumed intimations from Sir Robert, James sent Thomas Carte to the Minister with a formal request that he serve as the Monck of a new restoration: Add. MSS. 34522, f. 13.

[3] Coxe, *Walpole*, i. 670–1; Hardwicke, *Walpoliana*, p. 7; MS. Journal of Mrs. Charles Caesar, ii, cf. the comments in *H.M.C., Egmont MSS.* iii. 191–2.

[4] Mrs. Caesar's journal (especially vol. v) brings out clearly the Jacobites' respect, almost amounting to fondness, for the Chief Minister. Cf. Coxe, *Walpole*, i. 672.

For political purposes Sir Robert nevertheless continued to hold up Jacobitism publicly as an awesome bogy and to insist that all who voted with its adherents in Parliament were guilty by association. The Opposition protested bitterly against the false imputation: in 1731 Pulteney launched a savage attack on this ministerial policy, in which he asserted that Walpole had laid down in the following terms: 'When any known Whig who opposes me happens to concur with a reputed Tory, nothing can be more evident than that he hath deserted his principles, is turned a Jacobite, and hath a design of bringing in the Pretender.'[1] The extent of the malcontents' wrath may not be an altogether accurate measure of the effectiveness of the smear, but their anger was clearly matched by Hardwicke's anxiety about the counter-effect of Frederick's plunge into opposition. Thereafter Sir Robert did not withdraw his accusations, though perhaps he stated them in milder terms,[2] but one may doubt how seriously the political world could take the proposition that a deluded Prince was leading a movement calculated to upset his own succession to the throne.

These years also witnessed the growing inadequacy of Walpole's other major counter-measure—the purchase of able members of the Opposition who would submit to his leadership. For a time this policy worked as well as it had in the preceding period. In 1726 he deprived the malcontents of their leading lawyers by making Trevor Lord Privy Seal, Sir Thomas Pengelly chief Baron of the Exchequer, and Robert Price a puisne judge of Common Pleas. The rising young Thomas Winnington went over to the Court in 1729, and the next year Lord Bingley accepted the staff as Treasurer of the Household. Up to this point experience supported Sir Robert's famous boast that he knew the price of every man in opposition,[3] but during the remaining years of his Ministry desertions from the

[1] *An Answer to One Part of a Late Infamous Libel, intitled, Remarks on the Craftsman's Vindication of his two Honourable Patrons* (London, 1731), pp. 16–17.

[2] For examples, see *P.H.* x. 401; xi. 364–5. The words, of course, are those of the parliamentary reporter, but from the manner in which journalists composed speeches in this period, there would appear to be a strong probability that the points actually made by the speaker were generally reflected in the printed version: see Benjamin B. Hoover, *Samuel Johnson's Parliamentary Reporting* (Univ. of California Press, 1953).

[3] On Walpole's oft misquoted dictum, see Coxe, *Walpole*, i. 757; *H.M.C., Marlborough MSS.*, p. 18; Rose, ed., *Marchmont Papers*, ii. 76–77.

Opposition were few. The Duke of Marlborough accepted a place in 1738, but no other great coups dismayed the malcontents.[1]

There seems to have been a distinct hardening of attitude on both sides in the 1730's. Walpole firmly declined to parley with those who had blatantly defied him, and the King never indicated any willingness to take in parliamentary opponents, whom he repeatedly denounced as knaves and scoundrels. For their part the Opposition groups advertised the withdrawal of their virtue from the market. In a pamphlet of 1731 Pulteney thus addressed the Minister:

The distress in which you have involved yourself hath obliged you to tamper with several gentlemen in the Opposition, and to put your own vile glosses on these negotiations when you have failed in them. This hath induced them to consult one another upon this head. I believe the acquisitions which you have lately made among them will give you no additional strength or credit; and it will be vain for you to make any further attempts; for know, sir, that they are come to a determined resolution, and it is a measure taken amongst them, not to listen to any treaty of this kind whatsoever, or from whomsoever it may come, in which the first and principal condition shall not be to deliver you up to the justice of your country.[2]

The intended impression of Opposition solidarity was an exaggeration, and we cannot tell how severely Sir Robert put this declaration to the test.[3] The fact remains that no other of his noteworthy opponents accepted places until his fall in 1742.

Concurrent with the spasmodic desertions from the Court, therefore, came the decreasing effectiveness of Walpole's efforts to restrict and weaken the Opposition. Confining pressures

[1] There were usually a few unreliables, who switched sporadically from one side to another, but they were politically insignificant. Typical was Lord Tyrconnel, a ministerialist under George I, who went into opposition under George II, rejoined the ministerialist camp in 1732, then deserted Walpole over the Excise. George II called him 'a puppy that never votes twice together on the same side' (Sedgwick, ed., *Memoirs of Lord Hervey*, i. 162).

[2] *An Answer to One Part of a Late Infamous Libel*, p. 47.

[3] The dowager Duchess of Marlborough reported a rumour in 1735 that an emissary of Walpole 'has made great concessions to some of the opposing party, owning that the nation was now in a very melancholy situation and adding that if they would come in with their assistance to mend it, that everybody that had been turned out should be restored again' (Blenheim MSS. E. 13: Duchess of Marlborough to Hon. John Spencer, 31 May 1735). If ever sent out, this 'feeler' produced no results.

lessened as expansive forces continued to operate unabated.
Moreover, the crippling of ministerial counter-measures indicates that the malcontents did not play a merely passive role
in their own expansion. They were something more than a
reception committee at the cave of Adullam. The 'determined
resolution' announced by Pulteney reveals an endeavour to
erect defences against the Court's powers of disintegration. In
binding Prince Frederick to their cause, they displayed an
offensive energy, an aggressive tendency to multiply their
strength by exploiting the unavoidable weaknesses in Walpole's
political policies.

His public policies gave them openings as well. While the
'Court system' provided opportunities, eagerly seized, for
nobbling humiliated courtiers, disappointed place-seekers, and
a pouting Prince, Walpole's foreign and domestic projects
offered a means to widen the area of discontent by angry
protest. The *causes célèbres* are familiar: the administrative
reforms embodied in the Excise Bill, the social reform intended
by the first Gin Act, the disciplinary measures imposed upon
Scotland for Jacobite activities and the Porteous Riots, the
appeasement of marauding Spaniards, intriguing Austrians,
and faithless French. Not that popular storms could profit the
Opposition directly. Members might abandon the Court in
the midst of a tempest, only to return to their allegiance in the
ensuing calm. This held true of many on the excise issue. But
the indirect effect of widespread discontents, following rapidly
one upon another, and usually accompanied by some permanent defections, was to generate a feeling of uncertainty
about the solidity of the Government.

As the ground trembled, politicians cast about them for
secure footing. The half-hearted might respond to confident
assurances from the Opposition. Thus in 1738, as the malcontents blew upon the whirlwind they had raised over the
depredations of Caribbean *guarda-costas*, Lord Stair urged the
consolidation of opposition about the Prince, who should be
brought to a 'steady and uniform conduct'; for Stair insisted to
Marchmont,

There are gentlemen of figure in the House of Commons who have
good stakes in the nation, who, I know, think of Sir Robert and his
administration just as you and I do, and who own that whilst Sir

Robert is Minister, things can never take a better turn, and yet for one consideration or other they have all along voted with Sir Robert. I do not know but that some of these gentlemen may think that this is a proper time to change their conduct.

I think such folks should be talked to by proper persons in a proper manner; in my own knowledge I know some in that situation, and to be sure there are more that I do not know. To be sure, Mr. Pulteney will speak to somebody that he knows. I have spoken, and I shall speak to other persons, possibly not without effect. But there is another class, much more numerous indeed, who have voted all along with the Minister, not out of affection to him or because they thought his cause was right, but because they thought it was useful to themselves to do so. A great many of such wise men, whenever they can calculate that there are more chances for Sir Robert's falling than for his standing, will vote on [the] opposing side without any ceremony; such people should be talked to likewise in their own way.[1]

Like all bodies of men who feed upon hopes deferred, the grumbletonians underestimated the strength of their adversary. They made too little of the interests which attached men to the Government and too much of Walpole's political insecurity and flagging health. Not until the final crisis did the Opposition detach significant numbers of conscientious objectors or calculating mercenaries. Now and again anticipation of Walpole's fall brought in small accretions like George Bubb Dodington, who withdrew from the Treasury Board in 1741 to join a movement he rightly thought on the verge of triumph. But as the eventual climax of 1742 drew on, a sense of the Government's impending doom became a critical factor. In the assurance of victory, the Opposition threatened reprisals against some who would not come over to them, and abrupt shifts of allegiance upset all ministerial calculations.[2] Young Horace Walpole saw his father's Ministry defeated by 'men who would not care to find themselves on the weaker side contrary to their intent'.[3]

The Nature of Expansion

In sum, the Bolingbroke–Pulteney Camarilla of 1726 owed its expansion to a variety of impulsions. All partook of the same

---

[1] Rose, ed., *Marchmont Papers*, ii. 92–93.

[2] Coxe, *Walpole*, iii. 582–4, 590–1; *Horace Walpole's Correspondence with Sir Horace Mann* (New Haven, 1954), i. 244–5, 254, 299.   [3] Ibid. 243.

nature, the reaction of political sensibilities to Walpole and his 'system'. The great Minister's skill and courage, upheld by consistent royal support, had so prolonged his tenure that he became the inevitable butt of all criticism, the culprit to whom were attributed all failures and frustrations. This single, un-qualified, all-embracing negative fixed the character of the malcontent coalition. Uniformity of denial accounts for both its strength and its weakness. Men draw naturally together in the face of common affliction. A sense of grievance shared en-courages a league of redress and retribution. Concentration upon one prominent object makes for clarity of aim, strength of purpose, and economy of effort. Exploitation of these advan-tages gave the opponents an appearance of unprecedented solidarity. Hence the temptation to see in the coalition 'the characteristics of a modern parliamentary Opposition party'.[1] Hence also the tendency to view every disagreement as a 'party split'. But unity upon a principle of negation does not guarantee uniformity in positive aims and methods. Satan's adversaries do not all worship at the same shrine. Each 'interest' reacted in its own particular way from its own particular grievance. All carried their private convictions and prejudices into opposition. Close association gave rise to frictions, fears, and jealousies. Antagonism to Walpole sometimes obscured but never obliter-ated the very real differences among them.

This persistent heterogeneity meant that expansion could not take place by the absorption of new elements into the original Camarilla. As time would show, the *entente* of 1726, an unstable union at best, did not possess sufficient powers of assimilation. To say that the Opposition became a 'modern' political party is to misread the evidence. All large parties are coalitions, but 'modern' parties have come to be coalitions within a pre-existing ideological and institutional framework, which, how-ever imperfect, contains and co-ordinates divergent forces. When the framework breaks under the strain, a 'party split' occurs. A conventional alliance of eighteenth-century groups, such as that formed by Bolingbroke and Pulteney, did not consti-tute a comparable structure. The will to create one was not lack-ing, in some hearts at least, but resources were inadequate. Consequently, the Opposition expanded, not by any organic

[1] Realey, *Early Opposition to Walpole*, p. 158.

process, but by the extension and regrouping of the malcontent cliques of which it was composed. Some underwent striking metamorphoses through the adhesion of new members and the defection of old. Breaches and *rapprochements* frequently transformed their relationships to each other. The constituent parts of the coalition grew and changed, and the whole increased in numbers but not in homogeneity. The Opposition remained a loose confederacy, for ever on the verge of dissolution.

To this lack of solidarity the letters and memoirs of the time bear abundant testimony. One could quote at great length the records of endless *tracasseries*. A few examples may suffice to show how contemporaries saw the coalition. Describing the failure of their opponents' parliamentary campaign in 1734, Lord Hervey observed,

Nor ought anybody to wonder that things were no better concerted or managed against the Court when those who naturally ought to have acted in concert for the management of these affairs were most of them as ill with one another as with those they opposed. Lord Carteret and Lord Bolingbroke had no correspondence at all; Mr. Pulteney and Lord Bolingbroke hated one another; Lord Carteret and Pulteney were jealous of one another; Sir William Wyndham and Pulteney the same; whilst Lord Chesterfield had a little correspondence with them all but was confided in by none of them.[1]

Four years later Horace Walpole commented, '. . . The opponents being a body composed of men of different principles and of different views are much disjointed and have not any set scheme of opposition',[2] and Charles Howard detailed evidence which convinced him 'that the schemes of those who are in the minority are very much divided and broke this winter'.[3] Bishop Hare could not forecast how the malcontents would behave in 1740, 'they not being well united among themselves or agreed in their measures to distress the Ministry'.[4] The next year Egmont thought them so 'disunited' that they might never make

---

[1] Sedgwick, ed., *Memoirs of Lord Hervey*, p. 256. At this same time Dodington urged Dorset to refrain from open opposition upon the ground that it would be 'extremely disagreeable . . . to act with a number of gentlemen, united in one point indeed, but from different views and motives, and consequently liable to vary as those motives and views may cease or be satisfied' (*H.M.C., Stopford-Sackville MSS.* i. 154).

[2] *H.M.C., Trevor MSS.*, p. 10.   [3] *H.M.C., Carlisle MSS.*, p. 193.
[4] *H.M.C., Hare MSS.*, p. 254.

common cause again.[1] Such observations found confirmation in
cries of distress from among the malcontents themselves. During
these same years the correspondence of Bolingbroke, Chesterfield, Stair, Montrose, and other leading figures abounds with
reference to the 'jumble and confusion' in an Opposition
'seemingly united but really divided', 'broken and disjointed'
because 'the views of individuals are too different for them to
draw together'.[2] Despair often beset those who strove for steady
and consistent union.

3. THE PRINCIPLES OF THE OPPOSITION BLOCS

Yet the Opposition never reached the depths of utter frag-
mentation. There was form within the seeming chaos. Factors
which produced discord also imposed a rough pattern upon the
process of extension and regrouping by which the coalition
expanded. The divisive 'views' and 'principles' seen by contemporaries denoted three large bodies of collective opinion. In
each the essential element was a theory of the function of
opposition. Theories sprang from calculations of advantage,
that is, from estimates of the means required to achieve political
ambitions. Calculations in turn were based upon the position
and purpose of their authors. Differences therein account for
variations in theory, while community of interest, fortified by
personal sympathy, prejudice, or passion, gathered malcontents
about sets of 'views' and 'principles' which justified their actions
and promised them success. In this manner the opponents
cohered into three major blocs with distinctive political
attitudes.

The Tories

The largest bloc was the Tories. Despite confusion resulting
from persistent feuds and desertions, the old party name still
had a meaning. Men knew a Tory when they saw one. No Tory
peers were admitted to the Rumpsteak Club.[3] When in 1739
Lord Cardigan and Sir William Wyndham were blackballed
for membership in the non-partisan Whist Club at White's,

[1] *H.M.C., Egmont MSS.* iii. 193.
[2] Rose, ed., *Marchmont Papers*, ii. 99–102, 177–91, and ff.; Graham, ed., *Annals of
Stair*, ii. 208, 268–9; Dobrée, ed., *Letters of Chesterfield*, ii. 448–9, 462, 467.
[3] *H.M.C., Egmont MSS.* ii. 14.

Egmont reported that 'it is said the Club has separated, the Tories resolving not to meet more with the Whigs'.[1] Tories clung to their traditional soubriquet. Bruce discoursed to Dartmouth upon measures 'proper for we Tories to support'.[2] Courting the country folk about Cirencester, Henry Bathurst wrote, 'I go out hunting to show I am a Tory and drink bumpers to show I am a Churchman.'[3] Carmarthen once exploded, '. . . As there is a just God in heaven before whom I must appear I most solemnly declare I have no Whig principles in me, neither will I ever espouse the interest of such cattle.'[4]

Inveterate prejudice accounts in part for the continuing distinction. Few but successful placehunters would disavow a badge they had long worn so proudly. Election mobs still shouted, 'No redcoats, down with the Rump!' under the direction of their landlords in provincial towns where venerable loyalties fed upon bitter memories. Jacobitism, though subsiding into wistful sentiment, had lost none of its fervent righteousness. Walpole's policy of exclusion, accompanied by his diligent fostering of the myth that identified the Whigs alone as the authors of 1688 and the saviours of the Protestant Succession, kept alive the idea of a deep cleavage between the 'parties'.

The general concept of 'Tory principles' lingered on. Tories still thought themselves, as did others, the defenders of the Church and the landed interest. To them the Mortmain Bill of 1736 was 'a kind of sacrilege'.[5] Once when Sir Robert received lukewarm support from the 'true blues' upon a motion to reject a Dissenters' petition, the Minister left his seat and settled down beside their leader, Edward Harley, with the jocular remark, 'I may now [sit with you]. See, I take care of the Church when some of your own friends leave it.'[6] Walpole also knew the Tories' sensitivity to the land tax. His excise scheme was designed in part to soften their hostility because it would lead to the abolition of the impost on their estates.[7] Long years in the wilderness had added traditional grievances to traditional 'principles'. Tories could be counted upon to vote for any place Bill, any reduction of the army, any move to repeal the

[1] Ibid. iii. 48.
[2] *H.M.C., Dartmouth MSS.*, p. 154.
[3] Add. MSS. 41354, f. 8.
[4] *H.M.C., Wentworth MSS.*, p. 411.
[5] Add. MSS. 41354, f. 8.
[6] MS. Journal of Mrs. Charles Caesar, v.
[7] Coxe, *Walpole*, i. 377 ff.; Paul Vaucher, *La Crise du Ministère Walpole.*

Septennial Act. The 'Country party programme' had become theirs by prescription.

There was something deeper too. A Tory still cherished a Cavalier reverence for the King. Monarchy, even with the stain of Hanover upon it, had not lost its aura of sanctity. Despite their political proscription, Tories flocked to kiss hands at Court upon the accession of George II in 1727.[1] Even Jacobites were to be found among the train of squires who had not entered the royal presence for half a generation. The true nature of their sentiments is hard to come at. Tories were not eloquent. They seldom paraded their feelings. The Jacobites perhaps shared the view later expressed by Dr. Johnson that 'they have only lent, not sold, their principles; . . . they make His Majesty tenant-at-will of their loyalty' because 'various circumstances induce us to an acquiescence in what *is* without abandoning our opinions of what *ought to be*'.[2] The Hanoverian Tories may have seen the dawn of a new day, the advent of a king who would more fully deserve their abiding homage.[3] Tory veneration of the Crown seems comprehensible in part as romantic tradition, not to be dissolved by inner contradictions or destroyed by disillusion. George II never requited the Tories' affection, yet they suffered no change of heart. Events were to show also that with the elements of romance were mingled Conservative convictions on the nature of the Constitution, which were reinforced both by the Tories' political situation and by their relationships with Sir Robert Walpole.

The most significant test of their convictions came upon the famous 'Motion' of 1741. The routine stuff of parliamentary

---

[1] Realey, *Early Opposition to Walpole*, pp. 219–20. Seventeen years later a Whig pamphleteer derisively recalled that the Tories 'went to Court in a body at the beginning of this reign, in such a numerous body as to leave the Cocoa Tree empty of all but Martha single in the bar. . . . Failing of such reception as they expected at Court . . ., they returned again to Martha and the Cocoa Tree, and again to their complaints of grievances, were again all patriots, all for restoring the Constitution now [that] they themselves were not restored': *Warning to the Whigs and to the Well-affected Tories* (London, 1744), pp. 25–33. Cf. *Mist's Journal*, 17–24 June 1727.

[2] Portland Papers (Nottingham University Library): William Burke to Portland, 26 July 1779. Strafford, one of the Jacobites who went to Court, expressed Johnson's view in more practical terms in a letter to the Pretender on 21 June 1727: Stanhope, *History of England*, ii, app. xxv.

[3] See the justification adopted retrospectively by Hanoverian Tories in [John Campbell], *The Case of the Opposition Impartially Stated* (London, 1742), pp. 15–16.

debate rarely touched the fundamentals of political belief, but here was an issue that forced every politician to search his heart. On 13 February Pulteney's henchman Sandys moved that the Commons should address the King to remove Walpole 'from His Majesty's presence and counsels forever'. After a debate lasting from noon until three the following morning, the Address was lost, 290 to 106. The Tories split three ways. Shippen and Harley led thirty-two 'true blues' out of the House before the division. Twenty-two others supported Cornbury in voting for the Minister. Most of the remnants of Bolingbroke's coterie stood by the Whig malcontents.[1] The last occasioned no surprise, but why had the first two groups withdrawn from the pursuit of their arch-foe?

Some detected a shrewd political move. 'It is thought', wrote Egmont, 'that the Tories took this opportunity to distinguish themselves from the Anti-courtier Whigs and to show His Majesty that they are the better subjects of the two.'[2] There was perhaps reason to believe that this was a bid for favour. Tory speakers followed Walpole's own line of defence by declaring 'the motion' extra-legal and unjust. With bitter reference to the persecution of Oxford, Edward Harley warmly avowed his pleasure at 'this opportunity to return good for evil and to do that honourable gentleman and his family that justice which he denied to mine'.[3] Others perceived a Tory preference for Walpole's régime to one that might be set up by the dissident Whigs. Shippen openly professed indifference as to 'who was in or who was out'.[4] But Mrs. Caesar jubilantly recorded that her husband's friends took to themselves 'immortal honour' for defending Sir Robert against both Pulteney's hateful crew and 'those that left us'.[5] One need not seek the explanation in rumours about formal Tory pledges to support the Minister on a 'personal question' in return for relief from prosecution for Jacobite activity.[6] They had never made any secret of their

[1] On the same day Carteret moved the same address in the Lords, where it was defeated 108–59. For accounts of 'the motion' and the conduct of the Tories thereon, see *Gentleman's Magazine*, xi. 106, 232; *P.H.* xi. 1153–1388; *H.M.C., Egmont MSS.* iii. 191–3.

[2] Ibid. 192.

[3] *P.H.* xi. 1269.

[4] Ibid. 1375.

[5] MS. Journal of Mrs. Charles Caesar, v.

[6] Coxe, *Walpole*, i. 671.

aversion to the coalition leaders or of their private affection for the Minister.[1]

Yet the Tories justified their action in terms of principle. The Opposition indictment rested upon two points: that Walpole had arrogated to himself the position of Prime Minister, an office unknown to the Constitution, and that his policy had sacrificed British interests at home and abroad.[2] In Tory eyes neither of these charges warranted the address. Let Walpole's measures be condemned utterly, ran the argument; none had opposed them more vigorously than Tories. If bad policy involve crime, let crime be investigated and punished according to law. Since the evidence suggests no more than stupidity and poor judgement, the only legitimate recourse is continued opposition. But opposition to measures not men. The choice of ministers is in the Crown. Shippen would not 'pull Robin down upon republican principles'.[3] To infringe upon the prerogative with such a 'bloodsucking motion' is to court disaster. Cornbury reminded the House of the consequences of the assault on Strafford: 'the usurpation of authority, the subversion of our Constitution, and the murder of the King'.[4] Moreover, continued the Tory rebuttal, Britain's affairs have never gone so well as when the King entrusted his administration to one chief minister. Though the fundamental laws may be silent upon the matter, reliance upon a good premier is sound practice. Their defence of Walpole, the Tories concluded, was a necessary consequence of consistent 'Tory principles'.[5]

So complex are the motives of men that one can rarely attain to certain knowledge of the decisive impulses behind their actions. In 1741 interest, sentiment, and principle alike urged the same conclusion upon the Tories who refused to drive

---

[1] 'Our case is hard,' Strafford once said to Caesar, 'being forced to help support them [the Whig malcontents] against Sir Robert Walpole, who has not ill nature enough to use us so ill as they would do if in power.' (MS. Journal of Mrs. Charles Caesar, v.)

[2] See the summation of the Opposition's case in *Reasons Founded on Facts for a Late Motion in a Letter to a Tory Member* (London, 1741).

[3] Feiling, *Second Tory Party*, p. 37.

[4] *P.H.* xi. 1374.

[5] The most thoroughgoing exposition of Tory doctrine is *The Sentiments of a Tory in Respect to a Late Important Transaction and in Regard to the Present Situation of Affairs*, inspired by Cornbury's group in April 1741. See also the defence of the Tories' conduct on 'the motion' and their justification of 'measures not men' in [John Campbell], *The Case of the Opposition Impartially Stated*, pp. 18–21, 55–56.

Walpole from office. Their decision was in keeping with the position they had occupied during their years in opposition. 'Measures not men' was but a happy slogan to justify opposition within the orthodox interpretation of the Constitution. The decision to abstain or to vote against the motion must have turned upon the subleties of individual consciences. The split cut across family lines and dynastic loyalties. Distraction amid agreement had long been a Tory characteristic. It was the broad lines of agreement that marked out the Tory bloc in the malcontent coalition.

Bolingbroke had hoped to commit this group to his leadership, 'to render this generation of Tories of much good use to their country'.[1] He and his following strove constantly to maintain liaison with them. Suspiciously they kept him at arm's length, and he reacted in periodic bursts of exasperation at their narrow intransigence. Their defection on 'the motion' left him solemn and savage: 'The conduct of the Tories', he wrote to Marchmont, 'is silly, infamous, and void of any colour of excuse.'[2] For, in truth, if he had ever sympathized with their attitude, he had long ago cast off his allegiance to the name of Tory and its ideological associations. Since 1726 he had pursued a career shared by most of his old clique, which wound a devious course through the shoals of conflicting policies and clashing personalities. His alliance with Pulteney spun out a precarious existence for nearly a decade. Weakened perhaps by Daniel Pulteney's death in 1731, it collapsed in 1735 when, peevish and disappointed, Bolingbroke flung off to eight years of self-imposed exile in Touraine. From Chanteloup, where tracts on politics and philosophy flowed from his pen, he furnished oracular counsel to Wyndham, once again his designated successor, and to his loyal few, now augmented by a band of new-found friends.

The recruits came largely from among the haughty dispossessed, the victims of Walpole's ministerial discipline. There were the remnants of the Roxburghe 'squadrone' and other Scottish opponents of the Argyll interest, Aberdeen and Queensberry, Stair and Montrose, Erskine, Hamilton, Tweeddale, Marchmont and his able sons. Chesterfield threw in his lot with them, as did the amiable Waller, and they drew upon the

---

[1] Rose, ed., *Marchmont Papers*, ii. 247.   [2] Ibid. 245–6.

influence and pugnacity of the septuagenarian Sarah, dowager
Duchess of Marlborough. Bound to them by gossamer threads
were Cobham's party—the arrogant cousinhood of Grenvilles,
Pitts, and Lytteltons—and the expanding interest of the youthful Duke of Bedford. The deaths of Wyndham and Marchmont
in 1740 were a discouraging loss, but about the same time came
some testy support from Dodington and Argyll, the latter now a
strange bedfellow with his lifelong rivals from north Britain.
Proud outcasts, for the most part, they were attracted to the
ideas of the stormy, half-forgiven exile. They too hungered for
fame and preferment. They found inspiration and justification
in his high-flown metapolitics, which, as will become apparent,
made a radical departure from the principles of the Tories. It
was in Bolingbroke's pronouncements, practically interpreted
for practical operation, that this new bloc saw a course to their
destinations more certain than an uncharted journey in the
company of William Pulteney.

The Pulteney–Carteret Bloc

The reason was not far to seek. As he drew away from
Bolingbroke, Pulteney moved into a new partnership with
Carteret. Each brought along a modest following: Carteret the
Finch interest, Pulteney a variegated assemblage of minor Whig
malcontents like Sandys, Rushout, and Gybbon. This was a
small bloc, but its wealth of vigour and debating strength gave it
a pre-eminent position among the elements in opposition. Like
most such Camarillas, the union of Pulteney and Carteret was a
mariage de convenance, based primarily upon common principles
of action.[1] Their tactics in many ways paralleled those of the
Walpole–Townshend Opposition of 1717–20, in which Pulteney
had taken part. By every means which opportunity offered or
ingenuity could devise they sought to drive the Ministry to an
accommodation, a treaty which would bring them into office.
They were political opportunists with a limited but definite
objective. Circumstances, a few convictions, and some rash
pledges, fixed their views and set their course.

Knowing that Walpole would never take them in except
upon his own terms, they concentrated their attack upon him.

[1] If Hervey is to be believed, Carteret made no effort to conceal his personal
dislike of Pulteney: Sedgwick, ed., *Memoirs of Lord Hervey*, pp. 752–3.

They would, as Pulteney grandiosely declared, 'pursue Sir Robert to his destruction'.[1] Always with an eye to a breach at Court, they steered away from incriminating his colleagues. All odium fell upon the 'sole minister'. The precedents of parliamentary assaults on evil favourites provided their justification. They would not trench upon the Prerogative, at least not in form. Their constitutional doctrine was epitomized in Hoadley's dictum, once quoted approvingly by *The Craftsman*, 'that, although no man has a natural right to a place at Court, yet every man has a right to get one if he can'.[2] The usurpation of overweening power by 'one monopolizing favourite' prevented an equitable distribution of the royal bounty and so inevitably brought on maladministration, corruption, weakness, and tyranny. The removal of the chief adviser alone guaranteed a change of measures.

In speech and action the Pulteney–Carteret bloc kept this programme always to the fore. One searches their surviving words in vain for any subtler view or any deeper purpose.[3] No adventurous theorizing leavened their flatly conventional attitudes. They carried on their campaign as public prosecutors in a presumptive case of 'the People *v.* Walpole'. Each emerging issue entered a new count in the indictment, to which they

---

[1] Add. MSS. 18915, f. 29.

[2] *The Craftsman*, no. 22, 20 Feb. 1727.

[3] See their speeches as reported in *P.H.* viii–xii. There are no collected editions of the correspondence of Pulteney, Carteret, or any of their close followers. Their letters are scattered about in such volumes as Coxe's *Walpole*, *Marchmont Papers* (ed. Rose), *Correspondence of Jonathan Swift* (ed. Ball), *Annals of Stair* (ed. Graham), *H.M.C.*, *Mar and Kellie MSS.*, *Letters of Chesterfield* (ed. Dobrée). Carteret published no significant political tracts while in opposition to Walpole. Pulteney produced many, of which the most pertinent are *An Answer to One Part of a Late Infamous Libel intituled Remarks on the Craftsman's Vindication of His Two Honorable Patrons* (1731), *A Proper Reply to a Late Scurrilous Libel intituled Sedition and Defamation Displayed* (1731), *An Enquiry into the Conduct of our Domestic Affairs from the Year 1721 to the Present Time* (1734), *An Humble Address to the Knights, Citizens, and Burgesses elected to Represent the Commons of Great Britain in the Ensuing Parliament* (1734). There are interesting summations of Pulteney's political views in *The Patriot and the Minister Reviewed by Way of Dialogue* (1743) and *Review of the Whole Political Conduct of a Late Eminent Patriot and his Friends* (1743). Pulteney wrote extensively for *The Craftsman*, and Carteret probably made occasional contributions, but the methods of identifying the authors of articles therein are so haphazard that little reliance can be placed upon them. There is no scholarly biography of Pulteney or any of the lesser figures in his clique. Carteret's three biographers (Archibald Ballantyne, W. Baring Pemberton, and Basil Williams) make no constructive analysis of his political thought during this phase of his career.

spoke as from a prepared brief in a prolonged trial. Like many another political attorney, they sought not justice but a conviction. For, in plain fact, they had no real differences of principle with the Minister. Pulteney steadily insisted that he had broken with Sir Robert over foreign policy.[1] The Treaty of Hanover, he contended, had grievously ruptured traditional British relations with Austria and converted proud Albion into a pawn of France. However honest Pulteney may have been, international developments progressively weakened his position, in the light of which it is impossible to see such a dispute as a profound and basic cleavage. Moreover, the subsequent actions of Pulteney's party clearly indicate that they had no quarrel with Walpole's methods of government. After his fall in 1742 things went on much as before. When Perceval asked Sandys, who had become Chancellor of the Exchequer, what he proposed to do about the 'popular Bills' he had previous championed,

he said that all men knew that parties attempted many things of this kind in opposition which they never meant to carry, but it was necessary to amuse the people. But that these [popular Bills] in general he should oppose, and so must every minister, and that as Sir Robert used to say, they were but the flurries of a day.[2]

Such a philosophy could not, of course, be openly avowed. And the Pulteney–Carteret group in particular had to defend themselves against the Minister's unvarying taunt that their opposition proceeded not from principle but from 'rage and resentment'. They fell back upon appropriate professions of altruism. The Opposition performed a public service as a check upon bad measures. They had no aims but the restoration of British liberty, security, and prosperity. To this end they would co-operate with men of good will from all parties.[3] The reward of virtue would be theirs, but as true patriots they looked

---

[1] See Pulteney's two major pamphlets on foreign policy, *A Short View of the State of Affairs with Relation to Great Britain for Four Years Past* (1730) and *Politicks on Both Sides with Regard to Foreign Affairs* (1734). Cf. Lord Perceval's *Faction Detected* (1743) and Realey, *Early Opposition to Walpole*, pp. 165–6.

[2] P.R.O., Egmont MSS. 212, f. 2ᵛ.

[3] Pulteney professed publicly to rejoice that 'the senseless distinction of Whig and Tory is . . . almost sunk in a general concern for the national interest' (*Answer to One Part of a Late Infamous Libel*, p. 17). In private he insisted upon his adherence to 'Whig principles', which he thought irreconcilable with 'Tory notions' (*H.M.C., Mar and Kellie MSS.*, pp. 535–6).

to no other compensation. In an incautious moment Pulteney once pledged himself never to accept public office.[1] His colleagues were more circumspect but no less insistent upon their disinterested spirit.

In pursuance of their basic objective, however, this bloc kept a watchful eye upon the malcontents within the Ministry. Pulteney's declaration that the chief condition of a treaty must be the ouster of Walpole had been a clear if indirect invitation to an accommodation with his rivals at Court. Wilmington and Dorset ogled the inducement timidly now and then, but Sir Robert was too strong for them. When Prince Frederick came out in opposition, Carteret and Pulteney saw their chance to re-enact the events of 1720. They were to meet with fierce rivalry for control of the Prince, but for the most part, though others kept a foothold in his Court, they exercised the greatest influence upon his political conduct. Then about the time of the breach in the royal family the Pelham clique launched an active intrigue against Sir Robert, and Pulteney soon began to talk openly of the necessity for a 'Whig reunion'.[2] A *rapprochement* between these two groups of 'ins' and 'outs', with Frederick a *tertium quid*, paved the way for the triumph of 1742.

The New Doctrine of 'Broad Bottom'

Now at the outset of his opposition, Bolingbroke doubtless agreed with the programme followed by Pulteney and his allies. In the ensuing years he would probably have entered into any agreement that promised success. He privately urged Wyndham to 'cultivate . . . a coalition' with the fractious Pelhams as late as 1738.[3] But before the date of his second exile in 1735, Bolingbroke saw that he might well be excluded from a prospective treaty.[4] His fears increased till the project of a 'Whig reunion' resolved all doubt. The same suspicions weighed down the hearts of Chesterfield and 'the Scottish brigade', Cobham's group, Bedford, and later Argyll. From 1736 onward their

---

[1] Coxe, *Walpole*, i. 645; Add. MSS. 18915, f. 29.

[2] Rose, ed., *Marchmont Papers*, ii. 203–4; Coxe, *Walpole*, iii. 523; Dobrée, ed., *Letters of Chesterfield*, ii. 433.

[3] Coxe, *Walpole*, iii. 507. Wyndham disapproved of this project as a betrayal of his political ideals: Phillimore, *Lyttelton*, ii. 796.

[4] Rose, ed., *Marchmont Papers*, ii. 273.

correspondence groaned with the dread of treachery.[1] It appeared beyond a cavil that Carteret and Pulteney intended opposition only as a 'bubble scheme' to enrich themselves, leaving others holding worthless paper when the crash came.[2] No political punter would invest in a rival's stock with the foreknowledge that he was to be sold short. How could one set up the transaction so as to participate in the profit-taking? The answer came in the formulation of a new doctrine of Opposition.

Its basic elements first emerged as a coherent whole in Bolingbroke's *Letter on the Spirit of Patriotism*, dispatched from Chanteloup in 1736. Glosses and elaborations appeared over the next five years in the letters of the doctrinaires, occasional pamphlets, and a short-lived journal entitled *Common Sense*.[3] A rich flow of words bore the doctrine along on a high crest of moral fervour. Like most such ideological developments, its originality consisted in a recombination of old concepts modestly infused with novelty. And like other Opposition programmes, it was a dialectical argument, in which principles of action arose out of postulates derived from the contemporary scene at Westminster.

Walpole's 'system', of course, provided the gravamen that had necessarily to lie at the base of any malcontent theory. The 'all-engrossing favourite' received his full measure of obloquy.

---

[1] For examples, see Rose, ed., *Marchmont Papers*, ii. 106–8; Graham, ed., *Annals of Stair*, ii. 268–9; Coxe, *Walpole*, iii. 576–8; Dobrée, ed., *Letters of Chesterfield*, ii. 404–5, 433–5, 448–9, 462, 467–8.

[2] Phillimore, *Lyttelton*, ii. 796.

[3] Bolingbroke had laid the groundwork for his doctrine in *A Dissertation upon Parties*. In *A Letter on the Spirit of Patriotism* he developed his earlier ideas into a programme fitted to the immediate political situation. The *Letter* was probably sent first to Cornbury (Toynbee, ed., *Letters of Horace Walpole*, ii. 378; Sichel, *Bolingbroke*, ii. 345). It was not published until 1749, when it appeared in an authorized edition with other tracts dedicated by the author to George Lyttelton. Of the numerous letters in which Bolingbroke's ideas were developed, see particularly Blenheim MSS. E. 36 (Correspondence of Stair with the dowager Duchess of Marlborough, 1737–9); Graham, ed., *Annals of Stair*, ii. 197, 241–2, 266–71, 275–6, 279; *H.M.C.*, *Mar and Kellie MSS.*, pp. 544–5; Phillimore, *Lyttelton*, i. 153–6; ii. 796–9; Rose, ed., *Marchmont Papers*, ii. 80–81, 177–91, 209, 222–39, 262–3. For examples of pamphlets supporting the same thesis, see *The Fatal Consequences of Ministerial Influence: or The Difference between Royal Power and Ministerial Power Truly Stated* (1736); [George Lyttleton], *Letter to a Member of Parliament from a Friend in the Country* (1738); *The Importance of an Uncorrupted Parliament Considered in Three Letters Addressed to the Electors of Great Britain* (1740). *Common Sense* appeared in 342 numbers between 1737 and 1739 under the direction of Charles Molloy, Lyttelton, and Chesterfield.

The emphasis, however, rested neither upon the office of 'Prime Minister' (unknown to the law, perhaps, but not perforce illegal) nor upon Walpole's specific measures (evil as they were conceived to be), but upon his derangement of the constitution. 'Remember', wrote Bolingbroke in the *Letter*, 'that the Opposition . . . is not an Opposition only to a bad administration of public affairs, but to an administration that supports itself by means, establishes principles, introduces customs, repugnant to the constitution of our Government and destructive of all liberty'.[1] Corrupt use of the legitimate influence of the Crown had upset the balance by concentrating all effective power in the executive. Of the frequent reiterations of this point, none put it more forcefully than Chesterfield in a letter to Stair in 1739: '. . . While the House of Lords and Commons are absolutely in the power of the Crown, as they visibly are now, we have no Constitution, and the Crown alone is, without a mystery, the three branches of the Legislature.'[2] Ministerial tyranny not only ground down the inherited rights of Englishmen but threatened to extinguish liberty for ever by entailing a corrupt Constitution upon posterity.

The restoration of the balance therefore became a patriotic duty. Its achievement required an Opposition possessed of three characteristics. First, it should be vigorous and systematic. Weak and sporadic activity merely strengthens the Government. Opposition can surmount 'unforeseen and untoward circumstances, . . . the perverseness or treachery of friends, . . . the power or malice of enemies' only by a regular 'scheme of policy'.[3] Second, it should be positive. Oppose bad measures but also propose good. Let slip no opportunity to accomplish even the slightest reformation. Third, it should be prepared to take office. The patriot lies under obligation to study his country's welfare against the day when power may increase his responsibilities.

For the doctrine contained no self-denying ordinance. In view of the corrupt nature of the Ministry, Opposition can do little to reform the state. Since power makes virtue effective, duty binds an honest man to seek office. 'It is not necessary', ran an article in *Common Sense*, 'that patriots should not accept

---

[1] Bolingbroke, *Works*, ii. 364.   [2] *Letters of Chesterfield*, ii. 401.
[3] Bolingbroke, *Works*, ii. 360.

employments: on the contrary, as our Constitution is now changed, he may do his country more good in place than out of place.'¹ The Prerogative did not stand in the way. Bolingbroke and his fellows chose to ignore it. 'Wrest the power of government, if you can, out of the hands that have employed it weakly and wickedly,' exhorted the *Letter on the Spirit of Patriotism*.² The citadel is to be taken, not by sap, but by storm. The introduction of a few patriots by negotiation will not produce a salutary change of measures. The Opposition must expel and replace the Ministry by means of parliamentary majorities. As Chesterfield told Dodington in 1741, they should 'force their way' into office 'by victory with numbers'.³

The serried ranks of the Court, the argument continued, can easily repulse the assaults of separate units. Success, therefore, depends upon the formation of an Opposition united in purpose and action. Ideally, nothing prevents 'concord and unanimity' but prejudices founded upon the obsolete 'names and distinctions of party'. The only true differences of principle now lie between corrupt ministerialists and their patriotic opponents. Party has always been an evil, and happily 'Whig' and 'Tory' have long since lost their meaning. Talk of a 'Whig reunion' is nonsense. Let the old labels be for ever extinguished, and with them all the bitterness they engendered. The Constitution can be saved by the earnest co-operation of 'wise men of different denominations'.⁴

The Ministry's fall shall usher in a Government formed on a 'broad bottom'. All those enlisted in the 'national union' of Opposition shall man the new garrison. None are to be excluded by 'backstairs negotiations'.⁵ When all true patriots have entered the service of the Crown, hitherto monopolized by a narrow faction, the royal family will be established 'on a

¹ *Common Sense*, 17 Oct. 1738.
² Bolingbroke, *Works*, ii. 364. In so far as he made any effort to justify such action in theory, Bolingbroke maintained that parliaments are 'essential parts of our administration', one of whose functions is 'to change every bad administration'.
³ *Letters of Chesterfield*, ii. 468.
⁴ Graham, ed., *Annals of Stair*, ii. 275; Bolingbroke, *Works*, ii. 363–70; Rose, ed., *Marchmont Papers*, ii. 188–91.
⁵ The 'broad-bottom group' did not, however, bar 'negotiations' as a method of entering the Ministry: see *Marchmont Papers*, ii. 172. 'Victory with numbers' had not yet come to imply a clean sweep of the old Ministry by a new one composed exclusively of the former Opposition.

broader and more solid foundation'.[1] Then begins the reign of
virtue. The King shall retain the discretionary powers wisely
lodged in him, but the new ministers will 'shut up, with all the
bars and bolts of law, the principal entries through which these
torrents of corruption have been let in upon us'.[2] The natural
balance of the Constitution is thereby restored, and the
liberties of Britain are once more secure.

As a supplement to this doctrine Bolingbroke turned out *The
Idea of a Patriot King* in 1738.[3] His obvious first intention was to
engage Prince Frederick. The heir to the throne, counselled
Bolingbroke, should participate in 'a legal course of opposition
to the excesses of regal or ministerial power'.[4] At least one of
two good results would follow. Princely opposition, it is to be
hoped, would 'blast many a wicked project, keep virtue in
countenance, and vice, to some degree at least, in awe'.[5] That is
to say, his presence should strengthen the patriot band both in
numbers and in prestige. Yet even if he failed in this he would
acquire the experience necessary to become a wise king. By
suffering with the people, he would make their cause his own.
'He would be formed in that school out of which the greatest
and best of monarchs have come, the school of affliction', and so
upon his accession he would be properly trained in the 'ways of
thinking and acting to so glorious a purpose as the re-establishment of a free constitution'.[6]

Thus Bolingbroke wanted Frederick to help his friends storm
the closet, but the 'reversionary resource' was not forgotten. It
could not profit the patriots should Frederick imitate his
father's career. George II had brought about a 'Whig reunion'
in 1720 only to fall back into sullen obscurity and then, upon
his accession, to continue his predecessor's Ministry in power.
Since 'victory with numbers' might never come, *The Idea of a
Patriot King* besought Frederick to carry out the programme of
reform upon a 'broad bottom' when he came to the throne. He

---

[1] Phillimore, *Lyttelton*, ii. 143–4, 194–200.

[2] Bolingbroke, *Works*, ii. 364.

[3] Bolingbroke made a brief visit to England in 1738, when he met Prince
Frederick. *The Idea of a Patriot King* was written shortly thereafter and dispatched
to England in December. It remained in manuscript until Alexander Pope brought
out an unauthorized edition *c.* 1743. Bolingbroke issued a revised and authorized
edition in 1749.

[4] Bolingbroke, *Works*, ii. 387.   [5] Ibid. 387–8.   [6] Idem.

must 'purge his Court', subdue party, and summon high-minded patriots to his administration.[1] The reward would be great. So firmly would his régime be rooted in the affections of his people that the King would govern 'with power as extended as the most absolute monarch can boast'.[2] Against him no factious Opposition could ever prevail.

Bolingbroke's doctrine was eschatological. Carried to its natural conclusion, it called for the extinction of Opposition as the result of its own success. Whether the patriots gained control through a parliamentary triumph or the advent of the Prince, the reign of virtue precluded the necessity of another patriotic Opposition. A wise king, ably served by well-chosen counsellors, would compose all genuine differences of principle, correct abuses, and punish evil. The régime would not be infallible, but within it would lie the remedies for its own defects. Henceforth discontent would be groundless, impotent, and evanescent. Bolingbroke did not conceive of Opposition as an enduring and beneficent institution but rather as an instrument for realizing a lofty unitarian ideal. This ideal, of course, was quite traditional. When had Britain not longed for a king who would heal divisions, redress grievances, and lead a united people to glory and prosperity? To dub this king a 'patriot' was, in the widest sense, to adjust the focus against the shifting background of rising nationalism and, more narrowly, to link the ideal with the cause of Bolingbroke and his allies.

It served their cause admirably. How sincerely they all accepted the dialectic is open to doubt, and in the final analysis, irrelevant. All political programmes need an altruistic keynote. 'Patriotism' met the need. Equally important, the goal of restoring the Constitution directed attention away from Opposition differences and toward the points upon which most Anti-courtiers agreed. In this respect Bolingbroke had cleverly raised the 'Country party programme' to the level of a transcendental imperative. The 'broad-bottom' doctrine had three distinct virtues. It condemned the narrow and exclusive policy of 'government by party' as allegedly practised by Walpole. It protested the Pulteney–Carteret bloc's intention to prolong exclusion by a new 'treaty'. It held out hope to all malcontents that they would be included in a new settlement. Bolingbroke's

---

[1] Bolingbroke, *Works*, ii. 398.　　　　　[2] Ibid. 384, 428.

creed thus skilfully combined the appeal of accepted values
with appeals to immediate advantage.

The Progress of Opposition Theory

In terms of contemporary political theory, the Tories were
conservative, Pulteney and Carteret were conventional, the
'broad-bottom' group was progressive. The first allotted to the
Opposition merely an unexceptionable function as passive
critic of the King's servants. The second insisted upon the
preservation of constitutional form—they would not infringe
upon the sacred Prerogative—but maintained the standard
subterfuges to evade its consequences. 'Broad bottom' surmounted the Prerogative, tacitly regarded as no more than the
means to an end, by its emphasis upon the overriding importance of the end. If the monarch would not voluntarily
choose a wise and popular ministry, the indispensable prerequisite to national welfare, Parliament must force him to do
so. The Legislative, therefore, had the ultimate right to determine the composition of the Executive. The Opposition then
became in a new sense a responsible body, constituted not
only to restrain the excesses of power, but also to propose constructive measures and to prepare to assume office.

One point all theories had in common. They acclaimed the
Opposition as the organ of 'the People'. The Anti-courtier,
uncorrupted because out of place, spoke the public mind. Tories
in general took their stand for the Country interest, the true
solid body of the nation, whose opinions ought to prevail in the
management of national affairs. Discontented Whigs went
farther. They professed to articulate the *vox populi* from a direct
knowledge of their constituents' wishes and an intuitive com-
prehension of the popular will. Since the King summoned the
'common council of the realm' that he might hear the advice of
his subjects, it followed that he must heed the words of the
Opposition.[1] In this contention the malcontents further developed a notion which had first emerged under George I, the
concept of Opposition as a new element in the Constitution to

---

[1] The Opposition pressed its claim most vigorously in the multitude of pamphlets
and speeches during the excise battle of 1733 and the war crisis of 1738–9. For two
noteworthy examples, see *Review of the Whole Political Conduct of a Late Eminent
Patriot*, pp. 72–73; and Sedgwick, ed., *Memoirs of Lord Hervey*, pp. 141–2.

restore the balance upset by the influence of the Crown upon the Lords and Commons. In a sense this was no more than an extension of the old role of the 'Country party'. The patriots tended to justify their view in historical retrospect, as did Lyttelton when he wrote, 'There is hardly a privilege belonging to us which has not been gained by popular discontent and preserved by frequent opposition.'[1] The corruption of modern times placed upon the Opposition the whole burden of protesting grievances and checking maladministration. Latent in the argument also was the idea of popular sovereignty. Walpole's opponents included no Levellers, and Chartism lay in the dim future. Yet in this period the Opposition, by grounding a forceful claim to legitimacy upon the representation of public opinion, gave initial strength to one of the forces that drove Britain in the direction of democracy.

None of the Opposition's theories gained general acceptance. The Courtiers disputed them all point by point. Patriotism, they retorted, was but a shallow disguise for the envy and rancour of disappointed office-seekers, who sought to invade the King's right to choose his ministers. Impeachment was the only legitimate means to deal with evil advisers. Scurrilous charges, which distracted Parliament and traduced loyal servants, were in reality directed at the monarch himself. The influence of the Crown did not corrupt, rather it secured the proper functioning of the balanced Constitution. No validity attached to the Opposition's claim to represent legitimate grievances. Discontent was the product of the low demagoguery of sham patriotism. Systematic harassing of the Government, far from correcting any supposed maladministration, actually contributed to it by interfering with the smooth functioning of the Executive. A 'general opposition' to the measures of a ministry was not to be distinguished from sedition. In the current case the malcontents had proved themselves unmistakably treasonous by their relentless opposition to a Government conducted by the 'Whig interest'. The Whigs had made the Revolution of 1688 and saved the Protestant Succession. They alone could

---

[1] *The Works of George Lord Lyttelton* (ed. Ayscough, London, 1776), i. 305. Cf. *Fog's Journal*, 13 Mar. and 11 Sept. 1731. Precedents for this line of thought are to be found in Defoe's *Legion's Petition* (1703) and Molesworth's *Principles of a Real Whig* (1705).

administer the Revolution settlement, to which only they were inviolably attached. The budding 'Whig myth', that hardy perennial, thus came to its first full flower in the Court's defence against the eloquent clamour of the Opposition.[1]

The Court made but one concession to the Anti-courtier. The historic right to resist tyranny remained indefeasible. 'Is all opposition to be discouraged and abolished?' wrote the Treasury hack Arnall. 'God forbid. Let oppression and oppressors and every unjust administration be for ever opposed.'[2] But this was a doctrine for extreme necessity, inapplicable to the normal course of events since 1688 and especially since 1714. In strict justice, Courtiers maintained, the King's measures should have to meet with nothing more than occasional objections raised out of conscience. Only the independent, in their view, played a legitimate critical role.

4. THE INSTITUTIONAL LEGACY OF THE PATRIOTS

Yet the Court slowly lost ground in the prolonged contest. The same Arnall complained in 1735:

Many people think there is an inherent virtue in opposition; nay, a sort of divinity in it; and are apt to treat such as are violent in it as something more than men, without ever distinguishing between opposition to unjust measures and opposition to just as well as unjust.[3]

---

[1] There is a plethora of material presenting the Court's views on Opposition doctrine. Walpole used the *Free Briton* and *London Journal* to reply regularly to *The Craftsman*, *Fog's Journal*, and *Common Sense*. The King's speeches usually reflected severely on Opposition: see particularly those of 1730, 1734, and 1737, cited in Tindal's *History of England*, viii. 77, 245, 336. The most noteworthy pro-Government pamphlets are *The Case of Opposition Stated, between the Craftsman and the People* (1731); [Lord Egmont], *The Thoughts of an Impartial Man upon the Present Temper of the Nation* (1733); *The Case Truly Stated; or The Merits of Both Parties Fully Considered* (1732); [Lord Hervey], *The Conduct of the Opposition and the Tendency of Modern Patriotism* (1734); *The Ancient and Modern Constitution of Government Stated and Compared* (1734); *The Sense of an Englishman on the Pretended Coalition of Parties and on the Merits of the Whig Interest* (1735?); [William Arnall], *Opposition No Proof of Patriotism* (1735); *A Coalition of Patriots Delineated* (1735); *An Impartial Enquiry into the Motives of the Opposition to the Ministry* (1736). The parliamentary speeches of Government partisans, reported in such sources as *P.H.*, *H.M.C.*, *Egmont MSS.* i-iii, and Sedgwick, ed., *Memoirs of Lord Hervey*, are replete with rebuttals of the Opposition's contentions.

[2] *Opposition No Proof of Patriotism*, p. 11.

[3] Ibid., p. 6.

The first great achievement of 'the spirit of patriotism' was to cast the malcontents in an heroic mould. Evoking the shades of Eliot, Pym, and Hampden, they made their political expediency a virtue. The world of Westminster knew the Opposition for what it was, a loose agglomeration of placehunting factions rent by conflicting views and principles. The patriots surmounted their own weaknesses to wring a grudging toleration from the Court and to stamp their image of themselves upon the face of politics. The future would bring disillusion and cynicism, but the Opposition was never to lose the acceptance it had gained in these years. Its acceptance was a long stride in the direction of its establishment as an institution.

Further evidence of growing institutionalization is to be found in the fact that at this time the Opposition acquired its name. Reference to the body of Anti-courtiers as 'the Opposition' begins to appear in contemporary writing about 1731. Thereafter the term crops up with growing frequency until, within six years, it had clearly become common usage.[1] It did not, however, replace all the earlier terms. 'Grumbletonians' dropped out, but 'Anti-courtiers', 'malcontents', 'the Country party', and 'the discontented party' remained customary synonyms. 'Opposers' and 'Opponents' also appear often. Because both the 'broad-bottom' group and the Pulteney–Carteret bloc flaunted their patriotism so flamboyantly, 'patriots' grew as a popular designation. But 'patriots' never included the Tories, who persistently rejected identification with the dissident Whigs. This probably helps to account for the rapid development of 'the Opposition', which could be employed to describe all the various factions of Walpole's

---

[1] 'Opposition' was still generally used to mean 'the act of opposing' until 1730. In that year there are suggestions of transitional usage. Horace Walpole, for example, spoke of 'the boldness and violence of the Opposition, where all the forces of the enemy from all quarters were united and collected' (Coxe, *Walpole*, ii. 687). Then in *An Answer to One Part of a Late Infamous Libel* (1731), pp. 47–48, Pulteney clearly employed the word to mean 'the collective body of those who oppose'. The gradual acceptance of the new usage can be traced in pamphlets (see p. 153, n. 1) and in diaries and correspondence. Hervey, who apparently began to compose his memoirs in 1733, employed it from the outset. Egmont, Stair, and Howard picked it up in 1734. Thereafter the new usage is to be frequently encountered in all forms of political writing. In the autumn of 1742 Richard Grenville indicated how firmly established it had become when, despairing of the prospects of the Anti-courtiers, he wrote, 'the very word Opposition may be struck out of the language' (*H.M.C., Denbigh MSS.* v. 237).

enemies. The very fact of a steady antagonism to all Court measures over a long period of time by a recognizable and uniform body of men doubtless encouraged the use of the term. What had previously been '*an* Opposition', raised sporadically by 'out' groups against short-lived governments, became indeed '*the* Opposition' to the extended régime of '*the* Minister'.

Concurrently with the acquisition of its name, the Opposition commenced the regular practice of taking seats on the Speaker's left. The first definite evidence of their struggle for position is an anecdote related by Sir Thomas Robinson, a Government supporter, about the opening debate on the Excise Bill. Apparently the patriot orators had come down early and taken places near the chair. Their opening gambit was to move that, upon a technicality, the Bill should be withdrawn. This motion went against the orders of the day, and in accordance with the standing orders, all those voting for such a motion must go into the lobby to be counted, whereas those voting against such a motion (and thus voting to sustain the orders of the day) must remain within the House. A division took place, whereat, Sir Thomas recounted,

As upon this division the minority were obliged to go out of the House, of course they lost their places, and they had no choice but the gallery or the bottom of the House, so that their speakers would have met with difficulties to have been heard in the debate that was intended; so the first thing they proposed was a question to adjourn, which we disagreeing to, it fell to our turns to be fairly jockeyed out of the very same places we had in the last division taken possession of, for we were obliged to go out of the House, this question being only calculated to gain this point.[1]

After this incident the antagonists apparently tried to reserve seats on the eve of great debates. A standing order of 1640 permitted any member who was present at prayers to 'keep his place' by depositing book, glove, or paper thereupon. To take advantage of this technicality some members came down to the House early and pre-empted seats for their friends by distributing papers along the benches. The House ruled against this practice in 1734 and again in 1737 and 1741, declaring 'That no member is to keep any place in the House by book, glove, paper, or otherwise, till after prayers, and then only for

[1] *H.M.C., Carlisle MSS.*, p. 109.

himself.'¹ Yet during these years the Anti-courtiers seem clearly
to have settled the custom of gathering on the Speaker's left, with
the leading orators occupying the lower seats directly opposite
the Treasury Bench. From 1734 until the fall of Walpole,
whenever an Opposition speaker can be definitely located, he
was facing the ministers across the House. Sandys and Wyndham, Barnard and Jekyll, Shippen and Cotton, Gage, Lyttelton,
and Plummer, all directed their assaults upon the 'gentlemen
over the way'.²

William Pulteney was the only exception among the malcontent leaders. During his seventeen years in opposition he
always took a place on the Treasury Bench near Sir Robert,
who apparently overlooked this insolence with his customary
good nature.³ Pulteney's motives are uncertain; doubtless he
wanted a good seat, perhaps he thought his presence inhibited
ministerial communications, and perhaps also he thought that

¹ *Commons Journals*, xxii. 406, 414; xxiii. 97; xxiv. 67.

² *P.H.* viii. 1220, 1267; ix, 218, 257, 263, 279, 304, 438, 441, 567, 1339; x. 294,
448, 591, 597, 694, 804, 980, 1271, 1346; xi. 201, 223, 1230. In the House of Lords
there seems to have been considerable confusion about the standing orders and
customs in regard to seating as late as 1741: Add. MSS. 6043, ff. 53, 68–70.

³ Pulteney's case is perplexing. The story that he sat on the Treasury Bench
while in opposition rests primarily on four authorities: (1) legend, as transmitted in
Hatsell, *Precedents of Proceedings*, ii. 88–89; (2) the assertion of Pulteney's friend,
Bishop Zachary Pierce, as recorded in *The Lives of Dr. Edward Pocock, Dr. Zachary
Pierce, Dr. Thomas Newton, and Rev. Philip Skelton* (London, 1816), i. 390–2; (3)
references in the parliamentary debates which make it clear that the reporters, who
often wrote up the speeches from the notes of others, thought that Pulteney sat
near the Minister and opposite his own friends: *P.H.* viii. 1203; ix. 218, 220; x. 448,
478, 591, 694, 852, 1271; xi. 135, 495–7; (4) the anecdote of the wager in 1741, in
which Walpole, having lost a bet with Pulteney about the correctness of a quotation from Horace, handed or tossed a golden guinea to his rival who sat on the
same bench: related in Coxe, *Walpole*, i. 644–5, on the credit of several reports.
Some accounts of the wager, however, are ambiguous, and both Cooke (*History of
Party*, ii. 276) and Porritt (*Unreformed House of Commons*, ii. 507–8) accept a version
in which Walpole throws the coin across the floor to Pulteney. Pulteney preserved
the guinea and wrote a description of the occurrence, both of which were later
deposited in the coin collection of the British Museum. The guinea may still be
seen there, but the description (MSS. Catalogue of English Gold Coins, p. 278,
no. 27) was blitzed in the Second World War, so Pulteney's own version has been
lost for ever. His case is further complicated by the fact that his claim to sit on the
Treasury Bench arose in the first instance from his being a Privy Councillor, but in
1731 George II struck his name off the Council list. Since the weight of the evidence
supports the legend that Pulteney habitually sat by Walpole, one can only conclude
that the House indulged this oddity as it has genially tolerated so many others.
Cf. Hatsell's notice of the courtesy accorded to Grenville, Pitt, and Fox in *Precedents
of Proceedings*, ii. 89.

sitting next to the Minister gave him some pretence to speak with equal authority. At all events no one ever imitated his conduct. After 1742 the evidence is overwhelming that the Opposition consistently occupied, and were by custom conceded, the benches on the Speaker's left.[1]

Thus within the brief span of a decade, the Opposition acquired a customary location and a standard designation. These achievements possessed a high degree of permanence, for both have endured to the present. One can, of course, over-emphasize their institutional significance. They did not mark the foundation of a two-party system, nor did they constitute irrefragable precedents from which there could be no deviation. Later generations could have discarded them altogether, and needless to say, the mere presence of name and form never guarantees that they will be filled with substance. Yet the establishment of standard designation and customary location tended to

---

[1] Anecdotes and prints of the House of Commons afford some useful information on seating, but the best evidence consists in the references in debate to 'the gentleman over the way', 'the honourable member opposite', &c., when the location of one is known. To enumerate all such references would require an inordinate amount of space; the following may serve as examples for forty years after 1741: *P.H.* xii, 429, 482, 721, 729, 746, 901; xiii. 646; xiv. 860, 974, 977, 1123; xvi. 97, 226–7, 597, 712, 790–1, 1344; xvii. 366–7, 547, 552, 648, 753, 825, 828, 1160; xviii. 69, 776, 982–3, 1060, 1154; xix. 13, 19, 272, 434, 951, 1204, 1373–4; xx. 49, 173, 189–90, 213, 251, 290, 331, 1130, 1214, 1219–22; xxi. 192, 328–9, 351–3. How far the convention had become established by 1778 is indicated in a complaint from the Independent Sir W. Gordon that 'he knew not where to place himself. If on the Ministry side, he should be called by the Opposition a pensioner; if on the Opposition, he should be called by the Ministry a factious man' (ibid. xix. 1097). In 1782 Fox thought he might defy convention by keeping his followers on the Speaker's left after the fall of North (*H.M.C., Carlisle MSS.*, p. 598), but every change of ministry in 1782–3 resulted in a corresponding change of sides (*H.M.C., Stopford–Sackville MSS.* i. 79; *P.H.* xxiii. 1263; xxiv. 226–8). Tracts on legislative procedure in the 1780's assigned the Opposition to the Speaker's left as a matter of long-standing tradition: see Samuel Romilly, *Règlemens observés dans la Chambre des Communes* (1789), p. 305; Jeremy Bentham, *Tactique des assemblées legislatives* (ed. Dumont, Geneva, 1816), i. 246–7. Of course, there continued to be occasional anomalies in seating owing to crowding of the House and the peculiarities of individuals: see *P.H.* xx. 632, 834, 1382; xxii. 417; Edward Topham, *The Life of the Late John Elwes* (London, 1790), p. 66; Nathaniel Wraxall, *Posthumous Memoirs of his Own Time* (1836), ii. 212. One such anomaly draws attention to what may be the first open acknowledgement of the Opposition's exclusive *right* to the left-hand benches: on 31 March 1806 Philip Francis, a ministerialist, 'who, on this occasion only, sat on the Speaker's left hand, commonly called the Opposition bench, began with making an apology to the gentlemen who now occupied that situation for committing such a trespass on their undoubted though recent right of possession' (*P.D.* vi. 599).

perpetuate the pattern of political conduct from which they arose. Names and forms, however hollow in themselves, mould thought and action. In this instance they contributed to the institutional development of the Opposition by giving recognition to its existence apart from the men who composed it. Henceforward the eternal malcontent, whose previous formal condition had bordered so closely upon outlawry, could find some measure of sanctuary within the walls of precedent.

In terms of institutional development the manner of growth in each case is instructive. The use of 'the Opposition' was a result of a common linguistic process through which men give specific meaning to an appropriate general term by applying it consistently to a particular existing practice. No one made any conscious effort to have the term accepted: it was not invented. Its growth was natural in that it was a functional appellation, descriptive of the action of its object.[1]

Persistent and determined effort, on the other hand, brought about the custom of seating on the Speaker's left. Not that the coalition had any intention of establishing a new convention. They were all conservative or reactionary, highly condemnatory of Walpole's 'innovations' and innocent of any desire for novelty themselves. Even the iconoclastic Bolingbroke (whose ideal was the reign of Elizabeth I) had no concept of constitutional progress through the introduction of enlightened practices. Nothing suggests that the Opposition had any end in view other than the short-term objective of a good vantage point from which to attack Walpole. Earlier factions may have occupied 'the right-hand of the House' sporadically. The coalition, Pulteney excepted, laid a steady claim to it session after session. In search of immediate political advantage, they settled a practice so well adapted to the business of the House that it soon became an accepted and indispensable part of parliamentary operation.

The permanence of the coalition's legacy, in conclusion, would seem to have been the result of two principal factors. First was simply its duration. These long years of fairly consistent

[1] Since the growing usage of 'the Opposition' coincides with the development of the convention of seating on the Speaker's left, one is led to wonder if there could be a connexion between the two. Did the position of the malcontents *opposite* the Ministry give *Opposition* a felicitous *double entendre*? The use of 'the opposite party' was not uncommon during this period.

practice left a deeper impress upon political life than the brief and shifting Oppositions of the recent past. Second was its patently multi-factional composition. The consequent need for leaders and publicists to stake their claims on grounds that comprehended most, and hopefully all, made their achievements the property of all who followed them, not the obsolete triumphs of a narrow clique. Bolingbroke had contended that a steady 'national' Opposition would entail blessings on future ages. In a sense other than he intended, he was right.

V

THE OPERATION OF THE PATRIOT COALITION

1725–1742

---

1. *Party Organization*

The Problem of Leadership. Opposition Journalism.
Electoral Activities. The Character of Parliamentary
Operations.

2. *Parliamentary Tactics*

Opposition to Government Measures. The Excise Bill
of 1733. Opposition Bills. Motions of Censure. The
Dunkirk Inquiry of 1730. Other Motions of Censure.
Parliamentary Craftsmanship. The Tone of
Parliamentary Proceedings.

3. *The Defeat of Walpole*

The Election of 1741. Dodington's Scheme. The
Opening of the Session. The Opposition's Plan of
Attack. The Assaults on the Conduct of the War. The
Decisive Struggle over Elections.

4. *Conclusion*

M

V

THE OPERATION OF THE
PATRIOT COALITION

1725–1742

1. PARTY ORGANIZATION

The Problem of Leadership

THE 'patriots'' contributions to posterity were by-products
of their campaign against Walpole. They were inevitably
pre-occupied, not with setting precedents for the future,
but with the many practical problems of political operations.
Owing to their multi-factional composition, the greatest of
these was organization. The major problem of organization was
leadership.

The conventions of party leadership were inchoate. The final
triumph of an Opposition did not yet require a parliamentary
leader who would take over the first post in government and
from thence distribute the spoils. Management of a malcontent
coalition usually lay in the hands of a junto or partnership,
composed of the chief figures in the combined interests, in which
no one necessarily stood pre-eminent. The function of management was to plot a campaign, marshal the troops, send or lead
(but not necessarily *lead*) them into battle, and arrange the
capitulation in the hour of victory.

Members of a junto normally sought rewards for success.
Many doubtless aspired to become the royal favourite. But their
goals were not always political office, nor did they necessarily
involve a continuance of political management. The satisfaction
of 'honourable pretensions' might terminate the political activity
of the recipients. The functions of management could be
performed by persons outside of Parliament and even by those
ineligible for office. Leadership on the floor and management of
a confederacy might be but did not need to be concentrated in
the same persons.

When considered with the nature of the coalition these facts explain much of the leadership problem. The traditional management-by-junto was condemned to weakness because neither the Tories nor the Pulteney–Carteret bloc would commit themselves to a firm alliance with the other groups. Bolingbroke and the 'broad-bottom' clique, who clearly understood this, clamoured incessantly for one pre-eminent leader. Stair, for example, plainly acknowledged that it would 'require great skill and great temper to make an army composed of so many different troops, who have different interests and different views, act together'. He was equally certain that Sir Robert would stand secure until a man was found to 'unite the different pieces that make up the opposing party to act together as one body and by one direction'.[1]

Yet Stair and his fellows did not equate party management with parliamentary leadership. The proscribed Bolingbroke thought himself eligible to take the reins of a political team. Far from seeing an anomaly in seeking the Prince of Wales as a party head, the opponents still thought him ideally fitted. Memories of 1720 were still fresh. Though the Prince's position barred him from office, they hoped it would enable him to draw all interests together and negotiate their entry into place.[2] They did not see the leader of the Opposition as the future Chief Minister. Rather, they expected to lose their leadership at the moment of victory because they would find a new head in the King or in a royal favourite whose designation they could not control.

What is more, parliamentary leadership in the eighteenth century was always a product of individual ability, not of choice. Politicians recognized excellence, they did not elect it. A man had to establish a claim by his position and talents, and bring others to co-operation by his skill and industry. The long struggle against Walpole did not turn up such a leader. None of the outstanding figures in the various blocs could win the loyalty of all; and each potential leader was disqualified from taking command of a united array by some marked defect.

Bolingbroke could not overcome the distrust evoked by his

---

[1] Blenheim MSS. E. 36: Stair to the dowager Duchess of Marlborough, 18 Oct. 1737.

[2] Idem, and Phillimore, *Lyttelton*, ii. 796–9.

erratic past. He had hoped that his long experience, great capacity for intrigue, and brilliant literary output would draw all malcontents to his standard. Perhaps he too readily assumed that politicians were 'sheep' or 'hounds' eager to follow a lead. Bolingbroke had twice before taken the direction of a lost cause. None denied his exceptional talents, but they inspired neither confidence nor loyalty. Even his closest friends did not truly lament his departure in 1735.

Sir William Wyndham, wrote Speaker Onslow, was 'the most made for a great man of anyone that I have known in this age'.[1] Nature and fortune had endowed him with important qualities of leadership: great connexions, long experience, and impressive presence, a high spirit, an effective if halting eloquence. He commanded respect far outside his own coterie. But he too suffered for bygone folly, and upon him fell some odium reflected from his *alter ego*, Bolingbroke. The secession fiasco of 1739 greatly lowered his prestige, and in the next year death robbed him of the great opportunities which lay just over the horizon.

The debonair and lordly Carteret despised the petty transactions of politics. He is said to have set his course by the maxim, 'Give any man the Crown on his side, and he can defy everything.'[2] He cared nothing for the art of party management, nor did he understand its importance in the struggle for place. Adept at administration and diplomacy, he was well fitted to exercise power, but not to secure it. 'What is it to me who is a judge or a bishop?' he once exclaimed when Secretary of State. 'It is my business to make kings and emperors, and to maintain the balance of Europe.'[3]

Carteret took the same lofty view in opposition. He seems to have regarded himself as the chief figure, but too often evaded the sordid requirements of campaigning. In the planning of parliamentary attacks he displayed an aggravating delicacy. He 'could never argue in a point against his conscience' he told a meeting of Opposition magnates in 1735, but added that he would give a silent vote for such a question.[4] His aim being an

---

[1] *H.M.C., Onslow MSS.*, p. 467. On Wyndham's attitude to leadership, see J. B. LeBlanc, *Letters on the English and French Nations* (London, 1747), ii. 330–41.

[2] Toynbee, ed., *Letters of Horace Walpole*, ii. 59.

[3] Basil Williams, *Life of Pitt*, i. 99.

[4] *Marchmont Papers*, ii. 63.

accommodation with the Ministry, he was generally inclined to temporize, yielding only under pressure to vigorous measures. With mass gatherings of the malcontents he would have nothing to do—he 'never dined at taverns'.[1] Carteret may have been, as Chesterfield opined, 'the ablest head in England', but he was not made to lead a fractious coalition.

William Pulteney unquestionably stood foremost among the malcontent orators in the House of Commons. His speeches were brilliant compositions of wit and pleasantry, fire and elegance. Speaker Onslow, who had heard them all, concluded that Pulteney 'certainly hurt Sir Robert more than any of those who opposed him'.[2] Yet his character did not measure up to the task of managing the confederacy. Though wealthy, he was reputed mean and penurious. Though vigorous and determined, his balance often gave way in a crisis, when he fell under the sway of rash impulses. According to Hervey, Carteret once told the Queen, 'he knew Mr. Pulteney *very* well, that he was a very useful second in *opposition*, but a man who had such flights and starts that no minister could ever depend upon him, and such impracticable fits of popularity that no court could ever keep him long.[3]

Pulteney's instability became increasingly apparent as the possibility of a 'treaty' with the Pelhams opened up. When conditions seemed favourable, he slackened in his opposition even to the point of supporting the Court against his own colleagues.[4] A few weeks before the final push that drove Walpole from power, Pulteney refused all but the most nominal cooperation with other blocs, saying 'that he was weary of being at the head of a party; he would rather row in the galleys and was absolutely resolved not to charge himself with taking the lead'.[5] He wavered again at the very last moment, and then, with victory in sight, he once more flung himself frenetically into the struggle as the leading spokesman of the coalition in the Commons. This was to be his last 'impracticable fit of popularity'.

Prince Frederick inevitably occupied a unique position.

---

[1] Basil Williams, *Carteret and Newcastle* (Cambridge, 1943), p. 122.
[2] *H.M.C., Onslow MSS.*, p. 467.
[3] Sedgwick, ed., *Memoirs of Lord Hervey*, pp. 752–3.
[4] *Letters of Chesterfield*, ii. 433–4, 448; *P.H.* xii. 178–83.
[5] Coxe, *Walpole*, iii. 576–8; *Letters of Chesterfield*, ii. 467–8.

Feiling aptly calls him the centre, rather than the head, of Opposition.[1] Unlike his father, who had cast his lot with one connexion in opposition, Frederick dallied with all. He held out his hands to the Tories. His private secretary and most assiduous courtiers came from the 'broad-bottom' group. In political tactics he generally went along with Carteret and Pulteney. For its own purposes, each faction sought to use the Prince. Carlton House thus became their common meeting ground and Frederick himself their nominal liaison.

Much has been made of his frivolousness and ineptitude. Whatever his personal weaknesses, the inescapable consequences of his situation as heir to the throne do more to account for his failures. A royal personage without functions, he had nothing to do but dabble in politics, no other way to 'cut a figure'. To this conventional motive Frederick added only a desire for revenge upon his parents. He could pursue these ends, in which there was no positive or constructive element, only by remaining in opposition until he came to the throne. He was largely at the mercy of the malcontent groups, who planned to abandon him if they attained office before his accession. Their allegiance to him was strictly conditional, and any success they achieved, though it might give him passing satisfaction, left him in exactly the same position as before. Under these circumstances the Prince could hardly have become an effective party leader.

Lack of unified leadership left the Opposition to work as best it could through temporary agreements among the magnates. They behaved like a feudal array without a recognized commander-in-chief. They could co-operate reasonably well for a battle, but not for a campaign, still less for a war. The alliance, like Finnegan's train, was for ever 'off again, on again'.

For the most part the formal connexion of the three great factions was tenuous or non-existent. They followed their own interests, letting co-ordination come as it would in their mutual antagonism to Walpole. Moments of firm concord came only when one group secured the assistance of the others upon some particular issue or scheme of opposition. The organization of

[1] Feiling, *Second Tory Party*, p. 34. The Prince was, of course, a member of the House of Lords, and he appeared frequently at great debates in both Houses. He seems never to have addressed the peers or cast a vote. He sought rather to inspire the Opposition and to bring over waverers by canvassing and applause. For an example of the parliamentary reaction, see Coxe, *Walpole*, iii. 609.

the malcontents was fundamentally an irregular succession of *ad hoc* arrangements, made and dissolved time after time. The history of their career as a confederate Opposition is the record of their sporadic co-operative efforts in significant matters and at critical junctures.

Their only organizational framework was the structure of their society, the customs and habits of the gentleman's world. Many Opposition stalwarts met at social gatherings at the Prince's establishment or their own town houses. Idle hours at their favourite coffee houses and taverns often brought groups of them together. They visited each other in the country. The season might find many of them at Bath.¹ Though few were polite letter writers in the Augustan fashion, their surviving correspondence indicates frequent, sometimes frenetic, communication by the mails.² Out of these contacts arose their co-operative efforts, sometimes the product of chance, more often the result of conscious initiative on the part of individuals or close associates.

Opposition Journalism

The most consistent and well sustained of all Opposition activities was journalism. In this field the malcontents continued and enlarged upon the traditional practices of their predecessors. From the wealth of literary talent antagonized by Walpole poured forth a steady stream of political writing. Pope, Fielding, Gay, and Thomson turned out satirical verse and drama. Occasional pamphlet and pamphlet-war engaged the lordly pens of Bolingbroke, Pulteney, Chesterfield, and Lyttelton

¹ Not all, of course, travelled in the same circles. A private social gathering that included Shippen, Chesterfield, Barnard, Jekyll, and Beaufort is almost impossible to conceive. Even in a tavern, the broadest meeting ground, every type was not likely to congregate in the normal course of events, and clubs in the form later developed at Brooks's and White's had not yet come into existence. Yet there were arcs of each circle which intersected others so that contact was maintained among all. On Opposition inns, see the comments of LeBlanc in *Letters on the English and French Nations*, i. 195–9.

² The Government continued to open the letters of Opposition members (E. R. Turner, 'The Secrecy of the Post' in *E.H.R.* xxx (1918), 320–7), who were constantly worried about the security of their communications: e.g. Add. MSS. 27732, f. 49; Tindal, *History of England*, viii. 273; *Marchmont Papers*, ii. 259. In 1733–4 the malcontents worked out a scheme for a postal system of their own between London and Edinburgh (*H.M.C., Mar and Kellie MSS.*, pp. 529, 531–2), and they used private messengers whenever possible.

as well as their hirelings from Grub Street. Their periodical Press kept up a running fire of invective against the Minister and his policies. For the first ten years the burden of the assault was borne by *The Craftsman* and the *Weekly Journal* first known as *Mist's* and later as *Fog's*. When these disappeared in 1736–7 *Common Sense* and *The Champion* took their place.[1] Each normally carried a political leader, strong in tone and ably written, with a scattering of news items slanted to reflect upon the Government. The volume and persistence of the Opposition Press surpassed anything done by the Country parties of earlier times.

Several factors made this possible. The aristocratic opponents gave richly of their money and genius, which was uncommonly high, and they brought into their service many of the outstanding literary figures of the day. Their publications did not founder for lack of funds, nor did they suffer from a shortage of copy. Much depended as always upon the firm guidance of individuals, but in journalistic affairs the malcontents made common cause more consistently than in any other field. Because their efforts were so solidly grounded, they were able to withstand Government prosecution with considerable success. Also, though the Licensing Act of 1737 imposed both censorship and severe restrictions upon the Opposition's use of the stage, the Government took much less legal action against their prints after about 1730, and convictions for libel brought lighter penalties. The strong support given to the printer and editor of *The Craftsman* in particular discouraged prosecution and emboldened other Anti-Court publications. The Opposition journalism of this period made an important contribution to the freedom of the Press.[2]

Sir Robert professed to despise his enemies' effusions as an endless repetition of 'loud assertions', 'empty sophistry', and

---

[1] *The Craftsman* ran without a break from 5 Dec. 1726 to 17 Apr. 1736. Thereafter there were a few isolated issues and short runs, probably not produced by the original men. *Mist's Weekly Journal* ended with the issue of 7 Sept. 1728. *Fog's* ran from 28 Sept. 1728 to 22 Oct. 1737. The life of *Common Sense* extended from 5 Feb. 1737 to 16 Oct. 1742. *The Champion* appeared three times a week from 15 Nov. 1739 to 10 Mar. 1742. There were various short-lived journals of little note and sporadic efforts to run Opposition papers in Scotland. Typical of the latter was *The Thistle* (13 Feb. 1734—11 Feb. 1736) which carried a leader of its own and reprints from *The Craftsman* and *Fog's* each week.

[2] Stevens, *Party Politics and English Journalism*, pp. 128–34; W. L. Cross, *The History of Henry Fielding* (New Haven, 1918), i. 205–60.

'low conceit'.[1] He had much justice on his side. The gems which have continued to be good reading for later ages sparkle as tiny pinpoints amid a vast mass of dark dross. Opposition writers hammered away for seventeen years with deadly and often hysterical insistence upon the same points: the unconstitutional position, corrupt methods, and ruinous policies of the Minister. Wit, allusion, argument, and rhetoric were all devoted to the same theme. The good quality of the writing scarcely sustained the monotonous polemic, which often descended to mere scurrility and coarse abuse.

Yet these literary defects were political virtues. By the constant reiteration of charges against Walpole, the Anti-courtiers renewed their spirits, rededicated themselves to their aims, and persuaded others of their steadfastness. They upheld and spread a sense of public grievance which prepared the political world to accept their own accession to power as inevitable and the fall of Sir Robert as final. Their long tirade against the great Minister stands as the first example in British political history of an effective long-term propaganda campaign.

Electoral Activities

Since the malcontents' chief point of agreement was their common opposition to the Minister, co-operation in the field of journalism came with relative ease. Almost anything said against Sir Robert served the cause of all. In electoral affairs it was far otherwise. The long years of political stability did not resolve all conflicts of local interest into simple contests between Ministerial and Opposition candidates. The location of a man's property, rather than the colour of his politics, still determined to a great extent who his rivals would be. The coalition never sought to conduct a nation-wide electoral campaign. Yet common politics did produce some successful co-ordination of effort. On a small scale there were occasional endeavours to compromise conflicts between allies, to aid them against Government men, and to find seats for those who failed. Of greater dimensions were the concerts to 'pool interests', of which the best example was the union of Prince Frederick and the local Opposition magnates to carry 27 of Cornwall's 44 seats in 1741. Both in 1734 and 1741 the malcontents made a widespread

[1] *P.H.* xi. 881–2.

attempt to produce anti-Government addresses from constituencies all over the United Kingdom. On election petitions involving ministerial and anti-ministerial candidates the Country party often lined up solidly against the Court.[1]

Upon the evidence of their heated correspondence it would appear that the members of the coalition threw themselves into elections as strenuously as the opponents had done before 1725. Yet both contested and disputed elections were fewer. In England and Wales in 1727, 12 counties and 65 boroughs went to the poll, making 26 fewer contests than in 1722. The number rose slightly in 1734 to 14 counties and 71 boroughs, only to drop in 1741 to 8 counties and 61 boroughs. Doubtless the Septennial Act was permitting local interests to establish themselves more solidly, discouraging interlopers and persuading rivals to withdraw before the poll.

The number of election petitions declined even more spectacularly. Both in 1715 and 1722 roughly 80 per cent. of contested elections had produced petitions. The 53 petitions offered in 1727 and 1734 fell between 60 and 70 per cent., and the 30 petitions of 1741 were only slightly above 40 per cent. The high costs and slim results of such action probably exercised increasing restraint upon all but the angriest and the most determined. Of the 136 petitions stemming from these three general elections, 90 were dropped sooner or later, and 15 were denied. The odds lay heavily against the plaintiff, especially if he was in opposition. The election petition nevertheless remained a useful political manœuvre, as the fall of Walpole was to show.

The Character of Parliamentary Operations

In the long intervals between elections the Opposition had varying success at co-ordinating their forces for parliamentary assault upon the Minister. Their attack each session generally resembled the pattern that had prevailed in the first decade after the accession: a desultory beginning, the gradual development of a steady bombardment, followed by a major onslaught toward mid-session, then a fairly rapid withering of the storm and

[1] For clues to the various forms of electoral co-operation, see the following reports of the H.M.C.: *Carlisle MSS.*, pp. 125, 197; *Dartmouth MSS.*, p. 154; *Mar and Kellie MSS.*, pp. 534–6; *Somerset MSS.*, pp. 121–3; and Phillimore, *Lyttelton*, i. 64–67; *Annals of Stair*, ii. 208, 272–80; *Marchmont Papers*, ii. 233–4.

dispersal of the troops. Upon occasion the heavy assault carried a point against the Government—the defeat of a Ministerial measure or the passage of an Opposition proposal—but until 1742 the session always ended with the Opposition in retreat amid a flurry of mutual recriminations. Their failures and their violent expressions of disgust, however, should not make us overlook their real achievements. Despite their differences they were able to mount an offensive year after year, and despite some disastrous errors they developed very effective methods of parliamentary warfare and party organization.

A few weeks before each opening of Parliament the correspondence of the malcontent chiefs began to swell with calls for a meeting in London 'to consult on a scheme for the session'.[1] Their shattered forces had to be reassembled and new working agreements drawn up. The more vigorous leaders always wanted full attendance and a well-concerted plan of attack settled by the first day. They apparently never achieved their aim. No one had the authority to enforce a summons, and many concerns kept the jealous magnates apart. Chesterfield wrote to Dodington in September 1741:

I entirely agree with you that we ought to have meetings to concert measures some time before the meeting of the Parliament; but that I likewise know will not happen. I have been these seven years endeavouring to bring it about and have not been able. Fox-hunting, gardening, planting, or indifference having always kept our people in the country till the very day before the meeting of the Parliament. Besides, would it be easy to settle who should be at those meetings? If Pulteney and his people were to be chose, it would be only informing them beforehand what they should either oppose or defeat; and if they were not there, their own exclusion would in some degree justify, or at least colour, their conduct.[2]

In consequence, a sessional plan of operations had to be devised after Parliament got under way. First came cautious,

---

[1] For examples, see Graham, ed., *Annals of Stair*, ii. 221, 253; Rose, ed., *March-mont Papers*, i. 161–6; Phillimore, *Lyttelton*, i. 149–52, 190–4; P.R.O. *Chatham Papers*, 33; *H.M.C., Dartmouth MSS.*, p. 154.

[2] Coxe, *Walpole*, iii. 580–1. In a letter to Lyttelton a few weeks later Chesterfield said, 'I never could get 'em to meet in town two or three days before the Parliament' (Phillimore, *Lyttelton*, i. 194). His calculations of time were evidently rhetorical flourishes to impress upon his colleagues what they already knew, viz. that the Opposition never foregathered early enough to synchronize their attack with the beginning of the session.

tense, suspicious gatherings of the leaders, decried by the Government Press as 'private meetings with party clubs to form plans and deliberate a scheme'.[1] Once a *modus vivendi* had been worked out, invitations were issued to the rank-and-file for a large assembly at the 'King's Arms', the 'Crown and Anchor', or the 'Fountain', where the leaders sought general support for their programme. The sequence of meetings might have to be repeated several times during a session to keep up a united front. A revealing description of the difficult nature of this process is to be found in a letter from Marchmont to Montrose in May 1738: despite his utmost efforts over the last four months, wrote Marchmont,

the leaders could not be brought to act with vigour—scarce to have a meeting; and indeed there were very few, and none to any purpose. Other members were tried, who might have acted without the leaders; and they [the leaders] in that case must have joined them [the others] at last . . .; but they were unwilling to risk a breach among themselves, although desertion, the worst breach that can be, must ever be the consequence of inactivity. The reasons given for this management, though, I doubt, not the true ones, were the want of right points to push, and that points must arise from the other side . . . in their situation they would be glad to get the session over anyhow . . . in short, I look, as several others do, upon the Opposition as at an end.[2]

Marchmont's despair arose from his conviction that better organization could have achieved their ultimate goal—the 'broad-bottoms' and the Pulteney–Carteret clique hoped for final triumph every year and so desponded annually. Because they expected so much they failed to see that, awkward as was their co-operation, they were unwittingly developing one of the most important functions of an opposition. They were acting as 'watchdogs of the administration'. The Government knew their weaknesses as well as they, but incessant criticism and the potential threat of a vigorous offensive imposed caution and vigilance upon the Ministry. The attitude of Whitehall comes

[1] Laprade, *Public Opinion and Politics*, p. 404. Occasionally various groups established dining clubs during the session. In 1741, for example, an aristocratic clique of twenty-seven gathered every Tuesday at the 'King's Arms' to renew their spirits with food and drink (Torrens, *History of Cabinets*, i. 516).

[2] Rose, ed., *Marchmont Papers*, ii. 100–1. Cf. Chesterfield's parallel comments after the session of 1740 in Dobrée, ed., *Letters of Chesterfield*, ii. 404–5.

out clearly in a letter from 'old Horace' Walpole to Robert Trevor in February 1740:

The opponents continue in town [Walpole wrote], so that we are obliged to lie upon our arms. Several motions have been talked of, such as triennial parliaments, the prince's affair, in consequence of the meeting at the Crown and Anchor to stand by one another. However, they are extremely divided among themselves, and matters appear at present more calm.[1]

In sum, the coalition with all its infirmities served as a restraining and inhibiting force upon the Government with all the attendant possibilities of good and evil.

In their sessional attacks the malcontents improved significantly upon the 'Country party' tactics of the previous period.[2] The 'angry chiefs' had broader objects in view. They were not on the defensive, as the remnants of Anne's last Ministry had been, concerned to protect old idols and vindicate their own conduct in office. The sands of time drifted ever deeper over the ancient bones of contention, and with every passing year fewer of the coalition had any stake in politics before Walpole's rise to power. The whole tenour of the Opposition was offensive. They did not merely resist Government policy. Their aim being to shake the faith of both Court and Court party in the great Minister, they framed each issue to catch votes in Parliament and arouse sentiment outside its walls. Every point of dispute became a national grievance for which Walpole bore the blame. In sustained, audacious violence they far exceeded any of their eighteenth-century predecessors.

For this aggressive policy Bolingbroke and the 'broad-bottoms' bear the major responsibility. The Tories were passive opposers in keeping with the doctrine of 'measures not men'. Pulteney and Carteret were men of fits and starts, now rashly goaded into impetuous assault, now subsiding into moderation, in pursuit of their long-sought accommodation. The vigorous consistency of the Opposition offensive stemmed from those who would 'storm the closet' and gain 'victory with numbers'. They were the most eager to hold meetings and find

---

[1] *H.M.C.*, *Trevor MSS.*, p. 40. Walpole's apprehensions were correct. Ten days later the Opposition launched its major attack upon a surprise motion which he had not anticipated.

[2] See above, Chapter III, pp. 94–103.

'points to push' which suited all. Tories would not come out for repeal of the Test Act to please the Dissenters, Whigs were reluctant to vote for triennial parliaments to please the Tories, nor would the Prince court anyone's favour by supporting a reduction in the army. It was Bolingbroke, Wyndham, Marchmont, Stair and their group who for ever sought a ground of agreement and cast about for 'easy Whig points', 'liberty points', and 'popular points' with which to construct a programme.[1] Desultory sniping with an occasional major assault on some Government proposal did not satisfy them. They constantly urged a well-formed plan of campaign, organized to allow for contingencies and to carry on the momentum of the offensive. '. . . Nothing gives success like hope,' pronounced Bolingbroke in 1737, 'and nothing gives hope like the assurance of having a good second game to play.'[2] Tactical operations to their mind should be set in a strategic framework.

Thrown together in piecemeal fashion at meetings throughout the session, their programmes never attained the form and precision they desired. Too much depended upon the whimsy of allies, the opportunities offered by the enemy, and unpredictable shifts of opinion. Too often did the carefully planned manœuvre fail and the impulsive dash succeed. In no session did they ever bring themselves to formulate and execute a truly strategic campaign. Careful examination of debates and divisions over seventeen years nevertheless reveals the stereotypes in their plans and the remarkable ingenuity of attack which they developed.

2. PARLIAMENTARY TACTICS

Opposition to Government Measures

In their opposition to the routine measures of the Government the 'patriots' carried on the tradition of their predecessors.

---

[1] See above, p. 172, n. 1 and *H.M.C., Egmont Diary*, ii. 462; *H.M.C., Hare MSS.*, pp. 237–8; Rose, ed., *Marchmont Papers*, ii. 14, 72. Upon occasion Pulteney took an active part in sessional planning (*H.M.C., Mar and Kellie MSS.*, pp. 535–6; Graham, ed., *Annals of Stair*, ii. 221). He undoubtedly conceived some of the shrewdest strokes in the Opposition offensive, but his forte was tactics rather than strategy.

[2] Coxe, *Walpole*, iii. 479. As in his *Letter on the Spirit of Patriotism* Bolingbroke steadily insisted that the measures of the Opposition would be effective only if 'systematical': cf. ibid. 506–7.

They always debated the address on the grounds that the King's Speech was the speech of the Minister and thus subject to unlimited criticism.[1] Walpole admitted the propriety of considering the Speech as his but contended that 'it ought to be treated with decency, it having, at least, the stamp of majesty upon it'.[2] The patriots felt restrained only at the point of dividing. They risked a trial of strength in the Commons but six times and went down to decisive defeat on each occasion.[3]

More consistent was their opposition to financial and military measures. On the former they divided one or more times in every session; on the latter in every session except 1738.[4] Ministerialists came to regard a battle on such questions as an inevitable but minor nuisance. An 'opposition to the troops', wrote Hervey in 1736, 'is never anything more than the dispute of a day, which are [*sic*] never questions that distress most'.[5] Taxation was a more serious matter, but Sir Robert often avoided a major engagement by bringing on controversial Supply Bills late in the session when many country members had departed.[6] What distinguished the opposition to the routine

[1] *P.H.* ix, 224; Add. MSS. 6043, ff. 7–8, 23, 28, 98; *H.M.C., Egmont Diary*, iii. 338; Tindal, *History of England*, viii. 254, 296.

[2] Ibid. 206.

[3] The Opposition divided on the Address in 1727, 1729, 1730, 1735, 1739, and 1740–1. The Government carried the day by margins of 170, 162, 93, 80, 89, and 67. Egmont described the Opposition's more common tactic in 1734 when the 'patriots' raised bitter objections to the heads of the Address, then 'desisted from their opposition, only four or five gave a loud No to agreeing, that it might not appear the Address was voted unanimously, thus showing their teeth where they could not bite': *H.M.C., Egmont Diary*, ii. 8. 'Old Horace' Walpole thus complacently described the scene in the session of 1739–40, 'The question being put for agreeing to it, there would have been a *nemine contradicente* had it not been for one poor *no* out of the Tory corner which nobody would own' (*H.M.C., Trevor MSS.*, p. 36).

[4] These divisions are far too many to enumerate. Most are to be found in *P.H.* viii–xii, and *Commons Journals*, xx–xxiv.   [5] Coxe, *Walpole*, iii. 311.

[6] With some exceptions, major divisions on Supply did not take place before late March, and most occurred in April. The Opposition sometimes divided a very thin House: e.g. motions relative to Supply were carried by 36–23 on 16 Apr. 1730 and by 67–37 on 14 Apr. 1741. Walpole was usually content to put financial measures through late in the session, but obstructive tactics by the Opposition perhaps contributed to their tardy passage. Pulteney declared it his policy to frustrate any 'manifest design of hurrying on the session and precipitating the supplies' (*Answer to One Part of a Late Infamous Libel*, p. 19). When Walpole brought in his proposal to revive the salt duty on 9 Feb. 1732, the Opposition forced a lengthy debate and a division at every stage, including five divisions in committee on 8 Mar. alone, until the Bill finally was passed on 21 Mar.

measures of this period was its regularity. The Government knew that it must face a challenge, whose strength it could not surely anticipate, to most of its ordinary Bills.

To extraordinary measures the reaction of the Opposition was uneven. Sometimes the Commons approved proposals affecting the conduct of government, trade, or even foreign relations with little or no flurry, while the same issues produced a clash in other years. Much depended upon whose interests were involved and to what degree, what other issues were momentarily in the forefront, and the appeal of the issue to the various elements in the coalition. Economic matters often split them, and the Court party as well, according to particular interests of the members or their 'countries'. Religious issues were equally divisive.[1] The malcontents were most likely to make heavy weather when the dispute could be given a strong political tinge in line with the traditional 'Country party programme'. If Walpole stood firm, they must normally expect defeat. But debate and division allowed them to register one more stormy protest against the 'ruinous policies' of the Minister, and occasionally their efforts brought a heartening triumph.

The Excise Bill of 1733

Their most spectacular victory came upon the Excise Bill of 1733. It is a classic example of the malcontents' operations.

Two years earlier Sir Robert had brought in a Bill which imposed very stringent regulations to prevent frauds in the Excise. Without any recorded opposition this Bill passed into law.[2] The patriots apparently saw no issue worth a struggle. Walpole then set out to reform the Customs. In the spring of 1732 he first bruited his plan to levy import duties by excise.[3] Revenue calculations showed that the product of such a reform would make possible the abolition of the land-tax, a great

---

[1] The best examples of an economic issue that split both sides are the Wool Exportation Bills of 1731 and 1739. On the latter Bishop Hare reported 'a very motley division, people voting as their counties happened to be abounding in sheep or not' (*H.M.C., Hare MSS.*, pp. 246–7). The Opposition was sadly riven in 1736 by the Mortmain Bill for Universities, the Quakers' Tythes Bill, and the motion for repeal of the Test Act.

[2] 4 George II c. 14.

[3] *A Letter to a Freeholder on the Late Reduction of the Land Tax*, published in April 1732.

political stroke with the country gentlemen. This time, however, the malcontents determined upon a battle.

Anticipating the introduction of Walpole's scheme in the coming session, *The Craftsman* in October 1732 launched a series of attacks on 'a general excise' as destructive of trade and the liberties of the nation. These articles appeared in a collected edition on the London bookstalls at the opening of Parliament. Meanwhile the city merchants commenced widespread agitation against extension of the excise, and trading constituencies instructed their representatives to oppose any such measure.[1] Before the members had even assembled, the Opposition had aroused great public excitement over the coming issue.

On the first day, 16 January 1733, began a contest that lasted for three months.[2] 'Patriots' orators reflected severely on passages in the King's Speech that foreshadowed revenue reform. They challenged Sir Robert to bring in the scheme they were so well prepared to oppose, and dared him to introduce it before attendance waned at the end of the session. They proposed to amend the Address to state that the House would raise Supplies in such manner 'as shall be consistent with the trade, interest, and liberty of the nation and such as shall be consistent with the honour and justice of Parliament'.[3] Walpole accepted the amendment without a division.

Then he kept them dangling for seven weeks. The Press campaign against 'a general excise' went clamorously on, and the malcontents raised the issue whenever opportunity offered in the House. But not until 7 March was the Minister ready to act. Then he moved to consider improvement in the methods of collecting existing duties on wines and tobacco in a committee

---

[1] *H.M.C., Carlisle MSS.*, p. 95. How the Opposition decided upon its campaign is uncertain. In *Anecdotes of Distinguished Persons* (4th ed., London, 1798), pp. 338–9, William Seward gives the credit to Bolingbroke, who is said to have roused his desponding colleagues to oppose a Bill they all thought admirable. The long preliminary agitation shows this story to be apocryphal. Since the protest began in *The Craftsman*, still under the co-operative management of Bolingbroke and Pulteney, they must have had a hand in it. Sir John Barnard, the ablest and most consistent critic of Walpole's finance, may have been their chief inspiration.

[2] The chronology of the excise scheme can be followed in *P.H.* viii–ix; *Commons Journals*, xxii; and *Historical Register*, xviii. The best eye-witness accounts are to be found in *H.M.C., Carlisle MSS.*, pp. 103–14; *H.M.C., Egmont Diary*, ii. 307–67; Coxe, *Walpole*, iii. 129–36; Sedgwick, ed., *Memoirs of Lord Hervey*, i. 135–84.

[3] *P.H.* viii. 1170–6.

of the whole House 'this day sevennight'. The preliminary skirmishing over, battle was at last joined on 14 March.

Sir Robert brought in four resolutions to convert the Customs impost on tobacco to an inland duty. Opposition took its stand on the first. With mobs milling about in the streets and in the Parliament Houses themselves, the tumultuous committee, which had once to be brought to order by the chairman, heard a vigorous summary of the arguments so long presented in the Press against the excise. The theme was ever the same: Walpole's scheme would bring slavery and economic disaster. Near 2 a.m. the Government carried the division, 266 to 205, and the Opposition let the other three resolutions pass without dispute. Sir Robert needed help to fight his way out of the House through the irate rabble.

On the 16th the Opposition contested the report from committee till 1 a.m., then lost the division on the first resolution, 249 to 189, and defaulted on the remainder. A select committee headed by Walpole was ordered to bring in a Bill to effectuate the resolutions. The first stage had ended with the ministerial troops holding firm. The Commons marked time for a few days, then adjourned till 2 April.

Walpole brought in the Bill on the 4th. Now the patriots began to vary their attack. The first reading took place *nem. con.*, whereupon Gybbon moved that the Bill be withdrawn as inconsonant with the resolutions. Walpole countered by moving the second reading. Gybbon's motion was lost, 232 to 176, shortly before 5 p.m., and the Government renewed the call for a second reading, Pelham offering to postpone it a week 'that gentlemen might not say the Bill was precipitated'.[1] But Sandys pressed for adjournment and after much debate was defeated, 237 to 199. Finally at 1 a.m. Walpole secured a motion to read the Bill a second time on 11 April by 236 to 200. Ministerialists shook their heads at the ominous decline in their margin of victory but thought they might safely relax for the moment after so late a night.

In a thin House next day, however, Sandys moved to have the Bill printed. Walpole was taken by surprise. He knew the Opposition wanted copies to spirit up a fresh flood of expostulatory petitions, but he did not have a majority in the House

[1] *H.M.C., Egmont Diary,* ii. 349.

to stop them. Here the patriots made a tactical mistake. They let Sir Robert goad them into debate until his Whips gathered enough supporters to defeat the motion, 128 to 112.

It was nevertheless clear to him that he was running into very heavy weather on the Tobacco Bill, and the following day the Commons were due to go into committee on the wine duties. If the one could not carry, the other must fail. He saw no sense in having two struggles on the same issue at the same time. With a majority in hand, therefore, he quickly moved to discharge the Orders of the Day and postpone consideration of the imposts on wine for a week. The Opposition had hoped 'by the strength of their party . . . to knock it on the head immediately'[1] and so raised an angry protest. Sir Robert pushed hasty divisions and won, 124 to 73 and 118 to 76. He had out-manœuvred his enemies twice in the same afternoon, but he was now jettisoning cargo to lighten ship.

Out-manœuvred but undefeated, the Opponents somehow secured copies of the Tobacco Bill, which they distributed to trading communities. Within four days they had strongly worded petitions from London, Nottingham, and Coventry to present. A mere vote of the House could not halt the Opposition in their determination to give Walpole no rest and leave no means untried to increase the fury of the storm.

On the 9th the Minister privately decided to give up the excise scheme but for the time being kept his counsel. He wanted to hold his forces together for one more day to check the petitions. He would not truckle to the city merchants. Moreover, if the House were to admit and debate petitions against Money Bills, the granting of Supplies would be unduly prolonged. The sheriffs of London brought in the city's plea at 1 p.m. on 10 April, accompanied by a request to be heard by counsel. Walpole allowed the petition to be tabled but resisted the request. Debate went on till 10 at night, when counsel was denied, 214 to 197. 'This was a Pyrrhus's victory', thought Lord Egmont,[2] but Walpole, already resolved to accept defeat, had scored an important point for the future.

The second reading was set for the next day. While the Opposition, confident of success, came down to secure their seats at 8 in the morning, Sir Robert sent word to his supporters

[1] *H.M.C., Egmont Diary*, ii. 354.   [2] Ibid. 359.

that he planned to give up the Tobacco Bill but urged their attendance 'to prevent the coming of any ill-natured resolutions which the other party might in the height of their joy propose'.[1] The House first tabled the petitions of Coventry and Nottingham, then went to the order of the day for the second reading. To the astonishment of the 'patriots', Walpole moved that it be put off till 12 June when, it was expected, the House would have risen. Here at last was victory, but not in the form the Opposition had anticipated. They had not routed the Minister. He had retired from the field.

Unprepared to face this manœuvre, the Country party saw no counter-move but to try to force a fight. Wyndham moved the previous question. The House debated till after dinner, when the patriots gave in without a division. Now that Sir Robert had abandoned his scheme many of the Opponents, notably the Tories, would not force the issue further. Mrs. Charles Caesar recounted, 'Mr. Shippen gave it up, and Mr. Caesar going by Sir Robert told him he thought a father should have the burying of his own child. He laughing said, "But some of your party was so wise to have a mind I should have showed them my old majority." '[2] The Minister and his followers fought their way with difficulty through a vindictive mob that surged to the very doors of St. Stephen's Chapel, and for two days London rejoiced to the ringing of bells, the light of bonfires, and the sight of Sir Robert burning in effigy.

The Opposition still sought some means to capitalize on their triumph. They may have hoped for a struggle over the wine duties on the 13th, but the Government moved postponement till 14 June and carried it with little flurry. Walpole did not even come down to the House. A week later Sir John Barnard brought in a petition from dealers in coffee, tea, and chocolate, praying to be relieved of the excise. The Commons threw it out, 250 to 150.

Then the malcontents staked all on one shrewd stratagem. Sir Edward Stanley seconded by Sandys moved for a select committee to be chosen by ballot to inquire into the frauds in the Customs. The Minister could not oppose without denying the principle on which the excise scheme had been based. Yet a secret ballot would permit wavering ministerialists to desert

---

[1] Idem.   [2] MS. Journal of Mrs. Charles Caesar, ii.

him without detection, a most unwelcome risk; and a committee dominated by the Opposition would be a great source
of trouble. This was, wrote a Government official, 'a matter
indeed of greater consequence than even the Excise Bill itself.'[1]
Walpole decided to meet the challenge. The motion passed
nem. con., and each side drew up a strictly partisan slate. The
night before the ballot Sir Robert summoned the Court party
to the cockpit where he, Pelham, Yorke, and Speaker Onslow
harangued them on the gravity of the situation. The Opposition
also mustered their forces effectively, for on 24 April, 503
members appeared to cast ballots. The completed count next
day gave the Court list a margin of 85.

At the crisis Walpole had showed them his 'old majority'. The
defeat of the Excise was nevertheless a remarkable example of
what the malcontents could do when well organized behind
a well-framed issue. Despite Walpole's strategy of delay, the
'angry chiefs' had held their forces together and kept them in
battle array for over three months. The timing, variety, and
dexterity of their tactics had strained the resources of Sir
Robert's parliamentary genius. In the end the storm they had
raised wrecked sound legislative proposals supported at the
outset by the King, the Minister, and the overwhelming
majority of the Court party. Within the political framework
of the 1730's parliamentary opposition could accomplish no
more.

Malcontent resistance to other extraordinary Court measures
was but a pale reflection of the Excise agitation. Few Bills
offered so great an opportunity, and none was ever so fully
exploited. Walpole's caution made it difficult to turn his
measures into *causes célèbres*. The offensive spirit of the 'patriots',
therefore, often impelled them to select their own ground for
attack. They did not simply await the Court's moves. Each
session they hit upon at least one grievance serious enough for
conversion into a major parliamentary issue. Their tactics in
this aspect of battle were also varied and ingenious, but in
general they chose one of two angles of assault: Bills designed to
remedy the alleged grievance, or motions that reflected upon
ministerial policy.

[1] Coxe, *Walpole*, iii. 134.

Opposition Bills

Bolingbroke made it a cardinal point in his doctrine that the Opposition should 'propose true, as well as oppose false, measures of government'.[1] Pulteney boasted in 1734 of the 'beneficial acts' achieved and intended by the 'patriots'.[2] They did indeed bring in numerous proposals, some of which became law in their own or later times, and their 'true' or 'beneficial' character was fairly uniform. With few exceptions, they were intended to reduce the influence of the Crown. The Opposition founded their Bills upon the contention that Walpole ruled by corruption, which sound constitutional measures would destroy. Thus the Bills were many, but the subjects were few.

From 1730 through 1742 Samuel Sandys, 'the motion-maker', brought in five Pension Bills and six Place Bills. They were unexceptionable in principle, consonant with existing law, and appealing to the political conscience of the governing class. Sir Robert consequently found these measures embarrassing in the House of Commons. To the Pension Bills, all designed to enforce legislation already on the Statute Books, the Minister thought it unwise to make any serious opposition. He took the Whip off the Court party and seldom spoke in the debates himself. Each Pension Bill, therefore, passed the Lower House, only to be killed by the Lords promptly after the second reading. Walpole knew that the Government peers, little concerned with popularity out-of-doors, would stand by him; so he defaulted to the Opposition in the Commons, giving them a hollow triumph at the cost of throwing 'the odium of rejection' upon the Upper House.[3]

The Place Bills were not at first quite so grave a threat to the unity of the Court party in the Commons. Some members developed qualms, but a reasonably good case could be made against a further extension of the Exclusion Laws. Though Sir

---

[1] Bolingbroke, *Works*, ii. 370.

[2] *An Humble Address to the Knights, Citizens, and Burgesses* (London, 1734), pp. 30–32.

[3] Coxe, *Walpole*, i. 321–2. Sandys offered his Pension Bills in 1730, 1731, 1732, 1733, 1740, and 1742: *P.H.* viii. 789–98, 841, 844–55, 882, 942, 987, 988–92, 1177–84, 1200; xi. 509–78; *Commons Journals*, xxiv. 52; Tindal, *History of England*, viii. 313, mentions a Pension Bill lost in 1736 but gives none of the circumstances of its history. There may have been others which attracted no attention in contemporary sources.

Robert usually gave a silent negative vote, he was less reluctant to risk a trial of strength. The original Bill of 1734 was, in Tindal's words, 'treated with a good deal of intemperate mirth by the ministerial party'.[1] The Courtiers gleefully rallied their opponents with charges of patent hypocrisy. One Government member moved for the insertion of a clause 'excluding all those who have asked for any place or employment or any other favour from the Government, and have been refused what they asked for'.[2] The House eventually threw the Bill out by the slim majority of 39, and the division apparently had a sobering effect. The Government defeated the three subsequent measures by margins of 24, 57, and 16, after prolonged and tense debates. In 1741 Walpole therefore fell back upon the tactics he used for Pension Bills: he let the Place Bill go up to the Lords for its destruction.[3]

Various other Opposition proposals were intended to curtail Ministerial influence upon members of Lords and Commons. In 1731 the Lower House denied a malcontent motion for leave to bring in a Bill to prevent the translation of bishops. Four Qualification-of-members Bills, all presented by the young Tory, Henry Rolle of Devon, provoked strenuous but vain debate in 1732, 1733, 1734, and 1740. Opposition made two futile attempts to limit the Crown's power over military officers. Sandys moved in 1731 to declare vacant the seat of any army officer who accepted a military governorship. After Walpole cashiered Bolton and Cobham over the Excise affair, the malcontents introduced measures into both Houses simultaneously to prevent the Crown from dismissing commissioned officers, not above the rank of colonel, except by court martial or upon a Parliamentary Address. Finally, the Tories made several fruitless efforts to check 'the influencing powers of the Crown' by moving for the repeal of the Septennial Act.

Still other Bills struck at the supposed sources of the Minister's strength out-of-doors, particularly with regard to elections. In 1734 Tweeddale and Bedford brought in motions designed to break Government control of the choice of Scots peers. Plummer's motion to repeal the Test Act in 1736 was an attempt to

---

[1] Tindal, *History of England*, viii. 225.   [2] *P.H.* ix. 374.
[3] Sandys introduced his Place Bills in 1734, 1735, 1736, 1740, and 1741: ibid. 366–92, 967–8, 1060; xi. 328–80.

turn the Dissenters against Walpole. Sir John Barnard sought nation-wide popularity in 1737 by introducing schemes to lighten taxation and reduce the interest on the National Debt. All these proposals failed, but with Walpole's sufferance the Opposition did carry two 'Country party' acts. The first was Sir Watkin Wynne's Bill of 1729 to tighten the laws against bribery and corruption in elections. To avoid controversy Sir Robert kept his hand off the measure, which ultimately passed with some Lords' amendments by two votes in a thin House, but its defects had to be remedied by a Government-sponsored explaining act seven years later. The second was the famous Stockjobbing Act of 1734, inspired by the malcontents' belief that the Minister manipulated the funds to the advantage of himself and his friends. Tindal thought the 'patriots' were disappointed when Walpole let it pass 'with a becoming disdain'.[1]

The Bills not aimed purposely at the Crown influence were all by-products of particular situations, endeavours to capitalize upon circumstances embarrassing to the Government. Two examples may suffice. In 1735 a petition from five imprisoned Scots magistrates revealed apparent defects in the laws protecting liberty of person in north Britain. Having supported the petition in vain, the Opposition brought in a Bill 'for preventing wrongous imprisonment and against undue delays in trials'. An agitated Commons passed it over Walpole's objections, but the Lords threw it out. Amid the excitement over Spanish depredations in 1738 Pulteney tried to drive Britain closer to open hostilities by reviving Acts which offered high rewards to the captors of enemy ships, prisoners, or property. The Ministry mustered enough strength to defeat him, but after the declaration of war in 1739 Pulteney renewed his proposals with success.[2]

The coalition obviously accomplished very little legislation. Even when they carried the Commons with them, the Court could block their Bills in the Lords. The Crown's control of the Upper House, by the way, probably contributed much to the

[1] Tindal, *History of England*, viii. 227–8.

[2] It would seem unnecessary to devote a great deal of space to specific references to all the Bills mentioned in the text. Notice of them can be found in the standard annals of Cobbett and Tindal, and further comment in such sources as Hervey's memoirs, Egmont's diary, Coxe's *Walpole*, &c.

disuse of the royal veto under the Hanoverians. There was no need to resort to *le roy s'avisera* when the peers could usually be made to accept the 'odium of rejection'. But then it was not the intention of the Opposition to legislate, and their failures, which lived on as grievances, served their purpose as well as success.

Motions of Censure

The same may be said of the motions introduced to harass the Ministry. There were several main types, of which the most common was an address to the Crown for papers on a controversial subject. A pamphlet of 1743 recalled:

> Motions for papers were always favourite ones with the gentlemen in opposition to the late administration because they are agreeable to the Constitution; and they put the Court under great difficulties in refusing them in the debate since, in their very arguments for refusing them, some part of the reasons why they want to keep them a secret must perspire [*sic*]; and even the defeat of such motions have [*sic*] been looked upon as a matter of triumph to the minority.[1]

Sir Robert, of course, knew what his opponents were up to. On one occasion he derided such a motion as 'a piece of management . . . a sort of parliamentary play', the purposes of which were to provide an opportunity to declaim against the Government, to allow the movers 'to make a figure in the votes, which are sent out to all parts of the nation', and to render the ministers odious by forcing them to refuse papers time after time. The malcontents retorted that this was 'unparliamentary language': the House had a right to demand any papers it pleased at any time.[2]

The documents most often called for related to foreign affairs: diplomatic and military instructions, copies or extracts of treaties and other international agreements, statistics on foreign and colonial trade, official records of Spanish depredations, and so forth. The Opposition also frequently requested accounts of expenditure and the disposal of Crown properties. If pressed to a division, Walpole usually met the challenge squarely and defeated the address. Sometimes, to avoid direct

---

[1] *Review of the Whole Political Conduct of a Late Eminent Patriot and his Friends,* pp. 14–15, cf. [William Pulteney], *The Conduct of the Late and Present M——ry Compared* (London, 1742), pp. 15–16.

[2] *P.H.* ix. 205–13.

refusal of a superficially reasonable request, the Government moved the previous question, thereby effectually destroying the motion without putting a negative upon it.[1] On the rare occasions when Sir Robert allowed an address to pass, the King's answer provided no information worth having. Addresses for accounts could be evaded with the reply that the money had been expended on matters so secret and delicate that no disclosure could be made 'without manifest prejudice to the public'.[2] The accounts and papers actually produced were either innocuous or creditable to the administration. Thus Walpole always managed to escape censure, but this manoeuvre proved effective by forcing the Government time and again to a prolonged and often embarrassed defence of its policies.

Akin to an address for papers, though less frequently employed, was a motion for a committee on the State of the Nation. When shrewdly managed, this move gave the Opposition a peculiar advantage. The motion implied a general arraignment of the ministers, who could not anticipate the precise point upon which the attack would land. If the malcontents called for papers at all, they could disguise their intent by requesting documents of common knowledge. By this device, therefore, the Opposition could set up an opportunity to fall well armed upon a Government without prepared defences. The session of 1730 affords an outstanding illustration.[3]

The Dunkirk Inquiry of 1730

In their relentless probing for weak spots in Walpole's foreign policy, the malcontent leaders hit upon two situations that

[1] A negative vote on the previous question technically postpones a motion but generally puts an end to it (Hatsell, *Precedents of Proceedings*, ii. 109–10). 'The previous question is parliamentary jockeyship', remarked Lord Talbot in 1740 (Add. MSS. 6043, f. 49). Tindal observed that the previous question was a method of defeating a proposition while giving a 'tacit admission' of its truth (*History of England*, viii. 479). [2] For examples see *P.H.* viii. 550, 646.

[3] The following account of the struggle in the committee on the State of the Nation in 1730 is put together primarily from *Commons Journals*, xxi. 407–91; *H.M.C., Egmont Diary*, i. 34–78; *H.M.C., Carlisle MSS.*, pp. 67–69; Sedgwick, ed., *Memoirs of Lord Hervey*, i. 116–18; Coxe, *Walpole*, i. 323–4; ii. 668–71; Tindal, *History of England*, viii. 71–72. Of the many pamphlets on the issue, only the two following shed light on the parliamentary proceedings: *The Joint and Separate Accounts or Narrative of George Collcott and Robert Jones, Mariners, relating to what passed at their several meetings with others about the affair of Dunkirk* and *The Case of Dunkirk Faithfully Stated and Impartially Considered* (attributed to Bolingbroke).

offered promising lines of assault. The first was the provision in the Treaty of Utrecht, confirmed by the Triple Alliance, binding France to demolish the port and defences of Dunkirk, that nest of privateers which had taken a heavy toll of British shipping. The execution of this provision was a delicate matter. Early in 1714, when directing the appointment of inspectors to view the demolition, Bolingbroke had urged the selection of men of the most reliable character, for, he remarked, 'you know when faction is strong and government weak how little foundation will serve to raise a clamour'.[1] Now in 1730, with this in mind, he sent his secretary, Brinsden, to gather information about the state of Dunkirk. Brinsden reported that the French were restoring the port, and before long he turned up several sea captains to corroborate his evidence. Here was explosive material indeed.

The other situation existed in the Caribbean. Britain and France had long disputed the possession of St. Lucia, St. Vincent, and Dominica. The French had frustrated the most recent British attempt to colonize St. Lucia in 1722. Upon his return the leader of the ill-fated expedition had published a full account of the venture, exposing the humiliation of Britain and warning of the French threat in the West Indies.[2] In 1730 the two Courts were acrimoniously working their way toward a temporary agreement, of which the Opposition leaders apparently gained some knowledge, for joint evacuation of these 'neutral islands'. Here in a thick tangle of conflicting claims and treaties, where loss and disappointment aggravated the national fear of France, was fuel for an incendiary raid on the Government.

Their evidence carefully prepared, the Opposition moved warily to the attack. When Sir William Wyndham called on 22 January 1730 for a committee on the State of the Nation, only a select group of the leaders knew the plan. Lest Walpole should get wind of their intentions, the 'angry chiefs' kept their plans a secret from their own followers, and they did not address for papers. When the Orders of the Day for the committee were read on 10 February, Speaker Onslow reminded members that

---

[1] Egerton MSS. 2618, ff. 215–16.
[2] [Nathaniel Uring], *A Relation of the late Intended Settlement of the Islands of St. Lucia and St. Vincent in America* (London, 1725). This work was reprinted in 1727.

the House must call for and refer to the committee any documents to be used in the debate. The malcontents saw the trap. If they demanded papers relevant to the issue, they not only gave away their secrets but provided the Government with an excuse for delay, since time must be given to make the necessary copies. The Ministry equally feared an ambush, being particularly concerned that the Opposition might use the journals of past parliaments as grounds for censure. A long altercation ensued. At length the House found a way out of the impasse. William Pulteney called for copies of the Treaty of Seville and the Dutch accession thereto, which were readily available and had nothing to do with the issue; and the malcontents promised not to found any impeachment upon the journals. The House thereupon went into committee.

Wyndham opened the debate by deploring ten aspects of foreign and domestic policy, customary complaints that had often arisen in recent years. Then he startled the committee with the statement that Dunkirk was being restored. He flourished a paper which he said was a full account (probably Brinsden's) of the condition of that port, announced that seven ship masters who would confirm the report waited at the door, and moved that they be called in for examination. The thunderstruck Ministry struggled for delay. Their situation was the more embarrassing because Colonel John Armstrong, the chief engineer who regularly checked on the French observance of the Dunkirk provision, had recently departed on an inspection trip and could not be summoned immediately to counter the malcontents' accusations. Grumbling at Sir William's 'unkindness' in springing such a surprise, Horace Walpole urged that the Government be allowed to produce papers in its justification before taking evidence from the sea captains. The committee, aroused to a high pitch of indignation, would have no postponement. In an attempt to bow gracefully before the storm, Sir Robert agreed to hear the captains 'provided no resolution should pass'. Without any such guarantee, the committee called in the witnesses and questioned them till early evening. It became apparent that the inhabitants of Dunkirk, with the connivance of the Government, had made great progress in rebuilding jetties and clearing the harbour. The members, reported Hervey, were 'in a flame'.

The Opposition had struck a stunning blow. The Pulteneys and their henchmen were all for delivering the knock-out punch immediately. Though the hour was late, they wanted to proceed to debate and a resolution of censure. But with his opponent reeling, Wyndham suddenly showed a disposition to temporize. He apparently sensed the unwillingness of the Tories to damn the Minister without hearing any evidence for the defence. Accordingly he consented not to press for a decision that night, if gentlemen would continue the inquiry to a conclusion without the interruption of other business. Sir Robert promptly took advantage of this opening and persuaded the committee to postpone further consideration of Dunkirk for two days. The great question was whether this brief respite would suffice for the Minister to erect defences against the next assault.

The following day, 11 February, the House called for a copy of the Triple Alliance of 1717 and for all papers relating to Dunkirk and St. Lucia. On the 12th Henry Pelham, Secretary for War, announced that the King would order the papers requested, and Wyndham, after giving a lengthy summary of the evidence on Dunkirk, demanded to know when they would be produced. Sir William Strickland, supported by Walpole and Pelham, moved for a two-week postponement. It would take that much time, they contended, to copy all the documents and recall Colonel Armstrong. Knowing full well that the Ministry was playing for time, the malcontents ridiculed the motion. William Pulteney said he wanted to hear no more 'of wheelbarrows of papers to be brought in, which ended in two or three papers only'. Moreover, he added, outraged mercantile opinion would brook no delay. The House then fell into wild and bitter debate in which members raked up old scores back to 1708. The Speaker called Caesar to order once and Shippen twice. Vernon 'brought in the Pope, the Devil, the Jesuits, the seamen, etc., so that the House had not the patience to attend to him, though he was not taken down'. At last the motion was carried to adjourn the committee on the State of the Nation till 'tomorrow fortnight'.

The Opposition had now lost the initial value of surprise. They had nevertheless made so strong a case for the prosecution that the burden of proof lay heavily upon the Government. In the ensuing two weeks they strove to press this advantage. To

ensure full attendance when the committee met again, the
malcontents secured an order for a call of the House two days
in advance. When Walpole delivered the first 'large bundle of
papers' on 19 February his integrity was called into question.
He admitted the disappearance of some documents, and Daniel
Pulteney suggested that 'the administration were willing they
should not be found'. William Pulteney protested at the
presentation of copies and extracts instead of originals, leading
the House to believe that Sir Robert was 'cooking the evidence'.
Sandys' motion for original papers fell only when his close
friend Gybbon declared he would read the documents before
condemning them. As in the case of Wyndham's opening
accusation, the 'angry chiefs' found their followers reluctant to
attack the Minister *à outrance*. A strong disposition to fair play
again restrained the leaders from extreme action. The remaining
papers were laid upon the table during the next week with but
little further acrimony.

On the appointed day, 27 February, the House went into
committee between 12 and 1 p.m. The reading of the papers,
punctuated by disputes about the accuracy of the translations,
occupied a large part of the afternoon. Contrary to expectation,
the evidence of the Government supported the accusations of
the Opposition. The papers left no room to doubt that the
French were restoring Dunkirk. Britain had protested often and
in vain. The Government had no defence but a renewed
promise from the French Crown, hastily procured within the
fortnight, to demolish all the works contrary to treaty.

The tense and agitated committee then awaited Colonel
Armstrong's testimony, which everyone expected to be the
central point of debate. To the utter astonishment of both sides,
Walpole refused to produce the chief engineer. Sir Robert
condemned the Opposition's witnesses as rogues and smugglers
but candidly admitted the truth of what the committee had
heard. He would not allow his own witness to confirm the
disclosures of his opponents. With that he left the next move to
them.

This unexpected manœuvre clearly disconcerted the 'angry
chiefs'. Surely the great Minister did not intend to default on so
critical an issue. What was his game? Wyndham had three new
witnesses at the door ready to refute Armstrong's non-existent

evidence, but why confirm what the committee believed and Walpole admitted? Sir William elected to pile Pelion upon Ossa. After severe reflections on the Ministry for procuring a postponement in order to produce testimony now withheld, he summoned his 'fresh evidence'. The committee listened till early evening to corroborative detail, including the demonstration by a wooden model of the machinery employed to cleanse Dunkirk's harbour. The Opposition's case was now complete and irrefutable. As the dinner hour approached, Wyndham moved a resolution to the effect that France had violated her treaties with Britain by carrying on the restoration of Dunkirk.

The Opposition now stood on the verge of triumph. The resolution could not fail. At this point Walpole showed his hand. Before Sandys could rise to second Sir William's motion, a ministerial janissary named Sayer moved an Address to the King, expressing thanks for his vigilance in procuring a promise from the French Crown to demolish the works carried on at Dunkirk 'without authority of that Court', and declaring satisfaction at the happy state of the Union between the two kingdoms. Sir Robert's ploy was to shift the ground of debate from the undoubted perfidy of France to the importance of maintaining the French Alliance, upon which depended the structure of peace erected over the last fifteen years. The issue now hung in the balance, for the committee would vote upon whichever motion was seconded.

Bromley for the Government and Sandys for the Opposition leapt to their feet, Sandys being perhaps a little ahead. The chairman of the committee, Richard Edgcumbe, was Walpole's man. As pre-arranged he pointed to Bromley. The malcontents protested bitterly. There ensued a lengthy wrangle over the power of the chairman to select a speaker, the Opposition contending that the committee had a right to overrule him and should do so in this case. In the end Bromley was allowed to second Sayer's motion. Walpole had tricked his enemies out of certain victory. It remained to see if he could turn the trick into a victory for the Government.

The debate was as disorderly as the session of the 11th. The Opposition concentrated their fire upon the subjection of British policy to French interests. In reply Sir Robert attacked Bolingbroke for having instigated the inquiry, and Wyndham's defence of his friend threw the committee into a prolonged orgy of recrimination that had nothing to do with the resolution on the Floor. According to Egmont, the outcome turned on two points. Many Ministerialists could not stomach the proposition that the French Crown had been ignorant of the works at Dunkirk, so Walpole picked up their support by deleting 'without authority of that Court'. Then near the end of the debate both Wyndham and William Pulteney made it plain that the intent of the inquiry was to bring down the Ministry. These declarations, thought Egmont, drove several of their previous supporters over to the Court. There may also have been a good deal in the estimate of Colonel Charles Howard, who said the majority were convinced that, though France had played Britain false, Parliament should not follow the Opposition in measures certain to rupture the Triple Alliance. Shortly before 3 a.m., after more than fourteen hours in session, the weary members divided. They carried the Government's resolution by the overwhelming majority of 270 to 149.

The whole affair finally ended in an addled anti-climax. The day before the committee on the State of the Nation resumed on 10 March, the Ministry learned that the Opposition intended to take up the business of St. Lucia. Floor and gallery were crowded as John Chetwynde moved to address the king to assert his claim to the 'neutral islands'. But the 'angry chiefs', finding the Ministry well prepared, had no stomach for another major engagement. They did not press the question. Government speakers asked derisively if they wished the committee kept open for any further revelations. The Opposition sulkily declined. The Ministry then easily carried a motion that the chairman leave the chair. Sir Robert had as usual proved too adroit for his enemies, but Hervey, who experienced the anxieties of the Court throughout the affair, admitted that 'this Dunkirk storm' came 'very near shipwrecking the administration'.

Other Motions of Censure

Struggles in committees of the whole House always became tests of the solidity of the Court party. The Opposition leaders knew that, as long as Walpole could hold his troops together, no resolution of censure would pass. Hence they reserved the grand committee for spectacular issues which might split the

Courtiers and win over Independents. To censure the administration in lesser matters the 'angry chiefs' often moved for a select committee. They clung to the hope, as in the last stage of the Excise battle, that a small investigating board, upon which they might place some of their partisans, would bring in a damning report. At various times the Opposition called for select committees to inquire into such subjects as the public debt, the navy estimates, the erection of new offices, the affairs of the South Sea Company, Spanish depredations, and the negotiations leading to the Convention of the Pardo.[1] No findings damaging to the administration ever came to light. Walpole controlled the membership of the few committees that were appointed. In other cases he either defeated the motion or contrived to have the matter referred to a grand committee. The Opposition had to rest content with claims to moral victory for having shown that the Government must have had something heinous to hide.

Motions for select committees and papers called for the production of evidence with which to indict the Ministry. Another common form of attack, the presentation of a petition, was in fact a ready-made indictment in itself. Most petitions came from economic interests aggrieved by Government policy, but since they very often appeared in connexion with some measure upon which the Opposition had determined to make a stand, it seems likely that the malcontents encouraged or perhaps inspired the worded protests. The multifarious petitions from soapmakers, bakers, tea dealers, city financiers, East and West Indies merchants, American colonies and the like, brought in by Anti-courtiers, usually formed part of a concerted assault on the financial or foreign policy of the Government.[2] This tactic being normally a 'set piece', the debates were long and heated. Walpole generally had such petitions either rejected at once or tabled, which was called 'decent riddance' because tabled

---

[1] *P.H.* viii. 501–2; ix. 151, 823–38, 1005–16; xi. 491–509; *Commons Journals*, xxi. 233, 411; xxiii. 473; *H.M.C., Trevor MSS.*, pp. 40–41; *H.M.C., Carlisle MSS.*, p. 58; *H.M.C., Hare MSS.*, pp. 255–6. Oglethorpe's famous Select Committee on Gaols of 1729–30, though it included several malcontents, had nothing to do with partisan politics. The death of a debtor friend imprisoned in the Fleet impelled Oglethorpe to press for the committee.

[2] *Commons Journals*, xxi. 423, 654, 657; xxii. 66, 79, 230; xxiii. 248–9, 514; *P.H.* viii. 800–2, 859–60, 1261–5; ix. 236–62; x. 561–73, 1050–90, 579–82. *H.M.C., Egmont Diary*, i. 65–71, 340–1; ii. 19–20.

petitions could not be reconsidered in the same session. The Opponents nevertheless achieved their main goals. They gained favour with important interests, and they spread the impression that the mighty Minister would not suffer the House to redress the grievances of the people.

Motions designed to produce a similar effect were resolutions or addresses to the Crown requesting a change of policy, not for the benefit of particular groups, but for the supposed welfare of the whole nation. The 'angry chiefs' employed these tactics to raise issues of a particularly critical nature. Outstanding examples were the addresses to increase the Prince's allowance in 1737 and to remove Walpole from office in 1741. On several occasions the malcontents moved to ask the King to reduce the army or to dismiss his foreign troops. All met defeat. During the negotiations for the Treaty of Seville, the Opposition demanded a clause requiring the King of Spain to renounce his claims to Gibraltar and Minorca. The sensitivity on this point obliged Sir Robert to let it pass after he had 'softened' the wording by amendment. He accorded the same treatment to Pulteney's resolutions concerning the freedom of the seas in 1738, but after the declaration of war in the next year he allowed Wyndham's strong resolutions on the same subject to pass unaltered.[1]

These motions always brought on major trials of strength. The significance of the issues, the shrewd wording of the questions, and the careful preparations of the Anti-courtiers made them crucial affairs for the Government. Sir Robert managed to survive them all, but at times only by narrow margins, at other times only by bending with the wind.

Parliamentary Craftsmanship

Parliamentary procedure, as it had evolved by the eighteenth century, offered many angles of assault upon the Government. Those reviewed above comprise the chief methods employed in the 'patriots'' prepared attacks, but they also regularly exploited every advantage offered by the rules of the House. The effect of their tactics was to increase the subtleties and

[1] For these examples see *Commons Journals*, xxi. 285, 749; xxii. 26, 542, 760; xxiii. 134, 648; *P.H.* viii. 1188–90; ix. 1016, 1352–1448; x. 643–728; xi. 213–47, 1223–1303; *H.M.C., Carlisle MSS.*, pp. 59, 66; *H.M.C., Egmont Diary*, ii. 227, 354–6, 475; *H.M.C., Trevor MSS.*, pp. 4–5.

complexities of parliamentary practice. The frequent disputes about procedure during tense debates show that the Opposition often made unusual or unprecedented use of standard forms and that the Government resorted to similar expedients in self-defence. The most interesting case, which clearly reveals the attitude of the members, occurred in 1731.

The Opposition moved to address the Crown for a copy of a supposed declaration sent by Spain to France, in which Spain declared herself no longer bound by the Treaty of Seville. The Ministry replied, quite rightly, that the House could not ask for papers which the Crown did not officially possess. Since their only purpose was to accuse the Government of neglecting Britain's treaty rights, the malcontents pressed their motion. The Secretary at War, Sir William Yonge, then proposed an amendment by which the address merely asked if the treaty were still in force. After much debate, the motion as amended was called for. Then, as recounted by Egmont, the old Anti-courtier, Sir Wilfred Lawson, who often spoke to points of order,

got up and opposed the amended question, as wholly unparliamentary to alter any question with intention declared to spoil it and throw it out. He said questions were to be amended to make them better and to pass them, but to alter them only to spoil them was a parliamentary artifice of late date to serve the turn of parties. He remembered when the House would not suffer such things, even when the design of altering a question to throw it out was concealed; when he had said this, he declared he was also against putting even the first question unamended, because it was also a rule of Parliament not to put a question after, on debate, such question had an amendment proposed.

Sir William Young [*sic*] said that as he had moved the amendment, he thought himself obliged to vindicate himself, since that gentlemen had called it a parliamentary craft. He acknowledged he meant it so, but parties had made it necessary, for craft has been so much used by great craftsmen (alluding to Will. Pulteney, who is allowed to have a hand in that anti-ministerial paper called *The Craftsman*), that it became necessary to encounter them with their own weapons.[1]

Further discussion led the Speaker to interpose. Yonge withdrew his amendment and proposed another. The House then threw out the reamended motion by a large majority.

[1] *H.M.C., Egmont Diary*, i. 147.

Intensive exploitation of procedural rules points up an important aspect of the campaign waged by the 'angry chiefs': their determination to press every advantage within the framework of established forms. In only two important instances did they depart from strict loyalty to parliamentary rules. First, against an ancient standing order of the House the 'patriots' caballed with foreign envoys to procure intelligence with which to attack the Ministry. It is beyond doubt that Pulteney and Wyndham kept in regular communication with Austrian agents and sometimes conspired with emissaries from Spain.[1] Second, in protest against the approval of the Spanish Convention in 1739 a large bloc of the malcontents seceded from the Commons for the remainder of the session. They were sternly reprimanded by the Speaker, who declared 'that this secession destroyed the rule of Parliament on which all government depended, which is that the minority should yield to the majority'.[2]

For both of these practices there was abundant precedent. Though highly questionable, neither was precisely illegal. But they were serious mistakes. Walpole's intelligence system kept him well informed of the meetings between Opposition leaders and foreign envoys. He once had an Austrian agent recalled for intriguing with Pulteney, and when sure of his data he taunted the malcontents in Parliament with their disloyalty.[3] Moreover, it is doubtful if they gained any information that seriously incommoded the Minister.

The secession produced a very unfavourable reaction. It was roundly condemned by the Court party as well as the Speaker, and many of the 'patriots' themselves did not favour it. At the same time it proved a boon to Sir Robert. He observed that 'many useful and popular acts . . . were greatly forwarded and

---

[1] The standing order laid down in 1643 reads, 'Resolved that this House do declare that it is a constant and ancient rule and order of this House that no member of this House ought to receive or give any visit to any foreign agent or ambassador or any other person that vows himself to be a public agent or ambassador without the leave and consent of the House': *Commons Journals*, iii. 384; For the intrigues see *H.M.C., Kenyon MSS.*, pp. 468–9; Sedgwick, ed., *Memoirs of Lord Hervey*, ii. 519–21; Coxe, *Walpole*, i. 258–60, 361, 442–4, 577–8; ii. 336, 687; iii. 138–40, 156, 202, 318; Realey, *Early Opposition to Walpole*, pp. 198–9; Michael, *Englische Geschichte*, iv. 54–55.

[2] *H.M.C., Egmont Diary*, iii. 43.

[3] Sedgwick, ed., *Memoirs of Lord Hervey*, ii. 358–9; Coxe, *Walpole*, i. 420–1; *H.M.C., Egmont Diary*, iii. 345–7.

facilitated by the secession of these gentlemen'. The Minister had one of his serious bouts of illness that spring, and some Courtiers thought that the absence of the Opposition saved his life.[1]

With these disastrous exceptions the malcontents played the game within the rules, even if they sometimes stretched the rules to cover their activities. Walpole's opponents set the tactical standards for all future Oppositions under the Hanoverians. No other politicians in this era ever improved upon their modes of attack, though weaker ministries and more propitious circumstances sometimes allowed greater success; and no others imitated their departures from parliamentary practice without suffering a similar fate. The Anti-courtiers of the 1730's fought a hard fight but a fair one. By showing what could be done under the established laws of procedure they pointed the way for the loyal Oppositions of succeeding parliaments.

The Tone of Parliamentary Proceedings

As political struggles were conducted along these lines for seventeen years, with only slight shifts in the personnel of the contesting sides, there came a gradual softening of the tone of the procedings at St. Stephen's. Much bitterness still existed, but it was no longer the deep, mistrustful, vindictive hatred so prevalent in earlier periods. Rarely did the Speaker think it necessary to enjoin two antagonists 'not to prosecute their resentment'. The duel between Hervey and Pulteney in 1731, occasioned by a satirical pamphlet, was the only celebrated engagement of the period.[2] Although critical debates sometimes produced strong language, outbursts of passion, and scenes of wild disorder, there were no parliamentary martyrs. The House, increasingly reluctant to send members to the Tower,

---

[1] MS. Journal of Mrs. Charles Caesar, v; Rose, ed., *Marchmont Papers*, ii. 111–15, 158–61; Graham, ed., *Annals of Stair*, ii. 250–1; *H.M.C., Trevor MSS.*, p. 26; *H.M.C., Hare MSS.*, pp. 245–8; *H.M.C., Egmont Diary*, iii. 32–48; Tindal, *History of England*, viii. 403, 405, 413, 444–5; Coxe, *Walpole*, i. 604–7, 628–30; iii. 519, 607–8. The Opposition probably intended their withdrawal to be a brief demonstration, like the secessions of the past. They expected to be summoned by a call of the House, set for a few days after they absented themselves, but to embarrass them Walpole had the call postponed. A few of the seceders reappeared to deal with Bills of interest to their constituents, but they did not return *en masse* until the next session, after they had brought out several pamphlets justifying their action.

[2] *H.M.C., Carlisle MSS.*, p. 80; *H.M.C., Egmont Diary*, i. 221, 263.

preferred to maintain its normal decorum by accepting lame 'explanations' of heated indiscretions. One cannot escape the impression that, despite the intense struggle for power, nerves were quieter and tempers calmer than they had been before.

It would seem that the expanding complacency of Georgian England, so evident in the universities, the Church, and the literary world, had invaded the chambers at Westminster. As Parliament grew in the conviction that it was the greatest of senates, a deepening sense of security tended to withhold members from extremes. The influence of individuals reinforced the *Zeitgeist*. Speaker Onslow, whose long reign began in 1728, sought constantly to impress the House with the need for 'civility', 'propriety', 'decency and decorum'.[1] The Treasury Bench presented a panel of mild and gentle orators. Men like Pelham, Horace Walpole, Strickland, and Yonge, who bore much of the burden of debate, inclined rather to timidity than to violence. And probably more important than any other single factor was the even temper and good humour of the great Minister.

Unlike Stanhope, Sunderland, Townshend, and the other leaders with whom he served his apprenticeship, Sir Robert never gave way to fits of ungovernable fury. He could be stern and biting when occasion demanded, but he bore insult with forbearance and took witticisms at his expense in good part. Recording a debate in 1730, Lord Egmont set down that Shippen remarked

it was good to rub ministers, for it made them brighter. Sir Robert answered, if so, he must be the brightest minister that ever was. Pulteney replied he knew nothing was brighter for rubbing but pewter and brass, alluding to Sir Robert's nickname of 'Brazen Face' —ribaldry unfit for the House.[2]

Three years later Lady Anne Irwin noted, 'Sir Robert continues to be every day affronted and exposed in the Parliament

---

[1] Hatsell, *Precedents of Proceedings*, ii. 224–5; *P.H.* viii. 1183–4; ix. 256. The Opposition prepared to nominate Sandys for Speaker in 1735, perhaps to bring on a trial of strength, but gave it up (Graham, ed., *Annals of Stair*, ii. 219–20). When the Government renominated Onslow in 1741, Horace Walpole reported, 'the Opposition, to flatter his pretence to popularity and impartiality, call him their own Speaker' (Lewis, ed., *Horace Walpole's Correspondence with Sir Horace Mann*, i. 220).

[2] *H.M.C., Egmont Diary*, i. 9; *H.M.C., Carlisle MSS.*, p. 65.

House, which he bears with patience because he carries his point in every question.'[1] His equanimity in defeat was equally striking. The Minister also showed great skill in turning the extravagances of the Opposition against themselves. In 1730 Shippen courted another sojourn in the Tower with some coarse remarks about Hanoverian militarism. As an angry dispute was about to erupt, Walpole rose to declare that, though a long debate had been anticipated, he thought members so shocked that they should go to the question without further discussion. An immediate division was taken. Numerous malcontents dissociated themselves from Shippen by abstaining or voting with the Government, and the Ministry carried its question by a large majority.[2]

The softened tone of proceedings thus produced by mutual restraint seems to have a significance beyond itself. It suggests that political opponents had come to a realization that the contest for power was taking place amid agreement on fundamentals. With the possible exception of Walpole himself, who ultimately escaped vengeance with the connivance of his enemies, members came to feel less and less that politics deeply affected the security of their lives, properties, or beliefs. Britons now regarded a divided House as a normal state of affairs instead of a lamentable aberration or a symptom of disloyalty. Not that they yet considered an office-seeking Opposition to be a permanent or desirable institution. Rather, with the sophistication of their time, they looked upon the parliamentary rivalry of professional politicians as a natural thing, and, since it was no longer war to the knife, a thing to be accepted.[3]

3. THE DEFEAT OF WALPOLE

Now, it is against the general background of parliamentary operations and attitudes that we must view the ultimate success

---

[1] *H.M.C., Carlisle MSS.*, p. 102.

[2] Ibid., pp. 66–67; *P.H.* viii. 771–3; *H.M.C., Egmont Diary*, i. 11–12.

[3] An interesting example of the polite regulation of party warfare occurred during the Dunkirk Inquiry of 1730. During the debate of 27–28 Feb., Egmont recounted, 'the lateness of the night obliged about thirty members to leave the House before the question was put, each taking away with him one of the contrary side' (*H.M.C., Egmont Diary*, i. 74–75). This is the earliest example I have discovered of 'pairing'. In 1743 the House rejected a proposed resolution against 'pairing' (*Commons Journals*, xxiv. 602), and thereafter it became an accepted practice.

of Opposition tactics—the overthrow of Walpole. The tactical pattern of the 'patriots'' victory was much the same as in the years of their defeats. They did not in the final hour develop new devices to shock the Government, nor did the Minister's defences suddenly crumble to make way for an easy triumph. Indeed, the Opposition started down the path to success when their morale had reached the lowest point in the immediate aftermath of the disastrous miscarriage of 'the motion' in 1741. What occurred in effect was this: the long irregular campaign against the Minister had produced a situation which, capitalizing upon their experience, the 'patriots' were able to exploit to the fullest advantage.

The Election of 1741

The first important element in the situation was the election of 1741. Parliament was dissolved in April, and within a few weeks the state of the new House became reasonably clear. So deeply had partisan spirit penetrated the Commons that for the moment there was no sizeable body of Independents. The rivals could reckon very closely how each member would vote on major issues, making allowance for only a small number of 'doubtfuls'. Dodington called this 'the most equally balanced Parliament that ever was returned in England, upon paper I mean'.[1] Other calculations approximated his. Majorities would depend upon the fullness of attendance, the behaviour of the 'doubtfuls', and the outcome of election petitions. The margins of victory, whoever carried the day, would be slight. Contemporary estimates founded upon optimum attendance varied from a majority of 9 for the Opposition to 16 for the Ministry. Owen's careful modern study indicates that, on the basis of 553 returns, the Government outnumbered its enemies by no more than 18.[2]

No election since the accession had given the Opposition such strength. The Government had not faced so precarious a situation since the days of the 'narrow-bottom' ministry and the South Sea crisis.[3] In the latter years of George I the malcontents

---

[1] Coxe, *Walpole*, iii. 565–6. Cf. Add. MSS. 35876, ff. 138–9; Tindal, *History of England*, viii. 499–500.   [2] Owen, *Rise of the Pelhams*, pp. 6–7.

[3] The following figures on the strength of Government and Opposition are based upon the divisions recorded in *P.H.*, *Commons Journals*, and the contemporary letters and diaries cited so frequently above.

normally mustered about 85. Minorities seldom passed 100. On major questions the Ministry swamped them with 225 to 285 votes. George II's first election reproduced the same balance of strength in 1728 and at the opening of the session of 1729. Then began an uneven but perceptible increase in the size of minorities. Before that session closed the Opposition had several times voted 110 to 140 on Country party issues. From 1730 through 1733 (setting aside the Excise struggle as an exception) their maximum strength stood at about 170, and in 1734 it reached 184. The average majority fell off slightly during this period, but at the end of the Parliament Walpole could still count on 250 to 260 in crucial matters. Thus it would seeem that the Opposition picked up roughly 100, partly from Government defectors and partly from better attendance (particularly on the part of the Tories) and that Sir Robert held his strength by whipping in a higher proportion of his loyal followers.

In the election of 1734 the Anti-courtiers held their gains, dividing 185 at the beginning of the new Parliament. Thereafter they approximated full strength only in the major drive of each session, but on two crucial issues they passed 200. 'The glorious 204' supported the address for an increased allowance to the Prince in 1737, and two years later the minorities on the Spanish Convention rose to 207, 208, 214, and 232. Against their greatest effort (setting aside 'the motion' as an exception) Walpole could still bring in 260 votes.[1] Since the Court party sustained its strength, it appears that the Opposition was drawing in absentees and Independents. And since the idea still persisted that a stable ministry should be able to count upon a minimal 60-vote margin of victory,[2] it was clear that the malcontents seriously threatened the security of Walpole's régime.

The election of 1741 then further narrowed the gap between the two sides. The turn-over in the constituencies was not spectacular. In the aggregate the Government lost only 12 seats, thereby reducing its margin by 24.[3] What was remarkable

[1] Owen (*Rise of the Pelhams*, pp. 5–6) estimates that immediately before the dissolution Walpole had a majority of 42 in a full House (300–258). But all members were never present. During the last session of the 1734 Parliament, when attendance was fairly strong, Government majorities on straight partisan issues ranged from 16 to 104.

[2] Rose, ed., *Marchmont Papers*, ii. 67; Coxe, *Walpole*, iii. 578.

[3] Owen, *Rise of the Pelhams*, pp. 6–7.

was that the Opposition could increase at all. Looking backward one may see a portent in the returns of 1734, when for the first time since the beginning of Anne's reign the Anti-courtiers not only held their own but carried more election petitions than the Ministry.[1] Three things may account for this result. First, the hardening of attitude in the early 1730's which determined that malcontents returned by themselves or friends (and whom the Government had not tried to oust or had failed to oust) would persist in opposition. Second, the increased number of those permanently alienated by the policy and 'system' of Sir Robert, particularly the influential aristocrats dismissed or disgruntled after the Excise affair. Third, occasional seats gained by strenuous Opposition campaigns, especially in the more populous constituencies. Now all these factors were also operative in 1741. Old Anti-courtiers did not waver in their opposition. Walpole continued to lose support because of the unsuccessful conduct of the war and the unpopularity of his policy in *causes célèbres* like the Porteous riots. The Opposition victory at Westminster (finally achieved in a re-election when the Ministerial candidates withdrew) provides a good example of how a vigorous struggle sometimes gained new seats. As in 1734 these factors enabled the Anti-courtiers substantially to maintain their strength. A novel factor explains their increase.

In 1741 the influence of the Crown was divided against itself. The Prince of Wales threw his interest and his purse into the scales against ministerial candidates. The Government was thereby deprived of support upon which it could hitherto depend. One cannot estimate precisely the importance of the Prince's contribution, for the size and distribution of his finances is not known. The need for election funds is always so pressing that whatever he provided was a significant asset. In one area, however, Frederick's influence is clear. His Duchy of Cornwall, where he made his major effort, returned ten additional members for the Opposition.

There was a somewhat analogous state of affairs in Scotland. The Duke of Argyll, who with his brother Islay had previously managed the elections for the Government in north Britain, used the full weight of his influence and prestige on behalf of Opposition candidates. Though he could no longer dispense

---

[1] Sedgwick, ed., *Memoirs of Lord Hervey*, ii. 417–20.

royal patronage, Argyll evidently carried with him, in addition to his own interest, much of the support he had previously acquired with ministerial assistance. Thus he split the interest formerly at the disposal of the Court, and the malcontents won an increase of twelve Scots members.

In the rest of the United Kingdom the Government and its opponents traded small gains and losses to swell the total number of Courtiers by 10. The 22 new Anti-courtiers brought in by the efforts of Frederick and Argyll, therefore, account for the aggregate Opposition gain of 12.[1] These results would appear to discredit the old charge that Walpole, overconfident as a result of his victory on 'the motion', neglected the elections in 1741.[2] On the contrary, he must have made the most of the resources left to the Court, for, had he not lost a substantial part of the Crown's normal influence in Cornwall and Scotland, he would have obtained a majority greater than he had possessed at the end of the previous Parliament.

The closing of the polls was followed by an apparent political lull which lasted into the opening day of the session in December. Few documents survive to indicate the attitudes and activities of the different sections of the malcontent coalition. The little we know suggests that their behaviour was normal, quite consistent with their conduct in previous years. The Tories as usual made no move. Pulteney flatly declined to act.[3] Did he hope for an offer from the Government? Though there is no evidence to prove that at this time he was in communication with any ministerial dissidents,[4] the political world knew that the divisions in the administration were more sharply defined than ever. Given the uncertain equipoise of the two coalitions, one Court faction might seek to weigh down the balance by negotiating for additional strength from the Opposition. The completion of such a transaction before a trial of numbers in the

[1] This analysis of the election of 1741 is derived from the admirable study by Owen in *Rise of the Pelhams*, pp. 4–9.

[2] Coxe, *Walpole*, i. 683, 687.   [3] Ibid. iii. 576–7.

[4] In Add. MSS. 33002, ff. 95–96, there is a memorandum from Newcastle to Hardwicke, apparently drawn up in October or November 1741, consisting of a list of topics to be discussed against the opening of Parliament. The first two items are 'Mr. Pulteney and Ld. Carteret. The scheme of opposition for this session'. No sound inference can be drawn from such cryptic notes, and I know of no other document which even suggests the possibility of communication between the Pulteney–Carteret bloc and any ministerial group at this time.

House would make it appear that the Court acted from grace instead of necessity. Might not a quiescent instead of a bellicose Pulteney improve any spirit of accommodation? If he did not have some such idea in mind, Pulteney must simply have fallen into one of the irrational moods of his unstable temperament.

Among the 'broad bottoms' hope was mingled with despair. Chesterfield and Stair, for example, saw that the election results offered an unprecedented opportunity. As always they preached 'concert, concord, and unanimity'. But they feared their divisions would never heal, and they dreaded desertion by the Carteret–Pulteney bloc.[1] Only Dodington, the most recent defector from the Government, quickly evinced a spirit of strong determination. By mid-June he had worked out an elaborate plan of campaign, which for a time he propagated vigorously among Opposition leaders. His remarkable scheme, in essence a summary of lessons learned by the malcontents during their long years in the wilderness, merits careful attention.[2]

Dodington's Scheme

Dodington called first for a meeting of 8 or 10 chiefs 'with all convenient speed, at London, as the place of the least observation'. To be invited were 6 Tories, 3 'broad bottoms', Pulteney and Sandys, a city merchant, and a 'Prince's man'. At the outset they should correct and verify their lists of members, and, having identified the doubtfuls and waverers, determine the best methods of bringing them over to opposition. Next, they must select two major points of attack, one to be chosen by the Tories, for use at the opening of the session. No interval should be allowed for the coalition to disintegrate or for Walpole to steady his ranks. 'Those who give an ill minister time, give him everything.' Dodington would not contest the Speakership 'because it is not a point of the utmost consequence to carry but it may be so to lose'. He contended rather for the choice of 'popular and national' issues to be pushed immediately after Onslow's re-election.

Having taken these decisions, the chiefs should disperse to

---

[1] Graham, ed., *Annals of Stair*, ii. 274–80; Dobrée, ed., *Letters of Chesterfield*, ii. 467–9.

[2] Dodington expounded his plan in a letter to Argyll dated 18 June 1741: Coxe, *Walpole*, iii. 566–76.

effectuate them. The summer was to be spent in fixing doubtfuls and waverers and in imparting the tactical plan to all of
the Country party. At this point Dodington urged the correction of two traditional errors. First, private business and
pleasure must no longer absorb gentlemen between sessions.
Unless they take time for political preparation nothing can be
accomplished. Second, all sections and levels of the coalition
must be informed of proposed measures. 'I much doubt, in
Oppositions particularly,' he wrote, 'if there does not more
mischief arise by disobliging people and furnishing plausible
handles of desertion from want of communication than there
does from the indiscretion or treachery that may be the consequence of communication.'

The chiefs should then reassemble at Bath in the autumn to
evaluate the results of their summer's labours and to make
detailed plans for the session, so that they 'come to Parliament
armed and prepared against all events'. The usual haphazard,
unrepresentative meeting in town shortly before or after the
opening will not serve. The leaders must plan well in advance
to achieve the first requisite of success, namely, 'an entire
coalition'. They need fear neither that Walpole will regain
popularity by a change of policy nor that he will 'take off'
opponents with bribes and offices. But they must guard against
'his great talent at dividing and sowing dissensions'. Whereas
the Court party may be compared to a regular army, the Anti-
courtiers are but a militia, which the Minister can render
ineffective by exploiting old jealousies and suspicions. To attain
solid and lasting unity Dodington recommended that at the
autumn meeting the leaders prepare several specific measures
for implementation when members come to town.

From the first there must be a systematic effort 'to create as
total and entire a separation between the parties as possible'.
Dodington frowned upon private friendships between political
enemies. How could the world think the malcontents in earnest
if they shared their pleasures with those they attacked in
Parliament? What was worse, the amicable association of
courtiers with any bloc of the Opposition aroused suspicion
among the others. Therefore, let an impassable gulf divide
malcontent and ministerialist, and let there be a great increase
in 'our connexion and habitude with each other'. The lord

should entertain the commoner on a footing of equality and accept his hospitality in return. Those who have establishments in town should provide quarters for those who do not. Intercourse among the Anti-courtiers should be 'cheerful, communicative, and, above all, frequent'.

To this end the chiefs should also encourage the institution of 'clubs'. Dodington's use of the term is rather obscure. He may have meant assemblies of the entire Country party or simply convivial gatherings of various groups for common purposes. In either case he intended regularly scheduled meetings which took precedence over 'private engagements', and he was specific upon one aspect of their function. He would have a club 'instituted to watch over and defend elections: upon this the whole depends. . . . Therefore all earliest endeavours must be used to inculcate the attendance upon this club, and to make it infamous to desert an election.'

Finally, both in formal and informal association the chiefs should inculcate into all Anti-courtiers three vital precepts. First, Walpole is not invincible. The Opposition has the power to bring him down if zeal is not wanting. Second, the distinctions of Whig and Tory have lost their meaning. The 'charm' of the names alone divides the malcontents. To extirpate these invidious terms will be difficult, but in the interests of unity no effort must be spared to root them out. Third, all denominations shall share in the Opposition's ultimate triumph. The Tories must be given unmistakably to understand that they are considered, not a 'scaffolding' for the 'patriots'' climb to power, but 'brothers in pretensions'.

Clearly Dodington had adopted the 'broad-bottom' doctrine entire. The measures he proposed can be found scattered throughout the correspondence of Stair, Chesterfield, Marchmont, and their group during the preceding five years. Dodington's contribution was to bring their ideas and the long experience of the Opposition together in one coherent scheme adapted to the situation in 1741. His plan, though not original, comprehends the most advanced thought of the time upon the organization of an Opposition party. Until changes occurred in the structure of politics upon which it was predicated, no one could do more than adapt its proposals to the circumstances of other years.

The indifference and suspicion of the 'angry chiefs' blocked the initiation of Dodington's scheme. After several vain efforts to gain support from Pulteney and his friends, Dodington abandoned all hope in mid-July and retired disgruntled to the country. The various elements in the coalition thus faced the opening of Parliament in the usual state of disarray. Their conduct in the first days of the session revealed a growing but still imperfect co-ordination. Then, in a surprisingly short space of time, the Opponents drew their forces together and launched the united campaign that drove Walpole from office. It was a campaign shrewdly devised and cleverly executed, very close to the course of action which Dodington had previously urged with so little effect.

The Opening of the Session

On 1 December 1741 Onslow was re-elected Speaker without opposition. The first skirmish came three days later in the Lords, the secondary theatre of operations, where Chesterfield and Argyll forced a division on the Address. The Government's victory by 45 votes confirmed the anticipated alignment of forces in the Upper House. The Commons debate on the Address on 8 December made it clear that Pulteney, once more shifting his ground, had determined to resume the lead, but that 'patriots' and Tories, though inclined to co-operation, had not yet concerted measures. Shippen and Lord Noel Somerset pressed an amendment, the former declaring 'that he loved divisions'. Pulteney did not want to risk a trial of strength. Either he feared a defeat or hoped that restraint might encourage a negotiation with the Ministry. His witty remark that 'dividing was not the way to multiply' persuaded the Tories to drop their motion.[1] Pulteney nevertheless joined Gybbon in a savage attack on Walpole and his conduct of the war—'by way of brief and instructions to the new members', thought Tindal,[2] but also as a threatening portent of future intentions.

In the uncertain state of affairs Sir Robert showed equal caution. He accepted an amendment without a division, then challenged Pulteney to prove his accusations by calling for a committee on the State of the Nation. Pulteney took up the gage, Walpole seconded him, and the date was set for 21

[1] Coxe, Walpole, iii. 581.   [2] Tindal, *History of England*, viii. 527.

January. The Minister had thus driven his opponents to make their first positive move.

From this point forward the Opposition rapidly developed cohesion. The first mention of a general gathering appears in a ministerialist's letter of 10 December, in which was reported 'a hotch-potch meeting of Tories and "patriots" t'other day, 210 were present, and 25 sent excuses who were willing but not able to attend'.[1] Another general assembly took place on 16 December.[2] Thereafter, Tindal reported, the malcontents 'formed themselves into regular assemblies and meetings to concert the means of maintaining, improving, and pursuing their success'.[3] The results of their organization were to be seen in their parliamentary conduct: steady full attendance, augmented by a few recruits from waverers and absentees, and a systematic plan of attack.

The Opposition's Plan of Attack

In this plan as it unfolded there were three main points. First, to maintain a united front on election matters. How the House decided on the petitions involving 57 seats from 46 constituencies would determine whether Government or Opposition gained a majority.[4] Second, to concentrate a steady assault on the misconduct of the war. This was to be the main 'popular point' upon which to arouse public opinion. Third, to bring the attack home to Sir Robert by calling for papers upon which to ground a specific indictment of his policy. Mindful of their recent failure to convict him on general charges, the malcontents reverted to their earlier tactic of seeking evidence for a prosecution.

How the Opposition worked out this strategy we cannot say. There are no records of their private or general meetings. But their plan was doubtless the product of compromise, for its cardinal virtue is plain to see: all elements in the coalition could stand together on all three points. Each faction would gladly accept the support of the others in elections. The ill

[1] Coxe, *Walpole*, iii. 582.

[2] Lewis, ed., *Horace Walpole's Correspondence with Sir Horace Mann*, i. 243.

[3] Tindal, *History of England*, viii. 528. These meetings probably took place at the Fountain Tavern in the Strand which, we know for certain, was the scene of the celebrated gatherings in February 1742.

[4] The presentation of these petitions is recorded in *Commons Journals*, xxiv. 13–36.

success of the war made its management unpopular with all. Tories had deserted the Opposition on 'the motion' of the previous February because the general accusations were unprovable at law; but they made clear their willingness to support specific charges grounded on detailed evidence. Had the climax not come within five parliamentary weeks, one may well wonder how long the coalition could have sustained its unanimity. But the programme was sufficient unto its purpose.[1]

The malcontents' successes in electoral matters are generally considered to have been decisive. Certainly Walpole took his resolution to resign after a series of reverses in elections which culminated in a defeat upon the Chippenham petition. And, equally certain, the Minister had not found himself in a minority on any other issue. Nevertheless the Opposition's remorseless assault upon the conduct of the war played an important part in his fall. These attacks kept Walpole continually on a desperate defensive, and shrewd planning prevented him from scoring any spectacular victory which might retrieve his fortunes. Lengthy debates which frustrated financial legislation, brilliant oratory from the Speaker's left, narrow divisions, and reluctant concessions from the Ministry served to deepen the nimbus of doom that gathered about the Minister's head. Indeed, it was one of the offensives on this front that set up the Chippenham petition as the fateful issue.

The Assault on the Conduct of the War

On 18 December 1741 the Opposition made its first formal motion on foreign policy. Pulteney called for the presentation of all correspondence between Austria and Britain 'relating to the state of the war in the Empire and the support and interests of the House of Austria'. By 237 to 227 the Government carried amendments to omit personal letters between the two crowned heads, and the resolution passed. The Opposition then called

[1] The main printed sources for the parliamentary struggle of 1741–2 are *P.H.* xii. 188–404; *Commons Journals,* xxiv. 7–84; *Lords Journals,* xxvi. 3–54; Coxe, *Walpole,* i. 682–97, and iii. 581–94; Lewis, ed., *Horace Walpole's Correspondence with Sir Horace Mann,* i. 219–320; *H.M.C., Egmont Diary,* iii. 232–48. There is an excellent modern account and interpretation based on these and manuscript sources in Owen, *Rise of the Pelhams,* pp. 18–40. The analysis of Walpole's fall given in the text above is devoted exclusively to the battle in the Commons, the arena of decision; but the Opposition also carried on a vigorous offensive in the Lords to support the main action.

for all correspondence with France on the same subject. The Government carried the same amendments without a division, and again the resolution passed. When the malcontents next moved for diplomatic correspondence with Prussia, the Ministry carried the previous question, 232 to 208. On 18 and 20 January 1742 the papers were laid before the House. The next day, the day set for a committee on the State of the Nation, Pulteney moved to refer the papers to a select committee.

Taken by surprise with a minority in the House, Walpole struggled to avert defeat. While the front benches debated the establishment of a 'committee of accusation' designed to indict the Minister, Government Whips scoured the vicinage for votes. In came the lame and the sick, swathed in cloths and hobbling on crutches. Each side mustered every supporter within reach. The Ministry secreted two infirm members (later joined by a third) in the chambers of the Auditor of the Exchequer, intending to bring them in for the division, but some alert 'patriot' stuffed the keyhole with sand and dirt so that the door could not be opened in time for the vote.[1] The frantic duel went on till 11 p.m., when the Opposition lost its motion, by 253 to 250.

In previous sessions a defeat in a major trial of strength had normally been followed by the disintegration of the coalition. Some ministerialists apparently expected a recurrence of the familiar pattern. One, who estimated that 37 of the 50 absentees would support the Government, anticipated a larger majority on 'a proper question' which would cause significant desertions, notably among the Scots, from the 'starving and vanquished army' of the Opponents.[2] But now they stood firm, and even before they met with this repulse, they had commenced preparations for their next drive.

On 20 January the merchants of London, Bideford, Southampton, Liverpool, and Lancaster brought in petitions complaining of inadequate protection against Spanish privateers. The House ordered them to be heard by a Committee of the Whole on 27 January, and the petitioners were permitted to appear either in person or by counsel. The Opposition then called for a mass of papers relating to naval construction, the disposition

---

[1] Coxe, *Walpole*, iii. 590; Lewis, ed., *Horace Walpole's Correspondence with Sir Horace Mann*, i. 297–300.
[2] Coxe, *Walpole*, iii. 588.

of the fleet, and the appointment of convoys. Though the Government would normally have sought to check such an onslaught, Walpole allowed all motions to pass unamended and without a division. From that point until the adjournment, the Opposition flooded the House with more petitions from London and the outports and with further requests for accounts and papers concerning diplomatic, naval, and military affairs. The Committee of the Whole sat three times to hear these documents made the basis for savage criticisms of war policy. Sir Robert continued to avoid a show-down. With the same passivity he allowed the malcontents to push also such 'Country party points' as a Place Bill and a Bill for examining the public accounts. In the face of this mounting pressure the political world understood that the next division would be crucial. The next division came upon the Chippenham petition.

The Decisive Struggle over Elections

The struggle over elections began with a short run of Government victories. On 9 and 11 December the Ministry carried divisions on the Bossiney petition by majorities of 7, 6, 12, 15, and 36. Then abruptly the trend was reversed. The Opponents had a nine-vote majority in setting a date for the Denbighshire petition on 14 December. Two days later a Government majority of 23 in a thin House was overshadowed by the Opposition's triumph in electing their man as chairman of the Committee on Privileges and Elections by 242 to 238. St. Stephen's rang with Tory and 'patriot' cries of 'Huzza! Victory!' which spread to crowds in the Lobby, the Court of Requests, the streets, and the neighbouring coffee houses.[1] The tactical importance of this triumph has probably been somewhat exaggerated, for the Commons decided the fate of petitions, not in committee, but in the House. Nevertheless, Sir Robert's defeat in a major trial of strength unquestionably damaged his prestige and greatly inspired his enemies.

The protagonists then engaged in a prolonged contest over a petition brought in by the unsuccessful Opposition candidates for Westminster. The first to be presented, it had been considered by the House on 15 December. A second hearing set for

---

[1] *H.M.C., Egmont Diary*, iii. 232–3.

two days later was postponed till the 18th. On that date Walpole secured a further adjournment by 218 to 197. After another hearing, on 22 December the House voided the election in two divisions, 220 to 216 and 220 to 215. Overriding ministerial attempts to adjourn in two more close divisions, the Opposition proceeded to carry resolutions condemning Westminster city officials and the use of troops at elections, an implied censure of the administration. The Government could not find supporters willing to oppose the 'patriot' candidates at the ensuing re-election.

After the Christmas recess Sir Robert treated electoral matters with great caution. On 19 January he dared not press a division on the Berwickshire petition and so allowed a 'patriot' to displace a ministerialist.[1] The Opposition pressed home their triumph by summoning the sheriff to be reprimanded on his knees for making an illegal return. Thereafter during the strenuous attacks on foreign policy, every petition nearing a decision was withdrawn. The Minister at length determined to take a stand on the Chippenham election on Thursday, 28 January. 'Both sides made it the decisive question', wrote young Horace Walpole.[2] The malcontents carried a technical point by one vote, 236 to 235. Over the following week-end Sir Robert decided to resign.

Still he drove his enemies to one further effort. He probably chose to prolong his tenure until the royal assent could be given to the Malt Tax and other Bills then pending in the Lords. Since negotiations for alterations in the Ministry had already begun, he may also have hoped for a reversal of form that would strengthen the hand of the ministerialists. But on Tuesday, 2 February, the Opposition won another vote on the Chippenham petition by 241 to 225. As the tellers brought the results to the table the great Minister declared to some private members that he would now retire. Next day the King assented to the two public and two private Bills passed during the stormy session, and at the royal request Parliament adjourned for two weeks to permit a reconstruction of the Ministry.

---

[1] Lewis, ed., *Horace Walpole's Correspondence with Sir Horace Mann*, i. 294.
[2] Ibid. 318.

4. CONCLUSION

Sir Robert stated clearly the reason for his resignation. To the Duke of Devonshire he wrote on 2 February,[1] 'I must inform you that the panic was so great among what I should call my own friends that *they all* declared my retiring was become absolutely necessary as the only means to carry on the public business, and this to be attended with honour and security, etc.' The Minister still retained the King's confidence, indeed his passionate loyalty, but if Walpole could not get the 'king's business' done in Parliament, the machinery of state as constituted in 1742 would break down. Therefore, he must go.

The decision thus framed reflects important political and constitutional developments over the previous four decades. In earlier times, the Crown had optional courses of action. The Stuarts had often abandoned their 'business' rather than their ministers when the Commons proved intransigent. By 1742 administration required parliamentary sanction in so many spheres that the Crown could not govern independently. The imperative need for annual supply, all the greater in time of war, and the debt structure of the monarchy, made it impossible for the Crown to rule constitutionally without the passage of financial legislation. Nor could the King any longer maintain a military establishment by life grants, hereditary revenues, and foreign subsidies. Had the contest between Walpole and his opponents continued through the spring, the malcontents, who were loyal to the State, might not have refused Supply. The Malt Tax had passed easily. But indefinite postponement of other financial Bills, which the 'angry chiefs' clearly intended, carried the threats of confusion and inadequacy, if not of ultimate denial.[2] In 1742, even had there been no war, the King could not abandon his 'business'.

---

[1] Coxe, *Walpole*, iii. 592.

[2] In a private conversation on 24 Sept. 1742, Sandys told Perceval 'that Sir Robert . . . , if he had ever come to the Supplies, would have carried them. So that their [the malcontents'] only art was to defer them from day to day, and that he [Sandys] always said that if out of prudence or fear, he [Walpole] did not retire before, their endeavours had been in vain, and he would have stood his ground.' (P.R.O., Egmont MSS. 212, f. 2ᵛ.) Though Walpole intimated that he dared to call the bluff, those who persuaded him to resign were convinced, in Newcastle's words, 'that it was evident Sir Robert could not any longer answer for the success of the King's business in the House of Commons' (Coxe, *Pelham*, i. 473). In the

Another option sanctioned by tradition was a dissolution. The monarch's right to replace a refractory Parliament with one more likely to support him, so often exercised in the past, stood unchallenged. In addition to delay and inconvenience, two factors militated against this course of action. The political world had become attached to the 'Septennial Convention'.[1] A dissolution, however legal, would have been unpopular with both sides. It would certainly have come under attack as an unwarranted use of the Prerogative, a questionable expedient to save a royal favourite. The blame would have fallen upon Walpole, and so, in one sense, a dissolution might have defeated its own purpose by increasing his unpopularity. In another sense it was likely to fail of its purpose. Coming so soon upon the heels of the election of 1741, with the tide of opinion running against Sir Robert and no increase in the 'influence of the Crown' to support its own adherents, the Ministry stood little chance of improving its position. Both political convention and practical politics made a dissolution quite unfeasible.

A third option, much more in line with eighteenth-century practice, was to strengthen the Government by detaching some segment of the Opposition. Walpole had, in fact, tried to do so during the Christmas recess. Through intermediaries he had endeavoured to 'take off' the Prince of Wales with an increase in his allowance, payment of his debts, and a promise that his friends would be received at Court in return for Frederick's submission to the King. No stipulations were made concerning places for the Prince's faction, but had he accepted the offer, his following would have gone over to the Court by some form of 'treaty'. Frederick declined to negotiate until Sir Robert had departed from the King's counsels.[2] The failure of this manœuvre left the Minister with nowhere else to turn. If Pulteney and Carteret would deal with him, which seemed most unlikely by January, the Minister was no more willing to 'accommodate' them than he had been for so many years before.

There was thus no practical alternative to resignation. The parliamentary Opposition had by parliamentary methods numerous discussions of the situation by Opposition and ministerialists alike, there is no hint that anyone thought the crisis could be solved by sacrificing the King's business.

[1] Betty Kemp, *King and Commons, 1660-1832* (London, 1957), pp. 41–51.
[2] H.M.C., *Egmont Diary*, iii. 238–9; Coxe, *Walpole*, iii. 585.

brought down the King's Minister, and neither parliamentary nor extra-parliamentary devices could prevent his fall.

In the final session the malcontents did not outnumber the ministerialists, but the coalition had maintained the greater solidarity. Absentees from the Government benches accounted for the very narrow margins of victory and defeat. These were the waverers—'a parcel of such shabby fellows that will not attend', said Hartington[1]—'men, who would not care to find themselves on the weaker side, contrary to their intent', said young Horace Walpole.[2] The Ministry might perhaps have had twenty more votes, while the malcontents seem to have come much closer to mustering their maximum available strength for the crucial divisions.[3] What is more, the Opposition's offensive had *created* the waverers. By pressing Sir Robert so hard the 'angry chiefs' had forced the 'doubtfuls', who normally would have supported him, to stand like Derby at Bosworth to await the outcome. Finally, even had the waverers attended, Walpole would have remained in a precarious situation as long as the coalition held together. He would still have fallen short of the minimum majority of 60 deemed 'safe' by contemporaries. The Government would, therefore, have faced conditions which the 'narrow-bottom Ministry' of 1717–20 had found intolerable.

In sum, the Opponents had learned and applied so well the arts of party management and parliamentary tactics that they had driven out the greatest party manager and parliamentary tactician of the age. The victory had required much time, great effort, and not a little good fortune. Walpole's own intransigence had contributed significantly to his own fall—a fact not lost upon his successors. But it must not be forgotten that the malcontents had ousted a Minister, not a ministry; that the contest had been primarily one between men, not measures; and that the victors were a motley coalition, who had sunk their differences only momentarily to achieve their end. The conditions of victory were profoundly to affect its results.

---

[1] Coxe, *Walpole*, i. 590–1.

[2] Lewis, ed., *Horace Walpole's Correspondence with Sir Horace Mann*, i. 243.

[3] Owen, *Rise of the Pelhams*, pp. 20–34, carefully analyses all available data and concludes that it was the defection of these waverers that 'made it possible for the opposition to gain the upper hand'.

VI

BROAD BOTTOM

1742–1760

VI

BROAD BOTTOM

1742–1760

1. THE RECONSTRUCTION OF 1742

As soon as Walpole made known his decision to resign, the King authorized negotiations for a treaty with the Opposition. Thus began the conventional procedure for the reconstruction of a Ministry.

There were in the situation many elements similar to those present in earlier ministerial crises, particularly to the previous great crisis in 1720. To carry on the King's business the Court party was obliged to broaden its bottom by taking in some of its opponents. To make room for them some placemen would have to be sacrificed. The Court possessed the initiative in determining with whom to treat, but circumstances pointed strongly to those most prominent in the parliamentary Opposition. The Court had also to reckon with the Prince of Wales, for whom the malcontents would certainly make stipulations.

But years of conflict between the Minister and the Opposition blocs had introduced significant differences. The Anti-courtiers had concentrated their fire upon Walpole, whose position corresponded more closely to that of Clarendon or Danby than to that of Sunderland or Stanhope. The outstanding figure in the Opposition, Pulteney, was inhibited by an unprecedented pledge not to take office. In 1720 the groups in opposition had been neither co-ordinated in a common effort, nor (with the exception of the die-hard Jacobites) were they divided by antagonistic doctrines concerning the correct constitutional means of reconstruction. Now broad but imperfectly defined obligations bound the three malcontent factions, who were at the same time riven by the incompatibility of 'measures not men', 'broad bottom', and conventional accommodation. The open clash among these divisive 'views and principles', hitherto merely theoretical discord, made the reconstruction of 1742 a constitutional as well as a political crisis.

The surviving records of the negotiations, though they leave some points obscure, give a reasonably clear account of how the reconstruction took place.[1] To comprehend the position of the Opposition at this stage of constitutional development, it is necessary to analyse the significant incidents with considerable care.

On 1 February 1742 Newcastle, bearing a message from the King, sought a private meeting with Pulteney after dark 'at Mr. Stone's in the Privy Garden'. Did the ministerialists remember how, after the skilfully concealed negotiations that led to the treaty of 1720, Stanhope had joyously proclaimed that 'secrecy is always necessary to do good things'? Did Pulteney recall that secrecy had blighted his pretensions twenty-two years before? Perhaps, though neither mentioned it. Declining to meet the Duke 'by stealth', the 'patriot' leader insisted upon a conference 'at his own house by daylight in sight of all his servants' because 'it was necessary for a person at the head of a party to manage his reputation in this manner'. Newcastle quickly agreed to the wisdom of 'so much delicacy and precaution' and said he would bring Hardwicke with him for a conference the next morning. Pulteney then replied that he would have Carteret on hand 'to put himself on an equality with His Grace'.[2]

The four opened negotiations in the forenoon of 2 February at Pulteney's house. In the King's name Newcastle offered Pulteney the Treasury and asked him to nominate 'those other persons whom he would have put into power'. As a condition of acceptance Pulteney was requested to promise that the retiring Walpole should not be persecuted.[3]

At this stage of the transaction two points require comment. First is Pulteney's insistence that negotiations be formal and unconcealed. Though there would in the future be secret deals

---

[1] In *Rise of the Pelhams*, pp. 87–125, Owen provides an excellent synthesis of all the available material bearing upon the transaction. As far as the evidence permits, he has resolved uncertainties and reconciled conflicting testimony. I have relied upon his solutions to these difficulties.

[2] George Colman, ed., *Posthumous Letters from Various Celebrated Men; addressed to Francis Colman and George Colman the Elder* (London, 1820), p. 79.

[3] Ibid., p. 80.

between Courtiers and Anti-courtiers, Pulteney had set an important precedent for the removal of the politics of ministerial reconstruction from the backstairs, mistresses' boudoirs, and privy chambers, to parleys carried on with the avowed sanction of the Crown. Also, despite his equivocal personal and political position, his demand that the royal message be delivered openly to him as 'the head of a party' with a 'reputation' to preserve meant that he intended to live up to his professions. Here for the first time a successful leader of Opposition cast himself in the role of a responsible public figure.

Second is the Government's decision to solve the crisis by 'taking off' the most manageable and useful opponents. If the King's words are to be taken literally, there was at first some doubt in his mind about how to cope with the situation. He later told Pulteney,

> As soon as I found you were at variance among yourselves, I saw that I had *two shops to deal with*, and I rather chose to come to you because I knew that your aim was only directed against my Minister, but I did not know but the Duke of Argyll wanted to be King himself.[1]

Did George II, like his father in 1720, really misunderstand the character of the Opposition? When did he find out that the malcontents were 'at variance' among themselves? Had there been only one 'shop', how would he have dealt with it? The lack of any further evidence leaves the matter open to conjecture. The King may at first have thought it necessary to put his affairs into the hands of some Opposition leader in the hope that he would turn out to be another Walpole. If so, the Crown momentarily considered the distasteful course of capitulating to a storming party. In the event George II knew the true situation before negotiations opened, and it may well have been that Walpole put this speech in the King's mouth with a view to keeping alive the differences among the malcontents.[2]

George II's words also make clear why the Court chose the course it did. Argyll stood for the 'broad-bottom' doctrine of 'storming the closet' now that 'victory with numbers' had been achieved. The King feared that the Duke sought to 'be King himself' by usurping the Prerogative of the choice of ministers.

---

[1] Ibid., p. 77.   [2] Idem.

Though George grumbled then and later that Pulteney had 'forced' him,[1] clearly Pulteney represented the lesser evil, not only because of his conventional views, but also because of his own disclaimer of office. The Court acknowledged defeat but sought by this means a settlement short of unconditional surrender.

In response to the message transmitted by Newcastle, Pulteney repeated his pledge not to take office, insisted upon the necessity for a change both of men and measures, and refused to guarantee Walpole freedom from prosecution. This condition, Pulteney declared, he could not fulfil: 'If his Grace would read Cardinal de Retz he would find that *a party was like a serpent, that the tail pushed on the head;* so that if he [Pulteney] promised, he should engage for more than he could perform.'[2] He thus rejected specifically two of the three points in the royal offer but left open the possibility that, if the condition were removed, he would aid in the reconstruction of the Ministry.

Two days later on 4 February the four met again. In the interval Pulteney had been informed that Wilmington would go to the Treasury.[3] He now learned that the King did not insist upon an amnesty for Walpole but asked Pulteney not to 'inflame' any prosecution. Pulteney avoided a direct reply, saying that he was not 'a man of blood' but must consult his followers, and that 'he thought that some parliamentary censure at least ought to be inflicted for so many years of maladministration'.[4] Newcastle apparently found this answer acceptable, and the conference turned to the problems of reconstruction.

Newcastle opened the subject with a plea 'by authority from His Majesty' that the Opposition refrain from demanding 'too many alterations now in the midst of a session'. Would the Anti-courtiers 'be content for the present with the removal of Sir Robert Walpole and a few others'?[5] Pulteney agreed that many

---

[1] Sedgwick, ed., *Memoirs of Lord Hervey*, pp. 942–5; Rose, ed., *Marchmont Papers*, i. 174.

[2] Colman, ed., *Posthumous Letters*, p. 80.

[3] Owen, *Rise of the Pelhams*, pp. 93–95, explains the appointment of Wilmington as a 'double finesse', by which the Court obliged Pulteney to adhere to his disclaimer and prevented the nomination of Carteret.

[4] Alexander Chalmers, ed., *The Lives of Dr. Edward Pocock, . . . Dr. Zachary Pearce, . . . Dr. Thomas Newton, . . . and of the Rev. Philip Skelton* (2 vols., London, 1816), ii. 49.   [5] Ibid. 50.

changes necessitating new elections might distress 'the King's business', arouse undesirable ferment, and upset the balance of parties in the House of Commons. He then showed his hand:

He did not insist upon a total change of every person belonging to the Court; he acknowledged that he had no particular objection (for instance) to the noble Duke or the Lord Chancellor: but he said there must be an alteration of men as well as of measures; and for the present he insisted only upon the main forts of Government being delivered into their hands as their security for the rest, that is upon a majority in the Cabinet council, upon a Secretary of State for Scotland, upon a Board of Treasury and Admiralty, and upon turning out some other persons who are most obnoxious.[1]

After a debate of considerable length Newcastle reluctantly capitulated on all points. Pulteney proceeded to make his nominations of individuals. There is no complete record of them, and it is impossible to determine all his stipulations, partly because there was some haggling in the conference, and partly because he undoubtedly requested some deferred appointments. Beyond any question, however, the Pulteney–Carteret bloc was to dominate the 'main forts'.

Pulteney named seven for the Cabinet, four of his own group (himself, Carteret, Tweeddale, and Winchilesea) and three 'broad bottoms' (Argyll, Cobham, and Gower). Tweeddale would have the Secretaryship for Scotland. Sandys, as Chancellor of the Exchequer, and Rushout, Gybbon, and Waller would man the Treasury Board under the pliant Wilmington. Winchilsea would head the Admiralty Board, on which a Tory and two 'broad bottoms' would be included. In addition to the 'forts' specified, Carteret was to be Newcastle's colleague as Secretary of State.[2]

Though he had not previously advocated 'broad bottom', Pulteney now contended (and maintained for the rest of his life) that his ultimate aim was an administration that satisfied the pretensions of all parties. He insisted that, with reasonable co-operation from the Crown and the other groups in opposition, he could have achieved his goal. Few Tories were 'masters of numbers or of languages'; their leaders could be 'taken off' by

---

[1] Ibid. 50–1.

[2] Ibid. 51–52. See Owen, *Rise of the Pelhams*, p. 93, n. 3, for correction of Newton's error concerning the nomination of Carteret.

a few Court posts, Lords Lieutenancies, and 'some other marks of royal favour'.[1] In the process of time the most considerable of the 'broad bottoms' could be insinuated into suitable positions. His intentions, as recorded by his friends, seem eminently fair and intelligent. Yet why this sudden change of front?

The answer lies partly in the circumstances of February 1742. Pulteney, Carteret, and the Prince (who was soon to join in the reconstruction) could muster only about forty followers in the House of Commons. None appear to have been men of outstanding political calibre, and some owed their seats to the influence of the members of the other Opposition groups. Had the Government sought to take them off in a period of calm, a minor crisis, or between sessions, their accommodation could probably have been arranged without serious difficulty. But the fall of Walpole was a major crisis. The Court party needed a real accession of strength, and forty (not all of whose seats were secure) was a small number with which to bargain. Moreover, to make the position of his own bloc secure in the Government, Pulteney thought it vital to man the 'main forts' with enemies of the late Minister and to extend his influence as widely as possible in the garrisons of the lesser redoubts. His own bloc did not possess the numbers, ability, or position. To project a broad bottom and to endeavour to make clients of those for whom he secured places was clearly the course best calculated to gain the requisite strength.

The other part of the answer probably lies in Pulteney's complex temperament. His enemies and many historians have condemned him as self-seeking, irresponsible, and deservedly unsuccessful. His friends portrayed him as high-minded, moderate, and defeated by the malice of others. In fact, the conflicting qualities of ambition and altruism, cool calculation and impulsive quixotism, were constantly at war within him. To do him justice it must be said that throughout the negotiations he seems to have tried to act the part of a man of honour. His first obligation was to his own friends, those who had stood loyally by him through 'the heat and burden of the day'.[2] No

---

[1] Chalmers, ed., *Lives of . . . Pocock*, ii. 61–62. In an interview with Perceval on 24 Sept. 1742 Sandys independently confirmed Pulteney's insistence that the Tories 'would have been fairly dealt with, if their private views had not turned them to act so hastily and madly': P.R.O., Egmont MSS. 212, ff. 2ᵛ, 3.

[2] Chalmers, ed., *Lives of . . . Pocock*, ii. 56.

contemporary politician could conceivably deny that he should serve his close followers as they had served him. Pulteney well knew, however, that to negotiate for his friends alone, as Walpole had done in 1720, would be considered a gross betrayal. The Tories and most of the 'broad bottoms' had also, albeit erratically, pursued the offensive against the great Minister. By current standards of political honour, they too deserved to share in the spoils. As he honoured his pledge not to take office, as he demanded open negotiations which fixed the responsibility for their outcome, so Pulteney spoke for the inclusion of his allies. Though he apparently did not consult them before the conferences, at the second he extorted Newcastle's unwilling consent to their being informed of his proposals before the King gave his approval.[1] The negotiations were in Pulteney's hands, and he intended to keep them there, but the manner in which he conducted them displays a sense of moral obligation to the other malcontents.

Pulteney's position was nevertheless seriously compromised by two factors. He had repeatedly sworn to bring Sir Robert to justice. In 1720 Walpole had been hampered by no such oath. He could enter the Ministry and screen his erstwhile enemies against his erstwhile allies. Pulteney had to face the possibility (and ultimately the fact) of allying himself with the friends of his former enemy while he continued to attack that former enemy, defended by his new friends, with the assistance of his old friends. Such an anomalous situation inevitably provoked misunderstanding and recrimination.

Equally important, Pulteney's professions and actions caused many to doubt his sincerity. How could 'broad bottom' be reconciled with his earlier insistence on 'Whig reunion'? The nomination of so many of his own bloc and so few others looked like the treachery his allies had long dreaded. And what of his pledge not to take office? True, he had refused the Treasury. But he had asked for a place in the Cabinet, and (as soon became clear) he had agreed to accept a peerage. Had he not evaded his commitment by declining emolument but taking honour and power? If this was a measure of his integrity, what reliance could be placed upon his assurances of satisfaction for all just pretensions?

[1] Ibid. 52.

Pulteney now began to reap the whirlwind. Prince Frederick agreed to follow his lead, as he had done so consistently for the past five years, but the 'broad bottoms' saw themselves betrayed. Headed by Argyll, Dodington, and Cobham, they set in train a series of moves designed to force Pulteney into 'storming the closet' immediately. First, they persuaded Wilmington and Dorset, who had long intrigued against Walpole within the Ministry, to resign in protest against the narrow terms of the treaty. This failed when on 13 February the King overbore the objections of the two peers and kept them in their posts.[1] Meanwhile, Argyll and the others had summoned a meeting of all segments of the Opposition at the Fountain Tavern, where they planned by strength of numbers to coerce Pulteney into demanding a comprehensive administration at once.

The 'Fountain' meeting was the most dramatic incident in the annals of eighteenth-century opposition. Over 200 commoners and 35 lords gathered at the tavern on 12 February to place Pulteney and his policy on trial. Carteret and Winchilsea would not come to support him on the excuse that they never dined at taverns. His political life and honour at stake, Pulteney was left to face his accusers with the assistance of no other able speaker but Sandys. Of those whom Pulteney had named for office, Waller had turned against him, and Argyll, Cobham, and Gower led the attack. Pulteney had evidently failed to make new clients from among the leaders of the rival Opposition groups. Could he hope to win over the rank-and-file?

Unfortunately we have no full account of the meeting. From the summaries recorded it appears that feeling ran high and that the debate was marked by brilliant sallies of wit and oratory. More important, here were expounded for the first time in open forum the conflicting constitutional doctrines which distinguished the different malcontent groups. The 'broad bottoms' bore down upon the sound principle and practical necessity of Bolingbroke's doctrine, coupled with bitter reflections upon Pulteney's 'betrayal'. He vigorously repudiated the tactics they recommended. The closet must not be stormed, he averred, because there was 'neither justice, decency, duty, nor moderation in dictating to the King how to dispose of every preferment in the State'. 'Broad bottom' would be achieved,

---

[1] *H.M.C., Egmont Diary*, iii. 251–4.

but it must come gradually and with the monarch's willing consent. To insist on violent and sweeping measures was the surest way to defeat their own ends. Patience, unity, and moderation would carry the day. Having captured the 'main forts', Pulteney insisted, the other bastions must fall if the 'patriots' stood faithfully behind him.[1]

The meeting finally submitted to Pulteney's practical arguments. The 'broad bottoms' did not forsake their principles. They still thought it right to 'storm the closet'. They simply and grudgingly admitted that in the circumstances they could not dictate terms. The doctrinal issue remained unresolved. They merely gave in to momentary necessity.

Still the struggle for a 'broad bottom' did not cease. The day after the meeting Argyll, Bedford, Chesterfield, Gower, Cobham, and Bathurst resolved upon a direct approach to Pulteney. The three last named called upon him with a plea for the inclusion of more malcontents in the treaty. The patriot leader was adamant. Feeling perhaps more secure after his victory at the 'Fountain', he stiffly declined to compromise.[2]

The 'broad bottoms' then directed their pressure upon the Prince. Though it seems to have been understood that his allowance was to be raised to £100,000 and that his followers were to be preferred, nothing had yet been done. If Frederick could be detached from the Pulteney–Carteret bloc, the 'narrow treaty', made narrower still, might well collapse.

Pulteney saw the danger in time to meet it. He asked the Prince for an opportunity to defend his policy against his rivals in the presence of His Royal Highness. Frederick obligingly summoned a meeting at Carlton House for 8 p.m. on 16 February. Once again the familiar points were rehearsed. Argyll, Chesterfield, Gower, Cobham, and Bathurst presented their arguments one by one, and Pulteney answered each in turn. At the conclusion 'the Prince said that he thought Mr. Pulteney acted from the best motives and delivered it as his resolution

---

[1] For accounts of the meeting at the 'Fountain', see Lord Perceval, *Faction Detected by the Evidence of Facts* (London, 1743), pp. 41–44; Chalmbers, ed., *Lives . . . of Pocock*, ii. 55–56; Lewis, ed., *Horace Walpole's Correspondence with Sir Horace Mann*, i. 335–6; Add. MSS. 6043, f. 110; [John Almon] *Anecdotes of the Life of the Right-Honourable William Pitt, Earl of Chatham* (5th ed., 13 vols., London, 1796), i. 78–79.

[2] [Richard Glover], *Memoirs of a Celebrated Literary and Political Character* (London, 1813), pp. 5–6.

that he would go in with him'.[1] Frederick then wrote a submissive letter to his father, and the next morning King and Prince were reconciled at St. James's.

The 'broad bottoms' realized at last that they had failed. Pulteney had triumphantly countered their every move. They had no choice now but to co-operate or return to opposition. Argyll decided to give in. Since he had declared both to his followers and to the King that he would enter none but a comprehensive administration, he felt it necessary to justify his change of front; so on the evening of 17 February over 100 'broad bottoms' and Tories met at Dodington's house to hear his case. The conference was convinced. All agreed in urging Argyll to return to office, and next morning they accompanied him to Court to signify their consent to his action and to the terms of the treaty.[2]

Pulteney's victory now seemed complete. Both Court and Country had accepted his terms. It remained only to implement them. Here he encountered insuperable difficulties. On the one hand, George II so disliked the introduction of Tories into the administration that he was prepared to seize any opportunity to revise the treaty. On the other, the Opposition's pledge to prosecute Walpole exacerbated the tensions among the malcontents and between them and the Court. Within three weeks these factors had wrecked the prospects for a comprehensive administration gradually achieved, and driven the 'broad bottoms' and Tories back into a formed general Opposition.

The breakdown occurred abruptly in the short space of time between 8 and 11 March. Pulteney was at his country home, ill and distracted with grief at the bedside of his dying daughter. Sandys was at Worcester attending to his re-election. The firm and able hands which had thus far saved the treaty were powerless to act in the sudden crisis which began on 8 March when the new members of the Admiralty Board were to kiss hands. Limerick, Chetwynd, Granard, and Cotton stated that they accepted office only on the condition that other malcontents were to be taken into place. Though Pulteney had frankly stated that he intended to broaden the bottom, the treaty did not, so far as the records show, authorize others to extort

---

[1] Colman, ed., *Posthumous Letters*, pp. 82–83.
[2] *H.M.C.*, *Egmont Diary*, iii. 254.

promises in their own right. The angry King, evidently convinced that the Opponents intended to 'force' him beyond the terms to which he had already agreed, struck off the name of the Tory, Cotton.[1]

To the dismayed malcontents it now appeared that only a show of strength could keep the Court to the terms of the treaty and salvage their hopes for a 'broad bottom'. They resolved upon immediate action. The following day, 9 March, Limerick moved for a secret committee to inquire into the conduct of the administration for the last twenty years. The loss of the motion, by 244 to 242, convinced the 'outs' that they had been betrayed. Carteret's closest friends were absent. Several followers of the Prince, who had privately promised Walpole to defend him against any attacks on his life and fortune, also did not attend. Rumours had it that Pulteney had spread intimations that he would find it 'agreeable' if his friends were out of the House upon the introduction of such a motion, and his clients on the new Treasury Board gave only silent votes for the inquiry.[2] Pulteney had assured his rivals that unanimity would achieve their goal, but now his own bloc had broken the united front of the old coalition.

Argyll resigned in dudgeon the next morning. That evening the Tory and 'broad-bottom' chiefs met at Dodington's and decided upon opposition *à outrance*. On 11 March a general assembly of 184 malcontent M.P.s at the Fountain supported their leaders' decision.[3]

Upon his return, the sorrowing Pulteney tried in vain to retrieve the situation. On 23 March he and his bloc supported a second motion by Limerick to inquire into the conduct of the administration, this time for ten years past. The motion succeeded, and Pulteney himself drew up the Opposition's list for the secret committee of inquiry.[4] But nothing could heal the breach. The treaty had now to be concluded on a narrow bottom. By the end of the session most of the adherents of Pulteney, Carteret, and the Prince had been accommodated. Cobham accepted preferment but worked in secret with the Opposition.

[1] Ibid. 260.
[2] Idem; Chalmers, ed., *Lives of . . . Pocock*, ii. 59; Lewis, ed., *Horace Walpole's Correspondence with Sir Horace Mann*, i. 363-4; Add. MSS. 6043, f. 110; *P.H.* xii. 448-530.
[3] *H.M.C., Egmont Diary*, iii. 260-1. [4] *P.H.* xii. 532-90.

Of the other 'broad-bottom' chiefs only Gower and Bathurst were lured into office. No 'true blue' Tories came in. Nearly all of the Court party displaced by the 'new Whigs' were compensated.[1] Except for the fall of the great Minister, the reconstruction of 1742 was scarcely more extensive than that of 1720.

Thus concluded the second successful Opposition of the Hanoverian era. For the limited character of its success Pulteney has traditionally borne the blame. He is accused of cupidity, narrow-mindedness, and irresponsibility.[2] Yet in broad perspective it must be seen that he was acting within the framework of contemporary political conventions. To honour his own 'self-denying ordinance', made in accordance with the altrustic professions of early Georgian Oppositions, was politically unwise but morally correct. He still clung to the conventional doctrine that the closet should not be stormed. He believed in both the practicality and the constitutionality of a 'negotiated peace', whereby the Court took in a few who later introduced their friends through their influence with the King. As Carteret observed, Pulteney's treaty was

a prudent act, and considering His Majesty's temper, absolutely necessary, for it would have been impossible to have made the intended changes, if all at once a number of gentlemen whom Sir Robert Walpole had possessed His Majesty with an ill opinion of had offered to force themselves upon him before the aspersions cast on them were removed, and this could not be done but by degrees, and by some few new persons received by him, who would set their characters in a fairer light.[3]

In sum, Pulteney had to deal with a strong Court party and a resentful King who would make no more concessions than absolutely necessary. He had also to deal with allies whose constitutional thought was far more radical than his own. The reconstruction became perforce a messy and confused affair, complicated still further by the accident that removed Pulteney from the scene at a critical time. Despite seventeen years of bitter political warfare, it was nevertheless a peaceful reconstruction, accomplished without vengeance upon the fallen and

---

[1] See the summary in Owen, *Rise of the Pelhams*, pp. 115–20.

[2] For example, see the severe strictures in Lord Fitzmaurice, *Life of William Earl of Shelburne* (2 vols., London, 1912), i. 34–35.

[3] *H.M.C.*, *Egmont Diary*, iii. 251.

without serious derangement of the 'King's business'. All things considered, it seems the part of fair judgement to conclude that Pulteney's memorial plaque in Westminster Abbey is not undeserved.

2. THE ACHIEVEMENT OF 'BROAD BOTTOM'

The Opposition Controversy

The determination of Tories and 'broad bottoms' to oppose the reconstructed Ministry brought on a new debate over the purposes and principles of Opposition. For over two years the presses poured forth a spate of pamphlets and news-sheets in which each element of the old coalition justified its conduct in terms of personal morality, political wisdom, and constitutional rectitude. There was scarcely any novelty in the mass of assertion and counter-assertion, but the new situation produced significant shifts of emphasis.

Because of the limited nature of the settlement, the followers of Pulteney and Carteret found themselves upon the defensive. None but they had profited from the long years of struggle. Was it not evident after all that their opposition was a mere *fronde*, devoid of public principle, and motivated solely by resentment and thirst for power? Their ablest apologist was the new member for Westminster, Lord Perceval (later second Earl of Egmont), whose monumental *Faction Detected by the Evidence of Facts* was the most elaborate vindication of the Opposition before the publications of Edmund Burke.[1]

Perceval contended that the treaty of 1742 had properly fulfilled the aims of the erstwhile Anti-courtiers. The opposition to Walpole, he wrote,

was carried on upon Whig principles; that it was the grand principle of humbling France, and of assisting the House of Austria to which they adhered, and which they intended to maintain by the opposition. It was not a quarrel about particular laws or alterations of the constitution, as it is now falsely suggested to have been. Something of this kind is attempted in the course of every opposition, and

---

[1] Perceval's pamphlet, which appeared in September 1743, consists of 175 pages containing more than 76,500 words. For the amusing controversy over its authorship, see *A Letter to the Reverend Dr. Zachary Pearce, occasioned by his advertisement in the Daily Advertiser of October 28, 1743* (London, 1743).

something of this kind is from time to time necessary, within the bounds of moderation, to be done, to confine government to its first principles. . . . But these were secondary views; the grand point intended . . . was to remove the Minister and to bring the councils of this country to its true interest.[1]

The 'grand point' had been achieved amid popular ferment and against a ministerial party which had 'rallied' after a momentary 'retreat'. The discontented Whigs therefore accepted their obligation to take office in order to effectuate wise measures and to calm a disturbed people. In doing so they had not betrayed the other elements in opposition but, quite the contrary, had been deserted by them. Since Walpole had been guilty of no crime before the law, he was not pursued to the scaffold, nor would such vengeance have served their purpose: 'An administration founded in, or a party cemented by blood, would have been the loathing of this nation. . . .'[2]

The need for opposition was thus at an end. Still Perceval could not condemn opposition as such.

Opposition to the measures of government, whether good or bad, is no new thing in this or any other country where the people have any share in the legislature. . . . The discontented party of all denominations consist [*sic*] in general of men of no principle and of very unworthy character. Its root is always the same, but indeed its effects are very different. It becomes in some conjunctions of very beneficial consequence when it is led by men of honest views; and equally pernicious in others when conducted by men of different character. In the first case, it is an Opposition; in the second, it is a faction.[3]

The new party of malcontents—the Tories and 'broad bottoms' —deserved not 'the gentle term of Opposition' but the 'harsh appellation' of faction on two grounds.

First, the Anti-courtiers' attacks on foreign policy were treasonous in that they poisoned the minds of the people against

---

[1] *Faction Detected*, p. 17.   [2] Ibid., pp. 67–70.
[3] Ibid., pp. 5–7. In P.R.O., Egmont MSS. 212, ff. 2, 15, and loose sheets, are to be found several unpublished drafts of Perceval's views on opposition. He regarded the Court and Country parties as permanent bodies, each composed of good men and bad, each bent on pursuing its own interests. A man of public spirit must join one or the other, for 'no man can pretend to act a mixed part without rendering himself odious to all parties, contemptible in his character, and consequently useless to his country. This kind of character is what goes under the denomination of a trimmer, which by long experience has been found, tho' beautiful in theory, absurd in practice.'

Hanover and the royal family. Second, the principle and purpose of 'broad bottom' were unconstitutional.

> Was the pursuit of places [wrote Perceval] ever avowed to be the grounds of opposition? It has indeed been satirically imputed to be so upon all occasions, but it was never supported by the public upon that footing, nor ever was avowedly confessed to be so by any Opposition before this which now distracts this country.[1]

Perceval poured scorn upon 'the title of broad-bottom . . . a cant word . . . corresponding equally with the personal figure of some of their leaders and the nature of their pretensions'.[2]

The line of argument taken by Perceval was the standard defence employed in the general run of pro-Pulteney pamphlets. These writings, considered collectively, now made explicit the conventional view of Opposition previously implicit in the actions and occasional declarations of the old patriots. To them a formed general Opposition could be justified only by maladministration which could not otherwise be corrected. The perpetual existence of an Anti-court party bent on storming the closet constituted a threat to the stability of the State. One pamphlet pushed this point to its logical conclusion. If, wrote the anonymous author, you

> take it for granted that affairs will never go right till such time as all in the new Opposition have places, to which all in their high pretences of patriotism tend, then you must go on in a continual circle of changes and Oppositions; for if once opposing power appears to be the sole road to power, why then as men grow up who have or who imagine they have abilities to manage and consequently a good title to acquire power, they will immediately throw themselves into this path and persist in it till they come to their wished-for end. The bringing things into such a rotation has been the constant method by which all free states have been brought to their end. A certain progression of power in conformity to their respective constitutions is natural to them all, and may sometimes be quickened by party struggles without any very great detriment; but when through the force of faction this motion is increased to such a degree of rapidity, the machine of government is no longer able to subsist, but either stops in tyranny or shivers into anarchy.[3]

---

[1] *Faction Detected*, p. 50.   [2] Idem.

[3] *An Enquiry into the Present State of our Domestick Affairs, Shewing the Danger of a New Opposition* (London, n.d. [1742]), pp. 50–51. Other pamphlets defending the Pulteney–Carteret bloc are *A Compleat View of the Present Politicks of Great Britain. In a Letter from a German Nobleman to his Friend at Vienna* (London, 1743); *An Apology*

In private, of course, most of the old patriots were realists to the point of cynicism. They well knew that on one ground or another politicians would always contend for power. They knew equally well that political controversy would always be charged with some hypocrisy and disingenuousness, elements that were not lacking in their defence of themselves. But at no time, whether in or out, did they conceive of the beneficial operation of a two-party system, nor did they think it proper to admit that a formed general Opposition was a legitimate means to preferment. They simply believed in 'politics as usual'.

The Tories, whose publications were notably consistent and carefully written, clung steadfastly to their principle of 'measures not men'. To them a Country party was a vital element in the Constitution, the only effective curb upon the inevitable tendency of administration to abuse its power. A 'true Opposition' must be legal, loyal, and reasonable, but steady and determined. Its 'true function' must be

to repair those oversights which have been made at the different periods of our constitution; to settle those rights of the subject which are not rightly understood, to retrieve those that have been neglected, to acquire those to which they are entitled by nature, and to secure such as are too liable to perversion and abuse.[1]

In immediate terms, all this meant that the Opposition should support the traditional 'Country party programme': reduction of the army and establishment of an effective militia, reduction and control of public expenditure, retrenchment of pensions and salaries, an effective place act, a foreign policy that truly served the nation's interest. The Tories called in addition for the redress of specific grievances perpetrated upon the people by the administration since 1714: particularly repeal of the Septennial Act, the Riot Act, the Waltham–Black Act, the Smuggling Act, 'and a thousand coercive clauses in Acts relating to the Excise'.[2]

---

for the Conduct of the Present Administration. . . . In a Letter to a Noble Lord in Opposition (London, 1744); *Warning to the Whigs and to the Well-affected Tories* (London, 1744).

[1] *The Conduct of the Late and Present M——ry Compared. With an Impartial Review of Public Transactions since the Resignation of the Right Honourable the Earl of Orford; and of the Causes that immediately effected the same* (London, 1742), p. 24. This pamphlet has curiously been attributed by some to Pulteney, who could not have written such a condemnation of himself or such an encomium upon his current opponents.

[2] *National Unanimity Recommended: or, The Necessity of a Constitutional Resistance to*

Their pamphleteers maintained that a 'true Opposition' of this character was uniquely a Tory principle. They paid lip service to a high-minded desire for the abolition of odious party distinctions. They expressed a willingness to co-operate with 'moderate Whigs'. But in lengthy reviews of party politics going as far back as 1660, they gave all laud and glory to the Tories, 'old in a virtuous Opposition'[1] to corruption and tyranny in every reign. The Tories' virtue was the greater because, in accordance with their principles, they had never sought any reward for their public-spirited service to the Constitution:

> . . . the design of a faction [wrote John Campbell] is to bring those who compose it into power. . . . But an Opposition is quite another thing, it aims at a change of measures and not of men and therefore is never in a greater probability of succeeding than when such as compose it are bound to each other by no other tie than that of sameness of sentiment, and propound no more to themselves than obliging others to act right.[2]

It naturally followed that the Tory Opposition to the reconstructed Ministry would tread unwaveringly in the footsteps of its illustrious predecessors.

Yet here and there the Tories hint that, if given the popular support they deserve, their virtue need not go unrewarded for evermore. One pamphlet concluded with this exhortation to the subjects of Great Britain:

> Let us watch the notions of our open enemies, and guard against the machinations of our secret, by slipping no opportunity, not the most minute, of promoting the interest of those who have hitherto appeared to be our real friends. The Whigs have failed us constantly, deceitfully failed us, therefore have not the least title to our confidence. If we must depend on any, let it be on the Tories, who have not deceived us, and I believe never will deceive us.[3]

the *Sinister Designs of False Brethren* (London, 1742), pp. 52–54; *The Conduct of the Late and Present M——ry Compared*, pp. 16–24; *The Case of the Opposition Impartially Stated*, pp. 32–50; *Opposition More Necessary than Ever: or, A Review of the Principles, Designs, and Conduct of the Two Parties joined in Opposition to the late Minister* (London, 1742), pp. 52–54; *The Desertion Discussed; or, The Last and Present Oppositions Placed in their True Light* (London, 1743), pp. 53–60.

[1] *National Unanimity Recommended*, p. 37. In varying ways the other pamphlets cited in the previous note employ an historical approach in justifying Tory principles and conduct.

[2] *The Case of the Opposition Impartially Stated*, p. 56.

[3] *Opposition More Necessary than Ever*, p. 59. Cf. *The Desertion Discussed*, pp. 61–62.

To what end did the Tories seek the 'trust and confidence' of the people? To achieve the 'Country party programme', of course, but what then? Did they look forward to a future wherein the Tories conducted an unending, virtuous Opposition to an unending, evil Whig administration? This seems the obvious conclusion to be drawn from their public professions, but it is illogical to believe that they really expected the people to be governed always by those who had 'deceitfully failed' them.[1] The Tories' call for popular support, combined with their avowed willingness to co-operate with 'moderate Whigs', suggests rather that Pulteney had correctly estimated their pretensions: conscious of their deficiency in administrative talent, the Tories would be satisfied with a few honours, positions at Court, and posts in local government.[2]

The 'broad bottoms' left no room for speculation about their pretensions. They characterized themselves as

an association of all honest men to abolish all party distinctions, to embrace the common interest of the commonwealth, to free it from every yoke, to disencumber it of every load, to labour jointly, one and all whether in power or out, to restore the broken constitution of old England, and with the blessing of Divine Providence, render it unchangeable and immortal.[3]

Being out of power, they must pursue their noble aims by parliamentary Opposition, a time-honoured institution which they viewed as regrettable but necessary:

It is most fatally true that Opposition hath been of long standing in this kingdom: but then it is equally true that it hath always been authorized by the iniquitous conduct of those in power and the real grievances of the people. I make no distinction of Whig or Tory administrations. All have made themselves justly obnoxious, and therefore all have been justly opposed.[4]

The current administration, composed of false patriots and

---

[1] In ibid., pp. 25–26, the author expressed clearly the Tories' protest against the growing Whig myth: the Tories know and pursue the public interest, he wrote, whereas the Whigs are supporters of the Prerogative 'but pique themselves so much upon the title of Whigs and would arrogate to themselves a perpetual and indefeasible right to the administration barely from being called so.'

[2] Chalmers, ed., *Lives of . . . Pocock*, ii. 61–62.

[3] *A Defence of the People: or, Full Confutation of the Pretended Facts Advanced in a Late Huge, Angry Pamphlet called Faction Detected* (London, 1744), p. 98.

[4] Ibid., p. 8.

tools of the late Minister, is the worst in history. Consequently it deserves the most 'active', 'vigilant', and 'violent' opposition. The symbol of their determination was a weekly paper inspired by Chesterfield called *Old England, or the Constitutional Journal*, edited by 'Jeffrey Broad-Bottom, Esq.' who declared that he would carry on his publication in defence of the Constitution until the aims of Opposition had been achieved.[1]

Though these patriots proposed to do their duty on the Speaker's left, they declared that they could not save the Constitution until they came to power. A pamphleteer named Thomas Waller stated their objective most forcibly. With the support of the people, he wrote, the 'broad bottoms' proposed to 'root out a Ministry they detest for their perfidy and force a change of measures they don't like'. Nothing short of a 'total rout' would serve. By means of 'a well conducted unanimous Opposition' they intended to 'bring about another ministerial revolution which may be more favourable to the just demands of an injured people'.[2]

The screeds of this time dwelt upon the sombre rather than the bright aspects of 'broad-bottom' doctrine. The buoyant eschatology of the still unpublished *Patriot King* was altogether lacking. The dawn of a better day was a hope, not a certainty. The doctrinaires did not promise the King that an administration of 'all honest men' would achieve the peace and unity that must make him more powerful than an absolute monarch. They emphasized the primary need to expel the evil advisers from office, and with both King and Prince leagued against them, they made it clear, whatever the polite disguise, that they held the Crown responsible for employing a bad Ministry and pursuing a bad policy.[3]

No Opposition since the Revolution had exhibited a bolder effrontery in attacking the Throne. The 'broad bottoms' well knew the reluctance with which George II had accepted the treaty and the part he had played in the reconstruction. They then saw the ease and, in the case of Carteret, the affection with

---

[1] *Old England* was published from 5 Feb. 1743 until Dec. 1744.

[2] [Thomas Waller], *Public Discontent Accounted For, from the Conduct of our Ministers in the Cabinet and our Generals in the Field* (London, 1743), pp. 25–26.

[3] See Chesterfield's ingenious endeavour to distinguish the King's 'conduct' from the King's 'behaviour' in *P.H.* xiii. 102, 114, 131–2; *The Desertion Discussed*, p. 16; and *Public Discontent Accounted For*, p. 26 and *passim*.

which he embraced those whom he had lately denounced as knaves, puppies, and scoundrels. It is scarcely a matter for surprise, therefore, that in suiting their doctrine to the circumstances, they paid no regard to the susceptibilities of the King. 'The people', whom they nowhere defined, had brought down the great Minister, so they averred; and now through the 'broad bottoms', whose abhorrence of party distinctions guaranteed their cordial co-operation with Tories and all other honest men, 'the people' would again force a change of hands.[1]

Both the 'broad bottoms' and the Tories were uncomfortably aware that, in a sense, Pulteney's treaty had placed them as well as the 'betrayers' on the defensive. In the first issue of *Old England* Jeffrey Broad-Bottom, alias Chesterfield, expressed their concern:

I know that the conduct of those who sneaked and abandoned their principles upon the late change of ministry is sometimes made use of as an argument why Opposition must be fruitless, since all mankind, say they, employ it only as a means of their preferment or the instrument of their revenge.[2]

This dread of public disillusionment, this fear of being cast into the pit with the 'false patriots', accounts in large part for the strenuous justification of Opposition to 'the people'. One senses a feeling that this period, of which no one knew the duration, presented to their minds a crisis in the history of Opposition: could the public be persuaded again to accept the Country party as noble and disinterested, and so give it hope for the future; or would disappointment turn into cynical indifference so deep that no Opposition could expect support out-of-doors? These alternatives, unreal as they were, probably seemed clear enough at the time. As it turned out, 'broad bottom' was achieved by a devious twist in Court politics in which the public played no part.

---

[1] In the writings of this time 'the people' and 'the public' are rather elusive terms. One gathers by inference from the way in which they were used that they had a meaning slightly different from 'the country'. The writers express an awareness of the influence of popular sentiment in London and large open constituencies (sometimes in the form of mob violence) upon such affairs as the defeat of the Excise, the outbreak of the war with Spain, and the fall of Sir Robert. They understood also the importance of ministerial deserters, waverers, and Independents. With the immediate past clearly before the eyes of the Opponents, it seems reasonably clear that they meant to appeal to all these elements as 'the people' or 'the public'.

[2] *Old England*, no. 1, 5 Feb. 1743.

The Conduct of the Broad-Bottom Opposition

The reconstruction of 1742 produced a highly unstable settlement. Prince Frederick, despite occasional waywardness, remained faithful to the treaty; but having submitted to his father, he ceased to play any significant part in directing events. Pulteney and Carteret, however, soon appeared as rivals in the closet to the leaders of the 'old corps': Newcastle, Pelham, and Hardwicke. Pulteney, who became Earl of Bath in July of 1742, dropped into obscurity when Pelham defeated him in a contest for the Treasury in the summer of 1743. In the following winter Gower and Cobham threw up their places and returned to the Opposition. Where his friends had failed, Carteret succeeded— to his ruin. He became the royal favourite. His influence with the King, combined with his grandiose foreign policy, incurred the bitter jealousy and undisguised resentment of the 'old corps', who carried on frequent exploratory negotiations with the Opposition until they compassed his downfall in November of 1744.

In the event, therefore, Pulteney's treaty served only as a brief prelude to another reconstruction. During this short period the Opposition launched violent attacks in Parliament while the leaders entered eagerly into every intrigue for an accommodation with the 'old corps'. The possibility of a new treaty, however, did not modify the structure or strategy of the Opposition. The new was patterned quite consciously on the old. The experience of the past, as Chesterfield explained, offered the greatest hope for the future:

We have seen [he wrote] the noble fruits of a twenty years Opposition blasted by the connivance and treachery of a few, who, by all ties of gratitude and honour, ought to have cherished and preserved them to the people: but this disappointment ought to be so far from discouraging that it should lend spirit and life to a new Opposition. The late one laboured their [*sic*] point for a much longer term of years and against many greater difficulties than any Opposition at present can be under apprehensions of encountering. They became a majority from a minority of not above eighty-seven or eighty-eight in all: they fought against an experienced general and a national purse, and the questions they opposed were more plausible in their nature, and less dangerous in their consequences, than any that have yet fallen within the system of their blundering successors. At present, the friends of their country, who have already declared themselves, have advantages which their predecessors could never compass, even after twenty years' hard labour.[1]

Carteret replaced Walpole as 'an execrable, a sole minister', from whom the Opposition proposed to rescue the King with a 'rough but friendly hand'.[2] The 'deserters' as a group were held up to public abhorrence and marked out for vengeance. With a few other variations suitable to the changed circumstances, the Tories and 'broad bottoms' strove to carry on Opposition as they had known it under the leadership of their current enemies.

Organization remained the major problem. At the outset, the reconstitution of the Anti-court party was inhibited by the likelihood that Pulteney would bring in more of his former friends.[3] From February to July 1742 the old malcontents hung together reasonably well on election petitions, the prosecution of Walpole, and straight 'Country party issues'. In other matters, as Glover observed, 'every man shifted for himself'.[4] It was clear by autumn that no more would get places. The regelation of party lines led to closer co-operation among the Opponents during the session of 1742–3.[5] Then in the autumn of 1743 came a greater effort at co-ordination with the formation of an 'anti-ministerial Cabinet'.

It was composed of three Tory members, Cotton, Philips, and Wynne; and three 'broad bottoms', Dodington, Pitt, and Waller.[6] Though one source reports 'that the Opposition have entrusted their conduct in Parliament this session to a committee of six for the sake of secrecy',[7] we do not know how they

---

[1] Idem.

[2] Phrases attributed to William Pitt in Philip Yorke's Parliamentary Journal: *P.H.* xiii. 136, 142.

[3] For indications of the malcontents' irresolution, see Smith, ed., *Bedford Corresp.* i. 1–12; P.R.O., Granville Papers 1, Chesterfield to Gower, 15 and 22 July 1742.

[4] Glover, *Memoirs*, p. 6.

[5] Owen, *Rise of the Pelhams*, pp. 141 ff.; P.R.O., Galway MSS., Henry Pelham to Richard Arundel, 23 Oct. 1742.

[6] The evidence conflicts as to whether Philips or Lyttelton was the sixth member of the 'cabinet'. Owen, *Rise of the Pelhams*, p. 199, resolves the issue in favour of Philips because his inclusion accorded equal representation to both Opposition blocs. If the committee was to deputise for all interests, Owen's argument is strengthened by the fact that Philips was considered the leading Jacobite M.P., whereas Lyttelton at this time was Pitt's *alter ego*.

[7] Yorke's Parliamentary Journal: *P.H.* xiii. 146.

came to be chosen. There is no record of any formal compact among the chiefs or any open election at a general meeting. Most likely these six agreed among themselves to assume the leadership. They all attended regularly. They were among the most vigorous malcontent speakers. As each represented an influential group, they constituted a natural coalition of interests in the Country party.

Sometime in 1744 this 'cabinet' grew into, or was replaced by, a 'junto' of nine.[1] The new committee consisted of four peers, Bedford, Chesterfield, Cobham, and Gower; four of the old group, Cotton, Dodington, Pitt, and Waller; and one more 'broad bottom', George Lyttelton. The Junto came into existence, again probably by common agreement, primarily to deal with the Pelhams' endeavour to oust Carteret by reaching an accommodation with the 'outs'. If the Opposition had had to face another session, the nine may well have taken over the management of the parliamentary campaign. As it turned out, they did no more than conduct the negotiations for a new treaty.

Although the leadership of the new Opposition thus became more formal in character, the management of the party followed the familiar pattern. The chiefs issued circular letters calling for full attendance. They concocted measures for the session. When they thought it prudent or necessary, they summoned general meetings at the Fountain. But the task of making all the malcontents 'live and draw together' proved to be as difficult as ever.

It was not, as one might suspect, the differing constitutional views of Tories and 'broad bottoms' that caused the trouble. It was a matter of individual temperament and personal feelings. The arrogant Pitt adopted Carteret's old attitude that he would vote for but not speak for a motion of which he disapproved. On one occasion Pitt, Lyttelton, and a Tory member stalked out of the House to show their disapproval of a motion made by one of their colleagues. On another George Grenville brought in an address, said to have been framed by Waller, which was so

[1] Glover (*Memoirs*, p. 27), who obtained most of his information from Waller, is the sole authority for the formal existence of the Junto. The other accounts of the negotiations for the Treaty of 1744 nevertheless make clear that there was a co-operative agreement among the leaders of both blocs in Lords and Commons.

unsatisfactorily worded that Pitt, Lyttelton, and Grenville drew aside and amended it in the midst of the debate. On still another Pitt wanted to drop a question which Dodington and the Tories insisted on pushing to a disastrous division. Sir Francis Dashwood forced a vote upon the Address in 1743 after 'the anti-ministerial cabinet' had decided not to divide. Several times sizeable numbers of the rank-and-file deserted their leaders on major issues.[1] Despite the lessons learned in the campaign against Sir Robert, the Anti-courtiers would not agree upon or submit to rigid political discipline.

Their parliamentary tactics consisted largely of violent frontal assaults on simply defined issues. One discovers nothing of the shrewdness and ingenuity that had characterized the Dunkirk inquiry and the defeat of the Excise. The leaders seem to have believed that they could arouse 'the public' more effectively by vehemence and extravagance, and the 'young orators' were impatient of craft and subtlety. At the outset they gave their main efforts to the prosecution of Walpole and the passing of the 'popular Bills' of the Country party programme. After a spectacular defeat on 1 December 1742 the pursuit of the great Minister was abandoned.[2] The failure of a Place Bill two days later marked the end of their popular measures.[3] The major political issues in the sessions of 1742–3 and 1743–4 were all related to foreign policy.

Britain had been at war with Spain since 1739. After Prussia's attack on Silesia, the country became gradually involved in the continental struggle over the Austrian succession. Since both Britain and Hanover had guaranteed the Pragmatic Sanction, George II maintained troops in the field and entered deeply into the diplomatic tangle in support of the Habsburg cause. He led the 'Pragmatic Army' to a victory over the French at Dettingen in 1743, and at last in March of 1744 Britain became fully and openly engaged in European hostilities when France declared war upon her. In the formulation of policy the English

---

[1] These episodes are recorded in Yorke's Parliamentary Journal: *P.H.* xiii. 138, 384–6, 393, 472, 649, 673. See the comments on the operation of the 'cabinet' in Glover's *Memoirs*, pp. 13–22.

[2] The motion to revive the secret committee of inquiry was lost by 67 votes, 253–186, because the 'new Whigs' in the Court party refused to support further prosecution for fear of losing their places: *H.M.C., Egmont Diary*, iii. 267–8.

[3] Ibid. 268; *P.H.* xii. 873–906.

ministers had to deal with a highly complex situation which allowed many possibilities in the choice of measures. The malcontents viewed it all in very plain terms: they supported the Crown against its enemies, but to the conduct of the war in every aspect they objected without qualification.

In the two sessions that met during 1742–4 the Opposition brought on thirty major divisions relating to important points in the conduct of the war. They attacked the employment of troops, the method of paying troops, subsidies to foreign powers, treaty arrangements, the condition of the navy, the adequacy of naval intelligence, and the competence of the ministers—particularly Carteret—to manage foreign affairs.[1] Except in technical details, the critical theme was always the same: British interests were being sacrificed to those of Hanover. The general charge was laid down in the famous words which Dr. Johnson attributed to William Pitt: 'It is now too apparent that this great, this powerful, this formidable kingdom is considered only as a province to a despicable Electorate.'[2] Sandwich proclaimed the party line: 'A zealous Opposition ought to be made to all destructive, particularly all Hanoverian measures.'[3]

Thus it was the new Opposition that for the first time made Hanover a major issue in British politics. Rising national feeling made the English jealous of the foreign predilections of their princes. William III's obvious loyalty to Holland led to one clause in the Act of Settlement prohibiting the King from committing Britain to war in 'defence of any dominions and territories which do not belong to the Crown of England, without consent of Parliament', and another forbidding him to leave the realm without consent of Parliament.[4] Out of deference to George I the second prohibition was repealed in 1715.[5] Yet the prejudice remained. The Commons sent Shippen to the Tower in 1717 for anti-German sentiments 'highly dishonourable to, and injustly reflecting on, his Majesty's person and Government',[6] but the governing class little loved the King's determination to take an annual *Hannoverreise*. These summer visits of George I and George II to their 'country estate' caused

---

[1] Ibid. xii. 853–72, 906–1058; xiii. 1–44, 135–230, 232–74, 384–504, 636–9, 645–52, 675–83, 698–704. *C.J.* xxiv. 354, 362, 387, 406, 415, 416, 431, 441, 621, 624, 635–6.

[2] *P.H.* xii. 1035.　　　　[3] Ibid. 1061.　　　　[4] 12 & 13 William III, c. 2.

[5] 1 George I, stat. 2, c. 51.　　　　[6] *P.H.* vii. 511–12.

embarrassment and sometimes difficulty for their ministers. Still, any anti-Hanoverian feeling remained mostly dormant. During these early years Britain avoided entanglement in continental wars. Except for the minor dispute over Bremen and Verden, the interests of the Island and the Continental realms did not appear to clash. Then the outbreak in 1740 of the European war, in which there seemed to be a conflict of interest between the two states, puffed smouldering resentment into flame. Anti-Hanoverianism, considered Jacobitical in the early years of the dynasty, now became patriotic British sentiment. It was to remain so for many years.

The decision of the Cabinet in 1742 to take 16,000 Electoral troops into British pay provided the occasion for the first eruption in Parliament. A turn in the affairs of war having removed the French threat to Hanover, George II wanted to economize by reducing his German army to a peace-time contingent. The Cabinet feared that such a move would dismay their allies and undo their plans for future operations. A meeting attended by twelve ministers advised the King unanimously to keep these forces together with British funds and order them to join the rest of the 'Pragmatic Army'.[1] Diplomatically and militarily it was a sound move. Politically it was pie for the Opposition—a patent job to pay Hanover's bills out of British pockets.

The Opponents opened their assault on this issue at the outset of the session in December 1742. Hyperbolic speeches in both Houses, supplemented by highly coloured pamphlets, kept it constantly before Parliament and the country for two years. Carteret was vilified as 'a Hanover troop master' and an 'English minister without an English heart'.[2] Petty disputes between British and Electoral officers in the field were eagerly retailed.[3] George II's supposed preference for his German forces became a matter of common conviction. Scarcely any aspect of foreign policy could be discussed without consideration of the reigning prejudice, which infected Ministerialists as well as their enemies and the populace. Though the Opposition never got a majority on the 'Hanover question', it generally brought out their maximum strength of 180 to 190, and in a

---

[1] See Owen, *Rise of the Pelhams*, pp. 133–4. [2] *P.H.* xiii. 143, 465.
[3] For examples see ibid. 139–41, 274–5.

division on 18 January 1744 Government defectors swelled their numbers to the unusual figure of 226.[1]

A debate on the question always filled the ministers with anxiety. In each session all officers who were members of Parliament were ordered home from the British army in Flanders to support official policy.[2] The Earl of Orford (quondam Sir Robert Walpole) once made a special trip to London to hold the Court party together when the Ministry had resigned itself to defeat.[3] No Government ever faced a more deeply vexing problem than this violent outbreak of anti-Hanoverianism occasioned by an intelligent decision to hire a little German army which owed allegiance to George II.

In their anti-Hanoverian campaign the Opposition chiefs skirted close to the border of disloyalty. They contended, of course, that they aimed only at evil advisers, but since the popular prejudice arose from George's affection for his Electorate, they were in fact inflaming opinion against the King himself.[4] They also resorted to the questionable expedient of conferring with the agents of foreign powers to build a case against the policy of their own Government.[5] With the country at war and threatened by a Jacobite invasion, the Opposition certainly gave aid and comfort to the King's enemies.[6] But freedom of speech and the Press were so firmly established that the Government took no legal action, and provoking as Anticourt extravagance undeniably was, the ministers affected to despise its influence: 'Thank God!' exclaimed Winnington in Parliament, 'the insignificancy of opposition, when not founded on solid and right principles, is now as well known abroad as it is at home.'[7]

[1] Ibid. 463.

[2] Graham, ed., *Annals of Stair*, ii. 288; H.M.C., *Frankland–Russell–Astley MSS.*, 289, 295, 297.   [3] *P.H.* xiii. 467.

[4] The Speaker several times reproved Opposition orators for direct reflections upon the king: ibid. 141–2, 464.

[5] Rose, ed., *Marchmont Papers*, i. 20–69.

[6] In his *History of England*, viii. 595–7, Tindal doubtless exaggerates in making Opposition diatribes the primary cause of the '45. But there is no doubt about the encouragement the Jacobites drew from anti-Hanoverian sentiment. In April 1743 John Murray thought the fury against 'the Duke of Hannover' worth 10,000 troops to the Pretender's cause: W. B. Blaikie, ed., *Origins of the Forty-Five* (Edinburgh, 1916), p. 24.

[7] *P.H.* xiii. 170–1. In February 1744 the Government arrested the Jacobite agent, Colonel Cecil, and Lord Barrymore, a Jacobite M.P., on suspicion of

The Government suffered only one defeat in Parliament during 1742–4, but it could scarcely be accounted a triumph for the Opposition. On 20 February 1744 Limerick, a follower of Pulteney and nominal supporter of the Ministry, carried by eight votes a motion to replace a tax on sugar, proposed by Pelham, with a tariff on imported linen. The Scottish members, hoping that this project would encourage linen manufacture in north Britain, provided the support necessary to upset Pelham's proposal. In the event, the defeat was a matter of no consequence. The First Lord of the Treasury had to abandon his sugar tax, but next day without a division he put through a move to employ the surplus revenue of the liquor duties instead of the linen tariff.[1] The loss of a finance measure still did not seriously disturb an eighteenth-century Government. The issue cut across party lines, and the Opposition did nothing to aggravate Pelham's minor discomfiture.

On the other hand, their repeated failures embittered the quarrels among the Anti-courtiers themselves. As had happened so often in the past, 'the Parliament broke up with a great deal of ill humour and discontent on the part of the Opposition'.[2] Chesterfield's prediction that the new Opposition would repeat the success of the old in a much shorter space of time seemed far from fulfilment. It was clearly not in their power to force the Ministry to an accommodation. Their one positive achievement was to infect so many of the old corps with a dislike of 'Hanoverian measures' and the 'Hanover troop master' as to increase the Pelhams' desire to be rid of Carteret.

The Fall of Carteret

Friction within the Ministry first led to negotiations with the Opposition in the late summer of 1743. Until that time the leaders of the old corps showed a determination to stand by the reconstruction of 1742. Orford had advised them that 'there can be no change but for the worse',[3] and during the parliamentary session of 1742–3 the Ministry followed the rigid political line that had characterized the last ten years of his régime. Then in July 1743 the death of Wilmington forced a

complicity in an invasion plot. Secret intelligence, not Opposition activity, was the basis for their apprehension. The ministers left the other Jacobites in Parliament free to declaim against them.

[1] *P.H.* xiii. 652–5.   [2] Ibid. 857.   [3] Coxe, *Pelham*, i. 35.

change. Pelham worsted Bath in the contest for the vacant Treasury, and the old corps began to view their situation in a new light.

As soon as he learned of Pelham's success Orford sent him on 25 August 1743 a lengthy proposal for a radical reorientation of his political tactics.[1] It was now clear, said Orford, that any peace terms offered by the 'new Whigs' would be 'false and deceitful'. He therefore advised a cautious campaign to oust them by a junction with the 'broad bottoms'.

> Your strength [Orford wrote] must be formed of your own friends, the old corps, and recruits from the Cobham squadron, who should be persuaded, now Bath is beaten, it makes room for them, if they will not crowd the door when the house is on fire, that nobody can go in or out . . . if they still meditate the fall of the great man [Carteret], the attempt, instantly, will be in vain, which time, management, and opportunity may bring about.

The Pelhams need not fear, Orford went on, that Carteret would beat them at their own game: 'Broad Bottom cannot be made for anything that has a zest for Hanover.' The retired Minister concluded by recommending a return to the tactics that had served him so well until the hardening of political attitudes around 1731: 'Whig it with all opponents that will parly; but 'ware Tory! I never mean to a person or so; but what they can bring with them will prove a broken reed.'

The old corps leaders followed Orford's advice to the letter. Negotiations were opened through Gower and Cobham, the two 'broad-bottom' peers in place, who provided a liaison with the malcontents. After a month of wary manœuvring Pelham and Chesterfield met at the end of September in a four-hour conference which touched upon all the major problems involved in reaching an agreement. Frankly and confidently, Chesterfield reported to Gower, Pelham laid down an 'ultimatum [which] in short may be reduced to this:[2]

> 1st that he is engaged in honour, though not in conscience, not to break with his new allys [Carteret and Bath] in case they will submit, as he believes they will do, and as, by what he told me, I believe they will.

---

[1] Ibid. 91–93.
[2] P.R.O., Granville Papers 1, C. to Gower, 2 Oct. 1743. The style and attitude of 'C.' identify him unmistakably as Chesterfield.

2dly that he will not take in the few Torys proposed, upon the coalition, but only upon a personal foot, and that even he would rather have 'em without their followers than with, for fear of offending the old Whig corps.

3dly that the places vacant at present were at our service, upon the foregoing principle, and that he saw no great likelihood of any more being vacant unless his new allies broke all measures with him, which he did not think they would.

4^{thly} that as to publick measures, a peace should be made if it could, but in case a continuance of the war was inevitable, a continuation of the Hanover troops was so too, and that upon their present foot without those correctives and qualifications which I hinted as the only expedients that could enable us (and that but awkwardly too) to vote for 'em.'

The Opposition chiefs found all these stipulations quite unacceptable, Chesterfield continued. He and Pelham concluded that, barring accidents, the negotiation was at an end.

This being the case, all that we have to do, in my opinion, is to prepare for battle, to procure an early and universal attendance of all our people, and to blow the Hanover flame to the height. The evidence of the danger may possibly prevail, where the strength of the reasoning could not persuade; and I am convinced that if a treaty [with the old corps] is concluded, it can only be done sword in hand and immediately before the battle.

The wily diplomat nevertheless urged Gower to let the other malcontent leaders believe that the negotiation had been suspended, not ended, for fear of 'consequences that would render the renewal of it more difficult if not impracticable'.

For two months more, leaders on both sides continued to think and talk of a possible accommodation. The Opposition insisted uncompromisingly upon the dismissal of the 'deserters', the inclusion of the Tories *en bloc*, and 'correctives and qualifications' to make the Hanover troops palatable. Nothing was said of popular Bills. The conditions were purely political, designed to bring the malcontents into office on the most favourable terms with a show of public principle. Yet it must be observed that, with the exception of the 'deserters', the 'broad bottoms' stipulated for a broad bottom.

Of the ministers only Newcastle appears to have been intimidated by the Opposition negotiating 'sword in hand'.

Early in November he drew up a memorandum giving five reasons for dropping the subsidy to the Hanover troops. His fifth and conclusive argument was, 'It will open the best door to a reconciliation with the present opposers and enable us to insist upon better conditions for ourselves and our friends; that is, not to oblige us to consent to every thing they shall ask'.[1] Political tactics aside, Newcastle wrote, 'Jeffrey Broad-Bottom's' diatribes in *Old England* had convinced him that the Hanoverians obstructed Britain's war aims. Pelham, stoutly backed by Orford, stuck by his ultimatum. Gower and Cobham threw up their places on 8 December, and both sides abandoned hope of an accommodation for the remainder of the session.

Meanwhile Carteret had made a bid for Tory support. We know little more about it than the bare fact. He and Bath may have heard of their rivals' negotiation, which seems to have been an open secret. They may have been unsettled by Bath's failure to secure the Treasury. At all events, toward the end of 1743 Carteret is reported 'to have offered *carte blanche* to the Tories in return for their support of his measures'.[2] They declined to parley. Perhaps, as Walpole had predicted, the Minister's 'zest for Hanover' proved too strong a repellant.

The divided ministers and their quarrelling opponents now struggled unhappily with their difficulties until the appearance of a *deus ex machina*. The god was Bolingbroke. Despite his steady opposition, he had long maintained friendly relations with Lord Chancellor Hardwicke. As soon as Bolingbroke realized that he would gain nothing from the reconstruction of 1742, he began sedulously to cultivate this friendship.[3] The two men carried on an extensive correspondence in 1743–4.[4] Then Bolingbroke decided to return to England. In July 1744 he settled in his house in Battersea, where, he told Hardwicke, he proposed to centre his existence, visiting London 'as seldom as it

---

[1] Coxe, *Pelham*, i. 107.

[2] Owen, *Rise of the Pelhams*, p. 190. The story rests upon a communication to Pelham's biographer, Coxe, from Philip Yorke, the parliamentary diarist, a good many years after the event. Yorke may have been thinking of the statement in his journal that in November 1744 Carteret 'proposed *charte blanche* to the Opposition' (*P.H.* xiii. 982). Owen nevertheless accepts the evidence for the offer of 1743, which is inherently probable and quite consistent with Carteret's cavalier political tactics.

[3] Yorke, *Hardwicke*, i. 310.

[4] A large portion of their correspondence is contained in Add. MSS. 35587.

becomes one to do who is marked out for having the cloven foot'.[1] Twenty years before, Bolingbroke's return to the political scene had been followed by an endeavour to work out an accommodation between his old friends and the Ministry, and, upon its failure, the formation of the Opposition to Walpole. Now, in his second advent the veteran intriguer set out to explore the possibility of forming a 'national ministry'.[2]

In the early days of his return, Bolingbroke's informants pressed upon him three cardinal points.[3] First, the Opposition must exploit the breach between Carteret and the Pelhams. To attack without making a 'distinction between the parts of the administration' would drive them to a unity sufficient to defeat their enemies. But, as William Murray insisted, 'the breach might be widened so as to force them to a rupture before the session was half over, could one part of them see that they [*sic*] would be supported by the Opposition'. Second, Chesterfield, who held the pre-eminent position in the malcontent Junto, was a weak and despondent leader. Though he spoke bold and fiery words, he acted timidly, indecisively, and in dread of his more hot-headed colleagues. He must be guided. Third, since neither the Pelhams nor the Opposition had changed their views, 'a treaty was impracticable'. To these advices Bolingbroke gave fair words and careful thought. Before long he perceived the necessary course of action. On 10 August he explained it to Chesterfield.

The 'broad bottoms' and the old corps must effect a 'junction' to oust Carteret and the deserters. To initiate a treaty the Opposition should communicate to the Ministry a message framed as follows:[4] 'This is our plan for home affairs, and this for foreign; will you and the Pelhams propose this and adhere to it in the closet? If you will, we support you in it, or fall with you.' The key to Bolingbroke's plan lies in the phrase 'in the closet'. He intended, not Chesterfield's design for a parliamentary triumph comparable to that of 1742, but a palace revolution. Initially Bolingbroke did not hint at any timetable

---

[1] Add. MSS. 35587, f. 271.   [2] Rose, ed., *Marchmont Papers*, i. 11.
[3] Ibid. 10–12.
[4] Ibid, 19. In Marchmont's disconnected diary there is no antecedent for the 'you' who is bracketed with the Pelhams. It may refer to Stair, who was then busily peddling gossip between Ministry and Opposition; but much more likely 'you' meant anyone who negotiated for the Ministry.

of operations. It is probably significant, however, that he first broached his plan shortly after receiving two pieces of intelligence from the Court: one, that Newcastle had bluntly told the King that there were still three months before the meeting of Parliament to 'lay aside' ministers whose advice he disliked;[1] the other, a broad hint from Pelham that events had made him more tractable.[2]

The fundamental simplicity of Bolingbroke's plan did not mean that it would be easy to execute. The leaders of the old corps must be persuaded to agree to a policy acceptable to the Opposition. They must be convinced that the Opposition would support them in the bold move of presenting their common policy as an ultimatum to the King. Bolingbroke was sure that the old corps loved their places so well that 'they could agree to no such measure unless they were quite sure of carrying it'. The malcontent chiefs must be brought to compose their differences. Pitt and the young orators must soften their harsh language. Chesterfield, as the pre-eminent member of the Junto, must be driven to resolute action. To achieve all this, Bolingbroke admitted, would require *astutia Italiana*.[3]

In the weeks following 10 August his fine Italian hand stirred the waters of intrigue to their depths. He carefully controlled his agitation according to his most recent intelligence of the attitudes and actions of Courtiers and malcontents, encouraging each to think well of the other, withholding information that might cause friction, endlessly urging a *rapprochement* to implement his plan. The record of his activities is far from complete, and upon occasion he was so devious as to raise doubts about his immediate objectives. It is nevertheless clear that he enjoyed the confidence of leaders in both camps, which made him better informed than either, and that in consequence he occupied a key position in effecting the 'junction'. That the operation did not proceed exactly according to Bolingbroke's plan was no fault of his.

[1] Ibid. 10. George II was in England, having reluctantly submitted to pressure from both factions in the Ministry to give up his annual visit to Hanover. 'I know what this is', the disappointed King said to a protesting Hardwicke; 'it is contention for power and from motives of that kind that I am to be confin'd' (Yorke, *Hardwicke*, i. 347). Certainly had George been abroad until near the opening of Parliament, as was his custom, the fall of Carteret could not have been achieved as it was.

[2] Rose, ed., *Marchmont Papers*, i. 16.   [3] Ibid. 15, 19.

The discord of the 'angry chiefs' constituted the major obstacle. Bolingbroke repeatedly insisted that

the pathetic style should be used to the Pelhams, and all particular bargains laid aside; but it should be tried to persuade 'em to act upon an English plan, and, in general, told 'em, they should be supported in it, and if they did not succeed in the closet, they should be supported in Parliament with facts.[1]

Chesterfield blew hot and cold. At one moment he agreed. At another his old distrust of the old corps overcame him, and proclaiming their professions of goodwill only a ruse to 'soften people', he called for a vigorous attack on the Pelhams. Pitt remained a determined *enragé*, eager to assault 'weak, insincere' ministers but opposed to the methods proposed by Cobham and the Grenvilles. They, in turn, alternated between despairing wrath and conciliation. Lyttelton took the opinion of the last man he talked to. Waller grew deaf and indifferent.[2] Bolingbroke could not bring this 'jangling junto' to open negotiations for a treaty. If anything were to be done, the old corps had to take the initiative.

Since midsummer Newcastle had been pressing Hardwicke and Pelham for action to oust Carteret. The Duke sought to provoke a crisis on the conduct of the war 'to remove the cause and author of all these misfortunes, or to continue no longer ourselves'.[3] Gently and artfully Bolingbroke encouraged Hardwicke and Murray to believe that they could count on the support of the Opposition. On 19 September Hardwicke drew up, for presentation to the King, a memorial embodying the Pelhams' criticisms of Carteret and counter-proposals for foreign policy. After some emendations Newcastle secured the approval of the old corps leaders, and Hardwicke submitted the memorial to Bolingbroke. The veteran intriguer replied theatrically, 'My Lord, I will seal it with my blood'.[4] With no further assurance, the Pelhams decided to act.

On 1 November 1744 Newcastle waded into the Rubicon by presenting the memorial to George II. The king returned it without comment. After Pelham had reported a sullen

---

[1] Rose, ed., *Marchmont Papers*, i. 38, 57, 71.
[2] These reactions are recorded in ibid. 38, 52, 57–58, 67, 71, 75.
[3] Coxe, *Pelham*, i. 175.　　　　　　　　　　　　　　　[4] *P.H.* xiii. 977.

interview in the closet on the following day, Newcastle began to
fear that the scheme would fail. The King and Carteret (now
Granville) would agree to the memorial, he thought, with the
intention of nullifying it later. 'This is what I most dread', he
wrote to Hardwicke, 'and I own I think nothing will prevent it
but a concert *entamé*, in a proper manner, directly with Lord
Chesterfield.'[1] Still, the Duke made no move to open negotiations but urged his colleagues to press their policy upon the
King. Then on 6 November Newcastle led the old corps to the
Rubicon's south bank: he informed the King in a 'peremptory
message' that they would no longer serve with Granville—
either he or they must go.[2]

An excited Bolingbroke told Marchmont 'that now we had
the thing in our hands . . . the Pelhams could not go back'.[3]
Even the suspicious Chesterfield quickly understood that 'there
was now no fear of the Opposition being in the power of the
Pelhams; but that these were evidently in the power of the
Opposition'.[4] Bolingbroke nevertheless dreaded, and rightly so,
that the members of the discordant Junto would 'spoil' a negotiation with the Ministry. Professing a completely disinterested
desire to serve the nation, he therefore began to coach their
leader and wheedle the others into line. He advised Chesterfield

not to talk with Mr. Pelham as treating with him, but as adjusting
a concert for the manner of carrying on a plan already agreed to
between 'em, and to express no jealousy or aversion to the old Court
party, but to assure him that the deserters were those whom the
Opposition abhorred.[5]

The malcontents must not, Bolingbroke insisted, stipulate for
places in the first instance. The details of reconstruction could
be worked out easily once mutual confidence had been established. A junction of 'broad bottoms' and the old corps could be
successfully achieved only upon the basis of a clear agreement
on foreign and domestic policy.

Though wavering and desponding at times Chesterfield
learned his lesson well. Bolingbroke set negotiations in train by
arranging a meeting between Pelham and the Junto leader on

[1] Coxe, *Pelham*, i. 186.   [2] Rose, ed., *Marchmont Papers*, i. 76.
[3] Ibid. 75–76.   [4] Ibid. 80.   [5] Ibid. 78.

11 November. At the end of ten days the concert had been arranged. The Opposition consented to a slightly modified version of the policy embodied in Hardwicke's memorial. Pelham gave way to Chesterfield's demand that all the deserters be dismissed to make room for the 'broad bottoms': 'the victims are at the altar already; let 'em bleed' was Chesterfield's vengeful statement. He conceded

that he would not insist on their being moved before the meeting of the Parliament, but that if nobody was wiser than he, he would not stir one step without a positive engagement that a sufficient number should be filled up at the recess; that else they might be deceived, which he would not be; that pledges were ridiculous; and that they [the Opposition leaders] must bring their party with them, who otherwise would say, this was Carteret and Bath over again.[1]

At 2 in the morning of 21 November Pelham and Chesterfield settled the general terms of the 'consolidation'. The latter then threw himself into the delicate task of discovering the pretensions of his colleagues so that he might present a full list of appointments to be demanded.

Meanwhile, the Court cast about for means to save Granville. The King quickly summoned Orford, who had solved so many of his problems for so many years. Restrained initially by illness and then by his brother's advice to procrastinate, the old Chief Minister did not reach London until the crisis had passed.[2] George II, left to his own resources, first tried to dissuade the Pelhams and their allies from executing their threat. They stood firm. Knowing that Granville could not manage the Government without the majority in both Houses controlled by the old corps, the King and the Prince next tried to divide those who had subscribed to the ultimatum. This also failed. The Court then turned to the 'broad bottoms'. At the very time that the 'concert' was being concluded, the Prince sent messages to Chesterfield, Gower, and Cobham 'desiring the Opposition to come in with Carteret, who would make room for 'em all'. The Junto leaders, now quite sure of preferment from the old corps, proudly declined, giving their refusal as proof that they opposed not for places but on principle.[3] Since George II was prone to

---

[1] Rose, ed., *Marchmont Papers*, i. 87.   [2] Coxe, *Walpole*, iii. 601–6.
[3] Rose, ed., *Marchmont Papers*, i. 88; *Memorials of the Public Life and Character of James Oswald of Dunnikier* (Edinburgh, 1825), p. 37.

strong and colourful language, it is a pity that no one preserved his reaction to this brazen imposture.

The Court had no resources left. Granville resigned on 24 November. Nine days later Chesterfield, Cobham, and Gower presented 'the names and numbers of our necessary people' to Newcastle, Pelham, Hardwicke, and Harrington. 'Several more meetings were held before the alterations could be settled', wrote Philip Yorke, 'and many rubs and difficulties intervened.'[1] The testy King objected to some changes. Cobham was truculent. Various pretensions clashed. Thinly attended, Parliament accomplished little while the leaders intrigued. At length on 22 December the major changes were announced, and a few minor appointments followed shortly after the Recess.

The complex work of reconstruction was carried out with delicacy and skill. Thirteen 'deserters' of the Bath–Granville connexion bled on the altar of 'broad bottom'. One of the Prince's followers chose to resign, but none was dismissed. Compensation was provided for the few members of the old corps who had to give way. Into the places thus made available went fifteen of the Opposition, five peers and ten commoners.[2] All the prominent leaders except William Pitt received preferment. The King detested Pitt, and the one place he would accept could not be opened up. He professed himself content with promises for the future. Included among the 'new allies' were Cotton and Philips, two Tories who were reputed Jacobites. The reconstruction, in sum, appeared to have achieved the major objectives of those who made it: they had reached a general agreement on ministerial policy; Granville and most of the 'deserters' had been ousted without alienating the Prince; the most avid place-hunters had been satisfied; and the old corps had re-established its ascendancy at Court.

Thus concluded the third successful Opposition of the Hanoverian era. The rift in the Ministry was the most important factor in the 'broad bottoms' triumph. It is true that the Pelhams disliked defending unpopular measures in Parliament, fearing that discontent might cause disintegration of the old corps. It is true that the Opposition had done much to make the unpopular measures unpopular. And it is true that the ministers,

---

[1] *P.H.* xiii. 987.
[2] See the summary of changes given in Owen, *Rise of the Pelhams*, pp. 243–50.

anxious not to raise up against themselves an Opposition comparable to the coalition that had brought down Walpole, wished to silence the bitter attacks of the malcontents in Parliament and the Press. But in 1744 the 'broad bottoms' could not have gained 'victory with numbers'. They had accumulated no additional strength during two sessions. Their own weaknesses and extravagance gave no fair prospect of growth or solidarity in the near future. As late as 10 November, the day before negotiations began, Newcastle thought that his problems might be solved by kicking Granville upstairs to the Presidency of the Council with the Order of the Garter.[1] If the old corps had made this move, there would have been no necessity to sacrifice the 'deserters' or to take in the 'broad bottoms'. The negotiations were initiated by a united old corps with a divided Opposition, who owed much of their success to the skilful tutelage of the proscribed Bolingbroke. Without his direction it is doubtful if the members of the 'jangling junto' would ever have overcome their own dissension to exploit the ministerial breach.

The malcontents of 1742–4 consequently made no contribution to the institutional development of parliamentary Opposition. Although the 'broad bottoms'' conduct in the two Houses played an important part in their leaders' accession to office, the ministerial reconstruction was fundamentally the work of a powerful group of Courtiers who feared one of their colleagues more than they hated their nominal enemies. Like so many place-hunters before them the 'broad bottoms' clambered into office by the back stairs.

The 'Forty-Eight-Hour Ministry'

'Broad bottom' fulfilled its promise in part. The great majority of active politicians had their pretensions reasonably well satisfied, and they were reasonably well agreed upon public measures. With little left to fight about, and few left to start a fight, 'broad bottom' may seem to have inaugurated the long-desired era of national unity. Shortly after the completion of the

---

[1] Coxe, *Pelham*, i. 187. It is difficult to accept in full the contention of Owen (*Rise of the Pelhams*, pp. 230–1, 238) that the continuance of Granville or his policy doomed the Ministry to defeat in the approaching session of Parliament. Newcastle's correspondence indicates that he was motivated primarily by fear of losing influence in the closet.

treaty, Hardwicke proudly told the King that a scrutiny of the House of Commons would 'find no man of business or even of weight left, capable of heading or conducting an Opposition'.[1]

The old corps leaders considered this a highly desirable situation. They had become firm believers in 'broad bottom' as the most feasible political formula. Though tenacious of their own power, they were men of goodwill, anxious to allay domestic strife. In the years ahead they went to great lengths to satisfy the demands of those who threatened to disrupt the general pacification. The Tories were promised places in the Commissions of the Peace.[2] Old animosities were forgotten whenever expedient—within seven years even Granville had been forgiven and taken back into the Ministry. Bolingbroke's programme for the Opposition was receiving a serious trial by the Government.

But the treaty did not achieve stability at the outset. So much friction still remained that Britain had to pass through one more crisis before the new régime was settled in power. The Tories and many of the 'broad bottoms' submitted no more easily to party discipline than they had in Opposition. Though the ministers suffered no defeats, they were irritated by the way-ward voting of their new allies and embarrassed by the revival of Country party motions.[3] The reconstruction was so patently another change of men but not of measures that public Prints poured disillusioned scorn upon the politicians who had put 'an end to public virtue'.[4] Much more serious than all else, however, was the undisguised hostility of the monarch.

The 'broad-bottom' treaty did not make George II a happy and powerful patriot king. Outraged at having been 'forced' a second time, he continued to consult Granville 'behind the curtain'. At audiences in the closet he cursed and damned the Pelhams, using 'such foul language that no one gentleman could take from another'.[5] Neither the reasoned blandishments of Hardwicke nor the meek forbearance of Newcastle and his

[1] Coxe, *Pelham*, i, 202.

[2] Add. MSS. 32993, ff. 289, 304, 308.

[3] *P.H.* xiii. 1051–2, 1056–1107, 1202–50. Chesterfield's letters to Gower at this time (in P.R.O., Granville Papers 1) reflect the Ministry's uneasiness.

[4] *An Address of Thanks to the Broad-Bottoms* (London, 1745) is probably the most devastating and certainly the most scatological political pamphlet of this period.

[5] Add. MSS. 32705, f. 187.

brother could placate the resentful monarch.[1] In marked contrast to his acceptance of the treaty of 1742, George II obdurately declined to recognize the finality of the accommodation of 1744. For the first time since the accession, a Hanoverian King became the leader of the Opposition.

Early in the autumn of 1745 George made the first move to change his administration. He invited Lord Harrington to reconstruct the Government, excluding the Pelhams. Harrington declined with the impertinent suggestion that 'Granville might be tried'.[2] The restless activity of William Pitt then brought matters to a crisis. His pretensions still unsatisfied, Pitt began to harass the Government when the Parliamentary session opened in mid-October. To suffer the annoyance of Tory Independents was an easy matter compared to enduring the onslaught of the 'young orator'. After several parleys the Pelhams decided to press for his admission to office. In January 1746 the King countered by turning to Bath and Granville. Their plan seems to have been to build up strength while the Ministry got the King's business done, then to reconstruct the Government after Parliament was prorogued.

The wily Pelhams forestalled them. Seeing Pitt held off and Granville's advice taken in a crucial matter in foreign affairs, the old corps leaders determined to resign. For over six months the foreign war and Jacobite invasion had inhibited their desire to quit under the King's abuse. Now they took the bold step. Pushing Harrington before him, Newcastle delivered up his Seals on 10 February 1746. The next day Pelham and four peers surrendered their offices, and then the royal closet was mobbed by placemen turning in their resignations. A total of forty-five are said to have quit or informed the King that they intended to.[3]

George II designated Bath for the Treasury, gave Granville the Seals of both Secretaries of State, and commissioned the two earls to form a Government. Winchilsea accepted the Admiralty, and the Privy Seal was given to Carlisle. There the appointments stopped. Despite the strenuous efforts of Bath, no

---

[1] Coxe, *Pelham*, i. 198–207, 227–9, 260–1. The original account of Hardwicke's celebrated audience with the King on 5 Jan. 1745 is in Add. MSS. 35870, ff. 87–91.

[2] Add. MSS. 33073, f. 229.

[3] See Owen's analysis of this transaction in *Rise of the Pelhams*, pp. 283–95.

other competent men could be persuaded to embark upon the venture. A wit remarked 'that it was not safe to walk the streets at night for fear of being pressed for a Cabinet Counsellor'.[1] Forty-eight hours after receiving his commission, Bath reported to the King that 'he had tried the House of Commons and found *it would not do*'.[2] George capitulated. Closing his door upon the host still endeavouring to resign, he sent Winnington to recall his old ministers.

Their terms were severe. They insisted upon the King's full confidence, both in appearance and in fact. He had to promise that he would no longer take 'private councils', that he would follow the Pelhams' foreign policy, and that he would in various ways give 'public marks' of his satisfaction with his administration. William Pitt must have 'some honourable employment', and all placemen connected with Bath and Granville must be dismissed.[3] George II held out on only two points. Pitt could have an office but not the one he wanted, Secretary at War; and two friends of Granville should be allowed to keep their positions in the Royal Household. Vengeful as ever, Chesterfield counselled 'point de faiblesse humaine, point de quartier', but the Pelhams let the King have his way.[4] All other stipulations were carried out to the letter.

Upon the demise of the 'Forty-Eight-Hour Ministry', wrote Horace Walpole, 'Lord Granville is as jolly as ever; laughs and drinks and owns it was mad, and owns he would do it again tomorrow'.[5] Another such venture would have been equal madness at any early date. During their long years in office the old corps leaders had acquired three powerful assets. First, they had learned the need for concord and united action, and they had grown skilful in the use of the strength thus acquired. George II, Bath, and Granville were clumsy intriguers compared with Hardwicke and the Pelhams. Second, the old corps had become so firmly entrenched that no realistic politician would believe

---

[1] Coxe, *Pelham*, i. 292.

[2] Lewis, ed., *Horace Walpole's Correspondence*, xix. 212.

[3] Add. MSS. 35870, f. 117.

[4] Sir William Lodge, ed., *Private Correspondence of Chesterfield and Newcastle, 1744–46* (London, 1930), pp. 106–12. Two years later Chesterfield professed to abhor the resignations and the severe terms imposed upon the Crown, both of which he had been the first to recommend, in *An Apology for a Late Resignation in a Letter from an English Gentleman to his Friend at The Hague* (London, [1748]), p. 15.

[5] Lewis, ed., *Horace Walpole's Correspondence*, xix. 213.

that they could be abruptly dispensed with. A lengthy period of careful manœuvring would have been necessary to undermine their position. Their rapid mass resignation denied their rivals the opportunity to destroy their solidarity and the general confidence in their indispensability. Third, the old corps had, as Hardwicke boasted, absorbed most of the leading talent in the House of Commons. When the Pelhams led their followers out of office, the King and his agents could not find men capable of the administrative and parliamentary labour to conduct the royal Government.

As leader of the Opposition the King did not, of course, intend to get rid of the old corps. He meant only to replace some of their leaders. Their solidarity prevented him. No combination of the remaining malcontents, even with royal support, could overbalance so powerful a coalition on short notice. George's capitulation confirmed the prevalent conviction that the old corps were practically irremovable. 'Things are now upon a right foot', wrote Chesterfield to Newcastle, 'and you are Minister for life if you please.'[1] Those who did not live too long bore out his prediction.

3. PRINCE FREDERICK'S OPPOSITION

Within a few months George II had become reconciled to the dominance of the Pelhams. Some thought his attitude merely the resignation of a tired old man, weary of political bickering after nearly twenty years on the throne.[2] This view doubtless has some truth in it. But George had proved himself a resilient king, capable of dealing realistically with realities when fully convinced that they were real. Long before 1746 he had learned that his personal wishes could not always prevail, and he never abandoned his principle that it was the business of a king, regardless of his own predilections, to maintain a stable Government. The fiasco of February persuaded him, in the best interest of his realm, to eschew the leadership of an Opposition to his ministers.

That role was now resumed by his eldest son. Frederick had given general, if wavering and erratic, adherence to the Govern-

---

[1] Lodge, ed., *Private Correspondence of Chesterfield and Newcastle*, p. 113.
[2] Coxe, *Pelham*, i. 366; Rose, ed., *Marchmont Papers*, i. 197.

ment since the fall of Walpole. Early in 1746 he clearly displayed his current position by dismissing his Attorney-General
for failing to support the Pelhams.[1] After the 'Forty-Eight-Hour
Ministry' he ordered his followers to vote against the Court, and
the first to disobey promptly lost his post in the Prince's household.[2] Frederick maintained a steady opposition for the
remaining five years of his life.

The Constitution of the New Party

His motives were a mixture of old and new. He frankly
admitted that he wanted 'to have the influence due to his rank'.[3]
The King had denied him a command in the '45, and the
principals in the February affair had ignored him altogether.
In turning to Opposition he again took the heir's conventional
route to prominence.

On public grounds, Frederick averred, it was his duty to
redeem the King 'out of those hands that have sullied the Crown
and . . . with my friends' assistance, to rescue, a second time,
this kingdom out of wicked hands'.[4] This declaration, much as
it sounded like the professions of a decade before, now had a
deeper meaning. The Prince saw clearly the significance of the
'Forty-Eight-Hour Ministry'. Despite his occasional bold predictions of approaching triumph—the necessary boast of all
party leaders—he did not hope to displace the Pelhams during
his father's lifetime; and he realized that unless he took effective
action he could not easily get rid of them after his accession.
Frederick's feelings emerged clearly in a statement reported
by a Court spy in April 1747:[5]

que s[a] m[ajesté] est entre les mains des Pelhams, qui ont toujours
été ses ennemis. . . . Qu'ils se tiennent s[a] m[ajesté] dans une espèce
d'esclavage. . . . Qu'un jour viendra pour les faire rendre compte de
leur conduite, ayant nourri la rebellion pour obliger le roi à faire
une mauvaise paix, et ayant forcé s[a] m[ajesté] à les maintenir dans
leur pouvoir dans le gouvernement. Que personne de bonne intention devoit s'étonner que s[on] a[ltesse] r[oyale] tâche d'en tirer

---

[1] Ibid. ii. 165–6.
[2] *H.M.C., Egmont Diary*, iii. 315; Lewis, ed., *Horace Walpole's Correspondence*, xix.
229.
[3] Rose, ed., *Marchmont Papers*, ii. 231.   [4] Coxe, *Pelham*, i. 492–3.
[5] Add. MSS. 32808, ff. 126–7 (italics mine).

raison, formant un parti pour délivrer le roi, le royaume, *et soi-même* de cette espèce de tyrans.

Clearly the Prince dreaded the prospect of inheriting the Pelhams. Hence his ultimate objective was[1]

to have it in his power, when king, to choose such ministers as he chose to confide in . . . he must begin by attaching to himself such men as had and were thought to have honesty and ability to carry on the business in Parliament and in office; and that the merit and not the number of such was to be considered, for this [the number] would follow the first [merit], as every one would follow another, as they saw those engaged in a probability of being able to carry on a ministry. . . .

The Prince's friends were to be chosen and organized so that they might become the king's friends in the next reign.

The new Opposition, Horace Walpole wrote maliciously, was 'composed of the refuse of every party'.[2] Frederick did indeed recruit from all available sources, and it is true that in five years he attracted few men of ability. His followers were 're-fuse' in the sense that, having rejected or been rejected by the groups in power, they placed their hopes in the future. There were, in general, four main blocs.[3]

The core consisted of the old 'Leicester House gang', the Household officers and other Courtiers who had attached them-selves to His Royal Highness before 1746. In number about thirty, they were for the most part country gentlemen of little distinction. Some, like Sir George Oxenden and Daniel Boone, had held minor offices in the Government. Thomas Pitt was the party's able manager of elections. Henry Bathurst reached the Woolsack a quarter of a century later. But as a whole the group was characterized by its reputed leader, the Prince's favourite, Lord Baltimore: genial and good natured, 'the best and honestest man in the world but not capable of conducting a party'.[4]

---

[1] Rose, ed., *Marchmont Papers*, ii. 231–2. Frederick also considered his party as a necessary support against any attempt to alter the succession in favour of Cumberland or to give Cumberland, by the act of a subservient parliament, such power in the next reign as to make Frederick 'une statue sur le trône, sans pouvoir ni con-sidération, et soumis à son frère cadet': Add. MSS. 32808, f. 263.

[2] *Memoirs of George II*, i. 47.

[3] There is a full list of the prince's party in the Commons as of April 1746 in Add. MSS. 33034, ff. 110–11.

[4] Lewis, ed., *Horace Walpole's Correspondence*, xix. 360.

A large portion of the Bath–Granville connexion naturally gravitated to the Prince. Names long familiar in opposition—Carlisle and Limerick, Rushout and Gybbon, Jeffreys and Rudge—were now found again on the lists of those voting with Leicester House. George Lee and the rising young Robert Nugent took Household offices and places of leadership in the party. Bath himself gave the Prince active support.[1] Granville and Winchilsea, however, dissociated themselves altogether from their old friends. Abandoning his insouciant inclination to undertake another 'mad' adventure, Granville swore that he would never again enter an Opposition. He rebuffed one of several overtures from Frederick with the frank statement 'that he did not wish the public to hold him responsible for the conduct of His Royal Highness; that, moreover, he was not made to play cards nor to accompany him in his other pleasures'.[2] But the Prince never ceased to long for the return of the old leader whose advice he had so long followed and to whom he had given such loyal support.

Once the new Opposition was well under way, another of the great opponents of Walpole reappeared. Bolingbroke made his third advent. Though increasingly infirm, he could not resist an opportunity to re-engage in the excitement of political intrigue. 'That man is at fourscore just what he was at forty!' the Prince once exclaimed.[3] Bolingbroke had gained nothing from the negotiations he guided in 1744, and now he seized one more chance to re-establish himself at Court. His role became that of senior adviser, to whom the plans of Leicester House were frequently submitted for the careful criticism he always delighted to give.[4]

[1] Ibid. 370; Coxe, *Pelham*, ii. 51.

[2] Add. MSS. 32812, ff. 382–3; see also ibid. 32808, ff. 306–8; 32809, f. 243; 32815, ff. 208–10. Chesterfield likewise refused to join the Prince. When he resigned in 1748, he vowed that 'he would not submit any more to the slavery of an Opposition' (ibid. 35337, f. 112); and nothing could shake his resolution.

[3] Walpole, *Memoirs of George II*, i. 223–4.

[4] Sichel, *Bolingbroke*, ii. 393, finds no evidence to support a statement of the second Lord Hardwicke that Bolingbroke 'went into connexions with Leicester House, and when the Prince of Wales died, was one of his first ministers'. Hardwicke probably exaggerates Bolingbroke's position, but for evidence of his place in the new Opposition see Coxe, *Pelham*, ii. 50; Walpole, *Memoirs of George II*, i. 209, n. 1; 223–4. In April 1751 Egmont noted 'that Bolingbroke acted weakly by showing a great deal of despair at the Prince's death, which showed he was not a great man, and that he was gone into the country and that it discovered his views': P.R.O., Egmont MSS. 277.

The Tories constituted the third bloc. Three major political crises in four years had done much to disconcert the 'true blues'. Gower's final defection to 'broad bottom' took off some of their number and left the faithful angry and disillusioned. When in early 1745 Lord Noel Somerset succeeded to the dukedom of Beaufort, and so to the nominal leadership of the Jacobite Tories, the group formally repudiated Gower and proclaimed their opposition.[1] The Government's conciliatory declaration concerning the Commissions of the Peace did little to placate them. Leicester House soon began to pay them court.

After months of careful negotiation with Lord Talbot and Sir Francis Dashwood, the Prince authorized them to issue a declaration 'to the gentlemen in the Opposition' on 4 June 1747.[2] This manifesto contains a large number of the 'Country party points' for which the Tories traditionally stood. His Royal Highness promised to establish a militia, exclude junior military officers from the House of Commons, and reform 'abuses in offices'. The Civil List would not be increased. The new reign would abolish 'all distinction of party'. All gentlemen paying £300 land tax would be admitted to the Commissions of the Peace, and the national administration was to 'be composed, without distinction, of men of dignity, knowledge, and probity'. Vowing never to come to an agreement with any administration unless he had previously secured these points, the Prince invited 'all well-wishers to this country and its constitution to coalise and unite with him'.

This declaration secured the nominal adherence of the 'true blues'. After eight months' hesitation a meeting of fourteen leading Tories, in response to a renewal of the manifesto, rather coldly guaranteed 'their utmost endeavours to support those his wise and salutary purposes'.[3] Another gathering in

[1] Lewis, ed., *Horace Walpole's Correspondence*, xix. 26. The Duke of Newcastle estimated that Gower brought forty Tories over to the Government: Lodge, ed., *Private Correspondence of Chesterfield and Newcastle*, pp. 40–41.

[2] The Prince's declaration has been often printed: e.g. Russell, ed., *Bedford Correspondence*, i. 320–3; Owen, *Rise of the Pelhams*, pp. 312–13. Manuscript copies survive in numerous collections including those of Egmont, Leeds, Shaftesbury, Granville, and Newcastle. Note the conspicuous absence of such 'Country party points' as reduction of the army and annual or triennial parliaments. Neither the Prince nor his Whig Courtiers could stomach these proposals.

[3] P.R.O., Shaftesbury MSS. 28, no. 65.

1749 renewed the alliance.[1] The Prince's steadiest Tory adherents came from their small group of placehunters, such men as Dashwood, Talbot, Mordaunt, Firebrace, and Powney.[2] The rank-and-file continued as independent as ever, but with occasional exceptions, their natural inclinations usually led them to divide against the Government.

The fourth bloc, if such it may be called, was made up of deserters from the Government. Among the most conspicuous were Lord Middlesex, Lord Doneraile, George Bubb Dodington, and Lord Chief Justice Willes, all of whom had long experience in politics. The most important was the second Earl of Egmont. Already well recognized as an able writer and speaker, he soon proved himself a talented organizer and party leader. He joined the Prince in March 1748, and within a brief time he assumed first place in the councils of Leicester House. Henry Fox's reference to him as 'Prime Minister Egmont' contained more truth than sarcasm.[3]

Had Frederick lived a few weeks longer an even more spectacular defection would have broken upon the world of politics. William Pitt, the Lytteltons, and the whole Grenville connexion had contracted to desert Government for Opposition.[4] Their restless ambition constrained by 'broad bottom', they prepared to pool their bets on the heir to the throne. Chesterfield had told Newcastle, '. . . If there is any considerable party left for them to retreat to, they will be eternally threatening you with such a retreat.'[5] The Prince's death postponed their desertion for another four years.

The four elements of the new Opposition never became formidable in numbers. Shortly after the 'Forty-Eight-Hour Ministry' Newcastle estimated them at 52, exclusive of the Tories.[6] The largest minority in the spring of 1746 was 122.[7] But

[1] Lewis, ed., *Horace Walpole's Correspondence*, xx. 50–51; Wyndham, ed., *Dodington Diary*, p. 93.

[2] P.R.O., Egmont MSS. 277. In calculating the reliable strength of the Prince's party, Egmont generally included the placehunters and specifically excluded the general body of the Tories.   [3] Coxe, *Pelham*, ii. 165.

[4] Ibid. 163–5; Walpole, *Memoirs of George II*, i. 12–13, 79–80, 201–2.

[5] Lodge, ed., *Private Correspondence of Chesterfield and Newcastle*, p. 114. The Pelhams were worried about the possible defection of Pitt ten days before the Prince's death: Add. MSS. 32724, ff. 175–6.

[6] Add. MSS. 33034, ff. 110–11.

[7] Owen, *Rise of the Pelhams*, p. 306, n. 1.

the Prince looked to a substantial increase of strength from the election due two years hence. As early as August 1746 Pelham was worried by the preparations of Leicester House 'against a new Parliament'.[1] Then in January and February 1747 the malcontents divided 143 and 150, leaving the Government with uncomfortably small margins of 41 and 47.[2] The Pelhams knew that their control of the House was not yet endangered, but they regarded with concern any indication of growing strength at Leicester House. Newcastle began to consider the wisdom of dissolving Parliament a year in advance. The current happy situation, he wrote to Cumberland in March, promised 'almost a certainty of choosing a good Whig Parliament this summer', but

any reverse of fortune, though not to be prevented, and any final conclusion of the war, by almost any peace that can be obtained, would undoubtedly give strength to Opposition, raise some flame in the nation, and render the choice of a Parliament more difficult. And I beg leave to add this, the present new Opposition is yet unsupported, unconnected, and not in high reputation. What the course of a year may produce, nobody can tell. Unfortunate public events or private disappointments, and personal views may render that Opposition formidable, which at present is far from being so.[3]

Just as their resignations in 1746 had forestalled the efforts of their opponents to unseat them, the old corps' leaders now upset Frederick's plans by a premature dissolution in June 1747.

The ruse worked. The dismayed malcontents put forth their best efforts,[4] but the election was one of the quietest of the century. In England and Wales there were only 42 contests in boroughs and 4 in counties—and only 16 petitions, one-half of which were soon dropped. Newcastle rejoiced, 'Our parliament is better than could have been expected'.[5] The Prince claimed, and the Ministry conceded him, about 215 seats, Tories included.[6] The figure proved to be high. After two parliamentary sessions Newcastle more realistically estimated 327 'for', 150

---

[1] Coxe, *Pelham*, i. 334.

[2] *Commons Journals*, xxiv. 256; xxv. 294. Horace Walpole wrote that the first of these divisions 'frightened the Ministry like a bomb': *Correspondence*, xix. 360.

[3] Coxe, *Pelham*, i. 491.

[4] Add. MSS. 32808, f. 281.

[5] P.R.O., Granville Papers 1: Newcastle to Gower, 18 July 1747.

[6] *H.M.C., Report 3*, p. 221; Add MSS. 33002, ff. 440–6.

'against', 74 'doubtful'.[1] At roughly the same time Egmont made an even more conservative estimate of those who could be relied upon to attend: 'We are not above 100 . . . composed of two sorts of men, about sixty country gentlemen and about forty servants or personal friends to the Prince of Wales.'[2] The Prince's Opposition divided 150 or over only twice: the greatest number was 184.[3] At the time of Frederick's death, Egmont recorded, 'Our party exclusive of the Tories consisted of about 60. But I would count only upon 40.'[4]

The Struggle over Policy

This small and disparate coalition had its headquarters, of course, at Leicester House. During its brief existence the Prince more than doubled the number of lucrative Household offices to provide places of honour and profit for his adherents.[5] He met occasionally with an inner circle whose membership was drawn from all groups but the Tories. Otherwise the Opposition acquired little party paraphernalia, except in the field of journalism. Occasional pamphlets attacked the Ministry.[6] As an inspiration to the malcontents Bolingbroke first printed in 1749 his *Letter on the Spirit of Patriotism* and *On the Idea of a Patriot King*. A hack-writer named James Ralph edited a weekly party journal, *The Remembrancer*, which Horace Walpole called 'the *Craftsman* of the present age', from December 1747 through June 1751.[7]

The writings of the malcontents merely adapted traditional ideas to fit current circumstances. 'Opposition is a counter-poison to misgovernment', said *The Remembrancer*. Its present duty is to pull down, not 'one over-grown minister', but 'a

[1] Add. MSS. 32994, f. 247. In the same document Dupplin calculated 302 'for', 153 'against', 97 'doubtful'.

[2] P.R.O., Egmont MSS. 220.　　　　　　　[3] *Commons Journals*, xxv. 696.

[4] P.R.O., Egmont MSS. 277, Journal. Waldegrave (*Memoirs*, p. 43) stated that the Opposition 'had been growing strong and formidable' till Frederick died. He probably knew of the prospective connexion with Pitt and foresaw further defections.

[5] A. N. Newman, 'The Political Patronage of Frederick, Prince of Wales', *Historical Journal*, i, no. 1 (1958), 73–74.

[6] Good examples are *A Letter from a Travelling Tutor to a Noble Young Lord* (London, 1747) and *An Examination of the Principles and An Enquiry into the Conduct of the Two B[rothe]rs* (London, 1749).

[7] Lewis, ed., *Horace Walpole's Correspondence*, xx. 73.

party-coloured junto' whose monopoly of offices threatens the Constitution. Support of the Prince in his laudable aims will establish a reign of virtue.[1]

The only unusual work of the period probably had no direct connexion with Leicester House. In 1747 James Hampton, a young divine fresh from Oxford, brought out *A Parallel between the Roman and British Constitution; comprehending Polibius's Curious Discourse of the Roman Senate; with a copious preface, wherein his principles are applied to our government.* Hampton espoused the usual 'Country party programme' as the only means to restore balanced government. In doing so, sardonically but seriously, he drew together three significant points in justification of Opposition:[2]

But whatever may be the success of the opposers, the public reaps great benefit from the Opposition; since this keeps ministers upon their guard and often prevents them from pursuing bold measures, which an uncontrolled power might otherwise tempt them to engage in: . . . In the meantime a thirst of power, irritated by disappointment, animates the application of the opposers to public affairs infinitely more than the languid impulse of national considerations: By this means they grow able statesmen, and when they come to be ministers, are not only capable of defending bad schemes, but when they please, of forming good ones.

Another great advantage that accrues to the people from this Opposition is that each party, by appealing to them upon all occasions, constitutes them judges of every contest; and indeed to whom should they appeal but to those whose welfare is the design, or pretence, of every measure? and for whose happiness the majesty of kings, the dignity of peers, and the power of the commons were finally instituted. . . .

Hampton intended his preface to be a work of political science, not a tract in favour of any parliamentary connexion. Although he inclined toward a rather naïve Tory attitude—annual parliaments and a more equitable land tax were his panaceas for Constitutional imbalance—he was the first man of the age to undertake a non-partisan appraisal of the actual operation of political parties in Britain.

In line with much of contemporary philosophy, he assumed the individuality of men and the selfishness of their motives—

[1] *The Remembrancer*, nos. 2, 3, 12, 172.
[2] *A Parallel between the Roman and British Constitution*, pp. viii–ix.

hence the inevitability of political parties in a free state. With a fair knowledge of history he observed that 'for this last century . . . an opposition to a ministry' has been 'made the road to a succession in it'.[1] He understood the achievements and the failures of malcontent coalitions, and he saw that Opposition tended to strengthen the democratic element in the Constitution. Hampton's analysis, obscured by the eloquent partisan polemics of later years, contained the nucleus of the nineteenth century's conviction that a permanent, loyal, ambitious Opposition was, in his words, 'not only the effect but the support of liberty'.[2]

The leaders at Leicester House did not concern themselves with such institutional theory. Within the framework of conventional doctrine, they struggled over the best means to achieve the Prince's announced goal. One school, led by Nugent and Dodington, favoured a cautious policy. Since the Pelhams could not be ousted, they argued, 'a settled Opposition was become impracticable'. The Prince had no need of a large parliamentary party, and motions embarrassing to the Government served no useful purpose. For any minority it was almost impossible 'to bring any considerable national abuse into absolute, undeniable proof, all the offices and documents being in the hands of the Court'. The true function of the Leicester House party was to set before the world the standards of the coming reign: 'Those attached to the Prince should already act as ministers, by carrying on the system which the Prince intended to follow when king, and therefore should not oppose.'[3]

Egmont and Baltimore, on the other hand, insisted upon vigorous measures. They had no illusions about defeating the Pelhams, nor did they seek an accommodation. Their aim was to establish themselves as parliamentary leaders capable of commanding the support necessary to conduct the future king's business in the two Houses. With the lesson of the 'Forty-Eight-Hour Ministry' before them, Egmont and Baltimore understood the importance of establishing their 'credit': Frederick's

[1] Ibid., p. x.

[2] Ibid., p. vi. The value of an Opposition in a balanced Constitution was also debated in an objective manner in the first dialogue of Thomas Pownall's *Principles of Polity* (London, 1752).

[3] Rose, ed., *Marchmont Papers*, i. 231–2; Wyndham, ed., *Dodington Diary*, pp. 54, 472–82.

advisers must teach the political world that they had his confidence and both the determination and ability to carry on his affairs. A policy of inaction would make it difficult or impossible to inaugurate the new 'system' in the new reign.[1]

This dispute over policy led to personal disputes and to impotence in Parliament. Impatient of quarrels in the Prince's councils, Egmont did not tell Dodington's group of his plans until it was too late for them to object. Dodington complained that he was never admitted to 'the first concoction' of measures and swore that he would not support any point on which he had not been consulted. The Prince's servants openly disagreed with each other on the floor of the Commons.[2] Their parliamentary opposition consequently amounted to very little. There were some hot debates on such stock issues as Supply, military forces, and the Mutiny Act.[3] The peace terms provoked a concerted reaction in 1749.[4] But the old corps' majority was never in danger. In 1750 the revival of the Dunkirk question 'to make the Ministry feel they had *la corde au col*' proved a dismal failure.[5] Shortly before the Prince's death the Tories raised an ill-concerted opposition to the land tax and went down to defeat, 109 to 43 and 229 to 28. 'They could not conjure up a spirited division now on the most popular points', wrote Horace Walpole: 'if they were not new, they would scarce furnish a debate.'[6]

Frederick did his best to smooth over the quarrels in his official family, but in fact he agreed with the aggressive school. Inaction in Parliament, he thought, would alienate the Tories by raising suspicions that he was entering upon another negotiation with the Government.[7] If his friends did nothing, how could he 'have the influence due to his rank'? He seems also to have been in firm agreement with Egmont upon the need to establish the 'credit' of his ministers. For during the last two years of his life he was deeply engaged in the most important task of all, the preparation of detailed plans for his accession.

---

[1] P.R.O., Egmont MSS. 277, Engagement Book; *H.M.C., Var. Coll.*, vi. 21.

[2] Wyndham, ed., *Dodington Diary*, pp. 49–56.

[3] *P.H.* xiv, 395–400, 621–69.   [4] Ibid. 353–95.

[5] Ibid. 669–723; Wyndham, ed., *Dodington Diary*, pp. 33–37.

[6] *Memoirs of George II*, pp. 32–33.

[7] Wyndham, ed., *Dodington Diary*, pp. 33–35. In March 1751 Egmont noted that the Prince talked 'angrily to Nugent . . . for his conduct in the House in

The 'Glorious Plan'

The 'great outline' or 'glorious plan' was drafted by Egmont in consultation with the Prince.[1] In essence it was a programme for 'the general ruin' of the Pelhams and the establishment in power of the Prince's friends. At Frederick's death it was practically complete: in his last words to Egmont, His Royal Highness gave his final instructions and a solemn promise that he would live to execute the grand design.[2] His demise on 20 March 1751 brought it all to naught, but the scheme still possesses a twofold significance. On the one hand, it shows how well the Prince and his confidant had learned the political lessons of the eighteenth century. They clearly understood what a king must do to prevent a repetition of 1746. On the other, although the details were never made public, a widespread knowledge of the Prince's intentions gave rise to a legend that George III and Bute were directly inspired by Frederick's plans.[3] Let us see what he actually had in mind.

Complete preparedness against every eventuality was the basic principle. Nothing that could be anticipated should be left to chance. In the first place, the necessary technicalities must be arranged in advance:[4]

. . . all declarations, motions, speeches, etc. should be long before prepared and ready against the event. Even all the acts of Parliament should be ready drawn likewise. His Majesty will find great relief in this, for he will have enough upon his mind in the pursuit of the great outline without being embarrassed with such detail. It will give the King's servants great ease in a conjuncture of so much hurry, and perhaps of some perplexity, to have the plan of every step perfectly digested and settled in their minds, nothing being left upon them but the execution. It will save much precious time which they

opposing me and philosophy [?] continually to be well with the other side and to form a party'; and later Frederick told Egmont that 'the time would come when they should all follow me or shift for themselves': P.R.O., Egmont MSS. 277, Engagement Book.

[1] On the night of Frederick's death the Princess had the plans for his accession burned at Leicester House. Egmont kept his copies, which are preserved in P.R.O., Egmont MSS. 277.

[2] Ibid., Engagement Book.

[3] Burke, *Works*, i. 447; Walpole, *Memoirs of George III*, iv. 124, 136.

[4] P.R.O., Egmont MSS. 277, second and final draft of the plan of operations upon the accession. The description of the plan which follows is drawn entirely from this source. It is to be noted that the preparations for the accession described in the *Dodington Diary*, pp. 14–16, were abandoned.

may want for talking with and managing individuals. It will prevent disputes and inconvenient contests about the preference (which the principal men will all aim at) of being employed to draw up these papers. His Majesty having them in his hands and producing them as his own will stifle all contention of this kind.

Having studied carefully the accessions of Anne and the first two Georges, Egmont listed the prescribed oaths, drew up the King's declaration to the Privy Council, and drafted the King's speeches to open and close the first session of Parliament. He outlined the Bills to be passed immediately, and after a careful study of the Crown's income, he prepared a Civil List Act, complete in every detail except for dates and the official name of the new king.

In the second place, the removals and appointments of ministers and Household officers must be settled and placed upon an exact schedule:[1]

It is likewise of the last consequence that as far as possible (for absolutely it cannot be done, because some men from whom it is least expected, and others to whom it would be inconvenient to give any intimation of what is intended for them, may scruple to accept) the most perfect list of the persons to be employed in the respective offices should be framed and looked upon as sacred, not to be altered in one single instance without the most unavoidable necessity. For a system of this kind is a sort of chain, the whole of which depends upon every single link, so that the alteration of a single person may cause unforeseen and incredible confusion in such a crisis of affairs.

To carry out this step, Egmont compiled four lists of officers for the new reign—no two are precisely the same—and three calendars for effecting the changes—none of which differ in any important aspect.

The 'glorious plan' was then laid out on a time-scheme like the schedule for a military assault. Upon the news of the King's death the Lord President was to summon the Privy Council 'instantly that there may be no time for cabal'. After the formalities the leaders of the Leicester House party were to be

[1] P.R.O., Egmont MSS. 277. The lists bear no general headings. In Add. MSS. 33002, ff. 377–8, there is a curious 'scheme for a new administration,' drawn up some time between July 1746 and February 1747. It is primarily a composite of men out of office, predominantly Tory. Since none of the Leicester House favourites are included, this 'scheme' was probably never part of Frederick's plans. Perhaps it was a Jacobite dream.

sworn of the Council. Hardwicke would be relieved of the
Great Seal and perhaps dismissed. 'This evening His Majesty
will pass very privately in giving his directions, and in consultation with one or two of his most faithful friends', undoubtedly Egmont and Lee.

On the second day the King would dismiss Pelham, Hardwicke (if still in office), Newcastle, and perhaps Gower and
Sandwich. Carlisle would be appointed to the Treasury and the
other offices put in commission. Parliament was to undertake
its business, and political manœuvring was to begin. The plan
repeatedly stressed the importance of keeping all but the two
closest advisers out of the closet. Only they were to see Frederick
during the second evening, and the directions for the third
read,

This evening will be passed also like the former. None will be
admitted but the most faithful friends, and those most privately.
For tho' His Majesty will not be shaken in his resolutions, yet any
interviews or audiences will create some jealousies among his friends,
and doubts in the public, and will certainly be improved by the
faction to keep their tools together and their hopes alive.

Meanwhile those most entrusted and most active will be industrious
all this day with the members of both Houses to confirm their friends,
to manage artfully in discourse with the leaders of the faction not
yet dismissed, and to prevent despair in the underlings of office. The
result of all which will be from hour to hour communicated to His
Majesty.

This night will likewise produce a meeting and general agreement
with the Tories to let things go on without any interruption. In
which but two of His Majesty's friends can be employed.

While the King's advisers steered the necessary measures
through Parliament, Lee and Egmont were to proceed with
their 'artful management'. By the sixth day 'the Tories will be
entirely satisfied that they are not to be cheated and betrayed';
but trouble with the old corps must be anticipated. In the
succeeding day or two

the faction, notwithstanding the King's most prudent silence and
reserve, will infallibly have found out enough to suspect strongly
that their general ruin is at hand. The satisfactory assurances that
will and must be given to the Tories and to other individuals (tho'
never so secretly or cautiously conducted) must be so far known that

T

some of the party of the old ministers will certainly be set on to stir some mischief and to feel the pulse of the House. How far this will go cannot be ascertained, yet there is no kind of doubt but that with the King's old friends, the Tories and the bulk of the old party who will still retain their employments, any stir of this nature can produce no more than a discharge of malice and passion, and an endeavour to provoke imprudent speeches or declarations from the King's principal servants, which they will hope to make use of in the subsequent debates upon the Civil List or in future time. That will be seen thro' and consequently guarded against by them.

The King also must be on his guard against the wiles of 'the faction', who will try to ingratiate themselves both in an underhanded way 'by their secret friends in His Majesty's family' and openly 'by the most abject and fulsome speeches in the House'. These men must be kept dangling until future measures render them harmless. But if, upon the introduction of the Civil List, any should be bold enough to raise objections, 'one or two capital examples, made by an immediate dismission of such persons from their employments the very next morning, would have more beneficial effect upon the gross of that body than could be counterbalanced by any prejudice such persons could do afterwards by their most malicious Opposition during the course of that Bill'.

The 'great outline' then anticipates a fairly easy passage of the Civil List and accompanying legislation. The dangers of intrigue, however, will increase. 'Pretended friends', who feel that they have not been given sufficient weight in the royal councils, will try to force their advice upon the King and may even cabal with the old corps to strengthen their hands. Great 'steadiness' will prevent them from upsetting the programme. At the end of fourteen to eighteen days Parliament will complete its work, and the King will prorogue the Houses with the promise of an early dissolution. Thereupon the 'glorious plan' reaches its climax. On the day after the prorogation,

> *His Majesty will make the great change of his administration at once—appointing at the same time a new Privy Council.*

A measure of this *éclat*, so general, done with so much vigour and in one moment, will have a surprising effect. It will raise the spirit of his friends to a degree that will render them irresistible, and so utterly confound the faction that they will be able to exert no power or influence at the ensuing elections in any corner of the kingdom.

Of Egmont's four lists of ministers, two are rough, and two appear to be finished.[1] All are undated. None corresponds in every detail with the final draft of the schedule of operations upon the accession. Egmont never divulged the Prince's last instructions. Hence it is impossible to determine which was the definitive list. Three of the four, however, are substantially the same, and they differ from the fourth in only three significant items. In the fourth Egmont is to be First Lord of the Treasury and Chancellor of the Exchequer, Prince George Lord High Admiral, and Granville a Secretary of State. In the others Carlisle is to have the Treasury, Lee the Exchequer, Baltimore or Limerick the Admiralty, and Egmont Secretary of State. All four fill up the other offices almost exclusively with men out of place from 1749 to 1751. For example, they designated Willes as Lord Chancellor or Lord Keeper, Bath as Lord President, Rutland as Lord Steward, Oxford or Northampton as Privy Seal, Harrington as Secretary of State, Chesterfield as Lord Lieutenant of Ireland, Chandos as Groom of the Stole, Middlesex as Master of the Horse, and Henry Bathurst as Secretary at War. Tories, Leicester House Courtiers, and minor men were to fill the boards and Household offices. With a few exceptions like Marlborough, who would be retained 'while he behaves well', the Prince intended a clean sweep of the old Ministry.

He also outlined a disposition of the royal family to eliminate any focus for a new Opposition. The 'glorious plan' included a Bill to allow Prince George to become Lord High Admiral without taking the oaths. As a member of the Ministry, George would be restrained from setting up a rival court at Leicester House. Prince William was to be married into the House of Orange and sent to live at The Hague. The personal union of England and Hanover would be dissolved and Prince Edward dispatched to be Elector. Prince Henry, created Duke of Virginia, was to be settled on 'an island near Antigua'. Even young Lady Augusta would depart to marry the heir to Wolfenbuettel and reside at that Court.[2]

[1] P.R.O., Egmont MSS. 277.
[2] Ibid., Engagement Book. The Prince also intended the immediate dismissal of Cumberland from the army, but the plan says nothing further about the

The general election would then seal the doom of the former ministers. Egmont drew up a complete survey of the constituencies which displays a very good knowledge of members and 'interests', voters and returning officers.[1] By careful work Egmont calculated that he could bring in 413 members definitely committed or generally favourable to the new Government. He also compiled 'a list of particular friends who are to be brought into Parliament for the most secure boroughs where no contest can happen' (a rather undistinguished roster of forty-two brute votes), a new Court list of Scots peers (among whom only Bute and three others were new names), and a 'list of those who must if possible be kept out of the House of Commons'. These enemies fell into two categories. 'The most obnoxious men of an inferior degree', eighteen in all, included three Finches, Lord George Sackville, old Horace Walpole (but not his celebrated nephew, who 'will do'), and William Murray. Among the more important were Pelham, who should be 'obliged (if he can be made) to go up to the House of Lords'; Fox and Pitt, who should be offered 'some profitable employment inconsistent with a seat in Parliament'; George Grenville 'as likewise all his brothers together with Lyttelton'; Legge, Barrington, and Speaker Onslow (who would be a great nuisance to the new Speaker and committee chairmen). Obviously Egmont intended to eliminate petty hecklers as well as major opponents.

The 'glorious plan' thus envisioned the decapitation of the old corps but not its destruction. The new King would retain the 'underlings of office' who supported his ministers, and the scheme for choosing a new Parliament makes it clear that loyalty was to be required of the little Government officials who had influence or votes in the constituencies. The 'King's interest' in north Britain was to be kept intact. Though Tweeddale was scheduled for reappointment as Secretary of State for Scotland, Argyll was to be left 'as he is'. The new structure would rise upon the old foundation. Egmont did not doubt that he could convert most of those not marked for destruction. He had learned from the 'resigners' of 1746 that many had

Duke's fate. There is no disposition of Frederick's youngest children, one of whom was an infant and the other posthumous.

[1] P.R.O., Egmont MSS. 277, plans for the election of the new Parliament.

supported the Pelhams 'as of the strongest interest'.[1] The art-ful management of the first two weeks would make plain where the strongest interest lay in Frederick's reign.

The new structure, however, would not look like the old. Frederick did not intend to free himself from the Pelhams only to become the creature of a ministry of his own choosing. His attitude was clearly expressed during one session when Lord Doneraile failed to speak often enough for Leicester House measures in the Commons. 'Does he think I will support him unless he does as I would have him?' exclaimed the angry Prince. 'Does not he consider that whoever are my ministers, I must be King?'[2]

Two measures incorporated in the 'great outline' were designed to make the King master in his own house. One was the detachment of Hanover. Frederick wrote in his instructions to his son that, from the moment of the separation, 'Jacobitism will be in a manner rooted out, and you will not be forced then to court your ministers for one job or another: as unfortunately your predecessors have been forced to do.'[3] The other was the recruitment of the new ministers as individuals, not as leaders or members of connexions. For a while the Prince and Egmont thought of keeping the Duke of Bedford, but upon further con-sideration Egmont wrote: 'I am persuaded the Duke of Bedford will never be made to act as he ought to do upon a change, unless upon the terms of bringing in other men with him, which [who?] will confound the system.'[4] Just as he would make no distinction of parties in choosing his men, so Frederick would not allow others to make party loyalty a hindrance to his freedom of choice. All ministers owed paramount political loyalty to the Throne.

Not all, however, stood upon the same plane. Above the general run towered a First Minister, the royal confidant in all affairs, chief adviser and chief agent in the direction of the Government. Frederick's concept of this post appears to have had two inspirations. The first was the traditional Hanoverian

---

[1] P.R.O., Egmont MSS. 277, loose sheets bearing an account of the 'Forty-Eight-Hour Ministry'.

[2] Walpole, *Memoirs of George II*, i. 74–75.

[3] Sedgwick, ed., *Memoirs of Lord Hervey*, pp. xxxiv–xxxv.

[4] P.R.O., Egmont MSS. 277, plans for the election of the new Parliament, *sub* Tavistock.

employment of a Premier who took the responsibility for getting 'the King's business' done. Despite his opposition to Walpole, Frederick shared his contemporaries' admiration for the great man; but he wanted a Walpole of his own choice, a competent Compton, not one forced upon him by exigency at his accession.

The second inspiration was derived from a current historico-literary fad. In the late 1740's and early 1750's there developed what may be described as a 'cult' of Henri IV and Sully. Several editions of Sully's memoirs appeared in England during these years.[1] English writers saw the two great Frenchmen as patriot king and patriot minister. One pamphlet, dedicated to the Prince in 1750, described Sully as a minister 'inspired with a patriot zeal for the service of his king and country' who had freed the realm from aristocratic faction. The author urged Frederick to profit by this historical lesson and by similar means to restore 'the free exercise of the regal power'.[2] His Royal Highness showed the influence of the 'cult' in this excerpt from a letter written near the end of his life:[3]

Adieu, my dear Egmont, whom I know to be thoroughly mine and to be always the same, and I know that nothing will make him deviate from me and his country. Let us remember both Henry IV and Sully; in all things these are our models; let us follow them in most all, except in their extravagances. *Adieu, mon ami.*

There is no evidence to connect the plans of Frederick and Egmont directly with the actions of George III and Bute. The latter may have learned much from Princess Augusta and George Lee, but they probably never knew the 'great outline' in detail. Yet it is clear that the legend of a Leicester House plot

[1] In 1745 there were published a three-volume and an eight-volume edition of Sully's memoirs. The first was republished in 1747, the second in 1747 and 1752. Charlotte Lennox did an English translation in 1756, dedicated to Newcastle, which was reprinted four times in seven years. In its notice of this translation the *Monthly Review*, xiv. 561, observed, 'The original of this celebrated work is so well known, and so universally esteemed, that it would be ridiculous in us to think of either adding to, or detracting from, the public suffrage long since given in its favour.' F. A. Barnard, *Bibliothecae Regiae Catalogus*, i. 261, records that the royal library contained editions of Sully's memoirs published in 1638 and 1664, the three-volume edition of 1747, and the English translation of 1756. Barnard does not, however, give the dates of their acquisition.

[2] Henry McCulloh, *An Essay or Treatise relating to the Treasury* (London, 1750), pp. 99–113. Cf. *An Occasional Letter to the Rt. Hon. H. P.* (London, 1750), in which Pelham is urged to assume the character of Sully.

[3] P.R.O., Egmont MSS. 277, loose sheet.

had a basis in fact and that the ideas behind the plot informed the young Prince and his favourite. Bute aspired to be a modern Sully.[1] George III strove to accomplish much of what his father intended.[2]

4. THE TRIUMPH OF THE GREAT COMMONER

The Tranquil Triennium

Frederick's death inaugurated three years of unwonted political calm. The Princess dowager, who had helplessly disapproved of her husband's second Opposition, hastened to make her peace with the King. Egmont also thought peace the wisest course, but he hoped to maintain the influence of Leicester House by preserving the party. Augusta's only response to his efforts was the acid query, 'If the Prince could not keep them together, how shall I?'[3] Dodington struggled in vain to convert the core into a flying squadron which could drive the Pelhams to an accommodation.[4] The shaky coalition fell into fragments.

The Tories continued to act with their customary independence. The placehunters paid their addresses to Pelham. George Lee, shrewdest of all, accepted one appointment from the Princess, two from the Crown, and a knighthood shortly after. Egmont maintained friendly relations at Leicester House but played a lone role in Parliament.[5] Toward the end of 1751 death at last overtook the indomitable Bolingbroke. Thirty-seven years in exile and Opposition left the most imaginative politician of the century unrewarded and unregenerate. Despite his growing debilities he would still have embarked, with his usual philosophic disclaimers and his unquenchable zest, upon the first new adventure to offer itself. His *astutia Italiana* was now denied to questioning malcontents, but his doctrine for Opposition, sublimated in the volatile temperature of British politics, continued to serve many who would have denied him.

---

[1] Fitzmaurice, *Shelburne,* i. 110. Cf. *The Appeal of Reason to the People of England on the Present State of Parties in the Nation* (2nd ed. Edinburgh, 1763), p. 32.

[2] On the intentions and operations of George III, see Namier, *England in the Age of the American Revolution,* pp. 110 ff.

[3] P.R.O., Egmont MSS. 277, Engagement Book.

[4] *Dodington Diary,* pp. 102–20.

[5] *P.H.* xiv. 117; Coxe, *Pelham,* ii. 206–7.

During the tranquil triennium from 1751 to 1754 the only breath of opposition blew from Bloomsbury. Newcastle forced Bedford from office in June of 1751, and the head of the Russell clan shortly entered upon an intermittent campaign against the 'broad bottom'. For a time his tiny party produced a weekly paper, *The Protester*, written by James Ralph under the unlikely pseudonym of Issachar Barebone. Proclaiming that 'a spirit of opposition has been the guardian spirit of our constitution from the first hour of its establishment', this new organ heckled the Government with twenty-four issues in 1753; then lamenting that lack of popular response had turned patriotism into quixotism, Ralph abandoned the Constitution to irremediable degeneracy.[1] Bedford's parliamentary Opposition was equally futile. Pelham's majorities overwhelmed the malcontents. Under the Duke's leadership no minority even approached 100, and before long Bedford learned that he might profit more from intrigue than from defiance.

There followed three years of uneasiness and turmoil. Leicester House had again grown restless. Princess Augusta disliked the King's plans for young George's marriage. She dreaded the influence of Cumberland and chafed at her own presumed impotence. Cumberland became the focus of a rival interest. Ambitious young men, notably Fox and Pitt, fretted under the domination of the old corps leaders. Pelham's death in March of 1754 loosed the forces of discontent. Newcastle shrewdly engineered his own appointment to the Treasury; but though anxious to engross his brother's power, as a peer he could not fill his brother's place as 'Minister for the King in the House of Commons' and 'Minister for the House of Commons in the closet'. The preliminary hostilities of the Seven Years' War piled insecurity upon confusion. 'Broad bottom' started at the seams.

Pitt's Campaign for Power

Newcastle hoped to manage the Commons through lieutenants who had no effective voice in the formulation of policy

[1] Ralph professed to fear prosecution by the Government: *Bedford Correspondence*, ii. 135–6. Proceedings instituted against *The Remembrancer* while he was its editor had forced him into hiding for a time. Walpole thought that Ralph had been 'bought off': *Memoirs of George II*, i. 345–6.

or the distribution of Treasury patronage. Henry Fox, the ablest of Cumberland's set, was to be the ranking commoner as a Secretary of State. Legge at the Exchequer and Murray as Attorney-General were to give the Government added support. Promises and blandishments would 'settle' William Pitt, retained as Paymaster-General. As soon as Fox discovered his true position he declined the Seals and returned to his post as Secretary at War.[1] Newcastle replaced him with Sir Thomas Robinson, an experienced diplomat inexperienced in parliamentary affairs.

For a while it appeared that Newcastle's plan would work. The session of 1754 drew to a quiet close. The new First Lord then 'chose' a good Parliament with little difficulty.[2] In England and Wales there were 8 contests in counties, 50 in boroughs. Fox was returned for a Government borough. Newcastle brought in Pitt for one of his private boroughs. Most disputes occurred between rival interests which owed allegiance to the Ministry, a phenomenon that promised some embarrassment. Still, only 16 petitions were filed (the same number as in 1747), and since 9 were withdrawn, the Government had less trouble than usual. The political surface was serene.

But neither Fox nor Pitt was content. Fox, who soon came to believe that he had made a serious mistake, cast about for means to rectify it. The old corps' leaders could not soothe Pitt. On Pelham's death he had begun to grope for the best method to profit 'from the mutual fears and animosities of different factions in Court'. Thinking it wise to avoid action which might 'bear too plainly the indications of intending a third party or flying squadron', he chose to stay in office and conduct his manœuvres from within the administration.[3] They came to nothing. The King still loathed Pitt, and Newcastle distrusted him. Convinced that submission would not succeed, Pitt joined forces with the disgruntled Fox.

Their scheme was to wreck Newcastle's management of the Commons. By harassing his lieutenants, the vulnerable Robinson in particular, they hoped to overturn the Ministry or force

[1] Ilchester, *Fox*, i. 203–9.
[2] Newcastle's election papers are in Add. MSS. 32995, ff. 63–68, 75–135, 158–69, 213, 221.
[3] Phillimore, *Lyttelton*, ii. 448–81.

Newcastle to an accommodation. Fox aimed at the Treasury, Pitt at a Secretaryship of State, but for the time being they clung to their minor offices. Having witnessed Bedford's ineffectual opposition, they dared not risk defiance *à outrance*. The autumn session of 1754 thus presented an unusual scene. There was no pretence of a formed Opposition on the Speaker's left. Differences upon national policy were so conspicuously absent that men thought Newcastle might accept an offer of Tory support by providing for some of the 'true blue' placehunters.[1] The only major divisions took place on election petitions, in which the friends of Government voted against each other. And on the Treasury Bench the leader of the House was hectored and ridiculed time and again by two of his most distinguished colleagues.

At a moment when all men felt secure in their agreement on fundamentals and when there was no sense of national crisis to impose discipline, this political situation may be seen as the natural product of the Pelhams' 'broad-bottom' policy. Politicians had come to believe that Henry Pelham 'always bought off his enemies to avoid their satire rather than to acquire their support'.[2] They believed as well that 'he could live very well and treat with those who opposed, and even personally opposed him' and 'that he would take a blow from a strong man but not from a weak one'.[3] Newcastle was scarcely less pacific than his brother. Now, with most ambitious men employed, how were the most ambitious to secure promotion? The logical answer was, by using in office the methods of Opposition. Satisfaction was more likely than dismissal.

Still, given rival ambitions and personal jealousies, how was it possible for 'broad bottom' to satisfy all? Newcastle began by trying the usual Pelhamite means. He dismissed no one. The Cumberland group was more formidable than the Grenville clan, so he made a treaty with Fox. Upon a guarantee that he would cease opposition, the Secretary at War was promised admission to the Cabinet, and both he and Cumberland were

---

[1] Add. MSS. 41355, f. 28 and verso. 'Never was there so poor, so shabby, so insignificant a session of Parliament as this is', wrote the historian Guthrie. 'Our Courtiers are trumping their partners' tricks. Patriots we have none; all is election jobbing': *H.M.C., Laing MSS.* ii. 414.

[2] Walpole, *Memoirs of George II*, i. 231.

[3] *Dodington Diary*, p. 157.

made members of the Council of Regency. They closed the deal in April of 1755. Pitt reacted quickly. Though the negotiations were carried on with his knowledge he soon saw that he would gain nothing. Early in May he publicly repudiated his connexion with Fox.[1] Newcastle soon found that he had abated one nuisance only to aggravate the other.

Pitt's break with Fox was his first ostensible move toward the formation of a more formidable connexion—a pact with Leicester House.[2] The elevation of the dreaded Cumberland had driven Augusta to the uncongenial expedient of re-forming a party to protect the interests of her son. As soon as Bute learned of Pitt's 'disadvantageous, mortifying, and dangerous situation', he made overtures to the new 'patriots', and without giving up their offices, Pitt and the Grenvilles flung themselves into open alliance with the Prince's Court. For the Government this was an ominous development. 'It is my duty to tell you', said Newcastle to the King, 'that I find more difficulty from the notion of Opposition from that quarter, which affects particularly all the young men, than from all other causes whatsoever'.[3] The new party proselytized vigorously, even to the point of approaching the aged but still eager Dodington.[4] Of the younger men the most important addition was Henry Legge. His behaviour precipitated the next crisis. In August Legge, as Chancellor of the Exchequer, refused to sign Treasury warrants for a subsidy to Hesse–Cassel, and thereafter, flaunting his popularity at Leicester House, he proved a highly refractory colleague for the uncomfortable Newcastle.

The old corps' leaders had begun efforts to conciliate Pitt as soon as they had taken care of Fox. The development of the Leicester House connexion led to further overtures. As Pitt's strength grew, so did his demands. Legge's conduct encouraged him further. In early September Pitt demanded to be Secretary of State and 'the Minister' in the Commons with a full share of the power to recommend measures and appointments. The Court could not stomach so much. Leaving both Pitt and Legge in office, Newcastle promised these powers to Fox and went in quest of a new Chancellor of the Exchequer.[5]

---

[1] Ibid., p. 284.
[2] Sedgwick, ed., *Letters from George III to Lord Bute*, pp. xlvi–xlviii.
[3] Add. MSS. 32860, f. 16.   [4] *Dodington Diary*, pp. 374–7.
[5] Yorke, *Hardwicke*, ii. 237–49.

His search led him to the Prince's party. If he could draw in an able man from that connexion he might secure Leicester House and undermine Pitt's chief support. Newcastle reported with astonishment the result of his first exploration in October:[1]

Lord Egmont laboured to know of me whether, in case Sir George [Lee] and the rest would make *only* a slight opposition to the Russian treaty, *as it were pro formâ*, they might then be forgiven and negotiated with. And Lord Egmont told me expressly that he had talked to Sir George Lee upon that foot and would do the same to Mr. Pitt. That Sir George was disposed to it (and I think upon condition *then* to accept Chancellor of the Exchequer). I showed my Lord Egmont how impossible it was for me to enter into any such proposal, that I could say nothing as to the King; that such a previous stipulation was absurd in itself, and when known, was giving up our point. For everybody would expect the same liberty, and then the question was lost. To which he agreed himself. I think, but I will not be sure, that I particularly instanced the impossibility of making a man Chancellor of the Exchequer who had just opposed the measures of the Government.

Newcastle was unduly amazed. In 1742 and 1744 some of the highest offices of State had been filled by men whose anti-ministerial orations still echoed in the halls of Parliament. Why should Lee and Egmont think that a mild formal Opposition, to which they were already committed, could cause any real difficulty?

Having accepted the denial of his proposal, Egmont went on to explain that none of his connexion would serve with Fox. The Princess hated him and Cumberland. Still, Leicester House could be gained by minor concessions: places for a few of the Courtiers, more money for the younger children, and some influence for the Princess in the 'settlement' of her own family. To Newcastle's report, Hardwicke gave a typical Pelhamite reply. A 'feint Opposition' was, of course, 'impossible and absurd'. The Government wished to placate but not to encourage its enemies. To prevent their becoming a 'formed formidable Opposition . . .', it might be right (after they are beaten) to break them by taking in one or two at a proper time, but that is a different measure'. As for the price of Leicester House, '*If everything would come right*, 'twould be ridiculous not

[1] Add. MSS. 32860, ff. 14–15.

to give it.'[1] George II thought the old corps' leaders too much in favour of 'condescendances', and the negotiations fell through.

Sir George Lyttelton, who had broken with Pitt, was finally persuaded to accept the Exchequer. The First Lord and his prospective leader in the Commons flung their net wide to gather maximum support against the opening of Parliament. Still Newcastle could not bring himself to dismiss the rebels, and he approached the session lamenting, '. . . If we don't fix such a system of administration as may carry things through, we shall have attacks of different kinds every day, all tending to the same end.'[2] The debate on the Address at length brought about a decision. Pitt led the Prince's party, the Tories, and the Grenville clan to a brilliant attack upon the foreign policy of the Ministry. In a sitting concluded at 4.45 on the morning of 14 November 1755, the 'Opposition in administration' went down to defeat 311 to 105 and 290 to 89.[3] Political observers wondered in bewilderment how the Government should deal with such an anomalous situation. Horace Walpole, who thoroughly understood Pelhamite policy, wrote to a friend,[4]

You will want to know what is to be the fate of the Ministry in Opposition: but that I can't tell you. I don't believe they have determined what to do, more than oppose, nor that it is determined what to do with them. Though it is clear that it is very humiliating to have them in place, you may conceive several reasons why it is not eligible to dismiss them. *You* know . . . how easy it is to buy an Opposition who have not places; but tell us what to do with an Opposition that has places? If you say, Turn them out; I answer, That is not the way to quiet any Opposition, or a Ministry so constituted as ours at present.

The magnitude of his victory gave Newcastle the confidence

[1] Ibid., f. 31.

[2] Add. MSS. 32860, f. 269. It is usually said that Fox and Lyttelton did not receive their appointments until after the meeting of Parliament because re-election would have prevented their attendance at the debate on the Address. Actually Fox could have been re-elected in time. Newcastle's words and actions in this period suggest that Fox's appointment depended upon his success. The First Minister was so unsure of his 'system' that failure on the first test would doubtless have sent him in search of another. Cf. Fox's circular letter in Ilchester, *Fox*, i. 280–1.

[3] *P.H.* xv. 536–40. Newcastle's Secretary of the Treasury calculated that 76 of the 105 were Tories: Add. MSS. 32860, f. 471.

[4] Toynbee, ed., *Letters of Horace Walpole*, iii. 368.

to proceed. The highest flights of oratory had not shaken his followers: 'With these majorities', he wrote to Hartington, 'we have nothing to fear.'[1] Just a little competent management would keep the Court party intact. On the morrow of the great debate Fox had the Seals, and within a week the 'Opposition in administration' found itself an Opposition out of office. On 20 November Newcastle cleared the boards of Pitt, Legge, and George Grenville. He then picked up such useful strays as Dodington, and the administration faced the future with optimism:

The House of Commons will be a busy scene [wrote Stormont on 26 November 1755], though the Opposition there will not be near so considerable as was apprehended; it may and will be clamorous and virulent but cannot be formidable, as it has neither numbers nor popularity to support it. The majority is greater than ever was known, and the popular cry strong in favour of the Ministry and against the leaders of the Opposition, whose being turned out seems to have given general satisfaction.[2]

Stormont's prediction proved accurate. The new Opposition talked long and divided often. Members complained of late nights. Pitt revived the language and the tactics employed against Walpole and Carteret. For a decade Ministers had explained to the 'young orator' that his offensive remarks about Hanover had created the royal prejudice that barred him from the positions to which he aspired. His speeches now rivalled in audacity the most extravagant outbursts of his earlier career. Utterly heedless of the King's reaction, Pitt condemned foreign subsidies as foolish means to protect 'a place of such inconsiderable note that its name was not to be found in the map'. He expressed an ardent wish 'to break those fetters which chained us, like Prometheus, to that barren rock'.[3] In the best Country party tradition the malcontents brought in a Militia Bill and a Bill for strengthening the navy, while they poured scorn upon every military, diplomatic, and financial measure taken by the Government. Their most strenuous efforts brought nothing but defeat.[4] The ministerial majorities held together

---

[1] Add. MSS. 32860, f. 480. [2] *H.M.C., Hastings MSS.* iii. 111.
[3] *P.H.* xv. 704.
[4] The Government had difficulty with only one issue, a special levy on the possessors of silver plate. It was carried on the first two divisions by the slim

and swamped the small band of 'patriots'. Newcastle had calculated well.

The parliamentary triumph was succeeded a few months later by tactful concessions to Leicester House. On 4 October 1756 Prince George received what he most anxiously desired: a sizeable allowance, permission to reside with his mother, and the appointment of Lord Bute as his Groom of the Stole. Having reached 'a good understanding' with the rival court, the Ministry anticipated an easy accommodation with the isolated malcontents. 'If they remain still in Opposition', wrote Sir George Lyttelton, 'it may possibly be Opposition for life.'[1] Yet three weeks later the seemingly invincible Newcastle resigned, and before long the evidently beaten Pitt became First Minister of the Crown.

Two events upset Newcastle's system for managing the Commons. William Murray had been promised the Chief Justiceship of the King's Bench. The post was vacant, and Murray demanded his reward. Henry Fox, unhappy in his position and disgruntled by continual bickering about patronage, turned in his resignation on 13 October. The large ministerial majority now had no competent leaders, whereas the malcontents possessed considerable debating power, and, it soon became clear, their alliance with Leicester House had not been broken by the King's concessions. On behalf of the Government Hardwicke took the characteristic step of seeking an accommodation with Pitt. Though the old corps leaders had twelve months before protested that it was 'impossible and absurd' to make ministers of those who offered even a 'feint opposition', they were now willing to take in the most obstreperous 'patriot' of the century. The departure of Fox and Murray made it appear that Pitt had calculated better than Newcastle.

Pitt's price had risen. He would not serve with Newcastle. To justify his opposition he demanded an inquiry into past measures and the passage of a Militia Bill. To vindicate his anti-Hanoverianism, he insisted upon the punishment of one of the Electoral troops stationed in England, an unfortunate wretch

margins of 158 to 156 and 129 to 120. On the motion to commit, the Ministry mustered its strength to win 245 to 142. Thereafter no opposition is recorded: *Commons Journals*, xxvii. 494, 530, 538; Dickins and Stanton, eds., *An Eighteenth-Century Correspondence*, pp. 323, 326–7.

[1] Phillimore, *Lyttelton*, ii. 528.

who had by mistake taken more handkerchiefs than he had
paid for in a Maidstone shop. As a minister Pitt must be 'in the
first concert and concoction of measures', and he must have
the right to present his own proposals directly to the King.
The price was too high. On 26 October 1756 Newcastle and
Hardwicke resigned.[1] Strong as the Court party still was, its
aristocratic managers shrank from giving it leadership which
they could not control, even though the calamitous news of
Minorca, Calcutta, and Oswego discredited their direction of
national affairs. Disasters abroad, large as they loom in the
history of the Empire, seemed to be of no more immediate
political consequence to the old corps than crises in the distribution of petty patronage.

The King commissioned Fox to form a ministry. When Pitt
refused to join him, Fox abandoned the attempt. The court
then hit upon a viable expedient. With the approval of Leicester
House, the task of making a Government was given to the Duke
of Devonshire, a member of the old corps who had shown some
sympathy with the opposition to Newcastle's foreign policy. He
accepted Pitt's demands and patched up a precarious administration. Devonshire took the Treasury, but Pitt as Secretary of State was effectually 'the Minister'. A high proportion
of the 'patriots' were inserted into office, but there were not
enough of them to fill all the necessary positions; nor were there
enough, even with Tory support, to make a majority on the
Speaker's right. In consequence, many incumbents retained
their places, and ministerial measures could be passed only with
the acquiescence of the old corps.

Given the contemporary situation and the structure of
politics at mid-century, the new arrangement might in time
have acquired stability. The disastrous opening of the Seven
Years' War called for loyal support of the King's new servants,
who bore no blame for failure, and military successes would
surely bring popularity. Pitt was installed in office, and he was
in favour at Leicester House. With the 'attractive power' of
both Courts, he might gradually capture the loyalty of placeholders and placehunters. But the forces of instability proved
too strong. George II detested Pitt even more and wanted to get
rid of him at the first opportunity. As in 1746 the old corps

[1] Yorke, *Hardwicke*, ii. 277–8, 318–34.

believed that Newcastle still had 'the best interest'. The Duke apparently advised his followers to support the measures necessary for the war,[1] but he encouraged them to believe that he would soon be back in power. Throughout his first Ministry Pitt suffered badly from gout. Miserable and preoccupied with the conduct of the war, he maintained a cold reserve with his colleagues and attended Parliament infrequently. Such conduct could not build a majority.

Two months after Pitt kissed hands George II again undertook an opposition to his ministers. In February 1757 he initiated efforts to re-form the Government without Pitt, and when all failed, he disposed of Temple, Pitt, Legge, and George Grenville (5 and 6 April) without any plan for reconstruction. England possessed only a caretaker Government for the next ten weeks while a succession of futile and unedifying attempts was made to piece together a combination to govern the realm. Now, in effect, everyone was in opposition!

The caretakers, a miscellaneous collection in which there were numerous changes during this period, did not relish their lot and impatiently awaited the formation of a stable ministry. The King wanted to remove them as soon as he could find a satisfactory alternative. All the factions out of office opposed this 'mutilated, enfeebled, half-formed system',[2] but they opposed each other more; and while each had assets to offer a Government, each had too many liabilities to establish a Government on its own. The Fox–Cumberland group, the favourites at Court, was widely distrusted in Parliament and the country. Pitt's connexion had gained great popularity out-of-doors but little within, and of course George II still did not want them. The Tories would support Pitt but no one else, and being so deficient in talent, they could provide little more than four-score erratic 'brute votes'. The old corps had numbers but inadequate leadership in the Commons, and Newcastle suffered from the odium of the early failures in the war. Leicester House

---

[1] During Pitt's Ministry Government Bills were frequently subject to dispute and revision but, as far as I can determine, the Commons did not once divide on a public measure. The inquiry into Byng's conduct and the loss of Minorca produced the only major divisions, and on only one of these was even half the House present. For Newcastle's strength, see his calculations in Add. MSS. 32997, ff. 66–67, 101–12, 113–22.

[2] Yorke, *Hardwicke*, ii. 407.

was potentially strong but actually weak, and George II would not take an administration from his grandson and 'that puppy' Bute.

The prolonged crisis gradually softened factional antagonisms, and at the end of ten weeks the King decided that he must give up his prejudices. On 15 June he authorized Hardwicke to undertake negotiations without the proscription of anyone. Hardwicke threw out some feelers, then summoned a group which he called 'the four plenipotentiaries': himself, Newcastle, Bute, and Pitt. Two weeks of delicate parleying at length produced the great national Ministry which had the support of every faction.[1]

Opposition at Mid-Century

This settlement is traditionally regarded as a triumph for Pitt and public opinion. It seems to prove that a small Opposition, led by brilliant oratory and supported by national popularity, could force its way into office against the wishes of the King and the Court party. This generalization is true but superficial. Pitt could not have succeeded without his eloquence and high repute in the country,[2] but it must not be forgotten that only the peculiar circumstances of the time allowed him to capitalize on the first asset and to acquire the second. What if Britain had been at peace or if Newcastle's administration had conducted a victorious war? No mayor offered Pitt the freedom of the city when he first set out upon his opposition. What if he had had to face Charles James Fox instead of Henry Fox or Canning instead of Robinson? Extraordinary though Pitt's talents were, he was fortunate in having no extraordinary rival, as have so many other great orators. The comparative weakness of ministerial leadership, made weaker still by Newcastle's jealousy and timidity, enabled Pitt to make it practically impossible to govern without him. Moreover, his Opposition was supported by more than popularity. His little faction included able parliamentarians, among them a future Prime Minister, and his alliance with Leicester House gave him added strength.

[1] Yorke, *Hardwicke*, ii. 400–11.

[2] Upon the construction of the coalition Hardwicke wryly observed that it was necessary 'to put so much of the popular mixture into it as might be able to sustain some bad success, at least for the present. I say for the present, for what is unsuccessful can never be long popular': Phillimore, *Lyttelton*, ii. 575.

When this Opposition succeeded, the Government acquired more than Pitt's personal assets.[1] All these things taken into consideration, the perspective on his triumph may be finally adjusted by recalling that in the unreformed Parliament circumstances never permitted any other Opposition to duplicate his feat.

Yet objective analysis does not diminish the quality of the great commoner's triumph. There was nothing inevitable about it. Circumstances provided the opportunity, but he had to overcome powerful forces which had previously held him in check. Pitt's ruthless determination, the greater because his inner courage failed him now and then, surmounted the obstacles set by his opponents, his mistakes, and his bad health. No one repeated his success, but no one ever exploited his advantages more ably.

In most ways the great commoner epitomizes the development of the Opposition at mid-century. Devoid of original ideas, he echoed the cant and catch-phrases of *The Craftsman*, *Common Sense*, Tory pamphlets, and *Old England*—all in a jumble, without any concern for the contradictions among them. He championed the Country party programme and played upon current popular prejudices—indiscriminately and without believing in them for a moment. Proclaiming himself the tribune of the people, he resorted to the backstairs whenever he thought it would serve his purpose. He attacked the Government's policy, not because he thought it was altogether wrong but because he wished to execute it himself. Pitt steadily insisted that he would serve only if the King wanted him, but at the same time he continued to use his old metaphor about rescuing George II from the edge of a precipice.[2] Having violently proscribed his opponents, he finally showed himself willing to serve with anyone—on his own terms.

In the first tenure of office he paid little more than the customary lip-service to his promises. He promoted a Militia

[1] In the negotiations Pitt's followers may have been considered a liability. Hardwicke pointed out (ibid. 592) that 'there were not employments enough to satisfy such demands as were necessary to be complied with in order to come to any settlement'. The adhesion of Leicester House seems generally to have been thought essential to a stable Government: in addition to the sources cited above, see Newcastle's memoranda in Add. MSS. 32997, f. 135 and following.

[2] Walpole, *Memoirs of George II*, ii. 194.

Act, which did not prove altogether popular.[1] Though he disclaimed any direct responsibility, his actions caused the
Hanoverian soldier to pay for two handkerchiefs with 300
lashes. The inquiry into past measures became no more than an
investigation of the loss of Minorca, but he reluctantly risked his
popularity in urging clemency for Admiral Byng. In both his
ministries Pitt executed military and diplomatic policies that
differed rather in emphasis than in kind from those he had
attacked.[2] His rise to power, one may say, represented another
change of men but not of measures.

It does not appear, however, that Pitt's opposition and the
resulting crisis shocked the political world. The King cursed.
The factions traded hard words. Clever men commented with
sardonic amusement upon the self-seeking irresponsibility of the
politicians. Everyone deplored the confusion that deprived
England of strong leadership in the midst of a desperate war.
But one does not detect the angry disillusionment, the sense of
outraged public virtue, the feeling of betrayal, which followed
upon the reconstructions of 1742 and 1744. Nor did anyone
question the loyalty of those who caused the confusion. The
general attitude to the situation in 1756–7 seems to have been
that it was unusual but not unnatural. King, Prince, and Duke
were privileged to differ, and faction was inevitable.[3]

The comparative mildness of the public reaction may have
been due in part to the fact that all political groups were involved, and all accepted the final settlement. On previous
occasions the loudest outcries had come from the losers. But
also one cannot escape the conclusion that the open interplay
of faction since the fall of Walpole had prepared the political

---

[1] Add. MSS. 35353, ff. 222–3, 227; Pyle, *Memoirs of a Royal Chaplain*, p. 321.

[2] Pitt's strategic ideas, like his political philosophy, are difficult to analyse
because of the numerous contradictions in the declarations he made before,
during, and after the war. His pronouncements on what has been called 'blue-
water' strategy were, it seems to me, the traditional talking-points in the Country
party programme. When he came into office he maintained the alliance with
Prussia.

[3] For samples of the reaction in the political world, see Pyle, *Memoirs of a Royal
Chaplain*, pp. 245, 260, 270–1, 334, 358; Walpole, *Memoirs of George II*, ii. 260–76,
304–79; iii. 1–35; Waldegrave, *Memoirs*, passim; Dobrée, ed., *Letters of Chesterfield*,
v. 2071, 2145, 2181, 2187–9, 2192, 2206–7, 2209, 2213, 2217, 2220, 2223–32. The
full range of political charges was contained in two pamphlet series: *The Test*
(6 Nov. 1756–9 July 1757) edited by Arthur Murphy in support of Fox, and *The
Con-Test* (23 Nov. 1756–9 July 1757) run by Owen Ruffhead in defence of Pitt.

world for this kind of crisis. In the midst of war Pulteney had 'forced' the King once, the Pelhams had done it twice. Oppositions had not fulfilled their pledges. Fortune obviously favoured truculence and tenacity, not high moral sentiment. With these things in mind, what intelligent man could be shocked by this new crisis? Yet in its solution lay this happy irony: the ambitious Pitt, who precipitated and prolonged the crisis, who repudiated in word or deed nearly every charge he made as a 'patriot', carried out magnificently his determination to give Britain national unity and victory.

The solution represents the culmination of 'broad bottom'. Not every one had his pretensions satisfied—there were not places enough—but the factions all had a share. In contrast to previous reconstructions, no group was proscribed, and no group refused to serve with any other. The war and the length of the crisis unquestionably impelled the politicians to sink outstanding differences, and most differences turned out to be reconcilable. Two important aspects of the negotiations also reflect practices begun in the Pelhamite era.

One was the nature of Pitt's demands. He insisted upon power and control of national policy, and he would accept responsibility only for what he recommended. In the reconstructions of 1720, 1742, and 1744 the disposition of places had been the chief concern of the Opposition. But the Pelhams had made conditions similar to Pitt's in 1744 and 1746; and paying proper Constitutional deference to the royal Prerogative, they had proved that they could extort the official confidence of the King in the face of his personal disfavour. Pitt did not have the old corps at his back. He gambled upon his own indispensability and won. These lessons were not lost on the Oppositions of the future. The Dodingtons and Barringtons who would serve under almost any conditions did not disappear. There were still those who played the traditional game of seeking a place first and the King's confidence afterward. But those who aimed at power more than at the honour and emoluments of the King's service had these precedents for achieving their purpose by extortion.

The other was the King's approach to the formation of a ministry. In the first three reconstructions of the Hanoverian era the King had authorized the leaders of the strongest group in office to negotiate a treaty with the leaders of the group presumed strongest in opposition.[1] He endeavoured to keep the negotiations under his own eye and to interpose his own wishes and limitations. The resignations of February 1746 had driven George II to try a different expedient: to commission Bath and Granville, who were not in office, to form a Government out of the best materials they could find, exclusive of the old corps leaders. The resignations of October 1756 and George II's subsequent dissatisfaction with Pitt forced him to employ similar expedients several times. The only distinction to be drawn among his attempts was that in some cases he gave his commission to the man who was to be the real or nominal head of the Ministry, in others to an arbitrator who was asked to form some workable combination of factions. In no case did the commissioner receive *carte blanche*, but the successive failure of his efforts led the King to limit his instructions and reduce the number of his restrictions. George II accompanied his final, successful commission to Hardwicke only with a request that three men be appointed to specific posts.[2]

The employment of this device was a portent. The early method of reconstruction could succeed only when there was a strong faction in office which the King wished to or had to retain. When he went into opposition to his ministers, or when the factions capable of forming an administration insisted upon conflicting terms, the King had no recourse but to a commissioner. This practice tended to strengthen the hand of the Opposition.

If the commissioner were a mere negotiator, not intended for an important place in the Ministry, he was armed only with the King's authority, which never extended to *carte blanche*. He could not command the strength of a party already entrenched in office. As an individual, he was weaker than the leader of any faction. A treaty once concluded, he lost the King's authority and, therefore, all power to influence the course of future

---

[1] All three reconstructions took place with the King's reluctant consent. In 1720 and 1742 he chose the negotiators from the group which he wished to retain. In 1744 he found that he had no choice. Thus the King's attitude varied, as did that of the Oppositions, but the mechanics of reconstruction were roughly comparable.

[2] Yorke, *Hardwicke*, ii. 404. George II wanted Fox as Paymaster, Barrington as Secretary at War, and Anson as First Lord of the Admiralty.

events.[1] The factions knew that they had to deal only with an *ad hoc* emissary, to whom they had no obligations, and who had no power to circumscribe their demands or to enforce his own. The King, having delegated his authority, exercised less influence over the negotiations. He could attempt to modify a proposed treaty, but it was more difficult to make significant changes after the politicians had been brought to an agreement, especially if the agreement fitted the conditions he had set. If he could not make suitable modifications, the King could only accept or reject. Under these circumstances the factions obviously had greater freedom to insist upon their demands.

If the commissioner were a politician designated to lead the new coalition, his position was strong indeed. It was presumed that he had the King's confidence, that his stipulations had been accepted, and that he would have the support of the 'influence of the Crown'. His faction acquired pre-eminence over all others. But he could not command them. Not until the Fox–North coalition of 1783 was any Opposition party as strong as the old corps had been. The other groups knew that the commissioner must acquire support from among them, and they could adjust their demands to his necessity. It was even possible for a rival leader, by refusing all co-operation, to replace the one who held the King's commission.

In 1756–7 the factions had shown what an intractable Opposition they could make when their antagonisms, their terms, and royal prejudices clashed at so many points. Hardwicke succeeded, partly because of the perilous situation, partly because he possessed the strongest attributes of each type of commissioner. On the one hand, he could manage Newcastle, who controlled the largest party. On the other, he was experienced and disinterested. He refused to return to office, but he accepted responsibility for his handiwork by remaining as minister-without-portfolio to help keep the new coalition together.

Hardwicke might well have repeated his boast of 1745. His settlement had left no elements from which a formed general

[1] In his *Memoirs*, pp. 122–49, Waldegrave gives a vivid picture of his problems as a negotiator. When not designated for office, he was powerless to coerce the factions. When designated for the Treasury, he inspired no confidence because he had no political experience. Waldegrave concluded that on such occasions princes should 'do their own business' because of the weak position of any 'deputy' or 'commissioner'.

Opposition could be made. For the rest of George II's reign ministerial policy was rarely attacked. Parliamentary attendance was thin, and divisions were few. Members challenged the Government mostly when Bills affected particular economic interests: the taxation or regulation of commerce in grain, meat, fish, dairy products, ale and spirits, and cloth.[1] Minorities were tiny, seldom exceeding fifty, and the Ministry never had to muster its full strength. Once in 1758 two members called for a division only to find that there was not a quorum in the House.[2] The irrepressible Tories revived the old Country party Bill for repealing the Septennial Act in the same year, but it was 'a very cold scent', only 74 voting in its favour after a brief debate.[3] No ministry ever found Parliament so easy to manage. In December 1759 Pitt made the unusual request that the Supplies be voted before Christmas. To an objection that 'the House was not full enough to treat on such an important subject', the Minister replied 'that every member knew the business of the House and the times fixed for proceeding severally upon them [*sic*], that the immediate absence of the members proved only their confidence and acquiescence in the present design'.[4] The Commons passively accepted the proposition that abstention gave consent, and Pitt had his way.

Amid general rejoicing at the successful operation of an effective Government, voices were raised in concern. Horace Walpole recorded in his memoirs, 'Whatever was demanded was granted or allowed with such inconsiderate facility [in 1758] that Lord Mansfield, to stigmatize Pitt's measures and profusion, and the Parliament's condescension, called it *The South-Sea year*.'[5] Lord Bath inspired a pamphlet in which, it was asserted, the prevailing 'perfect harmony and union' threatened 'the ruin of our Constitution':[6]

The extinction of factious opposition, the unanimity of every party, and the acquiescence of every connexion in whatever scheme is proposed by His Majesty's servants, while it hath produced infinite

---

[1] *Commons Journals*, xviii. 74, 109, 167, 222, 240, 312, 446, 463, 475, 596, 788, 822, 829. The Scotch Militia Bill in 1760 apparently aroused some national prejudice, but the Government carried it easily: ibid. 872.

[2] Ibid. 309.   [3] *P.H.* xv. 870–1.   [4] Egerton MSS. 1719, f. 81.

[5] Walpole, *Memoirs of George II*, iii. 157.

[6] [John Douglas], *A Letter Addressed to Two Great Men* (London, 1760), pp. 1–2, 43–47.

advantages to the public, hath deprived those who direct the Cabinet of all such parliamentary instructions as their predecessors in power used to receive.

Even Pitt's strongest partisans worried about the failure of the two Houses, in the absence of a formed general Opposition, to act as a check upon the executive. Chesterfield was distressed that Parliament, taking it for granted that the Government's requests were 'necessary and frugal', voted supplies 'not only *nemine contradicente* but *nemine quicquid dicente*'.[1] The compiler of the statutes-at-large, Owen Ruffhead, searched medieval precedents for some way to 'restore the dignity and authority of parliament'.[2]

Pitt in Opposition had warned against the day when Parliament would sit only to 'register the arbitrary edicts of one too-powerful a subject'. Now he became the object of his own tirade. Many who had professed to long for an end of the 'odious distinction of party' found to their dismay that 'this new, this very new system' was in fact the 'prerogative administration' restrained by 'a mere cobweb limitation', which Pitt himself had taught them to abhor. 'Broad bottom' had enthroned, not a 'patriot king', but an 'overbearing minister' whose amazing success enabled him to dominate Parliament, his colleagues, and the Crown.[3] *Inter armos silent leges*, but had Britain sold her free institutions to buy military victory?

To those who expressed concern a worldly-wise pamphleteer offered this advice:[4]

Have a little patience . . . ; we shall soon, I trust, sir, have beat all our enemies, and then we shall perhaps again have leisure to quarrel among ourselves; we may then see more than one champion in the field; we may then list under that banner which our interest or our passions may direct us to.

The formation of the national Ministry had subdued but not

---

[1] Dobrée, ed., *Letters of Chesterfield*, v. 2085.

[2] *Reasons Why the Approaching Treaty of Peace Should be Debated in Parliament* (London, 1760).

[3] For these phrases see Ilchester, *Fox*, i. 228; *P.H.* xiii. 678, 701; Dickins and Stanton, eds., *An Eighteenth-Century Correspondence*, p. 368. Cf. Egmont's attack on the dictatorship of a 'popular faction' in his draft for a speech *c.* 1759–60: *P.R.O.*, *Egmont MSS.* 277.

[4] *Remarks on the Letter Addressed to Two Great Men* (London, 1760), p. 61. Cf. *An Account of the Constitution and Present State of Great Britain* (London, 1759).

erased the rivalry of faction. Men who were 'very attentive to the game', wrote one observer, thought that the ministers only 'play their cards together till fortune puts it in the power of some to over-reach the others'.[1] George II's advanced years encouraged the formation of a new 'flying squadron . . . of young men of ability and parts' early in 1760.[2] Ultimately the approach of victory, the accession of a new king, and internal stresses put an end to the unusual peace of parliamentary sessions.

[1] Egerton MSS. 1719, ff. 32–36. Cf. Dobrée, ed., *Letters of Chesterfield*, v. 2257, 2302.
[2] Add. MSS. 32908, f. 163.

VII

THE ROCKINGHAMITE ERA
1760-1782

---

1. *The King and the Parties*

2. *Party Doctrines*

The Chathamites. The Rockinghamites. The Constitutional Issues. Whigs and Tories.

3. *The Conduct of the Opposition*

Party Organization. Political Issues. The Opposition Campaign.

4. *The Fall of North*

VII

THE ROCKINGHAMITE ERA

1760–1782

I. THE KING AND THE PARTIES

THE formation of a stable ministry supported by Leicester House had the usual effect upon the position of the heir apparent. Prince George lost his party. His friends who took office became the King's men. The Prince found himself 'immured at home like a girl' in the company of his mother, Lord Bute, and the other members of his household.[1] Ministers with an eye to the future paid some deference to his wishes, but, as his father had learned, without a party he did not possess 'the influence due to his rank'. Nor did he have the materials from which 'to form a ministry who can have the opinion of the people' upon his accession.[2]

George and his favourite sensed their isolation keenly toward the end of 1758. Bute undertook exploratory investigations with distressing results. The Prince soon concluded that 'we must look out for new tools, our old ones having all deserted us'.[3] None came to hand. The intransigence of Pitt proved the greatest disappointment. After expressing a willingness to accept 'some honourable bystanding office', Pitt declared that Bute could never be 'the Minister', then refused to discuss plans without bringing in Newcastle and George II. The future King denounced his erstwhile ally and swore that he would accept any ministry 'provided the blackest of hearts is not one of them'.[4] Still, the men of Leicester House could think of nothing better than some Government headed by the impossible combination of Bute as First Lord and Pitt as Secretary of State. When George II died on 25 October 1760 his successor was prepared

---

[1] Sedgwick, ed., *Letters from George III to Lord Bute*, p. 27. Like his father, Prince George sought command of the army to re-establish his position, and like his father, he failed to get it.

[2] Ibid., p. 11.   [3] Ibid., p. 35.   [4] Ibid., p. 45.

only with a declaration to the Privy Council, some high principles instilled by his tutor, and a set of ideas inherited from
Leicester House Oppositions.

The absence of a 'great outline' did not mean that George III
had no plans. He knew well enough what he intended to do.
Bute was to be his Minister, in or out of office. Newcastle must
go, and the King must emancipate himself from the slavery
imposed by the old corps. He would replace the régime of vice,
faction, and corruption with the rule of virtue and virtuous
men. Experience taught George III to compromise with reality,
but he remained consistently true to his main ideas. He wished
to govern through a minister of his choice. He was determined
to maintain his 'independency' and to avoid domination by the
power of connexion. His struggle to uphold his position is the
central theme of his reign. The lack of a 'glorious plan' at his
accession meant only that George III did not yet know how to
achieve his goals.

Neither he nor his favourite had much political experience.
The Prince did not dwell in the world of politicians as his father
had done. Even after he attained his majority George lived a
remarkably secluded life.[1] He apparently understood the general
structure of politics, but most of his information came from his
mother and his tutor. His training led him to believe that he
could accomplish his aims simply by appointing Bute to the
Treasury and giving him steadfast support thereafter.[2]

The favourite had few qualifications for the post of First
Minister. After a brief term as a representative Scots peer from
1737 to 1741, Bute did not sit in Parliament until 1761. He
belonged to the Leicester House côterie for a short time before
Frederick's death, and so doubtless heard the common rumours,
which were generally accurate, about the Prince's intentions.[3]

[1] In addition to his frequent contact with politicians, Frederick occasionally
attended debates in the Lords. I have never seen a report that Prince George did so.

[2] Sedgwick, ed., *Letters from George III to Lord Bute*, pp. 3–6, 13–15, 18–22, 34–39,
43–45. In one respect the Prince was less naïve than his mentor. Bute seems to have
thought that he could be 'the Minister' without holding responsible office. George
wanted Bute with him on any terms but steadily insisted that influence should be
united to responsibility.

[3] Bute became a Lord of Frederick's Bedchamber in 1750, and in the 'glorious
plan' he was designated for election as a Scots representative peer. It is curious to
note, however, that Egmont did not set him down for any office, not even one in the
Households of the King, Queen, or Prince. Bute's name appears only once, in an

Bute had also taken part in the negotiations of November 1756 and June 1757. But compared to Egmont, he was the veriest tyro. He probably did not realize the need for a 'great outline', and to construct one was certainly beyond his powers.[1]

Circumstances did nothing to ease the task of inexperience. Egmont had drawn up the 'glorious plan' to meet the conditions of 1749–51, when Britain was at peace and prospects for a strong Prince's party were fair. In 1760 the war-time coalition enjoyed the general support of all factions and great popularity in the country. Was it right for the new monarch to wreck a ministry which he had originally approved and which so successfully fulfilled its purpose? Bute's inept conversations with Pitt, Fox, and Newcastle did not exploit the severe tensions within the Government.[2] King and favourite both realized that the 'bloody war' interfered with their objectives. Yet when saddled with responsibility, they had no programme to restore peace, virtue, and prosperity all on an autumn day. The accession of George III, therefore, was a damp squib. After years of bold professions, the King left his grandfather's Ministry intact. He pretended to think the war 'just and necessary'. Bute became Groom of the Stole. Some Tories were made officers of the Household. His Majesty began his reign in opposition to his Government, but he was helpless to change it.[3]

So for the time being he accepted his ministerial inheritance. Newcastle 'chose' the Parliament of 1761 in the most peaceful election of the century.[4] The coalition carried on with the same appearance of unanimity but with new frictions introduced by the presence of Bute. Eventually the King's enemies played into his hands. Outvoted in the Cabinet on the issue of war with Spain, Pitt resigned in October 1761. Newcastle withdrew after

unheaded marginal list which may be a catalogue of those designed for elevation to or promotion in the peerage.

[1] Shelburne recorded that Bute, knowing how Walpole had outmanœuvred Compton in 1727, prepared the new King's declaration 'several years before George II died'. Bute would have done better, Shelburne concluded, to have 'bestowed his time on thinking what measures he should pursue . . . instead of the composition of what he should say': Fitzmaurice, *Shelburne*, i. 33.

[2] Namier, *England in the Age of the American Revolution*, pp. 110–23.

[3] See the bitter chagrin expressed by the King in Sedgwick, ed., *Letters of George III to Lord Bute*, pp. 49–50.

[4] Namier, *England*, pp. 153–78. In England and Wales there were only 4 contests in counties and 37 in boroughs. Of the 11 petitions filed, 5 were soon dropped.

a departmental quarrel in May 1762. Bute took the Treasury, and the Government pushed on negotiations to end the war. As these progressed, the new Minister worried about the parliamentary strength necessary to approve the peace. The old corps still manned the administration, so Bute sought a reconciliation with Newcastle. When three months of parleying failed to secure the vacillating Duke, the Court summoned Henry Fox to head the House of Commons. George III considered this move a temporary expedient—'we must call in bad men to govern bad men'—to secure the peace that would permit him to inaugurate the reign of virtue.[1]

Under the King's eye Fox proceeded to break the old corps. By every means known to politics he set about detaching Newcastle's followers from him. The Duke tried to arrest defections by a programme of resignations designed to 'strike terror' as he had done in 1746. Few obeyed him, and those who resigned provided Fox with places to gain additional support. In December 1762 the Government carried all divisions on the peace preliminaries by overwhelming majorities. Fox and Bute then pursued their victory by a 'thorough rout' of Newcastle's friends and dependents. From the great lords to the humblest functionary, every appointee of the Pelhams who did not shift his allegiance was dismissed from the posts he held at the pleasure of the Crown. The Court had finally taken the one measure—clearly understood to be essential by Frederick and Egmont—to end the coercion of the King by the King's friends.[2]

The 'massacre of the Pelhamite innocents' effectively reconstituted the Court party. As long as the Government exercised proper discipline, it could count upon solid majorities.[3] But George III soon found himself beset by an unanticipated difficulty: the problem of leadership. In May 1763 Bute lost his nerve and resigned. The King was thus obliged to choose 'the Minister' from among the politicians, of whom most were

[1] Smith, ed., *Grenville Papers*, i. 452.

[2] For the political manoeuvres following the accession, see the detailed study in Namier, *England*, pp. 137–93, 331–482. Apparently George III was the first to express the need to cashier all recalcitrants, and his letters to Bute in 1762 show that he learned the lessons of politics with great rapidity.

[3] Newcastle exaggerated when he spoke in 1765 of 'the certainty of *any court* carrying any point' (Bateson, ed., *Newcastle's Narrative*, p. 42). The ministries of the 1760's were sometimes defeated—e.g. on the Land Tax in 1767—but only when they did not cultivate their majority carefully enough.

members of the factions he wished to annihilate, and few were personally congenial to him. The reign of virtue had to be postponed again. For seven years George III struggled to the limit of his sanity with short-lived ministries and shifting policies under Grenville, Rockingham, Chatham, and Grafton. No party had strength enough to govern alone, and mutual antagonisms put serious impediments in the way of coalition. To keep a Government in office the King had to make concessions as humiliating as any imposed upon his grandfather.

Factional antagonisms arose in part from the traditional sources: personal hostility and rivalry for place. The politics of the 1760's introduced new causes of friction. All but the followers of Bute dreaded his influence 'behind the curtain' and wanted him excluded from Court. Bedford, who had negotiated the Treaty of Paris, refused to co-operate with those who persisted in attacking his work. George Grenville kept the opponents of the Stamp Act at arm's length. Chatham professed great magnanimity about past measures, but his waywardness, his denunciations of faction, and finally his nervous breakdown made him an impossible ally. The remnants of Newcastle's following, re-formed under Rockingham, cared less than they pretended for their record in office. The sponsors of the Declaratory Act would have worked with Grenville, but they developed 'Constitutional principles' about the formation of ministries which were unacceptable both to the other parties and to the King. The politicians accused George III of employing a policy of *divide et impera*. That they could no more coalesce to form an Opposition than they could to form a Government makes it clear that they were responsible for their own divisions.[1]

Stability emerged gradually from weakness and confusion. Death or retirement swept away most of the figures who had dominated politics for so long in the era of 'broad bottom', and

[1] The parties and their 'principles' are excellently described in John Brooke, *The Chatham Administration, 1766–1768*, pp. 218–94; cf. Pares, *King George III and the Politicians*, pp. 90–92. The Rockingham Papers (Sheffield City Library, Index no. 4) contain Dowdeswell's 'Thoughts on the present state of public affairs. . . . Written the 23d and 24 of July 1767' in which the King is blamed for the weakness of the Opposition as well: 'The many divisions which have been the consequence of so many changes have so disunited men that though no Opposition can be successful, no Administration can stand.' George III dismissed both the Grenville and Rockingham ministries, but except perhaps for his interest in the Wilkes affair, he did not invent the disputes which divided the parties.

loyalties shifted as the younger men sought a winning combination.[1] By 1771 the Ministry had absorbed the active followers of Bute, Bedford, and Grenville. The King had found in Lord North a Minister who was personally satisfactory and capable of managing the Commons. With the inevitable defections and additions George III held this Government in office for twelve years.

Only two significant groups remained in the political wilderness: the Chathamites and the Rockingham connexion. They had few ideas in common. Over the years they alternately joined and repudiated each other. But each advocated a noteworthy Constitutional theory. Both sustained a consistent Opposition, comparable in length and intensity to the long struggle against Walpole. Together they demolished and replaced, more thoroughly than ever before, a Ministry with which His Majesty did not wish to part.

2. PARTY DOCTRINES

The Chathamites

From his resignation in 1761 till his death in 1778 William Pitt (who became Earl of Chatham in 1766) steadily proclaimed that he was an individual without a party, 'a man standing single and daring to appeal to his country at large upon the soundness of his principles and the rectitude of his conduct'.[2] His chronic bad health, both physical and mental, severely limited his political activity. He quarrelled with most of his old associates. He made no effort to cultivate a connexion, which he considered an 'encumbrance'. But there were always a few politicians who followed his lead, and those who survived him claimed to be his political heirs in the next generation.[3]

The most important of his heritors were the Earl of Shelburne and William Pitt the younger. Shelburne began his career as

---

[1] See Namier, *England*, pp. 69–71.

[2] Add. MSS. 32962, ff. 347–50.

[3] On Chatham's party see Brooke, *The Chatham Administration*, pp. 248–55. Pitt seems to have made some effort to re-form a flying squadron for a short time after his resignation in 1761 (Rockingham Papers, Sheffield City Library, Index no. 1, Sondes to Rockingham, 26 Nov. [1761]). Perhaps the results were discouraging. At all events, he never tried it again, although he and his friends sometimes attended meetings with the Rockinghamites.

an opponent of the great commoner in 1760, then three years later became his most devoted disciple. Personal friendships, county connexions, and two pocket boroughs provided Shelburne with a small following, which he chose not to call a party. Among its leading members were Isaac Barré, John Dunning, Lord Mahon, and Sir George Yonge, all able and aggressive politicians.[1] The Duke of Rutland brought the younger Pitt into Parliament at the general election of 1780. He immediately established himself as a brilliant speaker, and within a year he had gathered about him 'a small society of young men' drawn from relatives, friends and the Manners connexion.[2] Shelburne and Pitt were not formally allied until they were in office together; but they were on cordial terms, and both steadily proclaimed their adherence to the principles and policies of Chatham.

The political philosophy Chatham bequeathed to them was a strange compound of Tory phrases, Bolingbrokean ideas, old corps practices, and the lessons of his own experience. He never set it down in any systematic form. It emerged during the 1760's in sporadic utterances justifying his prejudices, his moods, and his conduct. He haughtily disregarded inconsistencies and apparent contradictions. He enjoyed mystery and cared nothing for logic. Any analysis must impose upon his thoughts an order which Chatham never gave them.[3]

A true patriot should oppose 'measures not men'. He should base his opposition upon his own convictions, 'independent of the sentiments of others'. If others agreed, let them join. Chatham praised 'that honourable connexion which arises from disinterested concurrence in opinion upon public measures'. He conceded that personal affections were virtuous, and in his more conciliatory moods he allowed 'the sacred bond of private friendship and esteem' a beneficent role in public life. But sound government could not be based on 'an exclusive system of family

---

[1] Ian R. Christie, *The End of North's Ministry, 1780–1782* (London, 1958), pp. 224–5.

[2] *H.M.C., Carlisle MSS.*, pp. 555, 575–6, 580–1.

[3] Chatham's frequent declarations of principle are recorded in numerous sources. The quotations in the following passages are taken from *P.H.* xvi. 1107–8; Phillimore, *Lyttelton*, ii. 763–4; Fitzmaurice, *Shelburne*, i. 263–4, 323; ii. 17; Add. MSS. 32962, ff. 347–50; 32974, f. 419; Rockingham Papers, Sheffield City Library, Index no. 38 (Newcastle to White, 19 June 1764).

connexions and private friendships'. Political friendship was faction. Any man who acted 'by the force of particular bargains' was mean and dishonourable. Chatham violently condemned 'the narrow genius of old corps connexion, [which] has weakened Whiggism and rendered national union on revolution principles impossible'.

He thus denied the legitimacy of party even as a temporary expedient to deliver His Majesty from evil advisers. Chatham seems to have thought that a connexion to oppose a wrong measure should terminate when the wrong measure ceased to be an issue. The group formed to oppose the next wrong measure might have a very different composition. Such parties did not intend to force a change of hands. The elderly Chatham no longer expressed the need felt by the young orator and the great commoner to rescue the King from the edge of a precipice. If His Majesty needed help, let him ask for it. He knew well enough where it could be found. Chatham repeatedly vowed that 'he would never force himself upon the King' nor be introduced into office by a cabal. At times he professed to be tolerant of other views, but he considered his own rule of conduct a model for others: 'The King's pleasure and gracious commands alone shall be a call to me; I am deaf to every other thing.'

If summoned from Opposition, however, he would serve only on his own terms. These were simply stated by Shelburne during a negotiation in 1778: 'Lord Chatham must be the dictator.' He would make concessions to the King's personal wishes, but he demanded the full use of the Prerogative in the formation of a ministry and in the conduct of the Government. With this power he proposed to make an administration from the best of all parties, destroy faction, and present the King with a happy and united people. George III allowed him to try his scheme in 1766, but even though he failed, Chatham clung to his principles for the remainder of his life.

The elder statesman obviously tailored his creed to fit his inclinations and his vision of himself after 1761. Only a man with equal self-assurance and a similar superiority to the opinions of others could make use of such a doctrine. Even Shelburne, who found it quite congenial, saw the need for some compromise. By 1779 he admitted that the Opposition must be based upon 'the great leading principle of new men and new measures'. The country could be saved 'only by a change of system'.[1] He did not insist upon the first place for himself in every conjuncture, and he never demanded dictatorial powers.

When he became First Lord of the Treasury in 1782 Shelburne confessed that he had made a great sacrifice for the good of the nation by serving under Rockingham, but in other respects he remained true to 'all those constitutional ideas which for seventeen years he had imbibed from his master in politics, the late Earl of Chatham'. The Sovereign had summoned him directly. The Earl defended 'the King's right to choose his own servants', declared that he had entered office uncommitted to any man, and repeated that government by faction would ruin the Constitution:[2]

he would never consent that the King of England should be a king of the Mahrattas, among whom it was a custom for a certain number of great lords to elect a peshaw, who was the creature of an aristocracy and was vested with the plenitude of power, while the King was, in fact, nothing more than a royal pageant or puppet.

The younger Pitt accepted his father's creed with modifications substantially the same as Shelburne's. Upon his first entrance into politics he proclaimed himself an 'independent Whig', unfettered by connexion. He joined in the assault on North because the ministers' disastrous measures had lost them the support of the people and made them unworthy of the Commons' confidence. In one debate Pitt justified his opposition in the language of Bolingbroke: the removal of the Ministry was[3] 'the only means of presenting to the eyes of the world, what he had read of with rapture, but almost despaired of seeing— a patriot king presiding over a united people'. Pitt nevertheless defended the Prerogative in orthodox terms. The House of Commons should 'watch and examine into the conduct of ministers' and withdraw its confidence from those unfit to govern, but 'the Crown had the undoubted right to appoint its own ministers'.[4]

As a political fledgling Pitt did not expect to take a place in a new administration, but 'were his doing so more within his reach', he declared to the House in 1782, 'he would never

[1] *P.H.* xx. 1165.   [2] Ibid. xxiii. 191–2.   [3] Ibid. xxii. 1199.
[4] Idem.

accept a subordinate situation'.[1] George Selwyn accurately interpreted this statement to mean that 'there is another *premier* at the starting post, who, as yet, has never been shaved'.[2] Like Shelburne, Pitt compromised at first. He became Shelburne's Chancellor of the Exchequer. Once he reached the top, he would never descend. His eminence as First Minister made his father's philosophy an almost perfect fit. He was considerate of the King—perhaps more so than Chatham would have been —and he never laid a formal claim to dictatorial powers. He steadily insisted, however, upon the effective direction of the Government and the freedom to bring in private members' Bills which embodied his personal convictions.

From 1770 to 1782 the Chathamites' Constitutional ideas kept them in temperamental and erratic opposition. There were wrong measures to be found whenever they chose to find them. Despite their resolute independence, they usually reached agreement among themselves without difficulty. Chatham did not always condescend to communicate his opinions to his followers, and when he did so, they sometimes could not fathom his Delphic utterances. Shelburne and the younger Pitt treated their friends much as other political leaders did their parties. The Chathamites 'consulted each others' sentiments'—they could not bring themselves to say that they concerted measures —and the leaders eventually took their men into office with them. But they were too independent to co-operate long with other parties. Their 'firm and indissoluble unions' with the Rockinghamites had short lives. A little more than a year before North's fall Shelburne declared in the House of Lords that any coalition of the 'petty squads' in opposition would be futile, factious, and inconsistent with the principles which guided his public life.[3]

The Rockinghamites

The events of 1762 turned Newcastle and his remaining friends into painfully reluctant 'patriots'. Young and old, they were Court Whigs at heart. Hardwicke recoiled from 'all the uphill labour of an opposition which we had never practised'.[4]

[1] *P.H.* xxii. 1149. [2] *H.M.C., Carlisle MSS.*, p. 593.
[3] *P.H.* xxi. 1025–6.
[4] Add. MSS. 35353, ff. 292–3.

Devonshire urged extreme caution.[1] The very thought of
Opposition brought from Newcastle cries of 'Most certainly not'
and 'God forbid'.[2] In his vague way he hoped at first to retain
his influence out of office by leaving his friends in place. Then
the programme of resignations, by which he hoped to terrorize
the Court in November, failed of its object. Five of the nine who
quit did so against their wishes.[3] With a young king on the
throne and Bute established at the Treasury, the prospects of
an Opposition were bleak. Most of those who wanted to be in
office thought it wiser to stay there. Most of those who were out
of office wanted to get back.

The threat of total impotence finally drove them to form an
Opposition. They were party men. They knew that without
concert and connexion they had no prospects at all, and a
party which did not act would soon disintegrate. Opposition
was the only form of action open to those who had been driven
out by Bute and Fox, or who would not serve on their terms,
or who had been dragged from place by old loyalties. The young
men pushed on their hesitant elders. The establishment of a
regular 'dining club' on 23 December 1762 marks the formal
beginning of the Rockinghamite party.[4]

This group took with them into the wilderness the ideas
upon which they had justified their tenure of power. In a very
short time they converted these ideas into a doctrine for
Opposition. Their experiences as a party led to modifications
and refinements. Professor Pares wittily accused Edmund Burke
of 'constructing a theory of politics out of generalizations . . .
on every incident in the career of the Marquis of Rockingham'.[5]
But in many aspects the new doctrine owed more to episodes
in the much longer career of the Duke of Newcastle.

[1] Add. MSS. 32944, ff. 317–18; Rockingham Papers, Sheffield City Library,
Index no. 0, Devonshire to Rockingham, 26 Dec. 1762.

[2] Add. MSS. 32915, ff. 336–7; ibid. 32939, ff. 264–5.

[3] Namier, *England*, p. 449. Of the 33 friends slated for resignation, 24 stayed in
office. Of these, 7 were later dismissed, 17 gave allegiance to the Court and kept
their places or were promoted.

[4] Ibid., pp. 484–5. The party chiefs began meetings on 2 Dec. 1762 to plan their
opposition to the preliminaries of peace (Add. MSS. 33000, f. 200). Not until
Fox's 'thorough rout' was well under way could the 'young Whigs' persuade the
old to consent to an organization which had the appearance of formed general
Opposition.

[5] Pares, *King George III and the Politicians*, p. 80, n. 1.

The Whig myth formed its basis. Anticipating Newcastle's departure from the Ministry in May 1762, Rockingham wrote to the Duke,[1]

Whenever it happens, I shall look upon it as a national misfortune, for indeed without flattering your Grace, I must look and ever shall upon you and your connexions as the solid foundations on which every good which has happened to this country since the Revolution have been erected.

Newcastle's remnant regarded itself as the old corps, the Whig party which had made the Revolution and saved the Protestant Succession when it was in danger. They were 'the old and true friends of His Majesty's royal family and Government', 'the great Revolution-principle families' to whom the King owed his crown.[2] Out of context, few would have recognized that the following declaration was a parody:[3] 'We are the true Revolution Whigs who set His [Majesty's] family upon the throne, and we will stand by the King who stands by the laws and employs such ministers as are acceptable to the nation.'

In point of fact the Rockinghamites had little right to their claim. Very few were of 'revolution lineage'. George Grenville once commented derisively on the supposed Whiggery of a party whose leaders were Rockingham, a descendant of Strafford; Conway, a descendant of Sir Edward Seymour; Winchilsea, a descendant of Nottingham; Dartmouth, great-grandson of James II's trusted admiral; Dowdeswell, member of a traditionally Tory family; and Richmond and Grafton, descendants of Charles II's bastards. A more correct ancestry could be attributed to the party members who had inherited the Dutch blood of Bentinck and Keppel. 'I should not have mentioned nor judged of any man by the party merit or demerit of his ancestors', concluded Grenville, 'if the *Whig families* had not been impudently urged to make up for their notorious deficiency in all other circumstances.'[4]

The high proportion of fiction in their case did not deter the

[1] Add. MSS. 32938, f. 123.

[2] Mary Bateson, ed., *A Narrative of the Changes of the Ministry 1756–7* (London, 1898), p. 4; Rockingham Papers, Sheffield City Library, Index no. 38, Devonshire to Rockingham, 30 Aug. 1763.

[3] *Patriotism. A Farce* (London, 1764), p. 13.

[4] *H.M.C., Lothian MSS.*, p. 261; cf. Namier, *England*, pp. 445–6. In fairness to the Rockinghamites it should be remembered that Grafton, Seymour, Nottingham, and Dartmouth turned against James II in 1688.

Rockinghamites from steadily reasserting it and extending its political significance. Their cause was 'the Whig cause', the cause of the Constitution, the cause of the Hanoverian line. As members of the illustrious families who had made and preserved the Revolution, they were the natural counsellors of the Crown. Who could govern better than those whose every tie bound them to the Constitution framed by their direct forbears? Also, as in 1688, their great families represented 'property, power, and popularity', which made them the natural leaders of society.[1] Finally, the monarchy stood for ever in their debt for services rendered. Newcastle once carried this idea so far as to say that, even though he was in Opposition, 'I should think it very hard that any administration under our present royal family should oppose or not assist my interest in the boroughs where I am concerned.'[2] All these considerations made it manifest that in justice to the Whigs, the Constitution, the nation, and the House of Brunswick, the King should employ the Rockinghamites.

Further considerations demanded that they should form the basis of every administration. They knew best how to govern. Years of experience had taught them the value of party in constructing a coherent and effective ministry. The Rockinghamites were 'the Whig party', consistent in principle and united by bonds of blood, friendship, and long association in office. Their group was not large enough to fill all the posts in the Government, but as Charles Yorke told George III in 1765, they were 'the *rock* on which he might engraft'.[3] The King should entrust them with the positions of greatest influence and, upon their advice, add such others as might be needed.

Since their claim to office was indefeasible, there had to be an explanation for their exclusion. They could not admit that the King exercised his Prerogative properly by choosing men whom he liked better. The Rockinghamites did not ask the

[1] See Charles Yorke's exposition of these views in his letters of 3 July and 10 Aug. 1765: Add. MSS. 45030 (unfolioed).

[2] Add. MSS. 32977, f. 398.

[3] Add. MSS. 45030 (unfolioed), Charles Yorke to [Lord Grey?], 10 Aug. 1765. The Rockinghamites' views of party in general and of their own party in particular are clearly expressed in Newcastle's correspondence with his colleagues from 1762 to 1768: Add. MSS. 32977, ff. 58, 209–11; 32978, ff. 11–13, 43, 281–3; 32987, ff. 363–4; 32988, f. 23; 32990, ff. 7, 61; 33000, ff. 99–100. See also Bateson, ed., *Newcastle's Narrative*, pp. 106, 111.

King to like them.[1] It was his *duty* to employ them. What caused the King to neglect his duty? The villain, of course, was Bute. He had manœuvred Newcastle into resigning. With Fox he had wrecked the old corps and driven out the faithful few. His advice, they came to believe, had prevented their return to office in 1763, and they convinced themselves that his influence behind the curtain had weakened and destroyed the Rockingham administration of 1765–6. To serve his own interests the favourite tried to keep every ministry feeble and divided. To maintain his own power he duped and misled the King into excluding his natural counsellors.[2]

Embedded in these articles of faith were the political lessons learned by the old corps since the Hanoverian accession. To acquire and retain power they needed an organized party whose leaders worked in concert. Their superior organization had given them a great advantage in the crises of 1742–4, 1746, and 1756–7. To sustain party morale, particularly in adversity, it was desirable to have a sense of solidarity, a faith in themselves, based upon a tradition of common achievement. Walpole's harangues in the cockpit had kept his 'old majority' intact till near the end of his career, and the Pelhams steadily preached up the unity of the old corps. To have the full exercise of power, they needed to occupy the chief offices of State, wherein they and they only, unimpeded by a Carteret or a Bute, should give advice to the Crown. The Treasury, of course, was the key position. Shortly after his resignation in 1762, Newcastle began to plan for his return to power by considering a 'new system or

---

[1] In the abortive negotiations of 1763 the Rockinghamites informed the King that 'they would never come into office but as a party and upon a plan concerted with Mr. Pitt and the great Whig Lords, as had been practised in the late King's time'. When George III objected, Hardwicke told his emissary that English kings sometimes had to accept ministers they disliked: the monarch must 'bend and ply a little' because the Rockinghamites would not (Yorke, *Hardwicke*, iii. 468, 513–15; Add. MSS. 32948, f. 291). The history of this negotiation shows how quickly the Rockinghamites had adapted their ideas to the circumstances of Opposition. For an early exposition, see *The Opposition to the Late Minister Vindicated* (London, 1763), pp. 16–17, 30–45.

[2] The Rockinghamites' hatred of Bute, which they shared with most other politicians, is constantly reiterated in their correspondence during the 1760's. In a summary of his party's credo Rockingham described 'our strong and unalterable determination of ever resisting and attempting to restrain the power and influence of Lord Bute' as the first 'fundamental principle': Portland Papers, Nottingham University Library, Rockingham to Portland, 17 Sept. 1767.

plan of administration' based on the principle 'that my great friends must make a principal part of any administration to be formed; and particularly to have a Treasury of friends'.[1]

Long experience in politics, however, had instilled into Newcastle and his experienced colleagues some attitudes uncongenial to the 'young Whigs' who made up the bulk of the party. The old Duke was never deeply concerned either about public policy or consistency in action. He could always persuade himself that he was right, and he loved office primarily because he loved to distribute patronage. Again and again during the 1760's he insisted that he sought power only 'to serve my friends'. He would play the political game with any partners—Pitt, Bedford, Grenville, the Tories—no matter how bitterly they had differed in the past. After forty-five years as a placeman, he found it agony to admit that, when opposing, he was in Opposition. Not until 1766 could he bring himself to say, with careful reservations, that 'Opposition is not only necessary but honest, popular, and I should hope even in these times (for venal times they are) will succeed'.[2]

Rockingham and the younger men were much more stiff-necked, particularly after their loss of office in 1766. The Marquis professed to despise jobbery—he had no object but 'the public service'. He prided himself on his friends' adherence to 'the upright principle of consistency'. He distrusted every party but his own, and he had no qualms about proclaiming his opposition.[3] In 1769 he viewed his party's situation in these terms:[4]

Our line of conduct is nice and requires much consideration. I think as a general rule we should constantly look back to what has been—and adhere to the same lines in the future.

I think we and *we only* of all the parts now in Opposition are so on system and principle. That we ought to avail ourselves of the other

---

[1] Add. MSS. 33000, ff. 99–100.

[2] Add. MSS. 32978, f. 478. Upon leaving office both in 1762 and 1766, Newcastle did not go into opposition until it was forced upon him. When the Rockinghamites formed a ministry in 1765, the old Duke recorded that, since George III had opened the negotiations, the Whigs were not guilty of 'forcing the Crown': Bateson, ed., *Newcastle's Narrative*, p. 2.

[3] See his letters to Portland of 4 and 27 Jan. 1768 in the Portland Papers, Nottingham University Library.

[4] Rockingham Papers, Sheffield City Library, Index no. 4, Rockingham to Dowdeswell, 20 Oct. 1769.

parties now in Opposition in order to effectuate good purposes, but that we should be cautious not even to throw the appearance of *leading* into hands whose principles we have no reason to think similar to our own and whose honour we have no reason to confide in.

The Rockinghamites' ideas were assembled for public consumption in the pamphlets of Edmund Burke. Between 1766 and 1770 he published three notable tracts. The first, *A Short Account of a Late Short Administration*, held up to admiration the virtue and consistency of the Rockinghamites during their term of office in 1765–6. The second, *Observations on a Late Publication intituled 'The Present State of the Nation'* (*1769*), concluded with a brief exposition of the party's views. The third, *Thoughts on the Cause of the Present Discontents*, was a full exegesis of the creed. Before publishing *Thoughts* Burke circulated it in draft among the party leaders and made revisions to meet their criticisms.[1] This pamphlet probably represents the consensus to which all Rockinghamites could subscribe.

To rehearse the gospel according to Burke would be to recapitulate in large measure the party views already presented. His primary achievement was to rewrite the articles of faith, hitherto recorded in awkward epistolary prose, with majestic and compelling eloquence. But his work was more than a summary of other men's ideas. He introduced novelties of approach and subtleties of argument beyond the capacity of the less articulate politicians. Under his pen the actions of individuals become systems, the elements of party strategy became principles, and political disagreements became differences between good and evil. The lofty quality of his exposition gave it the appearance of a work of political science.

Burke rests his thesis upon the proposition that 'every sort of government ought to have its administration correspondent to its legislature', which should be 'the express image of the feelings of the nation'.[2] The people cannot 'suffer their executory system to be composed of persons on whom they have no dependence, and whom no proofs of the public love and confidence have recommended to those powers upon the use of which the very

---

[1] T. W. Copeland, ed., *The Correspondence of Edmund Burke* (Chicago, 1958–), ii. 39–40, 52, 92, 104, 107–8, 113–14, 118–22.

The Works of the Right Honorable Edmund Burke (Boston, 1866), i. 471, 492.

being of the state depends'.[1] The Rockinghamites have such proofs to give. They possess, not personal and transient popularity, but 'a far more natural and fixed influence' arising from long experience, vast property, 'the name of Whig, dear to the majority of the people', and zeal for the royal family. They constitute a party bound together by mutual obligation, 'connexion of office', and ties of blood and friendship.[2]

A party, properly constructed, is a noble and necessary political instrument. It is properly constructed if united by 'common opinions, common affections, and common interests' and designed to promote 'the national interest upon some particular principle in which they are all agreed'.[3] It is noble because it brings the virtues of private life to the service of the state. It is necessary because individuals cannot act effectively. An inconsiderable party member, 'by adding to the weight of the whole', serves the state better than a great man in isolation. 'Connexions in politics' are 'essentially necessary for the full performance of our public duty' and only 'accidentally liable to degenerate into faction.'[4] As examples of wise and honourable party government, Burke calls attention to the Whig Junto in Anne's reign and the Rockingham Ministry of 1765–6.[5]

To effectuate its principles for the national interest a party makes the pursuit of office its 'first purpose'. The leaders demand 'the great strongholds of government' to insure the execution of their policies.[6] Other parties are not proscribed, but an 'honourable connexion' must preponderate in any ministry of which it becomes a part. To make this the goal is to engage in 'a generous contention for power on . . . manly and honourable maxims', not a 'mean and interested struggle for place and emolument'.[7] The king will be well advised to take the party into office on its own terms, 'but if this should not be the case, they may be still serviceable; for the example of a large body of men, steadily sacrificing ambition to principle, can never be without use. It will certainly be prolific and draw others to an imitation.'[8]

In this exposition Burke took a long stride toward the justification of party as a permanent institution in parliamentary

[1] Idem.   [2] Ibid. 452.   [3] Ibid. 529–30.
[4] Ibid. 526–7.   [5] Ibid. 467, 529.
[6] Ibid. i. 419. Compare Pulteney's insistence in 1742 on 'the main forts of government being delivered into their hands as their security for the rest'.
[7] Ibid. 531.   [8] Ibid. 426.

government. His predecessors generally tolerated parties as incidental evils, from whose clashes might come some incidental good.[1] Those who justified their own parties chose to regard them as temporary expedients to rectify misgovernment. Burke unquestionably looked upon the Rockinghamites as the current representatives of a party which, whether in or out of place, had a long past and an endless future.

The generalities in which he stated his concept appear to give it universal application. In reality it was limited by its derivation from the Whig myth. Though he spoke of 'a party' and 'every honourable connexion', he had only his own in mind. If all groups made occupation of 'the great strongholds' the condition of taking office, there could be no question of any one forming a ministry 'without a proscription of others'. Burke did not anticipate a perpetual struggle for power among equally well-intentioned parties. He looked forward to a Rockinghamite triumph which would re-establish the happy circumstances which supposedly prevailed in George II's reign: the great Whigs secure in the great offices, secure in the royal confidence, secure in their control of the influence of the Crown, broadening their bottom as much as necessary to man the government and render their situation comfortable. As in Bolingbroke's doctrine, so in Burke's, the victory of Opposition put an end to the need for an Opposition.

Burke dealt with his villains on the same plane as his heroes. He launched his attack, not on Bute the favourite, but on a 'system of favouritism'. It originated in a plot hatched in the court of Prince Frederick to enfeeble the men in office by placing all the sources of power at the disposal of one outwardly respectable minister.[2] On the accession of George III the plan was changed to the scheme of a 'double Cabinet', by which a secret cabal of 'King's friends' controlled the influence of the Crown while the ostensible ministers bore the responsibility of government. The pretext for this scheme was the factitious need to free the King from the tyrannous oligarchy which had oppressed his grandfather and to destroy the effectiveness of

---

[1] In the same year as Burke's *Thoughts* there appeared *Party Dissected* (London, 1770), a versified restatement of traditional attacks on 'demon faction' and 'the motly crew in opposition joined'.

[2] Burke, *Works*, i. 447.

any Opposition. The cabal sought to establish its system by demolishing all connexions and bringing all men to a direct dependance upon the Crown. Every ministry was kept weak and divided while the King's friends squandered his resources. In his new freedom the King found himself impoverished, his dignity lessened, and his repose ruined.[1]

The double Cabinet could not be damned as illegal. Burke offered no direct challenge to the Prerogative. He contended that the system operated against the 'spirit' of the Constitution because it prevented the Executive from being correspondent to the Legislature and the Legislature from reflecting the sentiments of the People. From the Revolution until 1760 monarchs had governed wisely by delegating the influence of the Crown to 'men of great natural interest or great acquired consideration'. George II was a royal paragon who knew when to 'sacrifice his private inclination to his public interest'.[2] Now the Court dispensed its interest 'under the sole influence of its private favour' and abused 'the discretionary power of the Crown in the formation of a ministry' by appointing mean and inconsiderable men.[3] The result was feeble, unstable government which gave rise to widespread public discontent.

Burke's invention of the Court rota was a new version of the old bogy of evil advisers. It was one of his cleverest strokes. The short-lived ministries of the 1760's and the current suspicions of Bute gave some verisimilitude to his charge. Even Shelburne publicly endorsed it.[4] By making the villain a secret system Burke strengthened his argument in two ways. Since the cabal was secret, its existence was hard to disprove. Since favouritism was a system, the charge did not hang on Bute alone, who might disappear from the scene at any time.[5] Burke also turned the

---

[1] Ibid. 447–50, 453–5, 467–8, 485–90.
[2] Ibid. i. 445–6, 456.
[3] Ibid. i. 446, 469.   [4] *P.H.* xvi. 974.
[5] Bute's influence came to an end in 1766, and the shrewd politicians knew it (Russell, *Memorials and Correspondence of C. J. Fox*, i. 35–38). Bute went on a continental tour in 1768, from which he did not return till 1771; so he was abroad all during the time Burke composed *Thoughts*. On 29 Dec. 1770 Burke wrote that 'Lord Bute is no longer the adviser, but that his system is got into firmer and abler hands' (Copeland, ed., *Burke Corresp.* ii. 176). Though 'the king's friends' are anonymous in *Thoughts*, Burke believed them to be the 'men of business', prototypes of modern civil servants, who occasionally 'discoursed in confidence': ibid. 209;

cult of Sully against its devotees. He found a passage in the Duc's memoirs which he interpreted to mean that Sully attributed the great disturbances of Henri III's reign to that monarch's 'system of favouritism'.[1]

To cure the ills of state, Burke used a slightly modified version of the traditional Opposition appeal to 'the people'. He rejected the usual nostrums: place acts, disqualification acts, and shorter parliaments. His remedy was a House of Commons composed of men undeceived by 'the cant of not men but measures', men who would not give indiscriminate support to any ministers simply because the King appointed them, men who would never accept office until the King's friends were 'entirely broken and disbanded'.[2] Only 'the interposition of the body of the people itself', by implication the unreformed electorate, could effect the cure.[3] If the voters chose only proved enemies to the cabal, the Commons would then reflect popular feeling, Parliament would resume proper supervision of the administration, and the Executive would correspond fittingly with the Legislature.

In recent years Burke's critics have found it amusing that generations of historians were 'taken in' by the elaborate fictions in his *Thoughts*.[4] The deception is to be accounted for only in part by the ignorance of the historians and the eloquence of the

---

N. S. Jucker, ed., *The Jenkinson Papers, 1760–1766* (London, 1949), pp. xxii–xxviii, 404–8. See also *H.M.C., Var. Coll.* vi. 266, where William Knox refers to 'the old system of Carlton House, which, since the Princess of Wales's death [8 Aug. 1772] have been distinguished by the name of the King's friends, or supporters of the administration for the time being, without regard to those of whom it is composed'.

[1] Burke, *Works*, i. 441. *The Present State of the Nation* concluded with a prayer for another Sully, which provoked Burke to a strong attack on the cult: *Works*, i. 412–16. From this point on (though it may well be coincidence) Sully ceases to appear as an idol in political pamphlets.

[2] Ibid. 524.

[3] Ibid. 521. Though Burke directed his appeal to the electorate, he really intended to influence the proprietors of electoral 'interests' and members of Parliament, not the mass of voters. He may also have had in mind the 'mercantile interest', whose support he had cultivated in 1765–6 (L. S. Sutherland, 'Edmund Burke and the First Rockingham Ministry', *E.H.R.* xlvii. 46–70). Rockingham originally wanted *Thoughts* published in time to be read 'by all the members of Parliament—and by all the politicians in town and country prior to the meeting of Parliament' in 1769 (Copeland, ed., *Burke Corresp.* ii. 92). The Marquis never considered a larger audience for the party manifesto.

[4] Sedgwick, ed., *Letters of George III to Lord Bute*, p. xix; Namier, *England*, pp. 182–3; Brooke, *Chatham Administration*, pp. 275–6.

author. Like Bolingbroke, whose work also survived his own career, Burke expressed himself in broad generalities and universal maxims which seemed applicable *mutatis mutandis* to conditions in later times. The Rockinghamites' political heirs made use of his party manifesto for years to come. Lord Archibald Hamilton applied Burke's arguments to the politics of 1804.[1] In 1818 Sir James Mackintosh called *Thoughts* 'a work which was, is, and in its general principles must ever continue to be, the creed of English Whigs'.[2] Lord John Russell saw it as 'one of the few standard works on the science of government which the world possesses'.[3] Such authorities helped to support the reputation of Burke's pamphlet among those who called themselves Whigs far into the nineteenth century.

From the point of view of those who recounted the history of George III's reign, it is probably of equal importance that the Rockinghamites kept their doctrine constantly on display. Year after year they blamed their exclusion from power upon the secret cabal. In every political negotiation they demanded the strongholds of the Government. They proclaimed each accession to office a triumph of their principles, and during the two brief Rockingham ministries they made a great parade of fulfilling promises given in Opposition. They evaded the issue of the royal Prerogative in parliamentary debate, but they never admitted, like so many 'patriots' before them, that their creed was merely an excuse to contend for power. In short, the Rockinghamites' apparent sincerity made it all too easy to take the whole of their convictions for the whole truth.

The Constitutional Issues

Thoughts on the Cause of the Present Discontents did not beguile Burke's contemporaries. The political world seems to have recognized it as a recapitulation of the old corps' creed which was well known by 1770. Horace Walpole judged it 'too diffuse and too refined: it tired the informed and was unintelligible to the ignorant'.[4] Perhaps the Government thought so too. A

---

[1] *Thoughts on the Formation of the Late and Present Administrations* (London, 1804).
[2] *Edinburgh Review*, xxxi. 170.
[3] *An Essay on the History of the English Government and Constitution* (London, 1823), pp. 229–30.
[4] *Memoirs of George III*, iv. 86. The attack on the Opposition in *The Political*

ministry usually produced a refutation of such a savage attack, but none appeared. Only Catharine Macaulay, 'the female patriot', undertook to expose this 'pernicious work' as a piece of mountebankery, designed to justify an aristocratic faction 'founded on and supported by the corrupt principle of self-interest'.[1] Burke himself was disappointed that the labour of many months had so little effect.[2]

During the ensuing twelve years Ministerialists frequently brushed off the Rockinghamites' protestations as Opposition commonplaces. Every Government had to face rival claimants for power who, said Henry Rosewarne, 'increased in violence in proportion to the length of time a minister continued in office'.[3] The 1770's seemed comparable to the 1730's: an able administration year after year withstood enemies whose accusations, Thurlow remarked, 'hardly deserve a single animadversion'.[4] The institution of Opposition was not condemned. John Courtenay went so far as to call the 'opposition of parties' a 'revolution principle'.[5] The case for the Court was well expressed by James MacPherson in a pamphlet of 1779:

In every popular Government Opposition is not only natural but, when conducted on liberal principles, useful and even necessary. There is a kind of charm in authority, which may induce the most virtuous magistrate to extend it too far, if subject to no control. The original object of a national representative was to watch over the political rights of the people and to check the encroachments of the executive power. The trust is great; and, strictly speaking, ought to be solely appropriated to the public good. Those who use it as an engine of private ambition and personal interest meet with forgiveness on account of the frequency of the practice. But the employing a weapon, given for the defence of our country, against its very existence is a species of political assassination which no example can justify, no state ought to pass without punishment.[6]

Conduct of the Earl of Chatham (London, 1769) shows how well the Rockinghamites' principles were understood before the appearance of *Thoughts*.

[1] *Observations on a Pamphlet entitled Thoughts on the Cause of the Present Discontents* (London, 1770). Cf. James Burgh's contemptuous dismissal of *Thoughts* in his *Political Disquisitions* (London, 1774), I, xvi.

[2] Copeland, ed., *Burke Corresp.* ii. 176. The Opposition complained about secret influence for years to come, but Burke's 'double Cabinet' was mentioned rarely, and then with little conviction: e.g. *P.H.* xviii. 1187.

[3] *P.H.* xxi. 1393.   [4] Ibid. 1049.   [5] Ibid. 1278.

[6] *A Short History of the Opposition during the Last Session of Parliament*, pp. 47–48. Cf. *A Short Defence of the Opposition*, pp. 3–4.

The American rebellion put the time-worn arguments over the use and abuse of opposition in a new context and reversed the traditional attitude of the Opposition to foreign affairs. Ever since 1726 malcontents had made a great show of their patriotism. In peace they demanded a policy better designed to protect British interests. In war they clamoured for more vigorous measures to ensure victory. Now both Chathamites and Rockinghamites espoused the cause of fellow subjects in armed revolt against the King. They rejoiced publicly in the triumphs of Britain's enemies. Military and naval officers with Opposition connexions refused to serve in the war. By the strict letter of the law the malcontents may well have been guilty of treason. In the political contest they laid themselves open to charges of hampering the war effort, seeking to dismember the Empire, and aggrandizing the power of France and Spain.[1] Dr. Johnson was not the only man in these years who thought this form of patriotism 'the last refuge of a scoundrel'.[2]

The open declarations of sympathy for rebels in arms testify to the security felt by the Opponents. They did not enjoy their unpopularity, but except when they contemplated secession from Parliament, they never worried about prosecution. Despite much harsh language and deep bitterness of feeling, it is doubtful if many regarded them as active traitors.[3] Parliamentary privilege protected most of their activities, for which the anti-Hanoverianism of the earlier decades furnished an excellent precedent. Pro-Americanism was perhaps a little more dangerous because it was a great deal more sincere. It was different in kind because the struggle involved ideology, the rights and liberties of the subject. The defence of the Colonies struck a

[1] The charges are too numerous to mention. Fox thus summed them up in 1780: 'As public men the Opposition had been . . . described as a faction of the most obnoxious kind: a faction who were enemies to the welfare of their country. At one time they were called Americans, at another time Frenchmen, at another time Spaniards, and now the phrase was that they were Dutchmen. In short, they were at all times any thing but Englishmen!' *P.H.* xxi. 517.

[2] *Boswell's Life of Johnson* (ed. Hill and Powell), ii. 348. Cf. *The Patriot* (London, 1774); *The Patriots: or An Evening Prospect on the Atlantic* (London, 1777); *Address to the People of Great Britain on the Meeting of Parliament* (London, 1779).

[3] Ibid., p. 14, voiced regret that false patriots who in fact were 'traitors and incendiaries have not been dragged forth to public view and sacrificed to public justice'. *Remarks on the Conduct of Opposition with Regard to America* (London, 1777) condemned them as 'active in sedition'. I know of no evidence that any responsible authority ever seriously considered prosecuting members of the Opposition.

new line for future Oppositions, which for years to come championed 'liberal' causes and objected to war except in defence of 'freedom'.

The success of 'broad-bottom' government from 1757 to 1761, which in long retrospect may seem a model for party conduct in time of war, could not be repeated during the American Revolution. That coalition was a measure of desperation, concluded only when all factions and the King realized that 'politics as usual' meant no Government at all. Weak as it became, North's Ministry got 'the King's business' done until its final collapse. The Minister nevertheless extorted the King's consent to three attempts to strengthen the administration between 1778 and 1780.[1] All failed because George III and the Opposition leaders disagreed on fundamental issues, which left no room for compromise. Only the capitulation of one side could resolve their differences, and neither thought it necessary to surrender. In addition to their conflicting views on American independence and domestic legislation, they were irreconcilably divided upon the Constitutional issue of the royal Prerogative in the choice of ministers.

George III stood firmly by his determination not to be 'forced'. During the first eight years of his reign he had waived his principles on numerous occasions in his search for a stable Government. He had suppressed his ingrained hatred of the old corps to give 'King Rockingham' his chance in 1765. He had loyally supported dictator Chatham in an effort to form a ministry from the best of all parties in 1766. After these failures George III grew more and more inflexible. He was youthful and vigorous—not the weary old man who had submitted to the Pelhams—and he flung his energy into supporting the reluctant North rather than betray the trust with which he was invested 'by the Almighty'. He permitted *pourparlers* with the Chathamites and Rockinghamites, but clung to 'my resolution never to treat with Opposition as a party, though ever ready to receive accessions to my present administration'.[2]

The King's interpretation of his Prerogative was, of course,

---

[1] See Russell, *Mem. and Corr. of C. J. Fox*, i. 206–23; I. R. Christie, 'The Marquis of Rockingham and Lord North's Offer of a Coalition, June–July 1780,' *E.H.R.* lxix (1954), 388–407.

[2] Add. MSS. 37834, f. 103.

constitutionally correct. As such it received widespread support in the political world. Lord Harcourt, for example, thought 'the very idea' of 'the government being taken by storm . . . was very alarming'.[1] In defence of the King, George Selwyn protested that the British Constitution 'is as different from what our present "patriots" or Whigs represent it as the government of the grand senior'.[2] The King's view was also endorsed because it made good political sense. After the failure of one *pourparler* in 1779 Lady Pembroke wrote,

Party here is such a thing that they [*sic*] will not suffer some to come in unless the whole party come in at once, and all the other set go out, right as well as wrong. . . . I do think it is a hard case upon our kings that, though they should wish to take a proper man into a proper place, he [*sic*] cannot generally do it without having out all his ministers, good as well as bad, and taking in all that belong to the others.[3]

At this stage even Charles James Fox expressed the same sentiments.[4] The malcontents' qualifications for office did not impress their peers, who mocked their presumed 'knowledge of business' and wondered why their ancestry fitted them to settle the problems of war and rebellion. Sandwich once asked in the Lords why 'the booby descendant of a Whig' should be preferred to 'the deserving offspring of a Tory'.[5] Their thirst for the emoluments of office was not only unconstitutional but altogether irresponsible. 'The Opposition seemed only anxious to push the Ministry out of place', said Lord Nugent, 'without taking any care previously to form a system of stability by which the country might be benefited'.[6]

After Yorktown the dismayed Ministerialists did appeal for a national coalition on the model of 1757. It is a further indication of the general opinion that in parliamentary debate no malcontent candidly avowed an intention to storm the closet. Fox declared that his friends desired a 'broad-bottomed administration' including every man of influence, popularity, knowledge, and experience except the men in office. When Dundas asked

[1] Add. MSS. 38206, f. 209.   [2] *H.M.C., Carlisle MSS.*, p. 587.
[3] Lord Herbert, *Henry, Elizabeth, and George* (London, 1939), pp. 149–50.
[4] Russell, *Mem. and Corr. of C. J. Fox*, i. 206.
[5] *P.H.* xvi. 1118. Cf. Weymouth's taunts in ibid. 1114–15.
[6] Ibid. xxii. 1134.

how one could form a comprehensive ministry 'which was to proscribe one-half of the ability of the Empire', Fox hedged. He stipulated for the exclusion only of the five or six authors of 'the present calamities', then talked vaguely about 'consulting the voice of the people without doors'.[1] Lord John Cavendish was more explicit. A vote of no-confidence, he asserted,

> by no means placed the Opposition in power and thereby prevented the coalition so ardently desired. They did no more than take the executive government from the present hands and leave it to His Majesty to form such an administration as His Majesty should think proper.[2]

As late as 1782 this was as far as one could go with Constitutional property. The Rockinghamites shrank from affirming in the House of Commons, as they had done in anonymous pamphlets, that a party might rightfully 'force' the King. In any event, they did not have to press their claim to office because the fall of North would leave George III but one alternative. They may well have thought it 'a matter of lamentation', as Fox once averred, that their opposition should triumph amid national disaster;[3] but even in such a case they would not abandon a doctrine which they dared not proclaim in Parliament. When George III finally capitulated, wrote Professor Pares, 'the failure of the American war enabled Rockingham, as the one acknowledged leader of the Opposition, to impose terms on the King which the generality of politicians would never have supported in ordinary circumstances'.[4]

The generality did not fail to observe, however, that North's was the third ministry since 1714 whose ill success in arms had contributed largely to its own disruption. Clearly, His Majesty could be forced when the political nation became convinced that his chosen servants had mismanaged a war. To the resolute, uncompromising Oppositions of the future it appeared axiomatic that their greatest hope of success lay in national misfortune.

---

[1] *P.H.* xxii. 1139–43.
[2] Ibid. 1197. On other occasions even Burke had brazenly denied that his friends opposed in order to get into office: ibid. xvii. 836–7, 1269; xx. 338.
[3] Ibid. xxi. 511.
[4] *King George III and the Politicians*, p. 121; cf. Christie, *End of North's Ministry*, pp. 355–6.

Whigs and Tories

In defence of their stand on Constitutional issues men occasionally declared that their principles were either Whig or Tory. There were still those who steadily repeated Bolingbroke's contention that these distinctions no longer existed—to use them was to 'revive' them for factious purposes.[1] Yet the party names continued to be regularly employed in particular contexts in which they possessed a generally understood significance.

In political altercation orators and pamphleteers made them terms of commendation and detraction. Chatham put this usage in classic form when he said, 'There is a distinction between right and wrong—Whig and Tory.'[2] No one could mistake him. Whiggism meant 'Revolution principles' in an all-embracing complimentary sense. Toryism meant royal tyranny, with historical implications of Jacobitism and treason. This was common cant, widely accepted as the essence of the well propagated Whig myth.

Deep prejudice supported the use of Tory as a pejorative. Whig politicians of the old school had no qualms about seeking Tory votes in elections and divisions,[3] but they distrusted any formal connexion with Tories in the Government. Their apprehensions may be seen at one level in the royal chaplain, Edmund Pyle. When Pitt took office with Tory support in 1756, Pyle warned, '*Timeo Danaos*'. He wrote to a friend shortly after the accession of George III,

You seem to mean Mr. Pitt by the 'unus homo qui nobis restituit rem'. And to rejoice in the boasted extinction of parties. This has always been the Tory method of getting into influence: to seem to wish for the extinction of parties. But what they really mean is to lull the Whigs into repose, whilst they are using incessant means to extinguish them. The game is playing now.[4]

---

[1] [John Douglas], *Seasonable Hints from an Honest Man* (London, 1761), pp. 28–33; Add. MSS. 33000, f. 96; 33035, f. 33; *P.H.* xvi. 1119.

[2] Ibid. 1107. Cf. Pares, *King George III and the Politicians*, pp. 55–57. For studied expositions of the stereotypes, see *A Letter from Albemarle Street to the Cocoa Tree* (London, 1764); *The Detection of Discord: or, The Whig* (London, 1776); *Characters of the Parties in the British Government* (London, 1782).

[3] P.R.O., Granville Papers 1, Sandwich to Gower, 21 Nov. 1764; Add. MSS. 32989, ff. 187–92; 34728, f. 89; Portland Papers, Nottingham University Library, Rockingham to Portland, 7 and 9 Oct. 1774; *H.M.C., Carlisle MSS.*, p. 443.

[4] *Memoirs of a Royal Chaplain*, pp. 283, 334.

At another level Whig prejudice may be seen among the politicians at Westminster. When the ever pliable Newcastle dallied with the offer of an alliance with the Tories of the cider counties in 1764, he was checked abruptly by Cumberland, Rockingham, and Albemarle, who reproved him for going so far as to consider negotiations.[1] Nicolson Calvert told the Commons in 1765 that 'whenever men of a particular cast of mind, known by the name of Tories, get any footing in the Government, violent measures ever ensue'.[2] Memories of 1710 were still alive. The old corps had been well trained to ''ware Tory'.

The ascendancy of Bute, a Stuart, and the favour shown to Tories led to charges that the Court had adopted their supposed philosophy of government. After the resignations of 1762, according to an Opposition pamphlet, 'the partisans of the Minister reassumed the old forgotten title of Tory and in like manner gave that of Whig (which has ever been the most respectable) to the opposite side'.[3] Thus measures to be opposed were called Tory measures. The Rockinghamites made the removal of the leading Tories a major stipulation in the negotiations of 1765.[4] A satirist accused the Opposition of endeavouring to fix 'the same mark of ignominy upon a Tory that the law of Moses fixed upon bastards'.[5]

The outbreak of the American Revolution increased the general usage of the party names as stereotypes. Taking their cue from English tradition, the rebels called themselves Whigs and the loyalists Tories. The Opposition followed a parallel line in Parliament throughout the war. In 1775 Fox denounced the ministers as Tories because they were 'enemies to freedom', and session after session the malcontents reiterated that the Tory administration sought to rivet despotism on the Americans, whose cause was based on Whig principles.[6] In reply Ministerialists pointed out the anomalies in the charge. North retorted to Fox

[1] Add. MSS. 32962, ff. 320–1, 341–2, 360–3; 32963, ff. 122, 364–8; 32964, ff. 93–95.
[2] *P.H.* xvi. 46.
[3] *Ministerial Patriotism Detected* (London, 1763), p. 31.
[4] Bateson, ed., *Newcastle's Narrative*, p. 28.
[5] *Patriotism, A Farce*, p. 10. Cf. *H.M.C., Laing MSS.* ii. 405–6.
[6] *P.H.* xviii. 769; xix. 543, 679; xx. 51, 399; xxi. 387, 1103; xxii. 612, 695, 823.

that if he [North] understood the meaning of the words Whig and Tory . . . , he conceived that it was the characteristic of Whiggism to gain as much for the people as possible, while the aim of Toryism was to increase the Prerogative. That in the present case administration contended for the right of Parliament, while the Americans talked of their belonging to the Crown. Their language therefore was the language of Toryism.[1]

Whatever their language, went on the ministerial rejoinder, the 'patriots'' principles led only to anarchy and republicanism. If the Opposition's distortion of Whiggism be taken for truth, North and Lyttelton said ironically that they preferred to be called Tories.[2]

Even more anomalous was the plain fact that self-styled Whigs and Tories stood on both sides of the American question as well as the other leading issues in these years. North and the majority of men in office called themselves Whigs, and they were supported by a sizeable bloc of Tories. Others frequently voted with Rockinghamites and Chathamites. It is little wonder that some historians have thought the party names meaningless. As images for use in debate, when they were considered to be stereotypes or caricatures, they did have significance. But their meaning in one context is not fully transferable to another. To see what they meant as guides to action we must examine the records of those who bore the labels. Their history is confusing but not inexplicable.

The Whigs made distinctions among themselves. The Rockinghamites commonly prefixed their party name with such modifiers as 'true', 'high', 'great', 'grand', 'constitutional', and 'revolution'. They were *the* Whig party with all the 'weight of Whiggism', as Charles Yorke expressed it, derived from the unbroken succession of leadership that extended from the Junto to Rockingham;[3] but they did not deny the title of Whig to others. Then there were those who liked to prefix 'independent' to Whig: the Chathamites and a large number of unattached members. The younger Pitt exaggerated when he wrote that 'an independent Whig . . . in words is hardly a distinction, as every one alike pretends to it'.[4] Most politicians boasted of their

---

[1] Ibid. xviii. 771. Cf. ibid. xxi. 1281; xxii. 818.
[2] Ibid. xix. 492; xxii. 615.
[3] Add. MSS. 45030 (unfolioed), Charles Yorke to Lord Grey [?], 3 July 1765.
[4] *H.M.C., Westmoreland MSS.*, p. 26. Charles Turner of York, who boasted of his

independence, but this description was generally assumed by Whigs who were neither Rockinghamites nor placeholders, whether or not they supported the Government. Finally there were the Whigs and Whig connexions in office. Whenever they employed the term they rarely prefixed an adjective. It was sufficient to say, 'I am a Whig.'[1]

In terms of historic 'principles', as expressed in the Whig stereotype, there was nothing to differentiate these three types or to bind together those in any one category. All professed devotion to the House of Brunswick and the Revolution settlement. In terms of state policy they differed according to their private convictions and political loyalties. Whig principles could be interpreted, quite sincerely and consistently, to justify positions on both sides of any question, partly because these principles were vague and adaptable, partly because the fundamentals of the Revolution settlement were never really at issue.[2] Moreover, perfectly honest Whigs might and did change their minds and their connexions without violating their principles.

True distinctions among them are to be found in their views on Opposition. We have already seen the ideological cleavage between Rockinghamites and Chathamites: the political storming party versus the independent who opposed measures while awaiting a summons from his sovereign. Among the ministerial Whigs there was a cleavage also, though it was not made apparent to all the world until after North's fall. On the one hand were Court Whigs of the traditional stamp, indifferent to political issues and anxious to stay at Court under any

independence, called himself 'an old-fashioned Whig': *P.H.* xx. 1250. For an elaboration of the views of 'a true independent Whig' see James Burgh's *Political Disquisitions* (London, 1774).

[1] *P.H.* xviii. 253; xx. 723; xxi. 98. To the Opposition these Ministerialists were 'renegado Whigs': ibid. xviii. 250; *A Letter from Albemarle Street to the Cocoa Tree*, p. 23.

[2] Politicians continued to assert that Revolution principles both supported and condemned the American war (e.g. *P.H.* xviii. 249–50, 595–9, 1170–80; xix. 690; xx. 1250–1; xxi. 1281). Since the makers of the settlement never thought of its possible application to a colonial rebellion, everything depended upon which Constitutional principle a speaker considered paramount. There were also debates about whether or not the Government had deserted traditional Whig foreign policy (ibid. xx. 79; xxi. 1087), and Fox pushed Whig principles to an extreme by declaring that the Marriage Act violated 'the true doctrine of Whiggism' (ibid. xxii. 400–1).

administration, and the equally traditional men of 'civil service mentality', who wanted to earn a living in the departments of the state. Officers of the royal Household typify the former, 'men of business' (alias the King's friends) the latter.[1] They often performed political duties, but they were not politicians in the usual sense. Whatever their private convictions—the 'men of business', in particular, held strong views on public affairs—they did not resign on issues of policy or patronage. Their primary loyalty was to the King, or, perhaps more accurately, to their positions and emoluments. As long as they remained true to type, they would not oppose if dismissed from their places. They might seek to return to office—they might give votes against ministers, especially those disliked by the King—but they would not join a formed general Opposition.

On the other hand were the politicians who held a conventional view of opposition. They were not wedded to any abstract doctrines about party or independency, but they had been in place long enough to understand the need for solidarity. They did not challenge the Prerogative, but they knew that the King could not govern without a majority in the Commons. They knew as well that the royal affection was not a prerequisite for office, and they had no scruples about alliances which offered a good prospect of preferment. They were heirs to the political philosophy of the old flying squadrons.[2]

These categories were not prisons, but there were significant bodies of self-styled Whigs who consistently made one of these views of opposition the guide to their conduct. If one knows the category in which a man belonged, one knows what Whig meant to him in practical political terms. One can see, therefore,

[1] The Courtiers are typified by peers like Hertford, Ashburnham, Pelham, Falmouth, and Bateman, who held Household offices through numerous political changes until the Rockinghamites ousted them in 1782. Lord Mount-Edgcumbe was several times removed but always managed to get back into some position after a brief interval. On the 'men of business', see Namier, *Structure*, i. 47–53; Jucker, *Jenkinson Papers*, pp. xii–xxix. Good examples are John Robinson, Sir Charles Frederick, William R. Earle, and Philip Stephens, who long held 'civil service' posts with seats in Parliament. There were others of the same stamp, like Andrew Wilkinson and John Pitt, who managed to retain their posts after they lost their seats; and still others, like Charles Jenkinson, Sir Grey Cooper, and Sir Gilbert Elliot, who were eventually drawn into politics in their search for preferment.

[2]. On the political groups in the Government, see Christie, *End of North's Ministry*, pp. 197–209.

why Rockinghamites and Chathamites could never co-operate for long but why, after Fox broke with Shelburne, the question before North's following was which of their former adversaries could offer the more advantageous alliance.

The divided allegiance of the Tories is to be explained by their history since the formation of the 'broad bottom'. A small group had crossed the Floor with Gower in 1744 and gave up the party name. There remained a number, variously estimated from 91 to 114, who continued to act as they had in Walpole's time.[1] The Cocoa Tree was still their rendezvous in town. They were fiercely independent, irregular in attendance, and generally opposed to the Government.

The formation of Prince Frederick's last Opposition marked the beginning of a change. Frederick courted their support and planned to give them places. His overtures received a cold, formal response. Their recognized head, the Duke of Beaufort, misliked any commitment to Leicester House, and the disappointment of the Tories' hopes by previous Oppositions made them generally suspicious. But the placehunters among them joined the Prince's camp. Bute and George III carried on Frederick's policy. Then in 1756 Leicester House formed a new Opposition, Pitt became its leader, and Beaufort died. Thereafter the Tories had no recognized head. They looked for leadership to the Prince's Court. Pitt took office with their support, and by January 1757 he had become 'the Cocoa Tree toast'.[2]

For four years the great commoner cultivated the Tories. The coldness which grew between Pitt and Leicester House does not appear to have affected them. They retained their affection for the Prince and were gratified by the measures taken to secure their support of the Government. Pitt summoned them to cockpit meetings, gave them commissions in the militia, and carried a Member's Qualification Act to please them.[3] For the first time in two generations the Tories became accustomed

[1] Lodge, ed., *Private Correspondence of Chesterfield and Newcastle*, p. 22; Add. MSS. 33001, ff. 357–63; Namier, *England*, pp. 227, 487–90. It is probably necessary to reissue the usual caveat about the difficulty of identifying a Tory and distinguishing one from an independent Whig. Namier listed Sir Edward Dering, 6th baronet, as a Tory upon his family reputation in 1761, but Dering, though still an Independent, called himself a Whig twenty years later (*P.H.* xxii. 818). The most important criterion, of course, was a man's own choice of label.

[2] Phillimore, *Lyttelton*, ii. 584.

[3] Walpole, *Memoirs of George II*, iii. 156–7, 184–5; Egerton MSS. 1719, f. 133.

to vote with the Ministry. When George III ascended the throne, they came to Court just as they had in 1714 and 1727, and this time they found a warm reception. Shortly after his accession the King added five Tories to his Lords and Grooms of the Bedchamber, and further appointments made Whigs grumble at the favour shown to those so long proscribed.[1]

Pitt's resignation in 1761 forced a crisis upon the Tory conscience. Some railed at his acceptance of a pension and a peerage for his wife, and the first cockpit meeting after his demission was crowded with 'old Tories', many of whom had never attended before.[2] Others went into opposition: 'honest and sensible men and by much the best of the corps', said Legge, who in a proprietary fashion called them 'my Tories'.[3] The eventual outcome was a four-way split which endured until 1782.

The placehunters became placemen. The Tory label clung to them for a generation, but otherwise they were quite un-distinguishable from Whig Courtiers and politicians. Except in local politics their Toryism ceased to have any significance.[4] A second group became regular supporters of the Government on all but Country party issues. Until his fall North could count upon about forty of them. A third were more favourably inclined to the King's ministers than their forbears but generally independent and unpredictable. Finally, a number voted con-sistently with the Opposition. Dowdeswell and Meredith, who became Rockinghamites, were exceptional. The others did not disavow the name of Tory.[5]

[1] Add MSS. 32939, f. 80.

[2] Russell, ed., *Bedford Correspondence*, iii. 52; Rockingham Papers, Sheffield City Library, Index no. 1, Lascelles to Rockingham, 2 Nov. 1761.

[3] Add. MSS. 32944, ff. 213, 223–4.

[4] Earl Talbot, Lord Steward from 1761 to 1782, is a good example of this type. Sir Francis Dashwood (15th Baron le Despenser, 1763) held both Household and political offices, except during the first Rockingham Ministry, from 1761 to 1781. Norborne Berkeley (4th Baron Botetourt, 1763) likewise took any post he could get. The 5th Duke of Beaufort served for a time in the Queen's Household, resigned with the Chathamites in 1770, but remained a Courtier and accumulated three Lord-Lieutenancies. Earl Bathurst became a Common Pleas judge in 1754 but continued to play the political game, rising to be Lord Chancellor 1771–8, and Lord President 1779–82. Sir James Lowther observed in 1770 that the Tories who took places 'have now lost all interest at the Cocoa Tree': Add. MSS. 38206, f. 201.

[5] On the alignment of the Tories, see Brooke, *Chatham Administration*, pp. 237–47; and Christie, *End of North's Ministry*, pp. 190–4, 209, 227–8. Because the Whig and Tory stereotypes were meaningless in terms of political conduct, Brooke and Christie quite properly classify Tories as 'independents' together with city Radicals

But because 'Tory' was so widely accepted as a pejorative it was applied to individuals with considerable care. A man might call himself a Tory if he chose, but rarely did any one else call him one except to insult him. The stock euphemism was 'country gentleman', often prefixed by 'honest' or 'independent'. This description was acceptable to the Tories, and politicians seeking their support always used it.[1]

This practice was employed by Pitt and carried on by Bute.[2] North was ever ready to acknowledge his debt to the country gentlemen. The Opposition alternately courted them under that title and damned them as Tories.[3] They represented such a considerable voting strength that *en masse* they could tip the scales in a major division. Toward the end of North's régime Lord Fielding declared that the country gentlemen held 'the balance of power' between the Government and the Opposition, and Conway alleged that the Minister was kept in place by

and independent Whigs. Since their blocs of Independents all include numbers of clearly identifiable Tories, their works provide the best descriptions of Tory conduct. See also Namier, *Personalities and Powers* (London, 1955), pp. 59–77.

[1] 'Country gentleman' was not, of course, an exclusive term. It was applied both to Independents and party men who were members of land-holding families. In 1782 Fox boasted of the support of 'the most respectable country gentlemen, both Whig and Tory', among whom he numbered Lord George Cavendish, a staunch Rockinghamite (*P.H.* xxii. 1196). When orators appealed to the country gentlemen, they meant to include men like Sir Edward Dering, who styled himself both a country gentleman and an independent Whig. In calling Tories 'country gentlemen' the politicians intended to compliment these men, who had so long been condemned and proscribed under their party name, by admitting them to the ranks of the loyal and respectable governing class. To the Tories who supported Wilkes a pamphleteer wrote, 'You, the worthy gentlemen of the Cocoa Tree, have honourably distinguished yourselves among the friends of liberty. . . . Welcome into the bosom of a free people and to be numbered among the best citizens.' 'You country gentlemen', he added, 'are miscalled Tories.' (*A Letter from Albemarle Street to the Cocoa Tree*, pp. 20, 40.) But sometimes politicians employed 'Tory' and 'country gentleman' interchangeably. Burke and Sir William Bagot used them as synonyms in a violent altercation over the principles of Toryism in 1770 (Copeland, ed., *Burke Corresp.* ii, 126–7; *P.H.* xvi. 919–21, 923–4).

[2] Walpole, *Memoirs of George II*, iii. 16–17; *H.M.C., Stopford–Sackville MSS.* i. 109; Add. MSS. 36797, f. 34.

[3] *Boswell's Life of Johnson* (ed. Hill and Powell), iii. 234. The practice of seeking the Tories' support by calling them country gentlemen goes back to the days of Walpole's Opposition, but for many years malcontents could also appeal to them as Tories because the ministries boasted of their Whiggism. When the Opposition condemned North's administration as Tory, they could not (except when Burke and Conway lost their tempers) apply the same term to the Tories they courted. Hence their increasing use of 'country gentlemen' in the 1770's.

'the little, despicable Tory party, which had deserted from our glorious Constitution'.[1]

What then were the principles of the three groups out of place who acknowledged the name of 'Tory'? On Country party issues they were the Country party still. They voted for annual parliaments in 1758 and in the 1770's, for the reduction of the land tax in 1767, for the Grenville Act in 1770, and for diminishing the influence of the Crown in 1780.[2] Such motions continued to appeal to their independence and their suspicions of Court corruption, but many voted against the King's Minister with regret. The end of their proscription had brought out their royalist sympathies. In a complete reversal of their conduct since 1715, the Country party tended rather to support than to oppose the Ministry of the day.

Not that they revived the principles of passive resistance. In moments of candour their most vehement detractors admitted that the Tory stereotype was a travesty.[3] It is extremely unlikely that even the most self-righteous Whig in the height of declamation seriously thought any country gentleman guilty of a desire to undo the Revolution settlement. The conduct of the Tories in all three groups is to be explained by this: in the reawakening of their traditional loyalty to the Crown they clung to the doctrine of 'measures, not men'. The final recognition of failure in America, like 'the motion' of 1741, revealed the true meaning of Toryism in practical politics.

When it became apparent that British arms had met irretrievable disaster, the Tories in general hoped for a change of policy but not necessarily of ministers. There was much uncertainty about what the new policy should be—even the Opposition Whigs were divided on this point—but sentiment strongly favoured an honourable peace in some form. The growing belief that the continuation of North's Ministry meant the prolongation of hostilities turned most of the Tories against him—not *en bloc* but, in their typical independent way, as individuals and groups of friends reached their own convictions.

---

[1] *P.H.* xxii. 149–50, 841. Cf. *The Revolution in MDCCLXXII Impartially Considered*, pp. 7–8.

[2] Dickins and Stanton, eds., *An Eighteenth-Century Correspondence*, p. 380; Rockingham Papers, Sheffield City Library, Index no. 5, Savile to Rockingham, 7 Jan. 1767; *Cavendish's Debates*, i. 582; Add. MSS. 35609, f. 169; *H.M.C., Stopford–Sackville MSS.* i. 119–20; *P.H.* xxi. 368–71, 628.

[3] Ibid. xx. 116, *H.M.C., Stopford–Sackville MSS.* i. 109.

They determined to oppose the war, and if a change of men was a prerequisite to a change of measures, North must go. An examination of the attitude of three different Tories will show how their doctrine directed them in this Constitutional crisis.

Sir John Rous, M.P. for Suffolk, was an Opposition Tory. On 15 March 1782 he moved 'that this House . . . can have no further confidence in the ministers who have the direction of public affairs', which he justified in these words:

No one . . . could suppose that he was actuated in any degree by a spirit of party; it was well known, and he was not ashamed to confess it, that he was descended from a Tory family and had been bred up in Tory principles: this circumstance alone, he hoped, would screen him from any imputation of being devoted to a party adverse in general to administration.

From the first dawn of the American war, he had felt the injustice, and impolicy of it; and he had come into that House its declared enemy on principle: but at the same time . . . he had come into Parliament highly prepossessed in favour of the noble lord in the blue ribbon [North]; and he had felt such a respect for his character that he would have gone to great lengths to support him; but when he found that the noble lord persevered blindly to pursue measures which had already reduced the country from a state of glory and prosperity to calamity and disgrace, he should deem himself an enemy to his country if he did not exert every faculty to remove him.[1]

The Tories who supported Rous's motion echoed his sentiments. Some favoured a coalition, but all took care to disclaim any intention of dictating to the King whom he should employ in a new Ministry.

Noel Hill, M.P. for Shropshire, was among those who gave North general but not unwavering support. On 27 February 1782 Conway moved that the House disapprove further prosecution of offensive war in America. In support of the resolution Hill said that he did not mean

to reflect on the noble lord in the blue ribbon. . . he assured them he had a favourable opinion of him, wished him well, and hoped never to give a vote against him again, because he flattered himself the noble lord would from henceforth adopt such measures as he could vote for with a safe conscience; but if he put the noble lord in one

[1] *P.H.* xxii. 1171.

scale and peace with America in the other, the latter would certainly preponderate; and the noble lord (though not a make-weight) would kick the beam.

He said he always wished to support Government, for he owned he was educated in Tory principles; but he could not support the present system.[1]

After Yorktown, Hill voted for every motion directed against the war. On motions for the dismissal of the Ministry he abstained.

Thomas Grosvenor, M.P. for Chester City, was pre-eminent in the Tory group which had steadily supported the American war. In the final crisis he voted to censure the administration of the Admiralty, but as far as the records show, he retained his faith in the Minister and his policy to the end. Yet it was he who inflicted the *coup de grâce* upon North. On 18 March 1782 Grosvenor delivered this message from his group to the Minister:

That, being now convinced that the present administration cannot continue any longer, they are of opinion that vain and ineffectual struggles tend only to public mischief and confusion, and that they shall think it their duty henceforward to desist from opposing what appears to be clearly the sense of the House of Commons.[2]

These sentiments convinced North that he must resign: the Government stereotyped as Tory fell upon the withdrawal of genuine Tory support. But Grosvenor's words make it clear that he and his friends had suspended, not surrendered, their principles to avert further disaster. They would not resist the majority, but they did not promise to support it. Like so many Tories since 1688, they yielded to a situation *de facto* which they did not approve as *de jure*.

There were other shades of opinion. Sir William Dolben, 'the staunchest Tory in the House', voted for one motion of censure but reversed himself on the next when the Government held out hopes for a change of policy.[3] But all made their decisions with reference to the principles which self-professed Tories called Tory. Their conduct revealed the untenability of

---

[1] Ibid. 1083.

Fortescue, ed., *Corresp. of George III*, v. no. 3566. In response to a personal appeal from North, Grosvenor stood by his principles in promising the Minister 'one other vote', provided that his support was asked for no other purpose than to gain time for the King to form a new administration (ibid. v, no. 3568).

[3] *H.M.C., Carlisle MSS.*, p. 561; *P.H.* xxii. 1083.

'measures, not men' in a severe political crisis under the conditions of 1782. When men and measures were inseparably joined, they had to be considered as one, and a vote against measures became perforce a vote against men. The Tories who deserted North knew perfectly well that they were 'forcing' the King and overriding his Prerogative, even though they were not doing so in order to get into office. The existence of a stable, successful ministry acceptable to the sovereign permitted a Tory to pursue his principles consistently, but he had to suspend them when ministers proved weak and unsuccessful. Then it was the matter of motive only that distinguished the actions of a placehunting Whig from those of a Tory in opposition.

3. THE CONDUCT OF THE OPPOSITION

Party Organization

Toward the end of North's Ministry, speakers in Parliament derided the Opposition as 'a rope of sand'.[1] They might have done so with general accuracy at any time from 1762 to 1782. The record of co-operation among the shifting parties out of office is the familiar story of working agreements attempted and dropped, or made and dissolved after a brief existence. The negotiations merely illustrate again and again the difficulty of obtaining concord on men and measures among aspirants to power who were rivals as much to each other as they were to ministers.[2] The significant developments of the period are all connected with the most doctrinaire and intractable of the groups, the Rockinghamites.

Burke's picture of the party in *Thoughts* is, of course, idealized, but no more so than most political self-portraits. The members' views did not automatically coincide nine times out of ten. On critical issues there were often several shades of opinion. But their correspondence shows that during their many disappointing years in opposition they dealt with each other cordially, sympathetically, and even affectionately.[3] Differences produced

---

[1] *P.H.* xxi. 537–8; xxii. 1098, 1113–14.

[2] The finest account of a negotiation, which may be taken as representative of all, is Brooke's description of the abortive Rockingham–Bedford–Grenville pourparlers of 1767 in *Chatham Administration*, pp. 295–324.

[3] On the Rockinghamites' cohesion, see Christie, *End of North's Ministry*, pp.

complaints but rarely recriminations. Desertions were few, and well compensated for by such able recruits as Charles James Fox and Richard Brinsley Sheridan, who became warm friends of the old guard. To outsiders the party was generally able to present a united front. A Ministerialist once observed in the House of Commons that the Rockinghamites opposed any motion not made by one of themselves, even when they agreed with it; and he warned that an Independent who joined them in the Opposition 'must follow a leader much more slavishly and implicitly than in any administration'.[1]

Rockingham was indeed their undisputed leader after his tenure of the Treasury. He sometimes took decisions on his own, but for the most part he consulted a 'conciliabulum'. This inner council was an extension of the old corps' practice of getting unanimity among the magnates upon important decisions. Newcastle summoned the first of the party's conciliabula in Opposition to consider his programme of resignations in 1762, and, largely upon his insistence, the leaders continued to hold meetings for the next few years. After 1765 conciliabula on critical matters were usually held only if called or consented to by Rockingham.[2]

The inner council did not have a rigid composition. A man's attendance often depended upon his availability. Essential to every major resolution, however, was the concurrence of the great electoral interests. In 1779 William Burke addressed Portland on the assumption that only the Duke, the Marquis, and the Cavendishes were 'fit' to determine party policy.[3] They

219–21. Of all the loyalties in the party the most touching is Newcastle's to Rockingham. The old Duke protested when his advice—usually very good advice—was repeatedly disregarded, but he never wavered in his support. After he was dropped from the party councils at the end of 1767, Newcastle instructed all his friends to transfer their allegiance to Rockingham; Add. MSS. 32987, ff. 257, 363–4; 32988, ff. 23, 25; 32990, f. 109.   [1] *P.H.* xviii. 1021.

[2] See Pares, *King George III and the Politicians*, pp. 83–84, 168–9. In their extensive correspondence the Rockinghamites used 'conciliabulum' in three senses: the group of leaders who directed the party; a meeting of this group and a confidential conference of leaders, all of whom were not of the inner circle, to decide a particular point. For examples, see Copeland, ed., *Burke Corresp.* ii. 159, 356; Rockingham Papers, Sheffield City Library, Index no. 31, Richmond to Rockingham, [n.d., Jan. 1771]. For Rockingham's views on his relationship to the party council, see Cavendish, *Debates*, i. 581.

[3] Portland Papers, Nottingham University Library, W. Burke to Portland, 22 Sept. 1779.

certainly became the core. In the early years Newcastle, Albemarle, Keppel, Dartmouth, and Bessborough belonged to the group, and Richmond played so active a part that he came to be regarded as deputy leader in Rockingham's absence.[1] Prominent commoners outside the noble families might be invited to attend. The magnates usually solicited the opinion of Sir George Savile. Dowdeswell, Edmund Burke, and later Fox seem to have been summoned frequently. The leaders deliberately kept the circle as small as possible. Newcastle advised the younger men that 'numbers . . . only create subdivisions'. The others were well inclined to his opinion. Richmond dreaded the ill effects of 'disagreements in large meetings'. Portland wanted all decisions made in secret by 'our great friends'. Most exclusive of all was Lord John Cavendish who equated the conciliabulum with the party: 'a snug chaste corps' of six or seven who lived in intimacy and mutual confidence.[2]

The lesser members of the party seem to have had no objection to taking their lead from a narrow clique. But they murmured when the directorate did not direct, and their complaints were frequent. Between sessions the grandees scattered to their estates, where personal and local interests engaged most of them more deeply than politics. Rockingham did not give the steady attention to business which had marked the careers of his predecessors in the old corps. When after his dismissal in 1766 he was importuned by Newcastle to maintain close communications with other leaders, the Marquis wrote Portland that he was overwhelmed with obligations in Yorkshire and 'so indolent at present upon the subject of politics that I don't know how to begin a letter to his Grace'. The next year he declared that if an advantageous treaty with the Bedfords could not be worked out, he proposed to 'stay all the winter in the country and mind his farming, which was much more fun'.[3] Rockingham did not like politics to intrude upon his enjoyment of the races at York and Newmarket. He never came up to

[1] Rockingham Papers, Sheffield City Library, Index no. 31, Richmond to Rockingham, [n.d., Jan. 1771] and 12 Feb. 1771.

[2] Add. MSS. 32798, ff. 53–54; 32964, ff. 191–2; Portland Papers, W. Burke to Portland, 22 Sept. 1779; Fitzwilliam Papers, Richmond to Rockingham, 1 Feb. 1771; Walpole, *Memoirs of George III*, ii. 92, 96.

[3] Portland Papers, Rockingham to Portland, 28 Aug. 1766; Add. MSS. 32985,

London a day sooner than he thought he had to, and any excuse would serve to postpone his arrival. It seems that he was a prey to staphylococcus infections, and frequent sore throats and outbreaks of boils did make travel very uncomfortable. By 1777 he professed himself altogether weary of public life and anxious to retire.[1] At times he bestirred himself to great activity in defence of his electoral interest, but he took a strong line as a party leader only when pressed by his friends. When he made a decision without their advice, it was usually a decision not to do something.

Except when political issues touched them closely the other magnates were scarcely more zealous. Conciliabula met between sessions only under the stress of crisis and clamour from the vigorous members of the party. As a result there was much confusion, uncertainty, and irritation among the rank-and-file, and the leaders passed up opportunities to strengthen their connexion.

One consequence of ill-co-ordinated leadership may be seen in their electoral activities. In traditional fashion each patron looked after his own interest. Some efforts were made to find openings for unsuccessful friends, and intelligence of seats on the market was occasionally circulated among the leaders. But in these as in other matters, Burke once observed, they wanted 'a spirit of adventure'. His own incursions upon Bristol and Fox's spectacular campaigns in Westminster were not typical of Opposition electioneering. The leaders generally shrank from strenuous and costly contests. Open seats sometimes went begging because none of the grandees considered one vote in the Commons worth three or four thousand pounds out of his own pocket, or because none would take the trouble to raise a subscription, or because none could think of a candidate deserving of the effort.[2] Newcastle, the most avid of electioneers, kept the party alert through the election of 1768. With characteristic enthusiasm the old Duke began his preparations more than two years ahead of time and bombarded the other

[1] Portland Papers, Rockingham to Portland, 7 Jan. 1777.
[2] For examples of their electoral activity and inactivity, see Add. MSS. 32986, ff. 329–31; 32988, ff. 196, 206; 32989, ff. 29–31; Portland Papers, Rockingham to Portland, 1 Nov. 1768, and 28 July, 15 Sept., 22 Sept. 1780; *H.M.C., Foljambe MSS.*, pp. 145–57; *H.M.C., Rutland MSS.*, 17, 26, 34, 37. Cf. Brooke, *Chatham Administration*, pp. 334–53, and Christie, *End of North's Ministry*, pp. 107–63.

magnates with reports and reminders.[1] The dissolutions of 1774 and 1780 both caught Rockingham by surprise, which left him 'vexed and perplexed' and quite convinced that the Government was unsportsmanlike.[2] The party held its own by vigorous last-minute efforts. Gains and losses were fairly evenly balanced. New strength came, not by the capture of new constituencies, but by the adherence of peers and M.P.s who turned against North.

The parliamentary policy of the party also suffered from lack of concert among the leaders. Each arrived for the opening of a session with his own ideas, which he may have communicated to others, but no common agreement had been reached. Year after year the correspondence of the Rockinghamites is heavy with complaints about 'want of plan' and 'lack of system'. 'We are in our usual disarray', Edmund Burke wrote to Rockingham in 1771. 'Nothing is concerted or disposed. I am totally at a loss what to do.'[3] Nine years later he and his kinsman William were still beseeching the magnates to come to some resolution. Even for the final attack on North in 1781–2 they came up to London unprepared.[4] The cause was not lassitude alone. Circumstances led them to genuine differences upon the most effective policy for an Opposition.

Since the prospect of defeating the Government usually seemed unpromising, there were always advocates of inaction. Divisions in Parliament, Portland wrote in 1764, simply set up 'a market for the sale of unsteady consciences'.[5] By displaying its weakness, the party invited defections. When in doubt, Rockingham thought in 1772, it was best to do nothing but attend Parliament to let the public 'see every appearance of the continuance of union, friendship, etc.'[6] The middle-of-the-road policy was to urge organization for assault on wrong measures.

---

[1] See his correspondence in Add. MSS. 32985–32989.

[2] Portland Papers, Rockingham to Portland, 1 Oct. 1774 and 1 Sept. 1780. The figures for these elections in England and Wales are: 1768, contests in boroughs 56, in counties 9, petitions 29; 1774, contests in boroughs 68, in counties 13, petitions 35; 1780, contests in boroughs 65, in counties 3, petitions 31. It is interesting to note that the Grenville Act of 1770 did not diminish the number of petitions.

[3] Copeland, ed., *Burke Corresp.* ii. 203–4.

[4] Portland Papers, W. Burke to Portland, 22 Sept. 1779, and E. Burke to Portland, 16 Oct. 1779. Christie, *End of North's Ministry*, pp. 268–70.

[5] Add. MSS. 32964, ff. 191–2.

[6] Portland Papers, Rockingham to Portland, 2 Jan. 1772.

This was not, as it may appear, a qualified Tory position. As a talking point, it salved the consciences of the old corps leaders who had to argue themselves into a new attitude. As practical politics, it meant attacking the Government only on points which enhanced party solidarity and bade fair to attract the support of other groups and Independents. Thus it was designed to conceal weakness behind occasional displays of strength and to keep the party in contention for power.[1] The most vigorous line of action, pressed by the young men in the Commons, was 'general opposition': a full and regular muster of the party, carefully planned campaigns on every issue, frequent divisions, and the introduction of salutary measures that kept the Government on the defensive and took the lead in Parliament away from the ministers.[2]

These conflicting views could be brought to practical reconciliation only after the leaders got to town, caught up on political intelligence, and found out the Government's intentions. Then, although disagreements did not vanish, affairs went more smoothly, and during the many years of opposition the organization of the party during a session took on an institutional form. The conciliabulum, meeting at the town houses of the great lords, laid down the major lines of policy. Larger gatherings, including those who were to speak in both Houses on a particular motion, plotted parliamentary tactics. The peers often gave dinners for this select group, which might number twenty or thirty.[3] The dining 'club' founded in 1762 maintained its existence throughout the period. To these dinners were invited all members of the party, those who usually supported them, and other connexions with whom they had alliances at the moment. Attendance over seventy was not uncommon. The Rockinghamite Whips had charge of the invitation list for each session.[4] For a long time the rendezvous was

[1] Add. MSS. 32978, ff. 235–41, 444–6; *H.M.C., Dundas MSS.*, p. 415.

[2] See the schemes of Charles Townshend in 1764 (*H.M.C., Townshend MSS.*, pp. 398–401) and of Burke in 1775 (Copeland, ed., *Burke Corresp.*, iii. 88–90).

[3] An excellent example of their procedures may be seen in the reports to the absent Rockingham in 1771: Rockingham Papers, Index no. 31.

[4] Portland Papers, W. Burke to Portland, 24 Oct. 1775. Apparently the leader in the Commons could issue impromptu invitations: on 7 May 1769 Dowdeswell asked all the minority in the division Lobby to a dinner scheduled for the next day (*H.M.C., Charlemont MSS.*, p. 294; Russell, ed., *Mem. and Corresp. of C. J. Fox*, i. 54–55). Cf. the memorandum 8 Jan. 1770 in Rockingham Papers, Index no. 8.

the Thatched House Tavern. In 1778 Brooks removed his gambling house to St. James Street, and within three years its patronage came to be drawn primarily from the Opposition. It was at Brooks's that Fox held his 'cockpit' before the session of 1781–2.[1] These meetings secured the unanimity which gave the Rockinghamites their reputation for iron discipline.

The party Whip was an important figure in the organization during a session. The chief role was assumed, apparently with general consent, by George Byng, whom Portland brought into Parliament in 1768. Byng had a passion and a talent for management. In the House he was called 'the ablest political mustermaster', who could foretell better than any other the outcome of a division.[2] No previous Opposition had enjoyed the services of so skilled an operator for so long a time. Byng held no title, but he created a recognized position which continued to be filled after he dropped out of politics.

Despite their weaknesses the Rockinghamites thus developed a structure more coherent than that of any other malcontent group. It owed much to the experience of the old corps when in office, and it outlived the men who produced it. Burke had some reason for his boast about their solidarity, and in another important aspect his picture presented a semblance of truth.

A party, he said, should be united 'upon some particular principle' for promoting public welfare. The leading principle of the 'true Whigs' who backed reluctantly into opposition in 1762 and 1766 was their repugnance to royal favouritism and secret influence, which they believed had shorn them of office and caused all the country's ills. As for other matters, they would act consistently with their past record. To the eyes of the twentieth century this appears a travesty of a programme. In 1770 it was quite in keeping with the traditions of Opposition and the conventional attitude toward the state. 'The Government existed, in those days,' wrote Professor Pares, 'not in order to legislate but in order to govern.'[3] Like the Opposition to

---

[1] *H.M.C., Carlisle MSS.*, pp. 371, 452, 470, 536. Cf. *Memorials of Brooks's* (London, 1907). In these years White's took on a stronger ministerial tinge, but neither club became altogether exclusive.

[2] *P.H.* xxii. 149. Frederick Montague was Byng's senior partner, and evidently a good share of party management was taken by Thomas Townshend the younger, who served as a teller more frequently than any other member of the party.

[3] *King George III and the Politicians*, p. 4.

Walpole the Rockinghamites distilled their grievances, not into a principle of law-making, but into a principle of administration based upon a partisan interpretation of the Constitution.

Secret influence, however, was neither so conspicuous nor so impervious a target as an overgrown minister. Tirades against the Court cabal, blowing upon a fantasm which frightened few, did nothing to increase the strength of the Opposition. The Rockinghamites concentrated more and more on the ostensible ministers and their failures, proved and presumptive. In line with the standard profession of all Country parties, the true Whigs were pledged to resist bad measures, and so were driven to take a stand upon leading issues, many of which, in this turbulent period, involved policies and principles of great moment. The Rockinghamites consequently developed a programme of measures designed to remedy the distempers of the Government.

Political Issues

In the days of Walpole and the Pelhams most of the issues between the Government and its opponents which deeply stirred the political world were artifacts. The Opposition created them by magnifying real grievances and inventing imaginary ones. In the first twenty years of George III's reign the greatest issues were raised by outside forces. Popular passions and widespread interests were involved. The expanding Press, whose growth was very marked in the 1770's, carried a knowledge of public affairs to a larger audience. During most of these years the Rockinghamites' major problem was, not to find grounds for attack, but to align their own convictions with the 'present discontents' and direct the outside forces to their own political advantage.

Their experience made them acutely aware of this problem, in principle as well as in practice. The leaders realized, more clearly than ever after 1767, that only a reversal of public opinion could return them to power. Burke's insistence upon the need for the 'interposition of the people' was quite sincere. He steadily maintained that the Opposition could never succeed until supported by opinion 'without doors'. Rockingham emphatically shared this view. With the party's prospects at a low point in 1772, he wrote that their only hope lay in this:

'The public at large sometimes make a sudden wheel and become violent against those who lead them into errors, notwithstanding they themselves had early adopted and even been favourable in the outset to those very errors.'[1] At the same time the leaders understood that it would be difficult 'to gain the minds of the people', as Charles Townshend put it in 1764, because of the dread possibility 'that Opposition by so often deceiving has lost the power of raising confidence'.[2] Taken together, these beliefs imposed upon the Rockinghamites a caution that was sometimes close to timidity. The members of the inner circle were naturally conservative, and knowing that success depended more upon the faults of administration than upon their own virtues, they refused to commit themselves to any proposition which they would not promote when in office. By adhering to 'the upright principle of consistency' they hoped to convince all men of their honesty. Then, when the Ministry fell, they would be the inevitable successors. They would take over the Government unhampered by impossible pledges, and being under no necessity of deceiving the people, they could rule with public confidence for an indefinite time.

Despite the appearance of radical and demagogic tendencies in some of its numbers, the party hewed closely to its policy of prudence. When serious differences developed, the leaders agreed to disagree, and the public was given to understand that the less conservative members spoke for themselves alone. To make profitable use of the outside forces was far more difficult. The discontented did not voice their grievances with any reference to Rockinghamite doctrine, and they did not look to the party for leadership. The most the true Whigs could do was to exercise as much influence as could be brought to bear upon the course of agitation and to support only demands agreeable to their own views. This approach produced the programme of measures with which they entered office in 1782.

In general, the leading issues fall into two categories: those raised by the complexities of Empire, which grew in magnitude after the peace of 1763; and those raised by radical agitators at home upon the rights and liberties of the subject. The former

[1] Rockingham Papers, Index no. 38, Rockingham to Murray, 20 Dec. 1772. Cf. Add. MSS. 32985, f. 307; *P.H.* xxi. 605.
[2] *H.M.C., Townshend MSS.*, pp. 398–400.

revolved about the difficulties of governing India, Ireland, and America. Wilkes and Wyvill personify the latter.

When Chatham's Ministry resolved to draw the affairs of 'John Company' back into politics in 1767, there ensued 'a weird dance of East India factions and parliamentary factions joining and parting hands in ephemeral partnerships of dazzling intricacy'.[1] The Company factions fought for wealth and power, but the main points in the public aspect of the India problem were the Company's finances, its administration of conquered territory, and its relationship to the British state. The Rockinghamites plunged deeply into all the controversies. For a time the Marquis himself played an active part in intrigue, and the Burkes took an increasing interest in Indian affairs. Private concerns and public views kept the party divided on specific measures, but they agreed that the issue should be settled on these principles: the rights of the Company as a chartered body must be protected; because of its great responsibilities Government supervision was necessary; this supervision must be exercised by Parliament, not the Executive, to prevent any increase in the influence of the Crown.

The Irish Parliament showed the first signs of serious insubordination in 1769. The Commons' resentment at Poyning's Law grew into a popular demand for legislative independence. Concurrently, economic distress led to proposals for a tax on absentee landlords and for the removal of restrictions on Irish trade. The Irish Volunteers grew so strong that there was real reason to fear they would take by force what was not granted by consent. Since Rockingham, Devonshire, and Shelburne were the greatest of absentee landlords, they did not wish to place power in the hands of men who might reduce their incomes—who might even overturn the whole landed settlement. In the end they came around to the view that concession to the political demands of Flood and Grattan was the only way to keep the peace and preserve the United Kingdom of Great Britain and Ireland.[2]

The Rockinghamites took their stand on the American question with the passage of the Declaratory Act of 1766. For

---

[1] Pares, *King George III and the Politicians*, p. 26. Cf. Brooke, *Chatham Administration*, pp. 72 ff.; L. S. Sutherland, *The East India Company in Eighteenth-Century Politics* (Oxford, 1952), pp. 138–364.

[2] See Fox's justification of their policy in *H.M.C., Charlemont MSS.* i. 369–70.

twelve years they maintained that the Colonies could be reconciled without repudiating that principle, and at no time would they countenance a motion to repeal it. Much as they deplored rabble-rousers and extremists, they justified American resistance to the harsh, oppressive, and inexpedient actions of the Ministry. They moved warily when hostilities broke out, dreading the imputation of treason which opposition must inevitably incur.[1] After Saratoga, however, they were convinced that independence was the only solution. It then became their position that since North had bungled an unnecessary war, only the Rockinghamites could make the necessary peace.

In the protracted Wilkes affair the party found an armoury of clubs with which to beat the Government. The exploits of 'the cross-eyed Casanova' raised important questions about general warrants, the law of libel, the privileges of Parliament, and the rights of electors.[2] The Rockinghamites gave conscientious support to most of the principles for which Wilkes stood—and thus aligned themselves with the cause of liberty—but for the man himself they had little liking. After his return to Parliament in 1774 they gave no support to his persistent campaign to have the resolution for his expulsion expunged. The uncontrollable libertine had served his purpose, and the party had no further use for him.

Christopher Wyvill brought the Yorkshire Association into existence in 1779. His agitation, originally directed against high taxation, soon expanded to include demands for stricter economy in the Government and parliamentary reform. The goal was to free M.P.s from the corrupting influence of the Executive. Similar movements followed in other counties, and delegates from local committees formed a general assembly in London to press their petitions to Parliament. The Rockinghamites tried in vain to forestall and then to capture the movement. Richmond and Fox favoured parliamentary reform, but most of the other leaders were opposed to it. They wished to reduce the influence of the Crown, but they would not do so by

---

[1] Portland Papers, Thomas Townshend to Portland, 18 Oct. 1776. For the Rockinghamite stand on the American issue, see G. H. Guttridge, *English Whiggism and the American Revolution* (Berkeley, 1942), pp. 58–137; C. R. Ritcheson, *British Politics and the American Revolution* (Norman, Okla., 1954), passim.

[2] See the summary of the Wilkes affair in Watson, *Reign of George III*, pp. 98–102, 131–43.

altering the structure of the Legislature or the electorate. From their efforts to direct the agitation to party purposes came Burke's celebrated plan for economical reform.[1]

The economical reform movement was a refurbishing of the old anti-corruption plank in the Country party programme. Although Burke had condemned the traditional nostrums in *Thoughts*, the Rockinghamites had not given them up. They had attacked pensions and other Civil List expenditures. They had brought in Bills to disfranchise revenue officers and to disqualify Government contractors from sitting in the House.[2] Outside the party Chathamites and London Radicals kept alive the Tory cry for shorter parliaments during the 1770's.[3] Thomas Gilbert called for reform of Civil List expenditure and a tax on pensions and official salaries in 1778.[4] Now at the end of the decade what had been, except among the Wilkeites, primarily topics for parliamentary declamation became the subjects of widespread agitation in the country. The discontent aroused by an expensive and unsuccessful war sought redress through measures which were at bottom a Radical restatement of Conservative ideas.

The Rockinghamite programme, as outlined by Burke, would have shocked the old corps but fell short of the specific demands made by popular reformers. He proposed to settle the issue by abolishing numerous places and laying strict controls upon public expenditure. His plan, he argued, would improve governmental efficiency and economy, and at the same time it would achieve the political goals of the movement: 'It extinguishes secret corruption almost to the impossibility of its existence. It destroys direct and visible influence equal to the offices of at least fifty members of Parliament.'[5] Burke intended to remove glaring abuses but to leave untouched the 'just and necessary' influence of the Crown and the constitution of Parliament.

The Rockinghamite programme was thus a parcel of expedients. By 1782, however, parliamentary opinion, which did

---

[1] H. Butterfield, *George III, Lord North, and the People* (London, 1949), pp. 181–333.
[2] For the Rockinghamites' proposals before 1780, see *P.H.* xvi. 833, 926; xix. 1088, 1103; xx. 124, 1255. Their numerous proposals for economical reform between 1780 and 1782 are reported in vols. xxi–xxii.
[3] Ibid. xvii. 176, 220, 322, 690, 1050; xviii. 216, 1237; xix. 873; xxi. 594; xxii. 357.   [4] Ibid. xix. 803, 873.   [5] Ibid. xxi. 67.

not hold the party or its Constitutional views in high regard, was prepared to accept these proposals as the most reasonable solutions to the problems of the moment, and unlike so many Oppositions before them, the true Whigs intended to put their measures into execution.

The Opposition Campaign

In their cautious way the Rockinghamites adapted the established techniques of Opposition for the exploitation of the leading issues. Burke, who had a good knowledge of parliamentary history, frequently cited the practices of Pulteney and Carteret as guides to the party. They did not invent any strikingly original tactics, but with one glaring exception the Rockinghamites made good use of the old.

To gain the public support they thought so necessary, the party had available the 'mature' eighteenth-century newspaper, which appeared in the eighth decade. The weekly-journal form which had served previous Oppositions—*Mist's* and *Fog's*, *The Craftsman* and *Common Sense*, *The Constitutional Journal* and *The Protester*—was given up toward the end of George II's reign. By 1780 there were eight metropolitan morning dailies and nine evening papers published thrice weekly. They were business enterprises financed by advertising and circulation, but most seem to have needed direct subsidies to keep afloat. The Government supported several, and as early as 1764 Charles Townshend urged the leaders to set up a daily paper of their own. Five years later the *Morning Chronicle* was founded 'in the Whig interest', and the old *London Evening Post*, which had taken a stand for Wilkes, came to favour the Opposition generally in its presentation of the news.[1]

The mature newspaper was made up of four pages with four columns to a page. Standard content included parliamentary intelligence, letters to the printer, and paragraphs of foreign and domestic news. Quite often there was a half-column or more of political comment—not an essay of the weekly-journal type, but a news item expanded by observations upon it. Here is an example from the *London Evening Post* of 23 January 1777:

[1] S. Morison, *The English Newspaper* (Cambridge, 1932), pp. 159–202; *History of the Times* (London, 1935), i. 23; A. Aspinall, *Politics and the Press* (London, 1949), pp. 6, 69–70.

following a paragraph on Howe's expedition to Rhode Island, the paper said,

In the reign of the late good old King, when Whig principles prevailed, the Americans afforded us their assistance. . . . In the present reign, when Tory principles prevail, the Americans are persecuted. . . . Would the old King have rewarded their assistance with making war on them; with hiring foreigners and beggaring this island for the support of such a war?

In a similar way the reputations of the party leaders were defended against misrepresentation in the Government Press, and praise was bestowed upon the noble aims of the Opposition. News favourable to the Ministry was not suppressed but reflected upon in a hostile manner. As an organ of Opposition the mature newspaper was much less crude than the weekly journal but not less partisan. The *Chronicle* and the *Post* made North as black as the *Craftsman* had made Walpole.

The *Annual Register*, founded by Burke and Dodsley in 1758, was not, strictly speaking, a Rockinghamite production. There is considerable doubt as to whether Burke exercised any influence on its policy after 1765.[1] But a perusal of the historical article in each issue during these years shows that the writer generally took a Rockinghamite view of national and world affairs. It is impossible to judge the effect of these articles upon contemporary opinion, but easy to see why the party received such favourable treatment from historians who regarded the *Register* as unbiased.

Given the nature of the issues, even Ministerial papers served the interests of the Opposition by reporting parliamentary proceedings and spreading news of disasters abroad. The 'Whig cause' was also aided by short-lived independent productions like the Radical *Middlesex Journal* and the Letters of Junius in the *Public Advertiser*. The provincial papers, which were increasing circulation in the 1770's, were not subsidized by the Government, and they were strongly inclined to treat ministers harshly. North complained in 1776 that taking all papers together, he was traduced in 12,230,000 issues annually.[2]

---

[1] B. D. Sarason, 'Edmund Burke and the Two Annual Registers', *P.M.L.A.* lxviii. 496–508.

[2] *P.H.* xviii. 1320. North based his estimate on the stamp tax revenue: cf. H. R. Fox Bourne, *English Newspapers* (London, 1887), pp. 225–6.

The pamphlet still had an important place in political journalism. In 1770 Burke urged upon Rockingham the need for unrelenting pamphlet warfare in this revealing letter:

> Something of constant and systematical writing seems to me of absolute necessity. We lost much of the advantage of the last pamphlet [*Thoughts*], because the idea was not kept up by a continued succession of papers, seconding and enforcing the same principle. For want of something of this kind, everything you have done or suffered in the common cause has perished as soon as it is known, and however it may have served the nation, certainly operates nothing at all in favour of the party. The more you are confined in your operations by the delicate principles you profess, the more necessary it becomes to push with the utmost vigour the few means that you have permitted to yourselves.

He went on to say that, though 'systematical writing' could not overturn the Ministry, the party must not lay itself open to the reproach of having omitted any means to destroy the 'mischievous system' of the Government. 'In all circumstances', he concluded, 'reputation is a great deal; in bad circumstances it is everything.'[1]

But the Rockinghamites never became assiduous pamphleteers. Except for Burke and later Sheridan, the party was not rich in literary talent, nor were there many of lesser stature who took an interest in writing. Consequently the party turned out few brochures, and, again with the exception of Burke's work, they had little distinction. Most of the great pamphleteering which served the Opposition cause was done by such men as Paine, Price, and Tucker, who had no connexion with the Rockinghamites.

The party made more frequent use of the time-honoured device of petitioning, as a means both of expressing and influencing opinion on popular issues. It was still a common practice to raise an outcry upon the prayers of some aggrieved body of His Majesty's subjects. More remarkable was the development of petitioning 'movements'. The Opposition to Walpole had set them a precedent in 1738–9 by bringing in a succession of inspired petitions from mercantile groups against the Spanish Convention. In 1769–70 the Rockinghamites made common cause with the Wilkeites in soliciting petitions from

---

[1] Copeland, ed., *Burke Corresp.* ii. 175–6.

towns and counties to the Crown for a dissolution of the corrupt
Parliament which had infringed the rights of electors. The
movement had a brief existence and an unhappy end. In the
framing of petitions the 'respectable' and 'radical' elements
struggled against each other. The King ignored them, and the
Opposition consequently found it difficult to exploit the discontent of the people in St. Stephen's. When the City of London
addressed a coarse and insulting remonstrance to George III,
North brought it before the Commons, where it was censured.[1]

In the movement of 1779–81 the petitions, praying for
economical reform, were presented to the Commons against
the mismanagement of the Executive and the influence of the
Crown. Several members of the party took an active part in
their meetings and became delegates to the general assembly
in London. They had to contend with opposition both from
Ministerialists, who wished to prevent the petitions, and from
Radicals who pressed for parliamentary reform. Though they
did not capture the 'anti-parliament', the Rockinghamites
dominated the agitation in the House of Commons, because all
reformers were anxious, in view of the Wilkes and Gordon riots,
to emphasize the sobriety and moderation of the petitioners.
The joint petitions were entrusted to Sir George Savile, who
enjoyed great respect among the country gentlemen, and other
party members took the lead in presenting and debating the
popular grievances.[2]

Largely for this reason the movement was far more successful
than that of 1769–70. Upon these petitions Dunning based his
successful resolutions for diminishing the influence of the Crown
and Burke his bills for economical reform. Parliamentary
opinion was thus prepared for the Rockinghamite legislation
which passed in 1782.

The campaigns at Westminster were carried on in other
respects much as they had been in Walpole's time. The pattern
of sessions varied little. Except in 1764, 1769, 1771, and 1773,
Parliament met before Christmas. The Opposition was at first
disinclined to divide upon the Address. From 1762 to 1774
amendments were offered only twice, in 1766 and 1770. Then

---

[1] *P.H.* xvi. 668 ff.; Cavendish, *Debates*, i. 534 ff.; Guttridge, *English Whiggism*,
pp. 36–41.

[2] *P.H.* xx. 1370; xxi. 285; xxii. 95, 138.

from the autumn session of 1774 onward the Opponents brought on a division each year. They did not, however, regard the Address as the occasion for a trial of strength. They never had all their members in town, and in the 1770's the Independents considered that the Address 'was become a business of course', a vote in its favour not committing a man to support the Government's measures.[1] The Opposition moved amendments, therefore, merely as gestures, to 'show their teeth' and to provide newspaper copy. All amendments, Shelburne wrote to Rockingham in 1779, 'should be *short* and at the same time such as will *carry* out-of-doors'.[2]

Onslow's long tenure of the Chair ended in 1760, and Cust succeeded him without opposition. In 1770 the Country party contested the Speakership for the first time since the Hanoverian accession. The Rockinghamites nominated Thomas Townshend, Jr. The Government elected Sir Fletcher Norton by 237 to 121.[3] Ten years later the Minister wished to replace Norton, who had expressed open hostility to North, with Frederick Montagu, a temperate and well liked Rockinghamite, whom the Marquis himself urged to stand. When Montagu declined on grounds of health, the Government put up Charles Wolfran Cornwall, and the Opposition supported the re-election of Norton. He was defeated by 203 to 134.[4] It is doubtful if the Rockinghamites expected to succeed on either occasion. The contests are to be explained by the decline in prestige of the Speakership under Onslow's successors, which offered a new opportunity to challenge ministers and to condemn them for placing a partisan in the Chair.

In their direct assaults upon the Ministry and its policies the Rockinghamites employed the old weapons with a new tactical objective. Reviewing the methods of 'experienced parliament men of former times' in 1780, Burke wrote

For as they never wished or proposed any real reformation, it answered their purpose if they showed the minister upon some preliminary or collateral point that they were strong enough to carry a more decisive question against him if they thought proper; and if

---

[1] *P.H.* xviii. 43.

[2] Rockingham Papers, Index no. 38, Shelburne to Rockingham [n.d., c. 24 Nov. 1779].

[3] *P.H.* xvi. 733–40.

[4] Ibid. xxi. 793–807; Christie, *End of North's Ministry*, pp. 235–7.

they succeeded, this was signification sufficient to that minister to make terms with them or to resign his place with all its *unimpaired* powers to persons who fought not *against* these powers but *for* the use of them.

The Rockinghamites did intend to implement their proposals, he went on, and their 'strength is without doors and not within'. Hence victories upon side-issues did not serve their main purpose. The party should try a question, in this case economical reform, 'upon its own merits and not upon collateral points'.[1] This was not mere self-righteousness. Throughout the period it was typical of the party to meet issues head-on and to force the debate on 'main principles'. They rarely resorted to surprise. Shock tactics were preferable to feints and ambushes because they wanted to defeat the Ministry, not upon an election petition, but upon a direct challenge to its right to power.

This is not to say that they took a division only upon stand-or-fall questions. They never despised an opportunity to expose a mistake, and they did not hesitate to divide a thin House. In 1778, for example, Burke spotted an item in the army extra-ordinaries for tomahawks and scalping knives. His motion to deny payment was lost, 56 to 21, but his oration against arming 'the savages of America to butcher, torture, scalp, and massacre old men, women, children, and infants at the breast' put him in the morally and sentimentally impregnable position so dear to a Rockinghamite.[2] In disregard of the advice of cautious members who wanted to 'lie by' and let other people fight their own battles, the party occasionally chose to be persistently obstructive. Historians have often noted that on 12 March 1771 the Opposition forced twenty-three divisions upon the prosecutions for printing debates. It should be added that there had previously been three divisions on the issue, and that the Commons divided upon it twenty-three times more in the two weeks following. The House was usually thin, and the minority once sank to seven. For their pertinacity the Opposition claimed the blessing of posterity.[3]

In proposing constructive legislation also the Rockinghamites

[1] Portland Papers, Burke to Portland, 16 Jan. 1780.
[2] *P.H.* xix. 971–2.
[3] Ibid. xvii. 58–163. In 1772 the Opposition divided fifteen times on the Royal Marriage Bill.

were more assiduous than their predecessors. After initial failure in 1768, they carried the Nullum Tempus Act in 1769. They made common cause with other Opposition groups to pass the Grenville Act in 1770 and to perpetuate it in 1774. These were singular triumphs over the Treasury Bench. Savile's Catholic Relief Act of 1778 was passed with Government consent. But most of their proposals, as was to be expected, were lost. The House denied leave to bring in all their Bills in pursuit of the Wilkes affair: Dowdeswell's Bill to declare the Rights of Juries in the Libel Cases (1771), and Savile's four Bills to secure the Rights of Electors (1771–4). In 1772 Dowdeswell introduced a plan for poor-law reform which came to nothing. Four years later Burke's scheme to prevent the plundering of shipwrecks was beaten on the second reading. All moves to disqualify contractors and disfranchise revenue officers were defeated or postponed. The only success in the economical reform campaign was a negative one: to forestall a concerted move by the followers of Shelburne and Rockingham for a Committee of Public Accounts, North admitted the validity of their complaints by bringing in a scheme of his own.[1]

The atmosphere of debate, which is so much determined by the leading speakers, took on a character of its own as the personnel of the opposing sides remained relatively stable after 1770. North never dominated the house as Walpole and Pitt had done, but 'the noble lord in the blue ribbon' was the ablest speaker on the Treasury Bench. Though he occasionally lost his temper and used strong language, he is famous for his amiability and easy-going nature. 'Patriot' orators condemned him roundly, but they could not dislike him, even when he closed his eyes to nap during their speeches. The qualities of his opponents varied greatly. Dowdeswell and Savile, plain and plodding, were always heard with respect. Barré was coarse and provocative, Dunning lucid and precise. Burke and Fox were the two most brilliant orators of the period. They were inclined to be long—once in 1774 Burke was interrupted by the hubbub of departing members when he said he would *try* to be short[2]— but on most occasions they captivated the House with their wit, finely turned phrases, and ingenious argument. As political

---

[1] The surviving debates on all these Bills are easily located in *P.H.* xvi–xxii.
[2] Ibid. xvii. 1314.

battles grew tenser from 1778 onward, the knowledge that Burke or Fox would make a major address filled the House. On the day Burke introduced his Economical Reform Bill, wrote the chaplain to the House of Commons,

the tumult was great; the swords of the deputy Serjeant-at-arms and the Speaker's train-bearer were broken in an instant, my gown and cassock narrowly escaped; every part was crowded; the reverend orator Wyvill and three or four hundred gentlemen could not gain admittance; more than six hundred persons were present when prayers were read.[1]

On less dramatic occasions the Commons often fell into disorder. Slips of the tongue provoked merriment, prolonged until the speaker recognized his error. The House once gleefully mocked Burke for saying that its membership was divided into three halves. Such incidents relieved the tedium of dull speeches and long sittings. Now and then the absurdity of a proposition broke up business. In 1770 the Clerk was seized with uncontrollable laughter while endeavouring to read a resolution to the effect that ballad-singing contributed to the increase in metropolitan crime. Infected by his hysteria the House postponed the matter indefinitely. A lame committee report in 1771 produced such hilarity that North interposed to carry a motion for adjournment.[2] More than ever conscious of its dignity as a great senate, the House tolerated much pomposity and bombast, dreary rhetoric and dull simplicity, but members' sense of the ridiculous inevitably broke through the crust of convention.

Violent altercations led to some ugly disorders. Speakers on both sides were shouted down by their opponents, and the Chair had difficulty restoring order when the House was in what reporters called a 'flame' or 'general ferment'. Feeling ran so high on 20 March 1782 that for a time it appeared that North would not be allowed to announce his resignation.[3] Hot tempers uttered violent threats. Burke promised to impeach ministers on the 'day of reckoning'. Fox declared they must expiate their crimes 'on the public scaffold' and lashed Dundas for smiling at his extravagance.[4] Several appointments on the 'field of honour' resulted from 'hard words' spoken in debate. The presiding officers of both Houses did their best to prevent bloodshed,

[1] *H.M.C., Graham MSS.*, p. 341.   [2] *P.H.* xvi. 943; xvii. 212–14.
[3] Ibid. xvi. 763, 807–11; xxii. 1214–32.   [4] Ibid. xxii. 693, 723.

but there were two celebrated duels toward the end of the period. Fox met Adam in 1779, and Shelburne met Fullarton in 1780. After the second, Sir James Lowther raised the matter in the Commons:

If this was to go on, [Lowther said] and the House did not inter-pose its authority, there would be an end to the freedom of debate and an end of the business in Parliament. The custom seemed to be growing upon gentlemen. . . . If free debate were to be interpreted into personal attack, and questions of a public nature which came before either House were to be decided by the sword, Parliament would resemble a Polish diet.

The House took no action, but from the absence of challenges in the immediate aftermath it would appear that members took the advice given by Rigby in the debate to learn 'better manners'.[1]

Political enemies nevertheless shared a large reservoir of good will. They sometimes rallied each other across the House in high humour. They privately expressed admiration for each other's talents—Burke once said that North had more wit than all his opponents put together. The Prime Minister bore them no rancour. Anecdotes collected shortly after his death contain this passage:

The natural civility and good humour of this nobleman left him no enemies out of the House of Commons. Even the principals of Opposition knew these qualities to be so predominant in his lordship that they frequently petitioned him as First Lord of the Treasury for little favours and indulgences for their friends and constituents, which he as readily granted when he could do it with propriety; and this they frequently acknowledged.[2]

Even in parliamentary warfare there was gentlemanly co-operation. Ministry and Opposition gave each other notice of important motions.[3] In 1780 the leaders on both sides worked out a common agreement upon the way to dispose of the Anti-Catholic Petition presented by Lord George Gordon.[4] Events subsequent to 1782 made apparent how shallow their super-ficial animosities had been.

---

[1] *P.H.* xxi. 319–27.

[2] *The European Magazine and London Review*, xxx. 84.

[3] Copeland, ed., *Burke Corresp.* iii. 115; Fitzwilliam Papers, Index no. 9, Rock-ford to Rockingham, 30 Oct. 1775; P.R.O. Granville Papers, Rockford to Gower, 30 Oct. 1775.

[4] Fitzwilliam and Bourke, eds., *Burke Corresp.* ii. 356–63; *P.H.* xxii. 702–14.

As the mood and temper of Parliament fluctuated, so the assault on the Ministry followed an uneven course. On the whole, it may be said that once the conciliabulum had decided upon a line of action, the Rockinghamite Opposition was steadier and more resolute than any of its predecessors. This is to be accounted for in part by the strength of the party organization, in part by the fact that there was more to oppose. The volume of legislation introduced annually was slowly increasing. Consistent with the theory of parliamentary supremacy, North embodied the major aspects of his American policy in enactments, and Indian affairs required an unprecedented number of Bills. But though the party showed remarkable perseverance in the settled plan for a session, they were not consistent from year to year throughout the period. The pattern of their operations resembles the profit graph of a business firm passing through an unsettled economy into an era of prosperity.

Opposition in the 1760's was much like that in the 1730's: the leaders lived on expedients and waited on the chapter of accidents. Major struggles were normally limited to two or three issues a session. Then the Rockinghamites and Chathamites drew together for a concerted and systematic campaign in 1770. Failure engendered talk of secession, and disagreements ruptured the alliance. From 1771 to 1774 opposition was sporadic and half-hearted. The malcontents desponded and considered secession again. Their weakness in the spring of 1773 led Colonel Barré to pronounce his comic obituary:

We only . . . came here [he said to the ministers] to know the hour when you order your carriages to be ready. Opposition is dead (here the Colonel folded his arm and reclined his head), Opposition is dead, and I am left chief mourner over her bier.[1]

The increasing trouble with the American colonies resurrected the corpse in the session of 1774–5 and 1775–6; but North beat off every assault with such ease that the Rockinghamites finally took the decision to secede.

By this measure they hoped to shock the people into a strong reaction against the 'corrupt' Government majority. They dwelt under the illusion that the secession of 1739 had produced 'great effects', and persuaded themselves that ministers dreaded

[1] *P.H.* xvii. 826.

such a bold stroke. Burke, who was less sanguine than others, thought the Court might be apprehensive and angry enough to proceed against the party leaders by way of impeachment or a Bill of pains and penalties.[1] All anticipations were unfulfilled. When George III heard of the secession plan, he calmly advised North to bring in measures with all appropriate speed 'as real business is never so well considered as when the attention of the House is not taken up by noisy declamations'.[2] The popular reaction was unfavourable, and the secession itself was badly managed. Some of the leaders arrived at the opening of Parliament in November 1776 to announce in solemn terms their imminent departure. Not all of the party did secede, however, and the followers of Shelburne would not co-operate. By mid-February 1777 the Rockinghamites conceded failure and drifted back to a policy of 'attendance and opposition upon great questions in a melancholy desponding way'.[3]

The news of Saratoga put heart into them again. From 1778 onward the pressure of the Opposition steadily increased, even though the leaders remained easily discouraged. In 1780 the Marquis made secret plans to secede again, and Fox threatened to leave the House.[4] They stayed to fight, however. Rockingham and Shelburne patched up another working agreement in that year, and in the last three sessions before North's fall the 'patriots', ill prepared as they were each time, hammered away at ministers with an ingenuity worthy of Pulteney.

All the most effective weapons available to an Opposition were hauled out and refurbished, notably demands for accounts and papers, motions for committees of inquiry and addresses to the Crown, resolutions of censure, and motions for a committee on the State of the Nation. The questions were well drawn to attract the Independent vote, for which the malcontents bid concurrently by their wide-ranging assault on the influence of the Crown. The crucial aspect of the campaign, however, was

---

[1] For Opposition views on secession 1770–7, see P.R.O., Chatham Papers 25, Calcraft to Temple, 12 Mar. 1770; Copeland, ed., *Burke Corresp.* ii. 138, 156, 343–6, 352, 362–9, 379–80; iii. 308–15. It is interesting to note that Fox, though he acquiesced in the decision, was strongly against it. He was to lead another futile secession later in the century.

[2] Fortescue, ed., *Corresp. of George III*, iii, no. 1929.

[3] Albemarle, *Memoirs of Rockingham*, ii. 309.

[4] Rockingham Papers, Index no. 38, Memorandum of agreement between Rockingham and Shelburne, 10 Mar. 1780; *P.H.* xxi. 527.

the negative, not the positive. The passage of a law or declaration for reducing waste and corruption would not pull down the Ministry. Many country gentlemen deserted North in 1780 to carry Dunning's resolutions that 'the influence of the Crown has increased, is increasing, and ought to be diminished' and that the Commons had the right to investigate and correct abuses in the expenditure of public revenue. The 'patriots' could not gather enough support to implement them, and even if Parliament had enacted reform measures, they would have had no more effect than the Nullum Tempus Act. The Opposition had to convince ministers, not that they could not block legislation, but that the House would no longer support them in office.

The final stage of the campaign in the session of 1781–2, therefore, consisted of a series of direct attacks on the Government and its American policy. Legislative proposals were abandoned. Fox's proposed amendment to the Address on 27 November called for 'a total change of system'. Three days later the Opposition voted against going into a Committee of Supply until an alteration of men and measures restored the confidence of the House. On 12 December Lowther moved the House to declare the American war a failure. Ministers held their own on the first two occasions by the comfortable margins of 89 and 95. Lowther lost his motion by only 41, so after the Christmas recess the Opposition first concentrated upon the misconduct of the war. In the first three weeks of February the Admiralty escaped censure by 22 and 19. The Government defeated Conway's motion for reconciliation with the Colonies on 22 February by 1. On the 27th ministers suffered their first defeat. Conway carried by 19 a motion to end offensive war in America.

While the Court cast about for an addition of strength, the Opposition tried to capitalize on their victory by turning condemnation of the war into direct censure of ministers. On 8 March Lord John Cavendish introduced a set of resolutions recounting Britain's losses, concluding with the statement that 'the chief cause of all these misfortunes has been the want of foresight and ability in His Majesty's ministers'. By calling for the Orders of the Day the Government escaped defeat by 10. A week later Rous moved the House to declare that it could have 'no further confidence in the ministers who have the direction of public affairs'. The Government met the issue squarely and defeated it by 9. 'Opposition say they will run us until they beat us,' wrote North's Whip, 'if they can but decrease our majority one at a time.'[1] His intelligence was correct. A motion for an Address to remove the Ministry was set down for 20 March. Meanwhile North saw his support crumble and finally persuaded the King that he must resign on that day.

Thus there came into being a situation bearing a close resemblance to the one for which the Rockinghamites had so long hoped. The public at large, as North confessed, had turned against the Ministry. The initiative in Parliament had passed to the Opposition. Feelers thrown out by the King for three weeks before North's resignation made it clear that the Marquis had the game in his hands. No new Government could be formed without 'the great party'. It cannot be said that they enjoyed the high public esteem to which they pretended, but in all other respects the eventualities upon which they had gambled came to pass. They were now to enjoy the rewards of their consistency and pertinacity.

4. THE FALL OF NORTH

For the first time since 1742 a shift of opinion in the House of Commons had in the midst of a session forced a change of hands. Except for the causal factor, however, the two ministerial crises were quite dissimilar.

The fall of North did not coincide with the conclusion of a general election. The common cause made by all malcontents upon election petitions in the new Parliament had been a major factor in holding together the Opposition to Walpole. In 1782 the Ministry was overturned by a House which had supported it for over two years. The Rockinghamites had no hold upon the country gentlemen, who deserted the Government upon a public issue and who did not expect to profit by a change of ministers.

Walpole had resigned on what Burke called a 'collateral' point. North's defeat on Conway's motion of 27 February was

[1] See Christie, *End of North's Ministry*, pp. 299–369, for a thorough description of the parliamentary crisis.

in fact decisive. The First Lord remained in office only to allow time for the formation of another Ministry, but he made no public statement to this effect. He simply promised to obey the resolution and stated that he would keep his place until the King commanded him to resign or 'the sense of that House expressed in the clearest manner, should point out to him the propriety of withdrawing'.[1] In the mind of the Commons, therefore, Conway's motion did not seal North's doom. At this stage, moreover, the country gentlemen thought it perfectly consistent to vote for a change of ministerial policy without wishing for a change of ministers, and enough of them kept their allegiance to provide the slim Government majorities on the next two divisions. By going out in anticipation of certain defeat on 20 March, North resigned on what must be called the main point, viz. the confidence of the House. He wished to avoid the stigma of an adverse vote recorded for posterity in the journals, but, as he told George III, 'The Parliament have altered their sentiments, and as their sentiments whether just or erroneous, must ultimately prevail', the King must acquiesce in 'the opinion and wishes of the House of Commons.'[2] The issue was as clear as if the vote had been taken.

By 1782 practically everyone but George III had come to share this view. Whenever North had found himself in a minority on Bills proposed by the Opposition, he had wanted to resign, and the King had kept him in office by insisting that defeat on Country party points did not mean a withdrawal of confidence from the Minister. Lack of confidence 'cannot be understood to exist', George wrote in 1774, 'but when the House coolly takes up a matter to distress him'.[3] Now that time had come, but as the crisis approached, George was reluctant to admit it. Those who would support Conway's resolution, he remarked, 'have lost the feelings of Englishmen': the House was 'wild' and 'running on to ruin'. He was 'mortified' that North thought resignation essential after the Opposition victory. When George came to realize that the closet might be stormed, his reluctance grew to the point of drafting a message of abdication.[4] In the

---

[1] *P.H.* xxii. 1108.

[2] Fortescue, ed., *Correspondence of George III*, v, no. 3566. Cf. North's declarations to the Commons in *P.H.* xx. 949–50, 1109; xxii. 1108–9.

[3] *H.M.C., Dartmouth MSS.* (rep. 13, app. iv), pp. 499. Cf. Fortescue, iv, no. 2536.   [4] Ibid. v, nos. 3522, 3534, 3536, 3601.

end he capitulated, without any change in his convictions, to prevent a breakdown of government.

Walpole had resigned under pressure from his colleagues, but they remained in office to deal for the King with one 'patriot shop'. The Opposition of 1782 had attacked, not one overgrown minister, but the whole Ministry and its policies. When it became apparent that no 'mixed system' or coalition could be devised, North told the King that the 'present Cabinet, except the Chancellor, must all be removed' as a preliminary to the formation of a new Government. This recommendation he accompanied by the advice to send for Shelburne or Rockingham.[1] To the House North announced 'that His Majesty's ministers were no more'—that they stayed merely to perform official duties until replaced.[2] The outgoing First Lord took no part, directly or indirectly, in the construction of a successor ministry. The final procedure of demission, therefore, was in broad outline much closer to that which prevailed in the mid-nineteenth century than to the resignation of Walpole.

In the minds of most contemporaries, however, North's fall set no rigid precedents for the future. Beyond a doubt the majority of Parliament men—Ministerialists, Opponents, and Independents alike—were agreed that the will of the Commons must ultimately override all other authority in the state. Yet a vote against one set of politicians implied no commitment to any other. The recorded speeches of several country gentlemen suggest that they would have supported a coalition that included some of the old Ministry. North expressed their attitude correctly when he wrote the King, 'Not that I suppose the minds of men in general exasperated against the individuals who compose the administration, but they are tired of the administration collectively taken, and wish at all events to see it altered.'[3] Coalition was impossible because the indispensable Rockinghamites would not co-operate and Shelburne stuck by his alliance with them. The force of particular circumstances thus dictated an unprecedented procedure which fulfilled the expectations of the Rockinghamites but to others seemed quite exceptional.

Especially did it seem so to the King. With all his scrupulous regard for the rights of the Legislature, he could not help but

---

[1] Fortescue, v, no. 3568. [2] *P.H.* xxii. 1215–19. [3] Fortescue, v, no. 3566.

feel that the Commons forced him to act unconstitutionally. He approached every step in the process of change with the agonized belief that he was being driven to sacrifice his honour, conscience, and principles; for the dissolution of North's Ministry obliged him, in a marked and unmistakable manner, to submit to the power of connexion.

VIII

THE AGE OF FOX AND GREY

1782–1830

VIII

THE AGE OF FOX AND GREY

1782-1830

1. THE CONSTITUTIONAL CRISIS, 1782-1784

THE dissolution of North's Ministry precipitated a political
and Constitutional crisis which lasted for approximately
two years. Lord Rockingham, frustrated by his debility
in the various *pourparlers* since 1767, was now determined to
exploit his new-found advantages to the utmost. In alliance
with Shelburne's following, the true Whigs seized the strongholds of government in March 1782. Feeling their grip weaken
when the Marquis died in July, several of their leaders withdrew, formed a coalition with North, and stormed the closet
again in April 1783. The outraged king dismissed them in
December, whereupon, in a vain effort to oust Pitt's minority
Government, they recorded their principles in resolutions of the
House of Commons until the election of 1784 broke the formidable 'Whig phalanx'.

The Rockinghamites looked upon each triumph as the
establishment of true Constitutional principles. Each downfall
they attributed to unconstitutional machinations: secret influence and the abuse of the Prerogative. Historians often concede that the true Whigs were fighting in the cause of responsible
government. Principles embodied in their resolutions of 1784,
ineffectual at the time, were later cited as Constitutional
precedents. The cause went down to immediate defeat, so runs
the common verdict, because the violence, animosities, and bad
tactics of the protagonists, who 'deserved to lose', drove the
majority of sensible men into the arms of Pitt and the King. The
general election simply confirmed the victory of the Court.[1]

---

[1] For examples of historical opinion, see Russell, *Mem. and Corresp. of C. J. Fox*,
ii. 87–92; Grant Robertson, *England under the Hanoverians* (10th ed., 1930), pp.
299–305; Barnes, *George III and William Pitt*, pp. 106–7; Watson, *Reign of George III*,
pp. 267–73.

There is no question about the facts of the crisis. The evidence is very full, and few points of consequence are open to doubt. It is clear that upon important issues the King and the Rockinghamites were directly at odds. But in the light of Constitutional doctrines avowed by Parliament men, as analysed in the previous chapter, did the crisis appear to contemporaries as a contest between the principles of responsible and personal government? If the issue was so clear-cut, why was there so much change and confusion? In these two years firm connexions cracked and cracked again. Old friends parted, and old enemies made friends. Is the outcome to be explained by the presumption that men voted out of disgust against those whose principles they shared? Was the denouement indeed a decision against responsible government? Let us consider the significant facts in search of the answers.

The Rise and Fall of the Rockinghamites

On 28 February 1782, the day after North's defeat on Conway's motion, the King undertook measures to reconstruct his Government. He wanted a ministry formed 'on a wide basis' from the best of all parties, their public policy to be the retention of all present possessions in America and the reacquisition by diplomacy of as much more as could be gained. Lord Chancellor Thurlow sounded Shelburne, and North communicated with Grafton and Gower, two of the most prominent peers who had deserted him in the 1770's.[1] When these moves failed, George III commissioned Thurlow on 10 March to make another effort for a 'broad bottom', and to the King's dismay the Lord Chancellor began in the 'most hostile quarter' of the Rockinghamites.

The Marquis, 'who avowed being able to answer for the different component parts of the Opposition', laid down his terms: negotiation with America on the basis of independence, disqualification of contractors, disfranchisement of revenue officers, and the essential parts of Burke's Bill of Economical Reform. Before any scheme could be proposed, the King must consent to these points, agree to part with 'obnoxious ministers'

---

[1] Fortescue, v, nos. 3537, 3542–5. Thurlow was originally authorized to see Gower and Weymouth, and he may have done so. It is clear that North tried Grafton and Gower on 7–8 Mar. Cf. *H.M.C., Abergavenny MSS.*, pp. 50–51.

and 'those who were deemed as belonging to a sort of secret system', and promise to accept the nomination of such persons as Rockingham considered essential for the service of the country. Then the party leader would see the King in person and present a 'plan of arrangements'. On 18 March George III rejected these propositions as an indignity. The next day Thurlow again tried Shelburne, who refused to parley with anyone but the King. George III flatly declared 'that my sentiments of honour will not permit me to send for any of the leaders of opposition and personally treat with them'.[1] Thus matters stood when North announced his resignation.

During these three weeks the King evinced a clear and consistent attitude. The state was in danger, and duty summoned all loyal men to rally around the Throne. The best hope for achieving unity of national action lay in a 'broad-bottom' ministry, agreed upon salvaging everything possible of the American Colonial empire. In addition to his scruples against delivering himself up to a party, he seems quite sincerely to have believed that 'changing from one party to another can answer no real good'. Only a comprehensive system could 'heal divisions', and the speeches favouring coalition persuaded him 'that the general wish was for "broad bottom"'. He also believed that politicians should give him advice after they entered office, not before, and he detested the content of Rockingham's stipulations as much as the form. Like the disgusted Thurlow, he had no regard for men who thought that excluding a contractor or disfranchising an exciseman was more important than the salvation of the country.[2] Nevertheless, he did not mean to disregard the voice of the House of Commons. The House had resolved against further offensive war, and none of the King's words suggest that he had any intention of frustrating their will. In short, the King differed from the Rockinghamites as much upon policy as he did upon their right to storm the closet, and he tried to find a ministry to govern in accordance both with his wishes and those of the Legislature.

After North's resignation George III gave ground step by step. On 21 March he summoned Shelburne and proposed that

---

[1] Fortescue, v, nos. 3551, 3553–8, 3563–7, 3571; Albemarle, *Memoirs of Rockingham*, ii. 451–60; Russell, *Mem. and Corresp. of C. J. Fox*, i. 286–7, 294–5.

[2] Ibid. i. 294; Fortescue, v, nos. 3563–4.

he 'take the administration with the Chancellor, Lord Gower, Lord Weymouth, Lord Camden, the Duke of Grafton, Lord Rockingham, &c., if the latter would agree to state what they meant by a "broad bottom", for the King's consideration'.[1] Shelburne, convinced that Rockingham was both indispensable and intractable, declined the commission. Next day the King tried Gower without success. The Marquis now seemed the only possibility, but George III absolutely refused to see him. The monarch had overcome his reluctance to negotiating personally with Opposition leaders. He had switched his tactics from the employment of a commissioner as an intermediary to the direct offer of a commission to a peer to form a ministry of which he was to be the head. For His Majesty this was 'unbecoming' enough.

Shelburne broke the deadlock by offering to act as an intermediary with Rockingham. Chatham's political heir made characteristically Chathamite stipulations:[2]

1. That His Majesty would give me every engagement I had already entered into; clear both as to men and to measures, at first setting out.
2. That the assistance and co-operation of the Rockinghams was to be procured, cost what it would more or less.
3. Full power and confidence.

On 24 March the King summoned Shelburne and pressed for some modification of these conditions. The 'ideas conveyed' and 'bounds prescribed' were never recorded, but he clearly tried to limit the concessions to be made to Rockingham.[3]

Shelburne wrote immediately to the Marquis, who adhered rigidly to the terms he had previously laid down. That night a meeting of sixty-four Rockinghamites approved their leader's action and 'resolved not to accede to any further adjournment of the House of Commons unless these terms were complied with, and to one not exceeding two days if they were'. The party obviously meant to force Shelburne and the King to negotiate under the heaviest pressure that could be brought to bear. Upon only one point did they soften their demands. Richmond and Fox persuaded the Marquis not to insist upon seeing the King in person until arrangements had been

[1] Fitzmaurice, *Shelburne*, ii. 87.   [2] Ibid. 89.
[3] Fortescue, v, nos. 3576, 3581.

concluded. After lengthy parleys on 25 and 26 March Rockingham and Shelburne reached an agreement to which the King
consented.[1]

The next morning, in a letter instructing the old Cabinet to
attend him to resign, George III wrote to North,[2]

At last the fatal day is come which the misfortunes of the times and
the sudden change of sentiments of the House of Commons have
drove me to, of changing the Ministry, and a more general removal
of other persons than, I believe, was ever known before; I have to
the last fought for individuals, but the number I have saved except
my bedchamber is incredibly few.

The great Whigs had driven a hard bargain. The Cabinet
consisted of six Rockinghamites, three Shelburnites, Thurlow,
and the Duke of Grafton.[3] In most departments of state and of
the royal Household there was a 'general sweep'. The party
even insisted upon the restoration of two Rockinghamite Lords
Lieutenant. The royal lament was well founded. To George III
the formation of the new Ministry was a violation of the Constitution, a defeat for his policy, and a personal humiliation in
which his enemies took too evident satisfaction.

To the 'patriots' victory had a compound meaning. In two
senses it was a justification of their long opposition. As the
Rockinghamites implemented their programme, they constantly drew attention to their sincerity and consistency. This
was no repetition of 1742 and 1744. They now proved themselves a responsible Opposition. As they filled up the offices at

[1] Ibid., nos. 3575–7, 3581–2, 3589, 3592; Russell, *Mem. and Corresp. of C. J. Fox*,
i. 290–3; Add MSS. 38218, ff. 45–46, 50.

[2] Fortescue, v, no. 3593.

[3] The previous and subsequent careers of some of these Cabinet members raise
questions about their true allegiance. Grafton had served with Rockingham,
Chatham, and North. 'The exasperating Conway' had served with Rockingham
and Chatham. Thurlow had served with North. Richmond, Keppel, Conway,
Grafton, Camden, Dunning, and Thurlow later served with both Rockingham
and Shelburne. At the time of the formation of Rockingham's Cabinet the most
accurate classification appears to be—*Rockinghamites*: Rockingham, Fox, Keppel,
Conway (who boasted his independence but who was sentimentally inclined to the
Old Whigs and who at this point was a member of the Rockinghamite inner circle),
Richmond, Lord John Cavendish; *Shelburnites*: Shelburne, Camden, Dunning.
Thurlow was a Court-party man. The errant Grafton might be regarded as a
repentant Shelburnite or Rockinghamite, but he did not have firm attachments to
any group. See Pares, *King George III and the Politicians*, pp. 74, 88 n. 2; Christie,
End of North's Ministry, pp. 210 ff.

the pleasure of the Crown, they rejoiced in the restoration of true, Constitutional Whigs to their natural places about the Throne. Britain's Government had been re-established upon a 'Revolution footing'. The evil of secret influence had been destroyed. The state was saved, and its saviours jubilantly reaped their long-deferred rewards.[1]

They nevertheless realized that theirs was not 'victory with numbers' in the full sense of the term. A majority against North did not necessarily mean a reliable majority for Rockingham. He represented the will of the Commons only in a negative sense, and his tenure depended upon gaining support for the policies he had forced George III to accept. The new ministers' awareness of this is shown by their anxiety both to attract the independent vote and to persuade themselves and the King that the division on Conway's motion was an endorsement of their programme.[2] At this stage, therefore, it seems impossible for the Rockinghamites or any one else to have considered their victory as a triumph for 'responsible' over 'personal' government. North had commanded a majority until the end, and throughout the crisis no one ever contended that the King's ministers, however chosen, could govern without the support of Parliament. The change of hands meant no more than a continuation of this principle. The true issue, at least for purposes of declamation, was the character of parliamentary support. The Opposition had steadily proclaimed that North's majority was secured by corruption—the majority of the new Government would be pure and independent.[3]

The victory was qualified also by the composition of the

[1] Their fullest apologia is *The Revolution of MDCCLXXXII Impartially Considered*, which boasts that government has been restored to 'the old tried friends of the Constitution' who are 'most worthy of the confidence of Parliament' because they possess 'great personal weight of character and fortune' and 'the hereditary purity of those principles and virtues which saved the country in 1688'. The central argument of *A Defence of the Rockingham Party* (London, 1783) is that both in 1782 and 1783 'the Rockingham connexion was the only connexion by which the country could be well served'. See also *The Present Hour* (London, 1782) and an absurd but pertinent piece of verse entitled *The Flames of Newgate; or The New Ministry* (London, 1782).

[2] *The Revolution of MDCCLXXXII Impartially Considered*; *H.M.C., Foljambe MSS.*, p. 158.

[3] In private Fox called the fall of North a 'revolution' and 'a complete change of the Constitution' (*H.M.C., Carlisle MSS.*, p. 604). In public he was strictly orthodox (*P.H.* xxii. 1220–1).

Ministry and the manner in which it was formed. Rockingham controlled the Treasury and the greatest strongholds, but he did not thereby acquire unrivalled control of the Government. The King did not disguise his dislike of 'the great party', whereas Shelburne, the architect of the coalition, enjoyed the royal confidence. The two leaders were continually at odds over policy and patronage. George III endeavoured tactfully to treat them as 'joint prime ministers'. This compromise apparently suited Shelburne, who would serve as Rockingham's 'colleague' but would not be 'reduced' to being Secretary of State under him. The Marquis, however, did not abate his determination to manage all measures and appointments, without which the true Whigs' aims were only partially fulfilled.[1] The struggle continued until Rockingham's death on 1 July 1782.

The King immediately designated Shelburne for the Treasury and instructed him to rearrange the Ministry. Inner tension broke into open conflict. Disputes with Shelburne over the peace negotiations had driven Fox to announce in the Cabinet that he intended to resign. Now he made an effort to strengthen the Rockinghamite position by insisting that Portland should have the Treasury. Without a party leader in command of the key stronghold, there would be 'a total end of Whig principles' and Fox would be reduced to a mere 'clerk' in the administration.[2] Inquiries led Shelburne to believe that he had sufficient strength in the Cabinet, and George III stood by his decision. On 4 July Fox and Lord John Cavendish resigned.

The four other Rockinghamite members of the Cabinet—Richmond, Keppel, Conway, and Thomas Townshend—thought it their duty to stay. There ensued a dramatic struggle for control of the party. Between thirty and forty members met and debated hotly for nine hours on 6 July. Fox and his friends, Shelburne heard, staged 'a monstrous scene of violence'.[3] Burke made a two-hour speech. Richmond was so bitterly attacked, wrote Lord Carlisle, 'that at length he burst into

---

[1] Pares, *King George III and the Politicians*, p. 123, n. 1; Fortescue, v, nos. 3627–8, 3632, 3637, 3639, 3646–8, 3664–6, 3677, and ff.

[2] Russell, *Mem. and Corresp. of C. J. Fox*, i. 457–9. As in 1762 and 1766 the party leaders had to decide whether they could fight their rivals better in or out of office. Burke's approach to the problem bears many resemblances to Newcastle's.

[3] Fortescue, vi, no. 3837.

tears, and so the meeting ended'.[1] The result was schism. A small number of underlings severed their ties with the party by remaining in place with Richmond and his Cabinet colleagues. Portland and Burke led a larger group out of office. The true Whigs returned to Opposition weaker than they had left it.

Victory, qualified as it was, had turned into unqualified disaster. Unlike the old corps leaders of the 1740's, the Rockinghamites could not hold their strongholds against a hostile King and a rival who enjoyed his confidence. The party gained little credit for its record in office, and the precipitate resignations drew upon them the odium of 'factious conduct'. Protests that the Opposition had again deceived the people were to be heard once more. To say with their enemies that they incurred universal reprobation would surely be an overstatement, but outside of their own partisan circle there was very little sympathy with their assertions of honour and consistency. The worldly wise had no pity to waste on the losers in a political quarrel. Those who conceded the King's right to choose his ministers saw no reason why George III should not prefer Shelburne to Portland. Whatever the vaunted moral stature of the great party in March, it was evidently diminished in July.[2]

In their discomfiture the 'Rockinghamite rump', now generally termed Foxites, bent the issue toward personal *v.* responsible government. First they rounded on 'the Jesuit of Berkeley Square'. Shelburne, they alleged, was shifty, untrustworthy, and a secret ally of secret influence. Then they assaulted his principles. At heart he was a Prerogative man, a Tory, who intended to re-establish the hated régime of rule by corruption. Altogether he was a Bute, a favourite, who owed his elevation to the prejudice he had inculcated in the monarch against worth and popularity. What had Shelburne contributed to the Opposition victory on Conway's motion? Five or six votes in a majority of nineteen. So what claim had he to the confidence of the people? Rockingham should have been succeeded by one of his own sentiments and principles, who commanded the esteem of England and the veneration of Ireland. Once more the King

[1] *H.M.C., Carlisle MSS.*, pp. 632–3.
[2] Russell, *Mem. and Corresp. of C. J. Fox*, i. 467–8, 472–3; Fitzmaurice, *Shelburne*, ii. 154; Hobhouse, *Fox* (1948), pp. 127–8; Lewis, ed., *Horace Walpole's Corresp.* xxix. 264–7, 269; *H.M.C., Sutherland MSS.*, p. 211; *Lucubrations during a Short Recess* (London, 1782); *A Vindication of the Earl of Shelburne* (London, 1782).

had been duped into defying the will of a loyal and discerning people.[1]

The new strain in the old song was the Rockinghamite claim derived from the division of 27 February. By reinterpretation the majority on that occasion now became a Rockinghamite majority and thus both an endorsement of Whig policy and a mandate for a Whig ministry. Those who took office were responsible to that majority, which had continued to support their measures since March. When the appointment of Shelburne signified a change in the principles of the Ministry, the Foxites honourably resigned because they could no longer be responsible to the House for the measures pursued. The clear implication, never flatly stated, was that the King should take back on their own terms the party supported by the majority.

This thesis was momentarily tenable because no trial of strength took place. Parliament was prorogued on 11 July. Shelburne reconstructed his Ministry, the most notable addition being the younger Pitt, and open hostilities were suspended until the next session opened on 5 December.

The Fox–North Coalition

The mythical character of the Foxite majority was quite apparent to practical politicians. Shortly after the resignations an estimate gave 130 to the Government, 120 to North, and 80 to Fox.[2] The new Ministry could not stand without the support of one of the other parties, and as long as Fox refused to serve with Shelburne, North held the key position. The central theme of high politics for the next seven months became the struggle for the conscience of the fallen Premier.

On 24 July North's old Whip, John Robinson, wrote to a friend that his lordship 'had had intimations and messages from Mr. F. through John St. John, why not be friends, why not join, &c., &c., and Mr. F. is certainly at work with every

---

[1] See the debates of 9–11 July 1782 in *P.H.* xxiii. 152–201; the following pamphlets published in London, 1782: *A Word at Parting to the Earl of Shelburne*, *A Defence of the Right Honourable the Earl of Shelburne* (ironically titled), *A Letter to the Right Honourable the Earl of Shelburne*; and *An Examination into the Principles, Conduct, and Designs of the Minister* (2 eds., 1783). Much was made also of Shelburne's reputed unpopularity on his own estates and of a report that he had advised the King to revive the use of the royal veto.

[2] *H.M.C., Carlisle MSS.*, pp. 633–4.

engine, but no harm done as yet, I think'.[1] Two weeks later George III asked North to back the Government and to rally the support of the country gentlemen. He replied vaguely that he was no longer sure of the Independents' allegiance but would see what could be done.[2] Amid attraction from both sides and uncertainty about his own position North remained for a long time irresolute. To his father he wrote on 12 September,

> As to my own conduct, I really do not see any plan that will quite satisfy my mind, and that appears honest and honorable, but *support to the general measures of government* and opposition to all innovations in the Constitution. I believe I shall speak openly in a few days, but I wish first to converse with some friends and learn what following I am likely to have. One would certainly wish to appear with as much dignity and importance as possible.[3]

Still he made no pronouncement. Early in November he informed George III that he thought the country gentlemen, upon whom he could exert no pressure, were generally favourable to the Government. At a meeting of his friends later in the month he declared himself free of all engagements.[4] The opening of Parliament on 5 December at last brought some clarification.

For once the King's Speech was in considerable part the composition of the King himself. George III expressed in his familiar style the agony with which he had 'sacrificed every consideration of my own to the wishes and opinion of my people' by consenting to the dismemberment of the Empire. In awkward but touching phrases he besought the loyal support of the nation in his efforts to uphold Britain's honour and restore her welfare. The Commons debated the Address for two days. The Opposition clearly realized that the King's words were in part his own but, to sharpen the attack, clung to the convention that they were the words of the Minister. Fox cut savagely at the Speech three times, terming it despicable, detestable, and unfit for the ears of Parliament. Burke sonorously condemned it in general, then subjected it to derision and ridicule line by line. But they betrayed their lack of confidence in their mythical majority by refusing to divide.[5]

---

[1] Add. MSS. 38567, f. 101.   [2] Fortescue, vi, nos. 3872–3.
[3] North MSS. (Bodleian), D. 26, f. 36.
[4] Fortescue, vi, no. 3972; Russell, *Mem. and Corresp. of C. J. Fox*, ii. 9.
[5] For the speech and debates, see *P.H.* xxiii. 204–78.

North had been prepared to oppose the Address if he found it objectionable in any part.[1] Some passages, he said, 'required explanation', but he was so moved by the royal appeal that he could not bring himself to offer any amendments. His speech made apparent the conflicting sentiments which kept him uncommitted. First was his loyalty to George III, whose suffering he well understood—'The sensations of that royal personage were truly those of a patriot king.' North's genuine sympathy for George's misery compelled him to testify to the sincerity and nobility of his sovereign's emotions. Second was his disagreement with Fox, whose tactless speeches revived many of their differences over national policy. North devoted the major part of his oration to refuting his old enemy. Third was his distrust of Shelburne. Unlike the Foxites, North cast no reflections upon the manner of Shelburne's rise to power, but, suspicious of the negotiations at Versailles, he threatened to oppose any treaty made upon 'timid and desponding principles'. He was highly sensitive about the peace terms because his honour as a minister was involved. Outlining the strength of Britain and the weaknesses of her enemies, he insisted that a bad peace must be blamed on bad diplomacy, not on the misconduct of the war.

The Address passed *nem. con.*, but no one could tell how North's friends would vote on a specific issue. On 18 December Fox tried the House by moving for the articles of the provisional treaty that related to the recognition of American independence. North expressed deep mistrust of ministers but declared against the motion because any interference would give them an excuse for making a bad peace. This speech decided the day, but the Treasury Bench, seeing no reason to rejoice in a victory won by such equivocal support, urged Fox to withdraw the question. He refused, rejecting the proposition that 'the smallness of a minority was a proof of the weakness of the cause', and was overwhelmed by 219 to 46.[2] The 'Rockinghamite majority' was now exposed as an imposture, but the Government lived under the threat of North's displeasure. 'Lord North's situation is singularly powerful', wrote the Irish politician Grattan: 'If

[1] *H.M.C., Abergavenny MSS.*, p. 56.
[2] *P.H.* xxiii. 311–22. The few subsequent divisions until 17 Feb. 1783 gave little indication of party alignments.

anything is to be collected from the papers, he manages it with much address.'[1]

Within each group subsurface tensions mounted.[2] Three of the four Rockinghamites in the Cabinet kicked up trouble over the peace preliminaries. Conway clung to office in obvious disgruntlement. Toward the end of January 1783 Richmond refused to attend Cabinet meetings, and Keppel resigned. Richmond began to intrigue for a reunion of Fox and Shelburne. North's followers knew that he could not balance himself indefinitely on the middle of the see-saw. One bloc urged an alliance with Shelburne, another a coalition with Fox. Meanwhile, the preliminaries of peace, laid before Parliament on 27 January, did not prove popular. Dissension within the Ministry increased. Carlisle's resignation as Lord Steward on 4 February was taken as a sign that the Government's 'system' was disintegrating. At last Shelburne, who seems to have thought the management of the Commons beneath him, came to realize that he must acquire additional strength.

Pitt was sent to try Fox, who refused to discuss any plan based upon Shelburne's remaining in office. Fox hated his former colleague, and, of course, the true Whigs must command the Treasury. The Minister then turned to North's friends. He sent Henry Dundas to demand their full and unqualified support of the peace preliminaries. Dundas had a treaty to offer if this condition was met, but of this he gave no intimation. Instead, he spoke vaguely of a possible accommodation at the end of the session and laid down an ultimatum: without North's support, Shelburne would resign. To North this threat clearly indicated an intention by the 'black Jesuit', perhaps in connivance with the King, to compass his ruin. Approval of the peace, which he and many of his friends disliked, would wreck his party and place him at Shelburne's mercy. Shelburne's resignation, on the other hand, would pave the way for a *rapprochement* between Pitt and Fox, leaving the Northites in impotent Opposition. Dundas's ultimatum was rejected, and as

---

[1] *H.M.C., Emly MSS.*, p. 175.

[2] The basic materials for an understanding of the fall of Shelburne and the formation of the coalition are to be found in Russell, *Mem. and Corresp. of C. J. Fox*, ii. 10–42; Fortescue, vi, nos. 4109–10, 4112–13, 4120–5, 4128–31; Fitzmaurice, *Shelburne*, ii. 230–5; Buckingham, *Courts and Cabinets of George III*, i. 142–59; *The Journal and Correspondence of William, Lord Auckland*, i. 7–47.

the only means to preserve his 'dignity and importance', the former Premier immediately decided to take the olive branch Fox had long held out to him. Within twenty-four hours the deal was closed. On 14 February 1783 Fox and North met in person to settle the terms of a coalition.

The basis of their agreement was disapproval of the preliminaries. Since the making of war and peace was a royal Prerogative, Parliament should endorse the fulfilment of the terms, but the Minister should be censured for having made too great concessions to Britain's enemies. This line of action, most of its proponents maintained, constituted opposition to measures not men. But the new allies knew perfectly well what they were doing. Censure must bring Shelburne down. At their first meeting Fox and North discussed the principles upon which a future administration should be based. 'There should be one man, or a Cabinet, to govern the whole and direct every measure', said North, 'Government by departments was not brought in by me. I found it so, and had not vigour and resolution to put an end to it. The King ought to be treated with all sort of respect and deference, but the appearance of power is all that a king of this country can have.'[1] No Rockinghamite could find anything to quarrel with in such a manifesto. The leaders then had a little discussion about places, but to avoid complications they left details to be decided when the outcome of their opposition determined their strength.

The political world learned of the coalition almost as soon as it was formed. Reaction was immediate and vehement. The issue, however, was not a simple judgement upon the rectitude of the conduct of Fox and North. Not only were there the conflicts of personal loyalty inevitable in any such situation but also the strife aroused in the breasts of those who preferred one set of politicians but not their stand on the peace. For some the issue may have been clarified by the fact that, no matter how Parliament voted, no matter who was in place, the treaties would not be altered. In the divisions of 17 and 21 February, which drove Shelburne out of office, the greatest number on each side probably found a correlation between their opinions of men and measures, but without question there were many torn by cross-purposes. The Tory Dolben, for example, liked North, loathed

[1] Russell, *Mem. and Corresp. of C. J. Fox*, ii. 38.

Fox, and considered the Crown's alienation of the Colonies unconstitutional. Sir Cecil Wray, an independent Whig, admired Fox, detested North, lamented the coalition, and thought the peace acceptable. Wilbraham Bootle, who said he did not know whether he was a country gentleman or not, damned the factions much but the treaties more. The old place-man Rigby voted for the peace but said he hoped the Opposition would win.[1] Since the margins of victory were 16 and 17, the votes of such men probably decided the question. It cannot be said objectively, therefore, that the Commons gave a clear majority to the coalition and, in consequence, instructed the King to call upon Fox and North to form an administration. But according to the conventions followed at the time of North's resignation, Shelburne must go, and no one could fail to see that the majority necessary to do the King's business could certainly be supplied by the coalition if placed in office and supported by the influence of the Crown.

The debates of February and March disclose the political character and Constitutional position which Parliament men attributed to the coalition. The unfavourable reaction was shock and astonishment that men of such opposite principles could form a union. The eloquent contention between the Rockinghamites and North, which had long attracted so much interest and excitement, and which the antagonists had steadily pronounced sincere and irreconcilable, was now seen to be a sham battle. Either the parties had no principles, or they were so lightly held as to permit facile apostasy. Such hypocrisy, said Wray, 'destroys all confidence between man and man'. One may question the candour of the fulminations of Pitt and Dundas—with their knowledge of ministerial intrigues, they should not have been surprised, and they themselves had gone in search of coalitions—but the moral outrage of Independents and even of some party men appears altogether genuine. To them the new confederacy was unnatural and scandalous, a contemptuous violation of political ethics.[2]

Their disillusion was the greater because the coalition was patently a storming party. Pitt called the leaders 'the self-created

---

[1] Russell, *Mem. and Corresp. of C. J. Fox,* ii. 39; *P.H.* xxiii. 484, 511, 514–15, 523, 555. See also the speeches of Powys (447–8, 520–2).

[2] Ibid. 457–8, 471, 491, 496, 511, 662, 673, 679, 705–6.

and self-appointed successors to the present administration'. They were broadly denounced as profligate place-hunters, imbued with factious malice and willing to sacrifice national honour and welfare to their own greed. They opposed, not the peace but the peacemaker, whose work they could not have improved upon. No good was to be expected from a Ministry composed of such disgraceful miscreants.[1]

It is significant, however, that no one in Parliament branded the coalition as unconstitutional. The attitude taken by Pitt in his speech of 21 February is particularly noteworthy. He flatly declared that no minister should be 'retained in power against the public approbation'. Right or wrong, the Commons might dismiss Shelburne 'from the confidence of his sovereign and the business of state when you please'. Pitt confessed his own ambition for 'high situation and great influence'; but as a minister, 'I am at the disposal of this House, and with their decision, whatever it shall be, I will cheerfully comply.' He was prepared to step down 'whenever the public are disposed to dismiss me from their service'. The Prerogative was not mentioned. Pitt poured scorn upon the self-creation and self-appointment of ministers because of the sordid motives which impelled their action, not upon the action itself. He would not seek office by such means, but he did not deny the right of meaner men to do so. Moreover, he assured his opponents that 'when they come from that side of the House to this, I will for one most readily accept the exchange', and 'I promise them, beforehand, my uniform and best support on every occasion when I can honestly and conscientiously assist them'. In short, bad as were the men, he would oppose only their bad measures. The repose of the country should not be disturbed by 'an indiscriminate opposition'.[2]

The coalition could have demanded no greater concessions from the son of Chatham and the colleague of Shelburne. His language can mean only that no ministry could stand without the confidence of the Commons, that the Commons might lawfully give their confidence to whom they chose, and that the Crown must accept their verdict. Pitt intended, however, to leave the King a wide area of discretion. Appointments need not be made only from those attached to a parliamentary majority. The House did not vote on a slate of ministers. Governments were put together by negotiation, in which the King's weight was felt. He was not expected to give *carte blanche* to those who controlled the majority. Thus, in speeches delivered near the end of the long 'interministerium' Pitt allowed 'that it was perfectly Constitutional to go up with an address to the throne on the subject of an appointment of ministers' but urged great delicacy 'in a case acknowledged on all hands to belong Constitutionally to the Crown'. The House might properly request the King to form an administration entitled to the confidence of Parliament and the People, but except upon a total breakdown of government, the interposition of the Commons in its formation was unwarrantable.[1]

The unfavourable reaction to the coalition, then, was derived from an ethical rather than a Constitutional code. Anticipating this, North and the Foxites at first took up an equivocal defence. In the debate on 17 February they refused either to affirm or deny the existence of an alliance. They maintained that they voted together out of conviction. No one had surrendered his principles. As men of honour they had submerged old animosities, for which there was no longer any cause, to censure jointly a humiliating peace. They were united for no other purpose, and on other points they differed as widely as before. They were not candidates for office, nor had they any other ulterior designs. In counter-attack they revived the old charges against Shelburne. Having sneaked into office by low and jesuitical cunning, he presided over a divided ministry based on a 'narrow bottom'. Reflections cast upon the supposed hypocrisy of coalition were characteristic of a hypocritical Government. Look at the Treasury Bench, urged Burke, where North's former colleague, Henry Dundas, sat between Pitt and Thomas Townshend, the renegado Rockinghamite.[2]

Evidently emboldened by success, the Opposition dropped the mask on 21 February. They proudly acknowledged the existence of a coalition based upon the principles professed 'by every sound Whig'. Fox, who had declared in December that he could best serve the nation in opposition, now confessed an ambition for office and announced his candidacy 'for a share in that new arrangement which the late neglectful, not to give a

---

[1] *P.H.* xxiii. 683–4, 690.   [2] Ibid. 468–9, 483, 486–7, 492.

worse epithet, conduct of the First Lord of the Treasury has rendered indispensable'. The administration having been 'destroyed through want of confidence', Fox went on, coalition became a patriotic duty:

Then let it not be said that such a combination against a minister is unconstitutional: and while it is acknowledged that the King by his prerogative possesses the right of ministerial appointment, let it be remembered that the people can by their privilege annul that appointment. It is only thus that we can derive the means of restoring the abused confidence of the people.

It is only coalition that can restore the shattered system of administration to its proper tone of vigorous assertion. . . . The obnoxious part of the administration must recede from the countenance of his sovereign. He has neither the sanction of people or [*sic*] Parliament, or, indeed, his wonted colleagues. . . . It is only from the coalition of parties for the honest purpose of opposing measures so destructive to the interests of the country that the spirit of Constitutional power can ever be restored to its former vigor.[1]

No other opponent so frankly expressed his desire for place. All emphasized the magnanimity of the leaders and the honourable nature of their connexion. The coalition of 1757, known to all and well within the memory of numerous Parliament men, was cited as a precedent. One essential difference was overlooked: the Pitt–Newcastle administration had been formed by a royal commissioner with the sanction, albeit reluctant, of George II; whereas the Fox–North coalition was a private political alliance, unauthorized by George III. But Government speakers did point out that the alliance of 1757 embraced all factions, not two in opposition to a third. The immediate retort was that, secret influence at Court having blocked the formation of a stable administration, the public spirit of the Opposition had impelled the leaders to provide for the nation's need. In a later debate North met the Government's criticism by saying that he would not object to the inclusion of Shelburnites in a new ministry, and Fox declared his willingness 'to shake hands even with those opposite to him as well as with the noble lord in the blue ribbon'. Pitt's scornful rejection of their friendship undermined his colleagues' position.[2]

[1] Ibid. 531–2, 541–2.
[2] Ibid. 522, 560, 596, 666, 681–6. The inevitable pamphlet controversy over the coalition followed the lines laid down in parliamentary debate. For examples, see

The uncompromising attitude of the Treasury Bench probably knit the coalition more tightly than before. At the outset
Townshend and Dundas seem to have hoped to win over North,
but while pleading for his support, Townshend made the gross
error of asserting that any fault in the treaties must be charged
to the former Premier's maladministration. Pitt followed the
same line.[1] In view of North's public warning, ministers had
made the move best calculated to alienate him. The bitter
contumely heaped upon the coalition then drove its leaders to
a strenuous common defence and declarations of union from
which there was no apparent escape. A dissolution of their
alliance would have seemed proof positive that it had indeed
been unnatural. It now remained to be seen whether agreements made in private and positions taken in public could be
sustained amid all the complex pressures involved in the
formation of a new ministry.

When the Commons refused to approve the peace on 17
February, all but the King and the Minister assumed that the
'system' could not continue. Shelburne was reported to have
thoughts of 'standing in spite of the House of Commons'. After
the direct censure of the treaties on 21 February, his colleagues
in the Lower House unanimously advised him to resign, and on
the 24th he retired.[2] George III now faced a situation more
galling than that of the year before. The most formidable
storming-party of the century meant to bind him in chains. The
key figure in this unconstitutional conspiracy was North, who,
despite their long and cordial association, belligerently defied
his sovereign's will. The royal 'horror of Fox', who made no
secret of his personal animus against the King, was intensified
by Charles's friendship with the Prince of Wales. Young George
had sided openly with Fox at the time of his resignation in 1782.
At Brooks's the Prince indulged regularly in riotous dissipation,
highly offensive to the puritanical King, and in coarse conversation which bordered upon *lèse-majesté*. The entry into Opposition of another heir to the throne reintroduced into politics the

---

*A Defence of the Rockingham Party in their Late Coalition with the Right Honourable
Frederic Lord North, The Coalition; or An Essay on the Present State of Parties, The
Ministerialist, Observations on a Pamphlet entitled A Defence of the Rockinghamite Party.*

[1] *P.H.* xxiii. 466, 470, 473, 570.

[2] Russell, *Mem. and Corresp. of C. J. Fox*, ii, 14, 18; Fortescue, vi, no. 4130.

usual bitterness of royal family quarrels sharpened by the King's conviction that Fox had debauched his eldest son.[1]

For more than five weeks George III wrestled with his conscience, his emotions, and the politicians.[2] The coalition insisted upon capitulation in the most stringent Rockinghamite terms: the King must in person designate the mute titular leader, Portland, for the Treasury and give him *carte blanche* both as to men and measures. To avoid such abject surrender George III tried three ineffectual devices. Pitt declined a commission to reconstruct the Ministry. North refused to be detached from the coalition. Gower, a 'neutral peer', failed to form a 'broad bottom'. The King then opened negotiations with the coalition through North, only to find that the storming-party could not agree on a Cabinet list. When the dispute had been settled, George III commanded Portland to submit his 'whole plan of arrangements'. The Duke refused to do more than present a Cabinet of seven, upon whom, he said, His Majesty could rely to propose nothing he could not acquiesce in. The startled King remarked that no man over forty could accept such a proposition and instructed the Duke to propose a complete system or give up the attempt. When Portland, construing this demand as lack of confidence, again refused, George III broke off the negotiation on 23 March. Again he tried Pitt, then North, and drafted his abdication.

After the rejection of Portland's terms, the Opposition determined to apply parliamentary pressure. On 24 March Coke of Norfolk carried without a division a motion requesting the King to form 'an administration entitled to the confidence of the people and such as may have a tendency to put an end to the unfortunate divisions and distractions of the country'. His Majesty in reply expressed a desire to do everything in his power to gratify their wishes, but at the end of a week no arrangement had been made. The Earl of Surrey then presented a resolution

---

[1] Ibid. i. 437; ii. 45–48, 57; Percy Fitzgerald, *The Life of George the Fourth* (London, 1881), i. 30–33. It is interesting to note that after the Rockinghamite resignations in 1782 George III wrote that the issue before the country was whether he or Fox should rule, and since he would never employ Fox again, 'the contest is become personal, and he indeed sees it also in that point of view': Fortescue, vi, no. 3872.

[2] The course of the negotiations can be followed through numerous letters in ibid. vi. 249–330; Russell, *Mem. and Corresp. of C. J. Fox*, ii. 18–62; Fitzmaurice, *Shelburne*, ii. 251–62.

'That a considerable time having now elapsed without an administration responsible for the conduct of public affairs, the interposition of this House on the present alarming crisis is become necessary', followed by a further address to the Throne. The debates upon these motions reveal the notions of 'confidence' and 'responsibility' current among Parliament men in 1783.

It was generally agreed that any minister, even though only a caretaker, was Constitutionally responsible for official advice given to the Crown. He was responsible in the sense that he was accountable to Parliament and thus liable to censure, removal, and impeachment for any wrongful act committed by him in the name of the King. After Shelburne's resignation Britain still had responsible ministers but not a responsible ministry. There was no collective body to advise the sovereign, who was presumed to act only upon advice, concerning general policy, which no departmental chief was singly qualified to decide. Thus there could be no general policy. Since the King could do no wrong, in the absence of a responsible ministry the Government was limited to office routine. Surrey's motions called for an administration to deal with the pressing affairs of state. His Address asked that it be 'formed upon principles of strength and stability', which implied the need for a parliamentary majority in order to be effective, that is in order to be responsible for the passage of necessary measures. It was never said that a ministry must have a majority in order to be Constitutionally responsible for giving advice upon general policy. Thus, though most men doubtless realized that a ministry of any permanence must possess responsibility of both kinds, the two were not yet thought to be fused in the law of the land.[1]

Inevitably the question arose as to where the King should take advice concerning the formation of a new ministry. The customary procedures had not yet permitted the development of the convention that an outgoing minister takes responsibility

---

[1] *P.H.* xxiii. 689–90, 693–4, 701, 705. The Opposition drew a distinction between the 'interministeria' of 1782 and 1783. In the first case, North and his colleagues remained in office until the appointment of their successors; ergo, they remained a responsible ministry. In the second, Shelburne left office, and without a Prime Minister there was no responsible ministry. During these debates nothing was said of the 'responsibility to a majority' which Fox had used to justify his resignation in July 1782.

for recommending a successor and that the new minister takes responsibility for the dismissal of his predecessor. Fox revived the old charge of secret influence to account for the long 'interministerium'. He first belaboured Jenkinson, who should have given advice as a Privy Councillor only in Council, not in private. Fox then attacked the Lord Chancellor, who, in the absence of a First Lord of the Treasury, 'was the person to be considered as the only official man from whom His Majesty could receive advice'. Others repeated the cry of secret influence, but neither of Fox's arguments received any endorsement. The general tenor of the motions and speeches was that in the formation of a ministry the King exercised his Prerogative without the protective shield of official advice. He was expected to employ his own wisdom, discretion, and judgement. Surrey withdrew his resolution when even North and Lord John Cavendish expressed doubts about the propriety of parliamentary 'interposition', no matter how desperate the crisis.[1]

The discussions of 'confidence' suggested factors which the King should take into consideration. No one quarrelled with the general proposition that administration should have the confidence of Parliament and the People. But, asked Pitt, what was the criterion of judgement? When the Opposition pointed out that Shelburne must be excluded because the votes of February expressed lack of confidence in him, Richard Hill retorted that the same Parliament had withdrawn its confidence from North the year before. Ergo, both were ineligible, or the proposition was absurd. Fox replied that it was not absurd but impractical because 'however respectable the Rockingham party were, they were not sufficient to stand alone'. Without a doubt, he continued, the people wanted an administration based on a 'broad bottom', which necessitated a coalition. One had been formed for the sole purpose of 'removing the political obstruction given to the business of state', an object which must be considered 'Constitutionally proper'.[2] No Foxite carried the argument beyond this point. The implication was unmistakable —the coalition possessed the requisite confidence because it had twice gained a majority in the House of Commons—but the Opposition still dared not offer a direct challenge to the Prerogative.

[1] Ibid. 667, 677–8, 691–3.   [2] Ibid. 659–60, 663–5, 677, 683, 707.

One of North's wavering friends, George Johnstone, outlined a constitutional theory which vaguely supported the Foxite implication. In a speech which touched closely on George III's personal ideas, Johnstone said,[1]

With regard to the Prerogative of the Crown in the choice of ministers, that matter, in his opinion, depended upon an equal balance: the King ought not to be altogether deprived of having some choice; neither ought he to consult his private feelings only. The public weal was the object that ought to operate solely in the appointment of ministers, and public considerations should alone guide the royal choice.

The case on the one hand was widely different from that of a private individual choosing and appointing his own personal servants, and on the other, the royal will ought not to be so far cramped, checked, and controlled that His Majesty should be rendered a mere king of straw.

No one disputed this declaration, for no one wanted another Bute, and the coalition would not avow its intention to concede George III only the appearance of power. Yet Johnstone did not bring the issue closer to definition because he left determination of 'public weal' and 'public considerations' to the King.

Another Northite, Charles Perceval, expressed an idea which best fitted accepted Constitutional doctrine. To Surrey's address he proposed to add[2]

'to assure His Majesty that the House would countenance and support any ministers he should be graciously pleased to appoint, so long as their conduct should entitle them to the confidence of the country.'

This amendment, he thought, ought to be inserted, as it would clearly evince that the Address did not proceed from any party motives, or that the House wished to point out any particular set of men to His Majesty of whom to make choice.

The weakness in such Constitutional correctness was that it did not fit the facts. The King's every expedient to avoid the coalition had failed. When Fox answered Perceval by saying that Parliament should not give confidence to men until it was known who they were, he meant by indirection to insist upon Portland's Cabinet list. As long as the coalition held together, there was no alternative combination which could get a parlia-

[1] *P.H.* xxiii. 669–70.   [2] Ibid. 700.

mentary majority. Surrey ultimately gave up his Address, but the King accurately observed that 'the House of Commons has taken every step but insisting on this faction by name being elected ministers'.[1]

The Royal Riposte

The success of the coalition was more complete than that of Rockingham. Despite desertions Fox and North controlled a larger bloc of faithful votes. The King had been forced to take them on their own terms, and having settled their internal differences, the leaders did not face a struggle for precedence in the closet. In form their 'victory with numbers' was a fulfilment of the ideal toward which Oppositions had been working for half a century. The coalition had played the game by the well-established rules, which even their rivals accepted, and by those rules Portland's Ministry could anticipate a long tenure of power.

George III, however, still would not recognize the rules and so considered the result of the game invalid. He capitulated because 'not a single man is willing to come to my assistance', and hoping that a steady demonstration of his dislike for the coalition would encourage 'the Grenvilles, the Pitts and other men of abilities and character' to rescue him from thraldom, he resolved to refuse any honours the Cabinet should recommend.[2] Once again a Hanoverian king stood in opposition to his ministers. This time he was a very experienced and very determined king. As the coalition had forced itself upon him by pursuing political conventions to their logical limit, George was prepared to employ his Prerogative to its Constitutional limit in order to get rid of them. Extreme, uncompromising action provoked extreme, uncompromising reaction.

Perhaps nothing could have turned George from his course, but certainly he was fixed in it by the conduct of the coalition in office. Apart from observing the strictest rules of politeness to the King, who was barely civil to them, the ministers appear to have made little effort to ingratiate themselves. What was worse, they misplayed the knave of trumps. Walpole and Pulteney had, at the conclusion of their successful Oppositions, effected a reconciliation between King and Prince. In 1784 there was no

[1] Fortescue, vi, no. 4272. [2] Idem.

open quarrel which called for the submission of the son to the
father, but Fox and Portland increased the bad feeling between
them in mid-June by bungling the delicate matter of an allowance for the heir. The King believed not only that he had been
misled but that ministers intended to favour his son at his expense. At the end of one letter to the First Lord, he wrote,[1]

I cannot conclude without saying that when the D[uke] of Portland came into office, I had at least hoped he would have thought
himself obliged to have my interest and that of the public at heart,
and not have neglected both to gratify the passions of an ill advised
young man.

George III came very close to dismissing the Cabinet in a fit of
fury, and when the affair was finally settled, declared he would
never forget or forgive his ministers' ill usage of him. The
Prince then alienated his father still further by openly showing
his favour to the coalition in the House of Commons and voting
with them in the House of Lords. Little wonder that George in
bitterness called them 'his son's Ministry'.[2]

Despite their precarious position at Court, which made them
uneasy about their tenure, ministers encountered no real
difficulties in Parliament. Attendance was thin for the remainder of the session, and after the Houses reconvened in
November, Fox's Whips mustered majorities of over 100 on all
critical questions in the Commons. Pitt's opposition was vehement but ineffective. When it became apparent that the coalition was firmly entrenched in the Lower House, the King
determined upon his celebrated *coup* of December 1783. Fox's
India Bill, framed upon the Rockinghamite principle of keeping
Indian patronage out of the hands of the Crown, had aroused
much criticism because it vested control of the Company in a
board appointed for a term of years. The Opposition interpreted
this provision as an attempt by the coalition to seize 'the im-
mense power of the East' through their own appointees. The
Bill passed the Commons by a comfortable majority, but when
it went up to the Lords on 8 December, George III let it be
known through Earl Temple that he would consider any peer
who voted for the measure his enemy. Concurrently, he had
John Robinson, North's old Whip, prepare a prospectus for a

---

[1] Fortesque, vi, no. 4384.   [2] Russell, *Mem. and Corresp. of C. J. Fox*, ii. 57.

new general election, from which it appeared that, despite the Rockinghamite reforms, the Court could gain a majority against the coalition.[1] On the 17th the Lords threw out the India Bill, and Pitt called upon the Cabinet to resign.

In his opinion [Pitt said] the servants of the Crown were worse than useless whenever they were without responsibility. For a situation thus dangerous and unconstitutional they were, indeed, strictly answerable. The moment they could not answer for their own measures, let them retire. They were no longer fit to occupy stations which they did not adequately fill.[2]

Fox and North waited for their dismissal, which took place the following night, and on the 19th Pitt accepted the Treasury.

For three months he headed an administration of the type which he had just condemned. He and his colleagues were in the technical sense responsible, but without a majority in the Commons they could not answer for their measures. The coalition defeated Pitt's India Bill and passed more than a score of resolutions censuring him and delaying the passage of necessary public Bills. *Pourparlers* with the Opposition came to nothing. Pitt absolutely refused to serve with North, but though that lord magnanimously withdrew all pretensions to office, Pitt and George III would not bow to the coalition's demands that the Minister resign prior to negotiations and that the King personally commission Portland to undertake an arrangement. A group of respectable country gentlemen, meeting at the St. Albans tavern, tried to effect a compromise which would produce a new 'broad bottom'. The debonair Lord Nugent, recalling that he had reconciled Pelham and Granville over a glass of wine, invited the antagonists to 'get gloriously drunk' at his house as the best means to settle their differences.[3] No suggestion, grave or gay, could persuade either side to abandon its position.

The Opposition were at first confident of a quick return to office. By the immediate passage of resolutions hampering the financial operations of the Government, they hoped to have

[1] W. T. Laprade, ed., *The Parliamentary Papers of John Robinson, 1774–1784* (London, 1922).

[2] *P.H.* xxiv. 202.

[3] Ibid. 634; D. G. Barnes, *George III and William Pitt, 1783–1806* (Palo Alto and London, 1939), pp. 71–100.

prevented a dissolution, and they did not see how Pitt could stand against their majority in the House then sitting. They grew increasingly surprised and baffled as the 'schoolboy Minister' time after time defied 'the uniform maxims' of the Constitution by remaining in office. Unlike North he quailed neither before the threat of censure nor censure itself. To their genuine astonishment the Opposition found that George and Pitt had changed the rules of the game without notice. Fox was wary of a 'snare', fearful of overplaying his hand. Calling for temper and moderation, he tried to wear down the Court by successive defeats, interspersed by brief adjournments to allow time for reconsideration. He postponed but would not stop Supplies or the Mutiny Bill, but Pitt's stubbornness drove him to stronger and more explicit resolutions. Finally on 8 March he brought in 'an humble representation' to the King, which was in effect a tract on the Constitution. Fox's majority, which had been declining sporadically since December, was now reduced to one vote. 'The enemy seem indeed to be on their backs', wrote Pitt, but though he still dreaded making some mistake that would give an advantage to the Opposition, the struggle was over.[1] Fox tried to forestall a dissolution by promising to let the Supplies pass, but when essential business had been concluded, Pitt dissolved on 25 March.

During these three months the Commons' attention was devoted almost exclusively to the Constitutional issue, and before the contest ended Pitt remarked that the debates had become 'a fatiguing and disagreeable reiteration of beaten themes and of hackneyed arguments'.[2] Certainly there was nothing left to add, then or for years to come, on the subject of the appointment of ministers, which was discussed with unprecedented poignancy and frankness. These debates and the conduct of the partisans have a peculiar historic importance as guide posts for Constitutional theory and political action for the remainder of the Georgian era.

The Opposition reapplied the traditional arguments employed

---

[1] *Correspondence between the Right Honble. William Pitt and Charles Duke of Rutland* (Edinburgh and London, 1890), pp. 7–8.

[2] *P.H.* xxiv. 708. The debates occupy roughly 500 columns. The fear of a dissolution may have discouraged the introduction of private Bills, but the journals nevertheless show that Parliament transacted a respectable amount of minor business.

against North and Shelburne. Portland's Ministry had taken office by Constitutional means, whereas Pitt had crept in by secret influence. North said with unblushing candour,[1]

if we became possessed of government, we are at worst charged with having carried it by storm, bravely, in the face of the enemy, not by sap; we carried on our advances regularly, and above ground, in view of the foe; not by mining in the dark and blowing up the fort before the garrison knew there was an intention to attack it.

The fortress of the Constitution, other speakers pursued the argument, should be manned by its 'natural defenders', the House of Commons, who speak for the people of England. An administration without a majority does not possess the confidence of the nation. The House, therefore, has the right and duty to negative the appointments of the Crown (without giving reasons, if such is its will), to hold ministers accountable for any misuse of the Prerogative, and to refuse Supply until the King chooses ministers who possess its confidence. He must take the advice of the Commons upon whom to dismiss and whom to appoint, for in this matter 'the Crown was endowed with no faculty whatever of a private nature'. The Prerogative, a public trust confided to the King for the common weal, is to be exercised in conformity with the popular will. If an administration can take office and govern in defiance of the House, the 'Constitutional remedy of opposition' will be annihilated, the Commons made 'a mere appendage to the Court', and the balance of the Constitution irretrievably destroyed.[2]

To buttress their position the 'patriots' appealed to Constitutional history as far back as the reign of Richard II. The powers of the Commons were 'hitherto undisputed', asserted Fox, except 'in those melancholy times which were still the opprobrium of our history, and involved a series of the most awful and affecting calamities that ever degraded and disgraced a great and brave people'. Since the Revolution no monarch

---

[1] Ibid. 255–6.

[2] The phrases quoted are to be found in ibid. 273, 460, 489, 694. Most of the speeches, as reported, are rambling discourses about the particular resolution on the Floor. The best succinct exposition of Opposition doctrine is Stormont's address to the Lords (ibid. 518–23). For examples of Opposition pamphlets published at this time, see *Vulgar Errors, Secret Influence Public Ruin!*, *The True State of the Question*, *The Source of the Evil*, and *A Vindication of the Conduct of the Late House of Commons with Respect to the Great Constitutional Question Agitated Immediately before its Dissolution*.

had overstepped his bounds. George III himself had until this crisis accepted the conventions on which the Opposition based its conduct. Now the House apprehended a 'dangerous innovation', unprecedented under the happy rule of the Brunswick line, which only Pitt's resignation or dismissal, considered as an acknowledgement of error, could correct.[1]

When challenged to carry his ideas to their logical extreme by stopping Supply, Fox showed his true colours. The rights of the Commons, like the royal Prerogative, must be exercised for the public welfare. The House should 'withhold the purse of the people' only upon a calculation of probable advantage to the community at large. To do so at present would plunge the nation into irreparable confusion. Why then had he voted against the Supplies in 1781? Because he knew that, if such a motion was carried, North would have resigned, but he feared that Pitt would not. In this case the Opposition should exert its power only 'in the last extremity', that is, at the risk of civil war. Because of this danger, Fox admitted, the right to withhold supply *entirely* 'was in a great measure gone from the House'— here he was thinking of the refusal of subsidies in Tudor and Stuart times—but the House retained the right to *delay* financial legislation 'which it might, and ought still to exercise, whenever a proper occasion should occur'. Delay was to be regarded as a menace, in the face of which a minister who loved the Constitution would retire; if the bluff was called, a loyal Opposition must waive, but not abandon, the use of this 'undoubted legal and Constitutional mode of obtaining redress'.[2]

Both in word and deed Fox thus rejected the *ultima ratio* to which politicians had for so long assumed that a determined Opposition would resort. The threat to stop Supply was now shown to be a hoax, a sham convention which could be ignored.

[1] *P.H.* xxiv. 440, 595–8, 679, 687–90, 736–9.

[2] Ibid. 460, 579, 582, 602, 619–21, 640–2, 657, 692–3, 735, 738. Fox's careful explanations that he meant only to delay Supply may have encouraged George and Pitt to persevere. The coalition had to tread warily, however, for fear of alienating support by rash and extreme measures, and though bitterly chagrined, they probably did not believe in their hearts that the King's defiance was a subversion of the Constitution that justified the use of violent measures. There is an interesting comment upon why the Opposition could no longer use 'the command of the purse' to coerce the King in a Foxite pamphlet entitled *We have been all in the Wrong; or, Thoughts upon the Dissolution of the Late, and Conduct of the Present Parliament* (London, 1785), pp. 3–4.

The most extreme of 'patriot' leaders had confessed that the Commons could not employ this means to compel the dismissal of ministers, which even some Tories accepted, or to designate their successors, which the true Whigs took for granted. It is among the greatest paradoxes in Constitutional history that this convention, defied by the Court and repudiated by the Opposition, should with the passage of time have again been received as a venerable usage by men of every political complexion.

In his defence Pitt refused to be drawn into debate over precedents or pointed references to his father's career. He often sat silent, maintaining that a minister was not obligated to answer 'the interrogatories of private individuals'. Only a question duly moved and seconded brought him to his feet, and his speeches were usually brief and guarded—evasive and sullen, said the Opposition. Continually stressing his own righteousness and integrity, he stayed cautiously upon the solid ground of recognized Constitutional law, rarely making a sally that might expose a weakness. His replies revealed some inconsistencies, but on the whole he and his colleagues presented a uniform argument.

The charge of secret influence was repudiated as nothing more than 'a fine catch-word of a party to amuse the credulous vulgar and to raise discontents against the sovereign or particular persons'. If there was any truth in it, let it be proven. The King had exercised his unquestionable right to appoint a minister of his own choice, and Pitt declared unequivocally that he took responsibility for advising His Majesty to keep him in office. The Commons might legally address the Crown for his removal, but their request was not binding. In the employment of the Prerogative the King followed the resolutions of the House only when, in his judgement, they charted the course best calculated to advance the public good. To the Commons' addresses George III replied that he could not see how Pitt's dismissal would be conducive to the formation of the 'firm, efficient, united, and extended administration' which everyone professed to desire. Acknowledging their right to advise him, he therefore rejected their advice. The King's answers also noted that the House had laid no specific charge or complaint against any of his ministers, and Pitt steadily challenged the Opposition to impeach him if he had in any way violated the Constitution:

impeachment was the one fair, legal, incontestable method of removing evil advisers.[1]

His retention of office, Pitt contended, was essential to preserve the Prerogative and the balance of the Constitution. He would neither incriminate himself by resigning nor admit the right of the Commons to nominate ministers by advising the King to dismiss him. It was most 'unfortunate' that he did not possess the confidence of the House, but no *law* forbade a minister to keep his place without a majority. What then of his injunction to the coalition to resign when they could not answer for their measures? On this point events forced him to shift his ground. First he asserted that he had come into office on the India issue. No ministry should be condemned untried. Let the House judge him by his measures. When his India Bill was defeated in January, he retired to his position as defender of the Prerogative and broadened the definition of confidence. A ministry must have the confidence not only of the Commons but also of the King, Lords, and People. The King (by accepting Pitt's advice), the Lords (by voting an Address to the Throne), and the People (by hundreds of addresses) had expressed their confidence in him. An administration not possessed of a majority in the Lower House, he admitted, could not last long. But how long? The question remained open. The Pittites simply referred to the prerogative of calling a general election, by which the wishes of the people would be truly reflected in the Commons, to bring all Constitutional authorities into harmony.[2]

The Dissolution of 1784 was an avowed attempt to secure endorsement of the views held by Pitt and George III. The King's Speech at the end of the session, in formal but unmistakable language, called upon the people to approve his use of the Prerogative. The Court's triumph was overwhelming. Roughly one hundred supporters of the coalition lost their seats. At the opening of the new Parliament Pitt carried by 282 to 114 an

---

[1] *P.H.* xxiv. 307, 433, 442–3, 610, 657–64, 678–9, 709–10, 717.

[2] Ibid. 233, 310–11, 589–90, 595, 609, 616–17. For tactical reasons Pitt himself refused to make any commitment on the subject of a dissolution, and his friends in the House treated the issue delicately. Pittite pamphleteers, however, showed no reticence: see *A Letter to a Country Gentleman*, *A Second Letter to a Country Gentleman*, *A Candid Investigation of the Present Prevailing Topic*, *Thoughts on the Idea of Another Coalition*, *The Whig-Catechism*, *Five Minutes' Advice to the People preparatory to the Ensuing General Election*.

Address which thanked the King for saving the Constitution. Ministerialist speakers declared that the election result was a correct public decision upon the Constitutional issue, which must now be considered as once and for all determined. Opponents talked glumly of 'popular phrenzy' and objected to the Address as 'adding a degree of insult to victory and exercising an arrogant and indecent triumph at the expense of the conquered'. Four weeks later Burke read to the House a lengthy 'representation to the King' in vindication of the coalition. It was negatived without debate or division. The feeble protests of the Opposition make it clear that the majority of Parliament men accepted the outcome of the election as the verdict of the people.[1]

No Opposition could yet hope to defeat the Treasury. Pitt's agents had been hard at work in the constituencies and with the holders of electoral interests since December. The Court had made efforts on an unprecedented scale to capture popular opinion. Numerous prints and pamphlets were widely disseminated, and Ministerialists secured 228 loyal addresses signed by thousands.[2] As in all the previous elections of the century, private men could not match the resources and organization of Whitehall. Yet there is good reason to believe that the result was, as most contemporaries thought, in accord with the popular will. No issue had ever been more fully publicized. The Opposition produced many screeds of its own, and the newspapers printed the debates, in which the orations from the Speaker's left were by far the more prominent. In contests where opinion could be tried, it appears that 'the cry of prerogative' had a powerful influence. As Pares has observed, 'the nation was not yet ripe to receive Charles Fox's doctrine that kings should reign but should not govern'.[3]

[1] Ibid. 829–43, 940–75. In the debate on the Address only Lord Surrey, a parliamentary reformer, challenged the verdict of the election. The other members of the coalition confined their criticism to the misuse of the prerogative of dissolution. The debate suggests that one reason the contest for Westminster was so hard fought was that Fox's return by that great constituency constituted the Opposition's sole claim to popular favour.

[2] Mrs. Eric George, 'Fox's Martyrs: The General Election of 1784', in *Trans. R. Hist. Soc.* xxi. 152.

[3] *King George III and the Politicians*, pp. 133–5, 196–7; cf. Watson, *Reign of George III*, pp. 270–2.

Coroner's Inquest

Thus was resolved the Constitutional solecism which Egmont had perceived in Walpole's time. A resolute king could not be distressed into taking ministers he did not want. The Opposition would not stop Supply, and the resources of the Crown were still great enough to destroy a majority against the Court. George III successfully defied the House of Commons and the Septennial Convention in 1784—a defiance which would have been inexpedient in 1742—because he made very skilful use of his assets in more favourable circumstances. The timid, inexperienced boy who mounted the throne had become a deft and courageous politician. After bowing to the coalition, he gave up despairing thoughts of abdication and determined to find men to help him restore the rights of monarchy. In Pitt he had a new man with recognized talent and a great name, not a Walpole who suffered from increasing jealousy and unpopularity, nor a North who had lost half an empire, nor a Shelburne who was distrusted even by his colleagues. The coalition, on the other hand, had since its formation been under severe attack as unethical and unprincipled, and Fox's India Bill was made to look like another 'power grab' by greedy placemen. The reforms of 1782 had not seriously impaired the influence of the Crown, and George III had trusty servants like John Robinson who knew how to use it. The King's cause, the Prerogative of choosing his ministers, rested on solid Constitutional ground, which his opponents had perforce to acknowledge. By every means he could employ with propriety he displayed his determination, so that waverers could locate the winning side. The public response to the royal appeal showed that the King could command greater loyalty than a loyal Opposition.

The 'system of opposition', in Wilberforce's phrase, had been undermined.[1] The closet might be stormed, but against the King's wishes it could not be held. What prospect, then, lay before the Oppositions of the future? Individuals and flying squadrons might strive for an accommodation because, with the exception of Fox, George III was willing as always to make accessions to a ministry in being. Since there was an adult heir to the throne, malcontents might cultivate the 'reversionary

[1] *P.H.* xxiv. 705.

resource'. Storming-parties had to return to Rockingham's long-term calculation that some unforeseen disaster must some day turn Parliament against ministers and force a change of attitude upon the King. Fox and North candidly avowed their hopes on this score by reminding Pitt that majorities were treacherous.[1] In short, the Opposition was thrown back upon the tactics in vogue before the fall of North.

The 'storms' of 1782 and 1783 had tested the assumption, nurtured by Rockinghamites since 1767 but hitherto untried, that a majority in the Commons could give the law to the King without exception or restraint. The assumption was derived from their concepts of the way in which Walpole, Pulteney, the Pelhams, and the elder Pitt had forced the hand of the first two Georges. The Opposition overlooked the fact that their pre-cedents were ministerial reconstructions in which a measure of compromise was involved. The King was presumed to possess some 'faculty of a private nature'. Both in negotiations and in office successful politicians, however overbearing in word and intention, paid some deference to the sovereign's personal wishes and took pains to make themselves palatable to him. In his resistance to Rockingham and Fox in 1782 and to the coali-tion in 1783 George III reasserted the private faculty which the Opposition called secret influence but which, though modified since the breakdown of Bute, the King had persistently striven to exercise. In this sense he 'restored' personal monarchy and checked the Opposition's assumption, never made by the shrewder politicians of earlier generations, that they could deal with the King as a disembodied institution rather than as a human being.

His successful resistance did not entail the destruction or delay of responsible government. Pitt was not a royal favourite. As Prime Minister he became fully as responsible, Constitu-tionally and politically, as any of his predecessors. The com-plaint of the Opposition was that he acquired office by misuse of the prerogative of appointment and was secured in office by the misuse of the prerogative of dissolution. Burke's 'representa-tion' in June 1784, which he called a 'coroner's inquest' upon the late Parliament, pointed out that if the events of 1784 were drawn into precedent, the House of Commons could be

[1] Ibid. 839–40.

new-modelled to support any ministry selected by the King. Thus, he contended, the law of the Constitution would be inverted: parliaments would be chosen for the approval of ministers, not ministers for the approval of Parliament.[1] Here again the Opposition disregarded the facts of history. Ever since Cowper had told George I that timely electioneering could always get a majority for the servants he favoured, Parliaments had been chosen to support the Ministry of the day. George III's innovation was to make a spectacular breach of the Septennial Convention in mid-session to get a majority for a ministry censured by the Parliament in being.

There was never to be a repetition of 1784, but George III's innovation did set an important precedent. Henceforward the King would grant a dissolution to a ministry which, for whatever reason, he wished to keep in office. The 'outs' of every description continued for a time to object. The Pittite Opposition condemned the Dissolution of 1806 as an unwarrantable use of the Prerogative. The Talents revived Burke's argument to protest the Dissolution of 1807.[2] But the progress of reform from 1782 onward gradually reduced the influence of the Crown, and the Court became increasingly less sure of obtaining a parliamentary majority by any means but the approval of a majority of the electorate and electoral interests.[3] In time, therefore, the Opposition acquired an equal chance with the Government to capture popular opinion, and a dissolution became an appeal to the people on a broader scale. The use of the Prerogative, condemned by the 'outs' as an instrument of personal government, was in fact, as the 'ins' had insisted, an instrument of responsible government.[4]

2. THE *ÂMES DAMNEÉS* OF MR. FOX, 1784–1801

During Pitt's first Ministry a declining Opposition laboured under the lengthening shadow of 1784. The coalition were the survivors of a lost cause, excommunicated for Constitutional

[1] *P.H.* xxiv. 960.
[2] Hansard, viii. 59–60, 80–81; ix, 615–16, 636–8, 648–9.
[3] A. S. Foord, 'The Waning of the Influence of the Crown', *E.H.R.* lxii. 484–507.
[4] See the comments of Lord John Russell, *Mem. and Corresp. of C. J. Fox*, ii. 245–6; Pares, *King George III and the Politicians*, pp. 134, 140–2.

heresy and damned for political ineptitude. The greatest experiment in Opposition had failed, and, as Fox later observed, that failure made them wrong in the eyes of the world.[1]

Defections began early. In 1785 William Eden, a prominent Northite, went over to the Government. Ministerialists gloated at this event, fine proof 'of what a set of rascals the Opposition is composed'.[2] 'Patriots' were still for sale. Yet for six years a band of about 115 reliables could be mustered on the Speaker's left, and to compensate for losses the coalition acquired such outstanding recruits as Charles Grey and Samuel Whitbread. Then the French Revolution tore the party in twain.

Fox and his *âmes damnées*, following the line taken by the Opposition in the 1770's, hailed the struggle of another people to assert their rights. From 1790 to 1794 the more conservative members gradually drew away from him. Burke was the first to break, renouncing even personal friendship with his old colleague. Portland faced in agony the prospect of wrecking the Whig party, in whose creed, as set forth by Burke, he believed with an almost religious fervour. After prolonged efforts to reach an accommodation with Fox, the Duke consented to the formation of a separate party at Burlington House in January 1794.[3] Six months later this group joined the Ministry.

With Portland went nearly every Northite and the bulk of those who vaunted their hereditary Whiggism. Fox now led a small Opposition comprised of his personal following, the Prince's coterie, and a few libertarian Radicals. In 1795 he struck up a working agreement with Shelburne (now Lansdowne),[4] and an occasional newcomer like George Tierney took his seat on the Speaker's left. Still, numbers continued to diminish. Only 63 voted for Grey's amendment to the Address in 1801. The change of ministry in that year looked like a deathblow to the Opposition. Upon George III's refusal to consent to Catholic Emancipation, Pitt resigned even though he commanded an overwhelming majority. The King replaced him with Addington, whose only recommendation was a respectable

[1] Russell, *Mem. and Corresp. of C. J. Fox*, iii. 135, 152.

[2] *H.M.C., Rutland MSS.* iii. 270–1, 277.

[3] Add. MSS. 33630, ff. 1–5, 11, 15–16; 33631, ff. 4–5; 36629, ff. 27–30; 37889, ff. 210–13.

[4] Fitzmaurice, *Shelburne*, ii. 408, 418; Russell, *Mem. and Corresp. of C. J. Fox*, iii. 112–13, 127–9.

tenure of the Speaker's chair, and within a short time it appeared that the new Minister was firmly entrenched in office. What limit was there to the power of the Crown? groaned Fox. The coalition had given George III a battle in 1784, but in 1801 the Commons supinely accepted a nonentity of the King's choosing in place of a great minister from whom they had not withdrawn their confidence. In May 1802 Fox wrote to Grey, 'All Opposition seems to be out of the question, perhaps for ever; and we may boast, I expect, that we were the last of the Romans.'[1]

Their continued existence in the face of such steady discouragement offers some evidence of the degree to which Opposition had taken root in the British political system. To an extent, it may be said, the Foxites carried on the struggle because, if they wished to stay in politics, there was nothing else to do. But they were fortified in their persistence in an apparently desperate cause by several noteworthy assets: their leadership, their organization, their sincere conviction of the need for an Opposition, and their hope, abandoned for a short time only in the darkest hours, that the traditional devices of opposition might bring the traditional reward in the unforeseeable future.

Charles James Fox possessed an unusual personal magnetism. Despite his ugly grudges, the open scandal of his private life, and the errors of his public career, his warm and generous personality attracted friends in a manner rare among politicans. His speeches as recorded are remarkably persuasive. Though he often spoke at length, he rarely delivered a set declamation after the fashion of Burke and Sheridan. He was a debater rather than an orator, adroit in directing his remarks to the specific issues under discussion, drawing his opponents' arguments into ridicule, and arranging in logical and witty form the reason on his side. A man could give his vote to Fox with pride and conviction. Bred to be a placeman, then schooled by the Rockinghamites, he learned superbly well how to employ his natural talents in the direction of a political following. One of his inveterate enemies, the Duke of Leeds, paid him this extraordinary tribute in 1792:[2]

As leaders of a party there is scarcely a competition (in point of

---

[1] Russell, *Mem. and Corresp. of C. J. Fox*, iii. 325, 367–8.
[2] Add. MSS. 27916, ff. 62–63.

management) that can possibly be urged. Mr. Fox is without doubt the best leader of a party that the memory of any man living or the history of this country (no bad climate for cultivating such a commodity) can afford us. . . .

[He] lives with as well as by his connexions, attentive to the discipline, even the smallest minutiae of the corps he commands; no local interest of an individual composing this corps is to him the object of indifference—witness the other day the attendance of Brooks' Club upon the question respecting the Rochdale navigation. Lord Derby's property was likely to be injured had the Bill passed. Mr. Fox himself attended, and numerous phalanx under his command disposed of the Bill without difficulty, for no other reason that I know of but the noble earl above-mentioned being interested in the event.

I do not mean the decision was wrong, but only mention this as a proof of good discipline in Mr. Fox's corps, and for which I think he himself is entitled seriously speaking to merit, and in this I sincerely wish Mr. Pitt would generally condescend to imitate him. I am aware that experience proves how much better the followers of opposition are drilled, and how much better they are collected and formed for actual operation than the supporters of ministry have usually been.

Fox's outstanding qualities gave him an unchallenged pre-eminence in the Opposition. The party was fortunate also in the adhesion of Charles Grey. This attractive Northumbrian squire early demonstrated talents which fitted him to be an effective aristocratic politician. His mind was quick, and he spoke brilliantly. Though sensitive and inclined to be irascible, he could charm when he chose. He became a firm believer in hereditary Whiggism, but the more Radical members of the party favoured him because of his espousal of parliamentary reform and his strong stand in defence of popular liberties. Grey rose so rapidly in stature that by the mid-1790's Fox appears to have regarded him as his first lieutenant, to be consulted on all important decisions, and as the coming leader of the party.

Brooks's Club remained the party centre. Its membership, consisting primarily of peers and Members of Parliament, became less socially exclusive and more politically inclusive.[1] Meetings were held there during sessions, and there the Whips had their headquarters. George Byng, the incomparable muster-master, lost his seat in 1784, but despite occasional

[1] *Memorials of Brooks's*, p. xii.

complaints about the lax discipline of the Opposition, his role was ably filled by Sheridan, Lord Maitland, and Sir James Erskine. The institution of a club as a focus of activity was an instrument, second only in importance to Fox's leadership, in securing the survival of the party.

The Whig Club was founded in 1784 by John Bellamy, a silk mercer, to assist Fox in the great Westminster election and to uphold Revolution principles in the metropolis. Members paid annual dues to an elected treasurer who was authorized to invest in consols to increase the club's capital. An elected secretary managed general activities, chief of which were eight monthly dinners, held at various London taverns from November through June. The constitution prescribed nine standing toasts to the most sacred symbols in the Whig tradition. In the 1790's it became the custom to schedule a great dinner on 24 January, Fox's birthday. The club proved such a success that by 1792 its membership limit had been raised from the original 100 to 700, composed for the most part of the Foxites in both Houses of Parliament and lawyers, merchants, and men of many trades in London and Westminster. Within a few years other Whig clubs sprang up in Southwark, several provincial towns, and even in Dublin. Their members when in town were accorded the courtesy of attending the dinners in Westminster. The Whig Club thus became the first broad party association of a more than temporary or local character.[1]

The club did much to spread the spirit of Whiggism and Opposition throughout the country. In 1794 a pamphlet observed, 'Its sentiments and even its toasts were industriously circulated through the kingdom; its resolutions not unfrequently claimed the attention of Parliament; it maintained from the capital a political correspondence with the distant counties.'[2] To aid in the parliamentary campaign of 1796 'The Declaration

[1] The rules, standing toasts, and a list of the membership are to be found in *Whig Club, Instituted in May 1784, by John Bellamy* (London, 1792). On the Whig Club of Dublin see Henry Grattan, *Memoirs of the Life and Times of the Rt. Hon. Henry Grattan* (London, 1849), iii. 428–38. For an account of a meeting, see *The Speech of the Right Hon. Charles James Fox. . . . Spoken at the Whig Club of England, Dec. 4, 1792* (London, 1792). Meetings were usually reported also in the *Morning Chronicle*.

[2] [Charles Pigott], *The Whig Club: or A Sketch of Modern Patriotism* (London, 1794), pp. 5–6. I am indebted to Mr. Donald E. Ginter for assistance in locating material on the club.

of and Form of Association recommended by the Whig Club'
against the Seditious Meetings and Treasonable Practices Acts
was widely distributed. Members of the club also founded
other extra-parliamentary organizations modelled on Wyvill's
Yorkshire Association. Thomas Erskine was the moving spirit
in the 'Friends of the Liberty of the Press'. In 1792 Grey
established the 'Friends of the People' to promote parliamentary
reform. The associators had little effect upon opinion at large
—like all evangelists they spent much of their time preaching
to the converted—but these were significant experiments in
forming pressure groups to support a party programme.

The Opposition also made increasing use of the Press, whose
influence upon the public mind was recognized to be growing
rapidly during these years. Politicians were more sensitive than
ever to attacks upon them in print, and they understood the
need to keep their views steadily before the country. Fox's
general policy was to have all important subjects treated at
length in pamphlets, then to carry on debate through paragraphs in newspapers.[1] Crises brought forth special efforts. A
Government screed thus described Opposition activity during
the Regency debates of 1788–9:[2]

. . . it is a principle of the party to hold in high estimation the
auxiliary powers of the public prints; . . . a subordinate committee
of themselves sits daily, and perhaps nightly too, at a well-known
tavern in Covent Garden to shape paragraphs, frame hand-bills,
and propagate falsehoods; in short, to do their utmost by any and
every means to inflame the people against the King's friends and to
influence the public mind in favour of their own masters.

Nay, so much do the Opposition seem to depend on this mode
of proceeding that a provincial newspaper in my neighbourhood
has been purchased to abuse government, and inflammatory hand-
bills seem to have been blown through the air to our market towns,
in order . . . to make people as glad as the writers of them that the
king was out of his mind.

The party became perforce involved in the deep game of
influencing the venal metropolitan newspapers. Sheridan, who
enjoyed the elaborate skullduggery of manipulating the Press,
took a prominent part in acquiring and directing Opposition

[1] Russell, *Mem. and Corresp. of C. J. Fox*, ii. 274–5.
[2] [William Combe], *A Letter from a Country Gentleman to a Member of Parliament on
the Present State of Public Affairs* (London, 1789), p. 48.

papers. Out of the welter of partisan journalism the *Morning Chronicle* emerged as a respectable party publication. James Perry, who became its editor in 1789, lived on terms of friendship with the Foxite front-benchers. He was their ally, not their hireling. He excluded scandal from the *Chronicle* and refrained from the vicious personal attacks which had hitherto constituted so much of political argument. His paper became a Whig institution, an organ upon which the party could rely as its public advocate.[1]

The importance which the Opposition attached to publicity stemmed largely from the events of 1784. The coalition well understood how much propaganda had done for Pitt, and they realized that they could not storm the closet with the country against them. It would do no good to defeat ministers in Parliament, Portland wrote in 1785, 'until the eyes of the public are opened to their own interest'.[2] For a long time Fox clung to the traditional hope that, if the Opposition remained united and vigorous, ministers would eventually hang themselves. He took comfort in recalling how the opposition to North had grown from small beginnings during the American Revolution, and when Pitt embarked upon war with Revolutionary France, Fox thought his party should gather new strength 'if anything happened as it used to do'.[3] Surely in a major war the Government must meet with some reverses that would enable the Opposition to repeat the successes of 1742, 1756, and 1782. Pitt's unprecedented ability to surmount every crisis deepened his opponents' conviction that they must strive to capture the public mind. 'Opinion itself is regulated from above', Fox remarked. After the change of Government in 1801, he wrote, 'It must be from movements out of doors and not in Parliament that opposition can ever gain any strength, I mean of course *as* opposition. What the King's death or illness might produce is another question.'[4]

[1] M. S. Hardcastle, *Life of John, Lord Campbell* (London, 1881), i, 179; Aspinall, *Politics and the Press*, pp. 270–98. Perry's independence and the impossibility of pleasing all when the leaders disagreed occasionally led to complaints that the *Chronicle* was unsatisfactory as a party organ. In fact, Perry steered a remarkably even course among the factions that developed among the Whigs.
[2] Portland Papers (Nottingham), Portland to Titchfield, 28 June 1785.
[3] *P.H.* xxx. 363–4; Russell, *Mem. and Corresp. of C. J. Fox*, iii. 80, 88–93.
[4] Ibid. iii. 190–1, 239.

The Prince of Wales was their only other hope. After Fox settled down in 1784 with the mistress who later became his wife, his personal intimacy with young George declined, but they remained close political friends. The Prince built a party under the leadership of his favourite, Lord Rawdon, later Earl of Moira and Marquis of Hastings, who considered this coterie as an auxiliary, but not a part of, the Foxite connexion.[1] They co-operated fairly well, even though the Prince declared his support of the French war at its outset. The Foxites joined heartily in the recurring parliamentary schemes to repair His Royal Highness's shaky finances, and the two groups voted together so frequently that political calculators generally lumped them both under the heading of Opposition.

When George III went mad toward the end of 1788, the Prince's friends thought their day had dawned. The Prince sent post-haste for Fox, who was vacationing in Italy. A shadow Cabinet was constructed, and the much denigrated coalition anticipated a gleeful revenge upon their traducers before the year was out.[2] Pitt meant to thwart them if he could. Upon the chance that the King might recover, he manœuvred to delay a regency as long as possible. To limit their triumph, he brought in a Regency Bill which forbade the Prince to dispense honours, restricted his disposal of patronage, and vested control of the royal Household in the Queen. The 'patriots' resisted vehemently. The heir to the throne had a Constitutional right, they contended, to assume a regent's full powers without legislation. He succeeded by the fundamental law of hereditary monarchy, and Parliament could not interfere. Restrictions upon his use of the Prerogative were unconstitutional, administratively unsound, and politically base. The King's ministers would surely go into Opposition to the regent's Government, a course which the coalition affected to approve, but 'as a pledge to the country for the sincerity of their Opposition' they should relinquish all share in the patronage and emoluments of office 'which fairly belonged to the servants of the Crown and to those who acted with them'. Nothing could be more scandalous than to allow

---

[1] *H.M.C., Knox MSS.*, pp. 203–8. Cf. William Knox's *Considerations on the Present State of the Nation. Addressed to the Right Hon. Lord Rawdon* (London, 1789) and *Extra Official Papers Addressed to Lord Rawdon* (London, 1789). There were some, notably Sheridan, who regarded themselves as members of both parties.

[2] Russell, *Mem. and Corresp. of C. J. Fox*, ii. 299–300; iv. 283–5.

Pitt to 'erect the standard of Opposition in the centre of the Queen's palace'.[1]

When Fox declared for hereditary succession, Pitt remarked, 'I'll *unwhig* the gentleman for the rest of his life.'[2] It has since been the general view that Fox gave the lie to all his previous professions by defending the Prerogative against the rights of Parliament. The situation was too complex for so plain a judgement. In the absence of exact precedents for the establishment of a regency in the event of the King's madness, whether temporary or permanent, each side used what arguments it could muster to support its own position. Pitt, just as much as Fox, was playing politics, and he was neither more nor less consistent in principle. He hoped that the Prince's friends could not hold the Government without the influence of the Crown, and to deny them this influence was to render ineffective the regent's choice of ministers. Fox had insisted that the Crown must choose servants who had the confidence of the Commons. For the regent to remove Pitt, who possessed that confidence, would have been inconsistent with the Opposition resolutions of 1784. But with the general election of that year in mind, Fox thought that the influence of the Crown and a strenuous propaganda campaign could get him the majority he needed. In one sense, therefore, Fox was playing Pitt's old game because 1784 had proved it to be a winning game; in another, he was playing the much older game of Townshend, Compton, Egmont, and Bute. Yet Fox continued to assert that, if he did not acquire the confidence of the House, he would retire in accordance with the Constitutional principles he had always avowed.[3]

The King's recovery in February 1789 shelved the regency issue for the time being. His health continued to be precarious, however, and Carlton House remained prepared for his death or the recurrence of his insanity. Upon assuming the regal power, the Prince intended to make a ministry under Moira from Foxites and their allies.[4] They did not, as far as the evidence

---

[1] *P.H.* xxvii. 1031, 1056–7, 1086.

[2] Stanhope, *Pitt*, ii. 5.

[3] *P.H.* xxvii. 1033. It was quite possible that under an unrestricted regency Fox could have got a majority without a general election: see the estimate of Pitt's secretary in *H.M.C., Rep. XII*, app. 9, p. 373.

[4] See the shadow Cabinet of 1798 printed in Fitzmaurice, *Shelburne*, ii. 428.

shows, construct a 'great outline'. The existence of an experienced, organized Opposition party in league with His Royal Highness made such an elaborate plan unnecessary. The future George IV had materials unavailable to Frederick in the days of 'broad bottom'. The assurance that the Prince's accession entailed their own, as long as they demonstrated their ability to replace the old King's Government, was a strong encouragement for the Foxites to sustain a strenuous Opposition.

Until 1797 the Foxites also persisted in their course out of a sense of duty. The leaders with a lust for parliamentary combat certainly enjoyed making a good performance at Westminster, but it became increasingly tedious to study Pitt's Bills, many of them very technical, and to go down to the House day after day to heckle an invincible majority. They did so, they asserted with evident sincerity, because only an Opposition, no matter how weak, afforded any hope of checking the excesses of power and maintaining the Constitution. Fox once pointed out sardonically that whenever the Government brought in unpopular legislation, the very men who kept Pitt in place looked to the 'Opposition as the standing counsel against the Crown in that House, ever to be resorted to in moments of difficulty, and therefore as necessary to exist as an administration'.[1] When the Portland group turned against Fox, Grey reaffirmed his faith in the leader of the Opposition:[2]

> The state of the country calls upon him to stand in the gap and defend the Constitution. He has said he will do so; and while I have power of body or mind, he shall not stand alone. A firm band of admiring friends, not the less respectable nor the less likely to prevail from the present disproportion of their number, will faithfully stand by him against all the calumnies of those who betray while they affect to defend the Constitution.

Such declarations usually evoked barbed retorts from the Treasury Bench. Sometimes the House rehashed all the arguments in the great debate of 1784. The Foxites were always condemned with the time-worn epithets—malignant, factious, greedy for power. As in the time of Walpole, however, the Government conceded a legitimate role to the Opposition in

---

[1] *P.H.* xxviii. 245–6. Cf. Sheridan's statement on the duty of the Opposition in ibid. xxix. 210.
[2] Ibid. xxx. 85.

the abstract. Of the many ministerial statements, this by Lord Camden in 1788 was typical:[1]

> Though in office himself, he declared he honoured an Opposition; and he had no scruple to say that he thought an Opposition of great service to the country when conducted on public principles. An Opposition awed ministers and kept them vigilant. It checked their career, put them upon their guard, taught them where error lay, and how to correct it.

A pamphlet written by Henry Mackenzie, 'the northern Addison', directly under the eye of Pitt, was even more emphatic. Unconstitutional ambition was reprobated in the usual terms, but said Mackenzie,[2]

> The Opposition in Britain is a sort of public body which, in the practice at least of our government, is perfectly known and established. The province of this ex-official body, when it acts in a manner salutary to the state, is to watch with jealousy over the conduct of administration; to correct the abuses and to resist the corruptions of its power; to restrain whatever may be excessive, to moderate what may be inconsiderate, and to supply what may be defective in its measures.

The Pittites thus took a short step beyond 'measures, not men'. They allowed the Opposition to be a body, i.e. a party. They granted it semi-official status. They required it to be constructive as well as critical. But the exercise of its 'functions', as Mackenzie called them, must not be inspired by ambition for office. During the regency crisis Pitt half-admitted that, upon a change of ministry, he would go into Opposition but not 'a factious opposition in order to disturb the necessary measures of government'. Considering the Minister's record, Grey commented, this meant no more than that Pitt affected to endow with virtue any Opposition in which he took part—a scarcely unique claim.[3]

---

[1] *P.H.* xxvii. 243.

[2] *A Review of the Principal Proceedings of the Parliament of 1784* (London, 1792), p. 174. Of the other Pittite pamphlets on Opposition the most interesting are George Chalmers, *Opposition Politics, Exemplified* (London, 1786), which makes extensive use of Perceval's *Faction Detected; The Letters of an Englishman; in which the Principles and Conduct of the Rockingham Party, when in Administration and Opposition, are Freely and Impartially Displayed* (London, 1786), which contains an attack on Burke's *Thoughts*; and [William Combe], *Considerations on the Approaching Dissolution of Parliament* (London, 1790), which defends party as an instrument both of the Government and the Opposition. [3] *P.H.* xxvii. 1007–8, 1016–17.

During the first few years of Pitt's administration the coalition conducted its operations very much in accordance with its own sense of duty and with the functions ascribed by the Government to the Opposition. Attendance was steady. Important ministerial measures were subjected to searching criticism clause by clause. Fox spun out the procedural stages for the passage of Bills of Commerce and Finance, and the fame of his obstruction was spread with a popular couplet:[1]

> Whenever a tax in the House was projected,
> Great Fox he rose up and always objected.

Sheridan once took nineteen successive divisions to block a Government resolution.[2] Petitions, questions, calls for papers, motions for investigation were moved so frequently that ministers complained of being teased and harassed by wanton attacks. The King resented the time wasted in getting Bills through Parliament and urged Pitt to persuade 'the friends of Government to speak merely to the point in future and try to shorten debates and bring if possible . . . the present bad mode of mechanical oratory into discredit'.[3] Ministerialists and Independents often grumbled at the length of speeches. In a debate on the slave trade in 1792, Lord Carhampton said,[4]

Gentlemen might talk of inhumanity, but he did not know what right anyone had to do so inhumane a thing as to inflict a speech of four hours long on a set of innocent, worthy, and respectable men. Gentlemen had continued this abuse day after day, both in their long and short speeches, some of which would have been equally proper for a house of commons, a pulpit, or a conventicle. If there had not been a back door behind the Speaker's chair for the infirm gentlemen to escape, he did believe they would have died on the spot.

The unrelenting pressure of the Opposition accomplished what in theory it was supposed to do. In 1790 Sheridan boasted of a long succession of Government measures defeated or modified by the coalition. Pitt in reply enlarged the list and

[1] Ibid. xxvi. 660–6; xxix. 840.

[2] [James Grant], *Random Recollections of the House of Commons* (Phila., 1836), p. 32.

[3] P.R.O., Chatham MSS. 103, George III to Pitt, 6 Mar. 1788.

[4] *P.H.* xxix. 1281–2. For other complaints see ibid. xxiv. 986; xxxi. 206. There are some amusing observations upon the verbosity of the orators of this period by the doorkeeper of the House of Commons in *Pearson's Political Dictionary* (London, 1792), pp. 16, 33, 51.

acknowledged their 'eminent success'.[1] The Opposition enjoyed its greatest triumph in the passage of Fox's Libel Act in 1792. Giving to juries the right to decide the fact of libel, this measure became a symbol of what could be accomplished in the face of entrenched legal opinion and a symbol of the 'patriots'' stand for the liberties of the people.

Pitt's leadership of the House allowed victories to his opponents which earlier ministers would not have tolerated. In keeping with his Chathamite principles, he drove his majorities with a loose rein, relying heavily upon his character and oratory to keep the Independents in line. Economical reform had deprived him of some of the patronage employed to strengthen the Court party, but though he created numerous peers to swell his following, Pitt went right on reducing the influence of the Crown by his own administrative reforms. He could afford to take so serene and virtuous an attitude because he knew that minor defeats did not weaken the House's confidence in him.

The coalition long wore the bend sinister which the Court had emblazoned upon its escutcheon. When country gentlemen planned to vote against Pitt on the detail of some measure, they often rose to assure him of their continued support as Minister. He was not indifferent to the need for consistent majorities, nor did he try to dispense with the machinery of the Court party. Indeed, in George Rose he had one of the finest Government Whips of the century. His position was so strong that he never suffered from the dread, which had haunted North, that defeat on a side-issue might bring down the Ministry. Thus his attitude encouraged Independents to incline to 'measures, not men', happy in the assumption that Pitt would remain in office despite an occasional failure. Politicians who thought they knew better how to manage the Court party worried about this new endeavour to conduct business in 'a loose, independent, and incorrupt parliament'. But Pitt proved shrewder than they, because, while his inspiration may have

---

[1] *P.H.* xxviii. 651–3, 708. At this time a group of manufacturers, who had appealed in vain to the Treasury for redress of grievances, asked the Opposition to present their case to Parliament. It is to be noted that such petitions differed in kind from those inspired by earlier Oppositions in order to foment discontent. Cf. Fox's pride in the Opposition's 'great influence on the measures of government' in 1792: ibid. xxix. 976–7.

been doctrinaire, he avoided Walpole's error of consolidating against him the votes of those who resented 'an overweening Minister'. Under the conditions prevailing after the election of 1784, concessions to a 'watchdog Opposition', theoretically endorsed by all men, proved a source of strength to the Government.[1]

The growing terror caused by the French Revolution enabled the Minister to strengthen his position still further. He accepted the adherence of Portland's schismatics and soon enticed them into office on conditions to which they had sworn they would never submit. With the passage of time many of them, angered by Pitt's blunders and weaknesses, returned to their old allegiance. The net result, however, was an increase of Pittites, the greatest of whom was Portland himself, the old standard-bearer of the closet-stormers, who lived out the last fifteen years of his life as the most faithful of the King's men.

The Foxites' outspoken sympathy with the Revolutionaries made it all too easy to damn them as opponents of dubious loyalty. Their blazing indiscretions added much colour to the imputation. In 1791, for example, Robert Adair, one of Fox's closest friends, made a visit to St. Petersburg, where, in the midst of a very tense diplomatic situation, he weakened Britain's hand by representing the views of the Opposition; and Fox himself set up a semi-official correspondence with the French Government. The infuriated Foreign Secretary, Lord Grenville, wrote to Auckland,[2]

> Is not the idea of ministers from Opposition to the different courts of Europe a new one in this country? I never heard of it before, and should think that if it could be proved, I mean legally proved, it would go very near to an impeachable misdemeanour.

The front-benchers on the Speaker's left consorted with agents from France, an imprudent course of action which appeared ominous in the light of Grenville's secret intelligence reports on

---

[1] On Pitt's management of Parliament, see Barnes, *George III and William Pitt*, p. 387; *H.M.C., Rutland MSS.* iii. 104, 129, 186, 192, 198, 203, 220–1, 283–5; Beresford, ed., *Beresford Corresp.* i. 302; *Pitt–Rutland Corresp.*, pp. 105–6; P.R.O., Granville Papers 384a, Pitt to Stafford, 31 Oct. 1789. On the strength gained by concessions to the Opposition, see the testimony of George Hardinge in *P.H.* xxvii. 155.

[2] *H.M.C., Dropmore MSS.* ii. 144, 149; Russell, *Mem. and Corresp. of C. J. Fox*, ii. 383–7. Cf. the views of Leeds in Add. MSS. 27916, ff. 33–34.

the expenditure of French gold to fortify the Opposition to Pitt. The Foxites' defence of those prosecuted by the Government and their speeches in favour of liberty convinced the King and his ministers that the Foxites were 'Jacobins' and 'open enemies' to their country, friends to sedition and abettors of high treason.[1]

The Government steadily pressed these charges in Parliament and the Press with great effectiveness. It became disreputable to be a Foxite. The *Anti-Jacobin*, whose leading contributors were brilliant young Pittites like George Canning, blackened the Opposition with a cutting irony and savage invective which rivalled the best efforts of Junius. In 1798 George III put a special mark of disgrace upon Fox by striking his name from the Privy Council. The 'patriots' protested in vain against the 'foul aspersions' of the King and his servants. The successes of the Opposition against Walpole and North were not to be repeated. Things did not happen 'as they used to do'. Military reverses and diplomatic failures abroad, discontent and mutiny in England, and riot and revolt in Ireland served rather to intensify the general loyalty to His Majesty's Government.

The success of Pitt's tactics led him to stiffen in his attitude toward Parliament from 1790 onwards. He often declined to argue about measures he proposed or opposed on the ground that the Legislature must give the Executive 'a reasonable degree of confidence'. Particularly in delicate matters relating to national security, the Houses must take it on faith that the Minister had good and sufficient cause, which his judgement forbade him to divulge, for such action as he had taken or intended to take. This 'necessary confidence', Pitt asserted, 'had been granted to all his predecessors in office', and he insisted upon its being given to him whenever he asked for it.[2]

The 'doctrine of confidence', as Parliamentarians came to call it, was a reversal of 'measures, not men'. It was akin to the contention of the 'hereditary Whigs' that Parliament should judge of measures by the men who proposed them. It was also a revival of the toplofty attitude of Chatham in the days of his

---

[1] *H.M.C., Dropmore MSS.* ii. 458, 473; iii. 323–4; Add. MSS. 37844, f. 274; 38231, ff. 298–9; P.R.O., Chatham MSS. 104, George III to Pitt, 9 Apr. 1796 and 27 Apr. 1797.   [2] *P.H.* xviii. 969; xxix. 75.

glory—the Legislature must place an enlightened trust in a Minister who had proved himself worthy of it. The son like the father pushed his advantage hard. Samuel Whitbread, scarcely a month after he had taken his seat in 1791, expostulated,[1]

In every debate on every subject, since the short time he had been sitting in Parliament, this doctrine of confidence had met him, and wherever it had met him, he had been alarmed; it had served in place of argument for every measure that had been proposed on the other side of the House; it had served in the place of an answer to every argument which had been adduced for any measure that had been brought forward on that side of the House.

How, asked another member, could Parliament counsel the Crown in arduous matters if reasons, explanations, and information were forever denied? Did Pitt think the House was summoned 'only to give our advice with respect to the construction of canals, the paving of streets, and the widening of the highways?'[2]

The Minister maintained his haughty reserve and, with the coming of war, increased his demands for confidence. The House regularly complied with them. Government Bills were seldom as drastically amended as they had been in the 1780's, and Opposition proposals critical of the Ministry had almost no chance of passage.[3] Not all those who supported Pitt believed in his policies. Of his strong majorities, Canning complained to a friend, 'part is composed of persons like you, *voting with* him but *thinking and talking against him*'.[4] But Canning's fear that such men would ultimately withdraw their confidence proved to be unjustified. Fox had little of hope of them. Anticipating a motion for peace with France in 1795, he remarked that, though there were not twenty men in the House who opposed it in their hearts,[5] 'The system of confidence has outrun all bounds and all

---

[1] Ibid. 198.   [2] Ibid. 228–9.

[3] George III delighted in substantial majorities and came increasingly to believe that concessions only led to further concessions and smaller margins of victory: see his letters to Pitt in P.R.O., Chatham MSS. 104, particularly that of 2 Mar. 1797.

[4] Dorothy Marshall, *The Rise of George Canning* (New York, 1938), pp. 94–96.

[5] Russell, *Mem. and Corresp. of C. J. Fox*, iii. 108. Pitt made an extraordinary use of the doctrine of confidence in Feb. 1801. While Addington, preparatory to taking over the Treasury, was awaiting re-election, Pitt pushed on the Supplies with a declaration that he would not retire until they were passed. The Opposition protested that the House should not take such a measure when the country was without a responsible ministry committed to a declared policy worthy of confidence.

former example, with this new circumstance, that it is now confidence without the basis of good opinion and without the pretence of success.'

From 1790 to 1797 the Opposition combated this 'monstrous doctrine' with every weapon at their disposal. They passionately denounced it as novel, destructive, and unconstitutional.[1] They resisted 'obsequious confidence-giving majorities', no matter how hopeless the cause, with wit, argument, eloquence, and obstruction. When in 1794 Pitt jammed the Suspension of Habeas Corpus through all its stages in the Commons within twenty-four hours, the Opposition took fourteen divisions, though the largest minority was thirty-nine.[2] Pitt's conduct of the war and his policy of repression were indicted with a persistent ferocity unsurpassed by the patriots of earlier times. To work an antidote to the poison of confidence—and, in the best tradition of Opposition, to the corrupting influence of the Crown—Charles Grey pressed his campaign for parliamentary reform both within and without doors. When his Reform Motion of May 1797 was crushed, 256 to 91, the Opposition abandoned the struggle and seceded from Parliament.

Fox had begun to talk of 'that habitual spirit of despondency and fear that characterizes the Whig party' as early as 1789.[3] Serenely content in the arms of his mistress at St. Anne's Hill, he gradually lost his zest for public life. In 1794–5 he, Grey, and Sheridan had contemplated secession but were deterred, partly by the remonstrances of their friends, partly by a fear that the public would think 'that, having lost all hope of place, we left the country to take care of itself'.[4] By 1797 the call to duty could command them no longer. The party would not consent to secession 'as a measure'. 'Secession means rebellion, or it is nonsense', pronounced Lansdowne, but even he finally admitted

To this Pitt replied that Addington deserved the confidence of the House because (1) he had been a good Speaker, (2) he was chosen by the King, (3) he would become responsible for expenditure upon taking office, (4) his principles were the same as Pitt's, and so he would pursue the same policies. The House accepted these arguments with little debate: *P.H.* xxxv. 958–70.

[1] For examples, see *P.H.* xxix. 60, 75–76, 175, 223, 230–1, 701, 889, 906, 1017, 1324.

[2] Ibid. xxxi. 521–5, 531, 573. On the persistence and futility of Opposition, see Barnes, *George III and William Pitt*, p. 325.

[3] Russell, *Mem. and Corresp. of C. J. Fox*, ii. 302.

[4] Ibid. iii. 105; *P.H.* xxxi. 387, 522, 546.

that circumstances permitted the Opposition to abandon the field. A 'voluntary dispersion' ensued. For four years the members of the party attended only if they chose, and there was no concerted campaign against the Government.[1]

Like Pulteney and Rockingham, Fox hoped that the absence of an Opposition might awaken the country to the scandalous servility of Parliament. The results were the same. The public was not impressed. The seceders were charged, then and for years to come, with retiring from the nation's service in an hour of peril and betraying the trust of their constituents. The Minister had to face only sporadic attacks by a tiny, unorganized band led by George Tierney, who kept up a regular attendance. Only once did the minority reach seventy-five, and it was often less than ten. The House was generally thin. In the absence of obstruction Pitt carried his measures with even greater ease. The seceders came to see the futility of their inaction and gradually drifted back to more frequent attendance. During the first meeting of the imperial Parliament in 1801 the secession came to an end.

This was the last time a parliamentary Opposition tried to gain its object by leaving Parliament. Secession had proved uniformly ineffective throughout the eighteenth century. It was an illogical move, motivated more by frustration than by expectation of success. Its failure finally settled for the future the position of the House of Commons in political warfare. An Opposition could accomplish nothing by passivity. Public opinion could not be rallied to support a party which did not hold up its standard in the lists at Westminster. The dispirited Fox professed to believe that the Crown was far too strong for any opponents. He wrote to Grey in 1801,[2]

The Constitution of this country is declining so rapidly that the House of Commons has in great measure ceased and will shortly entirely cease to be a place of much importance. . . . The only glimmering of hope I see is from the Court, when that shall fall into other hands, and the Court, without any invidious consideration of particular characters, is a miserable foundation to build a system of reform and liberty upon.

[1] Lord Holland, *Memoirs of the Whig Party in my Time* (London, 1852), i. 89–93; Russell, *Mem. and Corresp. of C. J. Fox*, iii. 136–8, 144–6, 273, 278, 295, 312, 319, 322–3, 339. Fox continued to be very lax in attendance until 1805.
[2] Ibid. 341.

But even had the prospect been as gloomy as it thus appeared, prevailing opinion evidently required the Opposition to do its duty in Parliament, to act as a 'watchdog of administration' in the face of all discouragement. The last seceders, like all their predecessors, came to realize that only by sustaining a regular attack at the centre of operations could they hope to gain the support, without doors and within, to accomplish anything at all.

For another three years Fox continued to talk in a desponding fashion, but once in a while his voice took on a sanguine note. Early in 1802, recalling how he had put new life into the Rockinghamites, he thought it possible that younger men could again revive 'an old, worn out, jaded Opposition'.[1] The trend of events after the secession invigorated his partisans much more than Fox. On 25 March 1801 Grey moved for a committee on the State of the Nation, which he lost after a debate lasting till 4.30 in the morning by 291 to 105. Young John Campbell, then a parliamentary reporter for the *Morning Chronicle*, wrote jubilantly to his father, 'There has not been such a minority since the year 1790, and I have little doubt it will increase on every division. There is no doubt that the eyes of the people are turned towards Fox.' Two weeks later Campbell was sure that the Opposition was growing in popularity, concluding happily, 'It is no longer a disreputable thing to be a Foxite.'[2] The youthful journalist saw pie in the sky a little too soon. None the less, the transfer of power from Pitt to Addington shortly precipitated another of those startling political re-alignments which so frequently occurred when a crisis upset a stable administration.

3. OPPOSITIONS OLD, NEW, AND PITTITE: 1801–1807

When Pitt retired in March 1801 he was accompanied out of office by followers committed to his stand on Catholic Relief. Some were friends and allies from the first days of his Ministry: his cousins the Grenvilles, the renegado Northite Henry Dundas, the hereditary Chathamite Lord Camden. Others came from

---

[1] Russell, *Mem. and Corresp. of C. J. Fox*, iii. 184–5, 197–9, 217–18, 239, 245, 325, 399.   [2] Hardcastle, *Campbell*, i. 66–67.

Portland's group, notably Lord Spencer and William Windham. There were the faithful men-of-business, George Rose and Charles Long, and a few rising youths like George Canning, Lord Granville Leveson-Gower, and Lord Castlereagh, who had grown up as Pittites. Most of them surrendered their places with great reluctance. They were fond of power. They believed in themselves as fit administrators, and the younger men were ambitious. They departed only in support of their leader. Had Pitt changed his mind about resignation at the last moment, as they almost persuaded him to do, they would joyfully have remained with him, and they went out in hopes of a quick return.[1]

In principle, they were sacrifices upon the twin altars of Constitutional rectitude and ministerial integrity. Since the King would not consent to Catholic Relief, to which they had become officially pledged without his knowledge, they could no longer be responsible for their measures. Convinced that it would be wrong to endeavour to force him, they had no alternative but resignation. Now what prospect lay before them out of office? They had been eloquent preachers against the sin of factious opposition, bold champions of the prerogative of the choice of ministers, strong advocates of 'measures, not men'. Consistently with these doctrines, Pitt had publicly expressed his faith in Addington, privately urged his friends to do likewise, and promised his personal support to George III's new Premier.[2] In theory, the Pittites could take no part but that of disinterested, constructive critics of ministers who, as His Majesty's chosen servants, merited their Constitutional confidence.

In fact, the Pittites were not a party in any way comparable to the Foxites. Like the old corps in 1762, they had been in place so long that the loss of the Treasury left them without organization. They had no party institutions, and loss of office sharpened the natural rivalries and differences among them. Their only tie was loyalty to Pitt. Despite failing health he took considerable pains to retain their goodwill, but he did little to concert action and nothing to weld them into a body. His

---

[1] *Diaries and Correspondence of James Harris, First Earl of Malmesbury* (London, 1844), iv. 5–45.

[2] George Pellew, *The Life and Correspondence of the Right Honble Henry Addington, Viscount Sidmouth* (London, 1847), i. 331–4; Stanhope, *Pitt*, iii. 276, 308.

leadership did not seem calculated to bring them back to Court. In the face of a Government with a stable majority, all aspiring patriots, except the elderly Chatham, had worked for an accommodation with ministers or coalesced with others for systematic Opposition. If Pitt imitated his father's example, would his followers violate this fundamental rule of politics?

The 'old Opposition', as the Foxites soon came to be called, was available for coalition on appropriate terms. The survival of the Whigs' institutions enabled them to revive the parliamentary party without difficulty, and in May 1801 the Prince of Wales renewed their alliance. It took some time for the Foxites to regain their old determination and solidarity. The leaders at first tended to look upon their return to Westminster as a formal act of duty, the end of secession rather than the re-establishment of a tenacious 'watchdog Opposition'.[1] Addington's majorities seemed invincible, and he deserved the 'patriots'' approbation for negotiating the peace which they had long urged. Consequently Fox and Grey, ever reluctant to be torn from domestic felicity, provided very erratic leadership, and party loyalty was weak. George Tierney, who had regularly resisted discipline, accepted an office in 1803, and Erskine and Sheridan generally supported Addington as a welcome improvement over Pitt. Despite the oppression of a gloomy lassitude, however, the leaders talked increasingly about the possibility of coalition with some group of Pittites as their only hope.

To Fox coalition was a basic principle of political action. As he had said in 1784, and as Burke and Rockingham had said so often before, the Whig party alone could never make a successful Opposition or a strong Government. Allies were necessary, and politicians who expected to achieve anything should not be too particular about their bedfellows. If a working agreement could be reached, past differences must be forgotten. He had no irremovable prejudices against anyone, not even Pitt. In 1802 Fox envisioned coalition in 'a distant view'. The next year he thought the possibility still remote but encouraged Grey to keep together 'our reliquiae, if it were only the Russells and

---

[1] Hardcastle, *Campbell*, i. 71; Charles Grey, *Some Account of the Life and Opinions of Charles, Second Earl Grey* (London, 1861), pp. 62–63; Russell, *Mem. and Corresp. of C. J. Fox*, iii. 184–5, 190, 197.

Cavendishes and a few more' for future contingencies. Early in 1804 he declared his willingness to resume vigorous leadership whenever he saw 'a chance of re-establishing a strong Whig party (however composed)'.[1] Fox made no secret of his views— his career afforded abundant evidence of them—but some of his friends and most of the Pittites needed more education in Opposition.

Pitt found himself in the role forced upon North in 1782. His course of action would determine the fate of Fox and Adding-ton, and the political contest was from the outset a struggle for his conscience. He began his new career in accordance with his lifelong professions. After resigning he took his seat on the third row above the Treasury Bench, affirmed his confidence in the new Government, and reserved his right to criticize bad measures. To Bathurst he thus outlined his position in October 1801:[2]

I see no reason to doubt that the system of government will be conformable to our opinions. If it should not, my sentiments on these points ['domestic precautions' and the maintenance of the 'high naval and military establishments'] are so fixed that nothing can prevent my declaring them and protesting in the strongest manner against any departure from them. But though I should feel this due both to my own character and to public duty, the same considerations would restrain me from making even this the ground for embarking in any systematic opposition with a view to changing the administration, which I think could hardly be effected, in any supposeable case, without leading to the most ruinous consequences.

But Pitt had lost none of his hauteur and self-righteousness. At the age of forty-two, he had spent most of his adult life as Prime Minister, and though weak with an ailment diagnosed as gout, he found it hard to assume the character of a benevolent senior statesman. In him Chathamite principles were to be put to their final test, the more severe and decisive because he was tormented by commitments, friendships, and a regard for con-sistency which had not inhibited his tempestuous sire.

From one direction Pitt was distressed by his connexion with Lord Grenville, Windham, and Spencer. Their friends and dependants hungered for places, and though the leaders at first had no great eagerness to resume the burdens of office, they

[1] Ibid. 222, 234, 376, 399.   [2] H.M.C., Bathurst MSS., p. 26.

looked sceptically upon Addington from the very beginning. Grenville and Windham had been the chief directors of Pitt's foreign and military policies, which in their minds could not be altered without endangering the nation. When the new Government moved toward peace with France, their hostility increased. Pitt urged all his friends to support Addington as far as conscience would allow, but the consciences of Grenville and Windham drove them to strong attacks upon the peace and the men who made it. The 'new Opposition' had come into being.[1]

Grenville tried for two years to draw his cousin along with him. It became apparent by the end of 1802 that Pitt was disillusioned with the Ministry, and within another year he and Grenville found themselves completely agreed upon their objections to Addington. The former Premier became convinced that his country's salvation depended upon his return to office. But he would enter into no concert for a systematic Opposition. In the House he displayed his growing antagonism in moves designed as 'signals emitted in order to attract the King's attention'[2]—good Chathamite tactics—but he took equal pains to dissociate himself from the old and new Oppositions. After numerous and lengthy conferences Grenville finally despaired of Pitt and sought an alliance with Fox in January 1804.[3]

The Prince of Wales had been urging such a junction for six months. Among others Grey was hesitant. To him the Grenvilles' 'opposition has appeared to proceed rather from personal disappointment than from public principle'. Fox instructed his lieutenant in the virtues of coalition, adding[4]

What you say of the unpopularity of the Grenvilles and Windham is, I believe, true, and especially among our friends, but they are the only part of the new Opposition with whom we can expect cordial and fair co-operation. You know I always thought among all their faults that they had one good quality, viz., that of being capable of becoming good party men.

[1] *P.H.* xxxvi, 565, 587, 671, 688, 737, 739. It is interesting to note that the 'new Opposition' signified their independence by taking seats 'at the bar end of the House': Russell, *Mem. and Corresp. of C. J. Fox*, iii. 449.

[2] Pares, *King George III and the Politicians*, pp. 136–7.

[3] Russell, *Mem. and Corresp. of C. J. Fox*, iii. 449–50. Grenville's course can be followed through his correspondence in *H.M.C., Dropmore MSS.* vii, and Buckingham, *Courts and Cabinets of George III*, iii.

[4] Russell, *Mem. and Corresp. of C. J. Fox*, iii. 417–18, 433; iv. 4–10.

Fox was ready for the offer when it came. He and Grenville soon reached a typically broad agreement for systematic opposition to turn out Addington and form a 'broad bottom' administration. Prejudices and fears on both sides prevented any more detailed arrangements. The leaders knew that they might be making a futile gesture. Pitt might turn their opposition into a stalking horse, behind which to bag the game they all knew he aimed at. Fox faced the possibility with a light heart: only a coalition could resist the tremendous power of the Crown, so, he wrote to Grey, 'Let the event be what it may, it is good to force the king to change.'[1] Such were Fox's powers of leadership and persuasion that the new alliance proved to be remarkably durable, both in success and adversity.

One segment of the Pittites thus took the traditional road to patriotism. Concurrently with the ineffective pressure from the Grenvilles, Pitt was tugged toward systematic opposition from another quarter. George Canning resented the ministerial change of 1801 with an almost hysterical passion. His resignation checked the rapid promotion to high office for which he yearned, and he cherished a virulent contempt for Addington. In the early months of the new Ministry, Canning would have accepted a Cabinet post, but none was offered. Thereafter his venom strained even his unsurpassed powers of vituperation. His correspondence was filled with savage condemnations of 'this wretched, pusillanimous, toadeating, beshitten administration'. Addington's incompetence made his retention of office 'an usurpation of the vilest kind . . . a conspiracy against all talents of all sides and sorts'. At Pitt's behest, Canning voted for the peace, then flung himself into a relentless campaign to drag his leader into open, uncompromising hostility to the Government.[2]

Canning's doctrine resided in the middle ground between Fox and Pitt, overlapping both but distinguishable from each. Temperate, liberal opposition to measures alone was sheer stupidity. Such conduct could not be understood by 'the plain, unrefining, down-right, fat-headed public'. Pitt foolishly 'chooses to calculate on principles which, he is every day finding, have no existence as motives of action in the House of

[1] Ibid. iv. 39–40, 45.
[2] Add. MSS. 38833, ff. 53–57, 79–81.

Commons'.[1] The function of the Opposition is to show the King 'the choice of the nation' and 'to make compliance with it on every account highly desirable'. In December 1802 Canning screamed in the House, 'Away with the cant of "measures, not men"! The idle supposition that it is the harness and not the horses that draw the chariot along.'[2] On the other hand, coalition in Opposition did not appeal to him. If Pitt would declare himself, he would have followers enough. Canning seized every opportunity to reinforce Grenville's pressure on their leader, and when the old and new Oppositions joined, he approved 'broad bottom' in principle. But, he wrote to Grenville,[3]

as it is impossible not to foresee that a successful Opposition *may* lead to arrangements on a more limited scale, I think it fair both to you and to myself to have it understood beforehand that I consider myself unpledged as to any connection with any new Government (however otherwise unexceptionable) in which Mr. Pitt shall not be included.

In short, he loved his Chathamite independence—in the election of 1802 he had bought himself an Irish seat so as to be beholden to no one—but he could be a much better Pittite if only the great man would take a more practical view of Opposition.

So he drove Pitt with passionate expostulation towards a break with 'the doctor', as Addington was scornfully nicknamed because his father had been a Court physician. 'The opposition to him', Canning urged, 'must be an opposition of contempt and derision—of the whip rather than the sword.' To 'bring Pitt forward again in spite of himself' and to demonstrate Pitt's strength, both to him and the King, Canning staged the famous birthday party of 28 May 1802. Two country gentlemen proposed 'that it would be a proper testimony to Pitt to have a public dinner on his birthday—why not on his as Fox's friends do on Fox's?' Canning grasped the possibilities before the idea went farther. 'It struck me as being capable of being turned to great account', he wrote, 'and the better if it were to *originate* in the City.' He introduced it tactfully into the proper quarters, and 'it spread like wildfire'. Before Pitt had heard a word, all was organized, and Canning had written 'The Pilot That

---

[1] Add. MSS. 38833, f. 152; Marshall, *Rise of Canning*, p. 261.
[2] *P.H.* xxxvi. 1080.   [3] Add. MSS. 38833, ff. 164–5.

Weathered the Storm'.[1] It was a *succès fou*. Over 820 people were present at the Merchant Taylors' Hall, and 200 more were denied admission. The crowning event of the evening was the enthusiastic reception of Canning's composition, the diners calling for a repetition of the last stanza:

> And O! if again the rude whirlwind should rise,
> The dawning of peace should fresh darkness deform,
> The regrets of the good and the fears of the wise
> Shall turn to the pilot that weathered the storm.

No one mistook the significance of this partisan verse. All understood it, Canning was sure, 'in its true intent and meaning'. He hoped the country gentlemen would see that 'a little *douce violence* might force a better pilot to the helm'.[2]

Pitt's cold nature was touched, but still he wavered. Would not the King be offended by his avowed opposition? Would it not exasperate the politicians so as to make any new arrangement impossible? Nonsense, replied Canning, the only fault they all find with you is that your opposition is 'not systematic *enough*'. Pitt steadily weakened, and Canning's hopes rose:[3]

He pauses and hesitates and shrinks and shuffles to avoid going into direct, open, avowed parliamentary opposition [Canning noted in November 1803], but it is all in vain. Go he must, like all ex-ministers before him, a little sooner or a little later, and if he will not let me go before him, I must wait his time.

While Grenville and Canning wrought upon Pitt's conscience, Addington strove to retain his goodwill. Pitt was informed of the Government's plans. His advice was taken, sometimes unwisely. He was given chances to return to office. But he would take no place but the first, and for two years 'the doctor' was unwilling to step down. The Government had a solid majority and Pitt's pledge of support. Why should the Minister cut his own throat? At length, dismayed by Pitt's displeasure, Addington offered the great concession. In April 1803, in a private conference and without consulting his colleagues or the King, he agreed to a reconstruction which restored Pitt to the Treasury. The arrangement was to be presented to George III after

[1] Add. MSS. 38833, f. 81.
[2] Add. MSS. 38833, ff. 110–13, 117; Stanhope, *Pitt*, iii. 379–81; Bagot, *Canning*, i. 197.
[3] Add. MSS. 38833, f. 163; Marshall, *Rise of Canning*, pp. 241–3.

approval by the Cabinet. The Cabinet balked—other men had their pride—and the King was very much annoyed by Addington's generosity.[1] 'The doctor' continued his efforts to appease Pitt in every way possible, but this extraordinary episode made clear that the Ministry was as secure in the royal confidence as it was in the confidence of Parliament.

More implacable than before, Pitt endeavoured to transmit his 'signals' with increasing power, only to reveal his own weakness. When he took divisions on motions made to distinguish him from the other 'outs' but to mark his dislike of the Government, it became apparent that he had only about sixty followers in the Commons. As the Peace of Amiens foundered, Addington lost the popularity gained by his brief truce, and, ill prepared, Britain plunged again into the storm of conflict with France. Still there seemed no general wish to recall the old pilot. His continued ill success and the formation of the Fox–Grenville coalition finally drove him to systematic opposition in everything but name. He regularly criticized the Government and its measures, and he surrendered his qualms about being in the same minority with Fox. In March 1804 he turned to offensive tactics by calling for papers upon which to found an inquiry into the navy. When ministers based their refusal on the 'doctrine of confidence', the House witnessed the amazing spectacle of Pitt fulminating against the device upon which he had relied for so long. To refuse papers was to demand blind, unlimited, false, dangerous, and alarming confidence, of which only perfidious ministers bent upon screening their own incompetence could stand in need.[2] No one could mistake his position now. He was determined to pull down the Government for the perfectly obvious purpose of returning himself to the Treasury.

In public Pitt insisted that his opposition was to measures. No matter how severe his strictures upon ministers, he avoided any statement which intimated a desire to force the King. To rally support, however, he had to admit his real intentions to his friends. On 29 March he wrote to Henry Dundas, now Lord Melville,[3]

I am strongly confirmed in the opinion that the present

[1] Stanhope, *Pitt*, iv. 32–37.   [2] *Hansard*, i. 874–928.
[3] Stanhope, *Pitt*, iv. 142.

Government cannot last for any length of time, and still more so in the full conviction that every week for which its existence may be protracted will be attended with increased danger to the country. I have therefore satisfied myself that the time is near at hand at which, if a change does not originate from the ministers or from the King, I can no longer be justified in not publicly declaring my opinion, and endeavouring by parliamentary measures to give it effect.

My present notion therefore is to take the first moment after the present recess, at which the state of the King's health will admit of such a step, to write a letter to His Majesty stating to him the grounds of my opinion, explaining the dangers which I think threaten his crown and his people from the continuance of his present Government, and representing to him the urgent necessity of a speedy change.

Another spell of the royal insanity postponed the proposed letter but not the parliamentary measures to effectuate Pitt's purpose. He made earnest efforts to secure votes and joined in the coalition's major assaults. He still stood off from any connexion or concert with Fox, but general knowledge of the business coming before the House made formal agreement unnecessary. Pitt knew where the attacks would land, and as he well understood, his volleys were as effective as if he were in league with the other besiegers. Canning's predictions were fulfilled. The ex-minister had finally gone into Opposition, and as soon as members understood what he was about, Government majorities dwindled.

The alarmed Addington then made one more effort at conciliation. In mid-April he asked Pitt to 'state, through any common friend, what his opinions were as to the present state of things and the steps to be taken for carrying on the King's affairs'. Pitt refused to communicate anything to the Minister, but took this opportunity to gain Addington's consent to sending his proposed letter to George III through the Lord Chancellor. The letter was sent on 22 April, and while Eldon awaited a propitious moment to present it to the slowly recuperating King, Pitt pressed on the attack. When the Government's majority dropped to 37 on 25 April, Addington declared in the closet that he could not continue, and on 27 April His Majesty read Pitt's letter. The present Ministry, it said, and particularly the present Minister, were unfit to rule, and having said so, he proposed to regulate his parliamentary conduct accordingly. Intimating that he possessed a personal opinion regarding the formation of a better administration, he asserted that he would never commit himself to any engagement which could cause the King the slightest 'dissatisfaction or uneasiness'. In his circumlocutory way Pitt thus manifested his intention to oppose till Addington fell, and his willingness to head a new system pleasing to the King.[1]

So it appeared at last that Chathamite principles were as hollow as all other doctrines invented to circumvent the royal Prerogative. If to oppose for the purpose of getting into office was by definition factious, Pitt was as factious as any other 'patriot'. He considered himself released from his pledge of support by his letter, but even though the King's illness had delayed its composition and then its delivery, Pitt had embarked upon systematic opposition, albeit unavowed, before he confided his intention to Melville. He pursued his course while awaiting the King's answer, prepared to execute his threat to avow his opposition if necessary. It was certainly a unique procedure to offer His Majesty a chance to capitulate before the final assault, but he meant to storm the closet just as surely as any Rockinghamite. Pitt's opposition nevertheless retained some notable Chathamite characteristics. His goal was the Premiership. No subordinate post was acceptable, and one cannot doubt the sincerity of his belief, a parallel to his father's conviction of half a century before, that only he could save the country. He expected to bring his friends in with him, but he had no organized party with a shadow Cabinet. He intended to force only himself upon the King, and out of consideration for George III's delicate health as well as out of principle, he would be very pliable about men and measures.

George III was at first inclined to resist as strenuously as he had done in 1782 and 1783, but Addington would not fight. Resentfully the King invited Pitt to submit an arrangement. After some manœuvring he received permission to try for a comprehensive administration, but with an absolute proscription

---

[1] Stanhope, *Pitt*, iv. 145–61, app. i–iii. In view of the intentions revealed in this letter, it seems quite extraordinary that a year later Pitt should have insisted that he did not 'cashier' Addington and that the change of ministry was made with Addington's 'free will and entire concurrence': *Hansard*, iii. 761.

of Fox. Neither the old nor the new 'patriots' would enter a ministry based upon 'a principle of exclusion', even though Fox himself offered to renounce his pretensions,[1] and the coalition took up a vigorous opposition to the weak second ministry which Pitt formed from his friends and a few hold-overs. Its fitful life was marked by repeated but vain endeavours to achieve strength and stability. Addington and his following were enticed back into office in January 1805, but there was so much bad blood that, after six months of quarrelling, they resigned in anger. Pitt then wanted to open negotiations with the coalition, but George III would not have it. The effort must have failed in any event because Fox and the Grenvilles were united in insisting upon Rockinghamite terms. Fox was still willing to waive his own claims, but Pitt must resign as a preliminary to any reconstruction, and the Treasury would have to be placed 'in proper hands'.[2]

The formation and structure of the new Government revived the Constitutional arguments of 1784. The Opposition again charged Pitt with using secret influence in a dark conspiracy to seize power in defiance of Parliament. The weakness of the Cabinet and its internal divisions provoked endless gibes at 'what is called the present administration', which was condemned as utterly deficient in the confidence necessary to govern the nation. Pitt called the Prerogative to his defence in the old familiar terms and declared that an unprincipled, factious coalition could never drive him from office. If his Bills were lost, he would lament them, but 'the hon. gentlemen opposite will be much mistaken if they think they will thereby be anything the nearer to getting rid of me'. He would persevere against all discouragement, impregnable in the royal confidence and in his own supreme merit. Fox once remarked that all Pitt's replies to criticism of the Government could be summed up in the phrase, 'look at me'.[3]

There was much speculation as to whether 'the refreshed giant' could repeat the triumph of 1784. After the resignation of the Addingtonians, Fox for one was sure that he could not, if

---

[1] Stanhope, *Pitt*, iv. 164–93, app. iv–xiii; *H.M.C.*, *Dropmore MSS.* vii. 221–3; *Bathurst MSS.*, pp. 34–41.

[2] Russell, *Mem. and Corresp. of C. J. Fox*, iv. 79–117.

[3] Hansard, ii. 744–51; iii. 482–511; v. 525–6. Cf. Lord Archibald Hamilton, *Thoughts on the Formation of the Late and Present Administrations* (London, 1804).

the Opposition played the game skilfully. Fox's tactics were to keep the coalition united against tempting offers from the Court and to draw Addington (now Viscount Sidmouth) to his side, so as to prevent Pitt from gaining any strength. This confederacy then should take a very moderate line of opposition to avoid the errors made on the previous occasion. If Pitt could get no additional help, he had no recourse but[1]

to get some *cause* with the public upon which he may be able to stand his ground against all parties. Now what cause can he get? no possible other than the old cry against storming the Cabinet, imprisoning and dethroning the King, aristocratical faction, interested coalitions, etc., etc., etc. Now, what method so good for the purpose of cutting him off from this his only resource as to show on our part every degree of moderation? to show that we would do everything possible to soften the King's prejudices, and would by no means adopt ourselves those principles of exclusion which we condemn in others?

This shrewd application of the lessons of 1784 did not mean, however, that Fox had weakened in his principles. Harsh intransigence should be replaced by more judicious 'professions and conduct' because the King could be forced more effectively if forced more gently. The Opposition remained a storming party which should act with vigour and concert, for in Fox's mind it was[2] 'very, very desirable that its power, strength, and union should appear considerable while out of office, in order that if ever they should come in, it may be plain that they have an existence of their own and are not the mere creature of the crown'.

Feeble as was his second Ministry, Pitt managed to get the King's business done by reasonably comfortable majorities, and after Sidmouth's desertion he never met Parliament again. His death on 23 January 1806 left the King to resolve another ministerial crisis. George III first hoped to reconstruct and strengthen the existing Government, but in a formal minute the Cabinet declared this course to be impossible. Portland advised the King, in the desperate situation after Austerlitz, not to engage in a protracted struggle with the Opposition but to call 'some *at least*' of them into office. Hawkesbury urged an end to the proscription of Fox. With surprising rapidity the

[1] Russell, *Mem. and Corresp. of C. J. Fox*, iv. 88–89.   [2] Ibid. iv. 68.

King capitulated. On the 27th he commissioned Lord Grenville to form a ministry, 'putting no exclusion upon anybody, but reserving to himself to judge of the whole', and despite some serious tensions within the coalition, the new Minister completed his task in four days. George III then extracted from Grenville a recognition of the royal right to accept or reject any advice from the Cabinet, and the coalition took office as 'the Ministry of All the Talents'.[1]

The manner of this change is worthy of remark. The Opposition had not won a decision in Parliament, but it appeared that they would soon defeat the now leaderless Ministry. The King sought and followed the advice of the incumbents. In forming a new Government he made no use of the old devices—the intermediate negotiator, the non-political commissioner, the neutral peer—as a means to control the operation. He laid his commands upon the least objectionable of the coalition's leaders as the future First Minister. The King had a general knowledge of what Grenville intended to do but made no specific recommendations or restrictions. Though the commission did not extend to *carte blanche*, George III could not have rejected Grenville's slate without prolonging the undesirable *interministerium*. In the event the King seems to have raised no difficulties about the new Cabinet. Grenville's acknowledgement that the Cabinet could not bind the monarch without his consent, however, strictly limited the success of the storming party. In 1783 Portland had required the King to accept his assurance that the 'patriots' would never make an unacceptable recommendation. Now the Opposition asked merely for the opportunity to advise. Beyond a doubt Grenville meant to ease the change for an old, upset, blinding sovereign. Malcontents would deny to strong masters concessions they would make to the weak, and also with 1784 still in mind, they understood the need to 'manage our cause', as Fox put it, in a fashion acceptable to public opinion.[2] The formal attitude of both King and Opposition had mellowed. The fundamental position of neither had changed.

All talents but Pittite were included in the new Government. Grenville had trouble enough to satisfy the hunger of his family

---

[1] *H.M.C., Dropmore MSS.* vii. 341–51; viii. 1–26; Barnes, *George III and William Pitt*, pp. 473–4.   [2] *H.M.C., Dropmore MSS.*, viii. 3.

and friends, Foxites, Prince's men, and Addingtonians. 'What a crowd of pretensions and pretenders', exclaimed Lord Glenbervie, to which Buckinghamshire added, 'The pressure of claimants for office, I hear, has been beyond anything ever heard of'.[1] 'Broad bottom', like all noble ideals, was very hard to implement and harder still to sustain. Aided by Fox's genial tact, Grenville did a remarkably statesmanlike job, but the Pittites quite naturally were not mollified.

With a ghost for a leader, the party which was not a party, inspired by ambition which was not ambition, looked on in dismay as the new Ministry took shape. Portland was sure that nothing[2]

could be so injurious and cruel to the King's feelings and situation as to force an Opposition prematurely, which should leave him without resource, and rivet the chains of his present thraldom, which he is most sensible of the burden of and yet thinks it an act of duty to submit to with temper and management.

Yet the Duke did not despair of living long enough to see the true friends of the Crown back in place. If they united to support Grenville against Fox's 'Jacobinical and republican notions and principles', the Minister would soon part with his new allies to recall his old. The Pittites generally favoured this plan. Charles Yorke, after lengthy conversations with the leaders in February 1806, reported that they proposed to act on

the fixed principle of giving no systematic or factious opposition to the Government of His Majesty . . . for all agree that nothing could be more *dangerous* at present than even the holding out to His Majesty *the idea* that a set of men are combining together to overturn the existing order of things and to abet him in his supposed wishes for a change.

The consensus favoured 'a corps of observation' to keep a jealous eye on measures and a cordial eye on the Minister. This course would attract the Independents, and upon the inevitable break-up of the Ministry the Pittite body would serve as 'a rallying point' for the Grenvilles, and together they would return to office.[3]

---

[1] *The Journal and Correspondence of William Lord Auckland* (London, 1862), iv. 271–3.
[2] Portland Papers (Nottingham), Portland to Titchfield, 17 Feb. 1806.
[3] Add. MSS. 35706, ff. 348–9.

With these sentiments but little else to bind them, the Pittites took their seats on the Speaker's left. It may have been a disappointment to them that Fox proposed no radical innovations, but they found sufficient grounds for vehement, if sporadic and fruitless, opposition. The country gentlemen were not impressed, and the Ministry's ostensible stability was discouraging. Early in March Castlereagh decried the reluctance of many members 'to assume even on a single point the appearance of opposition to the new administration before it has received a fair trial'.[1] His attacks, with those of Canning and Spencer Perceval, grew in steadiness and intensity as the session progressed, until by mid-June they had flung off the mask. The system of government was 'systematic absurdity', distinguished above all others for procrastination and futility. Every single one of their measures had deserved opposition, and so would all those that followed. Grenville was no longer spared. His 'all-wise, all-perfect administration' was a heterogeneous collection of pretentious bunglers, the worse for having been based upon 'the total exclusion and proscription' of every man who had preserved a political connexion with Pitt until his death.[2] These declarations closed the earth over the corpse of Chathamite principles. Now and then in the future circumstances made it appropriate to call up the wraith of 'measures, not men' and the sanctity of the royal Prerogative, but politicians substantially discarded the doctrine as a fit pretence for an ambitious Opposition.

Their experience during the session of 1806 also taught the Pittites the lesson learned by their political foes—the vital need for concord and unanimity. On 2 July the leaders held a meeting in which it transpired, Lord Wellesley told Grenville,

that the great portion of the present Opposition is personally well disposed towards you, and Canning particularly so; that, however, they are resolved to adhere together as a body, and the leading individuals would think it injurious to the public service, as well as to their own reputations, to form any connexion without the concurrence of the corps. That if any propositions were to be made to any of them, their first inquiry would be, whether it came from the king, without whose direct authority none of them would be disposed to enter into any discussions relative to the acceptance of office.

[1] *Hansard*, vi. 319.   [2] Ibid. vii. 618–47.

Perhaps they salved their Chathamite consciences by requiring the royal consent to any negotiations—except in the unusual situation of 1744, most malcontents had assumed it as a matter of course—but in Foxite fashion they also demanded the dissolution of the incumbent Government as a preliminary to the construction of a successor. If their conditions were met, they would allow Grenville to form the new system. They did not insist upon occupying the main stronghold of the Treasury, provided all other just pretensions were satisfied.[1] Opposition had made the Pittites a party at last.

Despite his knowledge of their terms, Grenville made some efforts to detach Canning and Perceval. Their ambition was well known, and Canning had with many misgivings joined his fortunes to those of colleagues for whom he cared little. He was a desirable successor to Fox, who was overtaken in June by the malady that bore him off in September. Though sorely tempted, Canning adhered to the party pact and advised Grenville to apply in future to Portland, the acknowledged head of the party. The Minister would not sacrifice the Foxites to admit the Opposition *en bloc*.[2] Convinced that he could not get outside help on satisfactory terms, Grenville reorganized his Government and sought new strength in a general election. The Parliament was only four years old, but the King seems to have raised no difficulties about granting a Dissolution, which was a public mark of the royal confidence in the Ministry. Canning raged, 'The dissolution itself is a death blow to all hopes of change —and is moreover a satisfactory proof that I have been the dupe of Messrs. Hawkereagh, Eldbury, and Castledon.'[3] The other Pittites were equally dismayed. It seemed as if their organization into a party was to result in a long period of exclusion from office.

They soon held up their heads again. Grenville took the Dissolution too hastily, counting upon the general popularity which he thought he had won after the breakdown of peace negotiations with France. Consequently the elections were not well prepared, and it became apparent how seriously Economical

---

[1] *H.M.C., Dropmore MSS.* viii. 212–13; Feiling, *Second Tory Party*, p. 249.

[2] A. G. Stapleton, *George Canning and his Times* (London, 1859), pp. 96–108; *H.M.C., Dropmore MSS.* vii. 210–337, 387–90. Grenville tried Canning again early in 1807 with equal lack of success.

[3] Add. MSS. 38833, ff. 216–18.

Reform had reduced the influence of the Crown. The Government gained only about thirty seats.[1] The Pittites went down to the opening of the new Parliament in December 1806 with an undisguised determination to hound the Ministry out of office. In the debates on the Address, Grey (now Lord Howick) complained of their 'low hostility of vexing and harassing by a warfare of details'. Castlereagh retorted that they intended to fulfil their obligations as public censors—the caitiff course of secession was not for them—'to watch and revise the acts of ministers in order to call them to account'. Perceval warned Howick,[2] 'If the noble lord thought that this kind of opposition, founded on public duty, was harassing, he frankly informed the noble lord in time that he could not expect much indulgence or sound repose during the session.'

Ministerialists treated such noble professions with much good-natured raillery. Sir John Doyle once acknowledged his awareness[3]

that in a free country like this, an Opposition is a wholesome check upon ministers: if so, the greater the talents in opposition, the more effectual the check. Now, as every man must admit the present Opposition to possess great talents, it follows as a natural corollary that the longer the present gentlemen remain in that state, the better for their country.

George Tierney taunted them with being 'young in opposition': after a few years' apprenticeship they might learn their trade.[4] The Pittites attacked as assiduously as they had promised, but the Government could afford to be light-hearted. Majorities, if not great, were sufficient to indicate security. Grenville managed his balky team with even-tempered skill, and the King was encouragingly gracious. Behind the scenes, however, the Cabinet was unwittingly preparing the ground for a Pittite triumph which bore some striking parallels to the changes of 1783 and 1804.

In mid-February George III reluctantly consented to the introduction of a measure permitting Roman Catholics to serve as officers in the English army and navy. King and ministers

---

[1] Buckingham, *Court and Cabinets of George III*, iv. 85; Add. MSS. 38737, ff. 163–4, 184; *H.M.C., Bathurst MSS.*, p. 54; Feiling, *Second Tory Party*, pp. 242–3.
[2] *Hansard*, viii. 62, 77–78, 83–84.   [3] Ibid. 538–9.
[4] Ibid. 769.

then became embroiled in a series of misunderstandings about how far the concessions should extend. On 11 March the King expressed his opposition to the Bill which Howick had already brought before the Commons, and after searching for a compromise, the Cabinet dropped the Bill. Meanwhile on 12 March the Duke of Portland, either knowing or anticipating the royal attitude, wrote the King a letter urging him to declare his opinion openly and assuring him that there was no shortage of able men to replace 'all the talents'. On 17 March George asked Grenville and his colleagues to give a written pledge that they would never again raise the Catholic issue. They refused, and the King commissioned Portland to form a new Government.[1]

The Pittite pact thus proved to be a boon to its adherents after all. In guaranteeing his ability to construct a ministry, Portland was in a much better position than Pitt had been in 1804. The party agreement enabled the Duke to create a talented Cabinet from his own friends, without deserters or hold-overs from other groups. Good fortune made him as strong with George III as Pitt had been in 1783, and stronger than in 1804, because the King saw eye-to-eye with Portland in his objection to the incumbent Ministry and its policy. There was no need of a threat to storm the closet. The Pittites' weaknesses lay in the aged Duke's growing infirmities, rivalries among the brilliant young men, and the difficulties of managing a Parliament chosen to support their adversaries. About the first two, nothing effectual could be done, but for the third there was the good Pittite remedy. The new ministers had a 'cause', or rather two: the Prerogative and 'no popery'. While the Opposition hurled charges of secret influence and defended the Privy Councillor's oath to give honest advice, loyal addresses to the Throne poured in from all parts of the kingdom, and the Treasury made vigorous preparations for a general election. A month after the fall of 'All the Talents' the King granted a Dissolution. The Address at the opening of the new Parliament was carried 350 to 155.[2] Portland had fulfilled his wish to live long enough to see the monarchy's true friends back in place.

---

[1] The voluminous evidence on the fall of the Talents is well summarized in Michael Roberts, *The Whig Party, 1807–1812* (London, 1939), pp. 7–34.

[2] *Hansard*, ix. 284–475, 608–59; Feiling, *Second Tory Party*, pp. 256–7; Roberts, *Whig Party*, pp. 29–31.

The Opposition success of 1807 was the last to be achieved by Pittite methods. During the short remaining years of his precarious sanity George III did not want to oust his ministers again. George IV, men soon discovered, was 'fonder of abusing his ministers than of changing them'.[1] There was never to be another Pitt, an overawing commanding figure, who could set all parties at defiance and bluff his way into power with private letters to the sovereign. Henceforward Oppositions frankly relied upon the more orthodox methods of the flying squadron and the storming party.

4. PARTIES AND CREEDS, 1783–1830

The construction of Portland's Government in 1807 established in power the administrative core that ruled Britain for twenty years. The original 'narrow bottom' was gradually broadened by reunion with others of Pitt's old friends—the Addingtonians in 1812 and the Grenvilles in 1822—by capable young recruits like Frederick Robinson and Robert Peel, and by the adherence in 1818 of the towering figure of Wellington. This long administration had periods of great weakness. Clashing pretensions and ambitions, notably Canning's, caused endless internal friction. Death and crisis necessitated numerous reconstructions. George IV was occasionally very troublesome. But Portland, Perceval, and Liverpool managed to hold the party together, to retain the confidence of the Independents, and to pursue policies that carried Britain through the darkest days of the Napoleonic wars and the post-war depression to the prosperity of the mid-1820's.

The Foxites, despite the loss of their allies, survived as the core of a regular Opposition. The party which looked to Grey for leadership still included many of the great aristocratic families of 'hereditary Whiggism'—Devonshire, Grafton, Bedford, Lansdowne, Albemarle, Fitzwilliam, Bessborough, Spencer, Holland—and from noble houses came such rising young men as Lord Althorp, William Lamb, and Lord John Russell. Less blue-blooded were their brilliant lawyers, Sir Samuel Romilly, James Scarlett, and Henry Brougham, who had connexions with the growing body of Benthamite Radicals. There

---

[1] Buckingham, *Memoirs of the Court of George IV*, ii. 395.

was little sympathy, and often open hostility, between the old guard and the 'mountaineers' or 'Jacobins', but being all malcontents they usually found themselves voting together in a division. All Radical M.P.s, even Sir Francis Burdett and Joseph Hume, were admitted to Brooks's and were sent the party Whip unless it was positively rejected. Opposition was thus composed of the materials familiar since the days of Wilkes: an alliance of political interests which brought in promising 'new men' and accepted the support of independent reformers.

The relative stability of 'ins' and 'outs' for twenty years gave each an apparent identity and solidarity which had lasting consequences. Professor Pares speaks of the traditional 'proprietary political groups' as 'melting away into the two great parties'.[1] The coalitions on both sides became more closely fused through habitual association and common action. They were not proof against rupture. No party ever has been. Each seemed more monolithic from the outside than from within. The very appearance, however, was important in itself. It led to a conceptualization of *the* two parties as elements in a system (others being 'third parties', flying squadrons, or fragments) and to the general use of the old party names to describe them.

How the Opposition acquired an exclusive claim to Whig and the Court party to Tory is in some ways an obscure process. Sir Lewis Namier has suggested that it may be explained by the obvious inconvenience of playing a 'two-party game' under a 'one-name system': the one being Whig, Tory 'crept in again' as a label for the other.[2] This is in broad outline a reasonably good description of what occurred, but there is much evidence to show that it was not a mere matter of brand marks. The ideological content of the old denominations was not without significance, and when the process was completed, the stereotypes of Whig and Tory had undergone considerable revision. To gain an understanding of the process from its beginning it is necessary to go back to the fall of the Fox–North coalition.

On 17 December 1783, the day the House of Lords defeated the India Bill, the Commons debated the Constitutional right of a peer to report the opinion of the King upon pending legislation. Early in his speech Fox took the Rockinghamite

---

[1] Pares, *King George III and the Politicians*, p. 191.
[2] *The Spectator*, clxiii (1939), 261.

line that his party was based on 'the most respectable Whig interest in the kingdom'. When he turned to the likelihood that Temple's intrigue would bring down the Government, Fox declared,[1]

> If . . . a change must take place, and a new ministry is to be formed and supported, not by the confidence of this House or the public, but the sole authority of the Crown, I, for one, shall not envy that hon. gentleman his situation. From that moment I put in my claim for a monopoly of Whig principles.

He was as good as his word. In the following years the Foxites steadily asserted their pure, exclusive Whiggism. They not only damned the ministers as rank Tories and high Prerogative men but, it appears, thought of them as such and persuaded others to do likewise.[2] In 1788 the Earl of Abingdon, proud defender of his rugged independence, spoke of 'the two grand armies of the Whigs and Tories' as if the observation were a commonplace.[3] The Pittites, however, did not grant Fox his monopoly. They flung back the familiar charges that the doctrines of the self-styled party were a perversion of true Whiggism, being no more than the absurd claim of an oligarchic junto to govern on its own terms, and during the Regency crisis others joined Pitt in his endeavour to 'unwhig' the Opposition.[4]

The disruption of the Fox–North coalition by the French Revolution precipitated a major crisis over the meaning of Whiggism. The dispute centred at first upon the applicability of the principles of 1688 to the establishment of Constitutional monarchy across the Channel. While Fox maintained that the National Assembly re-enacted the role of the Convention Parliament by exercising the right of a sovereign people to

---

[1] *P.H.* xxiv. 213, 222.

[2] For examples of Whig publicism, see *Three Letters to the People of Great Britain and Particularly to those who signed the Addresses on the Late Changes of Administration and the Dissolution of Parliament* (London, 1785) and [Thomas L. O'Beirne], *Gleam of Comfort to this Distracted Empire* (London, 1785).

[3] *P.H.* xxvii. 237. Abingdon had much to say of Whiggism and Toryism in these years: ibid. xxiv. 138–9 (where he condemns Burke's *Thoughts*); xxv. 1347; xxvii. 855–7.

[4] *The Whig Catechism* (London, 1784); *Political Letters written in March and April MDCCLXXXIV* (London, 1784), in which there is another attack on Burke's *Thoughts*; *Whig and No Whig: A Political Paradox* (London, 1789); *P.H.* xxvii. 777, 807.

cashier its governors and frame a new Constitution, Burke in his *Appeal from the New to the Old Whigs* exhumed the prosecutors' arguments from the Sacheverell trial to prove that the men of 1688 had ousted James II in order to preserve the original compact, which no people might lawfully violate. On 12 May 1791 the *Morning Chronicle* announced,

The great and firm body of the Whigs of England, true to their principles, have decided on the dispute between Mr. Fox and Mr. Burke, and the former is declared to have maintained the pure doctrines by which they are bound together and upon which they have invariably acted. The consequence is that Mr. Burke retires from Parliament.

Burke retired, not from the House, but from the party and the Whig Club. A year later he wrote, referring to his arguments in the *Appeal*,[1]

Whether they are allowed to be Whig principles or not is a very small part of my concern. I think them exactly such as the sober, honourable, and intelligent in that party have always professed. . . . If they are Tory principles, I shall always wish to be thought a Tory.

As the French Revolution progressed, Fox saw another application of his Opposition doctrine. It is 'most according to our Whig ideas', he wrote in 1792, that the French King should 'be forced to have ministers of the same complexion with the Assembly'.[2] The execution of Louis XVI and the declaration of war upon Britain, however, thrust refined argument into the background for those who sympathized with Burke. Windham precipitated the mass resignation of Portland's schismatics from the Whig Club, an act deliberately designed as a renunciation of Foxite principles. At roughly the same time Pitt, in response to renewed accusations of Toryism, declared that he 'held not the principles of some persons who had lately called themselves Whigs'.[3] In 1794, as Pitt and Portland drew closer together, Fox remarked, 'Our old Whig friends are many of them worse Tories than even those whom they have joined.'[4]

[1] *H.M.C., Morrison MSS.*, p. 485. Sir Brooke Boothby had analyzed Burke's principles as pure Toryism in *Observations on the Appeal from the New to the Old Whigs* (London, 1792).

[2] Russell, *Mem. and Corresp. of C. J. Fox*, ii. 368, 373–4.

[3] *P.H.* xxx. 602, 606.

[4] Russell, *Mem. and Corresp. of C. J. Fox*, iii. 70.

The Whig schism was an important milestone in the history of parties, but Portland's followers were not of a mind to concede a monopoly of Whiggism to those from whom they had parted. Fitzwilliam thought of the junction with the Government as a necessary act to infuse the 'true aristocratic spirit' of Whiggism into a ministry which had been formed and conducted on false principles.[1] Ministerialists of all shades, whether or not they alluded to party names, steadily asserted their devotion to respectable Revolution principles, and when they allowed the Foxites the title of Whig, it was usually with a sneer. So the exchange of charge and counter-charge continued throughout the period of the Napoleonic wars, the Pittites generally rising to resist all imputations of Toryism. As late as 1812 the Opposition newspapers pressed so hard the exclusive claim of Grey and Grenville to 'true Whig principles' that a ministerial memorandum laid before the Regent protested,[2]

It is almost unnecessary to observe that the British Government had for more than a century been and could only be a Whig Government; and that the present administration is, as every administration in this country must necessarily be, a Whig administration. For a Whig Government means now, as it has all along meant, nothing else than a Government established by laws equally binding upon the King and the subject.

In the post-war years one perceives the gradual adoption of the two names as standard labels for Ministry and Opposition.[3] From the innumerable references in letters, memoirs, debates, and the Press, it appears that the Whigs established their monopoly first. There might still be protests that their creed was not that of 'the ancient Whigs',[4] but in the neighbourhood of

---

[1] Fitzwilliam Papers (Sheffield), 30(*b*), Fitzwilliam to Portland, 15 June 1794.

[2] A. Aspinall, ed., *The Letters of King George IV, 1812–1830* (Cambridge, 1938), i. 143.

[3] The use of party terminology can be traced in the standard sources for the period, notably L. J. Jennings, ed., *The Croker Papers* (London, 1855), i; A. Aspinall, ed., *The Correspondence of Charles Arbuthnot* (London, 1941); F. Bamford and Duke of Wellington, eds., *The Journal of Mrs. Arbuthnot* (London, 1950), i–ii; Sir H. Maxwell, ed., *The Creevey Papers* (London, 1903), i–ii; L. Strachey and R. Fulford, eds., *The Greville Memoirs* (London, 1938), i; Holland's *Memoirs of the Whig Party* (London, 1852), i–ii, and *Further Memoirs of the Whig Party* (London, 1905); Buckingham's *Memoirs* of the reign of George III and the Regency and reign of George IV; the newspapers and the reviews.

[4] For example, see *A Letter to Earl Fitzwilliam on Recent Events* (London, 1819).

1818 it had become general practice to refer to Grey's followers by their coveted designation. Popular writers at this time described the Government as Tory; but Ministerialists themselves accepted the label very slowly. In 1819 the back-bencher Richard Hart Davis declared in the Commons,[1]

> He was not ashamed of avowing himself a Tory, or rather he gloried in the title, but not as frequently explained in that House. The only difference he knew of between a good old Whig and Tory was that the Whig apprehended the more immediate danger to the Constitution from the undue influence of the Crown, whereas the Tory conceived that it was as likely to arise from the encroaching and overbearing licence of the people. He was, however, convinced that both would be found fighting under the same banner whenever a real attack was made upon the Constitution [loud cheers].

The great men in office, while acknowledging the support of such as Davis, were less inclined to call themselves Tories. As long as the two parties remained fairly stable, it was sufficient to speak of the Government or the ministerial party. A 'one-name system' does not seem for some time to have been a serious inconvenience. But out of consideration for the self-styled Tories who voted with them, ministers' fierce renunciation of the title came to an end.

The disruption of the two parties in 1827 then served as a catalyst. The confusion attendant upon the formation of Canning's Ministry created an ineluctable need for brand marks to describe the groups jostling for power. The Whigs were Whigs clearly enough, though a variety of modifiers had to be employed to distinguish those who joined Canning from those who did not, and the supporters of the former Ministry now became unequivocally Tories, moderates or ultras.[2] After the junction of Canning Tories and Lansdowne Whigs, the old Government's Whips, Holmes and Arbuthnot, spoke of Wellington and Peel as the heads of 'the Tory party'.[3] It would seem that their descent into opposition made their formal adoption of the name given them by their opponents highly desirable as a

---

[1] *Hansard*, 1st ser., xxxix. 594.

[2] The use of nomenclature can be seen in Aspinall, *The Formation of Canning's Ministry* (Camden Soc., 3rd ser., lix, 1937).

[3] Add. MSS. 40340, f. 181; Aspinall, ed., *Correspondence of Charles Arbuthnot*, pp. 93 ff.

means of identification, which had not been strictly necessary while they were in office.

Now, one must ask, if there had to be another name for the convenience of a two-party system, why did Tory 'creep in again'? Was it simply because the term was traditional as the obverse of Whig and because the *soi-disant* Whigs insisted upon tacking the obvious appellation to their opponents? This was indeed an important part of the process. It is conceivable that the Pittites might have chosen a title of their own, as their ultimate successors chose Conservative. They did not do so probably because, in addition to the fact that they did not need a name while in office, they liked to think of themselves as servants of the Crown—not as a self-seeking partisan group but as the sworn enemies of the storming party. To have assumed a title would have been to admit that they were merely a rival faction. It was no part of their mentality, after taking office without a party label, to invent one as a matter of form. When the need arose, Tory was the inescapable choice. In this rather negative way the old name fell to their lot. There were positive factors as well.

One was personnel. Pitt had acquired the support of most self-styled Tories. It may be taken as symbolic that John Rous and Noel Hill, the two members who had trumpeted their Toryism most loudly in the crisis of 1782, became his devoted followers and were rewarded with peerages. In the 1780's we hear no more of the Cocoa Tree Club as an association of Tory squires. Many became members of White's and accepted the Government Whip.[1] As far as they retained any identity it was as Independents who generally gave to His Majesty's Government the confidence which Pitt demanded. These men and their political heirs supported Addington until Pitt's Opposition in 1804 divided their loyalty. After three years of confusion they settled down for twenty years as regular adherents of the King's servants. Upon occasion they voted against official measures but not with a view to turning their sponsors out of place. In short, the search for a Tory almost inevitably

---

[1] It appears that Independents developed a new club. In the 1820's John Campbell wrote that Brooks's 'is the stronghold of the Whigs. The Tories muster at White's. Boodle's is for the country gentlemen and is considered neutral': Hardcastle, *Campbell*, i. 409.

wound up in the Government Lobby. Where could the Tory party be except where there were Tories?

Another was ideology. The language and conduct of Pitt and his successors bore some resemblance to the old Tory stereotype. They were the defenders of the Prerogative, the public advocates of 'measures, not men'. During the French wars they carried on a policy of repression—suspension of habeas corpus, curtailment of the liberty of the Press—in contravention of the popular rights supposedly guaranteed forever in 1688. After Pitt's brief flirtation with Catholic Relief, all ministers (except, of course, 'the Talents') refused to press the issue as an official measure, whereas the Opposition stood pledged to break down religious barriers. 'The Church in danger' again was raised as a battle-cry by Ministerialists who opposed any tampering with the Test and Corporation Acts. In the post-war period the Government once more took stern measures to repress popular disturbances, and Castlereagh's foreign policy was broadly identified with divine-right legitimacy. The unfavourable version of the Tory stereotype was well expressed in 1821 by the liberal divine, Robert Hall, who lamented[1]

that the memory of the *son* of Lord Chatham, the vehement opposer of the American war, the champion of reform, and the idol of the people, has become the type and symbol of whatever is most illiberal in principle and intolerant in practice.

Why did court politicians accept so unflattering a characterization from their rivals? In the minds of Ministerialists Toryism gradually acquired a favourable connotation derived from the same facts. Tories were the props of Throne and Altar, the defenders of law and order, the enemies of dangerous innovations, the true champions of the principles of 1688. The Foxites had equated Whiggism with Jacobinism, atheism, licence, tumult, and treason. Let them have a monopoly of these doctrines. Modern Toryism resembled ancient Whiggism. The early protectors of the Protestant Succession had passed the Riot Act and stamped out seditious practices. They had refused religious concessions beyond the Act of Toleration. They had struggled for the balance of Europe. If these policies must

---

[1] Russell, *Mem. and Corresp. of C. J. Fox*, iii. 37; cf. William Hazlitt's scornful version (1819) of the party stereotypes in *Complete Works* (ed. Howe), vii. 17–22.

now be called Tory, then Tories must now be the upholders of Revolution principles.[1]

The Whigs, of course, denied any dereliction from their original creed. It was their mission, as it had always been, to uphold the rights and liberties of the subject and to extend the blessings of the British Constitution for the prosperity and contentment of all His Majesty's subjects. Not all the vices and follies of mankind, the upheaval of nations and the panic of timid functionaries could divert them from the cause for which Russell and Sidney had died on the scaffold. The shades of Newcastle, Rockingham, and Fox must have smiled with approval upon this pronouncement of Grey in 1820:[2]

In a public view I think the preservation of the Whig party in Parliament of the utmost importance. It is really in practice the only defence for the liberties of the country. By that party the Revolution was effected, the Protestant Succession maintained. . . .

Its utility, I think, cannot be denied by anyone who will calmly appreciate its efforts. How many unconstitutional measures have been checked, how many much mitigated in their character, by its exertions. Even the present session will furnish a striking proof of this in the alterations which the different Bills underwent in their progress through the two Houses.

Besides all this, the having such a body united, in the event of any change in the public councils, is a chance which, however remote it may appear, ought not to be lightly abandoned.

So as the Tories equated Revolution principles with the Government, the Whigs equated them with the Opposition. It is little wonder that in 1828 the Duke of Wellington, who strove to stand outside petty partisanship, declared himself unable to find any distinction between the principles of Whigs and Tories.[3] There were major differences upon legislative proposals which might be called opposing principles, but these were rather confusing. At this time, for example, not all Whigs favoured parliamentary reform, and the issue of Catholic Emancipation cut across party lines. The Duke was right in thinking that Whigs and Tories stood upon the same political ground, for, as each based its claim to power upon being the true

---

[1] There is an excellent summation of Tory views in *Quarterly Review*, lv. 197–219.

[2] S. J. Reid, *Life and Letters of the First Earl of Durham* (London, 1906), i. 129.

[3] *Wellington's Despatches*, 3rd ser., iv. 453.

heirs of the Revolution, the ancient dispute over the Constitutional role of the Opposition withered away.

From the time that Pitt abandoned 'measures, not men' in 1804, his followers gradually gave up the traditional aspersions upon unconstitutional storming parties. Ministerialists continued for years to reassert the King's right to choose his servants and to retain them despite defeats in Parliament.[1] But as the Pittites came to think of themselves as a party, they moved toward the position that rivalry for place was a wholesome thing. In 1811 a Government pamphleteer, John Ranby, described the British political system in these terms:[2]

> To begin with the ministerial party. This is composed of the officers in the Household or administration; of their relatives, connexions, personal or political friends; by these last I mean such as attach themselves to the Ministry because they believe them to be preferable, both on account of their abilities and their professed principles of governing, to the members of the Opposition or any other party. All the persons of the above description may be expected to support the members of the administration, both in and out of office.

> The Opposition is an exact counterpart of the ministerial party; composed of persons of the same description, having the same motives and the same objects; and equally influenced by the opinion and counsels of their leaders; with this difference, that the Opposition aspire to the situation which the ministerial party possesses. Of both these parties the leaders are almost always persons of high rank, extensive connexions, considerable property, disposed to do business, and some of them must be distinguished for superior political information and talents. Is it not natural, is it not laudable, that men thus qualified should aspire to have a share in administering the government of their country? Is it not desirable that they should do so? To some of them the emoluments of office may be presumed to be an object, and why should they not? . . .

> These two parties thus composed are to be considered as the principals in that legitimate warfare of parties in Parliament, from which much benefit is derived to the public.

Ranby's exposition is an obvious composite of old and new elements. The idea that party warfare produced some incidental good goes back to Walpole's time. It is to be noted that Ranby

---

[1] For example, see *Hansard*, 1st ser., xxiii. 252–81; 2nd ser., vii. 1307, 1314–16.

[2] *An Inquiry into the Supposed Increase of the Influence of the Crown, the Present State of that Influence, and the Expediency of a Parliamentary Reform* (London, 1811), pp. 37–45.

did not use Whig or Tory. The two parties are described in functional terms. The Opposition is not merely a Country party of passive critics, or an unprincipled flying squadron of place-hunters, or a storming party whose success will end the need for an Opposition. It is an alternative Government, a situation which may be occupied by either party, and since the parties are assumed to be permanent, the Opposition becomes a regular institution in national politics.

How far the concept expressed by Ranby gained general acceptance among the Tories may be seen in an article entitled 'The Opposition' in the *Quarterly Review* for 1822.[1] All of Ranby's assumptions are employed as Constitutional maxims. The authors, David Robinson and William Gifford, refer to the two parties automatically as Whig and Tory, a reflection of the development in the application of those labels over a dozen years, and the Whigs are condemned for failing to perform the proper duty of Opposition. Their principles and tactics are more likely, it was said, to produce a revolution than a mere change of ministry, their legitimate goal. Equally bad, 'they are disqualified by the want of talent and integrity from becoming the Ministry'. The country is without a 'genuine, Constitutional Opposition' because

There is no man of discernment in the nation who, whatever may be his politics, believes that the Whigs are capable of conducting the affairs of the Empire or ought to be entrusted with power; and therefore the sovereign and the country possess no longer an alternative in the choice of ministers, and the ministers no longer feel that powerful stimulant and effectual curb—the consciousness that men exist, anxious and able to replace them.

The Tory authors do not express a high opinion of the motives that actuate an Opposition, even if conducted by their own party. They admit that it is an institution unknown to the law, but they declare it essential to the welfare of the state. It is regrettable that the nation must be 'eternally embroiled in an election contest between two bodies for the reins of power', but happily Britain is 'the only nation that has hitherto been able to extract from factions more good than evil and to render their

---

[1] *Quarterly Review*, lv. 197–219; cf. the Tory Croker's memorandum on Opposition in Jennings, ed., *Croker Papers*, ii. 82–87; and to see how closely Whig and Tory views coincided, cf. *Edinburgh Review*, lix. 181–206.

G g

existence subservient to the general weal'. The strife for place and emolument, whether base or noble, is legitimate.

What, then, of the Prerogative, the ark of the Tory covenant? The authors are quite explicit. 'The favour of the Sovereign, whatever it once was, is now of inferior value' in the maintenance or change of an administration. It is the people who, through Parliament, 'virtually elect and depose ministries'. If an Opposition can obtain a majority in the Commons, the Ministry must be removed, and 'its removal constitutes in effect the election of [its] rival'. The King is the agent of the public. The Prerogative is the instrument by which the popular will is put into effect.

In view of the Pittites' historic defence of the rights of the Crown, it is startling that by 1822 Tory theorists had arrived at the doctrine which in basic essentials has since prevailed. Their views seem explicable, not as an exegesis of the law of the Constitution, but as an interpretation of contemporary facts. The influence of the Crown and the personal influence of the monarch had greatly declined. A repetition of the *coup* of 1783–4 was a practical impossibility. Ever since that time, except on the issue of Catholic Emancipation, the King had played a diminishing role in the formulation of policy. Ministers had occasionally suffered defeats, but not defeats which involved loss of confidence, and on the ground that they must satisfy a majority in the Commons, they had obliged the King to approve whatever measures they proposed. As long as the majority remained satisfied, ministers remained in office. If opinion changed, the King had no alternative but the Opposition. Only in the event of party ruptures, which the theorists did not anticipate, would His Majesty have any real freedom of choice.[1]

That they interpreted fact rather than construed law may be owing to a decline in the emotional involvement of King and politicians in the old Constitutional issue. George III ultimately accepted Fox in 1806 without any grumbling about being forced. Men in Opposition ceased to think of themselves as being unfairly excluded by the King, and consequently they got away from the idea, so strong in the minds of Rockingham and Fox, that the victory of the Opposition represented a triumph over

[1] See Pares, *King George III and the Politicians*, pp. 180–207.

the Crown. George IV was given to asserting his Prerogative and sometimes made serious trouble about appointments, but he did not try to form a Cabinet from his Carlton House favourites. With some glaring exceptions he treated his ministers as public servants whom he retained in office because they possessed the power and talent to do the work of state, not because he had any affection for their persons or their principles. In short, the defence of the Prerogative, particularly when it was in the hands of such a King as George IV, ceased to be a 'cause', and Tories could dispassionately take their observations upon the actual functioning of the political system as a correct interpretation of the Constitution.

The conduct of Tory politicians conformed to the views expressed in the *Quarterly*. In 1827 the Anti-catholics were at first demoralized by the party split and the loss of the Treasury, but by mid-July Peel had resolved to organize 'a systematic Opposition next session and keep no terms with the Government'.[1] The death of Canning and the collapse of Goderich returned the Tories to power before Parliament reopened. Their defeat in 1830 was followed by another period of confused hesitancy and then the formation of a resolute Opposition to Grey. In the following years Peel rebuilt the Tories into the strong Conservative party which stormed not only the closet but also the boudoir. The terms imposed upon the Crown by the old corps in 1744–6 and the Fox–North coalition in 1783 were not more severe than those imposed upon Victoria by Peel in 1841. The political heirs of Pitt established the right of a successful Opposition to dictate appointments in the bedchamber as well as in the offices of state. And so it turned out that the political heirs of Fox established their claim to a monopoly on the name of Whig but not to a monopoly of Whig principles.

5. THE WHIG OPPOSITION, 1807–1830

There was a large measure of truth in the Tory contention that the Whig Opposition did not constitute an alternative Government. The affairs of the party during most of this period were in a state of uncertainty and confusion. Out of a stern regard for Foxite principles the leaders forfeited several

[1] *H.M.C., Bathurst MSS.*, p. 640.

opportunities to enter the Ministry, and the effort to co-operate with Canning in 1827 proved a near disaster.[1] The Whigs' own partisans criticized them for lack of ambition and unwillingness to shoulder responsibility.[2] Fundamental differences of opinion, both on tactics and measures, made it difficult to sustain a united front in Parliament. Their divisions laid them open to the obvious jibe that they remained perpetually in Opposition because they regularly demonstrated their unfitness to govern:[3]

> Nought's constant in the human race,
> Except the Whigs not getting into place.

The weakness of the party was attributable primarily to weak leadership. Fox's mantle descended naturally upon the shoulders of Grey, for whom it was not well cut. He was soon removed to the Lords, where he could not carry on the role of 'the great captain', and after the fall of 'the Talents' he displayed in increasing degree his reluctance to storm his way back into office. He and Grenville, as the duumvirs of the party from 1807 to 1817, co-operated cordially, but they were rather like twin Rockinghams whose normal decisions were to do nothing. After Grenville's retirement Grey bestirred himself only on rare occasions, deprecated his own authority as leader, and wrote constantly of his wish to retire. By 1824 he had come to consider himself an aloof senior statesman, brooding in detachment upon the fallen state of the Whigs but quite unwilling to make any move to raise it. Thenceforward he instructed the party Whip to deal with Shelburne's heir, Lansdowne, 'as the person whom his friends were to look upon as their leader'.[4]

Lansdowne had been a well-liked and active member of the party, but the weight of responsibility induced in him a lethargic timidity that rendered him ineffective. Upon Grey's retirement he accepted perforce a position of pre-eminence, but he refused to take the post of leader.[5] He generally employed his authority to dampen the zealous spirits of the younger men

---

[1] Roberts, *Whig Party*, pp. 330–405; Holland, *Further Memoirs of the Whig Party*, pp. 400–3; A. Aspinall's 'The Coalition Ministries of 1827' (*E.H.R.* xlii. 201–26, 533–59) and *The Formation of Canning's Ministry*.

[2] For a summary of these criticisms, see *Edinburgh Review*, civ. 541–3.

[3] Trevelyan, *Lord Grey of the Reform Bill*, p. 242.

[4] On Grey's leadership, see ibid. 149–85; *Greville Memoirs*, i. 179.

[5] Aspinall, *Formation of Canning's Ministry*, p. 234.

for fear of causing a rupture. Under heavy pressure he negotiated a place for some of the Whigs in the coalition Ministries
of 1827, but his ineptitude nearly caused the total disintegration of the party. Back in Opposition Lansdowne grew 'sadly
lazy and supine', altogether unresponsive to demands and
pleadings for strong leadership. 'He is admitted by common
consent', said one exasperated Whig, 'to be the damnedest idiot
that ever lived.'[1] The party nevertheless continued to look upon
him as its nominal chief until the events of 1830 brought Grey
back to the forefront of politics.

The helplessness of the Whigs under Grey and Lansdowne
shows how little progress the Opposition had made in solving
the problem of leadership. In the absence of an outstanding
figure like Fox, whose talents and personality made him leader
by general acquiescence, the party clung to Grey as the ablest
man of rank who had served under 'the great captain'. It is
significant that his son-in-law, Lambton, who was too young to
remember the long struggle against Pitt, considered Grey the
only person capable of leading the party because he was 'Fox's
representative'.[2] The dead hand of the past lay heavy upon the
Whigs. When the squire of Howick declined all their entreaties
to remain at his post, they had developed no convention for
selecting a successor. They accepted the squire of Bowood *faute
de mieux* because Grey designated him, but when Lansdowne
would not lead, there was no means to replace him.

The problem was the more acute because the character of
the party was changing with the times. The standard image of
'the grand Whiggery' of these years—a cultured, witty, wealthy
clan of epicurean aristocrats—is largely accurate. The party was
still dominated by the great peers whose electoral influence returned a majority of its members, but it was no longer a snug
chaste corps which could hope to iron out its difficulties in a
conciliabulum at Newcastle House. From 1807 to 1818 there
were 150 names on the Whip's list; from 1818 to 1830 there
were 180.[3] Only powerful leadership, based upon a knowledge

---

[1] S. H. Romilly, ed., *Letters to 'Ivy' from the First Earl of Dudley* (London, 1905),
pp. 329–31; Maxwell, ed., *Creevey Papers*, p. 486.

[2] Reid, *Durham*, i. 105–6.

[3] Aspinall, *Formation of Canning's Ministry*, p. 78; Buckingham, *Memoirs of the
Regency*, ii. 280. On the basis of Wade's *Black Book* (1820), *Extraordinary Black Book*
(1831), Oldfield's *Representative History* (1816), and numerous scraps of information

of what measures would gain general acceptance, could manage effectively so extensive a group. A considerable number were of humble origin and radical bent. They did not disguise their impatience with the private quarrels and political indolence of the blue-blooded. Moreover, in company with several lordlings of the rising generation, the Radicals took a profound interest in social, economic, administrative, and electoral reform, and they recognized the growing popular interest in the mounting legislation passed by Parliament every year. The affairs of state, as Brougham once reminded Lansdowne, were no longer determined by the agreements and differences of the Russells and Cavendishes.[1] The party could not become an alternative Government until it acquired a chief active and persuasive enough to secure common agreement to a strong line of public policy.

The Whigs experienced comparable difficulties—only in part for the same reasons—with their leaders in the Commons. When Grey inherited his peerage in 1807, the duumvirs were pressed to arrange the selection of a deputy in the Lower House, who should manage the King's business there upon the party's return to office. Lord Grenville was hesitant:[2]

a leader of an Opposition cannot be chosen and appointed as a leader of a Government party may and . . . all the elections in the world would not have made Windham or Sheridan leaders of the old Opposition while Fox was alive. In opposition people will follow like hounds (according to Lord Bolingbroke's simile) the man who shows them game.

The obvious choice was Samuel Whitbread, a fine speaker who enjoyed the great advantage of being Grey's brother-in-law, but he was too Radical for the Grenvilles. To obviate his pretensions Thomas Grenville urged the choice of George Ponsonby, a little known mediocrity who was related to Lady Grey. Surely, wrote Grenville, 'any choice is better than none', and Grey cannot be offended if he 'is desired to recommend his wife's uncle instead of his sister's husband'.[3] With many

gathered from memoirs, I calculate that, in the elections of 1818, 1820, and 1826, 36 Whig peers returned 95 members by influence or direct nomination.

[1] Aspinall, *Lord Brougham and the Whig Party* (Manchester, 1927), p. 82.
[2] Buckingham, *Court and Cabinets of George III*, iv. 209.
[3] *H.M.C., Dropmore MSS.* ix. 147–59. Lord Henry Petty was also under consideration, but in little more than a year he inherited the Marquisate of Lansdowne.

misgivings the duumvirs accepted this solution, and by their nomination Ponsonby became the leader in the Commons.

Within a few weeks he had demonstrated his incompetence, and Grenville was urging his removal.[1] Ponsonby would not quit. For ten years the Whigs tried in vain to persuade him to resign. The chiefs had not the heart to depose him, and there was no other way to get rid of him. Under steady criticism and bitter ridicule he clung to his post until his death in 1817. Experience did nothing to sharpen his skill or improve his proficiency. Of the last year of his leadership Lord John Russell wrote,[2]

I remember being summoned to a meeting of the members of the party, both in Lords and Commons, early in 1817. Lord Grey, in a few clear, bold, and dignified sentences, sketched the policy expected from the Ministry and his own determination to oppose to the uttermost such of those measures as should be brought forward in the House of Lords. He ended by saying, 'Mr. Ponsonby will explain to you what is expected on the part of government in the House of Commons.' Mr. Ponsonby then addressed the meeting and declared that he knew nothing of the proposals to be made by the Government in the House of Commons or of the course that it was fit to pursue.

While such was the inability of the leader who had been set over us, there was little concord as to measures to be resisted or the motions to be brought forward by members of the Opposition.

For a year after Ponsonby's death the Whigs quarrelled over the selection of a successor. Lord Grenville retired, and Grey would take no positive action. All wanted a new Fox to step forward and solve the problem for them. Thomas Creevey, whose view was widely shared, declared that 'a man must make himself leader by his talents, by his courage, and above all by the excellence and consistency of his public principles'; but, as Charles Western observed, the party lacked a 'superior *mind* . . . to strike a line of policy and to command the *confidence* of the country'.[3] Sir Samuel Romilly was greatly respected by all

---

[1] Ibid. 282–7. Some despondent Whigs considered another secession at this time, but party sentiment was strongly opposed to a repetition of this futile tactic: ibid. 253–4; Fitzwilliam Papers 30(*e*), Sheffield City Library, Grenville to Fitzwilliam, 9 Jan. 1809.

[2] *Recollections and Suggestions, 1813–73* (London, 1875), pp. 30–31.

[3] Maxwell, ed., *Creevey Papers*, pp. 251–2, 290.

elements in the party, but he committed suicide in 1818. Henry Brougham was the most brilliant Whig commoner, but he impressed his fellows as being conceited, erratic, and intemperate. Lord Althorp was able and steady but indolent and a poor speaker. At length the Chief Whip, Lord Duncannon, and an active group of 'the busy bodies at Brooks's' took the problem in hand. In the summer of 1818 they drew up a petition requesting George Tierney to assume the lead.

Tierney had long stood on the fringe of the party. He refused to join the secession of 1797. He took office under Addington in 1803 and under 'the Talents' in 1806. Gradually he became a Whig stalwart, a capable and witty speaker who attended faithfully. It does not appear that he enjoyed any great personal popularity, but he had made no irreconcilable enemies. In short, he was rather a neutral figure, who, despite poor health, obviously possessed the vigour and competence to direct sessional campaigns. As was to be expected, the petition, circulated among the members in the Commons, met with general but unenthusiastic acceptance. Creevey jeered at the petition as 'a kind of a Luddite test' and declined to have anything to do with it.[1] Lambton thought Tierney a scallawag but signed in deference to his friends' wishes.[2] Finally 113 signatures were obtained, and Duncannon asked Tierney to take the post. He temporized, called the responsibility too great, professed a desire to refuse. After persistent urging he yielded with much reluctance.[3]

Despite this melancholy beginning Tierney's leadership proved an overwhelming success at the outset. Encouraged by gains in the general election of 1818, the party rallied strongly behind their standard-bearer. During the new session they had frequent meetings at Burlington House, and Whig dinners were held once a fortnight in public taverns. Members formally agreed to attend regularly and to remain at the House until released by Tierney.[4] Concurrently the Government was passing through one of its periodic states of disorganization. Castlereagh suffered severely from gout, and Canning was in

---

[1] *Creevey Papers*, p. 291.   [2] Reid, *Durham*, i. 106–8.

[3] On Tierney's election, see Holland, *Further Memoirs of the Whig Party*, p. 265; Olphin, *Tierney*, 182–92.

[4] Holland, *Further Memoirs of the Whig Party*, pp. 266–7. The dinners are reported in the *Morning Chronicle*.

poor health. Other official men objected to sitting out long debates when they had administrative work to do, and the country gentlemen who normally supported the Government declined to attend when ministers did not. The Government Whip, Charles Arbuthnot, wrote despondingly of late sittings 'with nearly empty benches on our side of the House, and with benches crammed up to the very corners on the Opposition side'.[1]

From January into early May, 1819, the Whigs defeated ministers on several minor points and occasionally forced them to give way without a division. Tierney skilfully exploited his strength to draw the initiative into his hands. Motions for inquiries into the criminal law and corruption in Scots burghs were carried despite official resistance. The Government had become so weak, it was reported to the Regent, that 'the Opposition has been allowed to originate every motion and have got possession of the committees upon the main questions now under consideration'.[2] It was widely believed that the Ministry must fall.

At length both sides determined upon a trial of strength. The Cabinet decided to make the revival of the malt tax a stand-or-fall issue, and the Regent promised them his full support 'to bear down the mischievous cabal to which we are now subject'.[3] Tierney took the matter out of their hands by bringing in a motion for a committee on the state of the Nation on 18 May. The occasion was dramatic. The Whips had rounded up every possible vote, and the House was more crowded than it had ever been. Tierney's opening speech was an appeal to the Independents to remove the feeble administration which they had 'kicked and cuffed about' all during the session. Could gentlemen have confidence in ministers who did not fill the Treasury Bench on a normal evening? If one looked to 'measures, not men' (the old Tory slogan might still arouse a response), let members compare the sound, consistent achievements of the Opposition with the wavering, ineffective policy of the Government. Other Whig speakers followed the same line. It all ended

---

[1] Aspinall, ed., *Correspondence of Charles Arbuthnot*, pp. 15–18. Passing Tierney in the Lobby one evening, Castlereagh remarked, 'I should like to learn the secret of your association': *Colchester Diaries*, iii. 72–73.

[2] Aspinall, ed., *Letters of George IV*, ii. 288. On the Opposition victories see Hansard, 1st ser., xxxix. 777–846; xl. 178–98.

[3] Aspinall, ed., *Letters of George IV*, ii. 289–92.

in disaster. The motion was lost by 357 to 178, the largest division before the Reform Bill.[1]

This defeat put an effective end to Tierney's leadership. So weak was his hold upon the party that his prestige could not survive one spectacular reverse.[2] For over ten years the Whigs had no head in the Commons. They did not want to risk another mistake, and in view of their apparently hopeless position, a choice did not seem imperative. The direction of their affairs, Lord Holland recorded, 'devolved to the guidance of three or four men of weight . . . or to that of chance itself'.[3] Then after the formation of Wellington's Government in 1828 a small group calling themselves 'the watchmen' gathered around Lord Althorp. His stature grew until early in 1830 a deputation of back-benchers urged him to lead the party. He asked for time to consult other prominent commoners and for formal petition by at least forty-five members. All turned out favourably, and Althorp took the vacant post. The remainder of the party silently acquiesced in the decision.[4]

Thus in these years the Whigs bore a good resemblance to de Retz's description of a party—a serpent whose head was pushed on by his tail. The vertebrae of the structure developed by the Rockinghamites and Foxites continued to function despite cranial debility. Now and then discouraged Whigs talked about breaking up the party, and it might have disintegrated under such uncertain leadership had not its institutions been so solidly established. The importance of Brooks's cannot be over-estimated. No matter what the fortunes of the party in the House, the club endured as a centre of common activity. Here, in addition to party meetings, members met informally, exchanged ideas, argued policy, announced the motions they proposed to make. The society was in effect the parliamentary

---

[1] *Hansard*, 1st ser., xl. 474–553. The total present was 568, adding the speaker, 4 tellers, 12 pairs, and 4 Grenvillites who departed without voting.

[2] Holland, *Further Memoirs of the Whig party*, p. 267; Olphin, *Tierney*, p. 208; Aspinall, *Brougham*, p. 95. Tierney did not disclaim the leadership till 23 Jan. 1821 (*Hansard*, 2nd ser., iv. 30), but he had ceased to exercise its functions since the great defeat.

[3] Holland, *Further Memoirs of the Whig Party*, p. 268.

[4] Sir Denis le Marchant, *Memoir of John Charles, Viscount Althorp, Third Earl Spencer* (London, 1876), pp. 243–6, 267. Althorp informed Grey of his election, but it does not appear that he sought the approval of Grey or Lansdowne in advance.

party out-of-parliament.[1] It was managed by the Chief Whip, Lord Duncannon, in whom the Whigs were singularly fortunate. He was, wrote Lord Broughton,[2]

a general favourite, and for the general transactions of a party and keeping a political body together, had a tact and success such as no man of my times possessed. He leant to the most liberal section of the Whig party, but being connected by birth and marriage with the most aristocratic and unpopular portion of it, he was of great use in going between the two and preventing dissension. He was exceedingly cool and collected in circumstances of difficulty, and was not to be deterred by scruples or trifles of any kind from steadily pursuing the object in view. He had an instinctive knowledge of mankind, and his manners being very pleasing and his understanding very good, though not of the higher order, he was an agreeable and welcome companion wherever he went.

The degree of solidarity achieved by the Whigs, despite all their differences, may be measured by the fact that those who joined Canning's Ministry in 1827 continued to meet at Brooks's and to receive their Whip from Duncannon, not from the Treasury.[3]

The Whig Club faded out of existence in 1811 to be soon replaced by the Fox Club, which performed the same functions.[4] Party zeal extended the institution of celebrating Fox's birthday far beyond the metropolis. The *Morning Chronicle* annually reported great gatherings at Chester, Norwich, Newcastle, Edinburgh, Glasgow, and many other towns throughout the realm. To these party rallies were admitted all who would pay the fee to drink Whig toasts. How such events appeared to non-politicians may be seen in this excerpt from the journal of Henry Edward Fox, the grand-nephew of 'the great captain', for 24 January 1823:[5]

Mr. Fox's birthday. I went with Lord Thanet to the Fox dinner. We sat for ever and I was bored. Lord Erskine, Mr. Lens, Mr.

[1] It should be noted that desertion from the party did not entail resignation from the club. In time Brooks's carried on its rolls a large number who were not Whigs. To make room for recruits the membership was gradually increased from the original limit of 150 to 575 by 1823. It does not appear that renegades took an active part in club affairs: *Memorials of Brooks's*, p. xii.

[2] *Recollections of a Long Life* (London, 1911), vi. 192; cf. Hardcastle, *Campbell*, i. 408–11.

[3] Aspinall, *Formation of Canning's Ministry*, p. 253; *Correspondence of Charles Arbuthnot*, p. 88.

[4] Ilchester, *Home of the Hollands*, pp. 284–7.

[5] Ilchester, ed., *Journal of the Rt. Hon. Henry Edward Fox* (London, 1923), p. 153.

Scarlett, Mr. Denison and many dirty, violent little black people, who talked about taxes, poverty, funds, war, peace, the wickedness of ministers generally, for they had no particular fact or person in view, and the usual prophecies of ruin, tyranny and revolution which wind up the sentences of speculative politicians. Good dinner at Grillon's Hotel.

The birthday parties represented a significant effort to keep the Whig spirit alive between elections and to incorporate the electorate (and perhaps some who were not electors) into the party. With reference to the celebrations in Edinburgh, Henry Cockburn wrote, 'These Fox dinners did incalculable good. They animated and instructed and consolidated the Whig party with less trouble and more effect than anything else that could have been desired.'[1]

The growing concern of 'dirty, violent little black people' with reform had a strong influence upon the conduct of the Opposition in Parliament. While still employing the traditional shock tactics and harassing manœuvres to weaken and pull down ministers, the Whigs turned their attention increasingly to measures for the improvement of Government and society. These were the years when members of the Opposition assumed a steady responsibility for constructive legislation. As long ago as 1731, of course, Pulteney had boasted of the salutary Bills introduced by the malcontents, and 'patriots' since his time had followed their example. Their proposals had been few, sporadic, and generally designed to reduce the influence of the Crown. The Whigs carried on this practice in their acts to end the grant of reversions and the sale of seats, in their unrelenting attacks on sinecures and unnecessary offices, and in their efforts to secure more effective parliamentary control of public expenditure. A study of *Hansard* from 1807 to 1830 shows also a long succession of Opposition proposals for reforming the criminal law and legal procedures, commercial and industrial regulations, the poor law and local government. Men on the Speaker's left made frequent efforts to improve popular education. The effect of early nineteenth-century humanitarianism can be seen in their motions for the preservation of wild fowl, the prevention of cruelty to animals, and the abolition of

[1] *Memorials of His Time* (Edinburgh, 1856), p. 425.

corporal punishment in the military services. Much was accomplished. The achievements of Brougham, Romilly, and Hume are distinguished in the annals of this time. The Opposition had no monopoly on the reforming spirit, and when their Bills did not conflict with the interests of the Government, Ministerialists often endorsed and supported them.

These measures did not, however, constitute a party platform. They represented the interests of individuals, who pursued them out of conscience—and probably also out of a desire to make a name for themselves. The Whigs had no general programme. All were agreed upon Catholic Emancipation, but their view was shared by many Tories, and during the 1820's there was generally a majority for the question in the Commons. The intransigence of the King and the Lords prevented any effective action and made it very dubious what the Whigs could do about the issue if they ever got back into place. They could not find any other national points to serve as a bond of union. On electoral reform they were divided by so wide a variety of opinions that the leaders dared not commit the party to it. Lambton and Lord John Russell made some progress in converting the more conservative peers between 1819 and 1822, but thereafter the question remained in the background.[1] Grey and the other magnates thought it unwise to pledge themselves to any measures which might create dissension and cause them embarrassment in office. It seemed most prudent to jog on as they were, allowing individuals to follow their own inclinations, and to issue the party Whip only on motions which did not stir up much controversy at Brooks's.

Such a cautious policy was doubtless instrumental in holding together an Opposition in which there were such broad areas of disagreement. It did not strengthen their putative position as an alternative Government. There was much truth in Brougham's observation in 1827 that the Whigs had 'ceased to act as a party, and the country has naturally enough given over talking about what has no existence owing to ourselves'. The time was

---

[1] On the Whigs' attitudes to electoral reform, see Reid, *Durham*, i. 130–2; *Life and Times of Lord Brougham*, ii. 340–1; Russell, *Recollections and Suggestions*, p. 41; Ilchester, *Chronicles of Holland House*, p. 8; Buckingham, *Memoirs of George IV*, i. 116; *Early Correspondence of Lord John Russell*, i. 223; *Edinburgh Review*, xxxi. 170–1; Hansard, 2nd ser. xi. 721.

overdue, he thought, 'rather to limit our numbers than to sacrifice union and vigour to numerical force'.[1]

When in the same year Lansdowne, Tierney, and Carlisle took places in the coalition ministries with the support of a large segment of the party, it appeared that there was nothing left of Whig principles. Lansdowne did not stipulate for Catholic Emancipation, their one measure. He neither demanded the strongholds of the Government nor staked a claim to his share in the distribution of patronage. In short, he accepted terms which would have shocked Rockingham and Fox, and which, considering the size of his following, would have seemed poor indeed to any of the old flying squadrons. Lansdowne had been driven to this course by 'the insurrection at Brooks's', led by Brougham, whose purpose was to keep out the ultra-Tories at any cost. Under his influence the party forced the leader, whose fault was 'being still in the year 1780', to the accommodation with Canning.[2] Once more the tail had pushed on the head. The negative principle of building a Government upon the exclusion of 'Eldon and Co.' proved a weak foundation, and the result was such as an old Whig would have foretold. The Ministry, rank with discord, was a prey to royal caprice and factious rivalry. Lansdowne had to give way on every point of disagreement with the Canningites and the King. Five months after Canning's death Goderich, unable to cope with unending dissension, resigned in a flood of tears, and the Whigs returned to their seats on the Speaker's left.

The confusion of political loyalties amid which Wellington formed his Ministry was increased by the passage of Catholic Emancipation. In 1830 the Duke's feeble Front Bench faced a large but unorganized Opposition of Whigs, Canningites, and ultra-Tories, which did not constitute an alternative Government. It was the prevailing sentiment for the first few months of the year that the King's Government could be carried on only by Wellington with some accession of strength from his opponents. Then the re-emergence of Grey as a leader made an alternative possible. He had condemned the coalition of 1827

[1] Aspinall, *Brougham*, p. 145.
[2] Maxwell, ed., *Creevey Papers*, ii. 114. On the coalition ministries, see Aspinall's, 'The Coalition Ministries of 1827' in *E.H.R.* xlii. 201–26, 533–59; and his *Formation of Canning's Ministry*.

and regarded the Duke with benevolent neutrality. Stimulated by the unsettled state of the country, the reform agitation of Attwood and Cobbett, and the election of Althorp, Grey came up to town in April to examine the political situation. After two months of careful probing he took his decision. In the House of Lords on 30 June he denounced the Ministry as unworthy of the confidence of Parliament. Grey found to his satisfaction that he had gained the favour of 'all parties not connected with the Government'.[1] He soon struck up a working agreement with the leading Canningites, and for the remainder of the session he harassed Wellington, not with a view to turning him out but to keep him weak and unpopular. All of Grey's words and deeds clearly indicate that he was working cautiously but consciously toward the leadership of a coalition which would storm the closet when the time was ripe.

The general election of 1830, made necessary by the death of George IV, took place in the midst of the great public excitement aroused by economic distress, reform agitation, and revolution across the Channel. The Press was filled with controversy over the result, but it was generally apparent that the Government's situation was precarious. Although Peel and the Duke put up a bold front, they knew that the Treasury estimates of a majority of 100 in mid-August had declined to a maximum of 26 a month later.[2] Wellington tried in vain to draw in the Canningites. They demanded a thorough reconstruction which included the Whigs, and during the first week of the new Parliament these two parties allied to turn out the Ministry.[3] Grey had succeeded in reconstituting a Rockinghamite Opposition united upon a programme of 'peace, retrenchment, and reform'.

In this programme traditional elements were mingled with some that were significantly novel. Peace had been a Whig cry since 1775. Retrenchment was another word for the Country party's anti-corruption plank, and now it included, not simply

---

[1] *Correspondence of Princess Lieven and Earl Grey*, ii. 20–21; *Hansard*, 2nd ser. xxv. 727–8.
[2] Planta's analyses are in Add. MSS. 40401, ff. 130–3, 138–40, 179–95, 228–67. Among the pamphlets on the election were *The Result of the General Election; or, What has the Duke of Wellington gained by the Dissolution?*, *The Duke of Wellington and the Whigs*, and *Government without Whigs*, which were commented upon in *Edinburgh Review*, ciii. 261–79. [3] H. C. F. Bell, *Lord Palmerston* (London, 1936), i. 90–94.

Place and Pension Bills, but a continuation of the legal and administrative reforms which the Whigs had long sponsored. Reform meant extension of the franchise. Grey had originally taken it up as a means to combat the influence of the Crown, but he endorsed it in 1830 'to prevent the necessity for revolution'.[1] He and his colleagues became convinced that electoral reform, introduced as a Government measure, was absolutely indispensable to restore public confidence in Parliament. Peel and Wellington, sincerely distressed at having been forced to reverse themselves on Catholic Emancipation, refused to be spun about again by Radical agitation. During the first debate in the new Parliament the Duke declared flatly against any change in the representation. By espousing reform, therefore, the Opposition for the first time performed the function of providing an alternative set of men prepared to pursue measures in accordance with the popular will to avert the possible overthrow of the state.

After Wellington's declaration the Whigs planned to challenge him directly on the reform issue. Brougham put down a motion for 16 November, but on the preceeding night the Ministry failed by 29 to defeat a proposal for an inquiry into the Civil List. The Duke resigned and advised William IV to summon Grey. The ensuing change of Government took place according to the procedure which the Whigs had been striving to establish since 1767. The King did not wish to part with Wellington, but convinced that he must, he called in Grey, assured him of the royal confidence, and gave him '*carte blanche* as to all offices both in Government and the Household but Brougham'. The restriction on Brougham was not an exclusion but a stipulation, with which Grey fully agreed, that the tempestuous orator must not be made Master of the Rolls, a well paid, lifetime appointment which would enable him to harass all ministries with impunity. In response to the King's offer Grey explained the principles of 'peace, reform, and economy' upon which he would form a Government, and when William IV assented to them, the new Prime Minister took up his commission. In four days he put together the strong coalition Cabinet that carried out his programme.[2]

[1] See Grey's declaration of principles in *Hansard*, 3rd Ser., i. 605–14.
[2] Trevelyan, *Lord Grey of the Reform Bill*, pp. 240–6.

By the time of the Whigs' success it is apparent that the major issues affecting in practice the Constitutional position of His Majesty's Opposition had been resolved. William IV and Victoria expressed just as strong personal prejudices about parliamentary politicians as had the four Georges. The Crown still retained much discretionary power in the formation of ministries when no party or coalition had a working majority in the House of Commons. But the Opposition was no longer considered disloyal, factious, or a threat to the royal Prerogative. The monarchs expected to yield to an Opposition which could defeat the Ministry-in-being, and, regardless of their private feelings, to embrace the men and measures proposed by the victorious party. Charles Greville probably expressed the general view in 1830 when he wrote,[1]

The King seems to have behaved perfectly thoughout the whole business, no intriguing or underhand communications with anybody, with great kindness to ministers, anxious to support them while it was possible, and submitting at once to the necessity of parting with them.

In short, the Crown had accepted the interpretation of the Prerogative which Fox had vainly tried to establish in 1783–4.

The old ideal of 'broad bottom' died hard. In 1830 the *Edinburgh Review* favoured a union of the best of all parties as a practical remedy for the weakness of Wellington's Government, and regretted that the result of the general election made it impossible.[2] A ministry of all talents, chosen by the King according to proved capacity, still appeared, even to some who acknowledged the valuable services of an Opposition, to be the most sensible and Constitutional mode of government. But except as a temporary expedient in a grave crisis, 'broad bottom' had been shown by a century of experience to be impracticable. It was not that personal and political differences cut too deep. Most politicians of the Georgian era, once dragged into harness, had been amazingly resilient in drawing together. It was rather that there was not enough room at the top. There were more aspiring talents than there were high offices to fill. Rivalry inevitably developed within comprehensive administrations and ultimately broke them up. Far better that Governments

[1] *Greville Memoirs*, ii. 62.   [2] *Edinburgh Review*, civ. 535–6.

should be united, that the contest should take place between 'ins' and 'outs', and that upon differences over national policy the nation should have a choice. Nor was it possible for the most astute of monarchs to select the best man for each post in the Government. Even if he could have acquired a detailed knowledge of the abilities of all aspirants, the decline in the influence of the Crown had deprived him of the power necessary to direct and sustain an old-fashioned 'government by departments'. The sovereign employed his Prerogative to implement the will of the House of Commons because he no longer possessed the means to affect or reverse its decisions.

With the removal of the Constitutional impediments, theoretical and practical, to the triumph of an Opposition, the politicians had developed the instrument to make it responsible and effective—the rudiments of national parties. The Whigs and Tories of 1830 were ill disciplined and loosely organized by standards of the twentieth century, but they were larger and far stronger than any political groups at the Hanoverian accession. Grey's resumption of the leadership was so successful because, despite all the confusion and dissension of the preceding years, the Whigs possessed a cadre which could be put quickly into fighting trim and, after the storm, even more quickly transformed into a powerful garrison. The development of a party structure invalidated Sir Walter Scott's generalization that 'an Opposition, howsoever headed or conducted . . . like a wave of the sea, forms indeed but a single body when it is rolling towards the shore, but dashes into foam and dispersion the instant it reaches its object'.[1] The fact that the Whig party of 1830 was still not powerful enough to constitute a Government forced Grey to rely upon the Foxite principle of coalition, but under his direction the Opposition was able to withstand the shock of success.

---

[1] H. J. C. Grierson, ed., *The Letters of Sir Walter Scott* (London, 1932), ii. 268.

IX

EPILOGUE

TOWARD the close of Walpole's long régime a French visitor to England described the Opposition as a force driving the country to distraction and ruin. 'A nation cannot make itself feared abroad', wrote Jean Bernard Le Blanc, 'but in proportion as it is united at home.' Surely, he thought, the struggle of faction would destroy the 'poise' of Britain's mixed Constitution. A civil war might well ensue and the Government he turned into either an absolute monarchy or a 'true republic'.[1]

There were to be times, notably the crises of 1755–7 and 1782–4, when the struggle of parliamentary factions seriously affected Britain's international position. In such times also men dreaded the derangement of the balanced constitution. The bitter tension and attendant confusion made it hard to perceive that the rivals of the Ministry were not enemies of the state—that the Opposition had already become in Le Blanc's day, what the Tory Drake later called it, 'the ventilator of the Constitution', a safety-valve rather than an explosive.[2]

In long retrospect it appears that several crucial periods in the uneven development of the Opposition are worthy of particular emphasis.

The first occurred in 1717–18. Parliament dropped the impeachments of the Tory ex-ministers, and an Act of Grace was passed. In close coincidence with the ending of political proscription, the Walpole–Townshend group, chivvied from office by Sunderland's intrigues, joined the Prince of Wales in the first loyal Opposition under the new dynasty. From these events emerged the pattern of politics that was to prevail under the first two Georges.

The events of 1720–2 confirmed the pattern. The destruction of the Atterbury plot eliminated Jacobitism as a serious menace. Upon his return to office Walpole screened his rivals from

---

[1] Le Blanc, *Letters on the English and French Nations*, i. 101–7; ii. 284–91.
[2] *P.H.* xxiv. 363.

retribution, and the treaty of 1720 set an important example for future Oppositions.

The fall of Walpole, succeeded in brief span by the rise and fall of Carteret, falsified Le Blanc's melancholy prophecy. For all their fierce Philippics and angry threats, the patriots revealed themselves as rather conservative politicians. Innocent of any revolutionary designs, they merely contended for power within the accepted framework of the Constitution. The one radical tendency, if such it may be called, was common to both ins and outs—an increasing determination to secure power in defiance, albeit usually deferential defiance, of the Prerogative of the Crown. This may be construed as an impulse toward the transition to a republic—in the sense that the directors of policy in a republican state are chosen in some form by its active citizens—but not a 'true republic' as Le Blanc meant it, for no one dreamt of dispensing with the monarchy.

By retaining the old corps headed by the Pelhams to stave off a storm of the closet in 1742, George II unintentionally made them indispensable partners in the management of the state. They 'forced' him in 1744 and 1746 because he could not find a way to reconstitute the Court party without its old leaders. He had allowed the Pelhams to take so firm a grip upon the influence of the Crown and the confidence of Parliament that he was unable to put an Opposition into office with a majority as his father had done in 1714–15.

George II soon came to accept the Pelhams with good grace, and they, gentle but jealous converts to 'broad bottom', became the arbiters of political fortune. Quiescence rather than Opposition seemed the safest road to office until Pitt shattered the political calm in 1755. Then was played out to its extinction the game constituted under the old rules. The coalition of 1757 allotted to each faction an appropriate share of the spoils, and for over four years, to the glory of Britain and the consternation of some Constitutionalists, the Government carried the King's business through Parliament without the let or criticism of a loyal Opposition.

The patriot parties under the first two Georges remained what they had long been—small groups which were weak except in alliance with others and which, upon admission to office, tended to merge into the old corps. The great coalition against Walpole, however, established ideas and procedures essential to the development of a two-party system. The Opposition acquired its name and its recognized position on the Speaker's left. The patriots worked out the parliamentary tactics that became the standard practice of their successors. The political world was brought to realize that, the Court party having become so strong an instrument for the control of Parliament, a vigorous loyal Opposition, whatever the personal motives of its members, served the excellent purpose of restraining the excesses of power.

During the calm era of 'broad bottom' the heirs to the throne grew restive at the prospect of governing as junor partners of the old corps. Frederick and Egmont formed the 'glorious plan' to recapture control of the Court party. George III and Bute, though incapable of making a 'great outline', acceded to power with the same intentions. Henry Fox helped them to decapitate the old corps in 1762–3, and it required nearly a decade to re-establish a stable and consistent administration.

The ouster of Newcastle and his most loyal colleagues turned the Opposition in a new direction. More deeply injured even than the haughty dispossessed of 1733, they assumed the tactical heritage of the Oppositions they had so long decried and the ideological heritage of the Whig myth which for so long had sustained their morale in office. Their failure to recapture their predominant position at Court drove the Rockinghamites to lay the foundations of an enduring party, whose undisguised intent was to storm the closet *malgré le roi*. George III frustrated them after their brief triumphs in 1782–3, but the party survived, as earlier parties had not, because it was supported by institutions which outlived both failure and success.

The Pittites, who professed to despise party and a formed systematic Opposition, came ultimately to adopt the Constitutional views of the Foxites. The summer of 1806, when Pitt's followers reached a common agreement to resist the allurements of Grenville, marks the commencement of the two-party system in its nineteenth-century form. The second party came into existence in the same fashion as the first: the dispossessed leaders of a Court party, regarding themselves as the true friends of the monarchy, formed a union for the purpose of restoring themselves to office.

By the mid–1820's it was generally accepted that 'His Majesty's Opposition' constituted an essential part of the state's political machinery, not simply as a check upon the Ministry and a 'ventilator' for the escape of irrepressible discontent, but as an alternative Government. An ambitious party on the Speaker's left was no longer regarded as a threat to the Prerogative but rather as a responsible body which provided both King and People with a choice of ministers and measures. So it turned out that the existence of a loyal Opposition prevented in Britain the disasters which Le Blanc predicted, whereas in his own and other continental countries, which developed no comparable institution, revolt and revolution became recurring plagues.

BIBLIOGRAPHICAL NOTE

ALL books dealing with British political history under the four Georges touch in one way or another upon the activities of the Opposition. The most significant volumes published before 1950 are noticed in Stanley Pargellis and D. J. Medley, *Bibliography of British History: The Eighteenth Century, 1714–1789* (Oxford, 1951). J. Steven Watson has commented upon some more recent studies in the bibliography of his *The Reign of George III* (Oxford, 1960). W. R. Fryer's 'The Study of British Politics between the Revolution and the Reform Act' (*Renaissance and Modern Studies*, i (1957), 91–114) provides an excellent survey and critique of current interpretations. There are valuable comments in William A. Bultmann's 'Early Hanoverian England (1714–1760): Some Recent Writings' (*Journal of Modern History*, xxxv (1963), 46–61).

The work of Sir Lewis Namier has exercised a pervading influence upon the current approach to the Constitution and politics of the eighteenth century. In *The Structure of Politics at the Accession of George III* (2 vols., London, 1929) and *England in the Age of the American Revolution* (London, 1930), supplemented by essays collected in *Personalities and Powers* (London, 1955), he set up standards of methodology and viewpoints of interpretation that all his successors have taken into account. With Namier's analysis in mind, Robert Walcott, Jr., delineated the background for the study of the Georgian era in 'English Party Politics (1688–1714)' in *Essays in Modern English History in honor of Wilbur Cortez Abbott* (Cambridge, Mass., 1941) and *English Party Politics in the Early Eighteenth Century* (Cambridge, Mass., 1956). Romney Sedgwick's introduction to *Letters from George III to Lord Bute, 1756–1766* (London, 1939) pursues Sir Lewis's hypotheses in an incisive study of the King and his favourite. Under Namier's aegis have appeared three important detailed monographs that are indispensable for a study of the political system: John B. Owen, *The Rise of The Pelhams* (London, 1957); John Brooke, *The Chatham Administration, 1766–1768* (London 1956); and Ian R. Christie, *The End of North's Ministry, 1780–1782* (London, 1958). The approach of the 'Namier school' is subjected to broad criticism by Herbert Butterfield in *George III and the Historians* (London, 1957).

Richard Pares's *King George III and the Politicians* (Oxford, 1953) is a brilliant synthesis, distinguished also by much original insight, of the recent scholarship in the field. *The Second Tory Party, 1714–1832* (London, 1938) by Sir Keith Feiling is not so much a monograph, as its title suggests, as a well-informed but rambling discourse upon the political annals of Britain under the four Georges. The political historiography of the early nineteenth century is dominated by the imposing figure of Arthur Aspinall. *Lord Brougham and the Whig Party* (Manchester, 1927) was the first of his many able books and articles (of which the most pertinent have been cited in the text) that have contributed to our knowledge of the reigns of the third and fourth Georges.

There are several volumes addressed directly to the history of Opposition. The broadest survey is John Carswell, *The Old Cause* (London, 1954), an endeavour to describe the development of the idea of a Constitutional Opposition through biographies of Thomas Wharton, Bubb Dodington, and Charles James Fox. In *The Early Opposition to Sir Robert Walpole, 1720–1727* (Kansas, 1931) Charles B. Realey has made a careful study of the antagonistic elements overcome by the great Minister in his rise to power. Kurt Kluxen, *Das Problem der Politischen Opposition: Entwicklung und Wesen der Englischen Zweiparteienpolitik im 18. Jahrhundert* (Freiburg, 1956), is essentially an analysis of Bolingbroke's political theory. Erwin von Wiese found the British politics of 1740–4 altogether bewildering in *Die Englische Parliamentarische Opposition und ihre Stellung zur auswärtigen Politik des Britischen Cabinetts während des Österreichischen Erbfolgkrieges* (Waldenburg, 1883). D. A. Winstanley wrote, with a strong Rockinghamite bias, a detailed political narrative of the first twelve years of George III's reign in *Personal and Party Government* (Cambridge, 1910) and *Lord Chatham and the Whig Opposition* (Cambridge, 1912). *Wilkes, Sheridan, Fox: The Opposition under George III* (New York, 1874) by W. F. Rae is another biographical approach to the subject, in which the characters appear as heroes. Michael Roberts, *The Whig Party, 1807–1812* (London, 1939) is a full chronicle of the Opposition in those years.

It would seem unnecessary to recite the long list of the standard printed source materials employed by all historians of the eighteenth century. Most of them are noted in the bibliography by Pargellis and Medley, and the value of those used for this volume will be apparent from the citations given in the text. Special mention should be made of two excellent compilations now in process: *The Yale Edition of Horace Walpole's Correspondence* (New Haven, 1937–   ) under the editorship of Wilmarth S. Lewis, and *The Correspondence of Edmund Burke* (Cambridge and Chicago, 1958–   ) under the general editorship of Thomas W. Copeland.

Surviving reports of parliamentary debates are fragmentary and often inaccurate. They should be used with the reservations indicated in Arthur Aspinall's enlightening article, 'The Reporting and Publishing of the House of Commons' Debates, 1771–1834' (*Essays Presented to Sir Lewis Namier*, ed. Pares and Taylor, London, 1956, pp. 227–57). Nevertheless, they represent the most that we can know of the speeches made at Westminster, and they can be very valuable when studied in conjunction with the journals of the two Houses, comments in contemporary memoirs and letters, and pamphlets which expound the views of the protagonists in Parliament. For general use the best compilation is *Cobbett's Parliamentary History of England . . . 1066 to . . . 1803* (36 vols., London, 1806–20), continued by Cobbett and later by Hansard as *The Parliamentary Debates* (1st and 2nd series) to 1830.

The abundant pamphlets, newspapers, and magazines are, of course, indispensable to the study of political history. Some items are scattered widely among various libraries. Most useful of the large well catalogued collections are those in the British Museum, the Yale University Library, and the Huntington Library in San Marino, California.

Manuscripts in English archives have yielded much useful information for this work. As will be evident from the citations, numerous collections contain only one or two relevant items, and so do not merit further attention. Bodies of significant and new material for the history of the Opposition are located in the two great London repositories. In the British Museum are the Egmont MSS.,[1] of which the most valuable are the second Earl's plans for the accession of Prince Frederick; the Newcastle papers, particularly the Duke's correspondence after his resignation in 1762 (Add. MSS. 32938–33000); the Hardwicke papers, especially the correspondence of the first Earl's sons in Add. MSS. 45030–2; and the Canning–Frere correspondence in Add. MSS. 38833, which reveals much about the Pittite Opposition of 1801–4. Of those in the Public Record Office the Cathcart papers throw interesting light on the Leicester House Opposition of 1717–20; the Granville and Shaftesbury papers supplement our knowledge of the Opposition in the

---

[1] I used the Egmont MSS. when they were in the Public Record Office. They have since been transferred to the British Museum, where new classification numbers have been assigned (Add. MSS. 46920–47212), and a 'Concordance of Old and New Egmont MSS. Numbers' (P.S. 1501. Handlists 1937) has been drawn up. Reclassification is incomplete, however, and it is not certain that the British Museum received the entire Egmont collection. A large number of the items I used in the Public Record Office cannot be located at present. The volumes in the British Museum have not yet been folioed, and some of the classification numbers are provisional. It has seemed best, therefore, to give citations of the old numbers in the Public Record Office and to advise the reader to use the 'Concordance' until reclassification is accomplished and a more accurate guide appears.

1740's; and in the Chatham papers the correspondence of George III and the younger Pitt gives important clues to their opinions on Opposition and parliamentary tactics.

The Portland papers in the Nottingham University Library contain useful materials for a study of the Rockinghamites from 1762 to 1782, but in the third Duke's correspondence there are distressing *lacunae* for the years 1783–93 and 1806–7. Valuable also for the Rockinghamite era are the papers of Rockingham, Fitz-william, and Burke in the Sheffield City Library. The correspon-dence of Sarah, dowager Duchess of Marlborough, with the 'Broad Bottom' leaders of the 1730's, in the archives of Blenheim Palace, deepens our understanding of the opposition to Walpole. The MS. Journal of Mrs. Charles Caesar, in the possession of Lt.-Col. John H. Busby of Harpenden, Herts., is the best single source on the Harley Tories from 1720 to 1740.

INDEX